The Texas Rangers

Wearing the Cinco Peso, 1821–1900

The Texas Rangers

Volume I

Wearing the Cinco Peso, 1821–1900

Mike Cox

A Tom Doherty Associates Book

NEW YORK

FORGE®

THE TEXAS RANGERS: WEARING THE CINCO PESO, 1821–1900

Copyright © 2008 by Mike Cox

A Forge Book
Published by Tom Doherty Associates, LLC
175 Fifth Avenue
New York, NY 10010

www.tor-forge.com

Forge® is a registered trademark of Tom Doherty Associates, LLC.

Library of Congress Cataloging-in-Publication Data

Cox, Mike, 1948–
    The Texas Rangers : wearing the cinco peso, 1821–1900/ Mike Cox.
        p.   cm.
    "A Tom Doherty Associates book."
    ISBN-13: 978-0-312-87386-8
    ISBN-10: 0-312-87386-7
    1. Texas Rangers—History—19th century.   2. Frontier and pioneer life—
Texas.   3. Law enforcement—Texas—History—19th century.   4. Violence—
Texas—History—19th century.   5. Texas History—1846–1950.   6. Texas—
History–Republic, 1836–1846.   7. Texas—Race relations—History—19th
century.

    F391.C7835   2008
    363.2092—dc22

                                                            2007044119

First Edition: March 2008

Printed in the United States of America

0 9 8 7 6 5 4 3 2 1

Again, for my granddad, L . A. Wilke, a longtime writer
who knew many of the old-time Texas Rangers and
first got me interested in their story.

✳

Also again for my mother, Betty Wilke Cox,
who taught me much about history and writing.

✳

And finally again, for my wife, Linda, who guarded
the cabin while I went word rangering (not to mention
helping with editing), and our daughter Hallie, already
developing as my family's fourth-generation writer.

Acknowledgments

I've always liked the story about a typically laconic Texas Ranger who killed an outlaw in the line of duty. When the lawman finally reached a town that offered telegraphic service, he wired Ranger headquarters in Austin: "We had a little shooting match and he lost."

Every month, Ranger commanders in the Frontier Battalion had to send a scouting report to headquarters in Austin. The report covered miles traveled, Indians or outlaws killed and wounded, arrests made and other statistical information. But early rangers did not much care for paperwork and, like the ranger who won the "little shooting match," generally did not waste words.

I've traveled a lot of miles and gotten help from a lot of people in the nine years since I began working on this two-volume history of the Rangers. Listing everyone who had a hand in helping me with this book would take a pretty long scouting report.

My wife, Linda Aronovsky Cox, as she has for all my books since 1990, gave this manuscript its first edit. My mother, Betty Wilke Cox, my other built-in editor for much of my writing career, got to read and comment on parts of this book before she died in mid-2006.

Beyond them, I can list the usual suspects whose names show up in many books about Texas: Donaly Brice and John Anderson with the Texas State Library and Archives; Ralph Elder, now semiretired from the Center for American History at the University of Texas at Austin; Chuck Parsons, writer and longtime member of the National Outlaw and Lawman History Association (NOLA); retired history professor Harold J. Weiss, Jr., of Leander; my many friends at various libraries across the state, from Amarillo to El Paso to San

Antonio to Houston. Particularly helpful were Suzanne Campbell with the West Texas Collection at Angelo State University in San Angelo, Evetts Haley, Jr., and the staffers at the Nita Stewart Haley Memorial Library in Midland, and Sue Soy, director of the Austin Public Library's Austin History Center.

Byron Johnson and his staff at the Texas Ranger Museum and Hall of Fame in Waco have helped a lot over the years, even prior to this project, as well as the officers and members of the Former Texas Ranger Association. Particularly helpful were retired Rangers Joe Davis, Joaquin Jackson, Ramiro Martinez, Captains Bob Mitchell and Dan North and current Ranger Sergeant Dave Duncan of Alpine.

Friend and avocational Ranger researcher Sloan Rodgers, a descendant (despite a difference in spelling) of Colonial-era American ranger Robert Rogers, read the manuscript and provided considerable enlightenment into the Captain Jack Hays era, his specialty.

As I worked toward wrapping up the editing and last-minute tweaks on this first volume, I had a stimulating visit in San Antonio with Texas historian T. R. Fehrenbach. The author of several enduring works, he graciously shared with me some of his insights on the Rangers. He also offered a very helpful tutorial on Mexican silver coins.

Finally, I appreciate the confidence shown by my editor, Bob Gleason, who gave me the go-ahead to write this book for Forge Books in 1999. This book was supposed to be finished long before now, but I just kept finding new material I couldn't pass up and Gleason remained (mostly) patient.

My sincere thanks to everyone listed here as well as anyone else I may have overlooked who helped out at any point during this long project.

A Note on the Title

Only ten days after Texas declared its independence from Mexico on March 2, 1836, George C. Childress, a signer of that declaration, offered a resolution to the general convention proposing that "a single star of five points" be recognized as the "peculiar emblem" of Texas. Childress's resolution also stipulated that "every officer and soldier of the army and members of this convention, and all friends of Texas, be requested to wear it on their hats or bosoms."

History does not record who, when, or where, but at some point a Texas Ranger, perhaps adhering to Childress's measure, pulled his long knife and carved a star in a silver Mexican eight real piece. (The Mexican government did not begin minting silver cinco pesos until 1947, but it produced two other silver denominations earlier, an eight real coin [1824–1897] and a one peso coin [1898–1909]). The story may even be apocryphal, but a photograph taken in 1888 of Ranger Walter Durbin shows what has come to be called a star-in-the-wheel badge on his chest.

Eventually, as Rangers evolved from Indian fighters (Comanches and other hostile tribes demanded no proof of authority from Texans with guns) to law enforcement officers, the star-in-wheel badge grew in popularity among Rangers. In addition to carrying a folded paper warrant of authority, some Frontier Battalion members paid out of their own pocket for a badge fashioned by jewelers. The state did not provide standardized, official badges to Rangers until the 1930s and not until 1962 did Texas Rangers begin wearing badges crafted from genuine cinco peso pieces.

Since then, Rangers have come to refer to their service to Texas as "wearing the cinco peso."

Contents

Preface

My late grandfather L. A. Wilke blazed several of the trails I have followed. He began his writing career as a Texas newspaper reporter during the days of the Mexican Revolution and then moved on to freelance writing. I hired on with a newspaper for the first time during the social revolution of the late 1960s and eventually started peddling stories to magazines and later writing books.

The urge to tell stories must be an inherited trait. I spent many hours sitting in Granddad's home office, listening to him reflect on his newspaper days and the colorful characters he encountered, including some famous Texas Rangers. The mental picture I have is of him turned around from his typewriter with thumbs twiddling over an ample stomach as he embarked on an always-interesting recollection. As I listened, my focus often settled on the considerable collection of Texas-related books on the shelves behind him.

One of those books had a yellow and blue dust jacket. The spine held its partial title, *The Texas Rangers*, followed by the single word "Webb" and the name of the publisher, Houghton Mifflin Company.

Written in the early-to-mid-1930s by Walter Prescott Webb, a Texas historian and longtime University of Texas professor, the book stood for decades as the definitive Ranger history. My granddad, who had personally known some of the Rangers who play prominent roles in Webb's book, had read this first edition and made notes in its margins.

Later, of course, I also absorbed the book. It is quite readable if at times racist, but Webb's history drops deader than an outlaw with a Ranger bullet in his heart, with the creation of the Texas Department of Public Safety in 1935. The book ends with Webb's incorrect prediction that the formation of the new agency marked the end of the Rangers. Webb intended to update his book, but his death in a traffic accident in 1963 ended that hope. Two years later, the University of Texas brought it back into print with a ghost-written foreword by President Lyndon B. Johnson but made no attempt to revise a history then more than three decades out of date.

In 1985, after spending nearly twenty years as a newspaper staff writer, I was fortunate enough to be hired by the DPS as public information officer. As the law enforcement agency's spokesman for the next fifteen years, I got to meet and become friends with many rangers. In 1990, I wrote a Ranger history for young readers. After writing two collections of nonfiction tales about the Rangers, I decided in 1999 to take on Webb and write the history of the Rangers from the beginning through 1935 to modern times.

I am an independent historian, not an academic. While this book is the result of years of research into everything from official documents, correspondence, and early newspaper coverage to theses and dissertations and unpublished manuscripts, I have tried portraying the history of the Texas Rangers through storytelling. As often as possible, I have included the Rangers' own words or other contemporary accounts. And what a story I found to tell.

Essentially, the Rangers evolved from a volunteer Indian-fighting force in 1821 to a paramilitary arm of government in 1835–1836 to a frontier law enforcement agency in 1874. The continuing evolution of the Rangers into the twentieth and twenty-first centuries will be the focus of the second volume of this book.

The Ranger tradition in Texas is a product of both American and European influences. In something of an irony, since Rangers sometimes were pitted against Mexicans, part of their tradition traces to Spanish-Colonial law enforcement in Texas. Rangers also learned—the hard way—some things about fighting from the early Indian tribes who laid claim to various parts of Texas. Texas did not invent rangering, but as a native son, I like to think we improved on it quite a bit.

As I say elsewhere in this book, the reality and mythology of the Rangers in our popular culture are as closely interwoven as a fine horsehair quirt. It is hard to separate the two strands, though I have tried with as much objectivity as possible to document both in this narrative.

Beyond myth versus reality, it has become increasingly popular among revisionist historians to label the Texas Rangers as racist practitioners of genocide, gun-toting tools of a greedy, land-grabbing Anglo establishment. While there is no question that men riding in the name of frontier protection or law and order killed some people who probably did not "need killin'," as the old Texas expression goes, those instances were rare and often exaggerated. To compare the Rangers to those who have systematically killed thousands and even millions of innocent people is not accurate and certainly not fair.

"Where I find the most fault with many of today's revisionist writers," bestselling Western novelist Elmer Kelton has written, "is in their penchant for seeing our forebears' pioneering experience only in the darkest terms. Surely it must be possible to exalt the minority viewpoints of the Western experience without automatically condemning the white male pioneers to perdition."

The early rangers did not all wear white hats, no question. As I have tried to show in this book, bad men sometimes did saddle up for Texas. More often than not, they either got kicked out of the Rangers or ended up getting killed. Some rangers, though neither dishonest nor holding themselves above the law, merely proved inept. Other rangers helped create their legend, and still others lived up to that legend.

The saying "the truth lies somewhere in the middle" has become a modern cliché, but it fits when it comes to the history of the Texas Rangers. The nineteenth-century Rangers can be labeled neither all bad nor all good. Though far from invincible, they did save lives along the frontier by scouting for hostile Indians bent on reaching the settlements, and they did eliminate many an outlaw—both figuratively and literally. It is hard to sustain an argument that the Rangers did not fall in the middle of what philosophers call the dichotomously variable continuum. With most issues, that bell curve has a small set—a group, belief, characteristic, whatever—on one end as well as a small set on the other end. But most of the set falls in the middle, whether the continuum is good versus evil or untruth opposed to truth. Or, as a Chinese proverb holds, "There is your truth, there is my truth, and there is the truth."

I will leave it to the revisionist historians to continue to duke it out with the mainstream over the amount of culpability the Rangers might have, but the simple reality is that the Rangers existed for only one purpose: to protect the people of Texas. At a governor's direction, they may have aided in strike-breaking or become enforcers of the majority's idea of morality, but most of the time, Rangers just worked to make Texas a safer place to live and raise a family.

The Texas Rangers played an important part in civilizing what in the nineteenth century and for much of the twentieth century was the nation's largest state, a huge hunk of land covering more square miles than France. In the process, they forged the words "Texas Ranger" into an internationally recognized icon. Their legend kept them alive when the frontier faded, and it continues to give them cachet today. This is their story.

—Mike Cox
Austin, Texas
2007

Part One

Indian Fighters

1

"Ten men . . . to act as rangers"

A RANGING TRADITION, 1821—34

Stephen Fuller Austin and his fellow riders broke camp in the short-lived cool of the late-summer morning and continued their trek to the southeast along a lake formed on the Colorado River by a large drift-wood raft.

The twenty-seven-year-old Missourian, a slim, noble-featured man with wavy brown hair and eyes the color of pecan shells, had crossed the Sabine River westward into Texas in July 1821. Folded in his saddlebag rested an agreement his late father, Moses, had negotiated with officials of the Spanish Crown to settle three hundred American families in this distant frontier province. Stephen Austin had vowed to follow through on his father's dream of bringing settlers to this new country, but Mexico's successful overthrow of Spain had placed the matter in doubt.

After meeting with the new republic's provincial governor in San Antonio de Bexar to assure that his *empresario* contract remained in force, Austin set out to see firsthand the territory he had permission to populate with men and women from the United States. A couple of times he had encountered friendly Tonkawas, but he knew that not all of Texas's Indian tribes had cordial feelings for those of European descent. Along the coast lived the Karankawas, tall Indians said to practice cannibalism.

From Bexar, Austin and his party traveled down the San Antonio River to Goliad, a small town near an old Spanish presidio and mission called La Bahia. With one of the town's councilmen as an escort and three Aranama Indians as guides, Austin's entourage rode southeast. When it became apparent after a few days that the locals did not know the country well enough to be of use, Austin talked them into going back to Goliad and pressed on with his own men.

Safely home back in Bexar, Manuel Becerra reported troubling news. Even though Austin's agreement stipulated that American colonists would have to practice Roman Catholicism, he had never seen Austin or any of his men perform any "religious act." Too, they spoke only English. Becerra found Austin's unabashed admiration of real estate clearly not a part of his grant even more disturbing. Assessing the coming Anglo immigration, the local official predicted, "They will be more harmful than beneficial."

The land clearly spoke to Austin. The grassy prairies and timbered river bottoms influenced him every bit as strongly as his father's dying wish that he continue with his colonization plans. "The country is the most beautiful & desirable to live in I ever saw," Austin wrote in his diary.

Now, on the second day of his journey along the Colorado, he heard a loud Indian war whoop. Startled back to reality, Austin reined his horse. A tall Indian, followed by fourteen warriors, emerged from the high, thick Arundinaria (bamboo cane) along the river and walked slowly toward the American horsemen.

"These Indians were well formed and apparently very active and athletic men," Austin later noted. Each warrior, his body smeared with alligator grease to ward off mosquitoes, carried a cedar bow nearly as long as he stood tall. Austin saw that the deerskin quivers hanging from the Indians' muscled shoulders bristled with arrows. Signing friendship, the Indian in the lead moved toward Austin and his party.

Telling his men to get ready to fight, Austin nudged his horse with his boots and rode about twenty yards ahead to meet the Indians. He had never fought Indians hand to hand, but as an officer in the Missouri militia during the War of 1812, Austin had learned something of military strategy and tactics. A show of determination, he knew, could be as effective as resorting to arms. Talk would come before gunfire.

In Spanish, the chief asked Austin where he was from and where he was going. Austin explained that he was an American with permission from Spain to bring families to settle between the Colorado and Brazos rivers. Accepting that, the chief identified himself as a Coco, which Austin knew to be a branch of the feared Karankawas. Wary of the chief's invitation to follow the Indians to their camp, Austin refused. Holding his flintlock rifle across his chest, the young American warned the Indians not to come closer.

Hoping to counter Austin's distrust, the chief made a show of laying down his bow and arrows. When five women and a boy walked into view, Austin's gaze shifted from the fierce-looking warriors and their weapons to the women. They wore painted animal hides that hung just below their knees, but, as Austin later recorded, "above the waist . . . they were naked. . . . Their breasts . . . marked or tattooed in circles of black beginning with a small circle at the nipple and enlarging as the breast swelled." All of the women, Austin continued, "were handsome & one of them quite pretty."

Not fully convinced by the Indians' demonstration of friendliness, Austin assumed their apparent conviviality came from a realization that they stood little chance against the mounted white men and their firearms. Finally deciding they posed no immediate danger, he gave the chief some tobacco and "a frying pan that we did not want" as tokens of friendship.

The chief told Austin that he and his followers were on their way to trade with "Spaniards and Americans" along the long road that stretched from Louisiana via Nacogdoches to San Antonio and then to Mexico, the Camino Real, or King's Highway. The Coco also said the downstream canebreak, which Austin later learned covered an area forty miles wide by seventy-five miles long and rose to thirty feet, grew too thick for Austin's party to reach the river's mouth. Besides that, the chief added, a large party of Karankawas had their camp nearby. Leaving the Cocos to their trading, Austin prudently gave up on seeing where the river emptied into the Gulf of Mexico and rode east toward the Brazos.[1]

This encounter, on September 17, 1821, marked the first significant contact between the man considered the Father of Anglo Texas and the Indians who lived in the area he intended to colonize. Austin's journal entry for that day not only summarized his views and the attitude of most of his countrymen, it presaged the next sixty years of Texas history:

> These Indians and the Karanquas [sic] may be called universal ene-mies to man—they killed of all nations that came into their power, and frequently feast on the bodies of their victims—the [approach of] an American population will be the signal of their extermination for there will be no way of subduing them but extermination.[2]

RAUNGERS, RAINGERS, RANGERS

The cultural collision that followed, the continuation of two centuries of European conquest of North America, constituted the problem for which the Texas Rangers evolved as a partial solution. In time, the ne-cessity of statewide law enforcement grew to be more important than protection from Indians, but Indian fighting stood as the first order of business for rangers in Texas. That conflict began an enduring tradition, giving rise to an earned reputation for effectiveness eventually enhanced by myth. Like a finely braided horsehair quirt, the story of the Rangers has many strands, an interweaving of reality and legend. Texans did not invent rangering, but they made the word usable as a verb and added to its meaning as a noun, over time forging *Texas* and *Ranger*—when used together—into a Lone Star icon recognized worldwide.

The word *ranger* dates to fourteenth-century England, when royal officers called *raungers* guarded the deforested areas on the edge of tim-ber. These men used dogs to keep game in the forest, ever available for royal hunts, to apprehend trespassers hunting illegally, and to take any-one they caught to court. Essentially, these representatives of the Crown amounted to game wardens. They patrolled the land—ranged it—and they had a semblance of law enforcement authority.[3]

When the first English colonists arrived on the east coast of North America, they brought the ranging tradition with them. By the first half of the 1600s, the common spelling of the word had become *rainger*, an *i* hav-ing replaced the *u*. By 1634, when one Edward Beckler served as a rainger on a Virginian island in Chesapeake Bay, the word had come to mean one of a body of men who afforded a community protection by scouting for enemies and engaging them when found. In 1647–48, the Maryland As-sembly weighed a plan to use "raingers or scouts" in the protection of the colony. Georgia colony records from 1733 reflect that "Rangers . . . protected the new Settlers." Nine years later, it was noted that "rangers who can ride the woods" were needed "for the defense of the colony."[4]

The early history of the American colonies is largely the story of a struggle for control of the land. The English and French vied for continental dominance, but both had to contend with the original inhabitants, the Indians. During the French and Indian War, a nine-year conflict beginning in 1754 between the British and the French and their Indian allies, the value of rangers as an irregular military force became firmly established.[5] "Our friends at Ft. Prince-George are in deplorable circumstances, the fort being blockaded Night & Day by the Cherokees," the Boston *News-Letter* reported. "Seven companies of Rangers are to be compleated forthwith to succour Ft. Prince-George, the garrison being greatly distressed for Provisions."[6]

Robert Rogers became the first American ranger to achieve lasting fame. His men, who assisted British regular soldiers by providing reconnaissance and serving both as advance guards and guerrilla raiders, came to be called Rogers' Rangers. In 1759, Rogers put pen to parchment and set down twenty standing orders for his men, a list of commonsense principles ranging from "Don't forget nothing" (No. 1) to "Don't never take a chance you don't have to" (No. 5) to "Don't use your musket if you can kill 'em with your hatchet" (No. 20.)[7]

Rangers later played a role in the Revolutionary War, and the ranger concept continued southward along the eastern seaboard before turning west. "Ranger-frontiersmen," a law enforcement historian later wrote, "had a distinctive role as soldiers: unmilitary dress with the firepower of a special weapon in irregular warfare. Citizen soldiers were an age-old instrument of British military policy that became embedded in American culture."[8]

England and France were not the only European powers with significant toeholds in North America in the 1700s. The land that would become Texas was part of the widespread Spanish empire. While the word *ranger* came of Anglo-Saxon heritage, the concept of an irregular fighting force of armed riders, available as needed, was not unique. If anything, the mounted tradition held stronger in the vastness of New Spain than the wooded lands along the Eastern seaboard, where *snowshoe men* served as an early synonym for rangers.

With brigands roaming the frontier provinces of New Spain as freely as the war-loving Comanches, a special court of justice promulgated a doctrine known as La Acordada. Agreed to by the Crown in 1719, the courts of Spain approved it three years later:

> Whereby the present courts of justice are insufficient to give protection to the country whose cities and villages are infested with thieves and bandits and, since Don Miguel Velasquez de Lorreo in Queretaro, Mexico, a member of the Holy Brothers, duly authorized, initiated summary trials without revision of the sentence has proven so effective, it has been accorded to extend the same procedure throughout the country.

In other words royal decree suspected criminals could be tried and summarily executed. An unpaid mounted law enforcement organization that ranged the frontier of New Spain, looking for trouble and troublemakers, carried out La Acordada. Those men, under the command of a captain based in Mexico City, were called lieutenants or deputies. They furnished their own arms, provisions, and horses. The riders wore no uniforms. The honor of serving the Crown and protecting life and property provided motivation enough.

By the time Mexico revolted against Spain in 1810, La Acordada—a one-stop criminal justice system—had resulted in the summary execution of more than eight hundred criminals. "It then became possible to travel throughout the country and to carry silver or money provided one had a small escort," one scholar later wrote.[9]

In addition to the men who enforced La Acordada, Spanish landowners had been ordered by the viceroy to organize "flying companies" of volunteer militia at the presidios of the northern frontier. The men of those companies could ride after Indians at a moment's notice, a tradition that would also take root in Texas. San Antonio–based companies under Salvador Flores and Juan Seguin (whose father served as alcalde, or civil judge, of Bexar), the Tlascalan Compañía Volante San Carlos de Parras, the Guardia Victoriana under Carlos de la Garza, the San Fernando Rangers under Mariano Rodriquez, and the Nacogdoches company of Vicente Cordova all amounted to rangerlike forces.

As a legal institution, La Acordada died with Spain's dreams of empire in the New World. But in Texas, the concept survived as an attitude. After Mexico won its independence from Spain in 1821, the spirit if not the letter of La Acordada continued in Texas with the emergence of the Juez de Campo, rural policemen vested with judicial authority. An officer's duties included the registration of cattle brands, regulating cattle sales, and arbitrating disputes among ranchers. He also ranged the countryside in pursuit of cattle thieves.

The Anglo ranging tradition mixed with a similar Hispanic tradition like straw in adobe. Texans would take a concept that came from two very different cultures and make it their own. That process began with a handful of Austin's colonists who arrived from New Orleans at the mouth of the Colorado on June 4, 1822, aboard the *Lively,* a chartered schooner.

"AND ORGANIZE THE MILITIA . . ."

The coming of the American colonists soon necessitated some form of home rule, but so soon after its revolution, Mexico's principal preoccupation focused on the development of national and provincial governments. In the fall of 1822, a new provincial governor, Jose Felix Trespalacios, authorized the creation of two districts in the Austin colony, one along the Colorado River, the other along the Brazos. Each district could elect an alcalde and a captain and lieutenant of militia.[10] On November 20 the colonists of the Colorado district selected North Carolina–born John Jackson Tumlinson as alcalde, Kentuckian Robert H. Kuykendall as captain, and Moses Morrison (he signed his name *Morrisson*, but all accounts of his activities use only one *s*) as lieutenant. Settlers living on the Brazos elected Josiah H. Bell as alcalde, Samuel Gates as captain, and Kuykendall's nephew, Gibson, as their lieutenant.[11] Tumlinson, a tough but affable frontiersman who had come to the colony in 1821 from Arkansas, also appointed a man to serve as constable, his duties being to "summon witnesses" and "bring offenders to justice."[12]

The two alcaldes had a tough job. They had to make do with delegated authority, not statutory power. They tried to act according to the Constitution they had left behind in the United States, reporting their actions to the governor and hoping for approval. If they had questions on an issue, they wrote the governor for instructions. Essentially, their power rested on their ability to persuade others.

Still, for all practical purposes, the Tumlinson-Kuykendall-Morrison triumvirate and their counterparts on the Brazos reigned as the sole protectors of law and order in the fledgling colony. Little more than a month after their election, Tumlinson and Morrison would investigate a double murder—the Anglo settlement's first recorded homicides.

Thomas Rogers operated a ferry on the Colorado where the river bisected the Atascosito Road, an old Spanish trail leading to San Antonio. On Christmas Eve, a settler named James Nelson stopped at Rogers's cabin, finding five other travelers sitting around the fire, four Spaniards and a U.S. citizen on his way to San Antonio to sell buttons and watches.

The next day, when Nelson had occasion to call again at Rogers's remote homestead, he found the place deserted. Supposing the travelers had moved on and that Rogers had gone visiting or hunting, Nelson left. Five days later, two other men came to the ferry and discovered two bodies floating in the river. One was Rogers, the other was the peddler Nelson had met. Both men had been beaten and stabbed to death.

As soon as Tumlinson learned of the slayings, he and another colonist saddled their horses and traveled to the crossing to investigate. After talking with Nelson and others, the alcalde believed that some or all of the Spaniards Nelson had seen had robbed Rogers and the American, taking not only their valuables, but their clothing as well. Tumlinson set down the details of the robbery-murders in a dispatch to the governor on January 7, 1823.

Before the end of the month, based on Tumlinson's information-gathering, two Spanish army deserters had been arrested in San Antonio. The governor sent a rider to Tumlinson's place on the Colorado with a rifle seized from one of the suspects to see if the weapon could be identified as having been owned by Rogers. After obtaining statements from several colonists who confirmed that the rifle had indeed belonged to Rogers, Tumlinson sent it back to San Antonio in the care of Lieutenant Morrison. Nelson went with the lieutenant to testify at the trial of the two men.

With Austin in Mexico City still negotiating his *empresario* agreement with the new government, Tumlinson had sent Governor Trespalacios a second letter on January 7. In this missive, also signed by Kuykendall, Tumlinson asked for help in protecting the new colony's settlers from Indians. The alcalde wanted authority to "raise fifteen hardy expert young men who are expert with the rifle by enlistment for the same pay that the troops of the Empire receive." In a postscript,

Tumlinson suggested that Lieutenant Morrison, a thirty-year-old U.S. army veteran with Indian-fighting experience in Mississippi, was "willing to take the charge of Commander of the troops."

The governor had been weighing the needs of the colony since December, when he had written Austin in Mexico City to inform him that he had "directed the inhabitants of the Colorado to appoint an alcalde of their own choice to administer justice, and organize the militia to oppose the Karankawas or other intruders."[13] The governor also envisioned the mouth of the river as a future Mexican port, and through his commissioner, Felipe Enrique Neri de Bastrop, had requested that Tumlinson reconnoiter the area.

In his letter Tumlinson described his plan for what amounted to a small marine force. He believed he could protect newly arrived settlers by constructing a series of blockhouses beginning near the mouth of the Colorado and using boats to move militiamen up and down the river. With fifteen men paid the same as regular troops, along with ten Mexican soldiers, "we have no doubt but the coast could be protected in such a manner that settlers could land with safety in our waters."

The need for some form of coastal protection had been clear since the previous September, when the schooner *Only Son* arrived at the mouth of the Colorado on its second trip from New Orleans with colonists and supplies. Protected by a party of men under Kuykendall, the immigrants moved upstream to join the other colonists, leaving three men behind to guard the provisions. When a party returned to the vessel to off-load the badly needed foodstuffs and other supplies, the men and most of the schooner's stores were missing. The loss of the supplies, presumed to have been the work of Indians, discouraged the colonists nearly to the point of giving up and returning to the United States.

Not long after being elected militia captain, the thirty-three-year-old Kuykendall–an experienced Indian-fighter who had come to Texas with his two older brothers—led fourteen men to investigate the disappearance of the three immigrants and the supplies they had been left to protect. Intent on chastising the Indians, the captain and his men rode to where the schooner's cargo had been left. But instead of tracking down Karankawas, they ended up conducting a criminal investigation. The militiamen could find no evidence that the men entrusted with protecting the badly needed supplies had been killed by Indians, but they did discover wagon tracks leading away from where the goods had been left

under guard. Since Indians did not have horse-drawn vehicles, Kuykendall and his men realized that someone else had stolen the goods. In
following the tire ruts, Kuykendall discovered a hidden cache of supplies from the *Only Son*. Eventually, Kuykendall and his party arrested
three men from Arkansas, determining that the Americans had found
the stores after Indians had carrried off the three guards and killed
them.[14]

The governor replied to Tumlinson on January 31, giving the alcalde
permission for the formation of the militia company and asking for an
estimate of how much it would cost to build the blockhouses and boats.
As for a military salary for the fifteen men who would serve under Morrison, "those troops," the governor wrote, "should not receive the same
pay as veteran troops whose duties have included a variety of operations
for which the new recruits are not being enlisted."[15]

Even though U.S. citizens had been involved in the *Only Son* cargo
theft, Tumlinson's request for a paid militia came as he and others in
the remote colony began to realize that the Indians saw the Anglo settlers not as neighbors but as an emerging natural resource: The white
newcomers gave gifts, they had a willingness to trade, and they owned
things worth stealing. "These Indians were beggarly and insolent,"
Mary Austin Holley, Austin's cousin, later wrote, "and were restrained
from violence for the first two years [of Austin's colony], only by presents, forbearance, and policy. There was not force enough in the colony
to awe them. One imprudent step with these Indians, would have destroyed the settlement."[16]

Though Holley included the Wacos, Tonkawas, Lipan Apaches, and
Karankawas in her ethnocentric observation, the latter tribe posed the
greatest danger. Kronks, as many of the settlers called them, were in the
words of one nineteenth-century chronicler "the Ishmaelites of Texas,
for their hands were against every man, and every man's hand was
against them." The Karankawas tended to stay close to the coast, living
on oysters, crabs, and fish, and "sometimes professed to be friendly to
the whites . . . when it suited their purpose."[17]

On February 23, 1823, Karankawas ambushed three men paddling a
pirogue full of corn up the Colorado. John Alley and H. W. Law (some
accounts give his last name as Loy) died in a flurry of arrows. John C.
Clark, the third member of the party, jumped from the canoe and, de-

spite an arrow in his back, managed to swim to the other side of the river. He hid in the dense vegetation at the water's edge and stayed put, fearing the Indians would find him. The Karankawas moved on, the following day attacking and wounding a messenger they encountered on his return from San Antonio.[18]

"I am extremely sorry to inform your excellency of another Depredation committed by a party of Indians . . . on Scul [Skull] Creek upon Robert Brotherton who was at that place on business," Tumlinson reported to the governor on February 26. The alcalde added that Brotherton had been "met by the Indians robbed of his guns and perceiving he was in danger of his life after making his escape was wounded in the back with an arrow—very severely."

Robert Kuykendall led a company of twenty-five men in search of the responsible Karankawas. They found a band of the Indians camped near where Brotherton had been confronted on Skull Creek, an appropriately named stream that flowed into the Colorado in what is now Colorado County. The Texans descended on the Indians without warning, killing nineteen by one account. Hearing the shooting, Clark emerged from hiding and reported the other attack. The Anglos scalped their victims, just to make sure any other Indians got the point. Then the frontiersmen helped themselves to some of the Indians' food and carried off any of their possessions that interested them.

"I have great pleasure in informing your Excellency that the part[y] of Indians was discovered upon Scul Creek and was immediately routed," Tumlinson concluded in his next letter to the governor.[19]

One of the men taking part in the colonists' retaliatory attack was John Henry Moore, a twenty-two-year-old Tennessean who had come to Texas two years before. He later wrote:

The fight was an entire surprise. We all felt it was an act of justice and self-preservation. We were too weak [as colonists] to furnish food for Carankawaes [sic], and had to be let alone to get bread for ourselves. Ungainly and repugnant, their cannibalism being beyond question, they were obnoxious to whites, whose patience resisted with difficulty their frequent attacks upon the scanty population of the colonies, and when it passed endurance they went to their chastisement with alacrity.[20]

The process of extermination foreseen by Austin only seventeen months before had begun.

In March, Lieutenant Morrison escorted one of the men accused of the cargo theft to San Antonio for trial by Mexican authorities. In another case, Gibson Kuykendall led militiamen nearly to the Sabine River, the U.S.-Texas border, in pursuit of horse thieves. Kuykendall's party took their prisoners to San Antonio and met up with Morrison on his way back to the Colorado settlements.

The lieutenant told Kuykendall how lightly the defendant in the previous case had gotten off—he had been ordered expelled from the country—and said he thought it a waste of the time and effort to take his prisoners to San Antonio for adjudication. Gibson presented the guilty party to his uncle, who, acting in Tumlinson's absence, summarily sentenced the two horse thieves to thirty-nine lashes. After the punishment was meted out, one of the men was released. The other, considered the more serious offender, was taken before the Brazos alcalde and sentenced to another whipping.[21]

By May 5, 1823, Morrison had nine men mustered into the company authorized by Governor Trespalacios three months before. Five of them farmed, one worked as a tailor, and another did carpentry. Two other men listed farming as their primary occupation, but Morrison's muster roll showed one as a currier and one as a schoolmaster.[22] Varying in age from forty-one to twenty-three, they wore no uniforms and furnished their own arms and mounts, but were hopeful of being paid for their service. The following month Morrison wrote the governor that he had scouted the mouth of a creek (named in honor of Trespalacios) flowing into the lower Colorado, finding no suitable site for a blockhouse or enough timber to build one. His next move would be to erect a fort at the mouth of the Colorado, he said. Instilled with the U.S. army's penchant for careful record keeping, the lieutenant reported he had 162 rounds of ammunition.

The militiamen's next criminal case would be a multiple murder.

A party of seven Mexican vaqueros driving a remuda of horses from Louisiana to Mexico was attacked on May 23 by five men who had joined them for the night at their camp near the already infamous Skull Creek. Though wounded, one of the only two survivors made it back to the settlements and reported what had happened. Robert Kuykendall led six militiamen in pursuit of the brigands and the horses they had stolen. After burying the five murder victims, Kuykendall took up the outlaws' trail, soon finding that the killers had split into two groups. Catching up with one of the factions as they crossed the Brazos heading east toward Louisiana, Kuykendall and his men killed three of them—Vicente Castro, Julian Chirino, and Felix Mendosa—and recovered the stolen horses.

Hoping to discourage further outlawry along the old Spanish road, Kuykendall ordered the three dead outlaws beheaded. He then told his men to place the severed heads on posts at the edge of the road as a warning to others who might contemplate highway robbery. (Another account of this incident has only one robber posthumously decapitated, and yet another account says Kuykendall executed the men after their capture.) Kuykendall had taken a page from the Spanish doctrine of La Acordada, seeding a Ranger tradition of occasional extralegal behavior. As one of Kuykendall's kinsmen later wrote, "After these examples, the border ruffians ceased their depredations within the bounds of Austin's Colony."[23]

To do their work, of course, the militiamen needed gunpowder and lead. By summer, the men of Morrison's command—who had to live off the game they could shoot—ran low on ammunition. With the company's supply down to only enough gunpowder for 111 rounds, Tumlinson and Joseph Newman agreed to ride to San Antonio to obtain more gunpowder. On July 6, 1823, along the Guadalupe River near what would become the city of Seguin, the two men encountered a party of Wacos and Spanish army deserters. Accounts of what happened next vary, but when Tumlinson leaned down from his horse to shake hands with one of the Indians, the Indian pulled him from his saddle and killed him with a thrust of his lance. Newman escaped and reported the incident to Kuykendall.

Giving an account to the governor a week later, Kuykendall wrote:

We . . . solicit that [Morrison] and his company may be drawn from [the coast] and placed in that part of the country where they are most needed, at least for three or four months, every man in our position is essential as the upper Indians are numerous and show strong symptoms of hostilities. . . . We feel it a duty we owe our countrymen to revenge his [Tumlinson's] blood, and the time is not far distant when we will teach those savage people better sence [*sic*] than to sport with the lives of our countrymen.[24]

Compounding the problem of defending the colony from hostile Indians, the early militiamen continued to have difficulties in getting supplies, particularly gunpowder. A letter Morrison dispatched to Kuykendall on August 3, 1823, from a place he called Camp Rascal explained that "we have no powder," and he did not feel "altogether safe" in attacking a Karankawa village he had discovered. "If you would come down and join us with a party of your men immediately I think we would be able to give them a good drubbing and clear them out from our coast," the lieutenant added. "As soon as our powder comes we shall go and spye them out and know where their place of resort is so that if you come down with a party you need not be detained long."[25]

Sparing "no labor or expense"

About the time Morrison sent his express to Kuykendall, Austin rode back to the colony after sixteen months in Mexico City, where he had been attending to matters related to his land-settlement agreement with the new government. He had a lot on his mind, particularly the clear necessity of keeping his colonists safe from Indians and highwaymen. He soon began to contemplate a paid corps "to act as rangers for the common defense." Remuneration would be $15 a month "payable in property."

After noting that he had spared "no labor or expense" on behalf of his colony, the *empresario* wrote:

> I have determined to augment at my own private expense the company of men which was raised by the late Governor Trespalacios[26] for the defense of the Colony against hostile Indians. I therefore by these presents give public notice that I will employ ten men in addition to those employed by the Government to act as rangers for the common defense. The said ten men will form a part of Lieut. Moses Morrison's Company, and the whole will be subject to my orders.

The *empresario* did not date this document, but he wrote it on the back of a land document dated August 4, 1823. That was the day he returned to his colony from Mexico, but not necessarily the date he recorded his thoughts about rangers. Historian Eugene C. Barker, who arranged and edited Austin's letters about a century after the *empresario* wrote them, labeled the document "Austin's Address to the Colonists." But as later historians noted, no record has been found that Austin actually delivered it as an oration. The document may have been the draft of a lost public notice, or simply blue-sky thinking reduced to writing. Whatever it was, the 177-word document, though unsigned, would come to be considered the "Magna Carta" of the Rangers. While that may be an exaggeration, it represents the first known use of the word *ranger* in any Texas document.

Whether Austin's ten rangers ever served has never been determined. No written orders or letters concerning his "rangers for the common defense" have been found in Austin's extensive papers. Clearly, Austin had been pondering how to expand Morrison's company, probably with men already serving under the Kuykendalls. Almost as certainly, he changed his mind, concluding his best financial interest lay in Mexico footing the bill for defending his settlers, not him.

In November 1823 (Austin did not put down the day of the month), he wrote a letter almost as ambiguous as the August document. Noting that the "roads are full of errant thieves united with Indians," the *empresario* said he could not protect travelers "without a small force of mounted troops." He needed to keep in service the fourteen men he had—presumably a reference to Morrison's command even though surviving muster rolls show only ten men in the unit—"and augment them with 10 more and a Sergeant." With that additional manpower, he said, "I can respond to the security of the roads."[27]

Despite Austin's early use of the word *ranger*, the men who defended the colony—and their own families—served as volunteer militiamen. They rode horses but they fought on their feet, not in the saddle. "These early fighters were not Rangers in the sense that they bore that name or that they constituted a permanent organization or a profession," historian Walter Prescott Webb would write more than a century later.[28] But neither could these men be considered militia in the traditional sense, particularly in their use for law enforcement purposes. In fact, many of Austin's colonists had an aversion to any service that smacked of military duty, even though Mexican law made every male citizen between eighteen and fifty years old subject to serve. While answering to

Austin and the alcaldes, the men chosen as captains had broad leeway to determine their own tactics. Operational flexibility plus captains who led more than they commanded became key aspects of the ranging tradition.

The militia company authorized during Trespalacios's brief service as governor was supposed to be paid, but despite repeated entreaties by Austin, that never happened.[29] By the fall of 1823, Morrison's company had been disbanded, no blockhouses ever built, and no boats ever constructed or purchased for militia riverine duty.[30]

"For several years," historian Barker later wrote, "[militia] service was fairly burdensome, and from time to time Austin had to subdivide the original districts to permit greater flexibility and local independence in dealing with marauding tribes."[31] Colonists who did take up arms desired to protect their families, and to exact revenge, as well as abide by Mexican government mandate. The prospect of plunder—from furs to livestock—offered a less noble attraction. Only later in the history of the Rangers would salary become an incentive.

A Body of Law

Early in 1824, Austin codified a set of laws for the colony, giving the settlers their first criminal justice system and formalizing the use of militia for law enforcement purposes. Of twenty-six regulations he set down on January 24, the first five dealt with Indians. The first article empowered "all and every person" in the colony to arrest any Indian or Indians "whose conduct justifies a belief, that their intentions are to steal, or commit hostilities, or who threaten any settler, or are rude to women or children," and convey them to the nearest alcalde or militia captain. But Austin enjoined colonists to avoid "the use of arms in all cases, unless compelled to resort to them."

Should a party of Indians be too strong for a citizen to arrest them, militia captains had authority to "call out as many men as may be necessary to pursue and take said Indians prisoners, always avoiding the use of arms if possible." An alcalde or captain also could examine any captured Indians to determine if they had been rude to or "ill treated any settlers without cause or provocation." If that were found to be the case, offending Indians were to receive "any number of lashes not exceeding twenty-five" and be returned to their chiefs.[32]

On the other hand, Article 5 of Austin's code stipulated that no colonist "shall ill treat, or in any manner abuse any Indian or Indians, without just cause, under the penalty of one hundred dollars fine for the first offense, and two hundred for the second."

Specifically listing murder, robbery, and theft, Article 6 authorized "the nearest militia officer or *alcalde*" to "raise men and follow the criminal or criminals" and to use deadly force should they refuse to surrender, resist, or try to escape. If the offenders could be arrested peaceably, they were to be brought before the alcalde for trial. Those accused of serious crimes faced hard labor until they could be tried by Mexican authorities. The problem was, the closest jail stood in San Antonio and the nearest judges presided in Monterrey or Saltillo.

Punishment under this system being neither swift nor sure, colonists tended to resort to extralegal proceedings in dealing with criminals. But crimes occured infrequently. The screening of prospective newcomers had a lot to do with that. The Mexican government wanted proof of an immigrant's good character, and Austin abided by the requirement "with the utmost rigour," asking for written testimonials from officials in a prospective immigrant's hometown. If someone of "infamous character and bad conduct" did manage to make it to his colony, Austin had no qualms about expelling him.[33]

In addition to the *empresario* contract vesting him with administrative authority, Austin held a Mexican commission as lieutenant colonel of militia. As the population of his colony increased and spread, starting in December 1823 and continuing through the spring of the following year, Austin approved the formation of additional militia companies. By June 22, 1824, he had a battalion of five companies. Though he had been reluctant at first to use force against the Indians, the *empresario* resorted to arms as depredations increased, particularly on the part of the Karankawas. When Austin used his militia, the penalty for "rude treatment" of settlers by Indians usually exceeded the laying on of lashes.

An older man, a settler known to history only as White, suffered some of that rude treatment. A party of Karankawas captured White and two Mexicans near the mouth of the Colorado. The Indians said they meant to release the Mexicans, but White must die. The Indians insisted they intended to kill all Americans they found, though the Mexicans pleaded in White's behalf. White finally saved himself by convincing the Karankawas he would go buy corn from the settlers upstream and return to give it to his captors. The Indians disingenuously agreed to that, and White made his way to the nearest settlement, reporting what had happened. As colonist William Dewees recalled, "We immediately collected about thirty men, elected Captain [Jesse] Burnham, commander, and marched down to the mouth of the river."

Burnham divided the men equally into two companies and set an ambush for the Indians, who White had agreed to attract on his return by setting a prairie fire.

As Dewees wrote:

We saw a large canoe filled with Indians, about a half mile below us, coming up the river. We were ordered to keep ourselves perfectly quiet, until they had come abreast of us, and we received orders to fire. We sat for a few moments, till the canoe had arrived opposite our midst, when we received orders to fire. We fired, and succeeded in killing all but one, who jumped overboard. We, however, were so fortunate as to kill him, on firing a second time.[34]

Dewees's recollection supports that the colony's early settlers referred to militia generically as companies, the word *ranger* seldom used. Men mustered for duty when needed, farmed or tended to their trade when they were not. Governmental control increased, but the model— men furnishing their own gear and electing their leader—would stand for decades.

"The government provided for their [the settlers'] protection as best it could with the means at its disposal," pioneer Noah Smithwick recalled, "graciously permitting the citizens to protect themselves by organizing and equipping ranging companies."[35]

On August 30, 1824, Austin led a force of nearly one hundred men, including thirty armed slaves, on an expedition against the Karankawas. He divided the men into three companies and moved them down both banks of the Brazos toward the coast and the villages of his quarry. Riding ahead were men Austin called "spies," an early synonym for rangers. Those men took in the lay of the land and scouted for Indian sign. The expedition pushed the Karankawas west without a fight. At Mission La Bahia near Goliad, Austin and others executed a treaty with the Indians, who agreed to stay west of the San Antonio River and not molest his colonists.[36]

The treaty did not hold long. On September 10, 1825, Austin wrote a Mexican official, Mateo Ahumada:

> In consequence of the continuous hostilities of the [Karankawas], and considering the treaty of peace we made with them . . . was broken by them without any cause whatever . . . I have been compelled in view of the security of our people to give positive orders to the Lieutenant of the Militia . . . to pursue and kill all those Indians wherever they are found.[37]

An address Austin gave in the spring of 1826 further reflected his position in regard to the Indians:

> The depredations of your enemies the W. [Waco] and T. [Tawakonis] Indians and their hostile preparations, has driven us to the necessity of taking up arms in self defense. . . . The frontier is menaced—The whole colony is threatened—under these circumstances it became my duty to call the militia to the frontier to repel the threatened attacks and to teach our enemies to fear and respect us.[38]

"Spies, or frontier guard"

With input from "a meeting of the people," Austin proposed on August 28, 1826, a detailed plan for reorganizing the colony's militia. The *empresario* wrote the latest Mexican official in charge of the province to suggest that the militia be grouped into twelve sections, "one section to be sent to the frontier every month, to do duty as spies, or frontier guard." He went on, "The object of the plan is to keep twenty or thirty mounted men continually on the frontier as spies; as well for the preventing of incursions of small parties of Indians, as to give timely notice should they come in force to make a formal attack."[39] Mexico had turned down requests for regular troops before, and there is no evidence Austin's concept of a larger militia and Ranger service got anywhere. As it was, by the summer of 1826 he had 565 men on the militia muster rolls, available when needed.

That winter, a company under Aylett "Strap" Buckner—a redheaded Virginian of Scottish-Irish ancestry who had been in Texas off and on since 1812—rode in pursuit of Indians who had massacred two families near Elliott's Crossing on the Colorado. To size up the Indians before the attack, the former lieutenant Morrison, now serving as a militiaman under Buckner, crawled out on a ledge overlooking the river and the Karankawas. The ledge crumbled and Morrison found himself on the riverbank, brushing off the sandy soil and surrounded by the Indians. Seeing what had happened, Buckner ordered a charge, and he and his men saved Morrison. Thirty warriors died in the fight that followed, the highest body count in any of the militia-Karankawa encounters.[40]

Another of the Kuykendall brothers, Abner, received a commission from Austin in February 1827 to muster eight men to "range the country between the Colorado and Brazos on the San Antonio road, in order to detect any inroad of the Waco or other northern tribe." He raised the men, the muster roll including two of his kinfolk.[41]

While Kuykendall and his rangers kept a lookout for Indians, more than four hundred other colonists marched under Austin toward Nacogdoches to assist a force of regular Mexican troops in putting down a short-lived separatist movement that came to be called the Fredonia Rebellion. But before Austin's militia reached the old Spanish town near the Louisiana border, the instigators fled across the Sabine and the armed colonists returned to their homes.

Whether men like the Kuykendalls considered themselves militiamen or rangers is unknowable, and the latter-day parsing of definitions is primarily an exercise in semantics. The descendants of those colonial Indian fighters certainly consider their forebears rangers, and not a few of them, such as the Tumlinsons, took up the same line of work. Newspapers of the era generally saw those men as militia, and their surviving official paperwork has a martial tone, but *militia* did not endure as a common word in the written recollections of men and women of Texas's Anglo colonial period. Early Texans viewed those men as Indian fighters and sometimes lawmen who played by their own rules in protecting the colony, romanticizing their role while tending to overlook or gloss over their abuses or failures.[42]

"We learn that the Carancawa [*sic*] Indians have lately made an attack on some of the inhabitants of Austin's Colony and killed one person," the

Natchitoches *Courier* reported on April 3, 1827, "when the Militia turned out in pursuit of the Indians and killed thirteen of them. These Indians have been at war with the inhabitants for some time past, in which their numbers have been so reduced that they give the settlers very little trouble at present."[43]

In less than a decade, bullets and disease had driven the Karankawas almost to extinction. The Wacos, Tawakonis, and other tribes continued to present occasional problems, but the settlers along the Brazos and Colorado had some elbow room, albeit bought with blood. To the west, though, lay land still firmly controlled by the Comanches, a culture that would prove more fierce, and far more tenacious, than the Karankawas.

"It is said by some who have been among the Commanchas [Comanches] that they have between five and six thousand Warriors," the Natchitoches *Courier* reported. "These Indians have been at war with [the] Spaniards ever since they have been in the country, but their warfare has been of late, carried on by small parties, whose principal object is plunder."[44]

As the end of the decade approached, another American secured a contract to introduce colonists to Mexico. Green DeWitt had a colony along the Guadalupe River, west of Austin's settlement. He also operated a militia, and also like Austin he sometimes used the word *ranger* in writing. On March 3, 1829, DeWitt wrote Austin to inform him of "outrages on the people of this colony" on the part of Indians and proposed a joint effort to raise and support a "Company of Rangers, or the public troops," to patrol their frontiers. Whether that happened is not known.[45]

From Mexico's point of view, a more serious new threat had arisen. By 1830, an estimated seven thousand Anglos and their slaves lived in Texas. Most Texans, including Austin, remained loyal to Mexico. But a few spoke for independence, a movement that soon gained momentum. The possibility of rebellion, however, was not Mexico's only concern. Its own government struggled in chaos, federalists challenged by centralists. Texans who cared about such things tended to lean toward the federalist side, since it had adopted in 1824 a constitution similar to the United States' organic law. In 1834, however, the other side carried the day and a centralist military officer, Antonio López de Santa Anna, assumed virtual dictatorial power. Problems with Indians in Texas would continue no matter who occupied the halls of government in distant Mexico City, but with the emergence of the centralists, trouble lay ahead like smoldering powder in a misfired rifle.

2

"Chastising . . . menaces to civilised man"

AN ARM OF GOVERNMENT, 1835—37

Daniel Parker, a rough-hewn man with a penetrating gaze, found political oratory not all that different from preaching. Both endeavors aimed at getting a man to change his thinking. Nor did the fifty-one-year-old Primitive Baptist, a spirited antagonist in theological squabbles, lack experience in espousing an unpopular opinion. Born in Virginia, raised in Georgia, and living in Tennessee as a young preacher, Parker had seen slavery firsthand. He opposed it. In Illinois, he argued with equal fervor against slavery and the growing Baptist missionary movement.

After coming to Texas, Parker spoke against revolution. Rising to address the rowdy assemblage of independence-minded Texans gathered at the log-cabin village of San Felipe in the fall of 1835 to organize a provisional government—many of them hungover from the previous night's revelry—Parker urged a peaceful course. He and other members of his family lived on land given them by the Republic of Mexico as part of its effort to encourage Anglo-American settlement in its northernmost province. He had no bone to pick with its government.

"The liberality of Mexico in her dealings with the colonists [has been] unparalleled in the annals of time," Parker said. "To the head of each family a league of land [4,428.4 acres] was given; exemption from all taxes, custom duties, etc. for ten years. To what land could they have turned for a more liberal tender?"[1]

While some may have agreed with Parker's sentiments, for all practical purposes the revolution had already begun. Mexican general Martin Perfecto de Cos had landed troops at Copano Bay on the mid-Texas coast on September 20, 1835, and marched to reinforce his country's small garrison at San Antonio. On October 2, an effort by a nervous Mexican military officer to reclaim a small cannon issued to the citizenry of Gonzales for self-defense had resulted in shooting, an incident soon heralded as the "Lexington" of Texas.

Parker did not favor war with Mexico, but he fervently believed in the force of arms. While perfectly willing to abide by God's will in all matters, he held just as firmly to the biblical teaching that God helped those who helped themselves. He would be the prime mover in the creation of a corps of Rangers by Texas's provisional government, his motivation both altruistic and self-serving. The summer before, in 1834, Parker's elderly father, his brothers, and other members of the family had settled on land near the Navasota River in Sterling C. Robertson's colony.[2] Being well beyond any other settlements, the Parkers cut timber and raised a twelve-foot-high stockade with two blockhouses on opposing corners. Inside the four-acre compound they built sturdy hewn-oak cabins. The family trusted that their walled fort, their weapons, and their faith would keep them safe from Indians on the exposed edge of the Texas frontier.

The Parkers and many other Anglo Texans had fathers or grandfathers who fought the British or Indians or both during the American Revolution. Just as an earlier generation had done in the thirteen original American colonies, the scattered centers of population in Texas as early as 1832 had begun organizing local Committees of Safety and Correspondence. Those committees primarily concerned themselves with defense from hostile Indians, but serving as information clearinghouses, they amounted to a first step toward self government.[3]

Though Parker would be a significant figure in the development of the Rangers, another man with equally strong convictions led the first Ranger company fielded by Texas's provisional government as the Mexican province moved closer to open rebellion. Brave but contentious, Robert Morris Coleman had come to Texas from Kentucky in 1831. Granted twenty-four labors (a Spanish measure, one labor equaled 177 acres) in Robertson's colony in what is now Lee County, the thirty-six-year-old Coleman did not shy from expressing his opinions or resorting to steel or lead in backing up his beliefs.

In the late spring of 1835, Coleman joined a volunteer force under Edward Burleson, a member of the committee of safety for Bastrop (for a few years called Mina), a community on the Colorado where El Camino Real crossed the river. A War of 1812 veteran who had settled in Texas in 1830, Burleson had been a lieutenant colonel of militia since 1832. He quickly established a reputation as a tenacious Indian fighter, but Coleman soon demonstrated an even sharper edge.

Burleson's company, augmented by men from La Grange under seasoned Indian fighter John Henry Moore, rode out on June 1 to find the Indians who had killed a Bastrop man and his son. Moore, thirty-five and married, had settled on a half league of land fronting the Colorado River at La Grange and built a double log blockhouse known as Moore's Fort. Adroit at telling a humorous tale, he had a more serious side, as evidenced by his wont to stand near the preacher in church during the sermon, sternly looking out at the congregants to make sure they stayed awake. Moore viewed Indians as Philistines in need of destruction. Sixty-one men strong, the Burleson-Moore contingent moved up the Little River in present Bell County scouting for sign.

About fifty miles above the Falls of the Brazos, a hunting party from Burleson's command ran onto a lone Caddo. The men brought the Indian, who made no attempt at flight or fight, to the colonel for questioning. The Caddo readily revealed the location of his fellow travelers. Burleson dispatched some men to find the Indian camp, which they soon did. The ranking member of the party identified himself as Canoma, a friendly Caddo who had assisted the Texans in trying to negotiate treaties with more hostile tribes. But when the volunteers discovered that the Caddos had two shod horses in their possession, they took the Indians prisoner.

Coleman practiced law when not trailing Indians, but he saw no need for trial by jury in dealing with the captives. To his mind, that the Caddos had two horses with forged metal on their hooves proved them guilty not only of horse theft, but of the recent double murder of the two Bastrop men. Canoma said he had collected the horses as strays, but Coleman thought otherwise and favored summary execution. A more reasoned volunteer prevented Coleman from immediate action, and

Burleson promised the Indians a fair trial in Bastrop. But Burleson and his officers could not control Coleman and the other hotheads in the ranging company.

With a slight nod to democracy, the volunteers put the matter to a vote. Forty rangers approved killing all the prisoners except for Canoma's wife, with only twenty-one men favoring less drastic action. Coleman cheerfully joined the firing squad.[4]

Back in Bastrop after avenging—at least in his mind—the deaths of the two local residents, Coleman received a commission from the committee of safety as "Captain of Mounted Riflemen." He entered service with command of his own company on June 12, 1835. The firebrand Kentuckian rode from Bastrop on July 2, having recruited a company of twenty-five men "for the purpose of chastising those menaces to civilised man," Indians who had perpetrated "wanton outrages . . . not only upon our frontier, but in the midst of our settlements." Two days later, Coleman and his men crossed the Brazos River at the new town of Washington, on the La Bahia (Goliad) road, scouting for Indians.

On July 9, Coleman's company encountered some one hundred Tonkawas, Caddos, and Ionis near Tehuacana Springs in present Limestone County. "We had a severe battle," he reported. "One fourth of my men killed & wounded. We took their encampment by a charge & the battle ended." Outnumbered four to one, Coleman retreated to nearby Fort Parker, the Parker family's wilderness settlement.[5]

From Fort Parker, Coleman rode to Sarahville de Viesca, the Robertson colony capital, where on July 20 he wrote Henry Rueg, political chief of the province's Department of Nacogdoches. Declaring that the Indians "must be chastised or this flourishing country abandoned, and again become a wilderness," the captain proposed levying a "general Tax on the citizens of Texas" to fund a force of two hundred men to be stationed in four garrisons of fifty men each "high up on the different rivers" and "under . . . a man calculated to command."[6] The Mexican government had no interest in collecting taxes to better arm its Anglo citizens, but Coleman's suggestion reflected an early awareness of a perennial Ranger problem: lack of funding.

As word of Coleman's bloody fight spread, the settlers raised four volunteer ranging companies to pursue the Indians. The rangers left Tenoxtitlan on July 31 for Fort Parker, where the men elected Moore as colonel in charge of all the companies, a unit considered the first Ranger battalion. The rangers, joined in late August by Coleman and his company, spent the rest of the summer in the field, traveling as far north as the forks of the Trinity River, the present location of Dallas. They seized corn, peas, pumpkins, and watermelons at a hastily abandoned Indian village they found on the Navasota River, but as one participant later wrote, the "main body of Indians was never overtaken; but . . . there was some skirmishing. The Texan forces kept daily diminishing, and in two months the expedition closed." Even so, most Anglos in the province saw Ranger companies as the best remedy for hostile Indians.[7]

That fall, one day after delegates convened as a Permanent Council in San Felipe pending the arrival of more members in two weeks, a resolution presented on October 17 by Daniel Parker authorized three Ranger superintendents to organize a seventy-man Ranger force. Each superintendent shouldered responsibility for one company of ten to thirty-five men plus providing their ammunition. One of the trio of superintendents would be Daniel's brother, Silas M. Parker. Rangers elected their own officers, but they reported to the superintendent.

"To secure the inhabitants on the frontiers from the invasions of the Hostile Indians," the *Telegraph and Texas Register* reported on October 26, "the General Council has made arrangements for raising three companies of Rangers."

With the arrival at San Felipe of additional delegates, the council reconvened on November 1 at what its members called a consultation, a description thought not as inflammatory to Mexican authorities as the word *convention*. Fifty-eight of ninety-eight credentialed delegates had shown up by November 4, allowing for a quorum. The problem of frontier defense loomed as only one of several major issues facing the members. The biggest was the situation with Mexico. But the men gathered in San Felipe also had to design a government, settle on the extent of its powers, and choose leaders.

Three different resolutions on the first, sixth, and ninth of November further refined the Ranger organization proposed by Parker. Men volunteering for service would be paid $1.25 a day. Each of the three companies would report their activities to their superintendent every fifteen days. The superintendents, in turn, had to send a rider in with a report for the council every thirty days.[8]

After approving a middle-of-the-road measure to establish a provisional government along the lines of the popular 1824 Mexican constitution, the delegates on November 13 agreed to an interim
governmental structure they called the Organic Law. Unlike the time-
proven system of government by checks and balances in place in the
neighboring United States, the Organic Law passed by the Texans vested
more power in the executive than in the legislative or judicial branch.
That would make for problems, but the Texans had taken another step
toward self-government.

On November 15, by a vote of thirty to twenty-two, the council
chose Kentuckian Henry Smith as "supreme Executive of the free and
sovereign state of Texas." His father had been a friend of Daniel Boone's,
and Smith favored blazing a new trail in Texas: independence from
Mexico. In delivering his first message to the council, Smith made fourteen major points, the fifth of which concerned the Rangers. Noting
that provisions had been made for a corps of rangers, he continued, "I
conceive it highly important that you should place a bold, energetic and
enterprising commander at their head. This corps well managed, will
prove a safeguard to our hitherto unprotected frontier inhabitants, and
prevent the depredations of those savage hordes that infest our borders."
In addition to most Indians' well-known aversion to Texans, Smith
noted that "the Mexican authorities have endeavored to engage them in a
war with us."[9] Smith also drew a clear distinction between a Ranger corps
and militia, which he said should also be organized as soon as possible.

"THERE SHALL BE A CORPS OF RANGERS . . ."

With Smith wielding the gavel, the delegates formalized the development of the Rangers on November 24, 1835 in passing an "Ordinance
Establishing a Provisional Government." First put down on paper by a
three-man committee on November 13, the ordinance included twenty-
one articles and an appendage styled "Of the Military." Article 9 of this
portion of the ordinance declared, "There shall be a corps of rangers under the command of a major." Other articles in the military section created a regular army as well as a militia. The framers of this ordinance
clearly envisioned the Rangers as an irregular force, distinct from traditional military units or volunteer citizen soldiers. The corps would con-
sist of three or more companies of fifty-six men each, rangers serving

one-year enlistments.[10] Rangers would furnish their own horse and tack, weapons, and powder and shot for one hundred rounds. Each company would be headed by a captain, backed up by a first and second lieutenant. The captains reported to a major. The major answered to the commander in chief of the regular army.

While the action taken by the men attending the consultation at San Felipe demonstrated how important they felt a ranging corps was to the defense of Texas, from the Mexican point of view what the delegates did amounted to rebellion. Four months earlier, preparing to move troops across the Rio Grande into Texas, Brigadier General Cos had published a broadside in Matamoras articulating his government's increasing concern over developments in the province. "If the Mexican Government has cheerfully lavished upon the new settlers all its worthiness of regard," Cos wrote, "it will likewise know how to repress with strong arm all those who, forgetting their duties to the nation which has adopted them as her children, are pushing forward with a desire to live at their own option without any subjection to the laws."[11]

Even as the provisional government's printer set in type the documents authorizing a Ranger corps "for the free and sovereign state of Texas," General Antonio Lopez de Santa Anna—having brutally crushed another separatist movement in the state of Zacatecas—busied himself with the organization of an army to put down this Anglo uprising. In the general's view, the Texans forging their own government amounted to pirates, not patriots. He intended to treat them as such.[12]

One of the members of the consultation, a body renamed the General Council after the passage of the Organic Law, was Robert McAlpin Williamson, a thirty-one-year-old Georgia-born newspaper publisher and lawyer. He had come to San Felipe in 1826 via Alabama and Louisiana after killing a man in a duel over a woman. In addition to whatever legal work he could do, from 1829 to 1831 he put out one of Texas's earliest newspapers, *The Cotton Plant*. Stricken as a teenager by a disease that left his lower right leg bent back at the knee, Williamson wore a wooden leg. In Texas, the prosthetic earned him a nickname—Three-Legged Willie. But his handicap did not impair his horsemanship or his skill with fists, knife, pistol, or rifle. He also showed himself to be as proficient at arguing a point of law before the bar of justice as he was leaning against another sort of bar and knocking back a tumbler of whiskey.

Three months before the General Council convened, Williamson had headed one of the ranger companies participating in Moore's fifty-day expedition into the heart of Indian country. Well aware of Williamson's experience and his attitude, on November 28 fellow members of the consultation elected him as major of the Rangers. William W. Arrington, Isaac W. Burton, and John J. Tumlinson won election as company captains. Officers, in addition to the per diem pay of privates, would be paid the same as officers in the U.S. Army Regiment of Dragoons. The companies would be based in Bastrop, Gonzales, and Milam.

On December 1, Smith passed on to the General Council a letter from Williamson. Smith said he had "concluded to accept" the "individuals named therein," presumably the men who would head the Ranger companies. "It is all important that the corps should be forthwith in service," he wrote.[13]

As Williamson organized the new Ranger corps, the provisional government's Federal Volunteer Army of Texas shouldered arms in San Antonio, where General Cos had been besieged since November. A Kentucky immigrant named Ben Milam finally succeeded in galvanizing an indecisive and dwindling Texas force into action, rallying them with "Who will go with old Ben Milam into San Antonio?" Those willing to "go with Old Ben" attacked Cos's troops on December 5, the beginning of a five-day battle that reclaimed the town and sent Cos in retreat and disgrace toward the Rio Grande. Milam inspired the victory but did not live to see it, falling with a Mexican musket ball in his head on the third day of the attack.[14]

"THERE WAS A SUSPICIOUS MOISTURE IN MANY AN EYE . . ."

One of the men who took part in the Mexican defeat was Ranger captain Tumlinson, the son of the alcalde killed by an Indian in 1823. After the fight, Tumlinson left San Antonio for Bastrop, where he began recruiting a new Ranger company. Enlisting in January 1836 was North Carolina–born, Tennessee-raised Noah Smithwick, a gunsmith who had been in Texas since 1827. Decades later, a nearly blind Smithwick wrote, with considerable help from his daughter, a memoir that constitutes most of what is known about the Rangers of the mid-1830s.

"We were assigned to duty on the head waters of Brushy creek, some thirty miles northwest of the site of the present capital," Smithwick wrote. "The appointed rendezvous was Hornsby's station, ten miles below Austin on the Colorado, from which place we were to proceed at once to our post, taking with us such materials as were necessary to aid us in the construction of a block house."[15]

The rangers arrived on time and settled into camp.

"Just as we were preparing for our supper," he continued, "a young white woman, an entire stranger, her clothes hanging in shreds about her torn and bleeding body, dragged herself into camp and sank exhausted on the ground. The feeling of rest and relief on finding herself among friends able and willing to help her, so overcame her overtaxed strength that it was some little time before she could give a coherent explanation of her situation."

The tearful woman, Sarah Hibbins, told the rangers a grim story. Her family had been attacked by Comanches on their way to their homestead on the Guadalupe River. The warriors killed her husband and her brother and took her prisoner along with her infant and three-year-old son, John. The Indians left the scene of the attack after tying Sarah, babe in arms, to one of the mules that had been pulling their wagon. Her son straddled the other mule. They rode to the northwest, their normal range well beyond the settlements. Soon the young mother experienced further horror—the loss of her baby.

"The poor little creature," Smithwick continued, "whose suffering the mother could not allay, cried so continuously that at length one of the Indians snatched it from her and dashed its brains out against a tree."

The Indians and their two captives made it to the point on the Colorado that would eventually become the city of Austin. When a strong norther blew in, the Comanches wrapped themselves in warm buffalo robes, bedded down for the night in a cedar brake, and went to sleep. They left their white woman captive unguarded, confident that she could not escape. While her captors slept, Mrs. Hibbins agonized over her slim choices. She dared not travel with her son, yet her only chance of saving them both lay in escaping and returning with help. She tucked her sleeping boy into a robe and slipped silently out of camp into the cold, dark night.

Covering her tracks as best she could, she followed the river, working steadily downstream to where the settlements lay. After a long, cold flight during the night and into the following day, she came up on several grazing milk cows. She realized settlers must live nearby, but fearful that the Indians might be trailing her, she did not call out for help. Instead, she hid until evening. Then, she knew, the cows would amble home. The cows did as expected, and following them, she soon discovered the ranger camp.

Moved by her story, Tumlinson ordered his men to saddle up. With Ruben Hornsby as their guide, the rangers rode most of the night, stopping only to rest their horses and get a few hours' sleep.

Not long after daylight on January 20, the rangers struck an Indian trail. The tracks led to a camp on Walnut Creek, where about nine o'clock that morning the rangers caught the Indians by surprise.

"I threw Lieut. Joseph Rogers, with eight men, below them—and with the others I dashed past and took possession of their route above them," Tumlinson later wrote. "The Indians saw that the route above and below them was in our possession, and struck off for the mountain thicket nearest the side of the trail. I ordered Lieut. [Joseph] Rogers to charge, and fell upon them simultaneously."[16]

Excited by the shooting, Smithwick's horse carried its rider right into the bunched Indians. One of them came out from behind a tree and leveled his musket at Smithwick, but the shot went wild.

"Unable to control my horse, I jumped off . . . and gave chase to my assailant on foot, knowing his gun was empty," Smithwick recalled. "I fired on him and had the satisfaction of seeing him fall. My blood was up and, leaving him for dead, I ran on, loading my rifle as I ran, hoping to bring down another."[17]

But the Indian still had life in him. He raised up and fired at Tumlinson. The bullet punched a hole in the captain's coat and then killed his horse. Ranger Conrad Rhorer grabbed the empty rifle from the Comanche and beat his brains out with the butt of the weapon.[18]

Counting the warrior Smithwick shot and Rhorer finished off (for good measure, he also scalped the Comanche), the twenty rangers killed four of the thirteen Indians in the fight. Two rangers suffered wounds—one shot in his arm, the other taking a bullet in a leg. Though the rest of the Comanches escaped, the rangers recovered the captured boy. The rescue, however, had been a close call. When the mule the boy had been tied to fled in terror during the fight, Rhorer shot twice at the child, mistaking him for an Indian. Each time his rifle misfired. With Rhorer about to try a third shot, another ranger realized the small figure on the mule was the little boy they sought, not one of his captors. Before Rhorer could squeeze the trigger again, his fellow ranger pushed his rifle aside, probably saving the child's life.

Collecting the Indians' horses and other plunder as the smoke cleared, the rangers rode back to Hornsby's Station. Tumlinson sent a detachment under his lieutenant to ride ahead with the child and brought up the rear with his wounded. The captain made the trip astride the best of the captured ponies, the prize selected and presented to him by his men.

"There was a suspicious moisture in many an eye long since a stranger to tears, when the overjoyed mother clasped her only remaining treasure to her heart," Smithwick concluded.

"Not an eye was dry," Tumlinson admitted in his later recollection of that day. "She [Mrs. Hibbins] called us brothers, and every other endearing name, and would have fallen on her knees to worship us. She hugged her child to her bosom as if fearful that she would again lose him. And—but tis useless to say more."[19]

Overshadowed by the revolution, the incident did not get much attention at the time, not even making the public prints. Nor has any official report of this engagement come to light. In later years, however, the rescue would be recognized as a prime example of what rangers could do for the people along the frontier. The published recollections of two of the participants, Smithwick and Tumlinson, preserved the essential details of the story, saving it from obscurity.

Despite Tumlinson's successful rescue of the Hibbins boy, Major Williamson had trouble recruiting rangers. The more contentious Texans preferred taking on Mexicans to scouting after Indians, though Robertson still had his own ranging company in the field. Remaining inside the boundary of the colony, the unit had no connection to the Ranger companies authorized by the provisional government. Other eligible men, perceiving no immediate threat from Indians and having no grievance with Mexico, seemed content to stay at home with their families. Because of that, Tumlinson had only thirty-four men, considerably below authorized strength. Worried, Williamson rode for San Felipe to plead for more money, hoping the prospect of better pay would net him more rangers.[20]

But the shaky provisional government had little money and less clout. For all practical purposes, Texas drifted in anarchy. Smith still held himself forth as governor, but the council hoped to see him tried for treason and had declared lieutenant governor James W. Robinson as his successor.[21] One faction of the council wanted to continue as a Mexican province under the constitution of 1824, while the hawks wanted full independence for Texas. No one person or group had full control of the volunteers-in-arms—what passed for a regular army and the Rangers. In fact, the Rangers largely existed only on paper, troubled by low pay, little money for supplies, and internal politics.

A week before the rescue of the Hibbins child, Acting Governor Robinson made a case for the Rangers. "The defenceless [sic] situation of our oppressed country call for your prompt attention and speedy relief," he wrote.

> Surrounded on one side by hordes of merciless savages, brandishing the tomahawk and scalping knife, recently red with human gore; and on the other by the less merciful glittering spear and ruthless sword of the descendants of Cortes, and his modern Goths and Vandals, make it in my opinion your paramount duty as a Council, to remain permanently in session until the Convention meets, as there is no other authority to provide for the speedy organization of the ranging corps, and particularly for the security and protection of the inhabitants of the frontier of Red River, where no force is yet stationed or raised.

Robinson suggested raising and "officering" detachments of rangers "from the inhabitants of the frontier where they are designed to range." He said he had little doubt that staffing the Rangers that way would "increase the activity and vigilance of the corps and promote their harmony."[22]

Led by Don Carlos Barrett of Bastrop, a committee of the General Council on February 4 sent the acting governor a report on the matter. Whoever wrote it down in ink could not spell very well, but the document got the point across: "This committee have Recd certain and correct information that A Law by the General Convention in November 1835 for the Organization of A Corpse [sic] of Rangers has tottaly [sic] failed of the disined [sic] effect." The committee reported that because of low pay, men could not be found to serve as rangers. Further, those who might be interested in enlisting did not like that they could not elect their own officers, an aberration from tradition.

"This Committee viewing it as A Matter of the first importance that our frontiers should be all means [be] procted [sic] from the incursions of hostile Indians and seeing no probability that A Core [sic] of Rangers will be Raised are clearly of the opinion that some prompt and decisive measures should be Adopted," the report continued.

Committee members then outlined a relatively complicated system whereby three commissioners would be appointed in the Gonzales and Milam districts, each charged with raising a fifty-six man company. The committee further laid out a method for the election of officers and set the pay at $1.25 a day for the services of privates "and that of his horse and arms and Ammunitions" plus $5 monthly for provisions. Captains would earn $60 a month, lieutenants $55, and second lieutenants $50.[23]

With General Santa Anna marching an army toward San Antonio, the provisional government had greater concerns. Still, no one could argue the need for rangers. "Having learned with regret of Indian depredations and murders committed on our frontiers," the committee in mid-February sent Robinson a series of orders for him to forward to Williamson. The major should maintain his headquarters at Bastrop, the westernmost settlement in Texas, while proceeding "to the frontier [to] make arrangements for the building [of] blockhouses and fortifications . . . at such points as he deem best calculated for the protection of the frontiers." Williamson needed to bring the "Ranging Corps" up to strength as soon as possible, the orders continued, reporting any vacancies to the governor and General Council. In addition, the committee instructed the major to arrange for a contractor to supply the corps with provisions.

The committee, through the acting governor, gave Williamson authority, "in case of emergency, or prospect of general engagement . . . to call on the mounted volunteers, to call out the militia of the county, and to concentrate his command at such points as may be necessary for the protection of the frontier." Complying with orders relayed by Williamson, Tumlinson and his men built a log blockhouse on Brushy Creek near what is now Leander, in present Williamson County. While those rangers guarded against Comanche incursions, the vanguard of Santa Anna's army reached San Antonio.

The Men from Gonzales

Whether acting on the February 4 committee report or simply in urgency, Williamson had gone to Gonzales to raise a ranger company. On February 25, a day after the formation of the Gonzales Ranging Company of Mounted Volunteers, a rider from Bexar brought a letter from Colonel William Barrett Travis reporting the arrival of advance elements of the Mexican army. Outnumbered, Travis and Jim Bowie had moved their men into an old Spanish mission popularly known as the Alamo. Williamson immediately issued a plea for assistance and dispatched a letter to Tumlinson ordering him to leave the frontier and reinforce the Alamo.

In Gonzales, Thomas R. Miller had joined the ranger company without hesitation. Until recently, he had all a man could hope for. One of the wealthiest men in town, at forty-one, the Tennessean owned a flourishing mercantile business and a productive farm. For sixteen months, he also had the fulfilling companionship of a teenage wife, a pretty Kentuckian named Sidney Gaston. But then his fortunes turned. The couple's only child died in infancy, and in the summer of 1833, Sidney left Miller for nineteen-year-old John Benjamin Kellough, a fellow Kentuckian.

His wife gone and a baby lying in a small grave in the town cemetery, Miller had no particular reason to stay in Gonzales when the call for help came from Travis. When George Kimball and Albert Martin gathered the newly formed ranger company on the town's public square about two o'clock that Saturday, Miller saddled up and threw in with the rangers. So did the teenager who had stolen his wife.[24]

Better known simply as "the men from Gonzales," the volunteers who rode to the aid of the besieged Texans in the Alamo did not fall under the command of Major Williamson and his widely scattered Corps of Rangers. But the men were rangers in the sense that they were mounted irregulars operating with governmental authority to meet an exigency. More important, they considered themselves rangers and stood ready to fight.

Twenty-two Gonzales men (some accounts say twenty-five) rode hard for Bexar, seventy miles to the west. Picking up a few more volunteers along the way, they arrived late at night on February 29. About one o'clock on the morning of March 1, they galloped inside the Alamo to the cheers of the weary defenders. Five days later Santa Anna's troops succeeded in storming the fortress, and the Gonzales rangers died to a man, along with all the other Texas combatants.

One of the 180-plus men killed in the unsuccessful defense of the old mission was George W. Tumlinson, Captain John Tumlinson's cousin. The Ranger captain might have died with his kin, but his orders from Williamson to proceed to the Alamo had been countermanded either by Burleson or General Sam Houston. Instead of going to San Antonio, Tumlinson had abandoned the log fort on Brushy Creek and returned to Bastrop.

When families learned the fate of the Alamo garrison, they began fleeing eastward toward the United States in advance of the Mexican army. Williamson divided his command, sending some rangers with the evacuees, leaving a few in Bastrop, and ordering the others to collect stray cattle to keep them from being used as food by the Mexican army. Some rangers chose to leave with their families, including Tumlinson and his first lieutenant, Joseph Rogers.[25]

With Anglo Texas unraveling like so much frayed homespun, most members of the Corps of Rangers had scattered. Left with only a small command, Williamson kept in touch with Houston via couriers and established headquarters at Washington-on-the-Brazos. The major in charge of the Rangers dealt harshly with looters and hanged two Mexican army deserters, an act that met the strong disproval of Houston and his secretary of war, Thomas J. Rusk. On April 13, Houston ordered Williamson back to his army "forthwith," but told him to keep his spies in the field.[26]

Eight days later, on April 21, Williamson participated in the eighteen-minute Texas rout of Santa Anna's army, the turning point of the revolution. Former Ranger captain John Tumlinson, his brother Joe, and two cousins also took part in the battle as privates in Houston's army, avenging the death of their relative in the Alamo. Former rangers Burton and Coleman fought at San Jacinto as well, along with two brothers whose names would be prominent in Ranger history, Ben and Henry E. McCulloch.[27]

Before, during, and after the revolution, the difference between ranger and regular army soldier was as thin as foolscap. The one exception was that rangers, generally tending to be more experienced, usually handled scouting or "spy" duties for the military. After San Jacinto, Williamson reorganized the Rangers as the provisional Texas government made another effort to separate the force from the regular army.[28]

"Good Lord, Dwight, you are not a going to run?"

As word of Houston's victory spread, the settlers who had rushed eastward after the Alamo began returning to their homesteads. The Parker
clan, which included eight families, had made it only as far as the Trinity River, where high water had kept them from crossing. But when
they learned of San Jacinto, they returned to their stockaded cabins near
the Navasota. Confident that their log fort offered ample protection, the
families set about getting a crop in and going on with their lives. For a
few weeks, as one nineteenth-century writer later put it, they enjoyed
"a life of Arcadian simplicity, virtue and contentment."

About nine o'clock in the morning on May 19, ten of the men and
more able boys left the fort to work in the fields. The other adults went
about their chores as their children enjoyed their play on what promised
to be a pleasant spring day. Mrs. Rachel Plummer, James W. Parker's
daughter, divided her time between work and watching her young son.
Her father, husband, and older son were among those working outside
the fort's walls.

"Indians!" Mrs. Plummer suddenly heard someone yell. "Indians!"
The settlers in the fort, "in a state of confusion," looked toward a rise
about a quarter mile away. Stretched out in a long line, hundreds of Indians sat silently on their horses. Mrs. Plummer watched as the Indians
rode slowly toward the fort, a white cloth tied to an upraised lance.

Not trusting the Indians, most of the men and women ran from the
fort, hoping to hide in the woods or perhaps catch a horse.

"Good Lord, Dwight, you are not a going to run?" Silas Parker asked
G. E. Dwight.

"No," Dwight replied, "I am going to take the women and children
to the woods."

"Stand and fight like a man," Parker said, but Dwight left, promising he would be back. Mrs. Plummer started to run to her father, husband, and son. But then she thought of her two-year-old son, John Pratt,
realizing she should not risk taking him outside the fort. As Silas
Parker, Samuel Frost, and his son Robert fetched their rifles and shot
pouches, Benjamin Parker strode out to meet the Indians, now only two
hundred yards from the fort.

"In a few moments uncle Benjamin came back to the Fort," Mrs.
Plummer continued, "and told those who were in the Fort, that he was

convinced that the Indians intended to fight, and told the people in the Fort to put everything in the best possible order."

Against Silas's advice, Benjamin walked back outside, hoping to forestall trouble by offering the Indians beef. "I know they will kill him," Silas said, "but I will be good for one, any way."

Hearing that, Rachel decided to take her chances outside the fort with most of the others. Clutching her toddler in her arms, she ran out the smaller back gate. Passing the corner of the fort, she could see that the Indians had gathered around her uncle Benjamin. "I saw them stabbing their spears into [him] and shooting him with their arrows," she recalled.

A warrior soon overtook the fleeing mother and struck her with a hoe, knocking her senseless. She came to with an Indian dragging her by her hair. "I heard one or two shots," she remembered, "and am confident that I heard uncle Silas shout a most triumphant huzza, as tho' he had thousands to back him."

In addition to Benjamin and Isaac Parker and the Frosts, the Indians killed seventy-year-old John Parker, the patriarch of the clan. The attackers also wounded three women, leaving them for dead. The Indians captured Rachel and her son, along with Elizabeth Kellog and two of Silas Parker's children, six-year-old John and his older sister, a blue-eyed eight-year-old named Cynthia Ann. After scalping their victims and ransacking the fort, the Indians rode off with their captives, studding the settlers' cattle with arrows as they left.

The men, women, and children who survived the Fort Parker attack hid in the dense foliage of the nearby river bottom until the Indians had gone. Then, led by James Parker, they started for the closest settlement, Fort Houston. A smaller party of survivors had been rescued earlier.

Mrs. Plummer, who spent thirteen months with the Indians before being ransomed to Mexican traders, never publicly revealed the full details of what she and the other captives endured. "I am confident it can be of no possible benefit to any person to read a full statement of their barbarous treatment," she wrote, "and I assure my sanguine reader that it is with feelings of deep regret that I think of it, much less to speak or write of it."[29]

Despite the massacre at Fort Parker, the Texas government continued to worry more about Mexico than Comanches. Secretary of War

Rusk ordered Isaac Burton—again a Ranger captain—to patrol the coastal plain from the Guadalupe River to Mission Bay near Refugio. Keeping an eye out for the retreating Mexican army, Burton and his men soon figured in an incident that contributed to the further misery of the Mexican forces in Texas, helped feed and equip the Texas army, and carved another notch on the shoulder stock of Ranger legend.

Maritime Rangers

On June 2, the Rangers learned a coastwise schooner had been spotted in Copano Bay, a landing place since Spanish colonial times. Burton's company rode some twenty miles and made cold camp so as not to be detected by anyone aboard the vessel in question.

At daybreak, the rangers saw the two-masted schooner riding at anchor in the shallow bay. The vessel flew no flag, but one of the rangers could make out her name: *Watchman.* Keeping his company concealed in brush on a bluff overlooking the bay, Burton dispatched two unarmed men to signal the schooner. When the *Watchman* ran up the Stars and Stripes, the rangers did not respond. Soon, her crew took down the American flag and raised the Mexican banner. The Texans' wariness had paid off. The two rangers signaled the schooner to send a boat ashore.

Careful to screen their actions from anyone aboard the schooner who might be watching, the rangers disarmed the captain and four sailors. Posting four men to guard the prisoners, Burton and the other rangers rowed to the *Watchman* and easily captured the rest of the unsuspecting crew.

Burton received orders to take the schooner to the port of Velasco at the mouth of the Brazos, but unfavorable weather delayed his departure. On June 17, two other vessels hove to in the bay. The Ranger leader ordered the master of the captured schooner to raise the Mexican flag and signal the other two captains to come aboard to "take a glass of grog." When the two schooners neared the *Watchman,* the rangers rowed out and captured the *Comanche* and *Fanny Butler* without a shot.

Two days later, Burton set sail for Velasco with his captured flotilla. From there, the vessels were escorted to Galveston for condemnation proceedings. The seizure proved to be a significant windfall for the cash-poor Texas government: $25,000 worth of pickled pork, beef jerky, rice, beans, and bread as well as gunpowder, ammunition, bayonets, and muskets.

The maritime rangering came to the attention of the U.S. press on July 28, when the Kentucky *Gazette* published a letter describing the incident. "On yesterday [news came] of the capture of three Mexican vessels by a troop of horses—these you will call 'Horse Marines' I suppose," wrote Edward J. Wilson, a Kentuckian who had come to Texas to fight for its independence.[30]

By the time the story made the newspapers, Burton had become major in charge of the Rangers. His ascension came after Williamson left the Rangers on June 24 to help organize the new Texas Republic's government.[31]

In mid-July, James Parker sought out Houston in San Augustine, where the general was convalescing from the leg wound he had suffered at San Jacinto. The distraught Parker urged Houston to mount a search party for his daughter Rachel and the other captives taken by the Comanches from Fort Parker that spring. Houston listened sympathetically, but told Parker he wanted to make peace with the Indians, not war.[32] Most of the provisional government's attention remained focused on Mexico and the possibility it would resume the war, even though Texas held Santa Anna prisoner.

The new republic—a nation more in name than reality—stretched from the Sabine River on the east to the high country of what would later become the state of Wyoming. Texas claimed portions of what would become five other states. Only the eastern third of the former Mexican province of Coahuila y Texas had any settlements, but even that area covered as much territory as big as all of New England and New York. The coastal city of Galveston lay three hundred miles from Jonesboro on the Red River, as far as Cincinnati from St. Louis. Texans had more land than they could handle. Still, the government did what it could for its citizens.

Frederick A. Sawyer, the new republic's acting secretary of war, ordered Coleman on August 12 to raise three companies of mounted men "for the Special purpose of protecting frontier inhabitants of upper Brazos-Colorado-Little-River-and-Guadalupe." Coleman's charge held no ambiguity: "You will at all times bear in mind the purpose for which you are detached, the complete protection of the inhabitants will not, it is hoped, be disappointed."[33]

The men, recruited for one year, elected their own officers. "Col. R.M. Coleman has left this place with his men, to go and protect the inhabitants of the Colorado from incursions of marauding Indians and to enable the farmers to attend their crops," the *Telegraph and Texas Register* reported on August 23, 1836, from its new home in Columbia, a town on the west bank of the Brazos that had recently become the infant republic's capital.

"A corps of between two and three hundred cavalry is now being raised in Texas," a New Orleans newspaper noted at the end of August, "to act as independent rangers in the west. They are to receive an additional compensation of one dollar per day while on active duty."[34]

Their base pay being $25 a month, rangers still had to furnish their own mounts, weapons, equipment, and clothing. The republic threw in powder and lead when available, and, on occasion, beef. Before the Rangers took to the field, as the *Telegraph and Texas Register* sarcastically noted, the Indians killed Texans. After the Rangers came, someone began killing the settlers' hogs.[35] A ranger did often have to live off the land, but if he stayed in service for one year, he could claim a bounty of 1,280 acres as his own land.

While the prospect of free land motivated some, others saddled up to ride after Indians simply because they considered them pests in need of eradication, no different from rattlesnakes, mountain lions, or bears. To their view, Indians impeded civilization's progress. One ranger who thought like that was Cicero Rufus Perry, a young Alabaman who joined a Ranger company commanded by W. W. Hill.

Hill's company soon left from Bastrop, riding to the northwest and scouting along the San Gabriel River. Finding Indian sign on a tributary, they moved eastward. Around sundown of their second full day on the trail, they spotted smoke rising from a campfire. The rangers dismounted and crept closer.

"A straggling warrior hastened the issue by coming out and meeting us accidentally," Perry later related. "Of course, we killed him immediately, but not before he had raised a war whoop, rousing his comrades to action. We continued to advance, not withstanding the fact of their being aroused and ready to meet us. We killed three and wounded several."

What happened next startled even Perry.

"We were somewhat surprised and puzzled just after the fight to see a member of our company, an old backwoodsman named Dave Lawrence, step up and cut off the thigh of one of the slain Indians," Perry continued. "I asked him what he intended to do with it."

"Why," he answered, "I am going to take it along to eat. If you don't get some game before noon tomorrow we'll need it."

Perry did not mention if they flushed any game, but they found no more Indians.[36]

Rangers soon established a line of forts that became the vanguard of settlement in the young republic. In September, Coleman supervised the construction of a log fort on high ground west of Walnut Creek about two and a half miles northeast of the Colorado River. Variously known as Coleman's Fort, Fort Coleman, Fort Colorado, and Fort Prairie, the outpost consisted of a pair of two-story log blockhouses and several cabins surrounded by a stockade. Coleman and other rangers also raised log forts in what are now Anderson, Bell, Falls, Henderson, McLennan, Tarrant, and Williamson counties.[37]

Still serving as commander-in-chief of the Texas army prior to his election as the new republic's first president, Sam Houston recruited friendly Indians as rangers. From Nacogdoches on September 18, Houston wrote a Shawnee chief named John Linney, saying, "You are allowed to raise twenty-five men . . . for six months as rangers . . . each one shall [be paid] at the rate of ten dollars [a] month. You shall receive double that amount." Houston directed the chief to "let the Texas rangers know when you commence" and that the "officer who will be in command along that frontier, will tell you from time to time what to do. The object in getting you and your warriors to ranger there is to prevent the Wild Indians from stealing Horses and murdering people on the frontier."[38]

"My highest ambition," Coleman wrote newly elected Senator Sterling C. Robertson on October 16, "is to give protection to this frontier and I hope you will sustain me. There are many who oppose me . . . but by the 1st of Decr. I will show to the govt. as well as all others what a Kentuckian can do. Give me men, ammunition, provisions and arms, and I pledge my honor with all that is sacred to check immediately all Indian depredations." Two days earlier, in a long piece laying out a suggested agenda for the First Texas Congress, *Telegraph and Texas Register* publisher Gail Borden urged that the "corps of Rangers . . . be made efficient."[39]

On October 21, Robertson, one of three members of the Senate's Standing Committee on Indian Affairs, introduced a measure "for the further protection of the Indian frontier."

Signed into law by President Houston—whose victory over Santa Anna had assured his election as the republic's first chief executive—on December 5, the legislation authorized creation of a battalion of 280 "Mounted Riflemen." This corps was "to be officered in like manner as the balance of the army." To operate under the same rules and regulations as the regular army, the Ranger force could be increased in size to 560 men at the president's authorization. These mounted riflemen would be paid the same as soldiers, though the act did provide an extra $15 a month "for the furnishing of the horses and arms." Enlistment would be for a year, and each man had to furnish his own horse, rifle, and a brace of pistol. Section 4 of the act authorized the president "to cause to be erected such block houses, forts, and trading houses, as in his judgment may be necessary to prevent Indian depredations." Five days later, the Congress set the pay scale at $25 a month for "every Mounted Rifleman who has entered the ranging service."[40] Officer pay ranged up to $75 monthly. Though the December 5 act referred to the corps as mounted riflemen and did not use the word *ranger*, an act approved on December 10 made it clear that "mounted riflemen" were the same as rangers by providing that "all officers and soldiers, who have actually been engaged in the ranging service since July, 1835, shall be included in this act, and shall receive pay for the time he is in the service."[41]

Neither of these acts mentioned anything about the enforcement of criminal laws. The republic's lawmakers clearly considered the rangers a component of the military, not a police force. For civilian peacekeeping, the Texas congress vested most of the power in the traditional office of sheriff. Each of the republic's twenty-three original counties, eventually expanded by the government to thirty-six, elected someone empowered to enforce the republic's criminal statutes. Also established was the office of constable, an elected officer who had authority only in his precinct. Though sheriffs and their deputies—or hastily assembled posses—at times chased marauding Indians, in the early days of the Republic the Rangers concerned themselves solely with Indian fighting and keeping a watchful eye on the roads leading north from Mexico.

For a time during the fall of 1836, Texas had two Ranger battalions in the field. The actual number in service at any time ebbed and flowed as terms of service expired. In comparison to the bloody rebellion that spring, followed by the Comanche attack on Fort Parker, the second half of the year proved relatively peaceful, largely due to the Ranger presence along the frontier.

But as settlers from the United States took advantage of Texas's newly obtained freedom from Mexico and streamed into the country, the Indian situation grew more troublesome. Nor had victory on the battlefield brought political stability. In May 1837, President Houston furloughed most of the regular army after its leader, General Albert Sidney Johnston, suffered a gunshot wound in a duel with Felix Huston, who believed he should be in charge of Texas's military. Leadership of the Rangers proved no less tenuous.

On December 19, the president relieved Coleman of command and had him arrested. The official reason was the death at Fort Coleman on November 8 of one of the colonel's men, Ranger Fee C. Booker. A heavy drinker, Booker had been tied to a post to sober up. Passing out during the night, the binding around his neck strangled him when his knees gave way. The lieutenant who ordered the harsh punishment, fearful of reprisal from the man's friends, had fled. To Houston's thinking, Coleman bore ultimate responsibility for the death. The president also had a personal issue with Coleman. The ranger had recently published a pamphlet, "Houston Displayed, Or, Who Won the Battle of San Jacinto?" that portrayed the hero of San Jacinto in not so heroic a light. Named as Coleman's replacement in the Rangers was Major William H. Smith, who established his headquarters on the Brazos at a community called Nashville.

While Coleman awaited the resolution of his legal troubles, in February 1837 a Ranger company under Captain Thomas H. Barron moved up the Brazos River to a longtime camping ground of the Waco Indians. Cutting a road and building a bridge over a bayou, the men took three weeks to get from a point known as the Falls on the Brazos to the old Indian village, which they found recently vacated. One of the rangers, George B. Erath, later wrote, "We built some shanties for barracks near the big spring on the river, but only remained there three weeks, when an order came . . . for us to return to the falls, as we were too far out to do good service. We went back, calling the place we had left Fort Fisher." In constructing the fort, named for Secretary of War William S. Fisher, the Rangers anticipated it would be a permanent outpost of the republic. After Erath and his company moved on, other rangers periodically occupied the fort through that summer. But only its name would last.[42]

With Coleman still under arrest in Velasco, the investigation into the death of Booker dragged on into the spring. Chief Justice James Collinsworth finally released the captain, who, having no Indians to fight, soon went fishing. His boat overturned in the Brazos River on May 12 and the feisty Kentuckian drowned.

Coleman had never been one to look for the good side of Indians, but the government did not consider all of them enemies. On June 12, Congress passed an act permitting Ranger companies to hire members of friendly tribes, particularly Cherokees, Choctaws, Delawares, and Shawnees, as spies or scouts. Lipan Apaches and Tonkawas also often went along with Rangers. Two Lipan chiefs, Cuelegus de Castro and Flacco the elder, led Ranger companies.

The Senate's Standing Committee on Indian Affairs, headed by ranger-turned-solon Isaac Burton, on October 12, 1837, issued a report on "the different tribes with their force, habits, Locality, Interests, origin and probable feelings in reference to this Govt." One long paragraph discussed the Keechi, Tawakoni, Waco, and Tawehash, which the committee described as "Indians of the Prairies." The Indians lived as nomadic hunters, "travel altogether on horseback," and primarily carried bow and lance. Their only firearms were "smooth bores or traders guns of little value and seldom used." The committee believed they numbered about five hundred warriors, "despicable soldiers but formidble [sic] rogues." These Indians, the committee went on, "have greatly annoyed our frontier" and "are now at war with this Republick [sic]."[43] Bows and arrows dated to the Stone Age, but in practiced hands they often were deadly, killing quickly with shock and loss of blood or slowly by infection. "Unless there was a cross-wind," one Indian-fighting ranger recalled in his old age, "you couldn't dodge an arrow at sixty yards."[44]

On October 13, 1837, a Ranger company under Captain William M. Eastland followed the Colorado in pursuit of a band of Indians who had raided a private fort on the Little River. They lost the trail, and Eastland and one of his lieutenants, A. B. Van Benthuysen, had a falling out. The lieutenant and seventeen rangers decided to keep looking for the Indians.

Riding north, they cut their trail again on November 1. Two days later, the Ranger command found a party of Cherokees and Delawares and one Keechi near the Brazos River in what is now Young County. When the Keechi raised his rifle a bit too hastily, the rangers took it as a threat and killed him as the other Indians, outnumbered, looked on in helpless outrage.

From the Brazos, the rangers rode on, still following a large band. On November 10, some 150 Taovayas, Kichais, Wacos, and Kadohadachos decided to halt and confront their pursuers. Though some of the Cherokees and Delawares riding with the rangers tried to prevent a fight, one of the rangers killed a Kichais. Reprimanded by Van Benthuysen, the ranger said he would kill any Indian for a plug of tobacco. To prove his point, he held up a plug he had taken from the dead Indian.[45] At that, the Indians attacked, sending the rangers scrambling for cover in a wooded ravine. When a well-placed shot from one of the rangers brought down the Indian chief, they pulled back.

"I flattered myself that the action was done," the lieutenant said in his report. But after picking a new leader, the Indians attacked again.

> Up to this time we had four men and six horses killed. In about fifteen minutes the savages again advanced and fired the woods on three sides of us. The fourth side was prairie, where their horsemen with bows & arrows were stationed. Our only alternative was to charge through those Indians who were armed with Rifles, in preference to those who were armed with bows and arrows. . . . [We] charged about fifty Indians and drove them before us. Six more of my party fell dead in making the charge. Eight came through alive but three out of the eight were wounded.

One of those killed in the fight was Lieutenant Alfred Miles, a veteran of San Jacinto and one of the men who had captured Santa Anna. Another casualty was a Mr. Bostwick, but he did not go easily. "After being shot through the body," Van Benthuysen wrote, "[he] loaded & fired his Rifle three times & had the fourth load in his gun when he expired in the act of drawing his ramrod from his Rifle." Seeking comfort in gallows humor, one of the men suggested that they prop the dead ranger up and let him go ahead and take that fourth shot.

The rangers succeeded in breaking through the Indians and "commenced our retreat on foot. We had just crossed the skirt of timber when we again came in sight of the Indians. They did not attempt to pursue us but stood and looked at us. They had enough of the fight for we had killed about fifty of their warriors."[46]

The eight surviving rangers made it back to the settlements on November 27 and soon joined another company.

Eleven days after the bloody fight, which came to be called the Battle of the Stone Houses because of three nearby rock formations that looked like houses to the Indians, President Houston made no mention of the incident in his message to the republic's congress. News of the engagement would not reach him until early December, but no matter, he had no interest in fanning the flames of conflict between the fledgling republic and the estimated fourteen thousand Indians within its borders. Indeed, judging from Houston's message, Texas had no Indian problem. "Measures are in progress with the several tribes, which, with the aid of suitable appropriations by congress, may enable us to attain the objects of peace and friendly intercourse," Houston wrote. "Apprized of these facts it is desirable that the citizens of Texas should so deport themselves as to become the aggressors in no case."[47]

The company that participated in the Stone Houses fight was one of more than three score Ranger companies or Ranger-like frontier militia units organized from June 12, 1835, to December 1837. Designations varied, including Ranger Company, Mounted Gunmen, Mounted Guards, Volunteer Rangers, Volunteers, Mounted Company, and Mounted Rangers. Ranks of company commanders included lieutenants, captains, and superintendents.[48]

By early 1838, enlistments for all the rangers who had served under Coleman or Smith had played out. Captain William Eastland, an officer under John Henry Moore in 1835, was now the republic's highest ranking ranger. On January 21, 1838, Eastland signed on twenty-nine men to range from San Antonio. That company amounted to the republic's entire Ranger force. Eastman resigned his commission on March 2, leaving a first lieutenant in command of the Rangers. By late April, the enlistments of all its men having expired, the Rangers had entered one of their periods of paper-only existence.

The record of John Bate Berry is illustrative of the on-again, off-again nature of the early Rangers and whatever they happened to be called at any given time. Inside three years, he served variously under Williamson as a private in "the permanent volunteer company of Texas Militia" (1835); under William W. Hill in "the ranging service on the frontier" (1836); under Jesse Billingsley in "the militia service of Texas" (1836); and under John L. Lynch in "the ranging service of Texas" (1838).[49] Nomenclature varied but function did not.

3

"Utterly fearless and invincible"

THE REPUBLIC'S INDIAN FIGHTERS, 1838—45

Whatever prejudiced President Mirabeau B. Lamar against Indians—possibly his earlier military service during the Creek wars in Georgia—his resentment ran strong. As Texas's second president, Lamar vowed not only to protect its citizens from the various unfriendly tribes, but to see the Indians forced from the country or killed.

"It is a cardinal principle in all political associations that protection is commensurate with allegiance," Lamar wrote the republic's congress, "and the poorest citizen, whose sequestered cabin is reared on our remotest frontier, holds as sacred a claim upon the government for safety and security, as does the man who lives in ease and wealth in the heart of our most populous city."

Lamar delivered that message on December 31, 1838, the same day the congress forwarded for the president's signature an act "to provide for the protection of the Northern and Western frontier." The measure created, at least on paper, an 840-man regiment of fifteen companies to serve the republic for three years at $16 a month.[1]

Secretary of War Thomas J. Rusk had already been creating Ranger companies. Working on Christmas Day at his field headquarters on the Trinity River, he wrote a sixty-two-word letter to Mark E. Roberts authorizing him "to raise a corps of rangers to range on the frontier of

Fannin county and picket it against Indian depredations, the company not to be composed of more than thirty men." Rusk further ordered Roberts to make monthly reports to Adjutant General Hugh McLeod.[2]

On New Year's Day, congress approved two other acts, one appropriating $75,000 to fund eight companies of "mounted volunteers," and $5,000 for fifty-six men specifically referred to as Rangers to "range on the frontier of Gonzales County and protect the settlements" for three months. A short time later, congress created two other companies of equal size for San Patricio, Goliad, and Refugio counties. By the end of the month, Lamar had signed various pieces of legislation committing the new republic to spend hundreds of thousands of dollars on self-defense.[3]

Battle-tested Indian fighter John Moore of Fayette County, commanding two volunteer ranging companies from La Grange and Bastrop totaling fifty-two men, soon rode to the northwest looking for Comanches. Forty-two Lipans and Tonkawa rode with the Rangers to strike their longtime enemy.[4] Moore's scouts found a Comanche camp twelve miles below the mouth of the San Saba River on February 15, 1839. Slipping as close as they could to the camp without detection, the rangers waited in the cold for daybreak.

"At length, when it was light enough, the order came to charge," former ranger John Holland Jenkins recalled. "Our men ran nearly through the village, driving the Indians before them—and by the way, the warriors were all at home this time, about 500 in number."

When the Texans charged, one ranger raced ahead. Screaming "run to me, run to me!" a desperate Andrew Lockhart thought his missing thirteen-year-old daughter Matilda—kidnapped by Comanches the previous fall—might be with the Indians. His hunch proved correct, but it would be months before he learned she had heard his voice and called for him, only to have her cries lost in the cacophony of gunfire, Indian war whoops, and Texas yells as the contest raged.

Meanwhile, Moore realized he had cut a bigger plug of tobacco than he could chew. His command dangerously outnumbered, Moore instructed his men to fall back into the protective cover of the timber. The Comanches charged repeatedly, but each time the rangers' rifles held them back. At one point, someone noticed Pat Moore, an Irishman, sitting on a bluff with his cocked but empty rifle pointed at the Indians.

"What are you doing, Pat? Your gun is not loaded."

"Hush," he whispered. "Bejabers, they don't know it!"

That momentarily gave the tired rangers a laugh, but none of the men saw any humor in what happened next.

"Our men left their horses without guards about two miles back," Jenkins continued. "The Indians, slipping around, stole them, together with all the baggage of the soldiers. Much to the vexation of a majority of the men, Moore ordered a retreat, and the band marched back home on foot, bearing their wounded on litters." Of those men, one later died. Moore claimed that he had killed or wounded eighty Comanches, but in his official report he neglected to mention the loss of his mounts and equipment.[5]

In retaliation, a large Comanche war party swept down the Colorado River into Bastrop County on February 24. The first cabin they attacked, about twelve miles above Bastrop, happened to be the late Captain Robert Coleman's homestead. The Indians killed his widow, Elizabeth, and two of her children. The raiders also struck the nearby cabin of Dr. James W. Robertson. The doctor and his family had not been at home, but the Indians captured seven of his slaves—a woman, five children, and an old man.

As word of the Indian incursion spread, fourteen Bastrop County men under Captain John J. Grumbles quickly rode in pursuit of the raiders. They soon overtook the war party but pulled back when they realized they were dangerously outnumbered. Following the arrival of more men, the volunteer rangers resumed the pursuit under the command of Jacob Burleson, one of Edward Burleson's six brothers.

Twenty-five miles from the scene of the Coleman massacre, Jacob Burleson and his men overtook the Comanches on the prairie near Brushy Creek in present Williamson County. As the Indians tried to reach a line of timber that would have afforded them a more defensible position, Burleson ordered his company to cut them off.

Fourteen-year-old Winslow Turner and the more experienced Samuel Highsmith followed Burleson's command and dismounted to face the Indians. But the other volunteers, seeing how many Comanches they faced, wheeled their horses to flee.

Knowing he could not face the Comanches with only one man and a boy, Burleson shouted to the pair to get back on their horses and retreat as well. Just as Burleson started to spur his horse into a run for safety, he saw the teenager struggling to get back astride his nervous mount. Burleson jumped from his saddle to lend a hand. Turner and Highsmith escaped, but Burleson caught an Indian bullet in the back of his head.

Edward Burleson, a brigadier general in the newly created Frontier Regiment of the Texas Army—rangers in function if not name—had been trailing his brother's company with more men and soon reached the scene. Assuming overall command, the general rode after the Indians who had killed his brother. Catching up with them about one o'clock that afternoon, he immediately attacked. But since the Indians had good cover, the engagement amounted more to a periodic exchange of gunfire over a four-hour period than a pitched battle.

The Houston *Telegraph and Texas Register* offered this account:

General Burleson, at the head of about 70 men, recently encountered a large body of Indians on the Brushy, and, after one or two skirmishes, finding the enemy numerous, retreated to a ravine in order to engage them with more advantage; but the Indians, fearing to attack him in his new position, drew off and retreated into a neighboring thicket.

Being unable to pursue them, he returned to Bastrop. It is reported that he has lost three men in this engagement; the loss of the Indians is not known; it, however, must have been considerable, as most of the men under Burleson were excellent marksmen, and had often been engaged in Indian warfare.

The newspaper had it mostly right. When the sun set, Burleson made camp for the night, planning to charge the Indian position at dawn. He did, only to find that the Indians had departed. The Comanches left behind the old slave they had captured, nine arrows in his body. Still alive, the slave told Burleson the rangers had killed about thirty Indians the afternoon before. Burleson lost only three men (Ed Blakey, John Walters, and James Gilleland) killed or mortally wounded.[6]

The day after the Bastrop County raid, at the capital in Houston, Lamar received a letter from fellow Georgian and San Jacinto veteran William T. Sadler. After the war, Sadler wrote, he had moved to Houston County, "commenced farming," and in March 1838 married. He had been "doing well until the 18th of October last, at which time my wife was murdered by the Indians." Even though a recent widower, Sadler did not dwell on his sorrow. Rather, "with great diffidence," he suggested to the president what needed to be done:

> We cannot check the Indians unless we follow them to their place of rendezvous or where they have their familys [sic] and visit them with the same kind of warfare that they give us. We should spare neither age, sect nor condition, for they do not. I know it will be said this is barbarous and too much like the savage. And it certainly is harsh, but it is the only means in my view that will put them down.[7]

"THOSE USURPING ADVENTURERS"

N ot long after reading Sadler's letter, the president learned of the raid into Bastrop County. On February 28, he called for six companies of mounted volunteers to alleviate "the suffering conditions of our North Western Frontier." Though he did not question the warlike nature of the Comanches, Lamar and others suspected Mexico of complicity in the Indians' depredations. Soon he would have damning evidence.

Out with another ranger along Onion Creek in present Travis County hunting deer for camp meat, Lieutenant James O. Rice saw a large, suspicious party of horsemen in the distance, riding north. Rice and the other ranger rushed back to report the sighting to their captain, Micah Andrews. Believing the riders to be Mexicans, the captain ordered a pursuit. Breaking camp at dawn on May 16, the rangers caught up with the party after following their trail about two miles.

Unsure how many they faced, one of the rangers cautioned against a headlong charge into the cedar brake where the mysterious riders had taken cover. Andrews agreed but most of his men did not. The captain soon changed his mind, but by that time the riders had left their place of concealment and gained ground on the rangers.

Early on the morning of May 17, Andrews's horse pulled up lame. Unable to go farther, the heavyset captain ordered Rice to stay on the trail. With sixteen rangers, the lieutenant finally overtook the riders and engaged them along the south fork of the San Gabriel River in what is now Williamson County, about twenty-five miles north of Austin.

In a running fight, Ranger William Wallace toppled the leader of the Mexicans from his horse, a rifle ball in his heart. Two other Mexicans also suffered fatal wounds, but the others escaped after abandoning their extra horses and loaded pack mules. His horses jaded and his men dead tired, Rice opted not to give chase. The rangers soon discovered that Wallace had killed Manuel Flores, a much sought after Mexican agent thought to have been recruiting Indians to fight against Texas.

In dividing the spoils, which included lead and gunpowder, the rangers found in Flores's saddlebags the outline of a Mexican plan for a "sudden and complete campaign against those usurping adventurers [Texans]." Flores's papers also included a circular published on February 27 addressed to seven Indian headmen, including Chief Bowles and Big Mush of the Cherokees. The broadside from General Valentin Canalizo of Matamoros urged the Indians to follow Flores's instructions and assured them "that nothing can be expected of the greedy adventurers for land who wish to deprive you even of the sun which warms and vivifies you, and who will not cease to injure you while grass grows and water flows."

When General Burleson forwarded the captured documents to Secretary of War Albert Sidney Johnston on May 22, he said he considered the papers important, adding that Lieutenant Rice and his "gallant men deserve the highest esteem."[8]

On May 26, eight days after rangers encountered Flores, Ranger Captain John Bird and one of his men rode up on a small party of Indians skinning a buffalo. Capturing one of their horses, Bird and the ranger returned to his company's camp on the Little River at an abandoned post known as Fort Smith in present Bell County. There, he learned that some of his men had seen more Indians near the fort. Quickly inspecting his men's arms, Bird called, "To horse."

That afternoon, Bird's trackers picked up pony prints. Following the trail about five miles, the rangers rode up on a small party of Indians. The rangers chased them several miles, not gaining any ground. Bird called off the pursuit and ordered his thirty-five men to dismount. As they followed their back trail, walking their exhausted horses, some forty Comanches descended on the rangers.

Bird's men remounted and got another six hundred yards out of their horses, riding hard to take cover in a ravine. At that point, more than two hundred warriors appeared. Formed in a single long line, the Indians rode down from a hill and surrounded the Rangers. A sub-chief who knew a little English taunted, "How do you do? How do you do?" When the Comanche posed his mocking question a third time, a German-born ranger stood and replied, "I dosh tolerably well! How dosh you do, God tam you!" At that, he squeezed the trigger of his rifled flintlock, dropping the leader from his pony. "Now, how dosh you do, you tam red rascal!" the ranger yelled triumphantly.

A Houston newspaper described what happened next:

This heroic band sustained their position for more than two hours against four times their own number of the enemy. Towards sunset the Indian chief, apparently enraged to be thus held at bay by a force so greatly inferior to his own, collected all his warriors and made one desperate charge, but fell when he arrived about 30 steps at the head of his men, and the remainder of the enemy seeing him fall, raised a hideous yell and fled, leaving him and about forty . . . companions dead upon the field.[9]

Firing their muzzle-loaders in relays to avoid being overrun, the rangers lost only four men, among them Captain Bird, who took a red-ringed Comanche arrow in his heart.[10]

"This victory will undoubtedly be of immense benefit to the citizens of the frontier settlements in that section," the newspaper concluded, "as these hordes of savages have infested that region for many months, and have hitherto held complete possession of the country. They will now be compelled to retire farther northward, and leave those settlers in the undisturbed possession of their improvements."[11]

As the killing of Bird should have proven, the Comanches posed a far greater threat to the new republic than the Cherokees. But Lamar, fearing further Mexican attempts to recruit the tribe in warring on Texas, wanted them gone.

"Recent events," the president wrote,

convince me of the necessity of the immediate removal of the Cherokee Indians, and the ultimate removal of all other immigrant tribes now residing in Texas . . . and unless they consent at once to receive a fair compensation for their improvements and other property and remove out of this country, nothing short of the entire destruction of all their tribe will appease the indignation of the white people against them.[12]

The republic fielded a force of five hundred regulars and volunteers under the overall command of Brigadier General Kelsey Douglass. When negotiations failed on July 15, 1839, Douglass ordered the Texans to action. What came to be called the Cherokee War lasted only a few days. Cherokee villages went up in flames and their residents fell before Texas bullets. Chief Bowles, the eighty-three-year-old tribal head who had led his people from Tennessee into Texas in 1820, fell fatally wounded on July 16 in the heaviest fight. "Some rude chaps scalped the poor chief after his death," the *Telegraph and Texas Register* later reported. By Christmas, the Cherokee expulsion had been completed.[13]

The Texans had made short work of the Cherokees, but faced a different situation on the frontier.

"Fire if they resist"

San Antonio was the republic's westernmost settlement. Comanches often picked off those foolish enough to travel alone, solitary herdsmen or those tending crops. Sometimes the Indians rode boldly into town, in one raid killing three people and capturing a little girl.

The bell in the tower of the San Fernando Cathedral called men and women to prayer, but it also pealed to warn of approaching Comanches. When the bell rang out at unexpected times, mothers herded their children indoors and men ran for their weapons and horses.

Though fierce and prideful, even some Comanches wanted peace with the Texans. On January 9, 1840, the tolling of the cathedral bell signaled the approach of three Comanche chiefs. The citizenry braced for trouble, but this time the Indians had come to discuss the possibility of a treaty. The ranking government official, Colonel Henry Karnes, received the Indians graciously, considering he was only recently recovered from a wound suffered in fighting them during the summer of 1838. He told the Indians a treaty could not be executed unless they returned all American captives in their possession. The chiefs left, assuring Karnes they would be back.[14]

More than three score Penateka Comanches rode into San Antonio on March 19 for a talk with two commissioners appointed by Lamar. But the Indians came with only one prisoner, the young Matilda Lockhart. Meeting in the old Spanish government building called Casa Reales, the commissioners said they would sign a peace treaty with the chiefs providing they returned others known to have been captured. When the Indians said they had no control over other bands with additional captives, the Texans decided to hold the chiefs hostage until their warriors returned with other prisoners.

What happened next involved regular Texas troops, not Rangers, but like a bloated carcass it poisoned the well for years to come in regard to Texas-Comanche relations. It started when one of the chiefs bolted for the door, stabbing a soldier blocking his exit. Another soldier shot down that Indian, as the other chiefs, drawing their knives, rushed to get outside. "Fire if they resist," Colonel William S. Fisher ordered. When the smoke cleared, Chief Muguara and thirty-four other Comanches, including three women and two children, lay dead. Violence only begat violence. Though seven of the known Comanche prisoners later found freedom, one of them recalled that after word of what became known as the Council House fight spread among the Indians, thirteen other captives had been "roasted and butchered."

In further retaliation for what the Indians saw as a betrayal in San Antonio, and probably egged on by Mexican operatives, that summer six hundred Comanches raided deep into Texas, cutting a swath all the way to the coastal village of Linnville on Lavaca Bay. Killing twenty-three Texans in the August 8, 1840, raid, the Indians destroyed the place so thoroughly no one ever felt inclined to rebuild it.

Three days later, a hastily organized force of two hundred Texans under General Felix Huston—regular soldiers, militiamen and Rangers—found the Comanches near Plum Creek in present Caldwell County, thirty miles southeast of Austin. With their captives and plunder, the Indians had been headed northwest, back to their home range—Comancheria. Seeing that they outnumbered the Texans, the Comanches arrayed themselves in a long line and prepared to attack, as one participant remembered, "exhibiting great bravado." Content to await the charge, Huston ordered his men to dismount. But Ranger Captain Matthew "Old Paint" Caldwell, a savvy Indian fighter, knew better. Men on foot had little chance against horsemen. The Comanches started picking off the horses of Huston's dismounted regulars, also wounding some of the men. Thirty mounted rangers rode up to the Indians exhibiting "personal heroism worthy of all praise."

The skirmishing lasted for about half an hour before a Texas rifle bullet dropped one chief from his horse and his warriors began howling in mourning. "Now, General, is your time to charge them!" Caldwell implored. "They are whipped!" Not waiting for Huston's consent, Caldwell and his rangers spurred their horses and rode toward the Comanches "howling like wolves," as Ranger Robert Hall remembered. Holding their fire until they closed with the Indians, the Rangers shot at least fifteen warriors from their ponies, sending the Indians into scattered flight. Eighty Indians died in a running fight that covered fifteen miles. Just a shave tail, Cornell Davis had been allowed to tag along with the Texan punitive expedition and witnessed the battle.

"When the Indians came to the creek," he recalled years later, "they had to cross the water and climb a steep bank. . . . Here the big pistols came into good play and the whites shot many Indians down as they scrambled up the bank. Those who were wounded severely enough fell backward. . . . This scene stands out more clearly in my mind than any other. I remember as we were pursuing them I saw one clay-daubed warrior writhing on the ground in agony and begging for his life, but a man dispatched him with a long knife, in order, I suppose, to save his shot and powder." Only one Texan died outright, though a second later succumbed to a wound suffered in the battle. As had been the case in the Cherokee War, the fight at Plum Creek had not been entirely a Ranger operation, but Caldwell's leadership carried the day.

"Old Paint Caldwell was equal to a thousand men," Ranger Hall recalled. "As soon as the bullets began to whistle, he seemed to grow taller and look grander." Too, the roster of those involved includes the names of many former and future rangers, most notably Caldwell, brothers Ben and Henry McCulloch, and John Coffee Hays.[15]

John Coffee Hays

The young Tennessean would shape the image of the early Texas Rangers as surely as a bullet mold turned hot lead into deadly rifle balls. Mary Maverick summed Hays up in her memoir:

Hays came. . . . [to] San Antonio he was nineteen years of age, at which time he was appointed a deputy surveyor. The surveying parties frequently had "brushes" with the Indians, and it was on these occasions that Hays displayed such rare military skill and daring, that very soon by consent of all, he was looked upon as the leader and his orders were obeyed and he himself loved by all. In a fight he was utterly fearless and invincible.[16]

Though Hays probably reached Texas somewhat later than Mrs. Maverick remembered, it was her husband, pioneer Samuel Maverick, who helped Hays gain employment as a surveyor in Bexar County, a sprawling district then covering all of western Texas. Being in the field with transit and chain on the sparsely populated frontier exposed him to the Comanches.

"Hays' party had on several occasions to defend themselves," one writer who had known Hays later wrote. "The little Tennessean would seem to be another man when the cry 'Indians' was raised. He would mount a horse and assume the appearance of a different being. With him it was charge, war to the knife, and the Indians were whipped every time they attacked his party."[17]

In the summer of 1839 Hays participated in an expedition under Henry Karnes that included an Indian fight in which Hays killed the first warrior. A year later he took part in the Plum Creek fight. His first Ranger command came January 10, 1841 as head of a company based in San Antonio. Texans soon marveled at Hays's ability to transform himself from Southern gentleman to fighter and leader.[18] When future California newspaper editor John Nugent met Hays in San Antonio, he later wrote, the captain was "thin to emaciation (he had just recovered from a severe fit of illness . . .); was dressed in black, and wore a fine Panama hat. He was extremely modest and quiet in his manner and his gentle laugh and soft voice were singularly winning. There was an entire absence of any of the roughness indicative of a life spent in the rude and desperate warfare of the frontier."

The next time Nugent saw Hays, he was "in red flannel shirt and soft felt hat, mounted on a superb horse . . . shouting orders. . . . Anything that might have been regarded as commonplace in his town garb and demeanor, had disappeared, and he sat his horse every inch a woodsman and soldier."[19]

Hays's "Spy Company," as German nobleman Prince Carl of Solms-Braunfels described it, never had more than forty men. The prince, who came to Texas in 1844 to organize a colony, noted that it was "[the company's] duty to patrol the entire southern and southwester border of

Texas . . . from the sea to the high mountains. . . . No comment need be made as to whether forty men are sufficient for such a job." Even so, the prince continued, "Whenever this troop . . . fought, it always came out victorious. They displayed great bravery, and their leader, Major Hays, was in his day known as the greatest Indian fighter."[20]

Older than Hays and a more experienced fighter, thirty-year-old Ben McCulloch, another transplanted Tennessean, soon evolved as Hay's right-hand man. Elected first lieutenant of Hays's "Ranger Spy Company" on April 26, 1841, the blond-haired, blue-eyed McCulloch was as tough as a cured buffalo hide, an accomplished bear hunter by twenty-one.[21]

John Forester joined Hays's company in San Antonio in 1842 as a private. More than a half century later, Forester described his fellow rangers:

The men were, in physical make-up, as fine a body of men as I ever saw, but the uniform was altogether new, unique and picturesque. Most of them were dressed in skins, some wearing parts of buffalo robes, deer skins and bear skins, and some entirely naked to the waist, but having leggings and necessary breechclouts. All were well armed and well mounted.[22]

As John C. Caperton later described the Rangers of the republic era:

Each man was armed with a rifle, a pistol, and a knife. With a Mexican blanket tied behind his saddle and a small wallet in which he carried salt and ammunition and perhaps a little panola or parched corn, spiced and sweetened—a great allayer of thirst—and tobacco, he was equipped for a month. The little body of men, unencumbered by baggage wagons or pack trains, moved as lightly over the prairie as the Indians . . . and lived as they did, without tents, with a saddle for a pillow at night, blankets over them, and their feet to the fire. Depending wholly upon wild game for food, they sometimes found a scarcity and suffered the necessity for killing a horse for food, when all else failed.

The men were splendid riders and used the Mexican saddle, improved somewhat by the Americans, and carried the Mexican riata, made of rawhide, the cabrista, a hair rope and the lariat, to rope horses.

Caperton did not need as many words to capture their behavior: "When they started after the Indians, if the force was large enough, they never went back until they caught them."[23]

Lacking Indians, rangers occasionally fought each other. In 1839, McCulloch ran for a seat in the republic's House of Representatives against Alonzo B. Swietzer, a doctor from Ohio. McCulloch won the election, but Swietzer showed himself to be a sore loser, charging McCulloch with "moral cowardice" for declining to debate him during the campaign.

Before the name-calling could play out one way or the other, Indians interrupted the political wrangling with a raid into McCulloch's district. The new congressman and his recent opponent both joined a Ranger company hastily recruited by Matthew Caldwell to pursue the Indians. When each man took credit for finding the Indians' trail, sparks flew between them like flint on steel. Swietzer challenged his ranger comrade-in-arms to a duel. McCulloch, focused on the job at hand, declined on the basis that the threat to the people of Gonzales County superseded their personal issue.

By the time their argument died down, the rangers lost the trail again. Camped for the night on the Blanco River on their way back to Gonzales, McCulloch walked up to "Old Paint" Caldwell's fire.

"Captain," the newly elected congressman inquired, "has your pursuit of the Indians ceased, and if so, do you have any reasonable expectation of a fight between this place and Gonzales?"

Caldwell reckoned they were caught up for the time being. At that, McCulloch, gripping his rifle, approached Swietzer and told him to stand and fight. Swietzer rose, but after looking into McCulloch's piercing eyes, he made a point of leaving his weaponry on the ground. The doctor, practicing preventive medicine, said he was not ready to defend himself. If he would not fight like a gentleman, McCulloch replied, he could not very well shoot him like a dog. Even so, McCulloch added, he considered him a "black-hearted, cowardly villain, in every respect beneath the notice of a gentleman."

Back in Gonzales, a man named Ruben Ross delivered McCulloch a formal challenge from Swietzer. But since Swietzer had already demonstrated he was not a gentleman, under the code duello, McCulloch could not accept his invitation to duel. The complicated code did allow the honor to default to Ross, he being a gentleman and McCulloch's social equal.

The ranger and Ross met in a field north of town on October 6, 1839. Facing each other at forty paces with rifles, Ross pulled the trigger a few parts of a second quicker than McCulloch. Ross's bullet struck McCulloch in his right arm just as the ranger got off his shot, which went wild. Honor satisfied, the two parted friends. Ross even sent a doctor to care for McCulloch's wound.

That November, a grand jury indicted McCulloch for "contriving and intending to break the peace of this Republic, setting at naught the quiet and good morals of this community" by engaging in a duel. Despite the true bill, the district attorney declined to prosecute.[24]

Rangers did not always abide by the law, and their fervor in chastising Indians did not always stem from altruism. Henry McCulloch, noting in a letter home that his brother had gone out after Indians, revealed Ben's other goal to be "plunder or anything that comes to hand in the mountains. Ben's principle object is to locate and survey some lands."[25] On the other hand, one woman later remembered that the Rangers "were in the habit of bringing into San Antonio game of various kinds, and it was freely distributed to all who needed."[26]

The Rangers elected their own officers, a manifestation of North American democracy later commented on by Solms-Braunfels. The prince, who brought many of his fellow countrymen to Texas even though he was not at all reluctant to set down its many faults, wrote that the Rangers "choose their own officers, but do not obey them."[27]

The prince may have had in mind Robert A. Gillespie, a successful merchant from La Grange. On the frontier, Gillespie quickly proved as adept at fighting as he was astute at business. When Major Mark B. Lewis led an expedition against the Comanches in the spring of 1841, Gillespie served as a lieutenant in Captain Tom Green's company. As was later reported:

> In one of the skirmishes a Comanche concealed himself in a thicket, which completely protected him. Capt. Green ordered a party of men to dismount and penetrate the thicket on foot and dislodge him. But Gillespie in the most daring manner . . . charged into the thicket on horseback alone and shot the Indian dead, although the latter probably discharged thirty arrows or more before being killed.[28]

While early Texans like Gillespie thought independently, they followed a good leader, and many of them went on to become good leaders. Men like Hays, who seemed to have a natural affinity for command, made the Rangers efficient. Similarly, mediocre leadership brought mediocre results.

Hays demonstrated his talent when he took on a superior force of Mexican cavalrymen near Laredo in the spring of 1841. Forty-six years later, Pasquale Leo Buquor, by then the only surviving participant, observed, "This fight established the fame of Jack Hays as a ranger."

Though Mexico never recognized Texas's independence, neither side of the border minded the economic benefits of trade. Mexican entrepreneurs smuggled beans, *piloncillo* (cones of sugar), flour, and leather goods into Texas. In turn, San Antonio merchants exported printed cloth, hardware, and tobacco to Mexico. The trade flourished until the fall of 1839, when roadside robberies of southbound traders became commonplace. Two groups, one led by Agaton Quinones and the other by Manuel Leal, accounted for the bulk of the robberies. In exchange for military protection, the bandits provided Captain Ignacio Garcia, commander of the Mexican garrison in Laredo, a percentage of their take.

Paying no attention to which side of the Rio Grande they happened to be on, the two brigands held themselves forth as Mexican customs guards and operated in concert with Garcia's troops. But as Buquor explained, the businessmen of San Antonio saw them as "unauthorized bandits and cutthroats, banded together for the purpose of pillaging and robbing the unguarded trader."

When two traders rode into San Antonio to report they had been robbed by Quinones and his followers near Laredo, Antonio Perez, "a daring Indian fighter and reliable citizen," recruited volunteers to ride south and "capture or destroy" Quinones and his gang.

In addition, the town's merchants sent a rider to Austin seeking governmental authority to raise a Ranger company to deal with the situation. President Lamar referred the matter to congress, but went ahead and sent an order to the chief justice of Bexar County authorizing the requested company with Hays as captain. Perez's twelve volunteers, all Tejanos, agreed to join forces with Hays's thirteen men.

The rangers and volunteers rode from San Antonio on March 15. Fifteen days later, Captain Garcia confronted the Texans with a company of cavalry ten miles east of Laredo. The Mexican troops, along with the

nonuniformed men the rangers deemed to be bandits, did some maneu-
vering, sounded a bugle, and opened fire on Hays and his men.

"After a short consultation, . . . Perez declaring that with ten chosen
men he could whip them, asserting that he knew their material, we
agreed to fight them," Buquor recalled. "Jumping over an ugly ravine
to our left, we reached a mott of Spanish persimmons, *chapotes,* when
Hays proposed that we dismount, secure our horses to the trees under a
guard of five men, and that the balance—twenty men—advance on the
enemy as near as possible before opening fire."

The rangers got within sixty yards of the Mexicans and then cut
loose with their muzzle-loading, long-barreled Kentucky rifles, weapons
deadly accurate within a hundred yards. In the hands of a good marksman, the rifles could kill at two hundred yards.

"Our shots were unerring," Buquor remembered. "On the first fire,
we killed two and wounded several, loading as we advanced. Upon nearing them, the cavalry and lancers who were on foot and firing from -
behind their horses, got demoralized and commenced retreating, being
soon followed by their citizen allies. We made a simultaneous charge,
got on their horses and charged them, a few of us using our pistols."

For a moment it looked to Buquor as if the Mexicans intended to regroup, "but being hotly pursued they threw down their arms and surrendered, only one escaping."

Hays and his rangers had killed or wounded nine, but Quinones and
Leal escaped across the river. Still, the rangers took twenty-five prisoners, with all their arms and ammunition, and twenty-eight horses.[29]
Hays would continue to deal with the bandits through the fall of 1843,
when someone finally killed Quinones.[30]

Though Hays had become the acknowledged leader of the Rangers,
they still existed officially only sporadically, from one congressional authorization to another. The young captain disbanded his company on
May 10, 1841. The Rangers of this era never enjoyed the status of being
a standing force, but the same men tended to serve time after time.

The same could not be said for the Texas presidency. The republic's
constitution prohibited the executive from serving consecutive terms.
When Lamar's term ended, voters returned Houston to office. Lamar
had left an empty treasury and a badly annoyed Mexican government.
As Houston explained in a message to congress on July 18, 1841, "For
the want of means it has been impossible to sustain any efficient force,

but for a few days, when emergency has called out men."[31] Houston did note, "Major Hays and Captain [Jose Antonio] Menchaca have received orders to raise men and act between the San Antonio river and the Rio Grande." When not scouting for Mexican brigands, Hays and his men looked for raiding Indians or cattle thieves.

Reporting that "Capt. Hays, of the San Antonio Spy Company" had arrived in the capital city after a scout to within twenty miles of the Rio Grande, the Austin *City Gazette* observed that while Mexican "Guerrilla Bands" continued to interrupt border commerce, "the Texian cow-thieves are playing the same game." The newspaper wondered why "some plan [could not] be devised by which a dozen or two of these cowboys could be caught and punished? They are doing far more mischief to the country than the Mexicans."[32]

"The Texas Rangers, under the gallant Hays and McCulloch, have for years held undisputed sway" over the real estate south of San Antonio toward Laredo, wrote the editor of the *Telegraph and Texas Register*.[33] In scouting the road from the Rio Grande to San Antonio, Hays and his men constituted an early-warning system for the republic, but the Rangers could not hope to stop a large Mexican force.

General Mariano Arista issued a proclamation on January 9, 1842, that Mexico would never acknowledge Texas's independence and would soon use the "persuasion of war" to regain its territory. On March 4, Ben McCulloch and another ranger discovered a force of seven hundred men under General Rafael Vasquez marching toward San Antonio. The two rangers watched from concealment as the soldiers, augmented by militia and a contingent of Caddo Indians, moved northward.

Vasquez easily took San Antonio one day before the sixth anniversary of the fall of the Alamo. Though it amounted to little more than a probe, the incursion and subsequent plundering of the town clearly came in retaliation for Lamar's Santa Fe expedition, a disastrous attempt begun in June 1841 to assert the republic's influence over New Mexico. Lamar had stirred up trouble with Mexico that his successor, who liked to pick his fights, did not want.

When the Mexican troops took control of San Antonio, Hays had been in the field with one hundred men. Returning to find the town in Mexican hands, Hays fell back to the Guadalupe River to await reinforcements he knew would come as word of the invasion spread. Before the Texans could counterattack, Vasquez left as suddenly as he had arrived. Hays, demonstrating that a wise leader knew when to exercise restraint, trailed the soldiers as far as the Rio Grande but refrained from engaging them.

In June, the republic's bellicose congress declared war on Mexico. But the pragmatic Houston vetoed the act. Still, a resumption of hostilities seemed inevitable. Indeed, three months later French-born General Adrian Woll, a veteran of Mexico's successful revolt against Spain, crossed the Rio Grande with fifteen hundred men. Once again, Mexico intended to assert its sovereignty over Texas.

Though clever, Hays could make mistakes. On the night of September 10, the ranger led a scout to check the road west from San Antonio. Finding nothing out of the ordinary, he returned to town on Sunday morning, September 11, only to discover it had once again fallen under Mexican control. This time Hays had been outsmarted. Woll had adroitly circled the town and swept in from the north. Their maneuvers cloaked by a dense fog, the Mexicans occupied the town with little resistance.

As he had done in March, Hays withdrew, again riding to Seguin for reinforcements. Within days, several hundred Texans—a mixture of volunteers, regular soldiers, and rangers—spoiled for a fight with the invaders. They did not have long to wait.

On September 18, Texans under Caldwell and Hays fought Woll's forces on Salado Creek in what is now Medina County. Both sides declared a victory, but the contest ended indecisively. No matter, Woll lost enough men to convince him that reclaiming Texas would not be easy.

Hays had made a definite impression on Woll. The general wrote a preliminary report on the Salado Creek engagement on September 20, but two days later, he expanded his account. In that document, he noted that while riding back to camp with his aide, he had seen a Texan emerge from the brush on the other side of the arroyo. The general recognized the rider as Hays.

"Taking off his hat," Woll wrote, Hays "hailed me. He called me by my name and title, requesting that I approach to speak to him." Woll's aide told the general to stay put, but Woll, removing his hat in reply to the friendly salute, walked his horse toward the ranger. The general continued:

I had gone a distance of about thirty yards, which is the breadth of the *arroyo*, when two Texans hidden behind some trees aimed and discharged their rifles at me. Fate determined that they should not hit their mark, and the whistling balls passed over my head: then ... Hays projected himself precipitantly into the most dense [area] of the forest, defaming God and insulting me and calling me a coward.[34]

Clearly, when it came to fighting Mexicans, the boyish Hays had no notions of chivalry. He stood prepared to kill them, and their leaders if possible, any way he could. This time it did not work.

By the time word of the Mexican invasion reached New Orleans, Woll already had begun his retreat. While not knowing the outcome, one newspaper put the matter in perspective.

"Never since the declaration of independence was Texas more unprepared for a vigorous contest than at this moment," the New Orleans *Bulletin* observed. "Her army is disbanded; her ships of war lie idle at New Orleans for want of funds ... her credit is utterly prostrate, and money she has none. Still, she has brave hearts and strong hands, and, when the crisis comes, we trust she will be found equal to it."[35]

Though the episode had not ended with the decisiveness of San Jacinto, for all practical purposes Texas had just concluded a second war with Mexico. The six-year-old republic had sustained its independence, but the rift between the two countries had only been dug deeper.

With the passage on January 16, 1843, of "An Act to Authorize the President to Accept the Services of One Company of Mounted Men to Act as Spies on the Southwestern Frontier," the Texas congress appropriated $500 to fund such a company. The legislation did not specify a commander, but the job again went to Hays with Ben McCulloch soon elected first lieutenant. Buquor, who had fought with Hays the previous year, joined Hays's company again.

New Yorker Nelson Lee, a thirty-six-year-old Black Hawk War veteran who had seen service in the Texas navy and ridden as a volunteer under Captain Ewen Cameron, also signed on to ride with Hays. Lee had come to San Antonio from Seguin, where he had been making a living capturing and breaking in mustangs.

"There were something less than fifty of us," Lee later wrote, "marshaled under Hays in the square of San Antonio, prepared to obey the order of President Houston, to scour the frontier in search of marauding bands of Mexicans and Indians." After the company had secured its provisions, he continued, "the citizens came out and filled the gourds which hung from our Spanish saddles with whiskey." Then, "reining into line, we waved our coonskin hats to the populace, and galloped from the city."[36]

James Wilson Nichols, another battle-tested fighter, had also enlisted for twelve months' service.

"We kept out scouts all the time," Nichols wrote in his journal. "When one would come in another would go out, and those not on a scout ware [sic] every day practising horsemanship and marksmanship."

The rangers set a post in the ground "about the size of a common man" and sank another about forty yards from the first. "We would run our horses full speed and discharge our rifles at the first post, draw our pistols and fire at the second," Nichols continued. "At first thare was some wild shooting but we had not practised two months until thare was not many men that would not put his balls in the center of the posts." The rangers could hit a ring on the posts "about the size of a mans head" before long.

> As for horsemanship, they tried Rideing like the Comanche Indians. After practising for three or four months we became so purfect that we would run our horses half or full speede and pick up a hat, a coat, a blanket, or rope, or even a silver dollar, stand up in the saddle, throw ourselves on the side of our horses with only a foot and a hand to be seen, and shoot our pistols under the horses neck, rise up and reverse, etc.[37]

The Council House incident still fresh on their minds, a contingent of forty to fifty Comanches warily came to San Antonio for more treaty-making. No matter their cultural differences, the Comanches and the Rangers shared one thing in common: skill on horseback. Pending the execution of an agreement, the Comanches and Hays's rangers agreed to face each other in an engagement where for once the stakes would not be violent death—a "riding match." John C. Duval, who witnessed it, described the incident years later in his book, *The Young Explorers.*

Practically the entire community turned out for the event, to be staged on open prairie just west of San Pedro Creek. Duval set the scene:

> Gaily dressed "caballeros" were prancing along the streets on their gaudily caparisoned steeds; rangers mounted on their horses, and dressed in buckskin hunting shirts, leggins and slouched hats, and with pistols and bowie knives stuck in their belts, galloped here and there among the crowd, occasionally charging "horse and any" into some bar-room or grocery, for a glass of "mescal" or "scorch gullet." All the strangers in the place, and all the citizens with their families crammed into all kinds of vehicles, were hurrying in hot haste, to reach the scene of action before the match began.[38]

When Duval arrived, the Comanches and Rangers—each set of horsemen drawn up in a line—sat their horses facing their old enemy. "After some preliminaries," Duval wrote,

> a Mexican lad mounted on a "paint" pony ... with a spear in his hand, cantered off some three or four hundred yards on the prairie, and dismounting, laid the spear upon the ground. Immediately a Comanche brave started forth from their ranks, and plunging his huge spurs into his horse's flanks, dashed off in an opposite direction for a hundred yards or so, then wheeling suddenly, he came rushing back at full speed, and as he passed the spot where the spear had been deposited, without checking his horse for an instant, he swerved from his saddle, seized the spear, and rising gracefully in his seat again, continued his headlong course.

The Indian rode some distance, turned his horse in a spray of sod, and galloped back to the point he had picked up the spear, dropping it in the same spot. "The same feat was then performed by every warrior, Ranger and Caballero on the ground, with a single failure."

Someone substituted a glove for the spear, and again, each rider picked it up and returned it at a gallop. Next came a shooting exhibition, first with bow and arrow by the Comanches, and then with pistols by the rangers and caballeros. The final competition involved breaking a wild horse, a feat that John McMullen, "a daring and handsome young ranger," performed handily enough to win first place. Long Quiet, a Comanche warrior, took second place.[39]

During the summer of 1843, while Houston and his administration continued an intense effort to persuade Mexico, as Anson Jones later put it, to "forego her phantasy of a nominal sovereignty" over Texas, the president and his secretary of war also cracked down on Mexican bandits preying on Anglos and Tejanos. In a letter to British consul Charles Elliott in Galveston, Jones said the killing of innocent Mexicans near Victoria had been perpetrated by "lawless robbers." Jones said Hays had authority "under the law martial," in the tradition of *ley de fuego* and the old Spanish system of La Acordada, "to execute without delay all whom he can arrest, and who are guilty of these infamous offences [*sic*]."[40]

Armed with extraordinary legal authority as well as rifles and pistols, Hays ordered three men he suspected of being spies for the Mexican bandit Quinones shot by firing squad.[41] "Upon interrogating the prisoners," the Clarksville *Northern Standard* reported, "their leader Rubio acknowledged that he and his party had, for a long time, been committing murders and stealing horses along the Colorado, the Guadalupe, and other western streams, and that he killed [a Texan] upon the expectation of getting his horse, which was a fine one. After hearing these disclosures, Capt. Hays immediately ordered the prisoners to be executed and they were shot forthwith." The Clarksville editor approved wholeheartedly: "A few such acts of retribution like this, will tend more to give peace and security to the frontier than all the 'letters' and proclamations the President can write during his term of office."[42]

William Bollaert, an Englishman who spent some time in Texas during the days of the republic, mentioned Hays several times in his diary. "He has been in command of the Western Rangers for a long period and lately the government has given him very extensive powers as regards the frontier," Bollaert wrote on September 30, 1843. "The Major is young, amiable, and exceedingly modest, and beloved by his followers. He has the reputation of an Indian fighter and good backwoodsman. Many have been his encounters with the Comanches and Mexicans."[43]

MOUNTED GUN-MEN

The Texas congress passed an act January 23, 1844, "Authorizing John C. Hays to raise a Company of Mounted Gun-men, to act as Rangers, on the Western and South-Western Frontier." The company's lieutenant would be elected by the forty privates Hays enlisted. Congress charged Hays's company with ranging "from the county of Bexar to the county of Refugio, and westward as the public interest may require." The Rangers would serve for four months, though the president could extend their enlistment in case of emergency. Each ranger would be paid $30 a month for his services. Hays earned $75 a month as captain. Ben McCulloch, again elected lieutenant, made $55 a month.[44]

In light of the recent Mexican incursions into Texas, on January 31, 1844, the congress—codifying what Hays had already done at least once—approved an act providing for the court-martialing of anyone "in arms" against the republic. That could be done instanter, with the ultimate penalty being execution.[45]

Though not yet at full strength, Hays's company rode that March in pursuit of cattle thieves. The rustlers had driven off nearly two thousand head of cattle and were believed headed north toward the Colorado River. If Hays caught up with the cattle thieves, the result did not make the public prints.[46]

That June, returning from a fruitless scout for Indians along the Pedernales River, Hays's company camped at a point he later described as "four miles east of the Pinto trace . . . nearly equally distant from Bexar, Gonzalez and Austin." The absence of Indian sign did not mean the absence of hostile Indians. Wise in the ways of the Comanche, Hays detailed one of his men to lag behind the rest of the rangers, alert to the possibility of their being backtracked. On June 8, the rear guard rode into the ranger camp and told Hays he had found ten sets of Indian pony tracks following the rangers' trail. Looking in the direction his ranger had ridden in from, Hays soon spotted several Indians in the distance, but they quickly faded into the brush.

Ordering his men to mount, Hays rode toward the trees. As the rangers advanced, three or four warriors emerged from the vegetation and made a show of surprise at seeing the rangers. Then they fled back into the cover on the east bank of a creek.

"Hays, however, was too old an 'Indian fighter' to be caught by such traps and made no efforts at pursuit," the Clarksville *Northern Standard* later reported. "As soon as the Indians saw this strategy was of no avail, they came out of the timber and displayed their whole force in line, some 75 in number."[47]

The captain had only fifteen men under his command. But a great equalizer rested in each of their holsters—the five-shot Paterson Colt revolver. Accordingly, Hays calculated his numbers differently from the Comanches: fifteen times five equaled seventy-five. Also, as the north Texas newspaper soon reported, "His men were highly disciplined, of tried courage, [and] their horses well broke."

Slowly, the rangers advanced on the Indians. Having higher ground behind them, the Indians fell back, moving to a position that would give them even more advantage over the approaching Texans. At the crown of the hill, the Comanches dismounted. Brandishing their feather-draped lances and raising and lowering their tough buffalo-hide shields, some of them knew enough English to taunt the rangers with cries of "Charge! Charge!"

Hays then demonstrated the genius for fighting that established his reputation. He knew the Indians could not see him at the base of the elevation. Rather than charge uphill, which was just what the Comanches wanted, Hays spurred his horse and cantered around the rocky prominence. The other rangers followed, circling to the Comanches' exposed flank.

Now the Indians got their charge, but from an unanticipated direction. Seeing the Texans galloping toward them on level ground, the Indians remounted. The shock of the charge broke the Indian line, but only for a moment. Regrouping, they split and attacked the rangers from two sides. On horseback, the Comanches considered themselves invincible.

"Back to back, the Texians received them and the close and deadly fire of their pistols emptied many a saddle," the Clarksville newspaper reported. "Thus, hand to hand the fight lasted fifteen minutes, the Indians using their spears and arrows, the Texians their repeating pistols. Scarcely a man of the brigade [*sic*] was not grazed . . . their gun stocks, knife handles and saddles perforated in many places."

Those Comanches still capable of sitting a horse tried to distance themselves from the rangers, but the Texans rode after them. At the end of a two-mile running fight, the chief rallied his warriors, enjoining them to turn and face the Texans. The Indians also had a brave leader.

"He dashed backward and forward amongst his men to bring them back to the charge," the newspaper continued. "The Texians had exhausted nearly all their shot. Hays called out to learn who had a loaded gun. [Robert] Gillespie rode forward and answered he was charged. 'Dismount and shoot the chief,' was the order. At a distance of thirty steps, the ball performed its office and, madly dashing a few yards, the gallant Indian fell to rise no more."

Losing their chief finally broke the spirit of the Indians, who fled in every direction.

When the last white clouds of gun smoke faded away, twenty Comanches lay dead. Another thirty had been wounded. Hays had lost one ranger, German Peter Fohr, his body full of arrows. Three other rangers had suffered wounds, including slim, redheaded Samuel Walker, pinned to the ground with a Comanche lance through his body.[48]

The rangers remained in the area, nursing their wounded. Three days later, four Indians probably intent on reclaiming their dead showed up at the battleground. Hays attacked again, killing three more warriors and raising the Comanche body count to twenty-three.

The Paterson Colts, Hays wrote on June 16 in his official report of the fight, "did good execution." In fact, he added, "Had it not been for them, I doubt what the consequences would have been. I cannot recommend these arms too highly."[49]

The fight represented more than a clash of two proud cultures. It demonstrated the power of nineteenth-century technology over primitive weaponry. With the Colt repeating pistols, the Texas Rangers had the frontier equivalent of nuclear bombs. In fifteen minutes, Hays and his rangers had changed the history of the West.

"Up to this time," Samuel Walker later wrote, "these daring Indians had always supposed themselves superior to us, man to man, on horse . . . the result of this engagement was such as to intimidate them and enable us to treat with them."

How long the Rangers had been carrying the Colts is not known. On March 28, 1839, Colonel of Ordnance George Washington Hockley reported to Secretary of War Johnston that he had completed an examination and test of the Colt rifle, carbine, and pistol. Hockley, the man who had so successfully overseen the use of the cannons called the Twin Sisters at San Jacinto, recommended against the new weapons. His six objections ranged from unreliable percussion caps to the revolvers being hard to keep clean.[50] But President Lamar thought differently, ordering a major purchase from Colt. The Texas navy requisitioned—on credit—180 five-shot Colt revolvers from the Patent Arms Manufacturing Company in Patterson, New Jersey, on April 29, 1839. The order also included 180 carbines. Three months later, the Texas army ordered fifty Colt pistols, then referred to as Patent Arms. The government requisitioned forty more revolvers on October 5. Though surviving records make it unclear whether all of those weapons actually made it to Texas, the .36-caliber revolver soon became the Rangers' weapon of choice. The Texian government bought "belt pistols" and Colt eight-shot carbines in 1840. The Colts were probably issued to the Rangers following Houston's disbandment of the republic's navy in 1843.[51]

Hays's rangers had brought awesome weapons to their fight with the Comanches that summer, but even with state-of-the-art technology, leadership had been critical to the success of the outnumbered Anglos in the fight near the Pedernales.

"I scarcely know which to admire most," wrote the anonymous person who first heard the story from Hays at Washington-on-the-Brazos, "the skill and courage of [Hays] or his modesty when giving the details here narrated. Concealing his own deeds, he did ample justice to his comrades and, at the close of his narrative, blushed to find himself famous."[52]

Chief Flacco, a Lipan warrior who scouted for the Rangers, said of Hays, "Me and Blue Wing not afraid to go to hell together. Captain Jack, great brave, not afraid to go to hell by himself."[53]

Not intending to be surprised by a third Mexican incursion, Hays kept regular patrols on the trails south of San Antonio. One of those scouts added considerably to the Ranger reputation for toughness.

LEFT FOR DEAD

Camped on the Nueces River on August 12, 1844, rangers John M. Carolan and James Dunn decided to take a dip in the cool, clear water. Resting in camp while their comrades splashed in the river, rangers Christopher Black "Kit" Acklen and Rufus "Rufe" Perry suddenly found themselves surrounded by Indians. Acklen got off one shot as he ran for cover in the nearby brush. Before Perry could get to his rifle, an arrow thumped into his shoulder. Running toward his horse, the ranger took another arrow in his face and a third in his hip. Firing his pistol as he ran, Perry managed to yank out that last arrow, pulling it out through the exit wound it had made. Moments later, weak from blood loss, he fainted.[54]

Assuming they had killed the ranger, the Indians moved on to find the others. When Perry came to, he hefted his revolver and considered shooting himself rather than face torture by the Indians. But when he realized the Indians had moved on, he struggled to stand and made his way to the river.

Carolan and Dunn had crossed to the north side of the river, but when they saw Perry emerge from the brush, they swam back to him. Acklen came out from hiding and joined his fellow rangers. They helped Perry across the river, but when he fainted again, the rangers thought he had died. They took his rifle and pistol, leaving him where he fell.

Unable to find Acklen's horse, Carolan and Dunn left him behind, too. When they rode into San Antonio, sunburned but otherwise un-harmed, the two rangers reported the deaths of Acklen and Perry. Hays sent scouts to bring back the bodies.

"The men who went to look for the unfortunate rangers did their duty but of course did not find them," an old ranger who had heard the story firsthand related years later. He said the rangers readily found the scene of the fight, well marked by dried blood, but not the two missing rangers. "They could not track as well as the Indians, for it is evident they . . . lost the trail there on account of Ackland's [sic] skill in cover-ing it," the ranger continued.[55]

Too weak to do anything else, Perry hid under a large pile of drift-wood on the riverbank. He used mud and leaves to staunch his wounds. At one point, the Comanches reappeared along the river, walking with their heads down as they looked for Perry's tracks. Either they never found them or once again decided that he must be dead. Perry sought refuge in a hollow tree and got some sleep.

Also supposing Perry dead, Acklen set out on foot for San Antonio. After resting for most of the first day after the attack, Perry, too, decided to move north. Eating mesquite beans and prickly pear tunas, the two wounded rangers walked and sometimes crawled through the blistering summer heat toward San Antonio.[56]

On the evening of August 18, a lazy summer Sunday, Perry reached the town, its residents quickly energized by the appearance of a nearly naked, sunburned ranger given up for dead. His arrival made such a stir that Prince Solms-Braunfels noted it in his diary: "Traveled 120 miles on foot; six and a half days without food. Has three arrow wounds." Three days later, Solms wrote, "[Acklen], the last believed to be dead, arrived. He has five wounds. In the evening the Dr. cut the arrow from his jaw bone."[57]

Learning that his scouts had failed to find the two men, Hays exploded. "Hays was so incensed at one of the scouts that he made him leave the company, but afterward took him back again. He was a good ranger and trailer, and was looked upon as being one of the most daring men Hays had."[58]

Solms-Braunfels did not use the word *ranger* in his diary, but their activities occasionally found their way into his daily entries. The German did not waste ink and paper with too many words, but his observations to some extent reveal the personality of Hays's men. A week before Perry startled San Antonio with his appearance, Solms had written about another ranger, Joseph A. Tivy, who had accidentally shot himself in his thigh. "The Dr.," Solms wrote, "wanted him held down during the surgery. They [some of his fellow rangers] said: 'No, we cannot do it, he is a free Texian.'" Unrestrained as the doctor probed his leg wound without benefit of anesthesia, the ranger recovered, serving under Hays until the following October.[59]

"My First Day With the Rangers"

Congress passed another act February 1, 1845, dealing with protection of the frontier. Again, Hays got the command of a company, with smaller detachments—each under a lieutenant—authorized for Bexar, Goliad, Milam, Refugio, Roberts, and Travis counties. (The men of the Goliad and Refugio company, with an authorized strength of fifteen, would report to the same lieutenant.) In addition to his company, the Bexar detachment, Hays would command all the detachments if gathered together. Pay would be $75 a month for Hays, $30 for the lieutenants, and $20 for the privates. The law also set aside $10 a month for each man to pay for ammunition, horseshoeing, forage and food, and medicine. Records do not indicate if any of the detachments were orga-nized, but Hays had his company formed by February 12.

The Ranger myth, already well-established in Texas, began to spread beyond its borders. A nine-page double-column article, "My First Day with the Rangers," written by "A Kentuckian" (Charles W. Webber), ap-peared in the March 1845 issue of a national magazine called *The Amer-ican Review*. If not the first, Webber's was one of the earliest stories about Texas Rangers to appear in a publication with a wide circulation. The author came to Texas in 1838, rode with Hays for a time, and also served under Captain John P. Gill in 1842.[60]

That rangers captured runaway slaves seeking freedom in Mexico did not get remembered in most of the recollections of old-timers from the 1840s. But slave owners usually paid bounties for their runaway property, San Antonio was the gateway to Mexico, and rangers excelled at tracking. The color of the man making the tracks mattered little. While Webber's story may be partially fictionalized, it has a ring of truth.[61]

Webber explained how the three races on the Texas frontier—white, Mexican, and Indian—lived "in a state of perpetual feuds in which the knife and the rifle are the sole arbiters." He added, "And strong men and unregulated passions exhibit their worst and best extremes in this at-mosphere of license."

He proceeded to illustrate his point:

Traveling from East Texas to San Antonio, Webber had thrown in with a Brazos River planter on his way to reclaim his chattel, a young black male who had been arrested "by the vigilant Rangers" and "thrown into chains."

After Webber and the slave owner found the San Antonio merchant who had been keeping the plantation owner's missing "boy," the two men retired to an inn on the market square. Inside they found eight or ten young men clad in a combination of Mexican and "ordinary Ameri-can dress." They wore sombreros, smoked Mexican *cigarittas,* and had pistols and knives tucked into their waistbands. Webber soon learned that the men belonged to Hays's Ranger company. After some cordial conversation, Webber wrote, "I announced my wish to Capt. Hays to be-come one of them and share the rough and tumble as well as their jolli-ties with them. I was welcomed with frank enthusiasm into the ranks."

Webber and his new comrades-in-arms talked and drank until two o'clock in the morning. He had not been asleep long before someone began pounding on the door of the inn. During the night, a messenger reported, the slave had escaped, making off with clothing, a rifle, food, a good horse, and a silver-mounted saddle.

When the slave owner offered $50 for the return of his chattel, and the merchant said he would throw in another $50 for his horse and saddle, two of Hays's rangers eagerly took the trail of the Mexico-bound slave.

Later that morning, Webber and the other rangers stood around the square, enjoying the sunshine on what had started off as a cold February morning. "Hays was said to be a wonderful shot, and gave us a proof that the report did justice to his skill," Webber continued. "He held one of my pistols in his hand, when he observed a chicken-cock some thirty paces off in the square, which was just straightening its neck to crow. 'Boys, I'll cut that saucy fellow short,' he observed as he levelled and fired quickly at it; and, sure enough, the half enounced clarion-note of Chanticleer was lost in the explosion, and it fluttered over dead with a ball through its head."

The chicken still quivered in the dirt when one of the rangers who had ridden out that morning came galloping back into town. Hays and the other rangers saw that he rode stiffly in the saddle, blood smearing the side of his buckskin jacket. Almost incoherent at first, he finally reported that he and the other ranger, hot on the slave's trail, had ridden into an ambush. After taking a bullet in his side, he had become separated from his partner and did not know what had happened to him.

Hays ordered his men to saddle up. Not far from town on the Laredo road, they found their missing colleague and his prisoner, a Mexican who had aided the slave's escape and then lay in waiting for the rangers he knew would follow. Asked why he had not already killed his captive, the ranger admitted that he admired the man's bravery.

Unimpressed, Hays ordered the Mexican executed on the spot. The rangers tied their prisoner to a tree and drew numbers to see which of them would get to do the honors. The rangers composing the firing squad raised their rifles and aimed, ready for Hays's command to fire. But before the rangers pulled their triggers, the Mexican yelled a warning: They aimed too low.

At that, the man's captor jumped to his feet.

"Jack! Hear that! Don't shoot this fellow! Spare him for my sake—could the devil himself beat that?"

Hays waved his hand, signaling the rangers to lower their rifles. The ranger who had captured the Mexican cut the thongs on his hands and legs "and he stood before us a free man."

He told the rangers that "attracted by a human sympathy for the Boy," he had assisted in the successful escape of the slave. He had hung back to ambush the rangers pursuing the fleeing slave to settle the score from a previous run-in with a sworn enemy.

"Such as it was," Webber concluded, "this was my first day with the Rangers, and we were soon afterward sound asleep on the grass."[62]

Webber's story no doubt had its fictional elements, but it demonstrated that Hays, as leader of the Rangers, could be flexible. In the summer of 1845, he even essayed to do the Mexican people a favor. Hays learned that 150 Comanches had been seen moving south from Torrey's Trading Post on the Brazos, intent on raiding into Mexico. The Ranger captain and others met the raiding party outside San Antonio. Hays gave the Indians $80 worth of beef and other provisions and tried unsuccessfully to talk them out of their planned foray south of the Rio Grande. Whether Hays was acting on orders or exercising his own judgment is not clear.

During President Houston's final term, and through the brief administration of his successor, Dr. Anson Jones, Texas had tried to get along with the Comanches. However, a willingness to let bygones be bygones did not extend universally. When Jones ran for office with Houston's backing, Edward Burleson sought the presidency with a promise to resume Lamar's more hawkish policy toward Indians. The frontier voted for Burleson, but not with enough numbers to defeat Jones, who had general support in the more populated eastern half of Texas—an area beyond the range of the Comanches. While Houston and Jones shared a more enlightened attitude toward Indians, Lamar and Burleson had a more realistic view. The two cultures—Anglo Texan and Indian—remained on a collision course.[63]

"This condition of affairs," former Hays ranger Lee later wrote, "necessarily resulted in bringing into existence the Texas Rangers, a military order as peculiar as it has become famous."[64]

The Texas Republic's near decade of self-proclaimed independence drew to a close. Through the years it had lacked enough money and consistent leadership to build a strong nation. The best that can be said is that its population growth and oft-demonstrated willingness to fight proved sufficient to prevent Mexico from reclaiming its lost province, although the Mexican Republic never acknowledged Texas's independence. The Rangers, although not single-handedly, played a vital role in preserving Texas's short-lived sovereignty. They had not eliminated Texas's twin threats—Indians and Mexico—but Hays, the Mc-Culloch brothers, Walker, and others had firmly established the Rangers' reputation.[65]

4

"Cleaning pistols and grinding knives"

STATEHOOD AND WAR WITH MEXICO, 1846—48

From a bluff overlooking the beach along Corpus Christi Bay, Captain D. P. Whiting sketched the scene below: Flapping in the Gulf breeze, nine rows of white canvas tents stretched toward the horizon. Blue-uniformed U.S. soldiers and their horses moved around looking as small as sand crabs. Five ships and three lesser vessels lay on the green water of the bay. Not since the War of 1812 had so many American men and arms amassed at one location—half the U.S. army had come to Texas.

Transformed from a rough sketch into a detailed engraving suitable for reproduction in a color lithograph, the army engineer's drawing appeared in print as a "Birds-eye view of the Camp of the Army of Occupation, Commanded by Gen. [Zachary] Taylor Near Corpus Christi, Texas . . . Oct. 1845."

Seven months before Whiting captured this image with his pen, Mexico had broken diplomatic relations with the United States in protest of Congress's approval of a joint resolution extending statehood to Texas. All the nearly ten-year-old republic had to do was adopt an acceptable state constitution. By May 1845, with Texas's admission to the Union nearly at hand, President James K. Polk ordered four thousand troops to Texas from Louisiana. A contingent of mounted dragoons crossed the

Red River from the Indian Territory and marched to Austin and San Antonio, while ships carrying infantry and supplies reached the Corpus Christi area on July 26, 1845.

When the first American troops arrived on the coast, a Ranger company under Peter Hansborough Bell rode up to greet them. The tall Virginian, who fought at San Jacinto, had first served as a ranger in 1840 with Jack Hays. Like General Taylor, whose military accomplishments would carry him to the White House, the events that followed would propel Bell into public office as well. What happened during the next few years also made the Texas Rangers internationally famous.

Though Polk hoped to reach an accord with Mexico through state craft, Mexico already considered the presence of American troops in South Texas an act of war. "As a precautionary measure," the president later told Congress, he had authorized Taylor to accept volunteers from Texas as well as Alabama, Kentucky, Louisiana, Mississippi, and Tennessee. Taylor reported to Washington that he intended to enlist three hundred rangers "as proper . . . for the protection of the frontier." The general wrote Texas president Anson Jones on August 16, 1845, that he would like to muster into federal service as militia any existing Texas volunteer or spy companies—rangers. Jones readily approved the request. Hays, who Taylor noted "has a reputation as a partisan," within a month had a commission to command four Ranger companies. Charged with reconnoitering for Mexicans and suppressing Indians, under federal law these men could remain active for only three months.[1]

Other Texans signed on with Taylor in short order. Captain John T. Price's company of Texas Mounted Volunteers, thirty-six men, mustered at Victoria on September 25. Seventy-three men of Robert Gillespie's company of Texas Mounted Rangers began federal service three days later. Gillespie's officers included Michael H. Chevallie as first lieutenant, John Adams, second lieutenant, and William A. A. (Big Foot) Wallace, first sergeant. Sixty-two men of David C. Cady's company of Texas Mounted Rangers went on the rolls at Austin on October 1. Near the end of the month, forty-seven men under Captain Bell's Texas Mounted Volunteers, the men on hand when Taylor's forces began massing, became federalized at Corpus Christi.

Texas officially joined the Union as the twenty-eighth state on December 29, 1845. Two days later, Hays and the republic's former secretary of war, William G. Cooke, arrived in Austin from San Antonio in time for a "very lively" New Year's Eve celebration. Citizens of the late Texas Republic lined Congress Avenue to watch a company of U.S. dragoons in full dress march up the capital's wide main street. That night they joined the soldiers at a grand cotillion, and as one resident later wrote, "a deputation of [Superintendent of Indian Affairs Thomas G.] Western's pets from the Ton-ke-wahs" got "most gloriously drunk."[2]

The festivities in Austin may have presented an opportunity for the friendly Tonkawas to go on a toot, but most Indians in Texas saw no cause for celebration. Good horseflesh meaning far more to them than flags, they had no interest in anyone else's sovereignty. Boldly striking San Antonio on the night of January 13, 1846, a party of Wacos and Keechies drove off thirty-five horses. Captain Gillespie and his "corps of Texas Rangers," as the *Texas Democrat* soon reported, "closely pursued" the Indians and caught up with them after a "hard and rapid march of seventy miles." When the rangers approached the Indian camp on the edge of a cedar brake, "they fled into the fastnesses of the thickets and defied discovery, or even pursuit." But the rangers recovered the stolen horses, returning to San Antonio January 16.

"Upon his arrival," the newspaper related, Gillespie "had the pleasure of restoring the horses to their respective owners, who were, as might be expected, highly gratified. The Captain deserves great credit for the alacrity and energetic promptness of his movements. Such men are invaluable upon a frontier, and the people of San Antonio would doubtless dislike very much to be deprived of his services."[3]

Following the organization of a state government, President Jones lowered the Lone Star flag and raised the Stars and Stripes over the whitewashed frame capitol in Austin on February 19. Jones then handed the government of the late Republic of Texas over to J. Pinckney Henderson, who took the oath as Texas's first governor.

The first session of the new state's legislature passed a resolution on March 14 in recognition of the "chivalry and many gallant and daring deeds of Maj. John C. Hays, Capt. Benj. McCullough [*sic*] and R.A. Gillespie." This "gallant band . . . are entitled to the gratitude of the people of Texas and the admiration of the world."[4] Though the lawmakers singled out only three men for recognition, the Rangers had been one of the republic's more successful governmental endeavors. Their forts became outposts of settlement; they rescued Indian captives; they discouraged Mexican incursions and took a part in rebuffing those that occurred; and they chased and dealt out summary justice to cattle thieves and bandits.

Taylor had, meanwhile, begun a staged removal of his army from Corpus Christi, marching toward the Rio Grande.[5] When the general crossed the Nueces River, which Mexico continued to claim as the true border between it and its runaway Texas province, the government of Mexico considered it an invasion. Within three weeks, Taylor's engineers had established a coastal supply depot at Point Isabel and busied themselves throwing up an earthen fortification above the Rio Grande across from the Mexican city of Matamoros.

Battle-scarred ranger Samuel Walker, who had recently resigned from Captain Gillespie's company, and about thirty former and prospective rangers had followed Taylor from Corpus Christi to the Rio Grande Valley, as one contemporary writer put it, "expecting to see a fight." Walker asked Taylor for permission to formally organize a company, but the general refused, calling it unnecessary. But when soldiers found the body of one his officers in the chaparral with its skull crushed, Taylor changed his mind. Clearly, he needed experienced scouts.[6]

The general wrote Texas's adjutant general on April 15 that he intended to authorize two companies of volunteers for "the purpose of keeping open our communication with Point Isabel, and relieving the regular cavalry of a portion of their duties, which are oppressive." On the tenth anniversary of the Battle of San Jacinto, April 21, a company of Texas Mounted Rangers under Walker went into federal service at Point Isabel.[7] This company never reached full strength, but it soon saw action.

For most of April, the two armies facing each other across the Rio Grande engaged in a battle of the bands. Every night, the U.S. musicians at the earthworks opposite Matamoros struck up "Yankee Doodle," the "Star-Spangled Banner," and "Hail, Columbia." The Mexican army's band shot back with music that one American termed "exquisite . . . surpassing anything ever heard from a military band."[8] But on April 25, a shriller note sounded. Investigating a reported river crossing by Mexican troops, a detachment of sixty-three dragoons under Captain Seth Thornton rode into an ambush. In the fight that followed, Mexican soldiers killed or wounded seventeen Americans, capturing the rest.

"I have this day deemed it necessary to call upon the governor of Texas for four regiments of volunteers," Taylor wrote Washington the day after the Mexican attack. War had begun.[9]

Two days later, scouting the road from Point Isabel to Matamoros, Walker and his rangers encountered fifteen hundred Mexican troops. To the captain's dismay, several of his men panicked and rode hell-bent for Point Isabel. Walker and twelve others stood their ground, fighting for fifteen minutes before following their colleagues, realizing they could run or die. Earlier the same day, April 28, Mexican *lanceros* had charged Walker's lightly guarded base camp, halfway between Point Isabel and Fort Texas, the new cantonment across from Matamoros. Sergeant Edward S. Radcliffe and five other rangers died in the surprise predawn attack. One ranger who managed to get on his horse did not make it far before a Mexican rope fell around his neck. The experienced Mexican horseman pulled the rope taunt and strangled the Texan.[10]

Mexican artillery began a bombardment of Fort Texas on May 3, and American gunners answered the fire. Later that day, the booming of artillery rolling like distant thunder across the salt prairie between his base camp and the fort, Taylor dispatched a company of dragoons along with Walker and ten rangers to assess the garrison's situation. Leaving the regulars behind, Walker and six of his men made their way through the brush toward the fort. Reaching the picket line around the star-shaped earthen redoubt, Walker continued alone, slipping into the fort and spending an hour with Major Jacob Brown, the commander. On his way back to Point Isabel to report to Taylor, Walker adroitly dodged Mexican patrols scouting the main road.[11] Not long after Walker left the fort, Major Brown fell mortally wounded, though the garrison held.

The day after the attack on Fort Texas, Hays rode into Austin. He soon learned that Taylor, somewhat ahead of his legal authority to do so, had requisitioned Governor Henderson for volunteers. The governor authorized Hays, whose earlier Ranger commission would soon expire, to raise a regiment designated as the First Regiment of Mounted Rifles. Henderson gave George T. Wood command of the Second Regiment, a body that came to be called the East Texas Rangers. From the capital city, Hays traveled east to Washington County to recruit former rangers.[12] At a gathering under the shade of an oak grove in Brenham, county residents listened to John Wilkins Sr. make a speech praising Hays and his men.

Barbecue followed, and then a dance. The next day, Hays departed to sign up more men.

"No mock show of the pomp and pageantry of war was seen—no tap of spirit-stirring drum, or note of piercing fife—no trumpet call or bugle sound," one observer wrote of the mobilization in Texas that spring. "But there was wiping of rifles and moulding of bullets— cleaning of pistols and grinding of knives—packing of wallets and saddling of steeds."[13]

It took Ben McCulloch only thirty-six hours to raise a new company of sixty men.[14] "This company," one of its members later wrote, "was perhaps the best mounted, armed, equipped, and appointed corps . . . in the ranging service; and from the time of its arrival at headquarters until after its disbandment . . . enjoyed more of the trust and confidence of the commanding general than any other volunteer company."[15]

Returning to San Antonio from his recruitment sweep, Hays formally mustered his regiment. Many of his men had ridden before as rangers, Texans eager for a fight.[16] The *Telegraph and Texas Register* reported on May 6 that "all the ranging companies on our western frontier . . . are on the march for the American camps." Hays's company, combined with McCulloch's, would probably amount to five hundred men, the newspaper said. "The rangers are all well mounted and have long been wishing for a brush with the Mexicans."

With Walker and his men serving as his scouts, Taylor decided to move his main force from Point Isabel to Fort Texas. "If the enemy oppose my march," Taylor wrote Washington, "I shall fight him." On May 8, at a point on the Matamoros road called Palo Alto, the twenty-three-hundred-man American force encountered four thousand Mexican soldiers. Though Taylor had instructed his assistant adjutant to inform the infantry "that their main dependence must be in the bayonet," well-trained American artillerymen carried the day, inflicting heavy casualties on the Mexicans during the five-hour battle.[17]

Taylor met the Mexicans again the following day at Resaca de la Palma. At the height of the fighting, Walker's horse took a bullet and tumbled to the grass. As the ranger got untangled from his screaming mount and struggled to his feet, he saw a Mexican *lancero* bearing down on him, the shining blade of his pike pointed straight at Walker's gut. The captain had no trouble remembering the last time he had been speared. With the elegantly uniformed cavalryman almost close enough to impale the dismounted ranger, Walker toppled him with a well-placed pistol shot. The ranger then grabbed the reins of the dead lancer's horse, swung into the saddle, and rejoined his company.[18]

Unaware of the two battles, army lieutenant Rankin Dilworth stood with his feet spread on the deck of the steamship *Galveston* to steady himself against the Gulf swell as the vessel made her way down the coast toward Taylor's supply depot. When the vessel hove to off Point Isabel on May 12, the young officer and others saw a group of horseman arrayed on the beach. Studying the mounted men through his telescope, the ship's captain feared they were Mexicans and that the place had been wrested from American control. As it developed, Dilworth wrote in his diary, "They proved to be Captain Price's company of Texian Rangers."[19]

Not yet apprised of the battles at Palo Alto and Resaca de Palma, President Polk on May 11 asked for and received a congressional declaration of war on the basis of the April 25 attack on Captain Thornton's command, in which "American blood had been shed on American soil." Two days later, Congress passed an act authorizing for one year a volunteer army fifty thousand men strong.

By midmonth, having heard that the war had begun, Hays and his men rode south to join the fray. From Corpus Christi, they followed the route Taylor's army had taken to Point Isabel. On June 22, Hay's men formalized the seasoned ranger's leadership by electing him as their colonel. Walker resigned his captaincy after being elected lieutenant colonel of Hays's regiment.[20]

Newly minted citizen-soldiers had begun descending on Texas from most of the other states of the Union, prepared to fight for their country. The men from Texas, while similarly inspired, had another motivation: revenge. In North Texas, the publisher of the *Northern Standard* in Clarksville believed all Americans should feel that way: "We trust that every man of our army, as he points his rifle or thrusts his bayonet, will think of his countrymen martyred at the Alamo, at Goliad, and at Mier."[21]

As volunteers gathered in South Texas, another army of sorts began to arrive: printers and journalists. Numerous typesetters from New Orleans volunteered for military service, ready to use lead any way they could, either by shooting it from a rifle or setting type for military orders or handbills. Newspapers, especially the fiercely competitive sheets published in the Mississippi River delta metropolis, dispatched representatives to write stories and sell subscriptions to soldiers and their officers. In addition to reports coming from staff writers, Texas and American newspapers gladly printed informative letters from soldiers and others. The Mexican War became the first U.S. conflict to receive extensive news media coverage from correspondents in the field. Texas Rangers, those scribes soon discovered, made good copy.

New Orleans *Picayune* correspondent George W. Kendall wrote one of the first stories as he traveled through South Texas toward Point Isabel with Hays's rangers. The dispatch featured one Bill Dean, a ranger under Chevallie. Dean told how tough it had been for him and his fellow rangers to get grub, relating that he once survived eight days on "one poor hawk and three blackberries." Finding the pickings slim, he continued, the rangers "couldn't kill a prairie rat . . . to save us from starvation." Their menu improved somewhat on the ninth day of their march, Dean continued, when a worn-out horse died. But the rangers could not find firewood to cook it. His story getting windier by the moment, Dean said he had solved the problem by setting the prairie on fire, impaling a chunk of horse meat on the ramrod from his rifle and chasing the flames for a mile and a half, finally settling for rare steak.[22]

Though troops now saturated the tip of South Texas, the new state's western frontier lay exposed to its perennial foe, the Indian. Army lieutenant colonel William S. Harney of the Second Dragoons, the ranking officer in the interior, requisitioned Governor Henderson on June 28 for five companies of "mounted rangers"—not for duty in Mexico but to remain in Texas and protect its citizens from hostile Indians. With Henderson on his way to join the fight against Mexico, Lieutenant Governor A. C. Horton ordered that the new Ranger companies be positioned "at or near" Castroville, San Antonio, the Little River in present Bell County, Torrey's Trading Post on the Brazos (Waco), and on the west fork of the Trinity River. Horton further instructed the company captains to keep in touch with their adjacent posts at least twice monthly, either by messenger or patrol.[23]

Taylor had moved unopposed into Matamoros on May 18 but could not penetrate deeper into Mexico without a better supply system. For the time being, the general concentrated on strengthening his hold along the river. Lieutenant Dilworth's company and several others received orders on June 4 to march for Reynosa, a Mexican city upriver from Matamoros. A company of rangers would accompany them. "The Mexicans dread the Texians more than they do the devil," the young officer wrote, "and they have good reason for it, if all the reports that we hear are true."[24]

"HAVE YOU A GOOD HORSE, SIR?"

Volunteers by the hundreds continued to stream into Texas. Lawyer Samuel Reid Jr. had sailed with the Sixth Louisiana Volunteers from New Orleans on June 5. "Long habituated to writing a journal," as he later explained, the words he set down while in Texas and Mexico would immortalize a scrappy bunch of Texans and their leaders.

Reid had not been in the theater of war long before he began hearing about the Texas Rangers. In Matamoros, he met the *Picayune*'s Kendall, who introduced him to McCulloch. The newspaper correspondent told the thirty-five-year-old ranger captain that Reid wanted to join his command.

McCulloch's clear blue eyes moved slowly up and down Reid's frame.

"Have you a good horse, sir?" the captain asked. "I have refused a great many because their horses would not do for our service."

Reid let the captain examine his horse. The animal "being pronounced 'a good horse,'" Reid recalled, "we were immediately made a Texas Ranger."

The next day, Reid arrived at the ranger camp to throw in with the Texans. A skillful painter of word pictures, Reid described the scene:

> Men in groups with long beards and moustaches, dressed in every variety of garment, with one exception, the slouched hat, the unmistakable uniform of a Texas Ranger, and a belt of pistols around their waists, were occupied drying their blankets, cleaning and fixing their guns, and some employed cooking at different fires, while others were grooming their horses. A rougher looking set we never saw.[25]

As Reid talked with McCulloch, a young ranger walked up with his rifle on his shoulder, his free hand gripping two dead ducks. The captain invited Reid to stay for dinner, the first of many occasions he would have to sit around a fire listening to the rangers tell of their experiences. The lawyer-turned-ranger enjoyed the stories as much as the roasted duck, and he made note of them in his journal.

Others, such as Lieutenant Dilworth, shared their observations in letters to family and friends. On June 21, he wrote, a company of rangers (McCulloch and his men) rode into Reynosa, having scouted to within eighty miles of Monterrey. During their scout, Dilworth noted, the Texans had gone a full day without water. Back in what passed for civilization, the rangers turned to something stronger than water to quench their thirst. Three days later, Dilworth heard a commotion and investigated. The young army officer found the rangers, who had been bivouacked in a cotton gin, on top of the building "dancing a war dance to the infinite amusement of the natives gathered below." Earlier in the day, the rangers had amused themselves racing horses.[26]

As Dr. S. Compton Smith wrote in his war memoir:

> The genuine Ranger may always be distinguished from the quasi-Texian, by the animal he rides. He is generally a cross of the mustang of the Texas plains with the Kentucky or Virginia blood–horse. He possesses all the fire and endurance of the one, combined with the docility, intelligence, and speed of the other; or rather, all the best points and characteristics of the two races are more perfectly developed in the half-breed horse of the Texas Ranger.[27]

The rangers rode good horses, and along with their gear, many of them carried a grudge. Some of the rangers, survivors of the Mier expedition four years before, had been treated harshly at Reynosa while on their way to the Mexican prison at Perote. Others had lost friends or family members at the hands of Mexicans. As Reid recalled:

> Our orders were most strict not to molest any unarmed Mexican, and if some of the most notorious of these villains were found shot, or hung up in the chaparral, during our visit to Reynosa, the government was charitably bound to suppose, that during some fit of remorse and desperation, tortured by conscience for the many evil deeds they had committed, they had recklessly laid violent hands upon their own lives! "Quien sabe?"[28]

Starting with Captain Price's company, the ninety-day Ranger companies called for by Taylor began mustering out on June 25. Some of the men returned to their homes, but most reenlisted in the newly authorized volunteer companies.

Busy planning his campaign into Mexico, Taylor lost patience with the rangers and threatened to have them arrested. The general's patriotism ran as strong as any man's, but he thought the rangers' behavior during the Independence Day observance in Reynosa had gone too far. Attempting to justify their actions, the rangers said the chickens and pigs they feasted on, though admittedly not their property, had died by accident during their firing of celebratory salutes. The stolen whiskey, carried off in two horse-buckets, could not as easily be explained. In a letter to Colonel Wood three days later, Taylor branded the rangers "licentious vandals."[29]

Most Texans tended to be more charitable in their assessment of the Rangers. An article in the *Texas Democrat* on September 9 marked the first publication of the line "A Texas Ranger can ride like a Mexican, trail like an Indian, shoot like a Tennessean, and fight like the devil."[30] Beyond that, as Dr. Smith wrote, "Nowhere . . . could one find such an assemblage of extraordinary and eccentric characters, as were to be met with in a Texas Ranger company. Here, men from all ranks and conditions of society were brought into contact."[31]

With U.S. forces finally moving toward Monterrey, McCulloch and fifty rangers confronted two hundred Mexican lancers at Ramos on September 14. They exchanged gunfire, but both sides withdrew, the Mexicans believing additional Yankees must not be far behind.[32]

A week later, Taylor's army camped within sight of the mountain-surrounded city of Monterrey, capital of the state of Nuevo León. In attacking the city of fifteen thousand, rangers fought as dismounted troops with the regulars and uniformed volunteers. Early in the battle, his hat replaced with a red bandanna wrapped around his forehead, Hays exhorted, "Here they come, boys, here they come. Give them hell!" The rangers did just that, fighting from hill to hill and house to house. The Mexicans surrendered on September 25 after an intense three-day battle.

Many more Mexicans than Americans died in the fight, but the Texans lost one of their most notable leaders: Captain Gillespie. In the assault on the Bishop's Palace, the Mexican defenders' final refuge, Gillespie caught a bullet in his stomach. Mortally wounded, he raised up, pointed, and yelled, "Boys, place me behind that ledge . . . and give me my revolver, I will do some execution on them yet before I die."[33] "Big Foot" Wallace, by then a first lieutenant, took command of Gillespie's company following his death.

John Salmon Ford, who served as Hays's adjutant, later wrote this assessment of the Ranger role in taking Monterrey: "This action had much influence in shaping subsequent events, for whilst it greatly elated the American forces, it produced corresponding depression on the Mexicans." Part of that depression could be laid directly to the Rangers. One regular army officer later estimated that Hays's men, running roughshod in the city after the battle, killed as many as one hundred residents, burned the thatched-roof *jacales* of peasants, and committed other atrocities.[34]

After securing the city, Taylor negotiated with the ranking Mexican general and signed an eight-week armistice. In his after-action report to Washington, General William Jenkins Worth praised the Texas volunteers, noting that "every individual in the command unites . . . in admiration of the distinguished gallantry and conduct of Col. Hays and his noble band."[35]

Though Worth went on to write that "we can desire no better guarantee of success than by their association," the three-month enlistments of the Texans would expire October 2. Openly disgusted at Taylor's decision not to prosecute the war, the Rangers made ready to go home. Before they left, General Worth requested that Hays's regiment assemble outside his quarters, a house the Texans had captured after fierce fighting.

"The regiment formed in front of the house," Ford later wrote, "and [the Rangers] were invited in to partake of wine with him [Worth]. One by one they entered by one door, passed by the table, and at the end of the table, near another door, stood General Worth with members of his staff, each Texian as he passed shook hands with the General." Afterward, flush with wine and victory, the Texans reformed and gave the general "three rousing cheers, to show their love and admiration for him."[36]

Major Luther Giddings of the First Ohio Volunteers had a somewhat different perspective:

The departure of the Rangers . . . would have caused more regret than was generally felt, had it not been for the lawless and vindictive spirit

some of them had displayed in the week that elapsed between the capitulation of the city and their discharge. . . . The commanding general took occasion to thank them for the efficient service they had
rendered, and we saw them turn their faces toward the blood-bought
state they represented, with many good wishes and the hope that all
honest Mexicans were at a safe distance from their path.[37]

After crossing back into Texas, McCulloch and his rangers had to
fend off a party of Comanches who tried to capture their horses near the
Nueces River on the road to San Antonio. Reid returned to New Orleans and began working on a book detailing his experiences. Hays and
Walker also traveled to the Crescent City, where they received a hero's
welcome. From Louisiana, Walker returned to his native Maryland
while Hays went back to Texas.

But the president of the United States did not consider the war with
Mexico over. Furious at the armistice Taylor had signed, Polk ordered
the general to resume the campaign, which he did on November 13. "He
had the enemy in his power," the president fumed in his diary, "&
should have taken them prisoners . . . and preserved the advantage he
had obtained by pushing on without delay."[38]

Back East, Walker soon received an interesting letter from Samuel
Colt. The inventive entrepreneur said that he envisioned making some
improvements in his revolver and wanted to talk to Walker about securing a government contract. Walker liked the idea. The fight he and
Hays had had with the Comanches three years earlier remained fresh in
his memory. Thanks to the five-shot Paterson Colts the rangers carried
in that engagement, fifteen Texans had killed or wounded roughly forty
Indians. Walker wrote the gunsmith back, saying he would be pleased to
discuss how the weapon could be made more effective. Too, he wanted
to equip his men with Colt revolvers. "With improvements," the ranger
added, "I think they [the pistols] can be rendered the most perfect
weapon in the world."

Walker met with Colt on December 2. Some say the meeting gained
ample inspiration from a jug of brandy, but Walker did not have a reputation as a drinker. Brandy aside, what came out of the meeting was the
concept of a sobering weapon that would help win the West: the six-
shooter.

After the redesign, Colt commissioned New York engraver W. L. Ormsby to etch a scene based on Walker's description of the 1844 fight. In a marriage of aesthetics and advertising, the engraving went on the cylinder of the new weapons. Like much advertising, the image was not totally accurate: Ormsby had Hays's rangers wearing the uniform of U.S. Dragoons.[39]

The government offered Colt a purchase contract for one thousand of his new revolvers on January 4, 1847. A virtual hand cannon, the weapon weighed four pounds, nine ounces. Its six chambers held conical .44-caliber bullets weighing 220 grains. Fifty grains of black powder made the weapon as deadly as a rifle up to one hundred yards and better than a musket out to two hundred yards.[40]

Requested by Taylor to return to Mexico to continue as his chief of scouts, McCulloch began recruiting another company in Gonzales. With twenty-seven Texans, he headed south again for Mexico, arriving at Monterrey on January 31. From there, he rode for Saltillo, reporting to Taylor on February 4. He found that most of the general's seasoned troops had been ordered to join General Winfield Scott at Veracruz for a push toward Mexico City. The majority of Taylor's command, which had moved south of Saltillo to Agua Nueva, now consisted of untested volunteers.

Unknown to Taylor, during the break in hostilities General Santa Anna—now back in power—had amassed a large army. Some were poorly clothed and equipped conscripts, but the general had nearly twenty thousand men under arms. The self-styled Napoléon of the West believed he could reverse the course of the war in favor of Mexico, crushing Taylor and then defeating Scott. That done, he would march north to reclaim Texas. From there, perhaps he would take the war to the United States.

"The victory is ours"

⬦ne Texas Ranger almost single-handedly prevented any of that from happening. On February 16, 1847, Taylor ordered McCulloch to reconnoiter Rancho La Encarnación, about thirty miles south of Taylor's camp. After questioning a captured Mexican picket, chasing another, and skirmishing with a cavalry patrol, the ranger began to suspect that more enemy troops lurked in the area than Taylor believed. Four days later, making another scout toward Encarnación, McCulloch encountered a deserter who told him Santa Anna had a large army nearby. The ranger rode on alone to confirm whether the Mexican told the truth.

That night after the moon set, McCulloch reined his horse five miles from Encarnación and took in an awesome sight—through the clear mountain air he could see hundreds of campfires twinkling in the distance. Now he had no doubt. Like a rattlesnake slowly slithering toward an unsuspecting prairie dog, a huge Mexican army was moving toward Taylor's smaller force.

Realizing he had to get word to the general, the ranger dispatched his lieutenant and all but one of his men to carry the news to Taylor. After the Texans galloped off, McCulloch and one volunteer, ranger William I. Phillips, slipped closer to the enemy camp. Near enough to see lances gleaming in the light of soldiers' cigars, the two rangers figured the camp to be nearly a mile long and a fourth of a mile wide. At dawn, after a cold and sleepless night, McCulloch watched the Mexican camp come to life.

"Ah cracky," he later wrote, "what an infernal din there was . . . every fellow seemed to have a bugle or drum and was going it on his own hook, fires were soon kindled and cooking commenced."

While Phillips held their horses, McCulloch observed the camp through his spyglass, his vision obscured by smoke from all the campfires. "This we did not give up until the sun was well up in the Heavens," he wrote. "It was now we found our position truly critical; below us . . . was 20,000 enemies, above a half mile distance on each road, was a picket of 20 well mounted men."

Not knowing for sure whether his men had made it past the enemy's various picket posts, McCulloch and his fellow ranger departed to brief Taylor. But first they had to get past the Mexican sentinels. At one point, riding up on twenty Mexican soldiers, the two rangers brazenly pretended to be Mexican mustangers. Holding their rifles against their legs on the opposite sides of their horses, the pair of Americans slowly rode through the enemy position unchallenged.[41]

Then, as Reid later summarized, "Freed from their late dangerous position, they took a long breath, and galloped on with light hearts towards the camp at Agua Nueva."

When the two rangers drew within sight of the American camp on the afternoon of February 21, they saw a long column of dust. McCulloch's men had made it to the American encampment with the news, and Taylor had ordered a fallback to Buena Vista. But the general had remained in camp, anxiously awaiting more details from McCulloch. After taking a long drink and watering his horse, the ranger presented himself to Taylor.

"Very well, Major," Taylor replied after hearing the ranger's report. "That's all I wanted to know. I am glad they did not catch you." Observing that McCulloch must be tired, the general told him to get some sleep. With that, Taylor swung onto his saddle and left with his staff officers for Buena Vista, a point midway between Agua Nueva and Saltillo.[42]

Later the following morning, February 22, a rider approached Taylor's position under a white flag. He bore a letter from Santa Anna:

> You are surrounded by 20,000 men, and cannot in any human probability avoid suffering a rout and being cut to pieces with your troops, but as you deserve consideration and particular esteem, I wish to save you from a catastrophe, and for that purpose give you this notice in order that you may surrender at discretion . . . God and Liberty!

The American general wasted little ink in his answer: "Sir: In reply to your note of this date . . . I beg leave to say that I decline."[43]

Though Santa Anna had been correct in his assessment that he had Taylor outnumbered more than three to one, it was his army, not the American force, that suffered catastrophe. Thanks to McCulloch's timely information, Taylor not only avoided a surprise attack but deployed to better ground. Good leadership on the part of Taylor's staff officers and good shooting, especially from his sixteen fieldpieces, enabled Taylor and his volunteers to prevail. With 267 soldiers killed and 468 wounded, Buena Vista claimed more American casualties than any other battle in the war. But Santa Anna's army lost some 1,500 killed and wounded.[44]

Watching from an advanced position as the Mexicans began to retreat, McCulloch observed to a Major Coffee, "The victory is ours."

Coffee asked the ranger if he really thought so beyond a doubt. "I told him I did," McCulloch recalled, "then says he, 'Here is a bottle of champagne. We will drink to the success of the American armies.' So saying, he took from his holsters I thought at the time, the best wine I had ever tasted. We drank it between the two Armies."[45]

In his report, Taylor acknowledged McCulloch's contribution to the American victory, noting, "The intelligence which they [McCulloch's rangers] brought caused us to leave the plains of Agua Nueva for a very strong and advantageous position." The victory would carry Taylor from the mountains of Mexico to the White House as the next president of the United States.

McCulloch left Mexico for Texas on March 5, intending to recruit more men and buy some horses. The month after Ben McCulloch returned to Texas, his brother Henry reached Mexico in command of another company. But neither Henry nor Ben would see any further service south of the Rio Grande. When Ben McCulloch got back to Monterrey with forty more rangers and a remuda of horses, he learned that Taylor had disbanded his company. The general put the rangers back on the muster rolls for one day so they could receive pay and travel money, then discharged them.[46]

Henry McCulloch's company belonged to a battalion of mounted volunteers led by Major Tom I. Smith. Two other companies, headed respectively by John J. Grumbles and Shapley P. Ross, rounded out the battalion. Having carried the day at Buena Vista, Taylor did not think he needed that many more Texans in his command. Accordingly, the general ordered the battalion back to Texas. Wanting to stay in the theater of war, Smith made an effort to change the general's mind, but Taylor remained adamant. The battalion marched back to Texas to take up station along its frontier under the overall command of Bell, now a lieutenant colonel.

At San Antonio, Bell gathered his captains and told them he planned to establish a string of temporary posts to defend Texas from the Comanches. Augmented by newly authorized companies under John Conner, Samuel Highsmith, and Big Foot Wallace, the Rangers began patrolling the western frontier in May and June 1847.[47]

Word of Santa Anna's defeat at Buena Vista had reached New Orleans about the time former ranger Reid put the final touches on a book he had been working on since his return from Mexico. Cribbing from newspaper reports, the Louisiana lawyer added a brief account of McCulloch's role at Buena Vista and then sent his manuscript to the publisher in Philadelphia. Reid dedicated the volume to General Taylor, but his *The Scouting Expeditions of McCulloch's Texas Rangers* amounted to a Ranger monument, the primary source for their enduring legend. The book stayed in print, through five editions, nearly forty years. While Reid's tome focused on the summer and fall campaigns of 1846, it presented the first biographical sketches of the Mexican War Ranger triumvirate: Hays, Ben McCulloch, and Walker.

Reid also gave considerable space to Hays and his exploits in Texas before the war. "Were an account of the Indian fights, skirmishes, and adventures of Col. Hays to be given to the world," he wrote, "it would fill a volume, and the work would be looked upon rather as the effusion of a fertile imagination, consisting of legendary tales, and the adventures of some fictitious knight-errant, than to be the faithful account of the achievements of a man, living and moving among us."[48]

As readers across the nation bought Reid's book on the Rangers, Hays busied himself recruiting a new Ranger regiment. He had begun the effort in April, signing up many of the men who had been with him the first time. At first, Hays expected to join the other Ranger units in patrolling the Texas frontier, but that summer he received orders to Mexico to assist U.S. regulars in dealing with Mexican guerrillas.

Perhaps Texas businessman James Morgan had read Reid's book on the Rangers. He saw the Rangers not only as a fighting force, but as the answer to a personal problem. Writing to his old friend Samuel Swartout in New York, Morgan expressed his frustration with a young man who had been staying with him, a "devil brute [who] cares not for Character . . . [a] Drunkard!" But Morgan had an idea. "[The] Texas Rangers . . . will be good for him. He is such [a] disappointment to me. . . . Don't you think he had just as well join the Rangers?"[49]

Meanwhile, some of the last fighting of the war cost the life of one of the shapers of the Ranger image, Samuel Walker. At the pueblo of Huamantla on October 9, 1847, Walker led four companies of mounted men against troops under Santa Anna. Trapped in a counterattack, Walker fell with a rifle round from a Mexican sniper.

"I am dying, boys," went one version of his final words, "you can do nothing for me now. I'll never see Texas again. Carry me back to San Antonio and bury me with Ad Gillespie."[50]

Gillespie, Walker, Hays, and the McCulloch brothers had helped build the Ranger mystique, but the nature of that reputation depended on a person's perspective. "The mounted men from Texas have scarcely made one expedition without unwarrantably killing a Mexican," General Taylor had written earlier in the war. "There is scarcely a form of crime that has not been reported to me as committed by them."[51]

Frank Edwards, in his *Campaign in New Mexico with Col. Doniphan,* related a conversation with a ranger who identified himself as John Smith. Smith told Edwards that since the U.S. army did not furnish the Rangers rations for man or horse, "they procured their subsistence out of the Mexicans." They did that, Smith continued, by riding up to "some rich hacienda" and informing the owner that in half an hour, the Rangers needed a certain amount of provisions. Smith quoted the ranger:

> Waal, of course he don't like that much, so he refuses. One of us then just knots a lasso round the old devil's neck, and fastens it to his saddlebow, first passing it over a limb of some tree; then mounting his horse he starts off a few feet giving him a hoist, and then returns dropping him down again. After a few such swings, he soon provides what we have called for.

After obtaining supplies, the ranger continued, they would "jerk him a few times more, and then the money or gold-dust is handed out. . . . We don't hurt him much, and he soon gets over it."

The hacienda owners shaken down for food and money, as well as most Mexicans who survived their contact with the Texans during the war, did not get over it. Neither, of course, had the Texans forgotten the massacres connected with the revolution nor the treatment of Texas prisoners following the Santa Fe and Mier expeditions. "It is said that the bushes, skirting the road from Monterrey southward, are strewed with skeletons of Mexicans sacrificed by these desperadoes," Edwards wrote.[52] The culture clash between Mexicans and Texans ran far deeper and wider than the river that separated their two countries.

The Rangers did not fight according to the rules, but few contested their effectiveness.

"Their knowledge of the character of the enemy and of the military frontier acquired in their long border struggle rendered them valuable auxiliaries in the invasion," wrote Major Giddings. "The character of the Texan Ranger is now well known by both friend and foe. As a mounted soldier he has had no counterpart in any age or country. Neither Cavalier nor Cossack, Mameluke nor Mosstrooper are like him; and yet, in some respects, he resembles them all."[53]

Albert Brackett, a soldier with the Indiana Volunteers, described the Rangers as "odd-looking" men whose intention seemed to be "to dress as outlandishly as possible. Bob-tailed coats and 'long-tailed blues,' low and high-crowned hats, some slouched and others Panama, with a sprinkling of black leather caps . . . and [a] thorough coating of dust over all . . . their huge beards gave them a savage appearance."[54]

"Hays' Rangers have come . . ."

General Scott attacked Mexico City on September 13, 1847, taking the capital the following day. The battle effectively ended the war, but Mexico would see more of the devil Texans. In October, four companies of Rangers raised by Hays boarded vessels at Brazos Santiago for transport to Veracruz, Mexico's principal port on the Gulf of Mexico. Until seasickness mellowed them, the rangers caused as much trouble aboard ship as they had demonstrated they could generate on land. The ship captains urged Ranger officers to restrain their men, but only nausea did the trick.[55] The rangers had their horses with them, and they, too, caused problems. To the delight of the Texans, one ranger's spirited mount bit off, chewed, and swallowed an Irish seaman's ear. Though that cheered the rangers up for a while, they remained generally subdued until land came in sight.

Once ashore in Mexico, Hays received orders to make camp at the inland village of Vergara. The Ninth Massachusetts Infantry already had its tents pitched there. Well aware of the Rangers' propensity for not getting along well with regulars, the boys from Boston sent over half a barrel of whiskey in the hope of getting their relationship off to a good start.[56]

Joined by Hays and the rest of his regiment on October 17, the Rangers left Vergara on November 2 for Jalapa and then Puebla. Their assignment was to eliminate the guerrillas who had been playing havoc with the American army's supply and communications lines and then join Scott in Mexico City, 260 miles inland from Veracruz.[57]

"Hays' Rangers have come, their appearance never to be forgotten," General Ethan Allen Hitchcock wrote on December 6. "Not in any sort of uniform, but well mounted and doubly well armed: each man has one or two Colt's revolvers besides ordinary pistols, a sword, and every man his rifle. . . . The Mexicans are terribly afraid of them."[58] When the rangers rode with the regular army into the nation's captured capital, some citizens hurled rocks at them. By way of response, the Texans shot and killed at least two of them. Most of the Rangers would kill a Mexican with less emotion than they would display in a snap shot at a coyote.

Near Agua Nueva on December 21, a raiding party chased several Ranger scouts for more than six miles until the Texans reached their better-manned base camp. Ten days later, the rangers found the Indians and returned the compliment.

"The Rangers reinforced and attacked the Indians," a surgeon with the Second Regiment of Mississippi Volunteers wrote in a letter to the Vicksburg *Daily Whig*. "The Indians and Rangers had a short engagement; the former were forced to retreat having nothing but bows and arrows."

One ranger died from an arrow lodged in his chest, the doctor wrote, and "three or four other Rangers were wounded . . . one of them was pierced through the hand with an arrow; he immediately drew it out, and killed the Indian."[59]

Meanwhile, Hays suggested to General Scott that he and his rangers be dispatched to seek out a band of *guerrilleros* led by Padre Caledonio de Jaruata. Operating from the valley east of Mexico City, de Jaruata's riders and other bands continued to harrass U.S. supply trains and small patrols. Realizing the job perfectly suited the Rangers, and happy to get them out of the capital, Scott readily approved the expedition.

THE WAR ENDS

On January 10, 1848, Hays led his rangers from their camp on the southern outskirts of the city in search of *guerrilleros*.[60] But within three weeks, with the signing on February 2, 1848, of the Treaty of Guadalupe Hidalgo, the war had ended.

News traveled slowly, however, and the cooling of blood took even longer. On February 25, rangers and dragoons under General Jo Lane took part in a guerrilla action at Zacualtipán, the last engagement of the war. The North Americans charged the village at sunup, with fighting continuing into the afternoon. Some of the *guerrilleros* and their leader escaped into the mountains, but roughly 150 of them did not. As one participant later put it, they had forever "ceased to feast on tortillas."[61]

Back in Mexico City, Hays hoped to resupply and finish the work with the *guerrilleros*. But the American army, its objective accomplished, had already begun moving out of the capital. To the immense relief of the populace, the Rangers left Mexico City on March 18 for Veracruz and the voyage back to Texas.

Except for Hays and Ford, all the rangers mustered out of federal service on April 29, 1848, and departed for home a few days later. If Hays and his rangers had not been held in check, they could have rekindled the war, bogging the United States in a protracted conflict against the Mexican people themselves. Fighting would have been street to street, house to house, in the largest city in the Western Hemisphere.

In another time, some of the Texans would have faced court-martial for what they did in Mexico. But Hays and the other rangers had served "not only [as] the eyes and ears of General Taylor's army but its right and left arms as well."[62]

As Ford would write, "If the Rangers themselves had indulged in a few excesses, it was because they were an intensely proud band of fighting men who wanted revenge; even if revenge became a cloak for pillage and murder, the Rangers were still honorable men."[63]

Most Texans saw it that way. The rangers who fought in Mexico returned as heroes. The Alamo and Goliad had further been avenged. What would take more time to realize is that the volunteers from Texas had given the words *Texas Ranger* worldwide cachet. Finally, since most of them had ridden off to war as relatively young men, Texas's Mexican War veterans made strong seed stock that would last the Rangers for years to come. Many who rode roughshod in Mexico would saddle up again as Rangers on the Texas side of the Rio Grande. Their attitude toward Mexicans, and the hatred it inspired on both sides of the river, would outlive them all.

The American military, with the help of the Rangers, had defeated the largest army in the Western Hemisphere, but the comanches continued their depredations on both sides of the Rio Grande.

"They have no idea of jurisprudence . . . and no organized and authoritative system of national polity," wrote former Republic of Texas president David G. Burnet, who had spent considerable time with the Comanches in 1818 and 1819. Burnet elaborated:

One captain will lead his willing followers to robbery and carnage, while another, and perhaps the big chief of all, will eschew the foray, and profess friendship for the victims of the assault. Hence treaties made with these untutored savages are a mere nullity, unless enforced by a sense of fear pervading the whole tribe and it is somewhat difficult to impress this sentiment upon them; for they have a cherished conceit . . . that they are the most powerful of nations.

Burnet had another troubling observation: "The Indians now use iron points to their arrows; but the use of the bow and arrow is gradually diminishing, and giving way to that of fire-arms."[64]

"OUR DUTIES WERE SIMPLE AND EASY . . ."

Under the Treaty of Guadalupe Hidalgo, dragoons and foot soldiers seasoned in battles south of the Rio Grande would be pulled back into Texas to garrison a line of military posts along the edge of settlement. But for the time being, only Rangers stood between the populace and unfriendly tribes. Leadership and personnel had changed, but Rangers had continued to scout the state's frontier throughout the war. Five companies operated, as Ford later recalled,

on a line near the upper edge of the settlements. They were required to send out scouts, in each direction, daily. The guard detachments from each company were to meet those of another company, and pass the night together, and return to their respective camps the next day, unless they struck an Indian trial, and followed it.[65]

Captain Henry McCulloch had established a post in Hamilton Valley near present Burnet about sixty miles northwest of the capital city. Mc-Culloch later described his camp as being "something over twenty log cabins—one for each mess of six men, one for the lieutenants and a good-sized one for quartermaster and community storehouse." In addition, he had a cabin for his family, as well as six cabins for other men with families. The camp also included a store where the proprietor had "cakes and ginger beer for sale to members of the company and others."[66]

"Our duties were simple and easy," company assistant surgeon John

Duff Brown recalled, "but necessitated constant scouting and watchfulness. . . . We had only one skirmish with the Indians."[67]

When a party of Indians managed to penetrate the Ranger line in present Gillespie County, McCulloch recalled, they "attacked and killed some citizens in the southwest portion of Gonzales county, which caused . . . Colonel Bell to conclude that they were once more on the war path and would reopen hostilities all along the frontier." The colonel ordered McCulloch to reorganize his company and continue to man the Hamilton Valley post until relieved by regular troops.[68]

Dr. Ferdinand Herff, author of a guide to help prospective German immigrants understand Texas, described "Texian Rangers" as "well-mounted and well-armed border troops . . . acquainted with the conduct of war against the Indians [who] count among their ranks Indian scouts (spies) from friendly tribes." He went on to assure European readers, "It is almost impossible that a small party of Indians, much less larger bodies, elude the watchfulness of those troops."[69]

Despite their well-deserved reputation for viciousness in dealing with their enemies, the more conscientious Ranger leaders believed in doing what they were told. Bell ordered Captain Highsmith to scout the San Saba River valley for any sign of Indians near the new German settlements along the Llano River.

With two lieutenants, forty-three privates, an interpreter, and a doctor, the rangers rode from their camp at Enchanted Rock the morning of March 13, 1848. Highsmith joined the company a day later after learning that Indians had killed a German immigrant near Fredericksburg.

Early on March 15, Highsmith sent one of his lieutenants and two privates to follow an Indian trail they discovered along the Llano. When the officer returned to report that he had found the Indian camp, Highsmith decided to attack.

"We immediately prepared for action," Highsmith later wrote, "and every eye flashed with animation at the prospect of inflicting merited chastisement on this lawless band, whose hands were yet warm with the settler's blood."

But when Highsmith "dashed down upon them," he ran into a problem he had not anticipated. Camped near the war party he had been trailing were a few friendly Lipan Apaches.

"My orders from Col. Bell were plain and specific—not to disturb the friendly relations with any tribe, unless satisfied that they had committed depredations, and, in this case, to chastise them," the captain recalled.

Before Highsmith had time to decide what to do, the Lipans solved his problem by quickly separating themselves from the hostile Indians, a band of Wichitas and Wacos.

The captain continued:

> Being scrupulously disposed to do no wrong, I called a talk with the chief . . . who, a minute after the parley commenced told his party to escape. He enforced his words with a corresponding motion of the hand. They instantly commenced to move off the ground, and when ordered to halt his men, he attempted to make his escape. To permit them to do so—allow them to go unpunished, required more forbearance than I possessed, or any of my men. As he retreated, I fired and killed him.

When Highsmith fired, so did his men, who he reported had "done their work with dispatch, and in a most satisfactory manner. The party numbered 35 or 40—but few escaped." Fourteen Indians died on the spot, with most of the rest shot as they tried to cross the river.[70]

Based on a letter from Highsmith to the *Texas Democrat* in Austin, the Galveston *Weekly News* reported on April 21 that the Lipans "expressed to Capt. H. their gratification at the result and informed him that Big Water, the chief of the hostile party who was killed, [less] than a year before, killed three or four Americans. . . . This band of Wichitas and Wacos (renegades from both tribes) intended attacking the German settlers of Castroville."

Later that spring, the people of San Antonio threw a grand ball for Hays and his rangers in appreciation for their Mexican War service. More than three hundred people attended, and dancing continued until midnight. Most of those on hand for the May 20, 1848, event assumed Hays would resume his role as protector of the Texas frontier, but the battle-weary ranger thought differently. He rode from San Antonio to Austin to meet with Colonel Bell, then traveled to Washington to close out the paperwork and accounting connected to his military command. "The gallant Hays," the New Orleans *Picayune* reported, ". . . is at length about to retire."[71]

Back in Texas, Hays agreed to take on another dangerous job, but not as a ranger. On August 27 he left San Antonio at the head of an expedition to map a trade route between San Antonio and Chihuahua City, Mexico. At Enchanted Rock, Hays joined Highsmith and thirty-seven rangers under orders to provide an escort. The party left the imposing granite landmark on September 5, crossing the Devils River, which Hays named, and the serpentine Pecos. They got lost in the mountainous vastness of the Big Bend, at one point going twelve days without food. Finally getting a meal at the village of San Carlos, the party reached the Rio Grande village of Presidio on the fiftieth day of their trip. Hays spent ten days at Ben Leaton's private fort before heading back to civilization. The beleaguered expedition and its Ranger escort arrived in San Antonio on December 12, by their reckoning having ridden 1,303 miles. Hays reported that wagon trains could make the same trip, the only difficulty being in crossing the Pecos. Highsmith's company mustered out at San Antonio on the day after Christmas. The hard trek gleaned information that would be helpful for future travelers, but it broke Highsmith's health. He got sick and died soon after returning to San Antonio.[72]

Texas newspaper editors applauded the renewed presence of Rangers along the frontier. "Four newly raised ranging companies, have all been organized, and taken their several stations," the Victoria *Advocate* had noted on November 16, 1848. The newspaper continued:

> We are much pleased. We know they are true men; and they know exactly what they are about. With many of them Indian and Mexican fighting has been their trade for years. That they may be permanently retained in the service on our frontier is extremely desirable; and we cannot permit ourselves to doubt [that] . . . such will be the case.

That sentiment not withstanding, permanence would elude the Rangers for nearly another quarter of a century.

Shortly after taking office as Texas's second governor, George T. Wood, who had shared equal rank with Hays as a regimental commander of Texas volunteers during the war, received a letter from a Ranger captain whose company had been operating in the vicinity of the headwaters of the Trinity River. The captain informed Wood that his company's term of service would expire on February 2, 1849, and asked for instructions. With the letter came a petition from settlers in the area urging that the Rangers be kept in service.

"The necessity for a ranging company for that section of the frontier is manifest," the governor replied on January 18,

> and as I am well pleased with your past services I desire that the same company be retained in the service or as many of you as may wish to do so. I have no direct orders from the War Department to have you re-mustered, I will, however, order it done, satisfied as I am that the General Government will sanction whatever may be done reasonably for the protection of our exposed frontier.[73]

Long after Wood's term of office ended, Texas continued to look to the "General Government" for protection from Indians, and for money to pay for companies of Rangers. So, too, would local citizens keep petitioning future governors for help from the Rangers anytime Indians threatened their area.

That summer, Brevet Major General George M. Brooke, commander of the U.S. army's Department of Texas, authorized three companies of Rangers to be paid with federal funds for six months' service in the Nueces Strip, the area between the Nueces River and the Rio Grande. Pay would be $23.50 a month, with rangers furnishing their own arms, equipment, and horses as usual. The term of enlistment was six months. Seeing plenty of work needing doing, the general soon requisitioned two additional companies.

Responding to another citizen's petition, Governor Wood on July 7, 1849, authorized J. W. Johnson to raise a company of Rangers to patrol the San Antonio River below Goliad. When Johnson heard that General Brooke had requisitioned three companies, he went to San Antonio hoping to get his men mustered into federal service. But all the companies had been filled. Not long after, someone killed him in what newspapers referred to as "a difficulty."[74]

Captain Grumbles's company operated seventy-five miles up the Nueces while Henry McCulloch, his former position on the frontier now garrisoned by U.S. dragoons, began scouting between Goliad and Corpus Christi. The editor of the *Nueces Star* in Corpus Christi had high hopes for results. "It is a matter of history," he wrote, "that Indians are disposed to give Texas Rangers a wide berth."[75]

The Mexican War had transformed the words *Texas Ranger* into an American icon. English-born Joseph Lancaster, who came to Texas in 1836 and had served as a ranger, established a newspaper at Washington-on-the-Brazos called *The Texas Ranger and Brazos Guard*. Published variously there and at Brenham, Independence, and Chapel Hill, it lasted for a decade.[76] The two words that gave Lancaster's sheet its bold title also came to hold significant political power. Having served as a Texas Ranger became as politically attractive as a log-cabin upbringing in presidential campaigns. Governor Wood had ridden his Ranger command into office, only to be defeated in his bid for reelection by someone with even more experience as a ranger, Colonel Peter Hansborough Bell.

As Bell assumed office, a nation heady with victory celebrated the exploits of the Rangers in story, book, and song. James T. Lytle, one of Ben McCulloch's rangers, had written a piece called "The War Song of the Texan Rangers" to the tune of an air called "I'm Afloat." Its chorus captured the attitude of most Texans:

> *Then mount and away! give the fleet steed the rein—*
> *The Ranger's at home on his prairie again;*
> *Spur! spur in the chase—dash on to the fight,*
> *Cry vengeance for Texas! and God speed the right.*[77]

5

"The captain believed in drilling his Rangers"

FRONTIER PROTECTION, 1849–59

A tall man with big ears and thick, dark hair over a high forehead, he stood stoically before the camera, one gloved hand slipped Napoléon-like into his fringed buckskin jacket. In his other hand he held a wide-brimmed, black stovepipe hat. A revolver in a snapped leather holster hung from his belt. His mouth set in a thin line, he looked serious and determined.

John Salmon "Rip" Ford filled Jack Hays's figurative boots as Texas's most notable Ranger captain of the 1850s. Ford fought as hard and smart as his predecessor, but unlike Hays, Ford left a lengthy memoir and much other written material. Hoping to be remembered as a modest man, in recounting his exploits he always referred to himself in the third person. Unassuming or not, what Ford did as a Ranger leader, and the stories he told, kept his name—and the Ranger tradition—alive.[1]

Though all of Texas's long frontier stood at risk of Indian attack, the area between the Nueces and the Rio Grande lay particularly exposed. On the authority of Adjutant General John S. D. Pitts, in response to a federal request Ford raised a volunteer Ranger company in Austin on August 23, 1849. He proceeded to San Antonio, picked up more men, then worked his way to Corpus Christi. From the coast Ford moved toward Laredo, making camp forty miles east of there at Los Ojuelos.

Ford's supplies came from the army, and he ran his company like a military unit, but his disciplinary style "had little that savored of that enforced in the regular army. It appealed to the pride and sense of honor of the men." A student of military history, the captain believed in drilling his rangers. As he put it in his eccentric way, "He exercised the men in the manual of arms, wheeling, changing front, and other maneuvers." That training and discipline soon proved its value.[2]

An intelligent man skilled in everything from medicine to editing a newspaper, Ford knew that preparedness evened his odds in a fight. But his men needed better weapons. Only he and his sergeant owned revolvers. The rest of his rangers carried single-shot, muzzle-loading pistols and one-shot army rifles. In May 1850, Ford and his men left camp for Fort Merrill, a federal post on the San Antonio–Corpus Christi road in present Live Oak County. Along the way he would look for Indians, but drawing a supply of modern handguns from the military constituted his primary objective.

In the interest of efficiency, Ford split his company in half. A third, smaller contingent led by a sergeant and a Mexican guide who had been a Comanche captive rode ahead of both commands. On May 12, the rangers began trailing a party of Indians and caught them by surprise on open ground. The Indians had only bows and arrows, but with most of his men carrying single-shot weapons, Ford realized he had only minimal advantage. To compensate, the captain ordered his men to stay close together and fire alternately, so those who had to fall back to reload would be protected.

Ford's leadership and the training he had imposed paid off. The rangers killed four Comanches and wounded seven, skirmishing with the Indians again on May 29.[3] Finally reaching Fort Merrill, Ford signed for Colt revolvers for his company.

Early the following year, the new pistols came in handy. A chance encounter on January 27, 1851, between a detachment of Ford's rangers under Lieutenant Edward Burleson Jr.—son of the man who had been vice president under Mirabeau B. Lamar during the days of the republic—resulted in what one nineteenth-century chronicler listed among "the most sanguinary and desperate fights with a band of Comanches that ever happened in Texas."[4]

Just south of the Nueces on the San Antonio–Laredo road, Burleson spotted three Comanches. Picking eight men to ride with him after the

Indians, he ordered the rest of his command to continue to Los Ojuelos. The lieutenant and his men galloped in pursuit for three miles before the Comanches turned their horses to confront the advancing Texans. As Burleson confidently charged, eleven other warriors stood up from hiding and began firing at the rangers. The young officer had led his men straight into a trap.

Burleson then made a second mistake. Contrary to Ford's training, he ordered the rangers to dismount and pull their horses to ground for cover. As the rangers picked targets, an arrow from the leader of the war party pinned Burleson's hat to his head. His wound did not affect his aim. With a shot from his revolver, the lieutenant brought down the Comanche before he could notch another arrow.

The outnumbered rangers killed four Comanches and wounded most of the others before the Indians retreated, leaving their dead behind. One ranger died in the fight and another suffered a mortal wound.[5] Only Warren Lyons, Burleson's interpreter, escaped injury.

When private James Duncan rode back from the main column to see what had delayed the lieutenant, he found his bloodied colleagues sitting on the ground, too tired to pursue the Indians or even to make it back to the road. Duncan left again for food and water. Burleson had his wounded men taken to the military post at Laredo, where an army surgeon treated them. The lieutenant ignored his own flesh wound until, as Josiah Wilbarger later related, "[his] swollen head bursted the [hat] band." A fellow ranger, using his knife, cut the arrow in two and pulled it from Burleson's scalp.

Down with a bout of malaria at the time of the fight, Ford visited the scene about a month later. He found the ground still covered with Comanche arrows, picking up more than two hundred shafts scattered over an area of less than a quarter of an acre. The Comanches, Ford surmised, had been preparing to waylay Mexican cart men along the heavily traveled road when the rangers rode up on them.

"What a difference . . . between murdering and scalping unarmed cart men, and meeting rangers in deadly conflict," the Brownsville *Sentinel* said several years later. "There was no plunder for them to divide—no captives for them to beat and drag through prickly pears at the end of a rope. There were death, and wounds, and escape from danger, to contemplate instead."[6]

Newly mustered ranger William J. Wills, a Pennsylvanian who came to Texas hoping it would cure his dyspepsia—a contemporary term for acid indigestion—realized the danger of Indian fighting. Even so, he thought dodging arrows would be just the medicine he needed. "There are several examples here in San Antonio of men whose lives were despaired of, who by leading [the life of a ranger] for six months or a year have been completely restored," he wrote in a letter home. "I am persuaded that, unless I get killed, my case will be another added to the list of cures effected by Ranging."

Wills fully expected his company to see action: "The Comanches are a brave and warlike tribe but the Texas Rangers are the most fearless and desperate set of characters I have ever met with."[7]

In Austin, the legislature's Committee of Indian Affairs collected data supporting Wills's view. "Authentic information had been adduced," the committee reported, "of the [recent] killing and massacring of seventy-one citizens of Texas by the Indians." Such "great destruction of life, attended by so many horrible circumstances . . . excited at once the liveliest and most painful solicitude of the citizens of our state; and requires, in the opinion of the Committee, the rise of all the resources of the state."[8]

The legislature also forwarded a memorial to Congress "Praying for Reimbursement for Defenses of Her Frontier." The document asked the federal government to underwrite payment of Ranger companies commanded by Benjamin F. Hill, J. M. Smith, Jacob Roberts, John S. Sutton, Shapley P. Ross, Henry E. McCulloch, Isaac W. Johnson, and Charles Blackwell "for frontier protection." Those companies, the resolution continued, had "promptly responded . . . stopping the further progress of murder and bloodshed by the ruthless savages who infested our frontier."

Texas politicians did not find it illogical to practically demand money from Washington on the one hand while at the same time complaining about the ineffectiveness of the federal military in Texas. From Washington's perspective, Texas looked well protected. Of the nation's 109 military posts, 19 stood in Texas. The Army had twenty-four hundred soldiers in the state—nearly a third of its strength. But infantrymen predominated at most of the garrisons. "The idea of repelling mounted Indians, the most expert horsemen in the world, with a force of foot soldiers, is ridiculous," one Texas newspaper editorialized.

Texas wanted more than a line of forts along its western frontier and the border with Mexico. It wanted the Indians gone for good, an economic issue as well as a consideration of public safety. The new state having retained ownership of its public land, and since that land could not be sold as long as Indians had free range, to the thinking of many Texans, the Comanches and other hostile tribes amounted to an encumbrance on the state's title. The *Texas State Gazette* put it more plainly: "The Indians must be pursued, hunted, run down, and killed, driven beyond the limits of the State."[9]

A Ranger force seemed the logical means to this end, but the state's treasury lacked sufficient funds to pay for one. Addressing the legislature in December 1851, newly reelected Governor Bell, who wore his hair long and still packed a brace of Colts when he walked around Austin, said it had been "abundantly shown that the system of military defense adopted by the General [federal] Government has failed to give peace and protection to the citizens . . . of our border." Bell urged the legislature to ask Washington for "ample military protection to every portion of our frontier" or demand the removal of all Indian tribes from the state. If the national government did neither, the former ranger continued, he wanted authorization "to employ such volunteer force from time to time as may be found sufficient for attainment of the end."

The legislature's Indian Affairs committee suggested a less bellicose solution: creation of reservations on state land near U.S. military posts. On December 16, 1851, the committee recommended that the state "could adopt no better or more humane plan to relieve our border citizens from the petty thefts and depredations committed by those Indians residing in our State in detached bands . . . [than] by setting apart small tracts or parcels of land . . . to be occupied by these Indians, subject to the pleasure of the State."

Representative Robert S. Neighbors, a Virginian who had served in the Texas army and ridden with Hays in 1842, signed the report on behalf of the House. Named the republic's Indian agent in 1845, he had continued in that capacity as a federal official after annexation. Creating an Indian reservation had been discussed before—the United States had proposed it shortly after Texas statehood—but Neighbors, his vision enlightened if flawed, made it happen. He believed that nomadic Plains tribes such as the Comanches would be content to "settle down, cultivate the soil, turn attention to stockraising" and forget about hunting buffalo and raiding, raping, killing, and scalping Texans. The United States would "take charge of said Indians" and peace would reign on the frontier, all at "no inconvenience to the wealth" of "our

State." In reality, the concept proved to be a considerable inconvenience to the people of Texas, not to mention the Indians. It would also cost Neighbors his life.[10]

In the meantime, Texas still needed Rangers. In Washington, with help from Senator Sam Houston, the upper chamber approved a House bill dealing with the Indian problem in various of the Western states and territories. An amendment authorized the president to "accept the services of as many companies of mounted Texan rangers as he . . . may deem necessary, the whole force not to exceed 500 men to be employed one year from the date of their muster into the service, unless otherwise directed by the President of the United States." These federal Texas Rangers would provide their own horses, clothing, and equipment, with the government furnishing arms and ammunition. Their pay would be the same as the regular army.[11]

Acting on the federal legislation, Governor Bell authorized state adjutant general James S. Gillett, another Texan who had ridden with Hays during the Mexican War, to organize three Ranger companies for service below the Nueces in Ford's old stomping grounds. Gillett recruited three captains: Owen Shaw, Gideon K. Lewis, and H. Clay Davis.

Shaw mustered his company on August 18, 1852, in San Antonio, picking up arms, equipment, and U.S. army manuals on the operation of a mounted rifle company from the federal depot in the Alamo City. Lewis filled his company roll with men from Corpus Christi and Brownsville on September 14. A week later, Davis had his company up to strength in Laredo.

The War Department dismissed reports of Indian problems on the border as nothing more than rumors, but Captain Shaw had no trouble finding hostile Comanches. The captain informed the adjutant general that he and his rangers had encountered a party of nineteen Indian men and two women. Of those, the rangers killed nine and wounded all but one. In addition, they captured twenty-three horses or mules.[12] Despite those results, beginning in February and continuing through March 1853, Shaw and the other Ranger captains received orders to disband their companies.

William and John Wright would not have agreed with the decision to muster the Ranger companies out of service. The two Irishmen, serving in South Texas with the U.S. Mounted Rifles, found the tenacity of rangers on the trail quite impressive. When a band of Comanches raided a settlement near Eagle Pass, "a party of Texan rangers . . . commenced trailing them up, as the expression goes." For twenty-one days, the brothers later wrote, the rangers "pursued [the Indians] without intermission, but to no purpose; in vain did they accomplish the most incredible distances, and explore the most inaccessible places, exercising at the same time a vigilance equal to that of the Indians themselves; still the wary Comanche eluded them."

About ready to give up, the rangers made camp for the night. For the time being, their preoccupation switched from chasing Indians to rustling up supper. One of the men rode out for meat, hoping to bring back some venison. Knowing that game would be coming to water, the ranger tied his horse near a creek and moved quietly through the brush, rifle in hand. As he approached the stream, he saw movement in the grass and froze. The ranger watched as an Indian crawled from cover on all fours. The Indian also had been looking for dinner, the ranger realized. Soon the Indian shot a deer, expertly cut some meat from its carcass and walked back to his horse, unaware he had become the hunted. When the Indian rode off, the ranger cautiously followed, staying just far enough back not to be seen. Three miles later, the ranger found the Comanche camp.

Forgetting his own hunger, the ranger spurred his horse to report to the captain. After weighing options, the captain decided to see if the Comanches would fall for one of their own tricks. He and the ranger boldly rode straight for the Indians. When they got close enough for the Indians to see, the two rangers feigned surprise and fear, jerking their horses around and galloping off. As the captain had hoped, the Comanches jumped on their horses and gave chase—straight into an ambush.

"A murderous fire," the brothers wrote, ". . . almost instantly emptied a score of saddles. With a wild yell of terror and disappointment, the remainder of the Indians wheeled round and fled; many more fell in the pursuit that ensued."[13]

Even as the state continued to periodically field Ranger companies to hunt down Indians, the legislature on February 6, 1854, took action on the earlier reservation recommendation and passed a bill giving the U.S. jurisdiction over twelve leagues of vacant public land in the state "for the use and benefit of the several tribes of Indians residing within the limits of Texas." Later that year, Neighbors and U.S. army captain Randolph B. Marcy picked two sites in what is now Young County, one on the Brazos twenty miles from Fort Belknap, the other on the Clear Fork of the Brazos, forty miles from the fort.

"NECESSITY KNOWS NO LAW"

On June 19, 1854, Secretary of War Jefferson Davis authorized General Persifor F. Smith, commanding the army's Department of Texas, to "call upon the governor of Texas for aid, should the exigencies of the service require it, in repelling Indian invasions." Mounted men requisitioned by Smith would be "supplied with ammunition, forage, and subsistence by the United States." Davis's action came in response to a request for more federal troops in light of reports of "constant outrages" by hostile Indians "on the defenseless inhabitants" of Texas. The secretary said the War Department did not have any additional troops to furnish "because of the slow progress of the recruiting service." But beginning December 1 and continuing for three weeks in 1854, five companies of Rangers, A through E, organized to operate along the southwestern frontier.[14]

When one of those companies rode from Weatherford in pursuit of Comanches, they carried a silk flag sewn by a group of local women. The banner bore a four-word legend: "Necessity Knows No Law." In other words, the Rangers would not be looking for the Comanches to discuss peace terms. The company had received a passionate send-off by a local clergyman: "Men, as the government has failed to give us protection, the only thing we can do is march upon these bloodthirsty savages and kill or drive them from the country." Hearing that, the rangers cheered and tossed their hats in the air.[15]

The army and the Rangers shared many of the same duties, but not always mutual respect. After a stay at Fort Clark, a post on Las Moras Creek in present Kinney County, U.S. Army Signal Corps founder Albert J. Myer and his escort rode up on two rangers. "Now," he wrote on January 7, 1855,

> don't picture to yourself the Ranger, as you read of him in newspapers, the personification of the brave and reckless-wild, perhaps but with a redeeming trait of lofty chivalry; but let me describe the animal and trust that you may have little to do with them. I have some under my control and can speak from experience. Rangers are rowdies; rowdies

in dress, manner and feeling. Take one of the lowest canal drivers, dress him in ragged clothes . . . put a rifle in his hand, a revolver and big Bowie knife at his belt—utterly eradicate any little trace of civilization or refinement that may have by chance been acquired—turn him loose, a lazy ruffianly scoundrel in country where little is known of, less cared for, the laws of God or man, and you have the material for a Texan Mounted Ranger, an animal—perhaps I should say brute—of which class some hundreds are at present mustered into service to fight Indians.

Appearances could be deceiving, of course. Myers added, "There are exceptions. My invective is not meant for all."[16]

That February, five Texas tribes moved onto the Brazos reservations, including more than five hundred Comanches. Though created to improve Indian-Anglo relations, the reservations made things worse. Plains Indians continued to raid into Texas, and the reservations became convenient sources for supplies or rest—places to disappear among friendly Indians when necessary.

Congress on March 3, 1855, authorized payment for the five companies of "Texas volunteers" raised the previous December. The last of those companies, Captain W. R. Henry's Company C, mustered out a month later. Federal funds expended for the operation of the companies came to $68,449.70.[17]

"FOLLOW THEM UP AND CHASTISE THEM . . ."

❶n July 5, 1855, Bell's successor—Governor E. M. Pease—wrote forty-year-old James Hughes Callahan, a veteran of the Texas army and an accomplished Indian fighter, authorizing him to form a company of Rangers (without the benefit of any supplies from the state) to pursue Indians and "follow them up and chastise them wherever they may be found." His term of service would be from July 20 to October 19.

When the U.S. army pulled much of its manpower from Texas to cope with growing sectional problems in Kansas, hostile incursions increased. Most Texans—citizens and politicians—still believed that the best Indians were the dead ones. Given that attitude, the line between self-protection and military excess could be crossed as easily as the Rio Grande.

With Callahan as senior captain, three Ranger companies comprising 110 men rode from Uvalde on October 1, 1855, intending to enter Mexico at Las Moras Creek. Finding the river too high, they moved downstream, crossing opposite Piedras Negras, Mexico. Callahan rode into town with an interpreter and called on the alcalde, the ranking government official. "To this officer he stated that he had not brought the forces under his command into Mexico for the purpose of making war or doing injury of any kind to its people," John W. Sansom recalled, "but that his sole object . . . was to punish the Lipans for their many crimes committed on Texas soil, and that all he asked of the *alcalde* was his moral support. Pleased and flattered, apparently . . . the *alcalde* was not slow in promising his moral support with every appearance of good faith."

Back in camp, Callahan lined up his rangers and led them "over a well traveled highway" toward the Lipan camp, supposedly about forty miles into Mexico. Late that day, after covering a little more than half that distance, the rangers reached a stream called Rio Escondido. Accounts of what happened next vary. One version has a Mexican peasant warning the rangers that they were about to ride into an ambush. Sansom remembered that four Indians appeared and galloped toward the rangers. Two reined their horses about three hundred yards away, but the other two came closer and let fly with arrows. A couple of the rangers fired on the Indians, wounding one of their horses.

When Callahan trotted up with his interpreter, he assumed a party of Mexicans, unaware of the alcalde's professed support of the Texas operation, had challenged the rangers. When no one came forward for a parlay, the captain formed his men in a line facing the stream.

"We had no sooner placed ourselves in battle array than, to our surprise and dismay 600 or 700 armed Mexicans and Indians climbed up the bank and formed in line parallel with the stream," Sansom wrote.

Before Callahan could react, the opposing force broke ranks and closed around the rangers in a V-formation.

"Those men are being handled by a man trained on the battlefield, and we are almost surrounded," Captain Henry told Callahan. "What shall we do, gentlemen?" Callahan asked.

Henry said they had to charge their right wing, push it back to the center, and then take on the other flank. Callahan agreed.

"With a yell such as only young fellows who had long breathed the pure air of West Texas could give," Sansom continued, "we followed, charging at full speed, and when our guns were emptied, using their butts as cudgels on such of the enemy as dared to await our approach."

The Mexican force sought cover and eventually fell back. The rangers had avoided annihilation, but Callahan had lost four men with seven wounded.[18] Concluding that he could not risk continuing his advance on the Lipan village, he ordered a return to Piedras Negras. The alcalde again treated Callahan with great courtesy, furnishing food for his men and forage for his horses.

"Prudence would have commanded the immediate crossing of the Rio Grande," Sansom recalled, "[but] pride, however, forbade any hurried departure, and only a few weak kneed counseled it."

Though lulled by the alcalde's hospitality, Callahan kept scouts on the roads out of town. On October 7, the captain learned of the approach from Piedras Negras of a contingent of twelve hundred armed Mexicans under Colonel Emilio Langberg. When his scouts confirmed the information, Callahan realized he had been duped by the alcalde. On his order, the rangers seized three Mexican cannons and ammunition, pulled back to the river, and took position "prepared to fight against any odds that might come."

Commanding a combined force of rancheros, Indians, and regular troops, Langberg arrayed his men between the rangers and Piedras Negras with "his flanks extending to the river above and below us." At that, the rangers opened fire with their small arms and captured artillery. The Mexicans appeared ready to charge when the commander of the U.S. garrison across the river had a battery of fieldpieces rolled out, the guns trained on the ground the Mexican force would have to cover if it advanced.

By then, the rangers had torched the town, though Sansom said they only fired the buildings nearest them to prevent them from being used for cover by the Mexican forces. The Mexicans stopped shooting and moved out of range. Callahan penned a note to the commander of Fort Duncan, requesting help getting across the river. The commander replied that if Callahan tried to attack the Mexicans, he would fire on him. That said, the military arranged for a boat to get the rangers back to Texas.

"The Callahan expedition accomplished quite a lot of good," Sansom concluded. "It showed the Lipans that Texas was awake to their crimes and did not propose to have its people murdered and scalped and their property pillaged and destroyed."[19]

Governor Pease said Callahan had been justified in following the Indians across the Rio Grande but should not have burned down a Mexican town. Though no conclusive evidence supported the thesis, many believed Callahan's real purpose in crossing into Mexico had been to recover escaped slaves.[20] Mexico argued through diplomatic channels that some Texans even envisioned a pro-slavery republic in the Rio Grande Valley.[21]

Whatever their motive, the Rangers had wrought their own pillaging and destruction. Eventually, the United States paid 150 Mexican citizens $50,000 in damages, including compensation for the theft of assorted produce and valuables ranging from gold jewelry to a silver-stuffed saddle worth $100.[22]

Probably because of the Callahan fiasco, that December the legislature voted down a measure from Senator Henry McCulloch, a former Ranger captain, to create a thousand-man Ranger service. In introducing the bill, McCulloch spoke eloquently in its behalf, offering grim descriptions of Indians raids along the frontier. But enough lawmakers to make a difference feared the force would be used for filibustering and prevented the measure's passage.[23]

As Callahan demonstrated, not all rangers of this era saddled up for strictly noble purposes. "They were western men that had suffered at the hands of Indians, either in the way of property or relatives," John N. Jones later wrote.

> Thar was a law in the State at that time that examped any man in the Service from arrest by the Civil Law. This forced a heap of tough men into the Service. Thar was several in this company that had a price on thar heads. However, I have never bin associated with any body of men that seemed to have more respect fur the rights of others. I was the youngest one in the company and it does seem to me that I must have been a pet of the hole outfit.

The Rangers' respect for the rights of others—at least those Jones served with in his youth—did not extend to Indians. In fact, the sixth legislature in 1857 practically declared open season on Indians with a statute making it "lawful to kill a public enemy not only in the prosecution of war, but when he may be in the act of hostile invasion, or occupation of any part of the State." The law went on to define a public enemy as "any person acting under the authority or enlisted in the service of any government at war with this State, or the United States," as well as anyone "belonging to hostile tribes of Indians who habitually commit depredations upon the lives or property of the inhabitants of this State, and all persons acting with such tribes." Merely "show[ing] an intention" to cause trouble made Indians legal targets. With a nod to fair play, the new law deemed the use of poison unjustifiable in eradicating public enemies.

Not long after Jones joined the Rangers, his forty-man company went on the trail of a large party of Indians and their stolen horses. "The men seemed to be as happy as they would have bin if they were going to a Mexican Fandango," Jones would write. When the rangers caught up with the Indians, five warriors died in the fight. As he remembered it:

> When we come to where the first Indian lay, he was not quiet ded but a shot from one of the boys sent his spirits to the happy hunting ground. A rope was put around the Indian's legs, then tied to the horn of a saddle. We dragged the Indian to camp, and so on til all five Indians were dragged into camp. The gards put out supper but I couldn't manage to eat a bite. The men then went on a spree of singing, dancing, cutting all sorts of shines. One man sayd he had to have a-nuff hair to tassel his bridle. He proceeded to scalp one Indian and tossel off his bridle in grand shape. Others, following, making tassels fur each bridle. They soon had them all minus thar wigs. One man was short a saddle stringe, so he commenst marking down a ould Indian's back with his knife, jest cutting through the skin with his knife in strips about one inch wide, then striping them off. It was not long till they were a gastley sight to look at. . . . I regarded the Indians as humans, and they deserve human treatment. I was disappointed with the Capt. He should not have allowed this action to take place.

Through rough country the rangers dogged the rest of the Indians to the Devils River, which they followed into Mexico. This time, the rangers respected the international boundary, though their horses being "rode down" probably had more to do with their decision than any considerations of sovereignty. Resting their mounts and themselves, the Texans spent their time hunting and fishing until riding back to the settlements.

After four months' service along the Rio Grande (with the exception of one expedition all the way north to near Waco), Jones's company received an order to disband. The rangers rode to San Antonio and drew their pay. Most of the men, Jones wrote, promptly went on a spree.

"A man that never seen these Western men on a tair don't have any eyda to what extent they go too," Jones continued. "The boys made it a point to nook every Mexican man down they could git in reach of. In fact, they completely housed up the town, had everything their way."[24]

About the time Jones and his fellows wrapped up their "tair" in San Antonio, *Putnam's Monthly Magazine of American Literature, Science and Art* offered its readers across the nation a portrait of the republic-era Texas Rangers, one that would still fit in the 1850s:

> Nowhere, perhaps, could one find such an assemblage of extraordinary and eccentric characters, as were to be met with in a Texas Ranger company. Here, men from all ranks and conditions of society were brought into contact. Here was the old, scarred hero of many a sanguinary Indian fight, whose head, for many months at a time, had not known the shelter of a roof, but whose only covering had been the "blue vault", and whose only food, such as his trusty rifle had furnished him.

Whoever wrote the article understood something about the Rangers that never got as much attention in the public prints as the Rangers themselves—their horses.

> The genuine Ranger may always be distinguished . . . by the animal he rides. He is generally a cross of the mustang of the Texas plains with the Kentucky or Virginia blood-horse. He possesses all the fire and endurance of the one, combined with the docility, intelligence, and speed of the other. . . . The true Texian, under all circumstances . . . whether on a march or in camp, is more regardful of the convenience and comfort of his steed than of himself.[25]

"A SUBJECT OF DEEP MORTIFICATION . . ."

The first significant use of Rangers for something other than Indian fighting occurred during what came to be called the Cart War, an outbreak of violence fueled by a volatile mixture of racism and economics: Mexican cart operators charged less to carry freight from the port of Indianola to San Antonio than their Anglo counterparts.[26] As surely as an ungreased wheel, that created friction.

At Manauila Creek in Goliad County on July 3, 1857, a band of horsemen swept down on a train of ox-drawn carts laden with bushels of corn and barrels of flour. Several *carteros* suffered gunshot wounds, and the raiders cut enough spokes of the man-high cart wheels to disable them. Eleven days later, fifteen to twenty Anglos attacked an even larger freight caravan on the edge of Goliad, damaging six carts. On July 18, more than a dozen white men struck another *cartero* camp. Three Mexicans lay wounded as the others fled. Again, the attackers made the carts inoperable before riding off. Another attack came on the night of July 31. This time the captain of the targeted cart train—an Anglo— suffered wounds along with three *carteros*. Another attack on September 12 left Antonio Delgado dead and two or three other *carteros* wounded.

Governor Pease visited San Antonio on September 23 to assess the situation. He concluded that local and county authorities had done nothing to stop the violence. Within the week, the governor called for a company of seventy-five "mounted volunteers to suppress certain outrages against the public peace." Pease selected Captain G. H. Nelson, San Antonio's city marshal and a veteran of Mexican War Ranger service, to lead the company. To assure impartiality, Pease stipulated that Nelson recruit his rangers in counties outside the trouble area. Even so, Nelson had difficulty getting volunteers.

Nelson and his company left San Antonio for Karnes County on October 26. Two weeks later, the captain wrote the governor from Lavaca to report on his activities, which had had mixed results. His company had escorted a cart train through Helena and past "a crowd of drunken rowdies" without serious incident. "I have no doubt from the demonstration made that if the train had been without an escort, some of the cart men would have been killed," he continued. On his way back north, Nelson ran into another train, but its operator declined his offer of an escort. A few days later, two of the cartmen died in an ambush.[27]

On November 11, Pease sent a message to the legislature concerning the cart train attacks and the general situation along the frontier. The western counties, he said, "have not been entirely exempt from Indian depredations during the past two years . . . [but] such occurrences have not been as frequent as at former periods."[28] Still, on November 23, 1857, Pease authorized three companies of from twenty to thirty "mounted men" to serve for three months in Brown, Erath, Palo Pinto, and San Saba counties as well as along the upper Blanco and Guadalupe rivers.

A week later, in another message to the legislature, the governor found it "painful to record such acts of violence" as the attacks on the *carteros* "and a subject of deep mortification that the law places no means in my power to prevent them." Perhaps, he suggested, the state could compel "citizens of a county that permit such acts to be done with impunity . . . to pay a heavy pecuniary penalty." The option of providing military escorts also remained on the table. But unless the legislature provided more money—Pease said he needed $14,500—the company he had commissioned to protect the freighters would have to be discharged when their enlistments ran out.

Legislative debate of the bill to fund Pease's use of rangers to protect the *carteros* showed some lawmakers had enlightened attitudes and that others did not. While one member referred to the attacks as "disgraceful outrages," a House member from East Texas carped that while Pease had acted quickly to do something about Mexican cartmen, he had been "callous to the sufferings of the men, women and children on the frontier when they were being scalped by the Indians."

After everyone had their say, the bill to pay for Pease's efforts passed with only one dissenting vote in the Senate and thirteen noes in the House. But lawmakers had not appropriated any money for further operations of the company, nor did they pass any law aimed at protecting the cart drivers. The sixty-day term of Nelson's company expired December 8.[29]

Indian raiding remained the state's most serious problem. On January 24, 1858, a frontier settler, Francis M. Collier, wrote a minister in Arkansas, "Perhaps at no time in her history has the frontier of Texas had greater cause for alarm than at present." Collier, the first clerk for newly created and ironically named Comanche County, continued:

> Bands of hostile Indians have been making descents upon us, drive off our stock in large hurds [sic], and murder & plunder our citizens in a brutal manner. Depredations was begun in Nov'r last, and they

have been continued in rapid succession ever since, and our property is driven off by wholesale and our neighbors murdered in the most brutal and shocking manner. In early life I have read novels describing scenes on the frontier that would chill my blood, but reading novels is nothing to compare with realities.[30]

Well aware of the situation along the frontier, on January 27, 1858, newly elected Governor Hardin Runnels signed "an Act for the better protection of the Frontier." The measure, shepherded through the upper house of the legislature by Senator George B. Erath—another former ranger in public office—authorized recruiting one hundred men for a six-month term of service, though it also allowed for the discharge of the men "whenever an efficient force shall be placed on the frontier by the Government of the United States." State lawmakers appropriated $70,000 for the Rangers.

"This is a step in the right direction," the Austin *Intelligencer* said the next day. "What with the Utah war and Kansas, the United States fails to afford Texas the protection necessary to save the scalps of our citizens. Let us therefore protect ourselves and charge the bill to Uncle Sam. The legislature has nobly performed its duty; let the governor see to getting the right sort of men."

THE BATTLE OF ANTELOPE HILLS

The same day, Runnels offered Ford a commission as senior ranger captain to lead a force against hostile Indians plaguing the state's frontier. "It is an excellent appointment," the Austin *State Gazette* commented. "He [Ford] is an old Indian fighter, and we predict that he will rid the frontier of all annoyance in the first campaign."[31]

Up to this point in Ranger history, most confrontations with Indians had been reactive: Rangers pursued raiding parties or followed an Indian trail they discovered on the frontier. But Ford's rangers would "provide better protection of the frontier" by going on the offensive.

Ford chose only the best for the expedition. He even mustered out some rangers already in the service under an earlier legislative act, including Captain John H. Conner, who had ridden into the capital city the same day the legislature passed the new Ranger law. Conner, commissioned by former governor Pease, reported having killed one Indian at the cost of one ranger wounded. Five citizens of Brown County had recently been killed, he told the *Intelligencer*, and 326 horses "driven off" by Indians.[32]

Asserting that federal troops had been ineffective in dealing with hostile Indians in Texas, Senator Sam Houston—elected to Congress following Texas statehood—rose on the floor of the U.S. Senate on February 10, 1858. Houston questioned the overall quality of the regular army and the institution that trained its officers, West Point.

Mississippi senator Jefferson Davis, former secretary of war, took umbrage at the honorable gentleman from Texas's opinion. When Davis praised the U.S. military's 1855 campaign against the Sioux in the Nebraska Territory, Houston dismissed it with Texas bravado.

"A single company of Rangers would have done all that," Houston told his fellow senators. "Jack Hays, Ben McCulloch and [Robert A.] Gillespie achieved more than that, and I believe they never had more than seventy-five men, and those for a few days only. . . ."[33] Give us one thousand Rangers and we will be responsible for the defense of our frontier. Texas does not want regular troops. Withdraw them if you please."[34]

Davis said he believed the U.S. army quite capable of protecting the Texas frontier, adding Houston "spoke in language well calculated to feed the vanity of his state, but not as a historian." Noting that General Zachary Taylor had said that the Rangers caused disciplinary problems during the war with Mexico, Davis continued, "If the General had gone further, and said that irregular cavalry [Rangers] always produce disturbance in the neighborhood of a camp, he would have said no more than my experience would confirm."

Rangers, Houston persisted, would "give more protection than all the regular Army of the United States." If Congress came up with the funding for a regiment of Rangers, he said, "every regular soldier of the artillery, infantry, and dragoons" could be withdrawn from Texas.[35]

Near the end of the month, Ford's rangers—each armed with two revolvers and a rifle—rode out of Austin. Rolling along behind the horsemen came sixteen mule-drawn wagons laden with ammunition and supplies. They marched up the Colorado River, then turned to follow one of its upper tributaries, Pecan Bayou. Under a large oak at the village of Chandler, a settlement that eventually became Brownwood, Ford set up camp to await additional recruits from San Antonio.

"Wild turkeys were very numerous," orderly sergeant R. Cotter recalled, "thousands in sight at a time. We would not while at this camp eat anything in the shape of meat but turkey steak."

Satisfied by his scouts that no hostiles lurked in the area, Ford left a small detachment at Chandler just in case and rode northwest, picking up more men from Comanche and Bosque counties. At Cottonwood Springs near the Young County Indian reservations, Ford established a base of operations he named Camp Runnels in honor of the governor. At the Brazos reservation, Indian agent and former Ranger captain Shapley P. Ross provided Ford with a hundred friendly Indians, mostly Tonkawas. Led by Chief Placido, the Indians would serve as scouts and adjuncts.

While Ford drilled his men on their marksmanship and military tactics, his scouts rode out to look for Indian sign. By spring, Ford knew the Comanches had spent the winter along the Canadian River, across the Red River in Indian Territory. Rested but well-trained, the rangers left Camp Runnels on April 22, moving north. Though they had no lawful authority outside Texas, on April 29, Ford and his men splashed across the Red River.

Slowed by rough terrain, Ford sent out hunting parties to replenish their larder with buffalo meat. As the rangers moved along the base of the Wichita Mountains, Ford's scouts discovered a wide, fresh Indian trail. Soon they came to a campsite only recently abandoned. Counting the fire rings, the scouts concluded that as many as four hundred Indians had passed that way not long before. Assuming he had found the Comanches, Ford did not have confirmation until his scouts rode in with two arrows pulled from a wounded buffalo. His Indian allies positively identified the feathered shafts as Kotsoteka Comanche.

On May 11, one of his scouts spotted in the distance a solitary Comanche leading a horse piled with fresh buffalo meat. His trail, the guide knew, would lead to the Comanche camp. Realizing the Comanches might discover his command at any moment, Ford ordered an attack in the morning.

At seven o'clock on May 12, led by Ross and Placido, the Tonkawas swept through the camp, killing or capturing nearly everyone. But two Comanches escaped on horseback, unwittingly leading the rangers and the Tonkawas to the main village at Little Robe Creek, just north of a wide, shallow stretch of the Canadian. Cotter reckoned the Texans and their allies faced six hundred Indians.

"It was a permanent camp and extended along the valley for a mile,"

Cotter remembered. "The bucks, upon seeing us, immediately began to hustle the women and children towards the hills, getting themselves ready for fight. Captain Ford rushed us over and we immediately formed for battle."

Ford watched as the Comanche's headman, seeking to make powerful medicine for his tribe, rode alone toward the Rangers. Known as Iron Jacket for the old Spanish armor he wore, Pohebits Quasho and his followers fervently believed in his invincibility. Pistol rounds "would glance off [his armor] like hail from a tin roof," one participant in the fight recalled. "The mail-clad and gorgeously-caparisoned Comanche chieftain moved in, seeming confident of being invulnerable," Ford wrote in his memoir. "About six rifle shots rang on the air; the chief's horse jumped about six feet straight up and fell. Another barrage followed, and the Comanche . . . was no more." As Ford and other rangers looked on, wisps of smoke began rising from the chief's bloody chest, the cotton backing behind the iron scales of his vest having caught fire from the multiple, close-range shots.[36]

"Captain Ford ordered us to charge and in a few minutes we were having a lively time of it," Cotter wrote.

With Iron Jacket dead, the battle deteriorated into a rout. Nearly four score Comanches died, a body count Ford thought conservative considering the high number of wounded. Only one ranger, along with one of the partisan Indians, died in the fight. One hundred rangers, aided by as many friendly Indians, had bested three times their number. They captured four hundred horses and forty Indians while freeing a Mexican boy and girl the Comanches had kidnapped.[37]

"The battle of Antelope Hills . . . was probably one of the most splendid exhibitions of Indian warfare ever enacted on Texas soil," observed Adam R. Johnson in his 1904 memoir, *The Partisan Rangers*. An old Indian fighter and former Confederate brigadier general, Johnson knew about fighting. Of course, the battle had been in Indian Territory, not Texas.

Ford's campaign solidified Texas's realization that it could not depend entirely on the federal government for protection along its frontier. That, in turn, supported the necessity of a permanent Ranger force. For both Texas and the U.S. military, Ford's victory showed that a defensive posture would never succeed in ending raiding along the state's frontier. "The Comanches," Ford reported to Runnels, "can be followed, overtaken, and beaten, provided the pursuers will be laborious, vigilant, and are willing to undergo privations." When Ford and his men returned to the capital city, the citizens honored them with a barbecue.[38]

While impressive, Ford's foray across the Red River had not ended Indian problems along the frontier. On October 3, Governor Runnels received a petition signed by "a large number of citizens" from Wise County asking for protection. The following day, the governor wrote James Bourland of Cooke County noting that he had read in the Dallas *Herald* that he "had taken the matter in hand, and, with a number of your fellow-citizens, had determined to follow up and punish the Indian enemy."

Runnels went on to commission Bourland to raise a company of seventy-nine men for up to three months' service. Mindful of Ford's success in pursuing Indians beyond the state's border, the governor further empowered Bourland to "pay no regard to treaty stipulations between them [the Indians] and the Government of the United States." If Bourland found it necessary to cross the Red River, the governor continued, he could cooperate with the United States in the effort "or not, as you think best."

The state would reimburse him for ammunition expended, Runnels continued, but the cost of food as well as pay for the men would be up to the next session of the legislature. Before sending a messenger to North Texas with the commission, Runnels reopened the letter and crawfished a bit: "I know not how far the legislature may be willing to justify the step, as its indorsement will be necessary in getting an appropriation."[39]

Despite their reputation, mounted Texans in the service of the state did not annihilate every band of Indians whose trail they crossed. Sometimes the Indians got the best of the Rangers. Years later, Benjamin Crawford Dragoo remembered a cool fall night in 1858 when clouds obscured a waning moon. Shortly after ten o'clock, armed with a shotgun, he started his turn at guard. He soon noticed that one of the company's horses had gotten loose. Watching as the animal slowly worked its way through high grass, grazing as it walked, Dragoo assumed the horse had pulled away from its picket pen. The ranger moved behind the horse, intending to retrieve the rope he believed it dragged.

Not finding a rope, Dragoo—by this time joined by another ranger—

circled to the front of the horse. Seeing the rope stretched out ahead of the horse, he realized someone had to be leading the animal.

"Our movements had been stealthy and noiseless as . . . a jaguar," Dragoo recollected. "When we found that there was an Indian at the end of the rope, although we could not see him on account of darkness and the high grass we determined on heroic treatment, as the doctors would say ."

Dragoo wanted to use his shotgun, but the other ranger won a whispered argument over who would do the honors. When Dragoo pulled back on the rope, the startled Indian rose. Presented with a shot, the other ranger fired but missed. The Indian escaped before Dragoo could shoot, but the report woke the entire camp. Assuming only one brave hoping to pull off a horse theft had been in the vicinity, the rangers went back to sleep.

An hour later, a war party rode down on their camp.

"Every man rushed to his horse but there was little time for fighting," Dragoo said. "The object of the Indians was to stampede our horses and run them off, but in this they failed as the horses were closely herded."

One Indian, riding a gray mule, ran into Dragoo and knocked him down.

"We fired right and left among them, but if we killed or wounded any of them they were carried away," he said. "They got none of our horses."

The raiders had more success when they struck Ranger captain Buck Barry's camp. The Indians got off with all but three head of Barry's remuda. Dragoo's company rode to help out, as did another company. The rangers trailed the Indians through the night, catching up with them at daylight. Seeing they were considerably outnumbered, the raiders abandoned the stolen Ranger stock and disappeared into the brush.

The incident did lead to casualties. On their way back to camp, a ranger saw a lone Indian rise up in the grass and quickly drop back down. The captain detailed eight men to ferret him out. "Keep your eye on the spot," he told the rangers. "Don't look at any other object." The rangers rode to the general area the Indian had been seen, then began a slow circle. "Presently one of the men cried out," Dragoo recalled. "He was shot with an arrow, and then another was hit. But while we could see from whence these arrows came, we could see no Indian."

The matter came to a head when one of the rangers spotted a buffalo trail in the grass. Following the trail to the point he calculated the arrows had come from, the ranger fired his rifle. "At the crack of the gun, [the] Indian jumped up and pitched forward—dead," Dragoo continued. "The shot had hit him squarely in the top of the head, and the ranger who had killed him took off his entire scalp and carried it home to show where the bullet took effect."[40] The rangers had killed only one warrior, but another company in the field about the same time had different results.

"THE BODIES WE OURSELVES BURIED"

Moses Jackson and his wife, Lydia, settled near a crossing of Pecan Bayou in 1855, the first family in future Mills County. On October 22, 1858, the couple and four of their seven children set out in their wagon to gather pecans along the stream. The Jacksons planned to meet two neighboring families, pitch camp, and spend a few days filling baskets from a bountiful fall nut crop. As the wagon bounced along under a canopy of trees only a few miles from their homestead, Jackson saw riders in the distance. He jiggled the reins and kept the wagon rolling, thinking that the horsemen must be people he knew. Too late he realized he had stumbled on a party of Comanches. Yanking leather hard to turn the wagon, Jackson whipped his team and tried to outdistance the Indians, but on horseback the warriors easily overtook the family.

Jackson and his eighteen-year-old daughter, Louisa, absorbed a barrage of iron-bladed arrows that shredded the white canvas covering of their wagon. With Jackson dying, the wagon careened into a tree. The Indians swarmed around, tearing Mrs. Jackson's screaming baby, I.J., from her arms. As she watched in horror, the Comanches threw the infant around like a ball before smashing his head on a log. Seeing this, ten-year-old Joshua began yelling at the Indians as his mother, desperately hoping to save someone in her family, tried to shush him. Her final prayer ended in an agonal gurgle as an Indian came up behind her and slashed her throat. Seizing Joshua and Rebecca, the boy's screaming eight-year-old sister, the Comanches rode off. Behind them they led the Jacksons' team and a string of horses stolen earlier in Brown and Coryell counties.

Rangers seldom became involved in situations such as the Jackson massacre until after the fact. But ten rangers from nearby San Saba

County under First Lieutenant D. C. Cowan had been in the field since October 16, hunting Indians. Five days into their scout, the rangers found unshod-pony tracks and began following them. After covering about ten miles, they rode up on parts of two cows obviously butchered by Indians. Making camp, the rangers got up early the next morning, October 22, and took up the trail again. The tracks led to a settler's cabin, but the rangers found no one home. Only a couple of miles from the homestead, the rangers discovered the wrecked wagon and the scalped, arrow-studded bodies of Lydia Jackson, her teenage daughter, and the baby. About 150 yards away, they found Moses Jackson's body. He, too, had been scalped.

None of the rangers recognized the bloody victims, but the Jacksons' horrified friends later identified them. Cowan's men laid Jackson and his wife in one grave and the two children in another. "The bodies we ourselves buried," Cowan soon reported in a letter to the governor. "Two of the family are still missing; probably carried off by the Indians." As word of the attack spread, people who knew the Jacksons began gathering at the bayou. By morning, more than thirty armed volunteers stood ready to join the rangers in searching for the missing children.

The Indians left a plain trail after killing the Jacksons, but Cowan's command had run out of provisions. No matter the eagerness of his men and the volunteers to give chase, the lieutenant knew he had to restock before he could follow the raiders beyond the settlements. "The supplies having just come," Cowan wrote Governor Runnels on October 25, "we will pursue the indians tomorrow with about sixty men." The rangers finally had enough food for a long expedition, but some of them did not even have a six-shooter.

A few days later, the rangers and volunteers discovered a recently deserted Indian camp "between the head of the North Leon and Pecan Waters." Seeing two sets of small footprints, the men dismounted and started searching the area, fearing they would soon find the bodies of the two Jackson children. Probing the brush with their rifle barrels, two rangers saw a small face and a pair of large, frightened eyes peeping from a thorny tangle of vines. Though scratched and bleeding, their feet swollen and blistered, the children had survived. They told the rangers that they had managed to escape the Comanches after the raiders had divided into two parties, a move Cowan recognized as a typical evasive tactic. When they saw the rangers approaching, Rebecca said, they hid in the thicket for fear that the Indians had relocated them. "The Children say they had not had any thing to eat for eight days," Cowan continued in another letter to the governor. "Humanity dictated the Children should be brought in they are doing well."

Not much of a hand at punctuation, Cowan nevertheless had saved two lives. Beyond that, he and his men underscored the value of having rangers on regular patrol, a level of protection the state did not maintain. Responding to pleas for assistance all along the frontier, the governor commissioned Ford on November 2 to raise another Ranger company to serve for six months, "unless sooner discharged," and "move without delay to a suitable point to protect the exposed settlements, which have recently suffered from Indian depredations."[41]

The forty-three-year-old Indian fighter recruited another company of young men in Austin and left near the end of the month for Comanche County. "The boys are all good riders and expert marksmen," the *Texas State Gazette* reported on November 27. "We are confident they will sustain the high character for chivalry, courage, fiery energy, daring enterprise, and obedience to orders, which in times past on many a bloody field, have distinguished the conduct of the young men of Texas."

His rangers may have been good shots, but Ford's second campaign hardly compared with his spring expedition. As he later wrote, "The results of that campaign did not satisfy Captain Ford," even though "his conscience did not accuse him of a failure of having done all he could to achieve success."[42]

Incidents such as the Jackson massacre only bred deeper hatred for Indians on the part of Texans. Two days after Christmas, a party of toughs under a gunman named Peter Garland ambushed a group of peaceful Caddos from the Brazos reservation. Garland's men killed seven Indians, including three women. Agent Neighbors called the Palo Pinto County attack "foul murder" and warned that if the state did not pursue a legal case against the killers, the reserve Indians would rise up and "seek satisfaction."[43]

Ford had been in San Antonio for the holidays when the incident occurred. Rejoining his company, the Ranger captain soon found himself in the middle of controversy: Were the Rangers paramilitary Indian fighters or peace officers or both?

After hearing the facts of the case, a grand jury presided over by Nineteenth Judicial District judge N. W. Battle of Waco handed down murder indictments naming Garland and seventeen others. The judge forwarded the arrest warrant to Ford. But Ford refused to make the arrests, insisting that as a military officer he did not have the authority to serve legal process.

"How did Judge Battle expect an organized body of men to be arrested except by force?" Ford later wrote in defense of his action. "Was his warrant anything more or less than a command to me to take my company and attack a body of American citizens? The sheriff had the power to call out the force of the county, and, backed by such members, could he not have been more effective than a company of 80 men?"[44]

Ford had correctly interpreted the letter of the law. Nothing in the state statutes gave a military commander the power to execute an arrest warrant, though the military could assist civil authorities if necessary. Whether Ford based his obstinacy on principle or prejudice, the warrant went unserved and the case unprosecuted. Even most of his friends thought Ford had been hardheaded and just plain wrong in refusing to take action.

The Caddo killings convinced officials that the reservation system could not work in Texas. The state abandoned the Brazos reservations on July 31, 1859, the remaining Indians marched under U.S. army escort to another reservation in the Washita Valley in what is now Oklahoma. On September 14, shortly after Agent Neighbors, who had accompanied his former charges to Indian Territory, returned to Fort Belknap, a rabid Indian hater named Edward Cornett shot him to death.[45]

"Death to the Americans"

The same month the last of the reservation Indians left Texas, trouble broke out on the other end of the frontier—the Rio Grande Valley. On July 13, Juan Nepomuceno Cortina, an outlaw who nevertheless had a strong sense of justice when it came to Anglo mistreatment of fellow Hispanics, saw Brownsville city marshal Robert Shears pistol-whipping a drunken Mexican-American during an arrest. Recognizing the man as a former employee, Cortina made it his fight. He shot the lawman, pulled the former prisoner up on his horse, and galloped out of town.

On September 28, from a stronghold at his mother's Del Carmen Ranch nine miles upriver, Cortina led seventy men in a predawn attack on Brownsville. Yelling "Death to the Americans" and "Viva Mexico," he and his men took control of the town, holding it for most of the day. Five residents and one raider died in the attack. Two weeks later, Cameron County sheriff James Browne formed a posse and rode for the Cortina ranch. The posse captured sixty-five-year-old Tomas Cabrera, Cortina's lieutenant and a participant in the September raid. Cortina soon demanded Cabrera's release, threatening to leave Brownsville "in ashes."

Learning of the tense situation in the valley, twenty-six-year-old William G. Tobin, a San Antonio businessman, on his own authority raised fifty men to ride for Brownsville. When he heard that Tobin already had an armed force heading south, Governor Runnels on October 13 formally authorized the young hothead to "muster into the temporary service of the State one hundred men, for the purpose of assisting the civil authorities in the county of Cameron in quelling the lawless and bloody disturbances at the city of Brownsville." Runnels also gave Tobin and his men the power to "promptly and at every hazard arrest the parties charged with the murder of peaceable citizens." Tobin's company would be expected "to arm and equip, furnish themselves, and look alone to the next legislature for such remuneration therefor, and for such pay as they deserve." Anticipating legislative approval of additional funding, Runnels told Tobin he could recruit more men in Brownsville if he found it necessary.[46]

As he moved south, Tobin added another forty volunteers to his force at San Patricio. Stopping at Richard King's ranch, the men got fresh horses and pressed on for Brownsville, where they arrived on November 10.[47] Skittish locals, hearing Tobin's bugler, assumed Cortina had attacked again and fired a cannon blast of grapeshot at the approaching rangers. Two pieces of shot perforated their guide's coat, but none of the projectiles penetrated anyone's flesh.[48]

On the night of November 13, parties unknown removed Cabrera from jail and lynched him on the Market Square. Tobin's rangers made no effort to prevent it and possibly even assisted.

Soon, a rumor hit Austin that Cortina had sacked Brownsville and now marched with more than a thousand men toward Corpus Christi. Walking down Congress Avenue in the capital city, Ford ran into a noticeably edgy Senator Forbes Britton, whose district included Nueces County. Ford tried to persuade the lawmaker that an attack that far from the border seemed highly unlikely. Having invoked common sense, Ford thought he had the senator convinced, but about that time, Governor

Runnels joined them. Seeing the senator almost in hysterics, Runnels told Ford, "You must go; you must start tonight, and move swiftly."[49]

Runnels followed up his spoken order on November 17 with written authorization for Ford to "enlist and organize a company of mounted men." Though clearly under state control, Ford's eighty-nine-man force would operate under the U.S. army's Articles of War and follow army regulations. Other Ranger companies raised in Bexar, Victoria, and Gonzales counties would be folded into Ford's command.[50] The same day the governor signed his order, a contingent of U.S. army regulars led by Major Samuel P. Heintzelman left San Antonio for the valley.

On November 21, the first contact between the Rangers and Cortinistas—an engagement on the Palo Alto prairie involving thirty men from Karnes County under Lieutenant John Littleton—ended in the death of three rangers and the wounding of four others, including Littleton. Ranger John Fox, also wounded, surrendered to the Mexicans. Never seen again, he either died of his wounds or faced a firing squad.

Tobin, his force augmented by a mixture of volunteers and militia newly arrived from Atascosa County, Indianola, and the local area, moved upriver from Brownsville on November 22 to "exterminate Cortina." Met by "galling fire," Tobin fell back. Against orders, sixty men left for Brownsville, their appetite for extermination apparently satisfied.

Tobin advanced again toward Cortina's ranch on November 24. Surveying the situation from high ground about a mile away, Tobin realized that Cortina had him well outnumbered. Again, the captain pulled back, this time returning to Brownsville. As many as one hundred of his men unvolunteered themselves and departed for north of the Nueces.

Heintzelman, his force bolstered by two companies of artillery and one company of the Second Cavalry, reached Brownsville on December 5. Two days later the major met with Tobin, later writing in his diary that the Ranger captain seemed "to be a clever man." The career army officer soon realized his first impression of Tobin had been wrong.

On December 9, army captain George Stoneman rode with Tobin to the Ranger camp, a mile and a half from town, and "gave them a drill & showed them a few things they wanted to know." Two days later, Tobin told Heintzelman that he believed Cortina had 620 men under arms. Heintzelman observed in his diary that Tobin "deals in round numbers." The following day, December 12, Judge Edmund J. Davis of Brownsville estimated Cortina's force at only 260 men and provided the major with a sketch of his position. "There is almost a mutiny in the Ranger camp," Heintzelman wrote. "Capt. Tobin don't appear to have much influence with them."

The major had no better luck dealing with the Rangers. "I cannot get the Rangers to do anything effective in the way of scouting," Heintzelman wrote to the governor on December 13. But the dynamics soon changed.

Ford and fifty-three rangers reached Brownsville on December 14. Hearing gunfire, Ford galloped his company upriver to find that Tobin and the U.S. troops had engaged Cortina.[51] "Captain Tobin with the rangers and Major [Heintzelman] with his regulars attacked Cortina's fortification and after cannonading the place for some time Cortina abandoned it and retreated up the road," a witness to the fight later re-called.[52] Heintzelman wrote, "The rangers dismounted and took the brush and fought them for several miles, but Cortina retained his cannon. It commenced raining and as night came on the fight stopped. We would undoubtedly have done better without the Rangers."[53]

With the arrival of Ford, Heintzelman thought the situation would improve. Ford and Tobin, however, did not get along. The governor had instructed Ford and Tobin to let the rank and file vote on who should assume overall command of the Rangers. "I hope by all means that Ford will be elected," the major wrote. "He is by all odds the better man. He controls his men & Tobin is controlled by his. I would rather have Ford with 50 than Tobin with all his men."[54]

Two days after Christmas, Ford led eighty rangers in a fog-shrouded fight with Cortina near Rio Grande City. After suffering heavy losses, Cortina escaped into Mexico with the rest of his men and what little equipment he had left. "There were several Rangers wounded & I don't know how many Mexicans killed—some 20 or more," Heintzelman wrote in his diary that night. "I hope now that the matter is ended."[55] For the most part, it had.

Ford had again demonstrated the effectiveness of well-led rangers, but nearly a quarter century after the provisional government of Texas first envisioned a Corps of Rangers, the state still had no standing force. Lack of funding and the perennial resistance of legislators representing the settled—and safer—eastern half of Texas kept the rangers from achieving continuity. When the government did commission rangers, the men who took on the job found the work difficult, dangerous, and relatively thankless. "Their pay while acting as rangers was indeed small," wrote land speculator Jacob De Cordova, "and, had it not been for the excitement attendant on military life and the essential service they were rendering to the country of their adoption, few, very few, would have ever joined these ill-paid and worse-provisioned companies."[56]

6

"So sad a face"

A Collapsing Frontier and Civil War, 1860–65

The young man climbing off his horse outside Isaac Lynn's double log cabin had been in the saddle all night.

Smoke rose from the chimney on the right side of the frontier home place. Likely Lynn had a pot of coffee on the hearth, and the traveler could sure use a cup. Twenty-four-year-old Charles Goodnight stepped up on the dogtrot separating the two cabins and walked in the open door. What Goodnight saw next burned into his memory as surely as if he had walked over to the fireplace and picked up a searing-hot poker. Lynn sat in front of the fire, roasting an inside-out human scalp hanging from the end of a long green dogwood stick.

"As he turned it carefully over the fire," Goodnight recalled, "the grease oozed out of it, and it had drawn up until it looked as thick as a buffalo bull's scalp. [He] bid me good morning, and then turned to his work. . . . I don't think I ever looked at so sad a face."

Lynn had every reason for melancholy. His daughter and son-in-law, Mary and Tom Mason, along with their baby, had been killed by Indians two years before.[1] Since their deaths, striving for the biblical balance of revenge set out in the Good Book, Lynn had made a habit of collecting Indian scalps. Now he busied himself smoking the latest addition to his gruesome holdings, a fresh scalp with long black hair adorned with small silver bells.

Lynn had not even heard the latest news: Ezra Sherman's pregnant wife had been repeatedly raped, stabbed, shot with arrows, and scalped by a war party that had attacked the couple's cabin on Stagg's Prairie, in eastern Parker County. No one expected Martha Sherman, suffering horribly, to live. Goodnight had ridden in a cold, driving rain all night to alert as many settlers as possible of the Indian raid. Eight men had agreed to meet him at the Lynn cabin to ride after the raiders, but the frontier needed more than vengeance-seeking volunteers.[2]

No one found word of the attack more frustrating than Governor Sam Houston, who had been trying for nearly a year to provide adequate protection along the frontier. After thirteen years in the U.S. Senate, in the spring of 1859 Houston had come home to Texas. He had tried to retire from Congress two years before, running unsuccessfully for governor against Hardin R. Runnels. Though at first reluctant, Houston challenged Runnels again, this time winning decisively. Assuming office on December 21, 1859, Houston addressed a joint session of the legislature the following day.[3]

"Called from retirement by the voice of my fellow citizens," the new governor told the lawmakers, "I am not insensible to the delicacy and importance of the duties which devolve upon me." None of those duties surpassed frontier defense in importance. "Depredations by the Indians are so frequent that to hear of them has almost ceased to excite sympathy and attention in the interior of our State," he said.

Though Texas rightfully looked to the military to defend its borders from hostile tribes, the buttons on the blue frocks worn by most of the U.S. troops stationed in the state bore the upraised *I* of infantry. As Houston had said while still a member of Congress, foot soldiers not being "calculated for that effective warfare which should be carried on against the Indians," Texas needed a mounted Ranger force. He believed the federal government should pay for them, but Texas had no time to wait on Washington.[4]

Four days after his inauguration, Houston wrote a confidential letter to forty-five-year-old William C. Dalrymple of Williamson County, a man with experience as a ranger, scout, and soldier. Asking to see him "so soon as your convenience will permit," Houston told him, "I wish to take immediate action for giving protection to the frontier."[5]

On January 2, 1860, Houston signed into law a bill providing for ten companies of eighty-three mounted men each to serve for one year under the direct command of the governor. Half the force would take the field immediately along a line from the Red River to the Rio Grande "to act as spies and minute men."[6]

Eleven days later Houston sent a message to the legislature informing the members that he had authorized Dalrymple, Edward Burleson Jr., and John H. Conner each to raise a company of sixty men "for immediate service" on the frontier. The legislature's frontier protection act, he went on, merely "affirms a constitutional power already existing." The measure provided no funding.[7]

"Without a dollar at his command," Houston wrote, "it is impossible . . . to sustain rangers on the frontier, or accomplish much for the defense of the State." Nevertheless, he would "endeavor to send to the frontier efficient and reliable protection" and hope for either a state appropriation or help from Washington.[8]

On March 8 Houston published an open letter "To the Citizens of the Frontier" in which he charged the chief justice of each county with immediately organizing fifteen-man minute companies to be led by an elected lieutenant. The state would furnish arms, but for funding, each company "must look to the next Legislature for relief." Houston also told the public that he had "mustered into the service of the State at least 500 men."[9]

Houston had more to worry about than getting the money he needed for frontier defense. On March 10, the governor wrote Captain Conner, "Commanding Texas Rangers," preferring charges against his company. Houston said he had reports that rangers in Burnet County had been charging $5 to $8 a head to return to their rightful owners horses recaptured from Indians. Also, contrary to orders, liquor had been allowed into the Ranger camp. The governor instructed the captain to "destroy every bottle . . . but one for medical purposes." He concluded, "You will report by return Express whether . . . such things have been done; whether or not it has been the custom to charge for reclamation of horses and you will see that every dollar thus obtained is immediately refunded or the men dismissed without honorable discharges."[10]

At least the trouble with Cortina had subsided. As Ford made his way back to Austin with his rangers, the ranking U.S. army officer in the Rio Grande Valley, Colonel Harvey Brown, left Brownsville on

March 8. "All was quiet on the frontier," Brown reported. "The disturbances were believed to be over, and Cortina to have given up the contest and to have retired into the interior of Mexico. Major Heintzelman
has officially reported the war to be ended."[11]

"I AM BOUND TO SEE HER"

With the situation on the Rio Grande under control, Houston could
turn his full attention to the problems along the state's western edge. As
the twenty-fourth anniversary of his defeat and capture of General
Santa Anna approached, Houston began planning a major offensive
against the Indians. The governor wanted someone with experience to
lead the campaign, and Middleton Tate Johnson of Tarrant County
seemed like a good choice. Fifty years old and a native of North Carolina, Johnson had come to Texas in 1839 from Alabama, where he had
served two terms in that state's legislature. He had been among the soldiers Houston had called up during his Republic of Texas presidency to
suppress an outbreak of violence in Shelby County called the Regulator-
Moderator War, won election to the republic's congress, rode with Jack
Hays during the Mexican War, and later commanded a Ranger regiment
raised to work along the Trinity River. Having settled on land granted
him for his military service, Johnson had become one of the more substantial men of the region. His biggest lack of success had been in politics, having run for governor four times during the 1850s. In 1859, in an
act that clearly endeared Houston to him, Johnson left his party and
supported Houston in his race for governor.[12]

Houston authorized Johnson on March 17 to "raise a sufficient number of mounted rangers to repel, pursue, and punish" Indians depredating the frontier settlements. Houston's orders gave Johnson "full liberty
to dispose of the force under your command at your discretion." Johnson immediately called for volunteers and soon had companies organized in his home county of Tarrant as well as in Collin, Dallas, Fannin,
and McLennan counties.[13]

With a "ranging force" of 720 men in the field, a body that could be
increased to 950 "upon an emergency," Houston dismissed the county
minute companies.[14]

Houston had high hopes that Johnson would produce results. But the
governor had not anticipated the effect a blossoming May-December

love affair would have on his plans. Writing his oldest son on April 3, the governor confided that Johnson and Louisa Power Givens "will make a match ire long." Houston continued, "The Colonel [Johnson] has gone on an expedition against the Indians. If he sees the Indians or comes upon them, Woe be to them, as he will wish to win laurels to lay at the feet of the fair one."[15] Unfortunately for Houston, and the people along the frontier, Johnson—a widower with five children—had a stronger interest in romance than in fighting Indians.

At his desk in the Governor's Mansion on April 14, Houston began a long letter to Secretary of War John B. Floyd in Washington. "It is entirely useless to think of rendering protection to Texas by the Regular Army," he wrote. "No one doubts the valor of our regulars or the skill of our officers. . . . But unless the Indians are fools enough to go up to a Garrison and be shot down, Garrisons will be of no use only to shelter the inmates." Even if cavalry did come to the frontier, Houston continued, army horses eat grain, a scarce and expensive commodity. Too, the federal horses would have to be shod.

On the other hand, the governor continued, Texas volunteers patrolling the frontier could immediately pursue any Indian trails they found and deal with them "before they have an opportunity to massacre and deprecate upon the people."

In the next paragraph, Houston specifically referred to these volunteers as Texas Rangers.

"I have, I think named reasons why the troops of the regular Army are not effective in Indian warfare," he wrote.

> I now propose to render reasons why the Texas Rangers are superior and the only class of troops fitted for such service. They are excellent horsemen, accustomed to hardship, and the horses of Texas having been raised on grass, can perform service without requiring grain . . . except to recruit their strength for a few days, when returned from a hard scout; The Texians are acquainted with Indian habits and also their mode of Warfare. They are woodsmen and marksmen. They know where to find the haunts of the savage and how to trail and make successful pursuit after them.

Motivated by a desire to protect their own families, as well as having the memories of past atrocities fresh on their minds, Houston reasoned that rangers would get results. "What are privations, suffering and danger to them, in comparison with the plaudits of their fellow citizens, which follow their successes," he wrote. Rangers "continually on the alert, will be a terror to the savage. The certainty of detection and punishment will keep him away from our settlements."

Having made his case for state Rangers, the governor got to the real point: "Justice would demand that the Government, to whom we have a right to look for protection, should not impose upon us the burden of maintaining this force in the field." In other words, Houston felt the federal government should fund the Rangers. The governor also sought in his fifteen-page letter to reassure the cabinet member that he had no plans to build a private army, as some in Washington apparently thought, to invade Mexico.[16]

Some evidence does exist that Houston flirted with the notion of conquering Mexico and perhaps becoming president of a vast new republic, but if so, it amounted to nothing but passing fantasy. The Ranger force he had put together could have been used against Mexico, but despite his history of sympathy for the Indians, the governor could not ignore the suffering going on along the frontier. He knew rangers could keep the Indians out of the settlements, and borrowing from the model demonstrated by Ford two years before, he believed another offensive thrust into their territory would solve the problem. Unfortunately for the people of Texas, in commissioning Johnson, the governor had picked the wrong man to make it happen.

Still, the campaign started with a flourish. One element of the command, Captain J. M. Smith's company, left McLennan County on April 23 riding under a ribbon banner presented by the ladies of Waco. Smith would rendezvous with the other companies under Johnson's overall command at Fort Belknap, a former U.S. cavalry post in Young County. The army had abandoned the garrison a year before with the closing of the reservations and the relocation across the Red River of the remaining Indians.

Smith's rangers elected young Lawrence Sullivan Ross as their first lieutenant. The company also had two second lieutenants, eight noncommissioned officers, a surgeon, and eighty-four privates. Ross, the son of Hays ranger Shapley P. Ross, had ridden ahead of the company to tend to some personal business, but rejoined the company at his father's Young County ranch on May 2. The following day, Smith's men met with Johnson's four other companies at a point three miles from Fort Belknap. A short time later, two other companies arrived, putting Houston's Ranger force at full strength.

All seven companies mustered on the parade ground at Fort Belknap on May 18. The rangers elected Captain Smith as lieutenant colonel, second-in-command to Johnson. The Waco rangers in turn promoted Ross to company captain.

A week later, rather than setting out after Indians, Johnson's Ranger regiment had a parade. Boredom began to take a toll as rangers filled their time with drinking and fighting. Food supply problems and bad water added to morale problems.[17]

Houston's young niece continued to dominate Johnson's thoughts. "There is no use talking," he wrote the governor on May 30 in a "strictly private" letter. "I am bound to see her, but will be back before I am missed." Johnson then headed south to Galveston, leaving the rangers under Lieutenant Colonel Smith.[18]

Finally, on June 10, the rangers took up the march. Three hundred strong, the various companies would operate as separate units, their next rendezvous point Camp Radziminski, an abandoned U.S. army post in Indian Territory. From there, the Texans would move against the Indians, striking a preemptive blow.

Five days later, with the rangers heading north, Indians raided several ranches to the south in Parker County. During their four-day spree, they made off with at least seventy-five horses.[19] Colonel Smith gathered his officers to tell them he had information that a party of Kickapoos had murdered two families and stolen horses. The officers decided to "wipe them out."

Apparently aware of the Ranger campaign, the Indians set fire to the prairie, sending much of the Texans' potential horse forage up in smoke. The fire spread over most of northwest Texas and up into Indian Territory. Not having found any Indians, and realizing he would have trouble feeding his horses, Smith called off the campaign on July 12.[20]

"We scouted that country about two months," ranger T. J. Vantine recalled, "and killed buffalo and antelope and hunted Indians for pastime."[21]

Vantine and his fellow rangers had much better luck shooting game than Indians. For all practical purposes, Houston's Indian offensive had ended. The effort cost the state about $1,500 a day and punished the hostile Indians not at all.

"At last dates from Fort Cobb (22d June) we learn that the Rangers were still in camp at the Wichita Mountains; that they had found no Indians and the belief was entertained that they would find none," the Austin *State Gazette* reported on July 21.

> We learn from information derived from the Camp of the Rangers, under date of 1st July, that Col. M. T. Johnson has not yet arrived; that the Rangers were sadly complaining of their being forced to stay in camp; and that Gov. Houston was charged by them with the shameful delay which had taken place in giving them no chance to fight the Indians.[22]

However shameful the delay, the rangers, itching for a fight, could not be faulted. The problem lay in Houston's choice of leadership. Johnson, a man with good credentials, had simply not been the right man for this job. As governor, Houston got most of the blame.

Among several resolutions drawn up at a public meeting in Parker County, one asserted that "the protection offered the frontier by the State government is a humbug, and deserves the condemnation of all honest men." Another resolution proposed a petition to Houston demanding that he "withdraw the Regiment of rangers from our frontier." That already had begun.[23]

The governor disbanded Johnson's regiment on August 26, an argument against later speculation that Houston had assembled the Rangers for some grander scheme.[24] Back in Waco, Ross mustered his men out of service on September 7.

Houston had lost faith in Johnson and had no money or political support to field another large force, but he still believed rangers constituted the best defense for the families along the frontier. Only four days after Ross released his men, Houston authorized him to enlist another company of sixty mounted volunteers to serve "in the neighborhood of Belknap." The governor charged Ross with guarding "the passes leading into the country, and should Indians get into the settlements . . . if possible destroy them."[25]

John R. Baylor, publisher of a racist sheet in Weatherford called *The White Man*, still fumed about Johnson's lackluster expedition. The Ranger regiment had been the "most stupendous sell ever practiced on a frontier people," he editorialized on September 13. To his mind, the regiment's failure had besmirched the image of the Rangers and "emboldened our enemies by demonstrating that Rangers are perfectly harmless." Baylor readily libeled Johnson and his new bride, hinting that Baylor and his followers would hang any rangers they could find.

Ross arrived at Fort Belknap on October 17. Ten days later, the company took the field and began scouting for Indians. The rangers encountered no hostiles, but Ross saw their efforts as good training.[26]

With the election of Abraham Lincoln as president, the national crisis over states' rights and slavery began to eclipse concerns about the frontier, at least among sectional firebrands and newspaper editors in the safer, more populated areas of central and eastern Texas. The Austin *State Gazette* warned, "The imminence of the danger resulting from the success of the Black Republicans in electing to the Presidency a man who is pledged to work against slavery . . . imposes upon the People of Texas the duty of taking prompt and adequate measures for the protection of their lives and property." The article said Texans could not expect help from its "executive," the governor. "Every able-bodied citizen . . . should enroll himself in some company."

Beyond relying on an armed citizenry, Texas could again look to its Rangers. "We believe the Texas Rangers will make the most formidable cavalry in the world," the newspaper writer continued. "In addition to their six-shooters and rifles, they should be armed with sabres, and instructed in the sabre exercise. They should also be thoroughly drilled in infantry tactics, so as to be able to dismount, and fight on foot whenever the ground might be too broken for the movements of mounted men."

Though the unnamed author of this saber-rattling piece clearly had in mind traditional military action in behalf of the Southern cause, he urged that the frontier counties, "being exposed to the joint incursions of Indians and Kansas ruffians, should be immediately furnished with the means of protecting themselves."[27]

By late November the horse-stealing raids had escalated into full guerrilla warfare, particularly on the settlers of Jack, Palo Pinto, Parker, and Young counties.[28] Learning of the bloodshed, Houston on December 6 authorized two companies of twenty-four men each to assist Ross, who remained in the field. But the companies never reached capacity, the likely reason being lack of money. An appropriation to pay for frontier defense—funds needed to cover Houston's unsuccessful spring deployment—remained tied up in an ongoing battle between the governor and the state comptroller. The governor had appointed a paymaster to go over the muster rolls and then inform the comptroller who should be paid and how much. The comptroller balked at issuing warrants, saying no statute authorized such a position as paymaster. An attorney general's opinion supported the comptroller's argument. Houston had, in turn, signed a proclamation voiding any other warrants issued by the comptroller unless certified by his paymaster.[29]

Houston continued to look to Washington for financial help. He wired the War Department on December 6, asking that a corps of Rangers be called into federal service to handle the Indian problem. Eleven days later, Secretary of War Floyd wrote Houston that with no congressional sanction, "this department is without the necessary power" to accept Rangers as U.S. troops.[30]

Floyd told the governor that "the number of regular troops [in Texas] has been recently much augmented, so that it now exceeds what it has been at any time before." The army, he continued, had five companies of artillery, ten companies of cavalry, and twenty-five companies of infantry stationed in Texas. "I cannot permit myself to doubt that these troops will be found efficient and ready for any active service the Indian relations in the State may demand."

Bogged down by political infighting, Houston could not pay the rangers who already had served the state nor those whose services he still badly needed. Assuming they would be paid eventually, and mindful of their great need, some rangers still patrolled the state's frontier. One of those companies soon solved a twenty-four-year-old mystery.

"ME CINCEE ANN"

Hoping to catch up with the Indians who had killed Mrs. Sherman and others, Ross left for the Pease River on December 14 in bone-chilling cold with fifty-nine rangers, ninety-three citizen volunteers, and a detachment of twenty-one U.S. soldiers. Two days later, they crossed the Big Wichita River, encountering a buffalo herd the rangers guessed at ten thousand head. They camped on the river's middle fork and resumed their northwesterly march the next morning. Seeing riders in the distance, a dozen rangers charged off at a gallop, thinking they had found some Indians to fight. The "Indians" turned out to be a party of surprised Anglo buffalo hunters.[31]

On the morning of December 17, the rangers awoke to a light rain. After rounding up several horses that had strayed during the night, the expedition broke camp about 8:30 a.m., still headed northwest. Two and a half hours later, they reached the Pease River, a wide, shallow stream of "gypy," foul-tasting water. When they made camp that night, someone discovered a freshly skinned buffalo hide. Knowing that American buffalo hunters took only hides, not meat, the rangers realized they had found the Indians.

The men drifted off to sleep listening to the howling of the wolves that followed the buffalo herds, patiently waiting to catch an unwary straggler. They awakened to the thunder of an approaching rainstorm that stampeded their remuda and left their camp soaked. At daylight, Ross noted with relief that most of their horses had wandered back.

With a guide from Fort Belknap, the Ross expedition headed up the Pease River Valley, crossing back and forth over the river as the terrain necessitated, avoiding quicksand by following the buffalo tracks. On the morning of December 19, the rangers noticed a white cotton pillow cover on the reddish sand. Inside they found a belt from a child's dress and a Bible. The owner had written her name on the flyleaf: Martha Sherman. Clearly, the rangers had cut the right trail. They could do nothing for the young mother who had put her faith in the book the Indians had taken, but they might prevent the shedding of more blood. The rangers moved on.

When a herd of buffalo appeared on the horizon, running toward the rangers, Ross realized Indians must have spooked the animals. Soon, he heard the screeches of the ravens that shadowed a large herd to compete with the wolves in feasting on the remains of the animals slain by the Indians. Topping a hill for a look-see, Ross found four sets of pony tracks. Riding hard to a higher hill about a mile away, the Ranger captain reined his horse and surveyed the area. Only two hundred yards below, on a stream later known as Mule Creek, he saw eight or nine grass huts. As Ross watched, the Indians casually worked to break camp, not having detected him. The captain signaled his men to advance.

The U.S. soldiers split off to block the Indians' escape while the Texans prepared to charge. About the time the rangers spurred their horses, the Indians finally noticed them. But the Comanches had lost their chance. As Ross later wrote:

The attack was so sudden that a large number were killed before they could prepare for defense. They fled precipitately right into the arms of the [U.S. cavalry] sergeant and his . . . men. Here they met with a warm reception and finding themselves completely encompassed, every one fled his own way and was hotly pursued and hard pressed.

When it came to Indians, gender made little difference to the Texans. They killed men and women with equal casualness, even shooting the dogs instinctively trying to protect their masters. When Ross saw two Indians on one horse and another Indian wrapped in a buffalo robe riding singly, he and Lieutenant Tom Kelliheir roweled their horses and chased after them.

Catching up with the rider in the buffalo robe, Ross had his finger on the trigger of his revolver when the Indian stopped running, threw back her robe to reveal her breasts, and held up a small child. "Americano, Americano, Americano," she screamed. Stopping only long enough to order Kelliheir to stay with the woman and her child, the Ranger captain resumed his chase of the Indians riding double. Galloping close enough to shoot, Ross dropped the hammer of his army Colt. The big ball from his pistol hit the Indian in the back, knocking him off his horse and pulling the other rider down as well.

The Indian jumped up and let fly with an arrow in Ross's direction. Other barbed missiles followed. One feathered shaft sank into the captain's horse, causing it to buck and scream in pain and fear. Somehow staying in the saddle, Ross fired a shot that tore into the Indian's elbow, preventing him from further use of his bow. His horse settling, Ross got off two more shots that hit the Indian in his torso. Startled that the Indian could take four balls and still be standing, Ross watched as the warrior slowly walked to a nearby mesquite and began his death chant.

Other rangers and Anton Martinez, Ross's manservant, rode up about that time. Martinez identified the Indian as Peta Nacona, a Comanche chief. The captain told Martinez, who could speak some Comanche, to tell the Indian that if he surrendered, he would not be shot again. But the Indian signed that he would not be taken captive. Martinez, whose family had been killed by Indians, took that as welcome news. At Martinez's request, the Ranger captain let him finish off the wounded Indian.[32]

Returning to Lieutenant Kelliheir, Ross found the officer still fuming that he had nearly lamed his favorite horse chasing down "an old woman." Looking closer at the woman, her hair cropped short in Comanche fashion, Ross figured her to be in her thirties. Then he noticed her blue eyes. The darkness of her skin, which the ranger had at first taken for the natural pigmentation of an Indian, came from long exposure to the sun. She was Caucasian, not Indian. The Ranger captain instructed Martinez to assure her that she would not be harmed. After that, she communicated her fear that her two sons had died in the battle. When Ross said that no young boys had been killed, she relaxed somewhat. Around the campfire that night, Ross told Martinez to ask the woman her name and where she came from. She said she was called Naudah and that she had been captured as a child, but did not know many details.

When the rangers got back to their base camp on Elm Creek near Fort Belknap, Ross detailed some of his men to escort the woman and her child to the military garrison at Camp Cooper in present Throckmorton County. There the wife of Captain N. G. Evans took them into her care. Ross also sent a letter to Isaac Parker of Weatherford, whose niece had, he knew, been captured years before by Indians.

Parker hastened to Camp Cooper, but the woman did not recognize him and Parker did not recognize her. Accounts vary, but in one context or another, Parker spoke the words "Cynthia Ann." "Me Cincee Ann," the woman blurted out, hitting her chest. When the military interpreter promised he would send her two sons if found, the woman agreed to go with her uncle to Fort Worth.

Ross sent Governor Houston a report on the Pease River fight and his recovery of the long-missing captive, along with assorted trophies taken from the dead chief, including his buffalo-horn headdress, shield, lance, and bow.[33] The Ranger captain's success gave the governor the ammunition he needed to mitigate Johnson's failure.

In his message to the legislature on January 21, 1861, Houston noted that Colonel Smith had sent only a portion of his rangers home. "The others," Houston wrote, "penetrated the Indian country beyond the line of Kansas, and after enduring many privations returned to Fort Belknap, where they were disbanded by order of the executive."

Houston claimed that the Ranger buildup during the first part of 1860 had caused hostile Indians to disappear from the settlements. Their leave-taking had been only temporary, of course. After outlining his response to "the most appalling outrages committed by the Indians in Jack and Parker counties," Houston said, "it affords the executive pleasure to state that the Indians who committed the late depredations . . . have been overtaken and killed by a force under the command of Captain Ross."

Since his inauguration, Houston continued, he had "devoted all the energies at his command to the defense of the frontier. He has called into service a number of the most experienced ranging officers in the state and given them troops obtained in counties capable of furnishing the best Indian fighters in the world."

What he had done, Houston claimed, had been "adequate to more than the reasonable expectation of the country."[34]

On February 6, Houston notified the Senate that Texas still had $300,000 in unpaid Texas Ranger claims. In all, the state stood $817,000 in the red. No less concerned about protecting the frontier than he had been the year before, the governor urged the Senate to take action before "the call for men and money comes laden with the dying shrieks of women and children."

In addition to financing a three-thousand-member militia, the eighth legislature approved funding for a company of forty "minute men" in each of thirty-seven frontier counties. To pay for this, the state would issue $1 million in bonds at 8 percent, redeemable after sixteen years.[35]

"I HAVE JUST LIVED OUT OF THE UNION"

But the coming war between the North and South rapidly overshadowed the issue of frontier defense. "Before this reaches you Texas will be a free and independent republic," S. G. Davidson wrote from Austin to his wife, Mary, at their home in Belton. "At half past six o'clock yesterday evening 29th inst. a vote was taken on the question of secession . . . the [roll] being called the vote stood thus: for secession 154, against 6 so you see the convention is nearly unanimous." Near midnight on February 1, the convention passed a final ordinance of secession. At 1 a.m. on February 2, Davidson wrote Mary, "I have just lived out of the Union."[36]

Davidson quickly volunteered to serve in a Ranger-like force organized to take control of U.S. military posts in the newly separated state.

On February 16, former ranger Ben McCulloch led eleven hundred men in bloodlessly taking control of San Antonio, forcing the surrender of General David E. Twiggs, the federal military commander. A week later, by a vote of 46,129 to 14,697, the people of Texas ratified the convention's secession ordinance. Nearly half the freeholders in the state's frontier counties, however, voted against secession. Some of those pro-Union residents—foreign immigrants—had no truck for slavery, but others who voted to remain a part of the United States did so because they realized that war would leave their families even more vulnerable to hostile Indians.

The day after the election, Davidson—now an elected first lieutenant in the ad hoc Ranger force—sent his wife a letter from near Camp Colorado to report that the cavalry post "fell into our hands by capitulation on the night of the 22nd."[37]

On March 4, Confederate secretary of war Leroy Pope Walker turned to McCulloch to raise a regiment of ten companies of mounted riflemen—Rangers—to guard the state's frontier from the Red River to the Rio Grande. But McCulloch, more eager for a command east of the Mississippi, passed the colonel's commission on to his brother Henry, also an experienced ranger.

The same day, Lieutenant Davidson wrote Mary from Fort Chadbourne, "a large pretty post" on a broad prominence above Oak Creek in present Coke County. With the federal troops waiting for wagons to haul off their supplies and equipment, the rangers primarily concerned themselves with the same thing the regulars had: Indians.[38]

No blood had yet been shed in Texas, but downstate in Austin, Houston knew that would come. Realizing the South had little or no chance in a war with the more populated and industrialized Northern states, Houston refused to be sworn in as governor of a Confederate state and resigned on March 16. Two days later, the lieutenant governor, Edward Clark, assumed office as the state's executive.

Though Henry McCulloch had the command of the new frontier regiment, brother Ben helped in the recruiting effort, attracting many men who had ridden before as rangers. He published a notice in the state's newspapers urging "those who wish to enter into the service of the State" to sign up. "Let it not be said that Texas cannot defend herself as she did in the days of the Republic," he said. Two Ranger regiments, he continued, could "drive the Indians from our borders and make them beg for peace." Volunteers needed "a good horse, a Colt's pistol, and a light rifle or double-barreled shot-gun that can be used on horseback." The notice concluded, "The Comanches will know 'The Ranger Is at Home on the Prairie' again."[39]

"The children are well and romping in the yard," Mary wrote to her husband on March 29. "If it was not for them I would be doubly lonesome. . . . George will sit in my lap and talk about papa. Says he wants to be a ranger."

After receiving a letter from Davidson that same day, she penned a second missive. "You say it is not a pleasure to stay away," she wrote. "I know it is not. It is duty that calls you." Still, Mary would have liked to see her husband back in Belton. "I noticed in last week's paper that there was a company of one thousand rangers being raised for the frontier," she wrote on April 9. "You all will be discharged, wont you?" But that would not be the case. In fact, Davidson would be part of that new Ranger force, receiving orders from McCulloch to raise a company for a year's service. "My evle [sic] star is still in the assendent [sic]," Davidson wrote Mary.[40]

By late April, McCulloch had his regiment in place, including Davidson's new company at Fort Chadbourne. While Henry McCulloch coordinated regular patrols along the West Texas frontier, the reputation of brother Ben—and of the Texas Rangers—caused near panic in the District of Columbia. Rumor swept Washington in May that the Mexican War hero had five hundred rangers in northern Virginia planning to cross the Potomac, kill or kidnap President Lincoln, and assume control of the nation's capital. Government officials, rather than dismissing the report out of hand, seem to have taken it seriously at first. The secretary of war even reported that McCulloch had reconnoitered military facilities in Washington and "said that he [McCulloch] expected to be in possession of the city before long." Playing into the hysteria, the New York *Herald* informed its readers on May 27 that McCulloch and his Texans bivouacked only fifteen miles from the capital. "Our distinguished fellow-citizen, Ben McCulloch, appears by all accounts to have achieved the difficult faculty of ubiquity," the Houston *Telegraph* observed with obvious pleasure. "If all reports are true, he is at one and the same time in the neighborhood of Alexandria, at Richmond, near Lynchburg, at Montgomery, at New Orleans, at or near Memphis, and in Texas somewhere."[41]

On the same page as the beginning of chapter 52 of Charles Dickens's new novel *Great Expectations*, the July 6, 1861, edition of *Harper's Weekly* featured an engraving of "A Texan Ranger." The drawing showed a long-haired, bushy-bearded man under a huge hat astride a big-footed horse. Visible in his belt are four pistol handles, a sword, and a tomahawk. In addition, he holds a rifle and a coiled rope. Tied to his saddle is a whiskey bottle. "We publish above a sketch, by one of our most reliable artists, of a Texan Ranger," the magazine explained. "A gentleman, just in from Richmond, gave the following account of these most redoubtable warriors." Rangers under Ben McCulloch, the caption continued, are "a desperate set of fellows." The force, the venerable national magazine continued, consisted of "1000 half-savages, each of whom is mounted upon a mustang horse. Each is armed with a pair of Colt Navy revolvers, a rifle, a tomahawk, a Texas bowie-knife, and a lasso. They are described as very dexterous in the use of the latter. These men are to be pitted against Wilson's Zouaves and M'Mullin's Rangers."

Ben McCulloch indeed busied himself working against the interests of the North, but he was in New Orleans to expedite a shipment of Colt pistols for use by his brother's frontier forces. Later, he spent time in the first Confederate capital of Montgomery, still waiting for a command.

Back in Texas, Henry McCulloch received reports of increasing Indian activity. In May, Indians had attacked a stagecoach stop only thirty-five miles west of Fort Chadbourne. "There is plenty to do in this section," now Captain Davidson wrote Mary from the fort on June 7. "The Indians are thick."

Ten days later, shortly before riding out on a planned scout to the headwaters of the Colorado River, the Ranger captain wrote another letter to his wife:

> We will be gone 20 days and I hope and trust that we may do something in that time. . . . The boys are all well and in high spirits. . . . Mary, I have no more to say now—no instructions to give, for I know that you will do all that you can. I will come home just as soon as I can but I wont neglect my duties to do it. . . . Kiss the children for me. God bless you all, Goodbye, S. G. Davidson.

On June 23, thirty-two rangers from Fort Chadbourne, under the overall command of Lieutenant Colonel T. C. Frost, spotted Indians near present Big Spring in Howard County. The Belton *Democrat* of July 12 told what happened next:

> Col. Frost formed the command in line and gave the signal for a charge, which was made in gallant style . . . but soon, from the unequal fleetness of the horses, the line was broken, and several of the boys got much ahead of the main body of the scout. . . . Capt. S. G. Davidson, being well mounted, was soon in the lead, and after running thus 5 or 6 miles, caught up with some of the Indians and dashed between two of them, and commenced firing upon them, when they dismounted and shot him—one in the heart just before he passed them, the other putting two arrows in his back immediately after he passed, killing him instantly.

After stopping briefly to see if they could do anything for the fallen captain, about half the rangers briefly continued their pursuit until they realized they had nearly galloped straight into a trap. Seeing that more than a hundred warriors waited in the distance, the rangers turned their horses around, met up with the rest of their company, and rode back to their camp. Fortunately for the small command, the Indians did not follow. The rangers wrapped Davidson in a blanket and used hatchets to dig a grave for him, covering it with piled stones.[42]

The rangers had killed one Indian and wounded two or three other warriors in the skirmish. Though state officials in Austin had high confidence in Henry McCulloch, his regiment answered to the Confederacy, not the state. Newly elected governor Francis R. Lubbock realized that the force could be moved elsewhere, leaving Texas' western flank unprotected. Even McCulloch believed his men should be on the coast to repel a possible federal invasion.

The Texas Confederate legislature on December 21, 1861, approved "An act to provide for the protection of the frontier of Texas." The measure authorized a Frontier Regiment of Rangers, which eventually totaled 1,089 men. Enlisting for one year's service, they would elect their own officers. As always, rangers had to furnish their own weapons and mounts. Nine companies of up to twenty-five men, each stationed twenty-five miles apart, would patrol eight frontier districts.

State officials forwarded a copy of the legislation to the Confederate congress with a request that the new regiment be included in the

Confederate army with a proviso that the Rangers remain under state control and not be subject to removal from Texas. The Texas delegation succeeded in quickly pushing through an act to that effect on January 17, 1862. The new law amounted to a sweet deal for Texas. The Confederacy would pay and feed its rangers, but the force would be under state control and not subject to out-of-state deployment. President Jefferson Davis, recognizing the measure as a new incarnation of Texas's long-standing desire to get national funding for its own frontier defense efforts, promptly vetoed it. Texas would have to foot the bill for its Ranger force.[43]

"Do Not Wait to Be Drafted"

Colonel James M. Norris assumed command of the new Ranger regiment on January 29, 1862. The forty-two-year-old lawyer soon provided further evidence that rangers could not be effective without good leadership. He tried to solve discipline problems not by setting good examples but by court-martialing unruly rangers. Even worse for residents of the far-western counties, the Indians quickly grasped the rhythm of the patrol system Norris set up between the sixteen Ranger camps and made their forays when they knew rangers would be elsewhere.

Handbills similar to one circulated by newly commissioned captain John J. Dix of DeWitt County appeared across the state. "Texas Rangers. Attention! Do Not Wait to Be Drafted," the flyer began, referring to a Confederate conscription act passed on April 16, 1862. Dix said he had been "granted the privilege to receive men from any portion of the State, with a view to select the very best material the country affords, that efficient service may be rendered."[44]

During the early months of the war, some Ranger captains found Union sympathizers more plentiful than Indians. "There are no Indians in this portion of the country," wrote Captain H. Y. Davis on July 25. "The patrol scouts have become worthless, they generally meet the Union men in larger numbers than themselves. . . . I think we will have to abandon Indian hunting and turn our attention to Yankee hunting, for it is apparent that no Indians are coming into a country where so much sign of white men is found."[45]

Colonel Norris resigned in early in 1863, leaving command of the regiment in the hands of a much more capable officer, former ranger

James E. McCord.[46] But the most experienced and vigorous officer in the Frontier Regiment was Lieutenant Colonel James Buckner Barry, far better known simply as "Buck" Barry. He had been one of Captain Hays's "boys," fought hard and well during the Mexican War, and had been with the rangers under Sul Ross when they recaptured Cynthia Ann Parker.

With six companies of Rangers along the northwestern frontier, Barry succeeded in cutting off several raiding parties despite frustrating supply problems. Short of ammunition and forced to use inferior gunpowder, he did not stop all forays by hostile Indians, but he did no harm to the Ranger tradition.

As the war dragged on and Southern fortunes ebbed, the Confederate military absorbed many of the rangers. Though Texas Rangers took no active part in the fighting outside the state, Southern generals, including John Bell Hood, Albert Sidney Johnston, and Robert E. Lee adapted Ranger tactics. Terry's Texas Rangers, formally known as the Eighth Texas Cavalry, used the Ranger name even though the muster roll showed its men as regulars.

M. B. Smith, a private in Company C, Second Texas Infantry Regiment, may have been one of those rangers who ended up fighting Yankees instead of Comanches. He wrote a song that told of the ranger's hard life:

> He's weary of scouting, of riding, and rustling—
> The blood-thirsty brutes thro' the prairies and woods;
> No rest for the sinner, no breakfast or dinner—
> No rest for a Ranger but a bed in the mud.

Smith's song reflected another reality, the perennial lack of state funding for its Rangers.

> Those great alligators—the State Legislators—
> Are puffing and blowing two-thirds of their time—
> But windy orations about Rangers and rations
> Never put in our pockets one-tenth of a dime.

The difficulties, from danger to lack of support, proved too much for some rangers. As Smith concluded:

Altho' it may grieve you, the Ranger must leave you,
Expos'd to the arrow and knife of the foe;
So guard your own cattle, and fight your own battles,
For home to the States, I'm determined to go.[47]

On December 15, 1863, Texas officials finally succeeded in getting the Frontier Regiment removed from the state's financial responsibility and into the Confederate military structure. That, of course, also removed the Rangers from state control. The same legislation authorizing that change created a Frontier Organization, with twenty frontier counties divided into three frontier districts, each to be commanded by a major. All men living in the frontier counties and qualified for military service faced compulsory enrollment in the new organization. By March 1, 1864, each county had to field a company.

Barry did not think much of the new system. "Unfortunately," he later wrote, "it was contended by some of the settlers, and no doubt suggested to members of the legislature from the frontier, that this defense [the Frontier Organization] would be sufficient. From eastern Texas, since early years, there came an element in the legislature which opposed the appropriation for any force of men that were referred to as Rangers."[48] As part of the reorganization under the new law, Barry received orders that August to take his four companies downstate to Columbus. En route, new orders came for him to proceed instead to the Houston area.

While the state government's commitment to frontier defense had not lessened, its ability to meet that commitment, and the quality of the men called on to fulfill it, had decreased as the rebellion drew increasingly more men into the regular Confederate army. Too, though Galveston had been restored to Confederate control following its brief capture by federal forces, Texas anticipated an attack by Union troops in Arkansas and Louisiana before long.

RAIDING UNDER THE FULL MOON

A full-scale federal invasion of Texas never materialized, but another foe swooped down on the state along its exposed frontier. On October 12, 1864, under a full fall moon, as many as seven hundred Comanches and Kiowas—some reports had the number at nearly a thousand—

crossed the Red River and thundered down the Brazos River Valley. The raiders killed any Texans they encountered, collecting scalps and live-stock. More than a dozen people—possibly more—died in the incursion, the largest Indian raid in more than twenty years. In addition, Indians captured seven women and children.

Despite Barry's absence from his normal station on the Brazos, a de-tachment of fourteen Company D Rangers under a Lieutenant N. Car-son, part of Colonel James Bourland's Border Regiment, managed to save some lives. The Indians, Barry later wrote, "would have done much more damage but for the opposition of the company of . . . Rangers who met them in a desperate fight."[49]

Breaking into two groups, at midday on October 13 the Indians be-gan striking ranch houses along Elm Creek, a tributary of the Brazos about a dozen miles northwest of Fort Belknap. Carson's rangers soon rode up on some three hundred warriors. Hopelessly outnumbered, the rangers whirled their horses around and galloped toward Fort Murrah, a private stockade in which many of the settlers had sought protection. Five rangers—nearly half of Carson's detachment—died in the running fight that followed. But as one of the settlers who survived the raid later recalled, the rangers killed seven or eight of their pursuers. During their retreat, the rangers also saved the widows of two men killed when the raiders attacked the McCoy Ranch. When Carson's men rode into Fort Murrah, the women clung behind two of the rangers, riding above the rumps of their horses. Among those seeking refuge inside the fort was Barry's father-in-law and several members of his family.

The rest of the Indians continued their attack on a smaller fortifica-tion, the stockaded ranch house of George Bragg. Only four men de-fended seventeen women and children crowded inside. Later that afternoon, one of those men made the best shot of his life, killing Little Buffalo, the leader of the raiders. Giving up on taking the fort, the Indi-ans pulled back to regroup with the raiders who had chased the rangers into Fort Murrah.

Expecting a dawn assault, the occupants of that fort realized they had to get help. "A Mr. Fields from Gainesville said he would go, and I volunteered, too," recalled Franz Peveler, one of Barry's brothers-in-law. "The rangers flatly refused their services, declaring they had had enough for one day."[50] Not knowing that only thirty-two men defended the fortification, the Indians decided not to attack.

When news of the raid reached Decatur, Major William Quayle, commander of the northernmost district, rode for Young County with 180 rangers. But by the time they arrived the Indians had left. Even so, some sixty rangers and volunteers chased the warriors a hundred miles before realizing they could not overcome their head start.

"All that autumn and winter," ranger R. H. Williams later wrote, "not only we, but all the other frontier Rangers, almost lived in the saddle, and still could not efficiently protect the lives of the ranchers and their property from the ubiquitous Indians. . . . All therefore that the few companies of Rangers could do was to establish their camps where best they could protect the widely scattered ranches, and follow up the raiding bands as soon as news reached them that they were in their neighbourhood."[51]

A set of nine general orders issued for Texas State Troops by Brigadier General J. D. McAdoo in the winter of 1864 codified what had become the accepted Ranger philosophy of dealing with hostile Indians, an approach that would endure until the problem ended along the Texas frontier. Under this system, squads of men would be kept in continuous patrol between the various camps or rendezvous points along the frontier. If Indians got past the regular patrols, "the different scouts will guard particularly the passes through which they usually go out with horses. All experience has shown that the most effective plan of operations against an Indian enemy is to head off the raiding parties as they leave the settlements with their plunder and booty. If they are able to get in through the scouting lines, see to it that they go out without spoils, and with severe punishment."

McAdoo's orders also reflected a familiar Texas suspicion, a paranoia dating to its days as a republic, that another government had a hand in stirring the Indians up against Texans. During the 1830s, the belief, not unfounded, was that Mexican agents encouraged Indian hostility. Now, the general wrote, he had "good reason to believe the Indians . . . are incited and perhaps led to depredate on the Frontier of Texas by White men, who are agents, if not officers and soldiers of the United States."[52]

The general's orders reveal another aspect of the situation along the frontier, something previous rangers did not have to cope with: bushwhackers and deserters. As Major Quayle, the ranking officer in North Texas, put it in the General Orders he issued from his headquarters, "All Officers and men will use their best endeavors to arrest all persons

who do not belong in the District who are of military age who are without leave of absence from a proper authority also all deserters from the
Army."[53]

Earlier that year, rangers under Captain Silas Totten, who reported
to experienced Indian fighter George B. Erath, had a daylong gun battle
with deserters barricaded inside a house in the county named in Erath's
honor.[54] Elsewhere, particularly along the Red River, Texans chased and
fought Texans in an ugly backwater of the much larger war between
North and South. Compounding the problem, especially toward the end
of the rebellion, Rangers and Confederate troops charged with rooting
out deserters sometimes joined their ranks.

"THE WORST MANAGED FIGHT THAT EVER WAS . . ."

Less than a year after his fight with deserters, rangers under Captain
Totten joined Confederate troops in one of the war's ugliest Texas incidents, a clash that came to be known as the Battle of Dove Creek. An
episode that concluded in many needless deaths began with an act of
desecration, the robbing of a grave.

When rangers under Captain N. W. Gillentine found an abandoned
camp on December 9, 1864, near the Clear Fork of the Brazos, they knew
from easily read sign that they had cut the trail of several hundred Indians. The Texans could not tell from the tracks what tribe had made them,
but Gillentine reckoned he had run across either a large party of Comanches or Kiowas or both. Following pony tracks that spread one hundred yards wide, the rangers discovered a fresh burial beneath a wooden
cross. Against the objection of some of his men, Gillentine allowed the
opening of the grave. That revealed the body of a recently interred Indian
girl. "Some articles in the grave and some of the decorative articles of
dress were taken and the captain stated that he intended to send me one
of the moccasins," Barry later wrote. Calling it "bad medicine," most of
the men had opposed digging up the body.

In a hastily written letter to Barry, Gillentine said he did not think the
Indians realized he had begun following them. The captain requested that
Barry hurry to join him with enough men to attack. Barry opted not to
take part in the campaign, but he sent reinforcements. With nearly three
hundred men from Bosque, Coryell, Brown, and Erath counties, Company A captain Totten rode west to catch up with Gillentine.[55]

From the ranger camp at Fort Chadbourne, a second command of 161 men under Captain John Fossett moved south, planning to cut off the Indians. These men—rangers transformed by statute into soldiers—belonged to the Frontier Regiment, now part of the Confederate army. Totten's rangers fell under the Frontier Organization. The original plan had been for Totten to meet Fossett at Chadbourne, but Totten changed his mind and kept after the Indians.

On January 7, 1865, Fossett's scouts discovered the Indians camped on Dove Creek, a tributary of the Middle Concho River east of present Mertzon in what is now Irion County. Fossett decided to attack the next morning. Later in the day on the seventh, Totten's Tonkawa Indian scouts found Fossett's men. Learning of Fossett and Gillentine's location, Totten left some men to guard his wagons and rode to meet the Confederate troops.

"[We] finally saw them coming across the prairie, in a long black line, nearly a mile long," wrote I. B. Ferguson, one of Fossett's men. Though technically a Confederate soldier, Ferguson saw himself as a ranger. He viewed Totten's command, "armed with all kinds of fire arms—shotguns, squirrel rifles, some with muskets and pistols," as "'The Flopeared militia.'" The two forces finally met about a mile north of the Indian camp at a water source later known as Ranger Springs about 9 a.m. on January 8.

Addressing his men that morning before the fight, Captain Fossett reminded the rangers and regulars that January 8 was the fiftieth anniversary of General Andrew Jackson's victory over the British at New Orleans in 1815.[56]

"We younger fellows did not need any enthusiasm injected into us," participant J. C. Cureton recalled, "for then the world was our oyster."[57]

The rangers waded the ice-cold water of Dove Creek and opened fire on the Indians. Outnumbered and outgunned, the Texans fought on for most of the day, one side's momentum vacillating in reaction to sundry maneuvers and retreats. Wasting no words in summing up the fight, one ranger wrote in his diary:

March on until day the 8th, dismount, load guns, mount and ride on across Spring Creek. Join Fossett with 200 men. Made the attack. Got whipped. Twenty men killed and 25 wounded. Fell back 6 miles to Spring Creek, a running creek.[58]

Captain Gillentine, the ranger who had a month before allowed his men to dig up the Indian grave, suffered a mortal wound early in the battle and died a few days later.

"All in all it was the worst managed fight that ever was," ranger W. R. Strong wrote. "Captain Fawcett [Fossett] was a good old man but no more fit for such a place than a ten-year-old child. He would stand off and cry, 'Come here my men, come here my men,' but they did not pay any attention to him and nobody being in command was what caused so many to be killed."[59]

Ferguson had become separated from his company during the fight and did not make it back to the ranger camp at Spring Creek until about ten o'clock that night.

"By midnight it was snowing heavily," he wrote. "All night long men were building fires and talking over scenes of the battle. The cry of the wounded men, the groans of wounded horses, with the white snow flakes falling through the fire light, furnished a weird picture of distress seldom seen in Texas."[60]

The Texans realized too late that they had taken on some 700 Kickapoos, not Kiowas. They learned the identity of the Indians from a warrior and two young boys they captured about three o'clock that afternoon. Fossett ordered the two shot, but his men would only execute the adult.

"The attack was undoubtedly a mistake," one writer later opined, "but those who participated in it are not to be blamed. They had long suffered from Indian depredations. . . . Each mind was fresh with the memory of some horrible deed the savages had perpetrated along the frontier and all red men looked alike to them."[61]

The Kickapoos had different memories. "I was out hunting horses, and . . . I was fired upon by soldiers. . . . The first killed was Aski," their leader, No-ko-aht remembered years later in Kansas. "Aski tried to shake hands and make peace with the Texans, but they shot him."[62] The battle kindled in the Kickapoos a long-lasting animosity toward Texans. The survivors splashed their horses across the river to Mexico, but armed with guns and bitter memories, they would fight again in Texas.

By the time the bluebonnets bloomed that spring, the South's dream of a separate nation had died, along with hundreds of thousands of its men. Confederate Texas governor Pendleton Murrah fled to Mexico. On a U.S. warship riding at anchor in Galveston Bay, Confederate general

E. Kirby Smith formally surrendered the Department of the Trans-Mississippi to the federal government on June 2, 1865. Fifteen days later, President Andrew Johnson named former U.S. congressman and secession opponent Andrew Jackson Hamilton as Texas's provisional governor. In Galveston on June 19, U.S. general Gordon Granger declared all actions of the Texas state government null and void. The general also proclaimed the freedom of all slaves in Texas.

Since most of the rangers who patrolled the frontier during the war knew they guarded their own families, the effort continued to some extent on a volunteer basis even after the collapse of the Confederacy. Some of the rangers deserted in the final few months, but most realized the end of the war with the North had no bearing on the attitude of the Comanches toward Texans.

"After the war they tried to get us to come in and give up our guns," Strong recalled. "But when we all went into the war we armed ourselves and so considered our arms as our individual property. Besides, we needed them worse than during the war. They were our sole protection against the Indians."[63]

Henry McCulloch, whose famous brother, Ben, had fallen early in the war during the Battle of Pea Ridge in Arkansas, ordered his rangers to keep up patrols until federal cavalry came to take their place. That done, with a well-armed escort, he left his headquarters at Bonham in North Texas and returned to his home in Guadalupe County.[64]

Governor Hamilton issued a proclamation on November 15, 1865, calling for a constitutional convention in Austin for the following February 7. The convention modified the charter Texas had approved with its admission to the Union in 1845, and voters ratified it on June 25, 1866.[65]

Even though Texas had thrown nearly ninety thousand men and boys into the rebellion, the state never abandoned its effort to protect its frontier residents.[66] Of eight Ranger-like state frontier defense units and Confederate forces fielded in Texas during the war, average strength ranged from three hundred to fourteen hundred men.[67] Many of those men had ridden as rangers before and would do so again. Most lived in the areas they saddled up to defend. While thousands of Texans died fighting federal troops out of state, Indians killed an estimated four hundred men, women, and children along the state's frontier during the war. In the disintegration of governmental control that came after the war, hostile Indians claimed roughly an equal number of victims through 1868.[68]

If the Civil War–era Rangers had not also had to deal with Union sympathizers and deserters, not to mention lack of supplies, modern weapons, and quality gunpowder, they could have been more effective in protecting their fellow citizens from Indians. Still, they had done about as well as the state had managed to do before the war and considerably better than it would do for nearly another decade.

Years later, an old man remembering his glory days as an Indian fighter, Barry offered this assessment of the Frontier Regiment Rangers:

Our regiment, perhaps it is not too immodest to record, had helped hold the frontier along the northern part of the line during the war. To be sure, there had been wavering at times, in a few settlements, but we had done fairly well. In less than two years after these frontier troops had been mustered out, the settlements were pushed back in many places more than one hundred miles.[69]

"Filling bloody graves"

RECONSTRUCTION, STATE POLICE,
AND RANGERS, 1866—73

The Indians called him Leathercoat.

In the waning days of the Civil War, Confederate brigadier general James W. Throckmorton, who often wore a beaded buckskin coat in the field, was one of two commissioners appointed to attend a council on the Washita River near Fort Gibson with Plains Indians and representatives of the Five Civilized Tribes. Having ridden as a ranger in Fannin County during the days of the republic, Throckmorton now crossed the Red River into Indian Territory hoping to achieve something others before him had tried and failed to do—a lasting peace between the Indians and Texas.

Citing their reliance on the buffalo for food, the various chiefs of the Plains tribes refused to agree to a Confederate request that they never again travel south into Texas. In the end, the commissioners and Indians settled on a mutual profession of friendship. That proved about as durable as the value of Confederate currency.

A Democrat, Throckmorton had been one of only eight delegates voting against secession in the convention of 1861. But when Texas threw in with the rest of the South, he served the Confederacy, spending most of his time in command of frontier forces in Texas.

Fourteen months after the council, on August 9, 1866, the forty-one-year-old Throckmorton assumed office as Texas's first elected postwar governor. Voted into office by a large majority, he knew he faced a tough job in restoring civil authority in Texas. The first step came on August 20, when President Andrew Johnson officially declared the insurrection ended in Texas. Even so, Texas and the rest of the South remained under military control.[1] Within a month, Throckmorton learned just how firm that grip continued to be.

Protecting the state from the Indians whose chiefs he had met with the previous year now stood as Throckmorton's more immediate problem.

"We have today a frontier many hundred miles in extent being desolated by a powerful and murderous enemy," he said in his inaugural address. "Our devoted frontiersmen [are] filling bloody graves, their property given to the flames or carried off as booty, their little ones murdered and their wives and daughters . . . carried into a captivity more terrible than death . . . unprotected by the government we support."

The governor referred to the recently victorious federal government, "with troops quartered in the interior where there is peace and quiet; unwilling to send armed citizens to defend the suffering border for fear of arousing unjust suspicions."

He would work to convince the U.S. army to do a better job protecting the frontier, Throckmorton continued, or he would raise a force of Texans to deal with the problem.

Not impressed by the federal response to his request for action, on September 21, Throckmorton signed a law passed by the eleventh legislature authorizing a thousand-man mounted Ranger force of three battalions to guard the "northern and western frontier." But the act provided no funding.[2] Even so, the measure marked the first time a piece of legislation in Texas had specifically used the term *Texas Rangers.*[3]

The governor had a letter from former ranger captain Reading Black, the state representative from Uvalde County, informing him that ten people had been killed by Indians in that southwest Texas county since May 1865. Three others had been taken captive.

"Our frontiers are rapidly depopulating from Indian depredations," Throckmorton said in a telegram to the president on September 26. "I am requested by the legislature, unless immediate assistance is afforded by the government, to call out one thousand men for its defense."

Throckmorton optimistically said he could have the Ranger force in operation within three weeks.[4]

Unfortunately for the settlers along the frontier, the U.S. military did not agree that Texas needed one thousand rangers. "I have no reason to believe that there is any necessity for these volunteers, except the reports found in the Texas newspapers and the representations of Governor Throckmorton," Major General Philip H. Sheridan wrote General U. S. Grant, commander of the U.S. army. Sheridan opposed the proposed Ranger regiment, viewing it merely as an attempt to get federal occupation troops out of Texas.

The leadership of the victorious U.S. army still harbored distrust and resentment for those it had so recently faced on the battlefield. As Sheridan pointed out in his letter to Grant, Rangers raised under the Texas legislation "would be of the element which fought against the government."

Planning to leave the next day for Jacksboro with a contingent of the Fourth Cavalry, Major George A. Forsyth wrote Sheridan from Waco on November 2, "If this border regiment is raised, ex-rebels will be the officers, and eventually, the State of Texas will call on the government to refund the amount expended in raising, equipping, and supporting it."[5] The major did allow that there was "no doubt but that the Indians have committed outrages, but not by any means to the extent that certain interested parties would like the United States Government to believe."

Forsyth also forwarded to Sheridan a notice from a Waco newspaper headlined "Volunteers Wanted for Frontier Protection." The ad, seeking a hundred able-bodied men with "suitable arms and good horse," had been placed by J. B. Barr Jr., captain pro tem of a company to be organized in Erath County. Forsyth noted that Barr had been a "Rebel lieutenant-colonel."

On November 11, Sheridan wired Throckmorton a thinly veiled cease and desist order: "I see by an advertisement in the Waco *Valley Register* of October 13, 1866, that you have authorized the calling out of troops under the provision of the act of the legislature of Texas. Now, as I have ordered to the frontier double the number of men the legislature thought necessary, I cannot see any good excuse for the employment of the volunteer force."

That ended Throckmorton's paper Rangers, but not the bloodshed on the Texas frontier. The *Texas Almanac* reported that from May 1865 to August 1867, Indians in the state killed an estimated 162 persons and wounded another 24. In addition, Indians captured 43 people. "These outrages still continue," the *Almanac* observed, "and many victims are yearly added to the bloody catalogue."[6]

In Washington, Congress reconvened and soon declared President Johnson's reconstruction plan null and void. In March 1867, it passed the Military Reconstruction Act, a measure that gave the army even greater power in its control over Texas and the other former Confederate states. On July 30, exercising that authority, General Charles Griffin, military commander of Texas, removed Throckmorton from office. Declaring the governor "an impediment to Reconstruction," the general named former governor E. M. Pease as Throckmorton's successor on August 7.[7]

With Pease only a figurehead, real control of Texas remained in the hands of the military. The Army had 1,500 cavalrymen at eleven garrisons along the frontier, another 726 at four posts on the Rio Grande, and 1,442 infantrymen scattered in twenty-two Texas communities. Though Texans did not like being under the federal thumb, their efforts at self-rule could hardly be called exemplary. Starting in June 1868 and continuing into February 1869, a constitutional convention in Austin wrangled over an assortment of issues. Delegates split along moderate and radical lines, the moderates led by former governor A. J. Hamilton and the radicals by Edmund J. Davis. They did agree that something should be done about lawlessness in the state.

With Hamilton and Davis standing as candidates for governor, Pease did not wait for the election. Aware that the military had rigged the contest in favor of Davis, Pease resigned. For more than four months, Texas had no governor. Not long after Davis's election in January 1870, many Texans began thinking that Texas had been better off when it had no executive.[8]

Born in Florida, Davis at the age of twenty-one came with his family to Texas. His government career began as a deputy customs collector in Laredo. He studied law, gained admission to the bar, and by 1853 served as district attorney in Laredo. Elected as district judge in Brownsville a year later, he held the post until the outbreak of the Civil War. A staunch Unionist, he recruited and commanded a regiment of federal cavalry. Though vilified by many, Davis clearly believed in the rule of law. Unfortunately for Texas, Davis did not mind bending those rules to make things go the way he thought they should.

The United States readmitted Texas to the Union on March 30, 1870, formally ending Reconstruction in the state. Recognition in Washington did not, however, alleviate all the state's problems.

"Whole families have been murdered and made captive," the San Antonio *Daily Express* raged,

> and whole communities talk of leaving their homes and seeking security in some other location.
>
> So common have these outrages become, so general these frontier complaints that few listen or take heed and even the gallant soldiers, in whose hands has been intrusted [*sic*] the honor of the Government make it a practice to discredit all news of Indian depredations until now, even if the wet scalps of all the men, women and children were hanging to savage belts and their homes laid in ashes, it would excite no sympathy or surprise and some wise Commander could easily account for the circumstance by saying it was not Indians or Mexicans but white men."[9]

One of Texas's most influential newspapers, the *Express* went on to propose a solution to the problem: "The old system has failed in every instance on our frontier. The . . . ranger plan seems best to us."[10]

Following Davis's April 28 inauguration, a legislature controlled by fellow radicals soon began handing him the tools he felt he needed to restore order in Texas. A law called the Militia Act designated Davis commander in chief of the state's military, vesting him with the authority to call all able-bodied men into state service. In addition, the law gave him the power to declare martial law.

"Where are the Rangers?"

On June 13, the legislature also authorized the governor to raise twenty companies of sixty-two rangers each for frontier protection. Rangers would be enlisted for one year of service.[11] As in previous legislative incarnations, the men had to furnish their own mounts, pistols, and equipment. The state would provide a breech-loading carbine, though the cost of the weapon would be deducted from each ranger's pay. Ammunition and food for man and horse would be furnished by the state at no cost to the rangers. Company captains would report to the state adjutant general, who in turn answered to Davis.

The day after lawmakers in Austin reconstituted the Rangers, Indians raided within two miles of San Antonio, making off with several mules and filling another with arrows. "This is growing rather bold," the San Antonio *Daily Express* understated. "We think it strange to say the least, that these red devils have been allowed to remain so long in this vicinity. . . . Where are the Rangers[?]"[12]

Members of the legislature, as had their predecessors, continued to see rangers as Indian fighters, not law enforcement officers. For the enforcement of the state's criminal statutes, the legislature on July 1 created an organization called the Texas State Police. Made up of 225 privates commanded by four captains, eight lieutenants, and twenty sergeants, the new force had statewide jurisdiction. The legislature had never before granted such broad authority. Unlike rangers, state policemen would be issued badges, uniforms, and weapons. Adjutant General James Davidson, appointed by Davis on June 24, would also be chief of police.

Though not rangers, the state police officers had the same authority the Rangers would eventually acquire. The new law actually gave the police force more power than the Rangers would have, including authority to conduct searches and make arrests without warrants. In addition, the law made all peace officers in the state members of the force, subject to call when needed. The unprecedented authority almost immediately began causing problems.

Even so, the legislation establishing the agency met a clear need. Crime in Texas had spiraled out of hand. Shortly after the new law went on the books, Davidson asked the state's sheriffs to send him the names of persons wanted for crimes in their county. The new state police soon had a list of 2,790 criminals on the loose in 108 of the state's 127 organized counties. Within a month, the fledgling force had arrested thirty-nine murderers or other felons. By the end of the year, the new agency had made 978 arrests. In attempting to make those arrests, state policemen had killed five persons.

While few could question the need for a state police agency in crime-ridden Texas, the federal government continued to be ill at ease over the legislature's creation of a Ranger force. The secretary of war pronounced on July 19 that "the State of Texas would not be permitted to make war upon the Indians, but that the United States military authorities would preserve the peace."[13] Colonel J. J. Reynolds, the new commander of the Department of Texas, got the word through his chain of command. Reynolds then notified Governor Davis of the War Department's edict.

Davis assured Reynolds on August 8 that the Rangers would be placed at his disposal to cooperate with U.S. troops. The state, he said, would provide rangers with food and forage for their horses if the army furnished supplies for the men. Reynolds agreed to that, believing he had the authority. On August 12, the legislature approved the sale of $754,000 in bonds at 7 percent interest to fund the Ranger companies. Styled Frontier Defense Bonds, they would be redeemable in twenty years and paid off in forty.[14]

"Many rumors are flying about . . . relative to the interference by the national government with the ranger force now being organized," the San Antonio *Daily Express* noted a couple of days later. "The War Department at Washington being informed that State troops are about to be employed against the hostile Indians on our border telegraphed Gen. [*sic*] Reynolds that no such force must be permitted to take the field and war on the Indians."[15]

Despite talk of federal opposition, company organization proceeded apace. Kendall County rancher John Sansom, who had ridden as a ranger under J. H. Callahan fifteen years earlier and during the Civil War had served for a time as sheriff of Kendall County, brought Company C up to strength within nine days of his August 3 appointment as captain. The men he and the other captains recruited under the new legislative act were rangers, but their organization would be military-like. Each company included a lieutenant, a medical officer, three sergeants, four corporals, a farrier, a bugler, and fifty privates. Most of the men in Sansom's company and the others had seen prior service as rangers or in the Confederate army.

Judging from reports from the frontier, the new Ranger companies would have plenty of work to do. "The counties of Llano, Mason, and Gillespie swarm with savages," the Austin *Daily State Journal* warned its readers on August 24. "The farmers are shot down in their fields, and their stock stolen before their eyes and in open day. Not for twenty years back have the Indians been so bold, well armed and numerous as now. At Llano the frontier is breaking up in consequence of these incessant and ferocious raids."

The day after the capital city newspaper made its grim observation,

Sansom's company rode through the streets of Austin to be sworn in outside the Capitol. From there, he led his rangers down Congress Avenue and across the Colorado River to hit the San Antonio road. Reaching San Antonio, they picked up their weaponry and other supplies. The greenest recruits soon understood that they had been issued military surplus of uncertain condition. Even so, only half the men ended up getting rifles. The others had to settle for pistols only. With some businesses refusing to accept state vouchers, Sansom had to pay cash for some items he needed, including horseshoeing equipment.

Company C set up camp in Kerr County. The enlisted men occupied twenty tents, while the officers stayed in an old house owned by Dr. James C. Nowlin, the company medical officer. By the third week in September, Sampson had his men on patrol.

By September 25 ten companies of Rangers, as the San Antonio *Daily Express* reported, stood ready "upon our frontier . . . to retaliate upon Mr. Redman for the evils he inflicts upon our borders and mete out to him the retribution he so justly deserves." The newspaper said it assumed the organization of the companies for the purpose of Indian fighting "will relieve the minds of those who distrusted the efforts of our Government in the matter."

The War Department found no such relief to its nervousness over the activation of what it saw as state troops, not a Ranger organization. Reynolds got orders on October 6 to revoke his authorization affording the Rangers federal subsistence. Though the U.S. military would not feed the Rangers, or even officially recognize them, the War Department stopped short of barring the new force from taking the field.

Six months shy of his eighteenth birthday, Samuel Coleman Lockett of Austin enlisted in Captain A. H. Cox's Company B.

"I had a burning desire to go," he later wrote, "but I felt sure that father & my brothers would oppose it. When the time came & Capt. Cox came down from Burnet County to be sworn into the Service, without telling anyone where I was going or what my purpose was, I . . . enlisted . . . and was soon on the march. . . ."

As the newly minted rangers rode northwest from the capital, two of them soon began getting on each other's nerves. A private who Lockett remembered only as Holmes had the reputation of being a thief and soon proved it. "He would not steal from any of our boys," Lockett related, "but would steal something every time he went to town."

Ranger Jack Singleton, an overbearing sort, had several profanity-laced disagreements and one fist fight with the sticky-fingered Holmes. Two days after their fisticuffs, Singleton "slipped up behind Holmes while he was . . . eating his breakfast & shot him in the back, the ball talking effect in Holmes' neck."

Screaming "Oh Jack," Holmes ran a short distance before Singleton fired again, this time killing him. The rangers buried Holmes beneath a mesquite tree and resumed their trek toward Erath County, where they would spend the winter. Though no one had cared much for Holmes, the rangers did not like the cold-blooded nature of his killing. Lynching Singleton for being a back shooter seemed in order. But before that could happen, Cox discharged him from the Rangers and turned him over to civil authorities. His later trial for murder ended in acquittal, no witnesses having appeared.

Company B, meanwhile, spent an uneventful if comfortable winter in split-oak, mud-daubed cabins they built. "Of course scouts were out most all the time & some of us go [sic] as gards [sic] for courts," Lockett wrote.

When not on duty, Lockett hired out at nearby ranches, cutting fence posts and splitting rails for spending money. "At that time," he explained, "the state was low in her finances. . . ."

Though Lockett did not participate, one of Company B's patrols did encounter a party of Indians in Palo Pinto County. Rangers captured fifty horses and killed five warriors, including one youth whose war paint obscured white skin. "It is probable that he had been stolen when a small child and raised by the Indians," Lockett theorized.[16]

Twenty-two-year-old Andrew Jackson Sowell also enlisted with the Rangers. He joined Captain David Baker's company, leaving Seguin for the ranger rendezvous point at Camp Salado, seven miles northeast of San Antonio.

"We were mustered into the State service on the 5th day of November, 1870, and were pronounced by our mustering officer, to be one of the finest looking and best mounted companies which had been sent out," Sowell later wrote.[17]

The Austin *Daily State Journal* reported in a page-one note on November 25 that eleven companies of Rangers "will be kept on the frontier, and if that number is not enough it will be increased at the next meeting of the Legislature." The Texas public and press, however, usually had more enthusiasm for fielding Ranger companies than budget-minded state lawmakers.

In troubled times, nostalgia can be comforting. Just before Christmas 1870, copies of John C. Duval's *The Adventures of Big Foot Wallace, the Texas Ranger and Hunter* reached Texas from Philadelphia. A quarter century before, Duval and Wallace served together as rangers, sharing the same mess. Though Duval clearly took poetic license, his book marked the publication of the first Texas Ranger biography. Wallace's exploits made for good reading, and he had not been particularly difficult to interview. In the right mood with congenial company, Wallace put on a good show. The old Indian fighter had learned that he could "come occasionally to San Antonio and by his talk draw such a crowd into a certain saloon that his own drinks were provided free."[18]

Only fourteen of the twenty authorized Ranger companies had reached the field by December. Hamstrung by lack of funding and mediocre leadership from Austin, the force nevertheless had some good men who worked hard. "They were mostly young, unmarried men, and anxious to be off and view the red man in his native wilds," Sowell wrote.[19] He went on to describe their equipment, how they dressed, and to assess their mettle:

> In the first place he wants a good horse, strong saddle, double-girthed, a good carbine, pistol, and plenty of ammunition. He generally wears rough clothing, either buckskin or strong, durable cloth, and generally a broad-brimmed hat, on the Mexican style, thick overshirt, top boots and spurs, and a jacket or short coat, so that he can use himself with ease in the saddle.
>
> A genuine Texas ranger will endure cold, hunger and fatigue, almost without a murmur, and will stand by a friend and comrade in the hour of danger, and divide anything he has got, from a blanket to his last crumb of tobacco.[20]

Two of the brighter stars among the company commanders were Captain Sansom and German-born Henry Joseph Richarz, captain of Company E. Mainly men from Medina County, the rangers under Richarz operated from Fort Inge, a recently abandoned army post in Uvalde County, southwest of San Antonio.

While rangers elsewhere on the frontier had to contend with

Comanches, Company E stayed busy scouting for hostile Kickapoos raiding from Mexico. The bitter recollection of Dove Creek still fresh in their collective memory, the Indians splashed their horses across the Rio Grande almost within rifle range of U.S. troops at Fort Duncan in Eagle Pass to steal and kill in Texas.

"I am at a loss how to protect 200 miles of frontier and 10,000 miles of territory with my fifty men," Richarz wrote the adjutant general, "if the United States Government allows these savages to hover on the banks of the Rio Grande watching my movements and crossing into Texas when they please."

Richarz split his command, sending some of his men on a scout led by the company doctor, S. E. Woodbridge. Demonstrating skills beyond the medical arts, the doctor and his rangers took on seventy "well armed savages," killing eight and wounding about fifteen. The Indians killed one ranger during the fight.

On the night of December 8, Richarz's scout rode into camp with hard news. As the captain promptly reported to headquarters, "Another band of Indians had appeared near . . . Fort Inge, [and] in overwhelming numbers had attacked two of my rangers at the Blanco [creek], sixteen miles east . . . and killed them. These . . . are Walter Richarz (my son) and Joseph Riff."[21]

The lack of effective coordination from Austin is reflected in one of Sansom's letters to Adjutant General Davidson. Noting that not a single horse had been stolen from his district since the organization of Company C, Sansom begged leave to report "that if Captain [John R.] Kelso, Richarz and my company could have acted in concert this last month, we could have got some Indians. . . . I should feel disgraced, were I to belong to the Frontier Forces service for eight or twelve months and killed no Indians, and they constantly coming on our borders."[22]

The mutiny of Company H

Not all Ranger captains had Sansom's grit, but results also depended on the caliber of the men in the companies. Bland Chamberlain certainly did not have much to work with. Of the sixty rangers in Chamberlain's Company H, only five hailed from Texas. The non-Texans included a Frenchman who had been in Emperor Maximilian's army in Mexico, a man who during the Civil War had ridden with Quantrill's guerrillas, eight Mexican-Americans, and, as one of the Texans later wrote, "the rest of the company was fished out of the slums in San Antonio by the first sergeant."

The company spent a few months scouting along the Rio Grande, but its service record amounted to only a few words: "Arrested several rustlers on February 25, 1871." Three days later, the company received orders to disband. That led to what proved to be Company H's most notable accomplishment—being the only Ranger company known to have had a mutiny.

As it developed, the men of Company H believed that Sergeant John Morgan, a former Yankee soldier, took his job way too seriously. He and other ex-soldiers in the outfit made up one faction, the less disciplined Texans and others composing the other side. On their way back to Austin for their official mustering out, some of the Texans, in strict violation of orders, got drunk.

The situation degenerated into a mêlée punctuated by gunfire. No one got shot, but one state-owned wagon ended up in flames. Order finally restored, the by-the-book sergeant had five rangers clapped into irons. When they reached Austin, he said, he would see them court-martialed for mutiny. The captain did not intervene, but when the lieutenant returned to the unit—he had been gone during the incident—he countermanded the sergeant's order and released the rowdy rangers.

Unreconstructed, when the rangers arrived in Austin on St. Patrick's Day, they pawned state-issued pistols and carbines for a keg of beer. When the brew ran dry, they started on whiskey.

The next day, those able to stand marched up Congress Avenue to the limestone capitol for discharge. Since the state did not have enough money to pay them all it owed them, the adjutant general told them they would be sent vouchers for back pay. He also offered them commissions in the state police, but most of the men had had enough of state service.[23]

The men of Company H had learned, as others would, that rangering did not always prove to be exciting and romantic. About all Pleasant Henderson Rice got out of his time with the state was a good story and an attack of rheumatism.

A private in Company A, the twenty-one-year-old Rice soon departed on a scout from Fort Griffin in northwest Texas. When the company reached the Brazos River that winter, he later recalled, "she was full to the brim and still a-coming with drifts as big as boats amid the stream." The flood left the rangers little choice but to "sit around camp, eat, drink, swap lies and warm the seat of our pants, with a short scout now and then to vary the program until the water fell to where we could ford it safely with the wagon and teams."

The wait lasted three weeks. Even after crossing the river, the rangers could not cover much country with the grass not yet green. Though still primarily concerned with protecting the frontier from hostile Indians, in an early example of the Rangers offering law enforcement assistance to local authorities, Rice and two other men escorted Erath County sheriff Fealdon H. Ross and a prisoner from Stephenville to district court in Jacksboro.

The most memorable event in Rice's brief state career came during a scout with another ranger nicknamed Old Forgit. Spooking a bunch of loose hogs in thick brush, the rangers shot the best-looking one for camp meat. Dismounting, they hung the carcass from a tree and had their knives out to start butchering it when they heard horses. The men could think of only two possibilities, neither good: either Indians or the ranch owner and some of his hands coming to claim their pork.

The rangers let the dead hog fall to the ground and lay down behind it, their rifles resting on the coarse hair of its still-warm back.

"When the brush parted . . . I recognized Jim O'Dorne of our company," Rice recalled. "I never was and never will be as glad, I don't reckon, to see anybody as I was him."

O'Dorne carried word that the captain had orders to report to Austin, where Company A would be mustered out of service. The rangers cut meat from the hog and rode back to camp to cook dinner.

On the way to the capital city, Rice came down with rheumatism. Unable to sit his horse, he made the rest of the trip in the back of a wagon. His fellow rangers pooled their money and gave Rice $3 to help him out. Back in Austin on May 18, 1871, each ranger got $100 in currency worth ninety cents on the dollar and state script worth seventy-five cents per dollar. Captain Cox reported that he had recovered nine stolen horses and killed three Indians, as proven by the scalps the rangers returned with.[24]

Captain J. M. Swisher's Company E had its headquarters at Camp Colorado in Coleman County. "We did not have much fighting to do,"

S. P. Elkins recalled, "but we followed a bunch of Indians six days and caught them on the seventh day and had a fight. We captured 28 head of horses, piled 10 Indians saddles on the prairie, and got a lot of blankets."

Rangers liked collecting souvenirs. "I had a few relics," Elkins remembered, "but most of them are gone." Years later, looking back on his rangering days, Elkins noted that all he had to show for his state service was "one scalp, an arrow and a bow string."[25]

Scarce money meant lean rations. During the first ninety days of Elkins's Ranger service, the state furnished the men hardtack bread "full of worms, weevils and spiders." Not hungry for that kind of protein, the rangers killed their own meat. "The next three months," Elkins wrote, "our rations were misplaced and we did not have a bit of bread for twenty-two days. We went to Comanche Town [seat of Comanche County] and secured a box of crackers, and they proved quite a luxury."

Money still tight, on February 4, 1871, the state reduced the number of ranger companies to seven. In addition to his existing company, Captain Sansom received orders to assume command of Companies B, E, and F and move his headquarters from Kerr County northward to the vicinity of Fort Griffin. In El Paso County on the far western tip of the state, Captain Gregorio N. Garcia's Company D (originally designated Company N) continued in operation, spending most of its time trailing Apaches. The forty-nine-man company had only two rangers with Anglo surnames, Charles Kerber and C. B. Miller. The rest were Mexican-Americans.[26]

"They never saw Rangers like these . . ."

Four days after officials in Austin cut the Ranger force in half, a detachment of eleven men from Baker's company found themselves in the hardest fight any of the frontier companies of the Davis era would endure. Notified that Indians had crossed the Red River to raid in Wise County, Sergeant Edward H. Cobb ordered his men with the best horses to saddle up. One ranger with a less spirited mount offered $5 to anyone who would loan him their horse, but got no taker.

The rangers rode hard for thirty miles before catching up with the warriors, finding they faced four times their own number. Just beyond rifle range, both sides studied and taunted the other for some time before Cobb, a Confederate veteran who had fought with Stonewall Jackson's division during the Wilderness campaign, said, "Boys, what do you say to a charge?"

The rangers galloped on their worn-out horses to within eighty yards of the Indians, a party of Kiowas and Comanches with red war paint daubed on their faces. As the Indians raised their rifles, Cobb ordered his men to dismount and take cover. The Indians charged several times, but the well-armed rangers repeatedly beat them back, managing to kill both chiefs and four warriors before the raiders decided to give up as daylight faded. Of the eleven rangers, only one suffered a serious bullet wound, but seven others had bullet holes in their clothing or cuts from arrows. The wounded ranger, only sixteen years old, recovered.[27]

"All the citizens say with one accord, and proudly too," Lieutenant A. C. Hill reported to Austin, "they never saw Rangers like these, to contend with such great odds."[28]

The next month, the citizens of Wise County staged a celebration to honor the rangers who participated in the fight. The grateful townspeople of Decatur laid out a big feed, presented Baker's company with its own flag—blue with a single white star in the center—and gave engraved pistols to the men who faced the Indians and drove them back to their reservation.

Sowell remembered:

Late in the evening the rangers mounted their horses and rode around the square, Ed Cobb in the lead, carrying the flag. In the wind-up, the boys gave a specimen of their horsemanship, charging furiously around the square, wheeling and turning at different points, and changing from one side to the other of their horses. Bill Archer's pistol was accidentally discharged, which killed his horse. By early candle light the ball commenced, which lasted until near midnight.[29]

Downstate, residents worried more about cattle theft than Indians. Texans had always taken a dim view of someone stealing their stock. But cow brutes had become cash on the hoof. Entrepreneurs made good money rounding up maverick longhorns in the South Texas brush country and herding them north through the state and across Indian Territory to the railhead in Kansas. The commerce stimulated the postwar Texas economy. Cattle, suddenly more valuable because of increased demand in the rapidly growing cities of the Northeast, became an even more attractive object to thieves.

More than anything else, protecting livestock ownership got the Rangers into the law enforcement business. Adjutant General Davidson wrote Captain Sansom at Camp Verde that he had received complaints of cattle theft, unlawful branding, and killing stock for hides. To deal with the problem, Davidson authorized the Rangers to arrest violators and hand them over to civil authorities for trial.

The news did not catch Sansom by surprise. One of his sergeants, Sansom wrote Davidson, had discovered a cache of one hundred cattle hides while scouting after Indians. The butchering had clearly been the work of Anglos, not Indians.

On February 20, a patrol under Lieutenant Charles A. Patton rode up on three men with a four-horse wagon piled high with cattle hides.

"All these I arrested and sent to Fredericksburg under charge of Sgt. [William] Caston with five rangers," Patton reported.[30]

Two days later, Patton's patrol followed a set of wagon tracks until they rode up on eight men camped on Paint Creek. The rangers found they had built a pen and had been gathering "beeves and mavericks. . . . I informed them that all illegal gathering, driving and branding was positively prohibited, they at once agreed to abandon their purpose and return to their homes."[31]

Rustling flourished along the sparsely settled frontier. "From what I have seen and heard from good sources," the Ranger lieutenant continued, "I think there are a great number of cattle being illegally driven off, killed and branded in Kimble and Edwards Counties."[32]

Captain Sansom had a notion of how he could deal with the problem.

"Allow me, General," he said in a letter to headquarters, "to express my opinion that the declaration of martial law in those unorganized counties, for the suppression of cattle stealing, would do much to intimidate, and help drive such lawlessness from the border."

Political influence on the part of some defendants seriously hampered the effect of the courts. Being judged by a jury of one's peers meant nothing if a majority of those peers supported themselves by stealing cattle. But those defendants, the captain projected, "would have a wholesome fear of a military court."[33] Though Governor Davis had declared martial law in Hill, Walker, and several other counties, the adjutant general took no action on Sansom's suggestion.

Having waited for the spring grass to come up before assuming his new post near Fort Griffin, Sansom sent a sergeant and eleven men to the San Saba River as an advance scout on March 13. The rest of his company left Camp Verde a week later.[34]

Cattle theft had a serious economic impact, but thieves did not usually get trigger-happy unless cornered. Indians preferred horses over cattle, but the more bellicose raiders considered it a bonus if they could collect a few scalps in addition to livestock.

In Austin, the Twelfth Legislature on March 15 passed a joint resolution urging Congress to send a joint committee to Texas to see firsthand the situation and look into ways "that the State of Texas may be protected by the United States against further invasion" by hostile Indians. During the last five years, the resolution said, Indians "have murdered several hundreds of the citizens of Texas, have stolen and destroyed property to the amount of millions of dollars in value, have not only retarded the settlement of the frontier counties of the State, but have almost depopulated several of the counties . . . most exposed to their invasions, and are at present actively engaged in their hellish work of murder, outrage and plunder."

Some in the army's lower echelons privately expressed the same sentiment in letters to their families. "Troops stationed here are outnumbered and overpowered," wrote First Lieutenant Cyrus S. Robert of the Seventeenth Infantry to a relative back home in Maryland. "Indians menacing our Western Frontier and gangs of desperadoes roaming throughout the northern portions of Texas . . . are making governing impossible."[35]

Lawmakers also passed a measure aimed at keeping Texans from killing Texans. Governor Davis issued a proclamation on April 13 directing "the officers of this State" to publicize "an Act to regulate the keeping and bearing of deadly weapons." The new law exempted citizens of frontier counties "liable to incursions of hostile Indians," but Texans elsewhere would be expected to hang up their six-shooters effective June 12. The statute prohibited "any person carrying on or about his person, saddle, or in his saddle bags, any pistol, dirk, dagger, slungshot [sic], sword-cane, spear, brass-knuckles, bowie-knife, or any other kind of knife manufactured or sold for the purposes of offense or defense." Those convicted of the misdemeanor violation faced a fine of not less than $25 or more than $100, plus forfeiture of the weapon.[36]

On May 15, with five Tonkawas and one civilian serving as scouts,

Sansom's company encountered and ran down two Indians. The first died in a volley of ranger fire after a broken saddle girth left him afoot. The second Indian led the rangers on a hard chase until they shot his horse out from under him. As Sansom's men closed in, the Indian fired at them with a revolver in each hand. Though seriously wounded, the warrior kept shooting until the hammers of both his pistols fell on empty cylinders. Dropping the weapons, he folded his arms over his chest in defiance as some thirty rangers on panting horses encircled him.

Sowell, a young ranger with a penchant for writing, witnessed the incident. His description of what happened next is a prose poem to bravery in the face of death:

> There was such a look of proud defiance in his features, and something so noble in the attitude in which he placed himself, that the rangers ceased to fire. He was bleeding from a dozen wounds . . . but still he stood erect and gazed far off across the prairie, not deigning to look at his enemies. . . . Presently the Indian began to sing, still looking far off. . . . It was, indeed, a touching scene, and one which is seldom witnessed on the frontier. . . . This lone Indian, standing on the prairie with his arms crossed majestically on his breast . . . singing his death song, with about thirty Texas rangers in a circle around him on their panting steeds. When his song was finished, he stood a few moments and then commenced swaying to and fro, and finally sank to the earth, dead.

As Sowell and the other rangers watched in silence, the Tonkawas moved in and scalped the fallen Indian. One of the scouts later showed Captain Sansom a lance with six notches in it. Each notch, the Tonkawa said, signified a slain white person. The rangers also recovered from the Indians a white canvas tent cloth decorated with drawings of Indians and whites fighting. Arrows studded the figures representing the whites.[37]

The new general-in-chief of the army, William Tecumseh Sherman, still did not believe that hostile Indians constituted all that serious a problem in Texas. But he did decide to tour the frontier to make a first-hand assessment. On May 17, he arrived at Fort Richardson, not realizing that he and his escort had been observed by a war party of more than 150 Indians, mostly Kiowa and Comanche, as they traversed an area known as the Salt Creek Prairie. The warriors wanted to attack, realizing they could easily kill the white soldiers. But Maman-ti, their medicine man, successfully argued against it. A better target would soon present itself, he said.

Maman-ti's prophecy proved correct. About three o'clock the next afternoon, a wagon train loaded with corn for the fort lumbered into view. The Indians swept down from high ground overlooking the road Sherman had traveled the day before and easily overwhelmed the teamsters, killing seven and making off with forty-one mules and a horse.

Two of five survivors made it to Fort Richardson before dawn on May 19. As the post physician treated the wounded men, Sherman personally listened to their terrifying story. The general immediately sent troops to the scene of the massacre to take up the Indians' trail.

"I reached here about dark," Colonel Ranald S. MacKenzie said in a quick note to Sherman, "and find statements concerning the wagon train not exaggerated."[38] Assistant post surgeon Dr. Julius H. Patski had accompanied MacKenzie's contingent. The Indians had left nothing for the physician to do but clinically assess the carnage.

"All the bodies were riddled with bullets," the doctor reported, "covered with gashes, and the skulls crushed. . . . Some of the bodies exhibited signs of having been stabbed with arrows, one of the bodies [was] fastened with a chain to the pole of a wagon lying over a fire with the face to the ground, the tongue being cut out . . . it was impossible to determine whether the man was burned before or after his death. The scalps of all but one were taken."

Soldiers trailed the raiders from Texas to the Kiowa-Comanche reservation near Fort Sill in Indian Territory. After arriving at the post, Sherman ordered the arrest of the three chiefs who directed the attack, Satank, Big Tree, and Santana. Convicted in Young County, Texas, Big Tree and Santana ended up in the state prison in Huntsville. Shortly after his arrest, Satank had been shot to death trying to escape.[39]

Davis's Rangers had no role in the pursuit of the Indians, but the incident marked the turning point in the U.S. government's position on Indian depredations in Texas. The army's highest-ranking officer had nearly lost his scalp to Indians he had not considered much of a threat. After hearing from the survivors of the May 18 wagon-train attack, and reading the surgeon's description of what had happened to the teamsters, Sherman changed his mind about the necessity for protection on the Texas frontier.

The army soon would bear all of that responsibility. Later that month, Captain Sansom learned from his scouts of an encampment of as many as four hundred Indians on the Pease River, northwest of Fort Griffin. The ranger made plans to strike the village with a combined force of thirty Tonkawa scouts, fifteen volunteer buffalo hunters, and more than two hundred rangers. Before Sansom could act, orders arrived from Austin to discharge his men, return his commissary supplies, and put the rest of the public property in his custody up for sale. The state's appropriation had played out. Texas could no longer afford to field any Ranger companies.

Sansom did not like leaving hundreds of hostile Indians camped within striking range of the state's frontier settlements. "I could have rendered great service to Texas, could my company have remained in service three months longer," he wrote the adjutant general in disgust.[40]

The sale of state bonds had proven too light to support the Rangers. Lacking funds to continue their operation, the state released all Rangers from service effective June 15. From the perspective of fiscal responsibility, this came as good news for the people of Texas. At a cost of $458,996.15, the Rangers (at a maximum strength of 868 men) had killed only twenty-one Indians (at an additional human cost of three of their own killed and five wounded) and recovered 134 head of stolen cattle and 94 horses.

The payroll records for Captain Sansom are illustrative of what must have been the case with most of the men who led the Rangers during this period. For nine months and sixteen days service, the state paid Sansom $920, less $28 for his Winchester carbine. But the captain had spent $737.50 of his own money on supplies and equipment for his men, making his net income only $154.50. Still, he came out better than many of his men. Some of the Rangers never got the money due them.[41]

Davis's Rangers had scouted hundreds of miles. Their presence on the frontier may have prevented some raiding and saved some lives. If nothing else, the Rangers had made the people of the frontier feel safer for a time. The force also proved to have been good training for future rangers. Elkins and numerous other veterans of the short-lived force would saddle up again in the name of the state.

Hoping to fill the void left by the disbanding of the Rangers, the second session of the Twelfth Legislature passed an act on November 25 providing for twenty-four companies of "Minute Men" to protect the frontier. These amounted to local ranging units. The state furnished arms and ammunition, but the companies lacked any central control. The men received $2 a day for their service, but they could not work more than ten days a month. If they did, they did so as unpaid volunteers. "Very often we were out twice that length of time, when Indians were in the country," recalled J. P. Heinen Sr. of Bandera County. The twenty-man company he led disbanded after two years, their weapons returned to the state.[42]

A letter written by eighteen-year-old, Mississippi-born Horace M. Hall to his younger brother Bill on November 13, 1872, demonstrates how many viewed the Rangers:

> Well I am still out in the mountains running wild beeves and ripping around generally . . . but I am going to join the Texas Rangers[. I] will be out a year, going right out where the Commanchee dwells not to make a war treaty neither. And have just put a Seventy Four Dollar and Ten cents $74.10 outfit of clothes in my trunk for the purpouse.[43]

The young man must have been disappointed when he found the Ranger force had been dismantled for lack of money.

In early March 1873, the legislature's Committee on Indian Affairs sent a House bill to the floor that would create a fifteen-company Ranger regiment to protect the state from hostile Indians.

"When Texas was a republic, with a population less than one hundred thousand souls, a few companies of gallant Rangers, under the control of experienced frontiersmen, kept our entire frontier clear of these red devils," the Austin *Daily Statesman* editorialized on March 13, 1873, "and the settlements were comparatively quiet to what they are now, with a large force of United States troops stationed at intervals along the frontier in comfortable quarters. There must be a change of policy in the mode of frontier protection soon, or the Indians, defying with contempt the United States forces, will penetrate and devastate the settlements heretofore thought to be safe from their invasions."

By this time, Texans had been fighting Indians for nearly a half century. The 1872 *Texas Almanac* included an article by J. H. Kuykendall on the Karankawas, a tribe long vanquished. "The Comanches being still a large tribe, with extensive hunting grounds, will last somewhat longer," Kuykendall wrote, "but they, too, are fast approaching the termination of their tribal existence." He concluded, "The child is now born who will live to say, 'The Comanches are no more.'"[44]

But for the time being it was the Rangers who were no more. Meanwhile, the state police continued its efforts to pacify Texas, though not all Texans saw it that way. The Austin *Daily Statesman* thought the force actually fostered crime. Killing a state policeman amounted to an act of heroism, the newspaper said on March 30, 1873. In reality, the effectiveness of the state police depended on a person's political leanings. The pro-Davis Austin *Daily Journal* noted on April 11 that twelve state police officers had been killed in the line of duty between January 22 and March 14, 1871.[45]

On April 22, 1873, the legislature repealed the law creating the force. The measure overwhelmingly passed the Democratically controlled body, but Governor Davis vetoed it. Both houses then voted to override the veto. The responsibility for enforcement of the state's criminal statues now rested squarely with local authorities, sheriffs, constables, and city marshals and their deputies.

Most Texas newspapers rejoiced at the demise of the state police, but not every editor. "Already the jail at Gonzales has been captured by organized ruffianism and the jail at Georgetown has shared the same fate," the Austin *Daily Journal* reported on May 12. The newspaper went on:

> Perhaps the 13th Legislature may be able to convince the people that it is not responsible for this condition of things! One thing, however, is certain. The people see that the police law has been repealed; that a new and unprecedented (for several years) array of organized bands of ruffians have appeared, and have run over the deputy sheriffs and their posses.

With the state police abolished, the legislature considered, but did not pass, a bill that would have resurrected the Rangers. Though no one questioned the need for frontier protection, many saw the proposed regiment as little more than a pension system for former Confederate soldiers. Had the regiment been fielded, the *Daily Journal* predicted, "heavy would have been the destruction of beef and the disappearance of other edibles, while scalps of raiding savages would have been few."[46]

Austin's other newspaper, the *Daily Statesman*, viewed the matter differently.

"The horrible massacres of helpless women and children, constantly taking place on our Indian border, is a disgrace to the civilization of the age," the newspaper declared. "Self respect and the sacred duty we owe to our hardy pioneers, demand that we should put a stop to it."[47]

The newspaper said fielding enough rangers to take care of the Indian problem would cost at least a million dollars a year. The state simply did not have the money, a problem not unique to Texas. The New York Stock Exchange reported numerous business failures on September 19, the beginning of the Panic of 1873. The economic depression that followed lasted six years, seriously affecting Texas businesses and tax revenue.

No matter the state's financial situation, on November 1, Governor Davis ordered the creation of seven "ranging companies" to assist the Minute Men in the field, but only four companies took station and they saw little if any service. Davis's two years in office nearly over, he soon had more to worry about than frontier protection.

By a margin of two to one on December 2, 1873, the voters of Texas said they wanted Richard Coke as governor and Richard B. Hubbard as lieutenant governor. Most Texans thought they had gotten rid of Davis, but on January 5, 1874, the Texas Supreme Court held the election unconstitutional. Armed with that ruling, Davis declared that he would not vacate the governor's office. Coke, in turn, said he would not be denied the governorship, no matter the findings of the state's high court. For two weeks, Austin verged on civil insurrection. The Capitol became an armed camp as two different sets of party partisans, legislators, and other elected officials tried to keep or gain control of the building.

The war of words nearly became a real war on January 16, when a pro-Coke party forced open the state arsenal and removed rifles and ammunition. Hearing of the action, Coke ordered the men to return the weapons. Davis, meanwhile, telegraphed Republican president U.S. Grant to ask for federal troops to back him up. The president recommended that Davis "yield to the verdict of the people." When Grant turned down a second request for Washington intervention, Davis reluctantly stepped down.

Coke took the oath of office at midnight and Davis left the Capitol about midday on January 19. Future governor John Ireland, newly elected to the Senate, managed to kick Davis on the seat of his trousers as he left the statehouse.[48]

Part Two

Frontier Peace Officers

8

"For the Protection of the Frontier"

THE FRONTIER BATTALION, 1874–75

About sundown, driver Bill Anderson neared Blanco Station, halfway from San Antonio to Austin. Only three more miles to go and it looked like the jouncing S. T. Scott and Co. stage would arrive right on time. But Anderson reined his team sharply and yanked on the brake as three men, all of them holding a cocked six-shooter in each hand, stepped from the brush onto the dirt road. No fool, Anderson raised his hands.

The gunmen ordered the passengers—eight men and one woman—to climb down from the coach and sit in a row on the ground. Two robbers stood guard, while the third busied himself collecting $2,500 in coin and cash, four gold watches, and a U.S. Mail pouch.

"After this," the Austin *Daily Statesman* reported a couple of days later, the bandits "proceeded to cut the horses loose from the stage, and rode off, leaving the bewildered passengers to proceed on their journey as best they could."

With fresh horses secured in Blanco, the stagecoach and its badly shaken driver and passengers made it to Austin by daylight on April 8, 1874. Later that morning, when the Fourteenth Legislature took up its business, lawmakers quickly passed a joint resolution authorizing the governor to offer a $3,000 reward for the arrest of the stage robbers. The

Post Office Department soon doubled that amount, and the stage line threw in another $1,000.

Such a bold robbery in a part of the state considered reasonably civilized set off a law-and-order frenzy in the capital city. The *Daily Statesman* applauded the quick posting of a large reward but suggested the employment "of some reliable detective, who will be shrewd enough to ferret out the rendezvous of the gang and their accomplices." The newspaper went on to stress the necessity of putting men on the case "who, like the hound, will follow cold trails patiently until the game is jumped."[1]

Three months earlier, in his first message to the legislature, newly inaugurated governor Richard Coke still believed county and local government bore the primary responsibility for protecting the public from criminals. But in pledging to provide for frontier defense Coke put the issue in a fundamental light: "Every citizen of Texas is entitled to demand of the State government protection for life, liberty and property, in return for his homage to the government. . . . Every consideration of humanity, justice and interest, demands protection for the people of the frontier."[2]

The stage robbery that spring may not have changed any votes, but at a critical time in the legislative process it underscored that hostile Indians and border raiders did not pose the sole threat to life, liberty, and property in Texas. On April 10, only two days after news of the holdup reached Austin, the legislature passed a considerably amended House Bill 128 by Representative Robert Bean of Grayson County. The new law, "An Act to Provide for the Protection of the Frontier of the State of Texas against the Invasion of Hostile Indians, Mexicans, or other Marauding or Thieving Parties," contained thirty-two sections.

The first seventeen sections of the bill authorized the governor to call up a company of twenty-five to seventy-five minutemen for any county "upon the frontier" furnishing evidence of infestation with any of the enemies listed in the title of the act. When the emergency ended, or whenever the governor ordered, the company would be disbanded. These provisions meshed with Coke's view that even frontier protection should be handled locally if possible.

But Section 19 of the act plowed new ground, authorizing the governor to organize "in addition to the force herein provided for . . . a battalion of mounted men" empowered both as Indian fighters and law enforcement officers. The police authority came in Section 28, which provided that "each officer of the battalion and of the companies of minute men . . . shall have all the powers of peace officers, and it shall be his duty to execute all criminal process directed to him, and make arrests under capias properly issued, of any and all parties, charged with offense against the laws of the State."

The next edition of the Austin *Daily Statesman* did not even mention the legislature's passage of this bill, but for the first time in the state's history, Texas would have a permanent Ranger force. At least that proved to be the effect of the legislation. The actual letter of the law read somewhat ambiguously on the point. Section 23 stressed that "this force is not designed as a standing force," but Section 25 authorized the governor "to keep this force in the field as long as in his judgment there may be a necessity for such force."[3]

Fixing the size of the battalion at six companies of seventy-five men each, the new statute vested overall command in a major who would report to the state adjutant general. In addition, the governor could appoint a quartermaster to obtain and disperse supplies and to handle the battalion's payroll. Command of individual companies rested with a captain and a first and second lieutenant. The major would receive $125 a month; captains, $100; lieutenants, $75; sergeants, $50; corporals and privates, $40. Recruits would serve twelve-month enlistments.

The new law continued the long-standing tradition that each ranger furnish his own horse, tack, and "six shooting pistol, (army size)." The state provided a breech-loading carbine, but the cost of the weapon would be deducted from a ranger's first month's pay. Magnanimously, the state threw in ammunition for both rifle and pistol as well as food for man and horse. The state also would furnish wagons, draft animals, tents, blankets, cooking utensils, and pack saddles.

The legislature had been cussing and discussing the issue of frontier protection for two months. Coke had pressed for a state-funded, county-based system of minutemen, not a standing state force. Senator David B. Culberson of Jefferson, a riverboat town in East Texas, had been a key player in working in the provision for a separate battalion under the control of the governor. Senator George B. Erath, a former ranger the *Daily Statesman* described as "a noble frontiersman of forty-two years standing," got the battalion's budget set at $300,000, though some lawmakers maintained that it would take at least $400,000 to get the job done.[4]

General Steele and Uncle John

The legislature had made the new law broader than Coke had intended, but in appointing fifty-three-year-old William Steele as adjutant general, the governor had someone who could make it work. A New Yorker, Steele had graduated from the Military Academy at West Point in 1840 and served with distinction during the Mexican War. After the war, he commanded federal troops at various points in Texas, Kansas, the Dakotas, and Nebraska until the outbreak of the Civil War, when he tendered his resignation from the U.S. army to fight for the Confederacy. By the end of the war, he had risen to brigadier general. Steele had been running a mercantile business in San Antonio when Coke asked him to take on a military role once again.[5]

Steele, in turn, made an equally sound choice in his selection of the battalion's leader. On May 2, Coke commissioned thirty-nine-year-old Corsicana horse-raiser and Civil War veteran John B. Jones as major in command of the new force.

A small man of medium height, Jones had big, dark eyes under a slightly protruding forehead, a narrow face filled out with a thick, drooping mustache. A contemporary newspaper said he possessed a "quiet, easy manner," spoke in a "soft and modulated voice," while communicating "almost free from gesticulation." A sharp dresser, he wore "black broadcloth, spotless linen, and dainty boot on a small foot."[6]

Referring to his Confederate service, in which he saw action in Arkansas, Louisiana, and the Indian Territory, the Austin *Daily Statesman* said Jones had been "scrupulously exact in the discharge of his multifarious and onerous duties, a good disciplinarian, and one of the coolest and most daring men that ever faced a battery or met a bayonet charge." The newspaper saw "his military service, unflinching courage, and indomitable energy as earnests of success in the future."[7] In addition to his combat experience, Jones had a college education.[8]

Young Helen Groce knew Jones as her doting "Uncle John," someone who "made every wish come true" for her and her little sister, Annie. Jones, then a bachelor, paid Annie to "sing childish songs for him," though he once sternly warned her that one popular tune she sang "is not nice." As Helen later recalled, "He was nice in every way—never anything but the purest motives, thoughts, language—clean and sweet to the core."[9]

Not everyone approved of Jones's selection, however. Some, including Burnet Senator W. H. Westfall and many other members of the legislature, thought the position should have gone to a hardened Indian-fighter, someone like William Jeff Maltby. Born in Illinois, Maltby came to Texas via Arkansas as a volunteer soldier during the Mexican War. After the war, he worked for the army along the West Texas frontier as a teamster and scout, settling about sixty miles northwest of Austin in Burnet County in 1857. He spent part of the Civil War in a state volunteer infantry company, but a health problem prompted him to resign his commission. For the rest of the war, Maltby led a Ranger company in the frontier defense force vigorously looking for "deserters and bushwackers" as well as chasing the Indians who frequently raided his home county. When he learned the frontier battalion legislation had passed, Maltby came to Austin armed with a petition recommending him as the man who should head the new frontier battalion.[10]

Out of courtesy, Coke agreed to met with Maltby, but the forty-four-year-old Indian fighter failed to convince the governor that his abilities exceeded Jones's skills. "His only apology," Maltby recalled, "was that he knew . . . Jones and did not know [me] and that he intended to give the appointment to Jones from the start, regardless of fitness, for he was his personal friend and that he had seen his bravery tested many times in the Confederate war."

After patiently listening to Maltby's argument that Jones had no experience dealing with hostile Indians, the governor admitted that Maltby did come well recommended and offered him one of the six captaincies. Pridefully, Maltby hesitated, asking for three days to think it over. Coke agreed and Maltby left his office. Not long after his interview with the governor, Maltby received a worrisome letter from his wife. It said, as he remembered years later, "Jeff, do come home as soon as you can; that Big Foot brute of an Indian who murdered poor Mrs. Johnson and her dear little innocent children almost at our very door has just been here in the neighborhood, and I am almost frightened to death for fear that he will come and kill me and the children or some other good family."

Maltby had been trying to catch up with the Kiowa headman known as Big Foot since 1863. He had nearly succeeded on several occasions, but the chief always managed to elude Maltby and his rangers. Not having

heard anything of Big Foot since at least 1871, Maltby had hoped his old
nemesis had died. Now, after rereading his wife's letter, he stuck it in his
coat pocket and hurriedly walked to the governor's office. On May 5, he
accepted command of Company E. If he could not lead the new battalion,
he swore, he would by God finally settle accounts with Big Foot.[11]

"He has shared the trials and dangers of pioneer life," the Austin
Daily Statesman said of Maltby a few days later. "He understands his
duty and will do it . . . as he did in times past."

The day after Maltby got his commission, Steele formalized the organization of the battalion in General Order Number One. The adjutant
general enjoined the company captains to use their discretion so "that
their commands may be as effective as possible for the protection of the
frontier." In doing so, the captains were to report each month any Indian depredations and the number of citizens killed or captured as well
as property stolen and recovered. Their report also was to include the
number of Indians they killed and the miles traveled on scouts. Seeing
to further organizational details, Steel also directed captains to "make
temporary arrangements to supply as economically as possible for furnishing the men with bread, beef, coffee, and sugar & salt."

In General Order Number Two, Steele set the standard for the kind
of men he wanted in the battalion: "As it is expected that this force will
be kept actively employed during their term of service, only sound
young men without families and with good horses will be received. Persons under indictment or of known bad character or habitual drunkards
will be rejected."

Rangering had considerable appeal, despite the low pay and danger.
"Among the original members of the battalion," one man who knew
many of its members later wrote, "were writers of note, young lawyers,
cowboys, soldiers of fortune, professional gamblers, and about as general a mixture of seekers of adventure as were ever drawn together in
Texas."[12]

The new Ranger organization quickly got down to cases. On May 7,
less than a month after the passage of the law creating the battalion, six
Company C rangers under Captain E. F. Ikard, a cattleman from Clay
County on the Red River, engaged ten Indians driving 150 head of stock
toward the Indian Territory in a fifteen-mile running fight. Ikard, the
Austin newspaper reported, "has been fighting Indians in self-defense

nearly all his life. Inured to fatigue and privation, [he] will do good service."[13]

Arriving in Burnet on a mule-pulled hack loaded with state-issued rifles and ammunition, Maltby quickly recruited twenty-five local men, many of whom he had ridden with before. On May 10 he left for Brownwood, where he would add twenty-five men from Brown County and another twenty-five enlistees from Coleman County. In addition to supplies for his men, he carried rifles, equipment, and food for Company A, then being organized by John R. Waller in Stephenville. A fifty-seven-year-old Confederate veteran, Waller had served two years as Erath County sheriff.[14]

Still in Navarro County, Jones appeared before a notary on May 19 to sign an oath of office asserting that he would "bear true allegiance to the State of Texas, and . . . serve her honestly and faithfully against all her enemies or opposers whatsoever." Texas had plenty enough enemies and opposers to keep him busy.[15]

A PREACHER'S KID GONE BAD

Captain Waller, having received his equipment from Maltby, mustered fifty-five men into his company on May 25. While his counterparts began scouting for hostile Indians, the county lawman turned ranger would soon be looking down the barrel of a shotgun in the hands of Texas's most notorious outlaw, a trigger-happy preacher's kid with a penchant for racehorses, cards, and booze named John Wesley Hardin. The day after Waller completed the organization of his company, the fuse leading to a clash between the newly created Frontier Battalion and the young gunman began burning when trouble broke out in the nearby town of Comanche. On a toot in commemoration of his May 26, 1853, birthday, Hardin and a couple of his cronies shot and killed Brown County deputy sheriff—and former ranger—Charles Webb. Only twenty-one, Hardin had killed his first man at the age of fifteen and could now claim one man for each year of his sanguinary life, plus eleven more. Webb had been the thirty-second victim of a Texas hard case who could be meaner than a stepped-on rattlesnake.

Though he had become more than handy with a six-shooter, Hardin claimed he made his living as a cattleman. Many a Texan did the same thing, but Hardin preferred making money off other people's livestock. Cattle rustling being a good way to get jailed or lynched, Hardin worked with his brother Joe, an attorney living in Comanche, to cover his tracks with paper. Joe Hardin made his brother's cattle thefts look nice and legal.

A need to discuss with brother Joe some legal matters concerning a recently acquired herd of cattle had brought Hardin to Comanche. With his friend Jim Taylor, he had ridden up from DeWitt County in South Texas, where he had been spending most of his time. One of the combatants in a worsening grudge fest that had come to be known as the Sutton-Taylor feud, Taylor had a $500 price on his head. The state had posted the reward for anyone who brought Taylor to face a murder charge stemming from the July 1873 murder of DeWitt County sheriff Jack Helm, a Sutton partisan and former state police officer. Hardin had emptied a load of buckshot into Helms before Taylor finished him off with his pistol, but no reward had been offered for Hardin's arrest.

Stone-cold killers, Hardin, Taylor and their associates—all youthful toughs and rustlers—had become known as the Hardin Gang. Shortly after the slaying of Deputy Webb, twenty-two business and professional men in Comanche petitioned Governor Coke for twenty-five to thirty of Waller's newly sworn "frontier troops" to deal with "a band of murderers and thieves headed by the notorious . . . Hardin and Jim Taylor that renders the lives and property of peaceable citizens unsafe." The petitioners wanted the Rangers "to be subject to the orders of the sheriff . . . and that they be especially charged with the capture of the said . . . Hardin and . . . Taylor and their coadjutors."[16]

The people of Comanche County got the ranger presence they wanted, but the state officers would be under Captain Waller's command, not their sheriff's. On May 30, three days after arriving in Comanche, five brush-popping rangers flushed Hardin and Taylor, but in an exchange of gunfire the two wanted men escaped. Captain Waller reported to Jones that he had "been in active service trying to arrest the John Wesley Hardin gang of murderers who are preying on the lives of citizens of this county." The captain added, "There is a great deal more danger from them than from the Indians."[17]

Frontier Texans welcomed the newly reconstituted Ranger force, but the people living on the edge of settlement could not be considered entirely defenseless. On the night of June 1, a party of twenty Brown County citizens rode to Comanche to spare the district court the time and expense of trying three of the men believed responsible for the killing of Deputy Webb—Joe Hardin and brothers Tom and William Dixon. Joe Hardin had not done any shooting, but his less than exemplary personal life had finally sunk in on folks. As for the Dixon boys, the way the Brown County men saw it, the mere fact that they had been with John Wesley Hardin at the time of the killing made them guilty. The Brown County delegation took the trio from the rock building being used as a temporary jail, carried them to a large oak a couple of miles from town, and lynched them. Captain Waller, continuing his search for John Wesley Hardin and Taylor, did not even consider the triple hanging worthy of mention in his report to headquarters. Jones, preoccupied with the operations of the entire Frontier Battalion, learned of the vigilante action through the newspapers.[18]

The major now had five companies in the field. Though many of the new rangers had yet to dull their first straight razor, when possible Jones preferred enlisting those with Indian-trailing experience, men like Cicero Rufus Perry. Most Texans knew the Alabama-born Perry as Old Rufe. Fifty-three, with eyes as gray as his hair had become, he had first ridden as a Ranger in 1836 when only fourteen years old. "He was one of the immortal band commanded by Jack Hays," the Austin *Daily Statesman* informed its readers. "They stood upon the western frontier like towers of strength. They fought whatever came in the shape of a foe to the Lone Star flag, no matter what the disparity of numbers." His body scarred by Comanche arrows, Perry eagerly hoped for another chance to settle accounts. After recruiting his men, he saddled up and left his home in Blanco County for Menard County.[19]

As Perry moved into position along the frontier, on June 9 a party of rangers under Captain Waller jumped Hardin and Taylor again and chased them to the Comanche–Brownwood road. The two wanted men easily outrode the rangers, but the savvy Waller had split his command. Hardin soon found himself riding hell-bent straight toward another group of rangers. He and Taylor pivoted their mounts, heading briefly toward the original party of lawmen, but then circled back and broke through the other rangers. Waller spurred his horse and galloped in pursuit. Seeing only one rider behind him, Hardin reined his horse and leveled his shotgun at the approaching captain. Just as he pulled the trigger, a gust of wind blew Hardin's handkerchief under the hammer, preventing the scattergun from firing. The Ranger captain got off a shot that grazed Hardin's horse, but he chose not to continue the pursuit. Waller later reported that he thought he had wounded Hardin but that he "made good his escape."[20]

Hardin and Taylor had eluded them, but when Waller's men concluded their operations in Comanche County on June 12, they had arrested twenty-two "Cattle Thieves and desperadoes." The rangers turned over seven of those prisoners, associates of Hardin's suspected in South Texas of cattle theft, to the new DeWitt County sheriff. That official had succeeded the man Hardin and Taylor had killed.

From his camp in adjoining Brown County, Captain Maltby wrote Jones on June 17 that he believed Hardin remained in Comanche County, "seeking the lives of the best citizens" to revenge the recent lynching of his brother and two other men.[21] Actually, Hardin had busied himself in planning a hasty move to Florida and may already have left. On June 21, Scrap Taylor, Kute Tuggle, and Jim White—three of the seven men the Rangers had transferred to the custody of DeWitt County—discovered their case on the verge of a permanent change of venue. A party of vigilantes, doubtless connected to the Sutton faction, removed the trio from the jail in Clinton and hanged them. None had yet been charged with any crime in DeWitt County, but simply being suspected of cattle theft seriously stained a man's reputation in Texas. Besides that, they all had allegiance to the Taylor crowd even though only one of them bore the surname.

While Maltby continued his fruitless search for Hardin and Taylor, Captain Perry had most of his rangers out hunting for Indians in Menard County. Company D did not come across any Comanches or Kiowas, but Perry's outfit soon made big news in Austin. A rumor swept through the city like a flash flood on the Colorado that a "disappointed [Ranger] appointee" had killed eight of Perry's rangers at the Company D camp. The tale became so pervasive that ranger Thomas P. Gillespie felt honorbound to write the *Daily Statesman* to report, "Nothing of the kind . . . has happened and that everything with them [Company D] is serene and lovely."[22]

Though Jones had quickly moved to set up a line of defense along the frontier counties, the state offered no protection to citizens venturing onto the High Plains of Northwest Texas, the unsettled area called the Panhandle. Those who dared go there, men like scout and buffalo hunter Billy Dixon, did so at their peril. "There was just a handful of us out there," Dixon later recalled, "each bound to the other by the common tie of standing together in the face of any danger that threatened us. It was a simple code, but about the best I know of."[23]

That summer, Dixon and twenty-eight others—mostly buffalo hunters, but some traders, a saloonkeeper, a blacksmith, and one woman—lived in a camp of sod-covered adobe buildings at an old trading post called Adobe Walls near the Canadian River in what is now Hutchinson County. Looking back on it, Dixon remembered the night of June 26 as being sultry, windless. The men, many of them drinking whiskey, sat outside or near open doors. "In all that vast wilderness," Dixon recalled, "ours were the only lights save the stars that glittered above."[24]

About two o'clock in the morning, a loud crack awakened all but the deepest sleepers. The ridgepole of their dugout had broken, and they set about shoring it up to keep it from caving in. Many of them, including Dixon, still were awake when the eastern sky began to lighten. Tossing his bedding in the back of his wagon, Dixon took in the view.

"Just beyond the horses, at the edge of some timber, was a large body of objects advancing vaguely . . . toward our stock and in the direction of Adobe Walls," Dixon remembered. "Though keen of vision, I could not make out what the objects were. . . . Then I was thunderstruck. The . . . objects suddenly spread out like a fan, and from it went up one single, solid yell—a war whoop that seemed to shake the very air of early morning."[25]

Dixon realized that if the ridgepole had not cracked, the camp would have still been asleep and caught by surprise by hundreds of Indians. Grabbing his .50-caliber buffalo rifle, he loaded a shell into the breech.

Quanah Parker, the Comanche son of Cynthia Ann, the little girl captured by his people back in 1836, led the charge. His mother, "rescued" by the Rangers in 1860, had since died, having to Quanah's mind succumbed to a broken heart at the forced separation from her Indian family. Now, guided by what he believed to be the strong medicine of a young shaman called Esa-tai (translations of the name vary from Rear End of a Wolf to Coyote Droppings), Quanah intended to save his people by exterminating those who killed their food. When he finished with these slaughterers of buffalo, he would strike deeper into Texas.

His face painted yellow like the sun, rattlesnake rattles hanging from his ears, Esa-tai watched in growing disbelief as his prophecies failed to come true. When a .50-caliber slug from one of the buffalo hunters slammed into the forehead of his pony, dropping the horse in its tracks, Esa-tai realized his medicine did not stop bullets, either.

Good shooting being the way they made their living, Dixon and the other well-armed hunters repulsed the initial attack and subsequent charges, despite the overwhelming difference in numbers. At least two hundred, possibly as many as seven hundred, Comanches, Cheyennes, and Kiowas took part in the Adobe Walls raid. Three whites died defending their camp, but the buffalo hunters killed seven Comanches and five Cheyennes before the Indians gave up and pulled back. What Quanah had seen as a new beginning for his people actually presaged the beginning of their end. The U.S. military soon began planning an all-out offensive against the Plains Indians, a conflict that came to be called the Red River War.

One of the Kiowas who rode against the buffalo hunters at Adobe Walls was a chief named Lone Wolf. His voice had generally been one of reason in dealing with the whites, counseling peace, but his attitude had changed. Two years earlier, his son Sitting-in-the-Saddle, had been killed during a fight with a U.S. cavalry patrol in South Texas.[26] Lone Wolf wanted revenge, and he would soon get it.

By July 10, all six authorized Frontier Battalion companies—some 450 rangers—had taken the field. Captain G. W. Stevens of Wise County (in appreciation of "efficiency and gallantry" in previous Indian fighting, the legislature had awarded him a rifle) headed Company B, with Neal Coldwell of Kerr County commanding Company F. The battalion would never have any more manpower than it did at this point.

Having some time on his hands, a member of Company D wrote a letter to the editor of the Austin *Daily Statesman* on July 12. In the fashion of the day, no name accompanied the missive, the anonymous correspondent's letter closing only with "Yours, truly, D."

"Our camp," D. wrote, "at present is near the village of Menardville, on the San Saba river, where we find the citizens generally greeting us with a friendly welcome. Capt. Perry proposes to let no grass grow up in an Indian trail that cross his line of patrol, until he has exhausted all means in his power to overtake them, in the event of which his many friends and acquaintances in Texas will not fear the result." Their scouting that summer had been "a little hard on our horses," the anonymous ranger continued. "If we can get forage after maturity of crops it will materially add to our efficiency."[27]

The officers and men of the battalion did a little better than their mounts when it came to grub. Jones, frugally leaving the quartermaster's position unfilled, bought subsistence for his rangers in sixty-day increments. His initial purchase from a merchant in Dallas included 802 pounds of bacon, 300 pounds of beans, 13 barrels of flour, 1 bag of rice, 3 twenty-five-pound sacks of coffee, 2 barrels of sugar, 1 sack of salt, 5 pounds of pepper, 16 pounds of soda, and a barrel of vinegar. Another order during the battalion's organization brought in 12 gallons of pickles. Ranger horses got shelled corn purchased at $1.40 a bushel. Not to overlook camp hygiene, Jones bought 40 pounds of soap for his men.[28]

Jones may not have expected his rangers to stay squeaky-clean, literally or figuratively, but he had high standards. When the major inspected Company E's camp later that summer, he found Captain Maltby absent from his command, having gone home to Burnet County. The company's first lieutenant had taken sick leave, and the rangers reported their second lieutenant away in Brownwood. Unsupervised privates idled around a messy camp, their horses not properly picketed or guarded. Six days later, Jones wrote Maltby and told him to shape up his company or resign.

Maltby may not have been the strictest of the battalion's captains, but his company included some skilled and tough young men. Ranger Henry Sackett, for one, always seemed able to put a bullet exactly where he wanted it. One day a snap shot saved his life. When a squad from Company E surprised a bunch of Indians they had been trailing, Sackett quickly outdistanced his fellow rangers in the pursuit, riding straight into the Indians' gunfire. But before Sackett could get close enough to shoot back, his horse stumbled on a rock and threw the ranger, leaving him temporarily stunned.

As fellow ranger G. W. Ellington recalled:

One Indian, thinking he had killed him, galloped back to get his scalp. In the meantime Sackett came to his senses enough to realize his danger. He grabbed his gun, fired at the Indian, and his bullet tore the lock off the gun in the Indian's hands and broke his arm. By this time the others of us had arrived on the scene. The wounded

Indian did not go far until he was shot off his horse, and two others were killed before they got away.

Two other Company E rangers, Bill Dunman and Andrew Mather, earned quite a reputation for riding down and roping a bear for camp meat. Later, Ellington saw Mather swing his loop around the neck of an iron-gray mustang, a horse he soon broke to ride. "Mather was without exception the greatest rider I have ever seen," Ellington declared, "and a great hand with a rope as well."

The men under Maltby and the other captains spent most of their time in the field. "Due to the outdoor life we followed," Ellington later wrote, "we were seldom ill." When a medical problem did arise, rangers usually had to fend for themselves. Those remedies, Ellington continued, "were sometimes extremely crude but effective."

A case in point, one also underscoring a young ranger's grit:

"I had been riding all day against a stiff wind and with an aching tooth that had reached a stage of intense pain," Ellington wrote.

When I reached camp I was in a mood to try anything for relief. There was nothing with which to pull the tooth, but one of the boys had an awl in his saddle pocket. He said he could heat the awl red hot and kill the nerve. If I hesitated, it was not long. He heat[ed] the awl to the proper degree and thrust it into the cavity of my tooth. It sizzled and burned, but cured the ache.[29]

The battalion did have a surgeon, Dr. S. G. Nicholson, but he could not be everywhere the need for medical treatment arose. Nevertheless, the doctor did get around. That summer, Jones set out with Nicholson to visit his field commanders and get the six companies positioned to his satisfaction along the frontier. Moving north up the frontier, Jones selected six men from each company to serve as his escorts, forming what amounted to a seventh company. Riding in a light spring wagon and trailing his horse behind, Jones traveled from camp to camp, making about twenty-five miles a day. The doctor preferred the saddle, walking his mount in tandem with the major's wagon. Behind them followed the rangers, riding two abreast, trailed by the supply wagons. An advance guard of two men rode a half mile in front of the column, with another two men flanking the column on each side. The major bounc-

ing along in the wagon had an office on the first floor of the white limestone capitol at the head of Congress Avenue in Austin and could have
left the fieldwork to others, but he did not enjoy being behind a desk.[30]

"They gave us fits"

On their way back to Company E's main camp in Brown County, a
twelve-man detail that had escorted Jones to meet with Captain Perry
in Menard County made camp on the Concho River. Posting one ranger
as a guard, they called it a night. "Just before the moon went down,"
ranger Ellington recalled,

> we were awakened by an appalling noise.
> A band of about thirty Indians were yelling and shooting and try-
> ing to stampede our horses. They lay on the sides of their horses and
> shot from under the animals' neck. They managed to get most of our
> horses, but only one man was injured in the attack.[31]

Excellent coup for the Indians, the theft left the detachment afoot
some forty miles from their base camp. While embarrassing, the loss of
their mounts would seem minor compared with the rangers' next contact with Indians.

On July 11, Jones and his escort reached Captain Steven's camp at
Flat Top Mountain in Young County. The major spent some time talking with the captain, then turned in. During the night, a couple of
horses wandered from the Rangers' remuda. In the morning, two men
left to bring in the strays. Whether the rangers located the missing
horses went unreported, but what they did find changed Jones's plans
for the day: Indian sign. With some rangers from his escort and some
from Captain Stevens's company, the major led a detachment of thirty-
five men to take up the trail.

The command followed pony tracks into a twenty-square-mile area
in present Jack County known as Lost Valley. Eventually, the trail played
out and Jones had his men scatter in the hope that someone would pick
up the tracks again. When a ranger detected two sets of impressions left
by unshod horses, Jones ordered that they be followed. The hoofprints
led straight into a trap set by someone far more experienced in plains
warfare than Jones's rangers—the vengeful Lone Wolf.

"We were charged by something over one hundred warriors, well mounted," ranger John P. Holmes later wrote. "And they gave us fits until we could all get together. They were all around, and so mixed up with the boys that it was nearly impossible to tell whom to shoot at."[32]

Recovering quickly from the surprise, Jones rallied his men and ordered a charge. Savvy fighters, Lone Wolf's warriors shot first to kill the rangers' horses. Thirteen screaming animals tumbled in the dust, leaving a third of the rangers without mounts. Realizing that any further attempt to pursue the Indians would be futile and deadly, Jones ordered his men to pull back. As Jones sat his horse watching the withdrawal, ranger William A. "Billy" Glass jerked from the impact of a fatal bullet.

"We charged," Holmes continued, "running them back into the mountains; then it was our time to fall back, which we did, to a strip of timber, and there dismounted and shot quite a number."[33]

For much of the time during the extended standoff, Jones stood exposed above the wooded draw, walking up and down behind the line giving orders and encouragement to his men. The major's bravado motivated the men, but it could have gotten him killed.

"I noticed him and become very much concerned," one of the rangers recalled. "At one point he leaned against a post oak tree directly behind me, while the Indians' bullets were cutting the limbs off the trees all around like a mowing machine. I remarked to him that I thought he was exposing himself unnecessarily, but he said he thought not, simply saying somebody had to be outside to observe the enemy's actions."[34]

Jones could tell that the Indians, having the higher ground, did not understand that downhill shooting affected trajectory. Almost all their rounds zinged harmlessly above the rangers' heads. The Frontier Battalion men fired more precisely, waiting to catch a glimpse of a face or torso when an Indian rose to fire before they squeezed a trigger.

But in the searing summer sun, the rangers faced another enemy: thirst. Some of the men began scooping mud from the draw, hoping to suck out a little moisture. As the afternoon wore on, ranger Dave W. H. Bailey volunteered to take everyone's canteen and move up the creekbed to a point about a mile away where he believed he could find water. At first, Jones refused permission. But seeing his men suffering from lack of hydration, the major relented. Riding low in the saddle, Bailey and another ranger made it to the water. They drank with their horses from the creek, filled their canteens, and headed back toward their thirsty comrades. Spotting the men, the Kiowas sent a party to cut them off. The rangers spurred their mounts to run for it, but Bailey's horse spooked. His companion got away, Bailey did not. As Jones and his men looked on helplessly, the Indians descended on the fallen ranger.

"They held Bailey up in full view," Ranger Jim McIntire wrote,

and cut him up, and eat him alive. . . .

They started by cutting off his nose and ears; then hands and arms. As fast as a piece was cut off, they would grab it, and eat it as ravenously as the most voracious wild beast.

We were all hardened to rough life, and daily witnessed scenes that would make a 'tenderfoot's' blood run cold; but to see Ed Bailey die by inches . . . made our hearts quail. We could see the blood running from their mouths as they munched the still quivering flesh. They would bat their eyes and lick their mouths after every mouthful. The effect of these disgusting movements on us was but to increase our desire for revenge, and we often had it later on.[35]

Lone Wolf rode up and finished off the young ranger with his tomahawk, finally getting revenge for his slain son.

Sick that he had given in to Bailey, a gamble that had wasted a life, Jones knew he had to hold his position and send for help. Finding that he had only eighty rounds of ammunition left, he ordered the rangers to hold their fire. Only eighteen miles away, federal cavalry stationed at Fort Richardson likely went about their routine duty, unaware of Jones's dire circumstances. But after what had happened to Bailey, the major did not want to risk any more of his men. Finally, ranger Holmes convinced Jones that he could keep his horse from panicking and make it to the fort. Jones reluctantly opted to let him try.

That night, the Indians stopped shooting. Doubling up on their remaining horses, the rangers quietly left the area. Those who still did not have mounts followed on foot. The Indians made no effort to pursue Jones, who made camp at a ranch about twelve miles from the scene of the fight.

Reinforced the following day by troops from Fort Richardson, Jones's weary men and the cavalry could not relocate the Indians. They did find the remains of ranger Bailey. "It was a sandy location where he lay, and we dug a grave with our Bowie knives and drinking cups and wrapping the body in a blanket we laid it away in the shallow grave," ranger Ed Carnal recalled.[36]

Since he had lost only two men killed and two wounded while killing anywhere from three to fifteen Indians (the numbers varied with the telling), Jones chose to call the fight a victory. "They are beyond doubt, strictly on the warpath," Jones reported to Steele. "All are well armed with improved breech loading guns, (they used no arrows in the fight) all well mounted, and painted, and decked out in gay and fantastic style."[37]

Jones's first Indian fight, only two months after the organization of the battalion, came close to being his last. At best, the confrontation with Lone Wolf had been a draw. Outnumbered more than three to one, without Jones's leadership, the rangers might have been killed to the last man.

As Jones had noted, the Indians used the same weapons as the rangers, .50-caliber Sharp's carbines. The heavy breech-loaders, firing cartridges filled with seventy to ninety grains of black powder, could kill a buffalo bull at six hundred yards. The rifles kicked like ornery mules and had to be reloaded after each shot, but they made deadly weapons in the hands of a good marksman. After the battle, one ranger counted nearly three hundred spent cartridges behind two large trees where several of the Indians had been concealed. The men found something else. All the blankets left behind by the Indians bore a two-letter stamp, *ID*. That stood for Indian Department and proved to the rangers what they had suspected, that the warriors they had fought should have been on their reservation at Fort Sill, not in northwest Texas.

"I am to-day all right, but thought for a while yesterday that I was gone up," ranger Holmes wrote home from Jacksboro, which he had reached without incident. His horse had been hit twice during the fight, but both wounds were minor. A rifle ball had punched a hole in his belt, but somehow missed his flesh. "You may tell them all at Austin that the Austin boys are all right, or were when I left them."[38]

The tenacity demonstrated by Jones and his rangers during the five-hour firefight probably saved some Texas scalps. As Governor Coke pointed out a few months later, "Lone Wolf . . . was within one day's travel of the most flourishing settlement in Parker county, and going rapidly to it when met by the rangers."[39] After the fight, the Kiowa chief and his followers returned to their reservation. In addition to preventing the raiders from reaching a center of population, the encounter solidified Jones's standing with the men of the battalion and the people of Texas. The rangers had no doubt as to the mettle of the man who issued their orders, even if his inexperience as an Indian fighter had nearly cost him his scalp.

Jones and the Frontier Battalion could deal with the Indian threat tactically, but a strategic effort needed federal troops. With a plan formally approved by Secretary of War William Belknap on July 20, the U.S. military undertook a major offensive against the Plains Indians. The campaign began on August 11 with the departure of the first contingent of troops from Fort Dodge, Kansas, under Colonel Nelson A. Miles. Backed by horse-drawn fieldpieces and ten-barrel, .50-caliber Gatling guns, some two thousand soldiers converged on the Panhandle from New Mexico, Kansas, the Indian Territory, and downstate Texas.

The army being better armed and better supplied, the outcome of the contest never hung in the balance. With most of the buffalo they depended on for survival having been slaughtered by white men, the Indians fought to preserve a way of life already gone. Still, before the Red River War ended, the Indians clashed with the cavalry in nearly twenty engagements. The most decisive fight occurred on September 27, 1874, in Palo Duro Canyon south of present Amarillo when Colonel Mackenzie attacked a combined Comanche, Cheyenne, and Kiowa camp. The soldiers captured the Indians' supplies and 1,414 ponies. After culling the best mounts, Mackenzie ordered the remainder of the horses destroyed and sent the captive Indians back to Indian Territory.[40]

While the Army dealt with the last of the hostile Plains Indians in Texas, Jones coped with a different issue: a rapidly depleting appropriation. On October 27, he issued General Order Number Five, prohibiting the sharing of rations with "camp followers and loafers" who stuck close to Frontier Battalion companies hoping to enlist. Warning that "it may be necessary to disband a portion of the command before a great while," Jones said that "no more recruits will be received until further orders."[41]

One of Captain Perry's rangers later described how the state paid the far-flung companies of the Frontier Battalion:

> Fifteen of us were detailed to go to Dallas with . . . our quartermaster. We stayed . . . about ten days while he made a trip to Austin.

Our headquarters were at the old Live Oak Hotel . . . and we kept
our horses in a good livery stable. While there we had a good time,
and when [the quartermaster] returned he brought with him two
good mules and an ambulance. He ordered us to saddle up and go to
a certain bank on Main Street, and when we reached there we found
the ambulance, with all the curtains fastened down, and the back
end open. Every Ranger was on his horse and took positions on all
sides of the vehicle, watching every move that was made. The bank
employees brought out several boxes of money and put them in at
the back . . . enough to pay the Rangers for six months service.

The rangers escorted the quartermaster, who slept in the wagon, to
Fort Worth and then to Captain Stevens's company, the northernmost
unit of the battalion. "We were not allowed to get over fifty yards from
the wagon at any time," the ranger remembered.[42]

Jones made it plain that he expected a full day's work for each day's
pay. The major reminded his officers and men to keep "in mind that we
are in the employment of the Government, being paid for our time and
services, and therefore should be constantly engaged in some sort of service." He ordered company commanders to "require of the men all the
service that can be performed with justice to their horses, in scouting
up and down the line, or on such longer scouts or expeditions against
the Indians as it may be expedient for them to make."[43]

For the Indians, their remaining days of freedom on the plains faded
like a dying campfire. On November 18, Lieutenant B. F. Best and sixteen Company E rangers trailed a party of Indians twenty miles from
Coleman County to a spot on Clear Creek, five miles west of Brownwood. The rangers killed three, wounded another, and captured what
the Adjutant General's Department called their "camp equipage." Best
reported two of his men wounded in the fight and one horse lost.[44]

Three days after this engagement, Captain Maltby and eight rangers
cut the trail of the surviving raiders. The Indians had ridden into San
Saba County, stealing a popular racehorse named Gray Eagle, gone back
into Coleman County and on to Valley Creek in Runnels County.
Maltby and his men found their camp that evening. Riding to within
two hundred yards of the Indians, the rangers watched as the Comanches cooked meat from a butchered stolen beef. Several other Indians, assuming a ranger pursuit, stood guard near their horses. Among

the Indians Maltby saw someone he had been looking for a long time: the Kiowa chief Big Foot. The captain ordered a charge.

"At the sound of the horses' feet Big Foot and his lieutenant sprang to their horses, but before Big Foot could mount, Captain Jeff's six-shooter spoke its voice of death and Big Foot's horse fell dead," Maltby wrote, describing the event in third person.

> Big Foot then turned and aimed his Spencer rifle, but before he could pull the trigger Captain Jeff's pistol spoke again and its leaden messenger of death went to the mark, knocking the hammer off of the Indian's gun and driving it into his cheek, then glanced down striking him in the jugular vein and breaking his neck. The blood spurted high and Big Foot fell to rise no more.[45]

"I WANT NO PRISONERS"

The Rangers could be every bit as vicious as the Comanches. One of Maltby's men, Caleb W. Grady, later recounted an incident that happened shortly before he joined the company. Though three Indians had died in the fight with Maltby and his men, including Big Foot, the Comanche woman riding the stolen racehorse escaped. Another warrior, however, lagged behind as a rear guard, periodically firing his rifle at the pursuing rangers. When the rangers stopped to rest their horses, so did the Indian. More than six hundred yards distant, he sat on high ground silhouetted by the setting sun, still pointing his rifle at the Texans. As Grady told it:

> Lieut. Best, watching him, asked if there was any one present, who thought that he could hit the Indian at that range. . . . Henry Thomas volunteered, threw his rifle to his shoulder, and after taking careful aim, fired. The bullet struck the Indian on the nose, taking it off as clean as a knife could have cut it, also shattering his rifle, and knocking him over. The Rangers then rushed up [and] captured the Indian.

The following day, Jones and his escort company rode into Maltby's camp.

"Major, we have a pet for you," one of the rangers said.

"Not for me," Jones replied, "I want no prisoners."[46]

The Indian could not speak much English, but the rangers' Mexican guide talked with him in Spanish. According to Grady, the Comanche boasted proudly of the various Texas families he had helped to kill. Indeed, his breastplate featured eighty-two joints from human fingers, and his headdress had eagle feathers interwoven with long strands of human hair.

Grady continued:

> They kept [the Indian] around the camp several days until they tired of him. The boys said he ate up all of the sugar, and they would have to get rid of him.
>
> One day they asked him if he would like to go back to his people at Fort Sill. He said, "Yes," and so they gave him an old poor horse, and told him to go. They let him get a good start, and then a bunch of them started after him.
>
> After a pretty good chase they overtook and killed him.
>
> Curly Hatcher scalped him, and threw his body into a thicket, where it lay and dried up. I saw it there many times after I went into the service.[47]

Another clash between Comanches and rangers resulted in the taking of another prisoner. On November 21, ranger Scott Cooley and one of his messmates, William B. Traweek, sent out to get some beef (whether the state intended to pay for it or informally "requisition" an animal passed unexplained in later accounts of what followed), rode up on nine Comanches along Elm Creek in southern Menard County. The Indians opened fire on the two rangers. Cooley and Traweek shot back but wisely spurred their horses and fled toward their camp. When the Indians saw more rangers coming, the chase reversed.

The pursuit lasted twelve miles at the gallop, a test of men and horseflesh. Occasionally, the Indians stopped and turned to fight. They succeeded in wounding three of newly commissioned lieutenant Daniel Webster Roberts's horses, but each time the Comanches broke and ran amid a flurry of ranger bullets.

The rangers killed five Indians and captured one, along with their horses and an assortment of arms and equipment. Roberts's men wanted to execute their prisoner, but the lieutenant ordered the Indian spared. A military detachment that had been accompanying the rangers continued the pursuit of the Comanches, but, his horses jaded by the long ride, Roberts had to stay put. The soldiers killed one more Indian in a second engagement.[48] As soon as his men and horses got some badly needed rest, Roberts detailed several rangers to take the captured Comanche to Austin "to be disposed of as the Governor may direct," as Jones later reported.

One of the rangers, S. P. Elkins, later described the trip:

We went through Fort Mason and stopped there a little while to let the people see our captive. The Indian was badly scared when the people began to crowd around, but as he could speak some Spanish we managed to make him understand that he would not be hurt. We then went on to Cold Spring . . . and there ate dinner, taking the Indian off of the pack mule, and giving his bow and quiver, and let him walk around. The next place we reached was Fredericksburg, where the men, women and children flocked to see the savage. We took him into a saloon and offered him whiskey, but he would not drink. . . . We went on to Austin and when we reached there we crossed the Colorado River on a pontoon bridge.[49]

The arrival of the rangers and their prisoner in the capital city created quite a stir. Austinites emerged from businesses and bars to stare at the somber Comanche. Most of the gawkers had never seen an Indian before. Obviously enjoying the attention, the rangers paraded up Congress Avenue toward the Capitol, their prisoner—"in wild Indian costume" that included a fox-hide headpiece—strapped to a mule.

"All eyes were turned to him," the Austin *Daily Statesman* reported the following day, "and large crowds of people followed him to the Capitol grounds, where the red warrior was gazed upon by hundreds of curious eyes."

The rangers took their prisoner straight to Governor Coke. "I don't know why you brought that Indian here," one ranger remembered Coke saying. "Take him back to camp."

Rather than do that, the rangers checked the Comanche into the Travis County Jail. The *Statesman* said it understood the Indian "perhaps [would be] tried by court-martial." In that case, the newspaper continued, "We wouldn't give much for his chance. The boys brought some fresh scalps with them, and they report that Scott Cooley . . . not only cut a wounded Indian's throat, but stripped a large piece of skin from his back, saying that he would make a quirt out of it." Jones mentioned none of that in his brief official report.

As it turned out, in the case of the captive, the nineteen-year-old Cooley had in mind more than making a quirt. The next day's *Daily Statesman* carried the following item:

> We learn from Mr. [Duncan J.] Murchison that "Little Bull," the captive Comanche . . . will be exhibited to-day at the Opera House, in full war dress, between 3 to 5 p.m. and also from 9 a.m. to 12 a.m. [*sic*] Monday. The admittance being but twenty-five cents, no doubt many will flock to the Opera House to see the wild warrior fresh from the bloody field of battle on the Texas frontier.

The public did indeed turn out for the show, but not everyone approved of the young ranger's entrepreneurial bent. If nothing else, some said, showing off the Indian on the Sabbath amounted to sacrilege.[50] The adjutant general thought it worse than that. The Sunday exhibition, the Austin newspaper noted,

> was made without the knowledge of General Steele. Yesterday handbills were circulated making the announcement that such an exhibition would be again made. As soon as these bills made their appearance General Steele promptly put an end to it. It seems as if the exhibition was a private arrangement between Mr. Murchison and the Rangers who brought [the Comanche] to this city.[51]

Governor Coke declared Little Bull (So-no-ya-na in Comanche) a public enemy and ordered him confined in the state penitentiary in Huntsville, where he later died. Cooley soon left the Rangers, but he would be heard from again.[52]

With assurances from General C. C. Auger, latest commander of federal troops in Texas, that the campaign against the Indians would continue that winter, and knowing there would be no real danger of any additional raiding parties until spring, Governor Coke took action on November 25 to conserve the rapidly diminishing funds available to maintain the battalion. In General Order Number Eight, Steele reduced the staffing of each company to one lieutenant, two sergeants, three corporals, and twenty-five privates. That cut the size of the battalion by more than half.[53]

Captain Maltby, who had probably remained in the doghouse with Jones over his lax enforcement of discipline, found himself relieved of his commission effective December 13 along with his first lieutenant. The second lieutenant, B. S. Foster, assumed command of the company.[54] Maltby at least had the satisfaction of having caught up with Big Foot. For the rest of his days, the old ranger had no reluctance in telling people about it.

Jones had written Steele on December 1 that even with the battalion "too small and the appropriation insufficient to give anything like adequate protection to so large a territory, the people seem to think we have rendered valuable service to them, and there is a degree of security felt in the frontier counties, that has not been . . . experienced for years before." In addition to its Indian-scouting duties, Jones wrote, "The battalion has rendered valuable service to the frontier people by breaking up bands of outlaws and desperadoes who had established themselves in these thirty settled Counties [of the state's western frontier]" and by "arresting and turning over to the proper civil authorities many cattle and horse thieves, and other fugitives from justice."[55]

The reduction in force had not gone unnoticed by Travis County sheriff George B. Zemplemann, who had work for the jobless lawmen. The sheriff placed a short notice to run in the *Daily Statesman* on Christmas Eve: "ATTENTION, RANGERS.—The discharged rangers of the frontier battalion are requested to meet at the court house Saturday afternoon, for organization, and to receive instructions from Sheriff Zemplemann in regard to the collection of taxes."[56]

If any of the out-of-work rangers showed up to help the sheriff, they must have seen tax collecting as a step down from what they had been doing. The adjutant general's report for 1874–75 noted that during its first six months of existence, the Frontier Battalion had fought fourteen engagements with Indians. Jones estimated more than forty war parties had operated on the state's western frontier, "being about the average, so the settlers say, of what it had been for several years past."[57]

When the legislature convened in special session on January 12, 1875, Lieutenant Governor Hubbard, presiding officer of the Senate, noted in addressing his colleagues the progress made by Texas since the days of Governor Davis. "Under your generous legislation," Hubbard said, "our gallant rangers have punished the savages, protected 1000 miles of border, and added a fadeless wreath of laurel to the traditional and historic fame of Texas arms."[58]

Governor Coke, in his legislative message, waxed equally complimentary of the Rangers. "The labors of the officers and men, have been severe and unremitting and well performed," he said. "While they have had but few opportunities of displaying their prowess in battle, they have shown themselves on those occasions fully equal to the task of maintaining unimpaired the historic fame of the Texas Ranger."

Though Jones had been forced to scale down the battalion that winter, Coke wanted its function continued. "I recommend that the law . . . providing for frontier defense be left unchanged, and that such appropriation be made as will place it in the power of the Executive, should the emergency require it, to fill the battalion to its original proportions," he said in his speech to the legislature. The battalion could do its job for about $150,000 a year, he optimistically estimated.

The governor then turned to the crime situation:

> Five-sixths of the population of Texas may be found in one-third of her territory. The remainder of the country is . . . frontier. The immense tide of immigration now, and for several years past, pouring into the State, with for the most part good, brings some bad people. Our railroad connections furnish easy access to Texas for lawless and desperate men from other States . . . and they are not slow to avail themselves of the inviting field of operations presented by the peculiar surroundings of society and the country. When to these considerations we add the demoralizing results of the late civil war, it becomes a matter of wonder, not that so much but that no more of crime and disorder prevail in Texas.

Despite that rhetoric, Coke still believed that the primary responsibility for law enforcement rested on the shoulders of local officers, especially county sheriffs. Though Coke said he had no problem with "furnishing an adjunct to the ordinary authorities for execution of the laws on extraordinary occasions, I would condemn [the concept of] the State police system."[59]

The new Ranger force not even a year old, on March 31, 1875, Jones had to cut its size again, this time reducing it by one company as the battalion's funds continued to shrink. Clinging to every penny he could, the major even renegotiated the price he paid to furnish his men coffee. He succeeded in getting the cost down from six bits to twenty-six cents a pound.[60] A month later, Jones mustered out another company, leaving the battalion strength at 124 men in four companies.

By June 1, the budget problem had become a budget crisis. With no money available to cover the battalion payroll at reenlistment time, Jones staffed four companies on a volunteer basis. With money he had saved by cutting companies in the spring, the major managed to pay for staples for the men and forage for their horses, but not salaries. "I induced the men to serve without pay and take chances of the next Legislature making an appropriation to pay them," he reported to Steele.[61]

The state might have been short of funds, but not paper. In General Order Number Ten, dated August 12, 1875, Steele required a monthly return to headquarters showing who had joined the companies by transfer or enlistment, who had been discharged and why, who had deserted and whether they were still responsible for their weapons, who had died and how. In addition, company commanders had to keep track of public property in their possession.[62]

Steele's next written order, issued August 21, reminded "all officers & soldiers of the State service" that they were "citizens subordinate to the law wherever they may be." Noting that "this fact appears to have been disregarded in some cases," Steele said rangers would be dismissed if they attempted to resist arrest or service of any warrant by a peace officer. Additionally, Steele declared it "positively prohibited that any officer, non-commissioned officer or private of state troops, shall go into the corporate limits of the town of Decatur . . . (or any other town) with arms in violation of the municipal regulations of said town."[63]

While rangers may have left their hardware in camp when they rode to town, in the field they knew no such regulatory encumbrance. Unexpectedly encountering "a squad of Rangers" in rural Kerr County on November 15, 1875, Dr. Charles E. Fisher of San Antonio—newly arrived in Texas after graduating from Detroit's Homeopathic Medical College—reported in a letter to the San Antonio *Daily Express* that he had never seen "a rougher more uncouth looking set."

They were twelve or fifteen in number, well mounted and armed to the teeth . . . dressed roughly, with hair and head [unkempt],

they . . . presented an appearance more like [guerrillas] than officers
of the law, and we were excusable therefore in wishing ourselves
well out of the neighborhood.[64]

The Rangers spent most of their time in the field, their weapons as
much a part of their getup as their boots. "All of our trips and rides were
not easy," one ranger later recalled, "for we had many hot, and hard
rides." Remembering a scout in the summer of 1875, former ranger
Grady wrote:

We suffered much on this trip; the August sun was hot and the water all gyp and alkali. We followed the trail to the head of the Brazos,
Wichita and Pease rivers, and rode for forty-five days, some days
without water, then finding a little running silver looking stream we
would quench our consuming thirst with a hearty drink, and within
a few minutes would all be sick.

But the young rangers soon recovered.

After a brief rest we would be as jolly and gay as ever. That was characteristic of the Texas Ranger. When he stopped and had a good feed
he could sing and dance and be as gay as you please, after enduring
hardships untold. Hot or cold, wet or dry, it was all the same. They
were real men.[65]

9

"Nothing short of an armed force"

THE WASHINGTON COUNTY VOLUNTEER MILITIA,
1874–77

Her late husband's child stirring in her womb, a grieving but gritty young widow angrily scratched out the text of an advertisement she intended to see published in the Victoria *Advocate* and Indianola *Bulletin*, two newspapers with wide circulation in South Texas.

"On the 11th of March last," Laura McDonald Sutton wrote,

> Wm. Sutton, my husband, and Gabriel Slaughter, whilst engaged in getting their tickets for Galveston, on board the steamer *Clinton* at Indianola, were murdered by James and Bill Taylor in my presence without any warning or notice, James Taylor shooting my husband in the back with two six-shooters. One of the murderers, Bill Taylor, has since been arrested by Marshal Brown of Cuero and is now in Galveston jail. James Taylor . . . is still at large and I offer to anyone who will arrest and deliver him inside the jail of Calhoun County, Texas, one thousand dollars in addition to the reward of $500 offered by the governor of Texas. . . . As to my ability to pay the $1,000, I refer to Brownson's Bank, Victoria, Texas.

James Taylor, the distraught expectant mother's ad continued, was twenty-three, weighed 165 to 170 pounds, stood five feet ten inches tall, had a dark complexion and "usually shaves clean about once a week . . . talks very little, has a low, dull tone, and very quiet in his manners."[1]

Manners during Reconstruction amounted to a very relative term, especially among those involved in Texas's most sanguinary feud, the five-year-old war between the Taylors and the Suttons. On June 20, 1874, sixteen days after the newspapers published Mrs. Sutton's card, a mob took the three prisoners that Captain Waller had transported to DeWitt County from Comanche County—one of them a Taylor—and lynched them. That outbreak of violence spurred Governor Coke to dispatch his adjutant general to take a firsthand look at conditions in the county.

Steele traveled the hundred miles from Austin to Cuero by stagecoach, arriving July 2. He talked with citizens and officials there and in Clinton, then the county seat. He also went to Victoria and down to the port of Indianola. Back in the capital city on July 10, he put his findings in writing for Coke. The general went into considerable detail on the state of affairs in the troubled county. Even decent citizens, he reported, feared standing up for justice. In one instance, the general said, the local criminal justice system could find "no information on which to base an indictment . . . in the case of a murder to which there was not less than forty witnesses."[2] Steele's assessment: "Nothing short of an armed force from Some other locality & having no interest in the feuds or quarrels of that county, and of sufficient strength (not less than 50) to ensure the safety of prisoners against mob violence and to aid in making arrests, will put a stop to the existing state of violence in DeWitt County."

The legislation creating the Frontier Battalion gave the governor authority to raise additional companies, separate from the battalion. To "assist the civil officers of DeWitt county in enforcing quiet and obedience to law in that desperado ridden section," Coke authorized the creation of a company to be called the Washington County Volunteer Militia. Technically it would be Company A, but there would be no additional companies and the letter designation saw little use. Nor did Texans generally refer to the unit as a military company. Though the terminology differed, and its authority came under a different section of the frontier protection act, for all practical purposes the Washington County Volunteer Militia amounted to a seventh company of the Frontier Battalion. But it could not be included in the force since the new law authorized the battalion only six companies.[3]

In seeking a leader for the new company, Coke turned to Leander H. McNelly, a thirty-year-old Civil War veteran. Born in Virginia in 1844, he came with his parents to Washington County via Missouri in 1860. McNelly had only a year of farm life before embarking on a vocation he proved much better at than raising cotton: fighting. Lying about his age to join the Confederate Army in 1861, he rose rapidly from private to captain. Seriously wounded in Louisiana during the Battle of Mansfield in 1864, at war's end in the spring of 1865 he had command of a cavalry detachment in his home county in East Texas, charged with hunting deserters.

A battle-tested officer, after the war McNelly returned to farming near the county seat of Brenham. He married, and fathered two children. With the creation of the state police in the summer of 1870, McNelly got a commission as one of the force's four captains. Seemingly as comfortable wearing the blue uniform and copper badge of a state police officer as he had been in the buttermilk gray of the Confederacy, McNelly served until the legislature abolished the force in April 1873. Back again in Washington County, he barely had time to get one crop laid by before Governor Coke asked if he would like command of the militia unit being raised to deal with the situation in DeWitt County.[4]

McNelly doubtless had read about the ongoing difficulties in his local newspaper, the Brenham *Banner*. It had reported on April 16 that the "reign of lawlessness and terrorism at Cuero continues unabated, and desperodism rules the county, trampling law and order under foot."

Coke commissioned McNelly as "Captain of Militia" on July 14, only four days after Steele's return to the capital from his fact-finding trip in the trouble zone. The governor ordered McNelly "to report to the Sheriff [of DeWitt County], and under the orders of that officer, to execute process of the courts, arrest . . . criminals, to preserve the peace, and render such assistance as might be desired by the local authorities, in conformity with the law."[5]

Most of his recruits came from Washington County, but McNelly had signed up as his sergeant one "T. Chanders," a young newspaperman who had been working for the Austin *Daily Statesman*. The name that McNelly wrote down on his muster roll turned out to be as phony as the name affixed to the pieces "Chanders" wrote for the newspaper,

"Pidge." Eventually, "Pidge" owned up to his real name, T. C. Robinson. He had come to Texas from Virginia following a confrontation with the protective older brother of a seventeen-year-old girl.[6]

"FOR THE SEAT OF WAR," the *Statesman* noted on July 22. "The members of Captain McNally's [*sic*] company now in the city intend leaving for DeWitt county immediately upon the receipt of orders from the Captain, which are expected daily; any one wishing to join can apply today at Dei's stable or at Cook's building, corner of Congress Avenue and Pecan street." With McNelly in Washington County, journalist-turned-ranger Robinson enlisted eight young men from Austin. The state issued the company fifty Sharps carbines, the same number of shoulder slings and cartridge belts, and three thousand rounds of ammunition.

"We bid a confectionary good bye to the young rangers who belong to Capt. McNally's [*sic*] company, and who took their departure last evening on the train for Burton [in Washington County] where the company is to rendezvous, preparatory to taking up the line of march for DeWitt County," the *Daily Statesman* saluted on July 25. "We trust that the boys may return home in due time to gladden the hearts of the girls who shed tears as the boys 'lit out' for the war in DeWitt County."

War well described the Sutton-Taylor feud. Though a writer for the Galveston *News* claimed the conflict between the two factions traced to difficulties in Alabama in the 1850s, the Texas trouble began when William Sutton, leading a posse, shot and killed two suspected horse thieves, one of them being Charles Taylor. "The county [DeWitt] is infested by a band of very bad people," someone had written the Galveston newspaper from Indianola on April 7. "They are so extensive as to render life and property insecure. . . . These outlaws do not hesitate to take the life of any citizen who favors law and order, when an opportunity to assassinate presents itself."[7]

The new company reached DeWitt County on August 1. Even though McNelly's title conjured the image of someone in command of a uniformed force, McNelly and his men showed up in South Texas wearing what they wanted to. A militia company on paper, in appearance and function they rode as Rangers.

McNelly, a thin man of medium build, had a receding hairline balanced by a brown Vandyke beard. He liked to chew cigars. One of the men who served under him later described his captain as "quiet, reserved, sedate." He "always had a pleasant word for those under him, and he was greatly loved by his men."[8] The captain looked and acted more like a Methodist preacher than a Texas Ranger.

The DeWitt County assignment, however, proved to be no brush arbor revival. The first shooting came only five days after the company set up its tents on the bank of the Guadalupe River near Clinton. On August 6, twenty or more of the Sutton party ambushed four of McNelly's men, a sergeant and three privates, as the rangers escorted John Taylor to Clinton on a district court subpoena. The fifteen-minute gun battle left one ranger suffering from a shoulder wound and two state horses dead. For a time after the smoke cleared, another ranger could not be found, leaving McNelly worried the man had been killed. He later showed up, uninjured, having gotten lost in the mêlée. "The Sutton party afterwards sent a man into our camp, who said they thought it was the Taylor gang they were firing into, and that they were willing to make all amends to Captain McNally [sic]," ranger E. A. Northington said in a letter to the Austin newspaper written the day after the incident. "We rather expect hot times down here, as the Sutton men say they intend to have the Taylor men we are protecting."[9]

For the rest of the summer and into the fall, McNelly followed a two-pronged strategy in trying to pacify the DeWitt County feudists— he kept small detachments on patrol along regular routes but at irregular intervals to prevent the gathering of parties bent on violence, and he and his men tried to get on friendly terms with both factions. This went to the extent of assigning a ranger to live with two of the more prominent feudists: Joe Tumlinson, a former ranger allied with the Taylors, and state senator Bolivar Pridgen, a key figure on the Sutton side.

"Everything seems very quiet at present," McNelly reported to Austin on October 18.

Even forty rangers could not solve the problem in DeWitt County. All they could do was keep the lid on a pot that would boil over as soon as the outsiders left. The rangers had proven to be tolerable peacekeepers, but they had fallen short in the manhunting category. Though McNelly had written Steele that "I feel quite sanguine of success" in capturing John Wesley Hardin and James Creed Taylor, the two killers remained at large. McNelly decamped in mid-November, leaving ranger-journalist Robinson, now a lieutenant, in charge.[10]

Not keen on official reports, the captain had written the recommendation that Robinson receive a promotion only to stick the letter in his coat pocket and forget about it for a time. At least he communicated to Austin with candor. McNelly did not try to inflate the results of his less-than-four-month occupation of DeWitt County. Back in the capital city the following January, the captain told a newspaper writer that he believed the troubles around Cuero had only been "temporarily allayed."[11]

TROUBLE IN THE NUECES STRIP

Created specifically to handle the Sutton-Taylor feud, by the spring of 1875 McNelly's company faced disbanding for lack of funding. But a perennial problem kept McNelly and his men in state service: the area south of the Nueces River known as the Nueces Strip. The sheriff of Hidalgo County, Alexander J. Leo, wrote the governor on March 4, 1875, admitting to being "entirely helpless in executing the laws in regard to criminals." This letter, other correspondence, and newspaper accounts convinced Steele to take "decided action." The general recommended that six companies—a force equal in size to the Frontier Battalion—be mustered and sent to South Texas. The state did not have enough money for that, though clearly something had to be done.[12]

On March 26, 1875, when raiders struck a store and post office in Nuecestown, a flourishing community on the Nueces thirteen miles upstream from Corpus Christi the need for state intervention became even more apparent. Thomas J. Noakes, a well-liked man with a wife and five children, owned the store, ran the post office, and served as the local justice of the peace.

"Opening the door, the first man who presented himself was shot twice by Mr. N," read one contemporary account. "Immediately afterward a man named Smith, in the store at the time, rushed out the front door, was met by the party and shot down, mortally wounded. Aggravated, it is supposed, by the unexpected resistance, the store was fired."[13]

The bandits did not kill the Noakes, but Mrs. Noakes suffered burns when she rescued her beloved feather bed from the second floor of the blazing building. The postal receipts, however, went up in flames, as did the calves in their pen.

The Nueces County raid amounted to the boldest outbreak in South Texas since Cortina's raid on Brownsville, but cattle stealing had been a problem for a long time. "Our officers are powerless to arrest the thieves," the Brownsville *Sentinel* had complained the year before.

"They come over in gangs of tens and twenties, armed with the best re-peating rifles. Our population is scattered, and are overawed. They are afraid to give information, for the thieves would not hesitate to murder anyone who made themselves officious in giving information on their movements."[14]

Reprinting the excerpt from the Brownsville newspaper, an Austin editor declared it "a humiliating statement. . . . Can it be possible that the United States cannot protect her citizens and their property? . . . Has it come to this?"[15]

It had, at least to the minds of Texas officials. The Washington County Volunteer Militia would be kept in service.

"Your object will be to get as early information as possible of such gatherings [of Mexican bandits], and to destroy any and every such band of freebooters," Steele ordered McNelly. "At the same time be careful not to disturb innocent people, who speak the same language with robbers." The general went on to caution the captain that people in "every town, ranch or village . . . will strive to convince you that their own particular locality is the one that especially requires protection." McNelly should exercise his own judgment, Steele concluded, "recollecting that the best way to protect all is to find the robbers and make them harmless."[16]

Meanwhile, the raiding continued. "The whole country from Brownsville to Rio Grande City, 120 miles, and back to the Arroyo Colorado was laid waste," a congressional document later noted.

> There was not an American nor any property belonging to an American that was not destroyed in this large tract of country. Their horses and cattle were driven across into Mexico and there sold—a cow with a calf by her side for a dollar. . . . Although cattle stealing was the original object of the raids, the lawless bands engaged in them have been necessarily led to the perpetration of other and greater crimes. The lawless spirit engendered by their trade, and their own protection, caused them to kill travelers who happened to meet them on their raids, and those whom they thought might inform against them. In fact these raids were soon turned into general robbery and slaughter.[17]

"Is Capt McNelly coming," Nueces County sheriff John McClure wired the governor on April 18, the operator who handled the message not bothering to add a question mark. "Five ranches burned last week by Mexicans." Steele replied to assure the sheriff that McNelly and his rangers had left for South Texas. Soon, Steele headed that way himself. Traveling with state senator Joseph Dwyer of San Antonio, who spoke Spanish, the adjutant general visited Corpus Christi to assess the situation firsthand.[18]

Arriving at the coastal town, McNelly found an appreciative local merchant willing to take signed receipts in lieu of cash and supplied his company with Sharps rifles, ammunition, and food. From there, the captain proceeded to Banquete, stopping at the ranch of William Woodson Wright. W6, as folks called him, had done pretty well in the cattle business, but he had a novel sidelight—wagering on the prospect of people passing through his property ever making it as far as Brownsville. Judging McNelly's men as thoroughly as he would a herd of beef on its way to market, W6 pegged nine of the rangers as not likely to "stick" with McNelly. As one of McNelly's rangers later recalled, W6 won his bets.[19]

South Texas, especially below the Nueces, gave Wright plenty of betting action. "The thieves and cut-throats, who have collected on the border," Steele wrote after his inspection tour, "think the killing of a Texan something to be proud of, and they kill anyone, even their own nationality, should he happen to encounter them with stolen cattle, unless they have confidence in his discretion."[20]

Nor did Anglos in that part of Texas feel particular remorse in dispatching a Mexican. "Soon after the raid of Mexicans in Nueces county," the adjutant general wrote, "some raids occurred of a different character. Bands of Americans went to a place called La Para, where a store was burned and several persons killed. . . . There is considerable element in the country bordering on the Nueces and west, that think the killing of a Mexican no crime."[21]

On April 27, McNelly published this statement in Corpus Christi:

In consequence of the most recent outrages committed in this portion of the country by armed bands of men acting without authority of law, I find it necessary to notify all such organizations that after the publication of this order I will arrest all such bands and turn them over to the civil authorities of the counties where they are arrested, and nothing but the actual presence of some duly accredited officer of the county or State will protect them from arrest.

The due process McNelly promised for any vigilantes, which he quickly and nonviolently succeeded in disbanding, did not extend to suspected bandits. In Jesus Sandoval, whose wife and daughter had been raped by bandits before the raiders torched his ranch and rode off with his remuda, McNelly had a vicious but effective means of acquiring information. Tying a rope around their neck and looping the other end of the lariat over a sturdy mesquite limb, Sandoval cheerfully tortured those thought to know more than they offered when first captured. Old Casoose, as the rangers called him, choked someone until he seemed interested in talking, then hanged him for good once he had provided useful information.[22]

Richard King, a former Rio Grande riverboat pilot vigorously building the sprawling ranch that bore his bold name, greeted McNelly and his men warmly, giving each a good horse. When an additional twenty-five rangers reached the ranch on July 9, King extended further aid. "He came forward and made us every proffer of assistance," Lieutenant James W. Guynn wrote in a letter to his hometown newspaper in Columbus, the *Colorado Citizen*, "furnishing us with food for ourselves and our horses, made your humble servant a present of a fine saddle horse for himself as well as four for the use of the company; besides changing horses with several of the company for their worn out and jaded ones, giving them the choice of his *caballada*."[23]

After giving three hearty cheers for King, the rangers left his ranch at Santa Gertrudis Spring and rode south to Edinburg (present Hidalgo) to join McNelly. He had set up a semipermanent camp at an abandoned ranch and met with the Frontier Battalion captain who had preceded him in the valley, Neal Coldwell. The captain would go on to establish a solid record as a ranger, but in the Nueces Strip, Coldwell had not been particularly effective. Though ready and willing to take action, he had not succeeded in finding any rustlers, primarily for lack of the kind of information McNelly would be able to acquire through the work of Sandoval and others. With McNelly in place, Coldwell moved his company upstate to resume duties along the western frontier.[24]

"We are expecting to have a fight with raiders," Guynn wrote, ". . . as soon as they set foot on Texas soil. The boys are . . . in good health and spirits, and anxious for a fight."[25]

McNelly got help in his efforts to find cattle thieves from Ben Kinchlow, the son of a slave couple who had escaped to Mexico. Kinchlow, as a cowboy on the Bare Stone Ranch in Cameron County, knew the Valley well and drew maps for McNelly and his rangers. When Kinchlow asked McNelly for a job as a guide, the captain replied, "I'd like to have you all right, but you couldn't come here on state pay, and under no responsibility." Recalling the incident years later, Kinchlow said he agreed to work for the Rangers for free. "I knowed I could more than make my wages after I got in that company, by gambling," Kinchlow said. He remained with McNelly for the duration of his command.[26]

Kinchlow's recollections, though more than a half century after the fact, shed light on McNelly's method of operation. Early each day, Kinchlow scouted the roads looking for places where riders from Mexico had crossed during the night. "If I found a trail, he'd [McNelly] ask me how many they was and which way they was goin' and I would tell 'im. He would give 'em two or three days to make their roundup [of stolen cattle] and then we'd always meet 'em or catch 'em when they went to cross back over the Rio Grande with the cattle."

One morning, Kinchlow cut the trail of more than a dozen horsemen pushing a large herd of cattle toward Mexico. "I knowed from the direction they was takin' that they was goin' to those big lakes called Santa Lalla . . . between Point Isabel and Brownsville." From there, Kinchlow realized, the riders would cross the river near Bagdad.

The rangers stocked up on food in Brownsville and rode for the crossing. After waiting about three hours, Kinchlow remembered, McNelly decided to let his men eat. While devouring their late lunch, they heard a distant yell.

"Boys, there they are!" the captain called.

Turning to Kinchlow, he said, "Ben, you want to stay with the horses or be in the fun?"

"I don't care," the guide replied.

"You better stay with the horses," McNelly decided. "You ain't paid to kill Meskins."

The captain stationed his men in the brush along the road, setting an ambush.

Soon, the cattle thieves came into view, "singin' at the top of their voices." The captain watched them splash into the river and then, in the old tradition of La Acordada, ordered his men to open fire. McNelly had probably never heard of the Spanish colonial system of justice, but Kinchlow did not mention McNelly's giving the Mexicans an option to surrender.

"They was in the water, and he just floated 'em down the river," he told the interviewer.[27]

Kinchlow's recollections, as might be expected of an old man, are not without ambiguity. Through most of the interview, he seemed to be describing a fight McNelly had on the Palo Alto Prairie on June 12, 1875, scene of clashes during the Mexican War and again during the Cortina troubles. In that June 12 engagement, only one of sixteen cattle thieves survived the running fight. "The Cap'n just piled 'em all in a pile and sent word . . . what shape they was in and where to find 'em," Kinchlow said. Since that is at variance with his memory of McNelly letting dead bandits float down the river, his recollection likely represents the intermingling of two separate incidents, even though the June 12 fight marked McNelly's highest reported body count in a Texas operation. One of McNelly's men, William Rudd, later remembered, "They [associates of the dead bandits] sent back word that they did not want dead men but were coming over to get four for one."[28]

In addition to "making harmless" fifteen bandits and wounding another, the rangers recovered 263 head of stolen cattle in the Palo Alto fight—a direct result of information gathered by Sandoval. The strike against Mexican cattle thieves did come with a price. One ranger, sixteen-year-old Berry Smith, died in the fight. The teenager's father also served in McNelly's company. Back in Brownsville that afternoon, McNelly made arrangements for a military funeral for the teenage ranger and got off a telegram to Austin:

> This morning I came up with a band of twelve raiders, after a forced march of twenty-five miles. They attacked me, when I overtook them. It was a running fight; after that I got seven men into the fight and killed the whole party. They fought desperately. I lost one man, Berry Smith, two horses killed and two wounded. I took 255 beeves. I shall be in the saddle tonight after another party. My men are all trumps.

The Austin *Daily Statesman* published the telegram the next morning, adding in an adjacent column, "Attention is called to the telegram to Governor Coke from Brownsville. Capt. McNelly has met a band of Mexican thieves near that place, killed the last one of them, and saved the stolen property. Our loss was one man."[29]

"Had a fight with raiders," McNelly wired Steele two days later, "killed twelve and captured two hundred and sixty beeves. Wish you were here."[30] In his written report, McNelly admired the tenacity of the bandits he had defeated: "I have never seen men fight with such desperation," the combat-proven Civil War veteran reported to Steele. "Many of them, after being shot from their horses and severely wounded three or four times, would rise on their elbows and fire at my men as they passed."[31]

McNelly realized his order of a public display of the dead bandits could well bring retaliation. When one of his men asked if McNelly intended to carry the fighting across the river in that event, McNelly testily asked the ranger if he wanted a discharge. That prompted the ranger to reply that he did not propose to fight Mexicans in their own country. McNelly then kicked him out of the company. Five other rangers not willing to cross the Rio Grande also accepted discharges, eventually enabling W6 Wright to collect on some of his bets.[32]

Governor Coke sent McNelly a congratulatory letter on July 9. The captain's work in "defending the Rio Grande border," the governor wrote, particularly his "signal blow struck the freebooters" on June 12,

> merit and receive the highest praise from the authorities and people of the State. . . .
>
> The pride of true Texans in the historic fame of the Texas ranger, is fully gratified in the record your command is making and the people of the State are confidently expecting that your combined efforts will contribute greatly towards the restoration of peace, and a sense of security to our long suffering border.
>
> Much was, and is expected of your command. . . . You have done well. Continue the good work.[33]

McNelly could dispatch bandits with celerity, but the captain had no jurisdiction over the killer microbes lurking in his lungs. The captain had "galloping consumption," more technically known as tuberculosis. He had been ill when he accepted his commission from Coke, and life in the field had not helped. Absent from camp most of the summer, the captain tried to regain his strength in a Brownsville hotel room paid for by one of his many supporters. The post surgeon at Fort Brown tried to make him comfortable, even sending fresh goat's milk.[34]

With Lieutenant Robinson assuming the hands-on leadership of the company, the rangers had a summer as unproductive as their captain's dry cough. Still, as he had done in DeWitt County, McNelly kept men in the saddle almost constantly. But considering the extent of the territory they covered, his rangers had little prospect of riding up on cattle thieves. To improve the odds, the captain developed a network of paid informants on both sides of the river.

INCIDENT AT LAS CUEVAS

The captain's intelligence-gathering bore fruit again that fall. Despite Governor Coke's admonition to McNelly to keep up the good work, Steele worried about expenses. With the adjutant general again on the verge of disbanding the company, McNelly received a dispatch from Rio Grande City informing him that Mexican cattle thieves had pushed 250 head across the river to the small community of Las Cuevas. After a hard ride, McNelly and about thirty rangers reached the crossing point about noon on November 18. He found that a troop of U.S. cavalry under Captain Joseph G. Randlett had engaged the thieves the day before, killing two in a firefight along the river. The Army captain had orders to follow the raiders into Mexico, but a high river would make that difficult.

Earlier on November 18, Randlett had been preparing to ford the stream when Major David R. Clendenin arrived with another troop of cavalry. Learning that Randlett had sent a messenger across the river demanding the return of the stolen cattle, the major opted for a more cautious course and told the captain to hold at the river.

Not part of the federal chain of command, McNelly believed he had authority to enter Mexico. The Ranger captain told Major Clendenin that he intended to recover the cattle from the other side. The major said his troops would stand by to cover the rangers when they returned to Texas soil but could not help them if he got into trouble in Mexico.[35]

McNelly gathered his men and delivered a speech reminiscent of William B. Travis's legendary line-in-the-sand talk at the Alamo. As ranger William Callicott later reconstructed his captain's remarks:

> Boys, you have followed me as far as I can ask you to do unless you
> are willing to go with me. It is like going into the jaws of death with
> only twenty-six men in a foreign country where we have no right according to law but as I have [gone] this far I am going to finish with

it. Some of us may get back or part of us or maybe all of you or
maybe none of us will get back. . . . I don't want you unless you are
willing to go as a volunteer. . . . Understand there is no surrender in
this. We ask no quarter nor give any. If any of you don't want to go
step aside.[36]

A thick fog shrouding the Mexican side, McNelly began trying to
cross the river late at night on November 18. But because of mud, the
rangers could only get five of their horses on the opposite bank. The rest
of the men rowed over in a small boat. In the dark, the rangers moved
inland, their rifles rustling the leaves of a cane-lined cattle trail.

About three miles from the river, the rangers approached a collection
of thatch-topped *jacales* that McNelly presumed to be Las Cuevas. When
someone snapped off a shot at the rangers, McNelly killed him as the
other rangers opened fire. The captain later claimed that he and his men
killed four people, but other accounts had the number much higher.
Whatever the body count, McNelly had attacked the wrong village.
Those killed may or may not have been cattle thieves, but they definitely
were not the Las Cuevas cattle thieves. That rancho lay farther inland.[37]

Though the action unfolded at one of the more remote points of the
lower Rio Grande, a military telegraph line extended upriver from Fort
Brown to Ringgold Barracks at Rio Grande City. An army telegrapher
had climbed a pole and tapped into the line, giving the field units opposite Las Cuevas instant communication with the ranking officer in
Brownsville. He, in turn, kept the Department of Texas headquarters in
San Antonio and the War Department in Washington informed of developments in a situation rapidly escalating into a major international incident. The tap also enabled McNelly to keep Adjutant General Steele
advised of his actions.

"I crossed the river on the eighteenth," McNelly wired Austin. "On
the nineteenth I marched on foot to ranch Las Cuevas. Killed four men
before reaching the ranch & five afterward."

Even though McNelly had been in pursuit of cattle thieves, the government of Mexico took his incursion as an invasion. Juan Flores Salinas,
a general in the Mexican *rurales*—that nation's equivalent of the
Rangers—gathered 250 men at Las Cuevas even as other armed men rode
to join his command. Indifferent at first to the numbers, McNelly charged
the village. A fierce firefight followed.

Reality sinking in, McNelly pulled back toward the river. At that point, thinking he had the Texans on the run, Salinas led a charge against the rangers. The general and several of his men fell in a volley of rifle fire, and the matter settled into an impasse.

McNelly summarized the situation in his next wire to Steele:

After a few shots, I retreated to the river as the US [forces] were ordered not to cross. The mexicans [sic] followed me to River and charged me. They were repulsed & as they seemed to be in force some forty US Soldiers came over.... The Mexicans made several attempts during the evening to dislodge us but failed. United States troops withdrew to left bank last night. I am in temporary earthworks and have refused to leave until the cattle are returned. The Mexicans in my front are about four hundred. What shall I do[?]

The answer came on November 20 from Colonel Joseph H. Potter, commander of Fort Brown, via wire to another of the U.S. cavalry officers on the scene:

Advise Capt McNelly to return at once to this side of the river. Inform him that you are directed not to Support him in any way while he remains on Mexican territory. If McNelly is attacked by Mexican forces on Mexican ground, do not render him any assistance.... Let me Know whether McNelly acts upon your advice and returns.

By some accounts, McNelly then scribbled a defiant reply that would become only slightly less famous in Ranger lore than the besieged Travis's 1836 "Victory or death!" letter: "I shall remain in Mexico with my rangers . . . and will cross back at my own discretion. . . . Give my compliments to the Secretary of War and tell him and the United States Soldiers to go to Hell."

If McNelly actually sent that message, no copy has survived. What is in the records of the Adjutant General's Department is a telegram the captain sent to Austin on November 21: "I withdrew my men last night upon the promise of the mexican [sic] authorities to deliver the cattle to me at Rio Grande City this morning."[38]

Though McNelly lost no rangers in Mexico, his lack of casualties could be laid not so much to his undisputed bravado as the efforts of a fellow Confederate veteran then living in Mexico, Dr. Alexander M. Headley. Militia commander of Camargo, the doctor rode up to the rangers under a white flag with a written communiqué stuck under the hammer of his rifle. If he had not succeeded in negotiating McNelly's withdrawal and the return of all the stolen cattle Mexican authorities could round up, the outnumbered McNelly and his men could have ended up as dead as the defenders of the Alamo forty years before. Had U.S. troops crossed the river in force, Headley said he would in turn have led an invasion of Texas.[39]

The Las Cuevas affair made the newspapers, but Texas editors devoted most of their attention to the just-ended Constitutional Convention in Austin and the submission of a new state charter to the electorate. A border incident that could have precipitated war got only a few inches of type in the capital city's two dailies.

"The big Indian hunt which the United States soldiers at San Antonio have been talking about is postponed in behalf of a much talked of advance, perhaps, towards the Rio Grande," the Austin *Daily Statesman* noted casually on November 20. "A war with Mexico won't make another President. In fact, wars, as President-makers, are only successful to the extent that they put the fellow in office."

"What Texas intends to do for her own protection," the New York *Herald* opined, "may be gathered from the recent action of Captain [McNelly.] She proposes to protect herself if the United States government will not."[40]

The incident resulted in the recovery of only thirty-five head of cattle out of thousands stolen, but coming so soon after Reconstruction, the Las Cuevas crossing made Texans feel firmly in control of their state again. Texas had won another fight with Mexico, and the Rangers had further added to their mystique. Finally, McNelly's demonstrated willingness to cross the river in pursuit of stolen stock and their thieves had a strong deterrent effect.

As for McNelly, though practically deified by his men, the Rangers had several young captains not lacking in initiative. While McNelly's leadership qualities and bravery could not be questioned, and though popular with the Anglo ranchers in South Texas, he periodically received reprimands from headquarters for not keeping his financial records in order and for failure to keep Austin abreast of his location and activities. No one could, however, accuse the captain of wasting state ink on the reports he did write.

Describing for the adjutant general an incident that occurred on December 18, 1875, McNelly wrote, "A scouting party came across a slaughterhouse for stolen beeves, about forty miles north of Las Kuscias. Ranchero in charge arrested. After an ineffectual attempt to bribe the Sergeant, he [the suspect] tried to escape, and was killed in the attempt."[41]

"This is King Fisher's Road"

Though dealing with outlaws from south of the border occupied much of McNelly's time, Anglo criminals living in Texas also needed attention. McNelly wired Steele that the situation between Castroville and Eagle Pass had become "critical," with more than a hundred outlaws on the loose. Of those, the most notorious was a fancy dresser with a regal-sounding name—King Fisher.

"Long . . . the terror of the people of the western border of Texas," the St. Louis *Republican* reported, "this king fishes for plunder and generally succeeds well in the catch."

John "King" Fisher had quite a reputation for someone only twenty-one. Some said he had killed one man for each year of his age, an exaggeration not supported by evidence. Still, Fisher had a record of lesser crimes. He stole a horse in Williamson County and at sixteen did prison time for burglary. After only four months behind bars in Huntsville, Fisher joined friends in Dimmit County, making a rapid transition from cowboy to rancher to "king" of a wide-ranging cattle-stealing operation. He watered his stock along Pendencia Creek, but a crudely painted sign on the trail leading to his place—"This is King Fisher's Road. Take the other"—tended to discourage the checking of brands.

The sign meant nothing to McNelly, who despite his worsening health orchestrated a raid on Fisher's ranch. After surrounding the place, the captain offered the outlaw two choices: surrender or death. Fisher took the first option and came outside with hands up.

"Have arrested King Fisher and nine of his gang and turned them over to sheriff," McNelly wired Austin from Eagle Pass on June 4, 1876. "Will camp at Fort Ewell and scout country between here and Oakville until otherwise instructed. Country in most deplorable condition. All civil officers helpless."[42]

Handing the prisoners over to local authorities, the rangers went back to the brush country to continue their work. Returning to Eagle Pass, the rangers could not believe it when they saw Fisher and his men riding toward them. Though charged with murder and other felonies, the outlaw and his associates had already bonded out of jail.[43]

Steele did not use many words summarizing the Fisher case: "On the 4th, arrested King Fisher and nine of his gang. On 6th, King Fisher and gang released, whilst Capt. McNelly was on his way with witnesses. Seven of the nine could have been indicted for murder in several cases. Had between six hundred and eight hundred head of stolen cattle and horses, which were turned loose."[44]

South Texas seemed to have as many outlaws as thorns in a prickly pear patch. "There was no difficulty in finding them," ranger Napoleon A. Jennings later wrote, "or in arresting them when found, for already they were beginning in that part of the country to have a wholesome respect for the Rangers, with their ever-ready six-shooters."[45] But as Mc-Nelly had seen in DeWitt County, the Texas criminal justice system functioned only when all of its components worked. Without the support of local officers, prosecutors, and judges, the Rangers could not accomplish much lasting good.

King Fisher continued his extralegal activities, but his frustrating ability to dodge judicial bullets at least gave weight to McNelly's testimony when he appeared before a committee of the Fifteenth Legislature on June 21, 1876, and said that little could be done for the advancement of law and order in Texas when an outlaw like Fisher had local officials in his control.

A month later, lawmakers passed "An Act to Suppress Lawlessness and Crime in Certain Portions of the State." This bill gave McNelly's company its own statutory authority, transforming a volunteer militia unit into a fifty-three-man body designated as Special State Troops. Mustered out on July 24, the Washington County Volunteer Militia reorganized the following day under its new name, funded with a $40,000 appropriation. An earlier version of the measure had specifically named McNelly captain, an unusual component that did not make it into the new statute. But the bill as signed into law vested the governor with the authority to appoint someone as commander of the unit. Each

Major Robert Rogers *helped establish the ranging tradition in the Colonies.* (Author's Collection)

Texas colonizer Stephen F. Austin *is generally credited as the father of the Rangers.* (Author's Collection)

Contemporary engraving of charging Comanche. *Rangers fought Indians for a half-century.* (Author's Collection)

Early Rangers learned to fight on horseback. *Texans gained insight from their foes.* (Author's Collection)

Robert M. Williamson, *better known as Three-Legged Willie, led the Rangers for a time.* (Author's Collection)

Captain John Coffee Hays's *exploits fanned the Ranger legend.* (Author's Collection)

Benjamin McCulloch *rode with Hays and acquired national fame in the Mexican War.* (Author's Collection)

Samuel H. Walker *suggested the six-shooter to Samuel Colt. He died in the Mexican War.* (Author's Collection)

Texas Rangers fought viciously in the war with Mexico. *Mexicans called them "Los Diablos Tejanos," the Texas Devils.* (Author's Collection)

John L. "Rip" Ford *commanded Rangers in the 1850s. His nickname stood for "Rest in Peace."* (Author's Collection)

William A. Wallace *rode as a Ranger and became far better known simply as "Big Foot" Wallace.* (Author's Collection)

Governor Richard Coke *signed the act that created the Frontier Battalion.* (Author's Collection)

General William Steele,
*Confederate veteran, organized
the Frontier Battalion in 1874.*
(Author's Collection)

Major John B. Jones
*commanded the Frontier
Battalion.* (Texas State
Library and Archives)

Leander H. McNelly
led the Special State Forces.
(Texas State Library and
Archives)

Lee Hall, *depicted in later*
newspaper engraving, replaced
Captain McNelly after his death.
(Author's Collection)

A Frontier Battalion company camped in the field. *Rangers conducted regular scouts looking for Indians or outlaws.* (Texas Department of Public Safety)

Cartoon engraving of Rangers raiding outlaw King Fisher's headquarters. *Drawing appeared in the old* Life *magazine in 1901.* (Author's Collection)

Company D, Frontier Battalion, *taken in 1888 at Realitos, Duval County.*
(Texas State Library and Archives)

Adjutant General Wilburn H. King *served from 1881 to 1891.*
(Texas State Library and Archives)

South Texas Ranger camp in the 1890s. *Engraving illustrated contemporary article on the Garza pursuit.* (Author's Collection)

Practically whole Ranger force converged on El Paso in 1896 to stop a prize fight. *Photo taken outside El Paso County courthouse shows, in front row, left to right, Adjutant General W. H. Mabry, Captains John R. Hughes, J. A. Brooks, William J. McDonald, and John H. Rogers.* (Texas State Library and Archives)

Ranger W. J. L. Sullivan *helped break up the San Saba mob. He served under Captain William J. McDonald.* (Author's Collection)

Rangers on scout in the Trans-Pecos high country. *Even after the railroad came Rangers still needed horses.* (Texas Department of Public Safety)

In tree-scarce West Texas, stacked brush made welcome shade. *Rangers used mules to pack their supplies.* (Texas Department of Public Safety)

Captain John R. Hughes *was promoted to company commander after his boss's murder.* (Author's Collection)

Rangers in camp near Fort Davis. *Apaches caused trouble in the area until 1881.* (Author's Collection)

Company E Ranger Charles August Johnson in Alice, Texas. *Johnson walked his horse inside a photography studio to pose for this 1892 image.* (Texas State Library and Archives)

Frontier Battalion Rangers (Texas State Library and Archives)

Captain Bill McDonald,
flamboyant but tough.
(Texas State Library and Archives)

Rangers furnished their own horses. *Advertisement on livery barn in background touts barbed wire.* (Texas State Library and Archives)

Captain George H. Schmidt and company *in Fort Worth during the 1886 railroad strike. As the turn of the century approached some thought Texas no longer needed Rangers.* (Texas State Library and Archives)

Company D, Frontier Battalion (Texas State Library and Archives)

member of the company would have "the powers of peace officers, and shall aid the civil authorities in the execution of the laws."[46]

The lawmakers also passed a measure that would have given county sheriffs virtually the same powers as the Rangers—specifically, authority to cross county boundaries in pursuit of criminals, raise a posse anywhere in the state, and ask for military assistance if they felt it necessary. One provision of the law even authorized a sheriff to shoot a fleeing suspect who did not stop in his tracks at a yelled command to halt. Governor Coke saw the bill as a recipe for one of the very issues the Rangers had been trying to deal with: vigilantism. He vetoed it as unconstitutional.[47]

Meanwhile, McNelly's exploits made recruiting easy. Some men enlisted because they wanted to help make Texas a safer place, some joined up hoping for action and adventure, and some saw the Rangers as their state's equivalent of the French Foreign Legion, a place to disappear. The October 14, 1876, Austin *Daily Statesman* carried this item:

> The Granbury *Vidette* tells that "Mrs. . . . the first wife of Mr. . . . , has heard of his whereabouts and is coming across the Mississippi, with the children, to claim support, etc., at his hands." The effect of this notice has been a rapid depreciation of farms and town lots everywhere in and around Granbury. Every old reprobate in those parts is crazy to sell out and get away and join McNelly.

"Red" Hall takes command

In January 1877, with McNelly's tuberculosis nearing its terminal phase, Steele informed the captain that he would be honorably discharged as of the end of the month.[48] Reducing the company to twenty men, on January 25 the adjutant general selected McNelly's replacement, twenty-seven-year-old Second Lieutenant Lee Hall. A big, blue-eyed redhead who had attracted considerable attention as a city marshal and sheriff's deputy in Grayson County, Hall had been a member of McNelly's company since the previous August. With John B. Armstrong as his sergeant, "Red" Hall took up right where McNelly had left off in maintaining the Ranger reputation in South Texas. A letter Goliad resident E. R. Lane had written to the governor on October 22, 1876, summed up the situation and the feeling of many:

Through the inefficiency of our Sheriff, our town and county had become a rendezvous of escaped convicts, cut throats, outlaws, and murderers riding through our streets at night shooting through business houses and private dwellings, imperiling the lives of our women and children. Human life had become frightfully cheap and this terrible realization had settled down on the hearts of our people, completely terrorizing and stupefying them and rendering them as passively submissive as sheep driven to the shambles for slaughter. . . . Lt. Hall had come, an entire stranger had taken in the situation at a glance and applied the remedy which caused the bad men to flee to parts unknown.[49]

That summer, with continued state funding for the company looking doubtful, the West Texas Stock Association met in Goliad and subscribed enough cash to keep McNelly's company in operation until the legislature could appropriate money. The private money, collected in twenty-four counties, rested in a Cuero bank account that could only be used by the adjutant general.[50]

Increasingly, though the Special State Troops and Frontier Battalion marched under two different statutes, they acted more in concert. One difference was that Hall reported to Steele, not Major Jones. Hall led one segment of the company, with another detachment under Armstrong. Both units coordinated law enforcement efforts in South Texas during the spring of 1877 with Company A of the Frontier Battalion.[51]

J. H. Swain gets a train ride to Texas

Two things stood out about Armstrong—his imposing physical stature and his limp. Named a lieutenant following Hall's promotion to captain, Armstrong's limp came from a still sore bullet wound, the result of an accidental shot from his own pistol in late May. The big ranger had barely recovered from the bullet wound when he suffered another, if not physically painful, embarrassment. Getting a tip that John Wesley Hardin—wanted for the murder of the sheriff's deputy in Comanche County in 1874—could be found in a certain saloon in Goliad, Armstrong decided to bring the man killer in alive. After enlisting the help of a local officer, the lieutenant approached the man and offered to stand him a drink. No sooner had the man said "much obliged" than the officer latched onto his right arm to keep him from going for his gun while the ranger stuck a cocked .45 in his stomach. The arrest had gone flawlessly, but the man proved not to be Hardin.[52] To save face, not to mention the incentive of a sizable reward, Armstrong resolved to get the real Hardin.

The price on Hardin's head had a lot of bounty hunters looking for him, but Armstrong and his boss realized the outlaw would not be captured unless they developed a way to get information from his family and friends. On July 15, Hall mustered into his company a Dallas policeman with a record as a successful manhunter, twenty-six-year-old John Riley Duncan, a dark-eyed native Kentuckian. The captain told Duncan he had heard from the DeWitt County sheriff that Hardin had relocated to Florida, calling himself Swain.[53]

Within a few days of his resignation from the Dallas city marshal's office, Duncan arrived in Gonzales County, posing as a farm laborer under the name of Williams. The undercover ranger soon managed to get himself close enough to Neal Bowen—Hardin's father-in-law—to briefly get his hands on a letter addressed to Mr. J. H. Swain, Pollard, Alabama, care of Neil McMillan. Duncan easily deduced from the letter's context that Hardin and his wife lived in Florida. Wiring Armstrong on August 15 to "Come get your horse," a prearranged code, Duncan hung around Gonzalez until several rangers showed up to "arrest" him and hustle him out of the county.

Three days later, the lieutenant and private Duncan left Austin by train for Montgomery, Alabama, arriving two days later. This time wearing ragged clothing to make himself look like a railroad bum, Duncan went to Pollard, a community on the Alabama-Florida border. There he located McMillan, a friend of Swain's, and chatted him up. Soon he knew that Swain lived in Whiting, just south of Pollard. Duncan next walked to Whiting, where a bit of idle talk with a local businessman netted him information that Swain had gone to Pensacola for a little gambling. From the Whiting depot, Duncan wired Armstrong to catch the next train and meet him there.[54]

When Armstrong arrived in Whiting on August 23, Duncan filled him in on some information about Swain that had fallen in his lap. Just like a certain John Wesley Hardin, Swain seldom turned down a drink. When drunk, also just like Hardin, Swain tended not to be pleasant company. In fact, on the very day the two lawmen stepped off the train in Alabama, a boozed-up Swain had pulled his pistol, intending to kill

railroad superintendent William D. Chipley, a fellow member of the local sporting fraternity. The quick-thinking superintendent got his hand
between the hammer and cylinder of Swain's pistol before it could go
off. The railroad man then used the weapon on Swain's head a few
times. In front of witnesses, Swain vowed to kill Chipley the next time
he saw him and departed.[55]

Accordingly, Superintendent Chipley happily cooperated with the
two rangers in their effort to return Swain to Texas. Soon, a special train
left Pensacola for Whiting to pick up the two Texas officers. The entourage included Chipley, twenty-seven-year-old Sheriff William H.
Hutchinson, and a local judge, whose most important role would be in
not taking judicial notice that the two Texas Rangers lacked a warrant
for Hardin's arrest. At Chipley's instruction, the Whiting telegraph operator wired a few contacts and learned that Hardin could be found at a
hotel in Pensacola, still busy at the gaming tables. With Chipley already
extending the rangers every courtesy in their preparations for his capture, the lieutenant decided not to disclose Swain's true identity.

In Pensacola, the rangers learned that Swain had bought a ticket to
return to Whiting that evening. They did not have much time before he
would be showing up at the station for the forty-four-mile commute
home. The sheriff, a Confederate veteran, offered to take Swain into
custody as soon as he reached the train station. Armstrong, familiar
with Hardin's history, prevailed in his argument that making the arrest
on the train would be less risky. Thinking ahead, the Florida sheriff deputized seven or eight citizens (accounts vary) to back them up in case
Swain somehow made it off the train.

As expected, the Texas fugitive appeared at the depot to return to
Whiting. He had several cronies with him, including Jim Mann, a
twenty-one-year-old hanger-on. The men toted shotguns, but when they
entered the smoking car they decorously stowed their scatterguns in the
overhead luggage racks. That done, Swain and his friends sat down, and
Swain started packing his pipe.

Hardin did not find it alarming when he saw the sheriff and one of
his deputies walking slowly through the car, making eye contact with
all passengers. He had made the trip often enough to know that the
county lawman routinely checked outgoing trains for wanted persons or
troublemakers. Too, Swain had gotten to know the deputy, having occasionally relieved him of a portion of his salary in games of chance. To al-

lay any suspicion, the deputy jokingly urged Swain to spend the night and give him a chance to win his money back.

The local officers left the railroad car, but unknown to Hardin, they quickly circled around and reentered behind him. Without further talk, the two Florida officers, possibly joined by another deputy, latched onto their unsuspecting target. Hardin recovered nicely from his surprise, fighting like a cornered panther.

Mann, not wanted for anything but possibly suffering from a guilty conscience, pulled a pistol and climbed out a window. When he did that, one of the Florida deputies started shooting, and the youngster dropped dead outside the train.

Armstrong had taken position in the adjoining express car while ranger Duncan stood outside, on the other side of the train from the depot. Pistol in hand, the lieutenant moved down the aisle of the smoking car as fast as he could with his stiff leg and weighed into the fight with Hardin as the outlaw desperately tried to get his pistol untangled from his suspenders. Duncan and Hutchinson joined the struggle a few moments later. The big Ranger lieutenant hammered Hardin's head with the barrel of his Colt, stunning him long enough for the officers to restrain him. For a few minutes, in fact, Armstrong thought he had killed the wanted Texan.

Once the rangers had Hardin tied to his seat, Chipley ordered the train to proceed straight to Whiting without stopping. As soon as he got off the train, Armstrong wired Adjutant General Steele:

Arrested John Wesley Hardin, Pensacola, Florida this P.M. He had four men with him. Had some lively shooting. One of their number killed. All the rest captured. Hardin fought desperately. Closed in and took him by main strength. Hurried ahead. Train then leaving for this place. We are waiting for a train to get away on. This is Hardin's home and his friends are trying to rally men to release him. Have some good citizens with me, and will make it interesting.[56]

Newspapers across the nation carried a 106-word telegram from Whiting dated August 24 that "the notorious John Wesley Hardin, who is said to have committed twenty-seven murders," had been arrested by the Pensacola sheriff and "two Texas officials."[57] In the strictest legal sense, the rangers and other officers had kidnapped Hardin. A Florida grand jury later indicted the sheriff for that offense, but the case never went anywhere.

"Hardin had wanted to return to Texas," the Galveston *News* reported a couple of days later, "but was warned by a letter, which was intercepted, that there was no peace here for an honest, enterprising man, on account of the disposition of Hall's men, the Frontier Battalion, and the State government generally, to disregard Magna Charta."[58]

Armstrong may or may not have heard of the Magna Carta, but he knew he had to have some official paperwork to get his prisoner back to Texas for trial. It took a while, and for a time it looked as if Hardin's friends and family would succeed in getting him released on a writ of habeas corpus, but the Ranger lieutenant finally received the documentation he needed to return his prisoner, a killer the Austin *Daily Statesman* proclaimed "the Grand Mogul of Texas desperadoes."[59]

By August 25, the two rangers were on their way to Texas with their notorious prisoner. When the state officers and Hardin changed trains in the East Texas town of Palestine, someone in the large crowd of onlookers shouted, "What have you got there?" Hardin snapped back, "A panther!" On August 27, the day before they arrived in the capital city, the Austin newspaper proclaimed, "This is one of the most important arrests yet accomplished in Texas, and Lieutenant Armstrong and Detective Duncan have made enviable reputations for themselves and rendered great service to the state."[60]

Paying no attention to the extralegal aspect of Hardin's arrest, the *Daily Statesman* saw the capture of the outlaw as evidence of improving law and order in the state. The editorial writer proclaimed, "The day is rapidly passing away in Texas when men can defy the law and still go unpunished, and by the time another twelve months has rolled around, Texas will be pretty well freed from desperadoes and lawless characters and leaders of organized bands of thieves and cutthroats."[61]

As the state's newspapers basked in their satisfaction with Hardin's capture by the Rangers, the health of Hall's and Armstrong's former boss continued to worsen. With his family at his bedside, former captain McNelly died at his home in Burton on September 4, 1877. "Able, gallant, faithful in all his enterprises against the enemies of a young and struggling society and civilization," the Galveston *Daily News* editorialized three days later, "long will his name be remembered and cherished with affection by thousands of beneficiaries of his skill and bravery."[62]

Not long after Hardin's capture, Adjutant General Steele opened a letter from Thomas J. Goree, superintendent of the state prison in

Huntsville. Goree wrote that an inmate, while in the Travis County Jail pending transfer to Huntsville, had seen a letter outlining a bold, violent scheme by a group of unknown outlaws. After first distracting the rangers by using Mexicans posing as Indians to stage a series of attacks along the frontier, the outlaws behind the plot would start breaking key colleagues from various county jails, including the castlelike lockup in Austin—right across the street from the Capitol.

If they got that far, the outlaws' next target would be the Huntsville prison. Then, with most of the bad men in Texas liberated from behind bars, they would "plunder towns, banks, etc." across the state. Further, they intended to assassinate Jones and several of his key officers, including Armstrong.

Not taking the purported plan seriously, Steele nevertheless saw to it that Hardin stayed under heavy guard. On September 19, six Company E rangers under Lieutenant N. O. Reynolds along with Comanche County Sheriff Frank Wilson transported Hardin from Austin to Comanche for trial. One of those rangers later recalled, "We had two factions to guard against, his friends and his enemies."[63] Following a weeklong trial, a jury found Hardin guilty of second-degree murder in the killing of Deputy Webb and assessed his punishment at twenty-five years in prison. On October 1, Reynolds and his rangers returned Hardin to Austin pending his appeal. That December, rangers transported the convicted killer to Huntsville.[64]

While only three years earlier the rangers under Captain Waller had tried their best to shoot him down, Reynolds and his men treated Hardin well. "I have Been in camps with the rangers ever Since I left austin and Have faired as they have in other words have . . . had a good time," Hardin wrote his wife, Jane, on September 24, the day his trial began in Comanche. In an undated letter written not long after, he elaborated, "I Had a Splendid time with the rangers for we went by Sansaba where they were camped and Staid 7 days in camps with the rangers there treatment to me was the very best for they done all in there power for my conveniences and tried to make me as comfortable as possible you can tell ma that they are a different Set of rangers to what Wallers men were." Had some of his many enemies tried to mob him, he continued, "They [the Rangers] would of Stood by me untill the last hour in the day."[65] Hardin could have used a little help with his capitalization and punctuation, but with a twenty-five-year sentence, he would have plenty of time to brush up on his grammar.

10

"Here lies a noted cow thief"

THE FRONTIER BATTALION, 1875—77

Adam Brayford held the reins loosely, his mind drifting, as his wagon rolled along on the road between Llano and Mason through some of the prettiest scenery in Texas, the Hill Country. Seeing a still form lying beside the road, he jerked the leather hard, stopping his mule in its tracks.

Jumping to the ground, Brayford ran over for a closer look. A young cowboy, Allen Bolt, lay dead in a pool of congealed blood. Someone had pinned a six-word note on the back of his coat: "Here lies a noted cow thief."[1]

Brayford found the body on February 17, 1875, the date generally accepted as the beginning of a bloody feud that came to be called the Hoo Doo War, *hoo doo* being a nineteenth-century expression for bad luck or what triggers bad luck. The rapidly escalating violence soon embroiled the not-even-year-old Frontier Battalion.

The trouble leading to Bolt's killing could be traced to festering resentments predating the Civil War. Mason County had a large German population, the 1870 Census listing nearly three-fourths of its residents as foreign-born. When Texans opted to secede from the Union in 1861, the Mason County electorate voted seventy-five to two not to join the Confederacy. After the war, that continued to stick in the craw of die-hard Southerners.[2] Cattle theft, as the note attached to Bolt made plain, added another critical ingredient to the cauldron. Texans took rustling personally, often taking the law into their own hands to stop it.

Company D's Lieutenant Dan Roberts arrived in Mason three days after the discovery of Bolt's body, but not to investigate the accused cow thief's murder. The ranger had come to town to buy grain for his company's horses. Roberts had just bedded down for the night in the Bridge's Hotel when newly elected sheriff John E. Clark, not bothering to knock, burst into the ranger's room "and yelled at me to get up, that a big lot of men were mobbing the jail."

Roberts shoved his feet in his boots, buckled on his gunbelt, grabbed his Winchester, and ran outside. Soon, Roberts, Clark, and one of his deputies faced more than three dozen armed men intent on removing five suspected cattle thieves from the Mason County lockup, an open-air stockade made of oak logs. The prospect of stopping the mob came down to simple arithmetic—the mob had the officers outgunned. While Clark ran for help, Roberts and the deputy could do nothing but watch as the mob gathered at the jail's gate.[3]

"Poor Mr. Wordly [Deputy Johann A. Wohrle] was choked until he had to give up the key," Lucia Holmes wrote in her diary entry for February 18. From the gallery of a neighbor's house, she "saw about forty men leading the prisoners . . . across the flat and go down the road. A lot of Mason men followed them but not in time to save the poor prisoners. . . . We were dreadfully frightened and horrified." A week later, Wohrle's wife, Helene, suffered a miscarriage Holmes blamed on "her fright the other night."[4]

Roberts, Sheriff Clark, and a small party of hastily recruited citizens followed the lynch mob to a point about a half mile south of town on the Fredericksburg road. By the time they caught up with the vigilantes, three men—Elijah Backus, his cousin Peter, and Tom Turley—hung from the limb of a big oak. A fourth victim, Abe Wiggins, had a bullet in his head. As the mob scattered, Clark cut Turley down in time for Roberts to revive him with a hatful of water splashed in his face. The fifth prisoner, Charley Johnson, pulled the noose from his neck and escaped.[5]

In the days following the lynching, a grand jury asked a lot of questions but handed down no indictments. Extralegal adjudication, meanwhile, continued. Following the killing of another suspected cattle thief, William Wages, Lieutenant Roberts reported to headquarters that the mob had "as yet . . . harmed no good man."[6]

On May 13, Deputy Sheriff Wohrle and county brand inspector Daniel Hoerster rode to a ranch near Castell in Llano County where thirty-two-year-old Timothy P. Williamson worked as foreman. A year before Williamson had been charged in Mason County with selling a yearling burned with someone else's brand. He may or may not have been guilty—the matter had not yet been set for trial—but he needed to make a new bond. Williamson's employer offered to sign a surety on the spot, but Wohrle said he would have to escort them to Mason to do the paperwork. On their way to the courthouse, twelve masked men ambushed them. Williamson implored Wohrle to let him make a run for it, but the deputy refused and one of the attackers shot him. Recognizing his assailant, the wounded Williamson begged the man not to shoot again.

"I've blowed my coffee and now I'm going to drink it," the gunman said, pulling the trigger again. Wohrle, folks said, did not try very hard to protect his prisoner. In fact, some believed that the whole thing had been a setup with Wohrle in on it.[7]

The violence continued. On July 20, parties unknown concealed by darkness fired on three German men camped on open, high ground near Streeter. One of them, Henry Doell, took a bullet in the stomach and died a few days later. Though some said the killing came in retaliation for Williamson's murder, Mason County attorney Henry M. Holmes (husband of diarist Lucia Holmes) wrote that there "was not a scintilla of evidence pointing to any conclusion . . . other than Indians did it." The Germans' horses had been stolen, Holmes said, and moccasin tracks found at the scene pointed to Indians.[8]

If Major Jones, following developments through Roberts and news-paper accounts, wondered if the situation in the county could get any more grave, he got his answer when former Company D ranger Scott Cooley, whose wrist had been slapped the year before for trying to make money by displaying a captured Comanche in the capital city, injected himself into the feud. "He was a small man but DYNAMITE," a woman who knew Cooley would recall, "and not afraid of anyone."[9]

Vengeance drew Cooley into the war. Williamson had befriended Cooley, left fatherless by a shooting in Jack County in 1870, on a trail drive to Kansas. Back in Texas, Williamson's wife Mary nursed Cooley back to health when he came down with typhoid.[10] Learning of Williamson's murder, as the San Antonio Herald reported, Cooley "sat down and cried for grief at the loss of one who he said was his best friend in the world." When he regained his composure, Cooley came to Mason County to exact retribution. Soon he had a pretty good idea of those involved in his friend's death—Wohrle and Peter Bader.

On August 10, the twenty-year-old ex-ranger found Wohrle and two other men digging a well in Mason. Cooley talked cordially with the deputy long enough to put him at ease, then said, "Wohrle, why did you kill Williamson?" When Wohrle replied, "Because I had to," Cooley said, "For the same reason I am killing you." When Cooley rode off, the twenty-nine-year-old, German-born deputy, a Union Army veteran, had six bullet holes in him and four stab wounds. Just to make sure people got the point, Cooley scalped the dead deputy and slashed a *W* on his forehead.[11]

Nine days after collecting Wohrle's scalp, in Llano County Cooley found Peter Bader's brother Karl working in his field and shot him down, mistaking him for Peter. By this time, Cooley had recruited a handful of young men more than happy to ride with him: George W. Gladden, brothers John and Moses B. Baird, and John Ringo.[12] After Cooley shot Bader, some accounts have Ringo adding a bullet from his gun for good measure.

When Sheriff Clark heard of the Bader killing, he set a trap for the Cooley crowd, sending James Cheyney to lure Moses Baird and Gladden to Mason. Clark gathered a fifty-man posse and waited in ambush near Charles Keller's store, a business on the Llano River east of Mason, on September 7. Baird died in the shoot-out that followed, Gladden suffering a serious wound. "Mr. [Baird] is a man of large connexions [*sic*]," attorney Holmes wrote Governor Coke. "If something is not done a civil war will be inaugurated."[13]

"H-ll has broke loose up here," the San Antonio *Daily Herald* reported a few days after the incident. "We fear this is but the beginning of a bloody solution of the difficulties about stock, that have become so serious of late."[14]

Revenge for Baird's killing came during a light rain on September 25, when Ringo and another pro-Cooley rider visited Jim Cheyney's rural home and gunned him down as he cooked breakfast for his family. In Mason the next day, Lucia Holmes baked a cake, but after relating the latest shooting, confided to her diary that she felt "so worried that I hardly know what I am about."[15]

A hundred miles away in Austin, Governor Coke also worried. Finally responding to a second urgent appeal from county attorney Holmes (the attorney had first written Austin for help on May 17), the governor had Steele order Jones and his escort company to Mason County.[16] Already in the field, the Frontier Battalion commander broke off a planned scout west to the Pecos River and hastened instead to Mason. Arriving on September 28 with twenty rangers, Jones went first to Keller's Store, where Sheriff Clark and fifteen or twenty men arose from behind a stone fence and nearly opened up on them before recognizing them as state officers. Clark said he had word that Cooley and his gang had headed for the community of Loyal Valley (so named for the pro-Unionist sentiment of the mostly German residents) to burn them out. Jones and his men hurried to Loyal Valley, finding everything quiet. It being late in the day, Jones ordered his men to pitch camp for the night.

Cooley and his cohorts, meanwhile, could have been found in Mason. They had ridden into town the same day Jones reached Loyal Valley. With the vengeance-seeking former ranger were Gladden, who had healed sufficiently to tote a gun again, and John Baird.[17]

"Came out on the gallery and heard a lot of shooting uptown," Mrs. Holmes wrote in her diary for September 29. "Poor Dan Herster [Hoerster] killed. Two men came riding to the house and we all went in and locked the doors. . . . We were all fearfully frightened."[18] In addition to killing Hoerster, Cooley, Baird, and Gladden exchanged shots with Peter Jordan and Henry Pluenneke, but no one got hit. Only a few hours after the courthouse square shooting, Jones and the rangers rode into town too late to do anything other than inspect Hoerster's body and marvel at what a load of buckshot could do to a man's neck.

Sheriff Clark filed on Cooley for murder, but the Rangers—some of them former colleagues—seemed to be having trouble finding him, despite a standing $300 reward for his "arrest and delivery . . . to the Sheriff of Mason County inside the jail door." Finally, Jones gathered his men and told them he understood that several regarded the wanted man as a friend. Anyone not willing to hunt Cooley down would receive an honorable discharge. Though one of the men present later recalled that fifteen rangers resigned, the official paperwork does not support that number. But three rangers did receive honorable discharges a short time later "for the reason that they say they cannot conscientiously discharge the duty to which they have been assigned."[19] Despite Jones's pep talk, the Rangers never located Cooley.[20]

Nor could the Rangers be credited with ending the Hoo Doo War. The basic issues and ever-compounding animosities in this feud lay as intractable as the granite outcrops scattered across the Mason County countryside. Rangers could only be effective with the cooperation of local authorities, and that would not happen as long as those officials remained as divided as the rest of the citizenry. When he wrote his memoir years later, Roberts offered his theory on the problems in Mason County: "The men supporting civil authority, needed no arrest, and those opposing it, urged equal claims, of being right, but would not submit their grievances to law."[21] The old ranger's misuse of commas makes that passage difficult to comprehend, but he made his point: The justice system only worked when people chose to rely on it.

Though Roberts later blamed a flawed local judicial system, the perception arose that the Rangers had taken sides in the feud. When Jones received a cautioning letter from the adjutant general advising him "of the necessity [of doing] nothing outside of the law" and giving "no cause to think you favor one or the others [sic] party to the feud," the Frontier Battalion commander fired back a long, indignant reply on October 20.

While not surprised "that reports have gone to the Governor that I had taken sides with one or the other party to the terrible feud in this county," Jones wrote he had been taken aback that Coke had "taken any notice of it." He continued, "Having had some experience in troubles of this kind . . . I knew the difficulty of steering clear of imputations of partiality when I came here and consequently was [as] careful as possible from the first not to act in such a manner as to give cause for such a suspicion. . . ."

Jones wanted to know who had accused him of taking sides, guessing it was the Mason county attorney, Holmes.

Steele wrote back and said he had shown Jones's letter to Coke, and that the governor had said no one had complained to him but that he had merely wanted "to remind you of the necessity of avoiding a semblance of taking sides."[22]

Jones left the county in late October, leaving behind a detachment under Lieutenant Ira Long that stayed until the following January. The Rangers had spent more time scouting for Indians between Mason and Menardville than they had in trying to mitigate the feud.[23] Jones's summary report listed twenty-two arrests and two shooting incidents resulting in wounded suspects, but the Rangers had not stopped the violence in and around Mason County.

"I am conscious of having done all that I could and in the manner best calculated, from a moral as well as legal standpoint, to restore peace and quiet and enforce the law in this community," Jones wrote Steele on October 26. Even so, eleven men had died violently inside eight months, and more would die before the feud settled into history, though the Frontier Battalion had no further significant involvement.[24]

The day after Jones sent his report to Austin, Steele wrote him that Cooley had been seen in the capital city, bragging that Sheriff Clark was the next name on his list. After spending a few days in Austin, Steele said, Cooley had left for Burnet.[25]

Sheriff Clark, under pressure from more peace-minded elements in the county, wisely vacated his office, leaving for parts unknown. Only death and the passage of time, not the Rangers, ended ill feelings in Mason County.[26]

The Hoo Doo War had been only one of Jones's problems in 1875. He issued an order that effective November 30 "commanders of companies will reduce the force of their respective companies by discharging all except two Sergeants, one corporal, and seventeen privates, giving to the men discharged final statements of their accounts, as had been done heretofore in similar cases."[27]

The Rangers would have been less active anyway. In the winter, particularly, company activity tended to slow except for emergencies. Without green grass or abundant corn, people dependent on horses for transportation did not move as often or as far. After spending the summer scouting for Indians, Roberts—recently promoted to captain—established camp for the winter on the San Saba River, about two miles below Menard and five miles from the federal garrison at Fort Mc-Kavett.

"We were never dull in camp," recalled Lucvenia Roberts, who as a newlywed spent time in the field with her husband and his company.

Several of the Rangers were musical, and had their instruments with them. Captain Roberts was a fine violinist. A race track was laid out, and there was horse racing. Card playing was not allowed, and it was not done openly. Betting on horse races was permitted, but the Rangers ran their races for amusement. We had a croquet set and that game was enjoyed.[28]

Hearing that local citizens needed to raise money to build a church, the rangers put on a minstrel performance and donated their profits— $60—to the effort. Rangers also enlivened occasional square dances, drinking steaming black coffee and do-si-doing into the wee hours with the local belles.[29]

Using their state-issued rifles for hunting, rangers supplemented their regular provisions with fresh meat. "The forests . . . abound with the finest game—deer, turkeys, etc. It is a wild and rugged country," one ranger said in a letter to the Galveston *Daily News*.[30] In the early fall and spring, many rangers turned to fishing in their spare time. "Such sport as we enjoyed!" Mrs. Roberts gushed. "As fast as a hook could be cast it would be caught up by a fish. I have often wondered whether a white man had ever fished there before us."[31]

On a scout that saw more hunting and fishing than anything else, rangers made an interesting discovery. "No live Indians were seen," Mrs. Roberts wrote, "but we found the skeleton of a dead one where he had been buried in a crevice of rock."[32]

Increasingly, the battalion focused on its law enforcement role, not Indian fighting. "The Brazos fairly vomit out Freedman and the whole state is lawless, armed to the teeth," one letter writer complained in 1876. "Robbers robbed fifteen men on the way to Dallas, cattle thieves are the worst ever, crime runs riot over the land. It is about time for Gabriel to blow his wind instrument, but God help him if he lays it down, for someone in Tx. will surely steal it."[33]

Adjutant General Steele noted, "The most important duties of this office . . . have resulted from the power given by law to members of the frontier battalion to act as peace officer, and the organization of a special company for the 'suppression of lawlessness and crime.' "[34] Indeed, during its second six months, the battalion had only four fights with Indians.[35]

Even so, Indians still occasionally left their reservation to raid into Texas. On July 10, 1876, Lieutenant B. S. Foster and eleven rangers followed an Indian trail they picked up on the Colorado. The rangers tracked the Indians thirty-five miles, finally finding their camp. Before daylight the next morning, the rangers charged. Succeeding in catching the Indians by surprise, the rangers made off with their horses. Realizing that they had the rangers outnumbered almost five to one, the Indians recaptured their horses and sent the rangers into strategic retreat.

But having lost most of their supplies, the Indians headed back to their reservation. Sustaining no casualties themselves, rangers wounded one Indian in the engagement.[36]

Foster's eagerness to take on more than his number in Indians reflected a Ranger tradition already forty years old. Rangers had a different attitude toward Indians than the regular army: "The soldiers did not go after the Indians the way the Rangers did," Mrs. Roberts wrote in her memoir. "Their movements were . . . regulated by a lot of red tape, and they couldn't catch them. The Rangers used no ceremony; they mounted their horses, ran down the Indians and killed them."[37]

A ranger private made $40 a month; a soldier started out at $13 a month. If a soldier quit before his enlistment expired, the army called it desertion. If a ranger wanted to give up his job, a captain would happily let him move on, rightly thinking that a disgruntled ranger offered no value to the company. Mrs. Roberts pointed out another significant difference between rangers and soldiers: "Rangers had their hearts in the service; they were protecting the frontier of their home."[38] Soldiers from out of state, many of the enlisted men immigrants from other countries, had no personal stake in frontier defense.

Elsewhere in the West, the U.S. army faced the Indian alone. The June 25, 1876, massacre of Colonel George Armstrong Custer and more than two hundred of his men along the Little Bighorn in Dakota Territory, though hundreds of miles from Texas, nevertheless had an impact on the state's frontier. Stunned at the loss of one of its brightest, if controversial, officers and so many men, the War Department began moving additional troops to the Dakotas to deal with the warring Sioux. Some of those soldiers came from Texas. At Fort Griffin, two of the post's three companies of infantry departed for Dakota. Other Texas-based troops joined the deployment to the new trouble spot. Even more discomforting to Texans, as the Fort Worth *Daily Democrat* reported, "Major Jones of the Rangers expects to disband his troops the last of this month unless the legislature makes an appropriation. Apprehension is accordingly being felt on the frontier because of the withdrawal of the U.S. troops and the Rangers."[39]

The legislature did not disband the Rangers, but it further reduced the Frontier Battalion appropriation. Jones informed his captains that effective September 1, 1876, each company could have only sixteen men plus two sergeants and two corporals.[40] Company A would continue as Jones's escort company, a unit almost constantly on the move.

Change overtook the frontier with the speed of a wind-fanned prairie fire. With the Comanches and Kiowas effectively bottled up north of the Red River, the hunting of bison in West Texas reached its zenith. A Fort Worth newspaper predicted that one hundred thousand buffalo hides would be shipped from there the next season. In a few words, the anonymous scribe summed up the closing of one era and the beginning of another:

> The buffalo are being hemmed up . . . and but a few years are sufficient to exterminate them. Such a result is to be desired by the people. With the disappearance of the buffalo vanishes the independence of the Indian. . . . Their destruction will render available a superb range country for the stockmen. Shorthorns or longhorns are a source of greater wealth than all the buffaloes.[41]

On March 20, 1877, in Special Order Number Fifteen, Jones instructed his captains to concentrate on "suppression of lawlessness and crime." From then on, the major said, the Rangers would discontinue routine scouting for Indian sign and only pursue raiding parties. Jones told his captains to pay particular attention to cattle theft, ordering them to start doing brand checks on trail herds.[42]

"As an Indian fighter," one state newspaper observed, "Major Jones has acquired a reputation unsurpassed, and now that a quietus has been put upon the red man, he is devoting special attention to the rest of the outlaws and lawless characters generally among more civilized classes. In this field he has so far achieved a success no less conspicuous than on the frontier."[43]

"Kimble County is a thiafs stronghold"

One place in particular deserved that special attention. Junction City, the seat of newly organized Kimble County, lay on the edge of the frontier and even farther than that beyond the law. Captain Roberts came to realize the extent of the problem when several of his men rode bareback into camp early one morning to report that someone had stolen their saddles. The boys had been attending a local dance and had left their horses hitched to a tree.

Sheriff Joe Clements did not know who helped themselves to the ranger tack, but he knew someone who might. The sheriff led Roberts and two privates fifteen miles up the Llano River to the man's place. Rather than immediately pressing him for information, the officers invited him to their camp for a friendly cup of coffee.

Not long after they had made themselves comfortable around the campfire, a stranger rode up. Roberts made a big show of having the man detained for questioning. After some discrete communication between the captain and his men, Roberts left camp for a walk with their guest. The captain and the man had not gone a hundred yards before they heard a pistol shot, immediately followed by moaning, and another shot. The wide-eyed man told Roberts it sounded as if his rangers had just killed the fellow they had been questioning.

Roberts agreed. The man must have been lying, the captain said. His men would never harm someone who told the truth. At that point, the captain casually brought up the matter of the missing Ranger saddles. His guest said he did know a little something about that. After Roberts promised immunity, the man revealed where the stolen state property could be found and named the principal participant in the theft.

When they got back to camp, the informant found the "executed" stranger in perfect health. The rangers recovered their saddles and arrested a suspect.[44]

In addition to taking on more law enforcement duties, the Rangers began carrying better weapons. The Winchester Model 73, a lever-action carbine holding eight .44-caliber rounds, soon would replace the old single-shot Sharps rifles. Not every Ranger had one of the new repeating rifles, but the transition had begun. A tight state budget remained a problem, however.[45]

Lack of money for the battalion frustrated the governor as well as Steele and Jones. In April, new governor Richard B. Hubbard replied through his secretary to one W. T. Cherry of Tyler. Cherry had written seeking a ranger appointment. The Frontier Battalion, the three-hundred-pound governor dictated tongue-in-jowl, had vacancies for anyone interested in being "shot at by the Indians and white cutthroats at forty dollars per month."[46]

Quite a few of those cutthroats lived in the Junction area. "I find that Kimble County is a thiafs stronghold," Ranger H. B. Waddill wrote Jones on February 27, 1877. "The County is unsafe to travil through." The ranger, who had spent time in the county quietly gathering information while posing as a settler, could have used some help with spelling, but nothing dulled his powers of observation. W. A. Blackburn, the judge whose district included the new county, wrote Jones on March 30 that he could not convene court there because of the prevalence of armed outlaws. "It is the home of a gang of the most desperate characters from all parts of the state, who are depredating upon all the adjacent counties," he wrote. The judge estimated that a hundred men could be raised "in a few hours to resist the execution of legal process." In fact, the lawless element of the county had made known "their determination to resist the holding of any court in that county."[47] Jones received a second letter from the judge, this one written April 6, in which he said he had decided to convene court in the county on April 30—if the Rangers provided an escort. "I do not think it safe for me to travel through that county without one," he wrote, "and I know I cannot hold a court without your assistance." Jones had already decided the situation had grown out of hand.

"Will have three companies in that county by the 15th of this month," Jones had written the judge on April 2, "and will scour it thoroughly before the time for your court."[48]

With a clear vision of the role the Frontier Battalion should play in any county, Jones coordinated a military-like campaign, planning to move rangers into the county from four different directions. "Our business is to enforce the law and keep the peace," he wrote Reynolds on April 8. "We must have no personal quarrels or feelings in the discharge of our duty, and should carefully guard against strife or ill feeling against either good or bad people."[49]

Intending to lead the operation himself, the major ordered Lieutenant F. M. Moore of Company F to meet him at Paint Rock, in what is now Concho County, on April 18 with three rangers "who know where everybody lives on both Llanos and Johnson Fork." Jones instructed the lieutenant to send the rest of his company into Junction City on April 20 with ten days' rations. "I will bring Coldwell's and Dolan's companies with me and will make a general 'roundup' of Kimble County, but want it kept secret until we are ready to make the break," Jones continued in his orders to Moore.[50]

Riding into Junction City on April 19, Jones succeeded in taking the county by surprise, later reporting that only three local residents knew of his planned sweep. Dividing his men into five detachments, he kept scouts in the saddle day and night, rounding up anyone who seemed suspicious and could not account for their good character. Constitutional guarantees of presumed innocence and due process meant nothing during the clean-up operation. Rangers surrounded houses and entered without warrants. Remote campfires drew rangers like moths. Anyone who could not convince the Rangers of his innocence went to Junction City for further interrogation.

No one got hurt during the cleanup, not that everyone submitted meekly. "Sometimes we came in contact with their women and were terribly tongue-lashed by them for searching their houses and arresting the men," Jones wrote.

During their first seventy-two hours in the county, rangers made twenty-three arrests. Junction City having no jail, the prisoners spent their time shackled in an area that quickly came to be called the "bull pen." By the time Jones wrote his report to the adjutant general, the bull pen's population had risen to forty-one, all but four from Kimble County.

"A grand jury of good men was secured who worked industriously and fearlessly," Jones reported. "They presented twenty-five bills of indictment and would have found many more but for the absence of witnesses and lack of time to procure evidence."

Despite the successful campaign, the jury commission appointed by the district judge could only find nine "good honest citizens" (other than the grand jurors, who could not hear the cases they had indicted) to serve as jurors. Because of that, the cases had to be continued until the next session of court.[51] Even so, the Rangers had made a definite impact on outlawry in Kimble County.[52]

In his 1877 legislative message, Governor Hubbard put the accomplishments of the Frontier Battalion into perspective:

Fourteen counties have been organized in Northwest Texas during the last two years. It is a fact that, for more than twelve years prior to the creation of the frontier battalion, and its service in the West, no new county had been organized. Three counties had been depopulated, and had lost their county organizations, and hundreds of citizens had been compelled by the Indians to abandon their homes in the other frontier counties. But if the same progress marks her future that now marks her present, many years will not elapse before the savage will be a stranger within our lives, and the State, along her border, will be securely protected by a living wall of her own hardy and patriotic people.[53]

Texas still seemed longhorn-tough to much of the nation. Adding to the perception, the St. Louis *Globe-Democrat* published a regular column headed "Texas Killings." The newspaper had no trouble filling the space. Though no one could argue against the accuracy of the Missouri newspaper's portrayal of Texas as a rough-and-tumble place, at least one Texan took offense at such out-of-state meddling. Expressing his opinion in a letter to the editor, he threatened to string up any *Globe-Democrat* staff member who ever dared come to Texas.[54]

The St. Louis newspaper received a fair amount of its Texas material in the spring and summer of 1877 from dispatches detailing the latest developments in an ongoing difficulty in Lampasas County that came to be known as the Horrell-Higgins feud.

"Yonder comes the Higginses"

A wild and wooly cattle town sixty-seven miles northwest of the state's capital, Lampasas lay along aptly named Sulphur Creek, its mineral-laden waters said to be good for what ailed folks. But the waters could not cure gunshot wounds. The sanguinary feud owed the first half of its name to the five Horrell brothers—Ben, Martin, Merritt, Sam, and Thomas. They had established their reputation four years before, when some of them forcibly prevented a posse from arresting two friends who had seriously wounded the sheriff when he interrupted a shooting spree they had undertaken. Local officials asked Austin for help, and a few days later a detachment of state police arrived with a freshly signed gubernatorial proclamation barring the carrying of pistols in the county.

The lieutenant in charge, seeing that the number of armed men in town considerably exceeded his four-man force, wrote headquarters to report that he thought it best to wait a few days for word of the proclamation to get around the county before he tried to enforce it. Following another round of indiscriminate street shooting, the officer asked Austin for more manpower. The governor dispatched Captain Thomas Williams and a larger contingent of policemen to see the no-pistol order carried out. On the afternoon of March 14, 1873, Williams noticed a man wearing a pistol enter a saloon on the courthouse square. The captain did not know it at the time, but the gunman was a brother-in-law of the Horrells'.

Intending to disarm the man, Williams and three of his men walked inside the saloon—straight into an ambush. Having come to town to enforce a handgun ban, the four officers ended up being slaughtered by a bunch of drunk cowboys armed with Winchesters. When the smoke-filled bar emptied, several police officers who had not gone inside managed to wound two of the fleeing cowboys, Martin and Thomas Horrell. Thomas got away, but Martin and three others got arrested and taken to the lockup in Austin as a precaution against jailbreak in Lampasas. Later transferred to Georgetown, midway between Austin and Lampasas, friends of Martin Horrell and his pals'—probably including his brothers—sprang the prisoners on May 2.

Not wanting to overburden the courts, the Horrell boys and several of their cohorts decided to vacate Texas for New Mexico Territory. Proving that their penchant for violence had nothing to do with environment, they soon got caught up in the early stages of the long-playing Lincoln County War. Five Horrells had made the ride west, but only four returned to Lampasas. Brother Ben died in a New Mexico gunfight.

Not long after the Horrells came home to Texas (a jury had quickly acquitted Martin of the quadruple police killing), cattleman John Pinckney Calhoun Higgins—better known as Pink—began having trouble getting his herd count to come out right. In the spring of 1876 he found one of his calves tied up outside a butcher shop owned by another of the Horrells' brothers-in-law. Higgins filed on Merritt Horrell for cattle theft, but a jury found him not guilty. The following January, Higgins checked a herd of cattle Horrell had driven into town and discovered thirty-six of his animals. Higgins cut his livestock from the herd and drove them back to his place.

This time, Higgins opted not to press charges. Instead, on January 22, 1877, Higgins approached Merritt Horrell in the same saloon where the four state police officers had been gunned down in 1873. "Mr. Horrell," he said as he raised his Winchester, "this is to settle some cattle business." When Higgins quit working the lever of his rifle, Horrell lay dead with four .44 slugs in him.[55]

The smell of burnt gunpowder now mingling with the stench of stale beer, Higgins fled the bar. A posse soon galloped after him, brothers Martin and Thomas Horrell among the riders. The citizens failed to locate Higgins, as did local officers, but they arrested four of his associates. On March 26, however, someone did manage to find the Horrell boys, ambushing them on a creek east of town. Both brothers sustained minor wounds. Soon the sheriff held arrest warrants for Higgins and Bob Mitchell, his brother-in-law.

Company C captain John C. Sparks, called to Lampasas to prevent further violence, did not find the wanted parties, but on April 22 Higgins and Mitchell came to the Ranger camp and turned themselves in. The two men soon gained their freedom on $10,000 bail each. Optimistic that the criminal justice system would work, the Lampasas *Dispatch* declared, "We are all civil now, nobody having been killed in a week or more. By the time the summer visitors make their appearance, we will all be on our good behavior."[56]

True enough, no one had been killed for a few days, but on June 4 parties unknown burglarized the county courthouse and removed all the legal documents pertaining to the case against Higgins and Mitchell. Hearing that their surety bonds had been taken and presumably destroyed by whomever had broken into the courthouse, Higgins and Mitchell came to town on June 7 to see about making new bonds. William R. Wren, another of Higgins's brothers-in-law, and a friend came along for the ride.

As the Higgins the party walked their horses toward the courthouse, they noticed the three Horrell brothers and four of their friends hanging around the square. "Yonder comes the Higginses," Thomas Horrell observed. Shortly, the lead started flying. By the time the last cap had popped, Bob Mitchell's brother Frank had mortally wounded Jim "Buck" Waldrup, one of the Horrell crowd. Martin Horrell had, in turn, killed Frank Mitchell. Wren had a bullet wound in his hip. More men on both sides would have died had not local officers and three hastily deputized citizens finally established control and disarmed the two factions. Even so, dozens of pistol and rifle shots had been fired on the courthouse square. Luckily, no innocent bystander had been felled.[57]

Though the Rangers had been in and out of Lampasas County all year, this time they came in force, with Jones on hand to oversee matters. Local residents, Jones reported, lived "in constant dread of another collision" between the two feuding parties. "This trouble is one of the most perplexing to me that I have yet had to contend with," the major continued. He knew that placing the two factions under bond pending trial would not stop a fight if they encountered each other. "That has already

been tried and failed," he wrote Steele. "So I am taking the responsibility
in the interest of peace and quiet, rather than in accordance with the dic-
tates of law, to intercede and endeavor to reconcile the difficulty and thus
terminate this long continued feud. I am on good terms with both parties
and hope to effect something towards the desired object in a few days."[58]
To do that, of course, the Rangers had to corral the Horrells—all of them,
along with three of their associates, having been charged with assault
with intent to kill.

Noting that the people of Texas "give us credit for much good work
and expect us to keep it up," Jones returned to Austin, leaving a detachment under N. O. Reynolds in Lampasas to bring in the Horrells and
generally keep the lid on. Reynolds handled other duties as well, including rounding up eight men charged with breaking Scott Cooley and John
Ringo out of the Lampasas County Jail, but he and his rangers kept alert
for any information on the whereabouts of the Horrells.[59]

About a month later, on the evening of July 27, Bob Mitchell rode
into the Ranger camp and said the Horrells could be found on School
Creek about ten miles from town. Now back in Lampasas, Jones ordered
Reynolds and six privates to go after the Horrells and the other wanted
men. Guided by Mitchell and another brother, along with the still-
recovering Wren, the rangers left at dark. Picking up more accurate information on the way, Reynolds changed direction and rode for the
residence of Martin Horrell on Mesquite Creek. About 5 a.m. on July
28, in a heavy rain, the state officers surrounded Horrell's house. The
sergeant and his men rushed in with guns in hand, catching the Horrells
and eight other men asleep.[60] Reynolds later wrote the local newspaper
to describe what happened next:

> The Horrells thus rudely aroused, and confused as to the character
> of their early visitors, sprang to their weapons and for a few mo-
> ments a desperate conflict was imminent. Sam Horrell seized upon
> my Winchester, and in wrenching it from his grasp the weapon was
> accidentally discharged, which added to the excitement.

Reynolds considered it only "fair and just" to note that the Horrells
"though assembled in force" surrendered "as soon as they learned and
fully believed that we were Rangers." As soon as the situation cooled

off, Reynolds deputized four friends of the Horrells to assist him as guards and then returned to camp with the three brothers. The other men he cut loose. Reynolds locked the brothers in the county jail and kept a guard until they made bond.[61]

On July 30, two days after their arrest, the Horrell brothers signed a four-paragraph letter addressed to Higgins, Robert Mitchell, and Wren. The letter, likely dictated by Jones, said the Horrells had "determined to take the initiatory in a move for reconciliation," holding themselves "honor bound to lay down our arms and to end the strife in which we have been engaged against you and exert our utmost efforts to entire-eradicate all enmity from the minds of our friends." Further, they promised to "abstain from insulting or injuring you and your friends, to bury the bitter past forever, and join with you as good citizens." The Horrell sentiment, however, hinged on a significant requirement: a similar promise from the opposition in the feud.

Higgins, Mitchell, and Wren responded on August 2, noting that Major Jones had hand-delivered the Horrell letter to them. "It would be difficult to express in words the mental disturbance to ourselves which the sad difficulties alluded to in your letter occasioned," their response stated. Noting that their passions had cooled, and reflecting sorrowfully on the past, the key players of the Higgins faction said they would "make every effort to do our part to restore good feeling and we lay down our weapons with our honest purpose to regard our former difficulties as bygone things." Both letters appeared in the August 9 edition of the Lampasas *Dispatch* under the exuberant headline "Peace Restored in Lampasas! The Higgins and Horrell Parties Have Laid Down Their Arms!!" The newspaper went on to point out who had done the good work: "We ascribe much credit to Major Jones for the unwearied patience and persistent efforts to appease the wrath and to unfold each party the wrongs and injuries they were inflicting upon society, each other and themselves by a continuation of so foolish a warfare." Too many children had been orphaned, "too many happy wives . . . widowed," the newspaper editor went on. "But we believe the troubles are over, and once more it can be said that Lampasas county is free from local broils and her population quiet and law-abiding."[62]

Later that month, Governor Hubbard presented the keynote address at the Lampasas County Fair. Hundreds flocked to town for the three-day

event, which featured trotting races and a balloon ascension. The fair proceeded peacefully with no further conflict between the Horrells and the
Higginses.[63]

No such joviality brightened state government in Austin. Funding
low, Jones had to reorganize the battalion again, reducing it to 150 men.
Though fewer in number, the Rangers at least had improved firepower.

"The entire command is armed with the new improved Winchester
carbine and the new improved Colt revolver," a ranger who signed his
name only as Mervyn wrote the Galveston *Daily News*. "The men are almost without exception brave, able-bodied, deadly shots, and perfect
horsemen. Major Jones is an excellent judge of horse flesh and will receive into his command nothing but sound, swift animals. He is also very
select in recruiting men, and has gathered into the battalion quite a number of scholars whose attainments would grace any position in life."

Mervyn waxed on about the Rangers' "perfect discipline" and "strict
obedience to orders," painting a word picture of them "sweeping like
the Tartars of Ukraine over the wide plains." One by one, the correspondent went on, "the desperadoes are being captured and handed over
to justice by these sun-browned, cartridge-girdled riders, captured or
sent to that place whence they return no more to trouble. Wes. Hardin
is in irons, Bill Posey is dead, Bone Wilson and Frank Taylor are sleeping
where the cayotes [*sic*] bark above their graves; a few more bullets must
be sped and beautiful Texas will bask in God's light free from the ruffians and thieves with whom she has so long been cursed."[64]

"A terror to evil doers"

THE FRONTIER BATTALION, 1877–79

Anyone capable of reading a map could see that El Paso County lay in Texas, but culturally it might as well still have been a part of Mexico. Six hundred miles of rugged, mostly dry terrain separated El Paso del Norte—the Pass of the North—from the more settled section of the state. Of the twelve thousand people living along both sides of the Rio Grande between the Franklin Mountains on the north and the Sierra Occidentals in Mexico, fewer than one hundred had Anglo surnames. Most of them lived in the small community of Franklin across the Rio Grande from the Mexican town of Paso del Norte (later renamed Juárez), though Ysleta, fifteen miles downstream, had the distinction of being the county seat. Ten miles below Ysleta lay the community of San Elizario.

A feud over control of a series of salt lakes seventy miles east of San Elizario near Guadalupe Peak had developed between two former friends, Italian-born, Spanish-speaking Louis Cardis, El Paso County's representative in the distant state legislature, and Charles R. Howard, a Missouri-born lawyer and Confederate veteran who came to Texas in 1872. A big man said to be half-Cherokee, the Mexicans called him El Indio. He won election as district attorney and later served for a time as district judge. On several occasions, Howard assaulted the short, stocky

Cardis. Soon he began threatening to do more than thrash him. But salt rights—a volatile local issue well before Howard arrived in El Paso County—constituted only one of the factors in the increasingly tense situation. Cultural conflict, religious differences, politics, and lack of strong local law enforcement all contributed to what came to be called the Salt War.[1]

Securing title to the salt lakes, a geographic amenity the people of both sides of the river had long considered public property, in September 1877, Howard had two Mexicans arrested for simply asserting that they intended to continue collecting salt at the lakes. That enraged the local Mexican population, a mob soon briefly seizing the county judge and justice of the peace who had handled the case. When the county judge refused to issue an arrest warrant for Howard in connection with an assault on Cardis, the mob went after him themselves. They found him at the adobe residence of Sheriff Charles Kerber in Ysleta. The mob surrounded the sheriff's house, took control of the county lawman when he came outside to talk, then waited for Howard and his business associate John McBride to give up.

When Howard and McBride finally surrendered, the Mexicans released the sheriff and took the two men to San Elizario to discuss the salt question and other matters. On the third day of his extralegal detention at the hands of the mob, given the choice of summary execution or affixing his signature to a document returning the salt lakes to the people pending a court ruling on the matter, Howard asked for a pen. Another provision set forth on the paper called for Howard to leave El Paso County. Released on October 3, he quickly departed for Mesilla, New Mexico.

"The sheriff has telegraphed to the Governor for assistance," a New Mexican newspaper reported on October 6, "and we have no doubt that the State of Texas will take prompt steps."[2]

After receiving the wire, Governor Hubbard checked with Adjutant General Steele about sending rangers to the pass. Steele said that it would take at least thirty days to get two companies to the area. Meanwhile, the situation in the El Paso Valley continued to deteriorate. Despite the agreement that he had been forced to sign, or the $12,000 bond he had posted to guarantee it, Howard returned to El Paso County with another remedy in mind.

On October 10, an orderly rushed into the Santa Fe, New Mexico, office of Colonel Edward Hatch, commander of the military district of New Mexico, with a telegram from Franklin:

Don Luis Cardis . . . killed this moment by Chas. Howard and we are expecting a terrible catastrophe in the county, as threats have been made that every American would be killed if harm came to Cardis. Can you not send us immediate help, for God's sake?

Howard had decided to mitigate the land dispute and his long-standing differences with Cardis with a double-barreled shotgun, blasting the legislator first in his stomach, then his chest. A week earlier, after learning of the mob's ouster of Howard, Colonel Hatch had sent a squad of cavalry to San Elizario. The colonel believed that a military presence would have a calming effect on the anti-Howard crowd, but the soldiers only had orders to prevent "armed bodies of Mexicans" from crossing into Texas—they could not enforce civil law. Accordingly, Hatch forwarded the plea for help from Franklin to Governor Hubbard. Local authorities duly charged Howard, who had gone back to New Mexico, with murder.

Two weeks went by before the governor finally ordered Steele to send Jones to El Paso County for a firsthand assessment of conditions. Jones left Austin by train on October 24. Arriving in Topeka, Kansas, he caught an Atchison, Topeka, and Santa Fe train to the end of the line in New Mexico. From there, the Frontier Battalion commander rode the stage to Mesilla, and then on to Franklin, which he finally reached on November 6, nearly two weeks after leaving the capital city. Jones soon wired the governor that things remained tense at the pass. Hoping to do the same in El Paso County as he had in Lampasas, the major had met with Howard in Mesilla, then called on the leaders of the anti-Howard faction in Texas. The major assured them that he had not come to meddle in the salt dispute, only to preserve law and order. Toward that end, a few days later, Jones notified Austin that he would raise a "three month's minute company." But when he recruited the men, he designated them as a detachment of Company C, Frontier Battalion.[3]

The major knew he needed solid leadership for the company, but he did not have much to choose from. Most citizens in the upper Rio Grande

Valley already had a position on one side or the other on the salt issue. The major settled on John B. Tays, an honest man, albeit someone who knew considerably more about digging wells than law enforcement. Jones likely made his choice because he knew Tays's brother, an Episcopal priest who had been chaplain of the state Senate before moving to El Paso County. Too late, the major would realize that he should have ordered one of his key officers to El Paso along with some of his veteran rangers, men who had experience and no stake in the feud.[4] "A company of rangers has been recruited and everything is quiet now," local merchant Ernst Kohlberg wrote his family from Franklin on November 12. "When you read about trouble on the border, always discount the stories by one-half."[5]

On November 16, Howard returned to Texas from Mesilla and surrendered to Jones on the charge of killing Cardis. The major took him before a magistrate, who set his bond at $4,000. Several of his friends having signed as sureties, Howard remained free on bond pending trial. The lawyer felt confident he could prove self-defense, easily winning acquittal.

Ten days later, having left Tays with detailed written instructions on how to run a Ranger company, Jones wired Steele, "The mob has disbanded and promised to submit to law. Lieutenant Tays and 20 men stationed here. I leave for Austin today via Coleman and Kemble [Kimble County.]"[6]

Led by Chico Barela and egged on by Father Antonio Borajo, an avaricious Catholic priest who lived on the Mexican side of the river, a militant group determined to enforce their own law quickly coalesced. No matter the sovereignty of the state, the junta outnumbered those who sought protection under civil and criminal statutes. Still, when Howard learned that a Mexican cart train had left to gather salt at the lakes, he filed a civil suit at Ysleta to sequester the salt collected pending final resolution of the land dispute. Then, escorted by the sheriff, Tays, and ten of his rangers, Howard rode to San Elizario to see that the writ got served on the Mexicans returning with the salt.

As word of this latest development in the dispute spread, armed Mexicans began pouring into San Elizario on December 12 from both sides of the border. Some saw it as time to avenge the murder of Cardis and reassert their right to the salt. Others simply took it as an opportunity for looting. The crowd soon grew murderous.

With a pistol in his boot, Charles E. Ellis, a generally well-regarded store proprietor and miller who also functioned as the new Ranger detachment's supply agent, walked outside to reason with the mob, some five hundred men strong. But the Mexicans quickly demonstrated they did not feel like talking. A horseman tossed a lasso around Ellis's neck and dragged him down the dusty street for a while before stopping and finishing him off with a slash across his throat.

Howard soon sought shelter at the Ranger compound, a stout adobe building with an adjacent corral. Six men, including former Ranger captain Gregorio Garcia, now a private under Tays, occupied Ellis's nearby store. As a crowd began surrounding the structures, Tays posted his men in defensive positions on the roof and behind the adobe walls of the corral. At that show of resolve, the mob withdrew. But during the night, an even larger number of armed men encircled the Ranger headquarters.

On the morning of the thirteenth, John G. Atkinson, another Anglo store owner and one of the men who had gone on Howard's bond, arrived with a grim message for Tays. The captain had three hours to hand over Howard or the junta would come and get him. As Tays pondered that demand, Sergeant Charles E. Mortimer tried to go from the Ranger adobe to Ellis's store. As soon as he exposed himself, someone shot him in the back. At that, both sides opened fire. Tays managed to get Mortimer back inside, but his wound soon proved fatal.

For the rest of the day and into the next day, the besieged rangers held off the attackers, killing several with no further losses of their own. At the nearby store, Garcia managed to hold out for a time, but wounded and with his son dead, he surrendered when he ran out of ammunition. For his part, Tays kept the attackers at bay until midday on December 16, when he called for an overnight truce.[7]

In the morning, the Ranger lieutenant and Barela met to talk. The junta leader assured Tays that if Howard came out and agreed to drop his claim to the salt lakes, he would be allowed to live. If not, Barela said he would use barrels of gunpowder quietly positioned during the night to blow his way into the Ranger compound.

Back inside, Tays filled Howard in on what Barela had said. Realizing that Barela had lied about intending to spare his life, Howard knew he was a dead man either way. Tays said he would defend him at all costs, but Howard made his first unselfish decision of the whole episode. He would surrender. Perhaps hoping that the situation could still be made to end peacefully, Tays escorted Howard to Barela and his lieutenants.

Realizing he needed an interpreter, the Ranger commander sent a runner back to his headquarters for Atkinson, who had taken shelter there with the cash assets from his store. But rather than being used to translate, Atkinson ended up in a private discussion with Barela. Thinking to buy Howard's life, as well as the well-being of the rangers and probably his own neck, Atkinson offered $11,000 to assure the safety of all. The junta leader accepted the deal and dispatched Atkinson to tell the rangers that all was well and that they should come to the junta headquarters.

When the rangers showed up, the Mexicans threw down on them and took their weapons, marching the men into a corral like so many obedient burros. Though Barela may have intended to honor his agreement with Atkinson, his men demanded that Howard and McBride die. For good measure, while they were at it they would kill Atkinson. Either way, the Mexicans had $11,000 to split.

Howard faced the firing squad first, opening his shirt and bravely giving the order to fire. Unfortunately for him, the rifle rounds did not kill him outright. As he lay groaning, several Mexicans descended on him with machetes and hacked him to death.

Then came Atkinson's turn. He, too, bared his chest. In Spanish, he cursed the Mexicans for not honoring their deal, then told the firing squad to aim for his heart. Their aim either affected by the heat of the moment or hatred, they shot low, hitting Atkinson in his gut. *"Mas arriba* [higher], *cabrones,"* he cursed. Shot twice more and still not dead, he managed to point to his head. At that, the "officer" in charge of the squad stepped forward and administered the coup de grâce with a pistol.

After seeing all this, McBride died quietly, his only offense having been working for Howard. Strong sentiment existed to kill all the rangers as well, but Barela prevented any further slaughter and eventually allowed Tays and his men to ride back to Franklin—minus their weapons. Meanwhile, the Mexicans looted Ellis's and Kohlberg's stores, taking assorted merchandise, grain, and flour across the border.

Sheriff Kerber found more guns for Tays and his company, but knowing he needed more manpower in a hurry, Kerber had wired Hubbard for authority to recruit a hundred men from New Mexico to restore order. The governor quickly agreed, empowering the El Paso County lawman to raise men "at once, to resist invasion, put down insurrection, and re-enforce State troops [the Rangers.]"[8]

Seeking help from New Mexico, however logical, only aggravated the problem. Not all the men from the territory who rode to their neighbors' aid qualified as law-abiding. Some merely sought a chance to raise hell in an official capacity, which they proceeded to do. Colonel Hatch, who had come to El Paso County with troops and a mountain howitzer, soon reported that the posse from New Mexico had committed "cowardly murder" in killing two suspected mob members at Ysleta and asked authority to arrest them. Generals Philip Sheridan and John Pope ordered Hatch to use necessary force to prevent further murders, but stopped short of giving him leave to take the rowdy volunteers into custody. Both officers did urge Governor Hubbard to prosecute those responsible. An El Paso County grand jury returned dozens of indictments, including true bills naming Barela and five other suspected henchmen, but they had fled to Mexico and never faced trial.[9]

Overlooking their poor showing, Jones kept Tays's company in service. Tays continued as lieutenant until April 1878, at which time his brother the preacher took over the command. James Tays ran the Ranger company until resigning in November.

Governor Hubbard had asked for a federal probe of the role of Mexican nationals in the incidents at San Elizario. Responding to that, President Rutherford B. Hayes directed the army to investigate. Two colonels came to El Paso County in January 1878 and began taking statements. Learning that the investigation was under way with no input from the State of Texas, Hubbard on February 9 told Steele to send Jones back to El Paso. Though Hubbard had requested an inquiry into Mexico's part in the events of the previous year, Jones found that the federal officers had taken it as their duty to investigate how county and state officials had comported themselves. The major finally gained formal appointment to the investigative commission, which produced a lengthy report published by the U.S. House of Representatives later that year as *The El Paso Troubles in Texas*.[10]

Jones believed that if the army had acted earlier, all the bloodshed might have been avoided. "Not a shot would have been fired, and the trouble would have been ended," Jones wrote Steele. That lack of cooperation did nothing for the already chilly relationship between the federals and the Rangers. "We hear it stated upon good authority," the

Grant County (New Mexico) *Herald* reported, "that quite an unfriendly feeling exists between the Rangers and United States troops stationed in El Paso County."[11]

The Salt War showed that despite the power in the words *Texas Ranger*, the mystique could be ridden only so far. Reputation did not stop bullets. Ranger effectiveness depended on good men, good leadership, and good communication. The lack of effective communication between El Paso County and the state capital particularly contributed to the pedestrian results in El Paso. Nothing came of the federal investigation other than a decision to regarrison Fort Bliss, virtually abandoned at the time of the conflict.

Despite the Rangers' poor showing in El Paso, on the first day of 1878, the San Antonio *Express* looked back on what it saw as a good year for Texas:

> If there is any one thing more than another the people of Western Texas have to congratulate themselves upon in connection with the progress of the year 1877, it is the breaking up and almost entire eradication of the bands of cutthroat desperadoes that infested our section a year ago. Strong in numbers and the self-interest that banded them together, they had defied the officers of the law, and laughed at the idea of arrest and punishment for the serious crimes almost daily committed. But the rangers entered in among them . . . and now the penitentiary and jails are almost crowded with the scoundrels; most of the ringleaders have been arrested, and the others have become demoralized; they are being hunted down and driven from the country. Crime in Western Texas has been almost paralyzed.[12]

The Alamo City newspaper's sentiments aside, Texas still fell short of being a utopian paradise. The Adjutant General's Department had distributed to the Ranger companies *A List of Fugitives from Justice*, a 227-page book containing the names and descriptions of thousands of men and women wanted for crimes in the state. The book listed fugitives by county up to page 153, when another alphabetical list began. In Travis County alone, the seat of state government, authorities sought eighteen persons for murder. In addition to the county listings, the book had seven pages containing the names of 228 persons for whom the governor offered rewards. Assorted bounties for unknown murderers, stage robbers, and perpetrators of a couple of arson cases rounded out the contents. Rangers called this publication, indexed by name and county, The Book of Knaves or simply The Book.[13]

Rangers carried the fugitive list in their saddlebags, often checking suspicious persons against descriptions their well-worn copy contained. Catching criminals not only made Texas safer, with rewards ranging from $100 to $1,000 it benefited rangers financially. When a ranger heard someone had been captured or killed, he made a mark against that person's name in his book and concentrated on finding someone else.

SAM BASS "WENT TO ROBBING STAGES"

When Sergeant James B. Gillett received his copy of the fugitive list, he had it bound along with blank notebook paper into a buckled leather case. A ranger since June 1, 1875, Gillett used the blank pages to note names and descriptions of wanted persons not included in the printed book he got from headquarters. In the early spring of 1878, Gillett made this entry: "Sam Bass . . . 25 or 26 years old 5 feet 7 in high black hair dark brown eyes brown mustash [sic] large white teeth shows them when talking has very little to say."[14]

Bass may not have been much of a talker, but he had become quite a doer. Orphaned in his native Indiana, he had drifted to Texas in 1870. Living in Denton County, he did odd jobs, worked as a cowboy, and raced horses. By 1876, as he later said, he "went to robbing stages." On September 18, 1877, Bass took up train robbery as well. In Big Springs, Nebraska, he and Joe Collins hit a Union Pacific train, escaping with $60,000 in gold.[15]

Though Bass managed to get back to Texas by November, he had been charged in the Big Springs robbery. At the behest of Nebraska authorities, Governor Hubbard issued an arrest warrant in his name. By December, the Rangers had picked up Bass's trail in San Antonio, where he had been living it up on what he had left of his share of the freshly minted gold dollars taken from the Union Pacific express car.

Bass succeeded in getting out of San Antonio and returned to more familiar territory in Denton County. Soon, he resumed his new avocation, introducing Texas to train robbery. On February 22, 1878, he and five colleagues held up a Houston & Texas Central passenger train at

Allen Station, about twenty-five miles north of Dallas. The gunmen escaped with between $1,200 and $1,600 in the first successful rail holdup in the state's history. Not one to rest on his laurels, the young outlaw and his gang struck again on March 18 (Hutchins, $616.80) and once more on April 4 (Eagle Ford, $233.95).[16]

After the second robbery, authorities suspected Bass. Scores of local peace officers, railroad agents, and private detectives, well aware of the price on Bass's head for the Nebraska robbery and a standing reward for the capture of the North Texas train robbers, began beating the brush for Bass and his accomplices.

"Detectives can do no more," the Dallas *Commercial* editorialized on April 9, "for they have traced the robbers to their hiding place, and can almost name the guilty parties. The local authorities are powerless to capture the robbers, therefore the matter should at once be taken in hand by our State authorities and a sufficient force should be sent into Denton to arrest the guilty parties or drive them out of the country."[17]

Plainly not preoccupied with the prospect of their capture, the Bass gang struck again on April 10, hitting a Texas & Pacific train at the depot in Mesquite. This time the robbery degenerated into a shoot-out with the train crew. Conductor Jules Alvord suffered a serious wound, and two of the robbers sustained flesh wounds. For all the zinging lead and gun smoke, the robbers netted only $162.50.[18]

The Dallas newspaper had been correct in its assessment that it would take help from the state to end the robberies. When word of the latest holdup reached Austin the next morning, Governor Hubbard increased the reward for each train robber to $1,000. The adjutant general, in turn, ordered Jones to Dallas by rail. Instructions, he said, would arrive via letter. With the concurrence of Hubbard, Steele wrote Jones on April 12 authorizing him to muster thirty rangers—their specific charge being the capture of the train robbers—for one month's service. The same day, not yet aware of Steele's actions, the Dallas *Daily Herald* criticized the administration for not sending Rangers.[19]

Reaching Dallas on April 15, Jones began raising the new unit, which would go on the battalion's muster rolls as a detachment of Company B. Realizing some aspects of state business had no place in the public prints, the major told the newspapers he had come to Dallas to obtain supplies for rangers in Coleman.[20]

Jones wrote Steele the following day asking that Junius Peak be named second lieutenant in command of the new company. Jones presented his brief: "He has been raised here, is very popular, is regarded as a terror to evil doers, is a man of fine courage, active, energetic, and efficient in arresting violators of the law." Hubbard made the appointment a day later, and Peak began raising men.[21]

The Bass furor verged on hysteria. Steele pulled Captain Roberts's company in from the frontier to Burnet County, closer to Austin, and ordered Captain Coldwell to dispatch five men to the capital for fear that Bass and his boys might make a raid on the $1 million in cash and coin on hand in the state treasury.[22]

Carrying arrest warrants for Bass, Seaborn Barnes, Frank Jackson, Henry Underwood, and "Arkansas" Johnson, Peak and his rangers scoured North Texas for the suspected train robbers. On April 29, rangers and a posse led by Denton County sheriff William F. Egan had a long-range, but short-lived gunfight with Bass after jumping him in a rural area of the county. The outlaw escaped, and the hunt continued.

More than a hundred miles to the east, on May 1 a federal grand jury in Tyler returned indictments against Bass and seven associates for mail robbery in connection with the April 10 holdup. The jurors named eight other men accessories. Two days later, a ranger and the sheriff of Grayson County arrested two of the alleged accessories, Henderson Murphy and his son Jim. Officers quickly transported both men to Tyler.[23]

Henderson Murphy, a pioneer Denton County resident, had no meaningful connection to Bass. But his two boys, Jim and Bob, had helped the outlaw convert some of his stolen gold into more easily spent cash. Son Jim, feeling bad about his father's arrest, approached Peak and a deputy U.S. marshal with a proposition: If they could get the charge against his father dismissed, he would throw in with the Bass gang and provide information to get them captured. Peak told Jones of the offer, and then the two of them met with the federal officer to talk it over. That led to an agreement drawn on May 21 by the U.S. attorney stipulating that if Murphy proved instrumental in the arrest of Bass and the other robbery suspects, the charges against him and his father would be dismissed. Brother Bob had no part in the deal.[24]

Bass, meanwhile, realized that he had to get out of Denton County. He could have gone north to Indian Territory, but he chose to ride to the southwest, passing through Tarrant and Parker counties into Stephens County.

On May 28, nineteen "gallant Rangers from Shackleford County . . . armed to the teeth" and other officers thought they had the Bass gang cornered in Stephens County. A correspondent for the Fort Worth *Daily Democrat* expressed the sentiment of Sergeant Jack Smith: "[He] stated that if they could find them, they would capture the robbers dead or alive, if they lost half of their men in the attempt."[25] But as one newspaperman put it a couple of years later, Bass "escaped his pursuers and outgeneraled them in the cedar brakes and rocky hollows of the mountains."[26]

The state had an intense interest in Bass and his accomplices, but the Rangers still had to live with fiscal realities. Their thirty-day enlistment expired, sixteen of Peak's rangers had been discharged on May 17. Jones said the remaining fourteen men could continue looking for Bass. The following day, the major also had to discharge the lieutenant in command of Company B and most of his men, leaving only five men under a sergeant.[27] Spurred by a sense of duty reinforced by the possibility of collecting a sizable reward, the Company B rangers stayed on the trail in Stephens County until it became clear that Bass had eluded them.

Peak, promoted to captain as of June 1, had better luck. Eleven days later, he caught up with the Bass gang on Salt Creek in Wise County. Both sides immediately started shooting. One of the outlaws, "Arkansas" Johnson, began concentrating his fire on Sergeant Thomas A. Floyd. In addition to being a member of Peak's specially raised company, Floyd periodically donned the uniform of the Stonewall Greys, a state militia company in Dallas. An excellent shot, Floyd quickly dismounted, dropped to one knee, and took careful aim at Johnson. When Floyd squeezed the trigger of his Winchester, "Johnson sprang into the air a corpse, a rifle ball through his heart."[28] Seeing their cohort go down, the other outlaws scattered into the brush like so many quail and got away.

Inside seven weeks, with Johnson's death and the flight of three others, Bass's gang had decreased to three members—himself, Barnes, and Jackson. The trio, lately joined by casual-friend-turned-informant Murphy, began drifting south. With Peak and his rangers camped in Dallas County, Jones awaited further intelligence in Austin.

Sitting in the adjutant general's office in the Capitol on July 17, Jones opened a letter from Murphy. Twenty-nine hastily scrawled words told the major what he had been waiting for: "We are at Georgetown on our way to Round Rock to rob the bank, the railroad or to get killed, so for God's sake be there to prevent it." Jones had only three rangers in Austin—Richard C. "Dick" Ware, Chris Conner, and George Herold—but they soon loped their horses north on the road to the small Williamson County community where Murphy said Bass intended to strike.

The nearest additional rangers, Lieutenant Reynolds's company, had last reported to headquarters from Lampasas, seventy miles northwest of the capital. With no telegraph service there, the major dispatched Corporal Vernon Coke Wilson, his clerk and the nephew of former Governor Coke, to ride with orders for Reynolds to leave immediately for Round Rock. The young ranger killed a horse getting to Lampasas, only to find that Reynolds had moved farther northwest to San Saba County. Wilson caught the next stage for San Saba, finally reaching the Ranger's pecan-shaded camp at dinnertime on July 18. Reynolds, who had not been feeling well, ordered an eight-man squad under Sergeant Charles L. Nevill to leave immediately. The lieutenant and Wilson would follow in a hack, leading the company's pack mules.

"We left our camp on the San Saba River just at sunset and traveled in a fast trot and sometimes in a lope the entire night," Ranger Gillett recalled. "Jack Martin, then in the mercantile business at the little town of Senterfitt, heard us pass by in the night, and next morning said to some of his customers that hell was to pay somewhere."

Meanwhile, Jones had taken the International and Great Northern to join his three-man detail in Round Rock. Maurice B. Moore, a Travis County sheriff's deputy and former ranger, accompanied the major on the short trip. When Jones and Moore stepped off the train, the major found his men and told them to lie low. He wanted to take Bass and company when they struck whatever target they had decided to rob.[29]

Back in Austin, on July 19 Steele pulled newly elected sergeant at arms Lee Hall from the state Democratic convention then in session and ordered the captain to proceed to Round Rock and report to Jones. Hall left as soon as he, Lieutenant Armstrong, and two of their rangers could get their horses saddled and cinched. Leaving his men to make camp three miles from Round Rock, Hall rode into town alone that afternoon.

"I found . . . Major Jones at the hotel in conference with Williamson County [deputy] sheriff [A. W.] Grimes . . . and . . . Moore," Hall recalled. "Grimes and Moore were instructed by Jones and myself simply to go down the street and remain on the *qui vive,* and that if they saw any suspicious characters to come and report to us. As they left the room Major Jones left also to go down to the telegraph office."

Tired from the hard ride from the capital city, Hall got a room, took off his boots, and lay down for a nap.

"It couldn't have been longer than fifteen minutes before . . . shooting began," Hall continued. "I jumped up, pulled on my boots, grabbed my Winchester and ran down in the street. As I got down I met people rushing away from the fighting."

Reaching Henry Koppel's Store on Main Street, the captain saw Deputy Grimes waver and fall on his face outside the stone building. "Moore staggered up against the wall on the outside and fell," Hall said.

Ranger Ware had been sitting in a barber chair, getting a shave, when he heard the gunfire. Not bothering to wipe the lather off his face, Ware pulled his pistol and ran down the street toward the shooting. As he approached, Bass, Barnes, and Jackson opened up on him and Ware returned their fire. The ranger did not yet know for sure whom he was shooting at, but it made no difference at this point. For a few moments, he faced the trio alone, one of their bullets striking a nearby hitching post and sending cedar splinters flying toward his face.

"I saw . . . three men shooting," Hall recalled. "There was considerable smoke and I could not tell one man from another."

Hall held his fire until he had a better target, but by now Jones, Herold, and Conner had reached the scene and started shooting at the smoke-shrouded outlaw trio as they ran for their horses. Laying the barrel of his carbine across a fence to steady his aim, one ranger dropped Barnes in midstride, a bullet in his head. As Bass and Jackson continued to fire their pistols at the state officers, a puff of dust rose off Bass's britches as a ranger bullet tore into his gunbelt just above his right hip. Clutching the bleeding wound, the outlaw kept running until he reached his horse. Somehow, despite all the lead in the air, Jackson unhitched Bass's steed and helped his friend onto his saddle. All the while he continued to fire at the rangers.[30]

Young T. J. William witnessed the shooting from a couple of blocks down the street.

"I . . . saw the two men, Bass and his pal, fleeing north at full speed," he remembered. "Bass, very badly wounded, could scarcely keep in his saddle and held one hand high over his head. One finger on that hand had almost been severed by a bullet."[31]

A short time later, Lieutenant Reynolds and his company rode into town after their forced march from San Saba. Despite their jaded mounts, they immediately took up Bass and Jackson's trail, easily following the fresh blood on the ground for about six miles. The rangers found a bloody glove with a bullet hole in it along with its clean mate, but not the two men. The exhausted officers hunted until dark without success, then returned to Round Rock. There they learned that Grimes, a former ranger whose brother still served in a Frontier Battalion company operating along the border, had died when he and Moore confronted Bass and his cohorts after noticing the men seemed to be carrying pistols. Moore, shot through one of his lungs, still clung to life.

Resuming their search early Saturday morning, July 20, nine rangers and Williamson County deputy James Tucker soon rode up on a man sitting under a big live oak near an old man's rural shanty. Drawing his pistol, Sergeant Nevill ordered him to put up his hands.

"Don't shoot, I am unarmed," the man said. "I am the man you are looking for. I am Sam Bass."

Too badly hurt to flee, Bass had urged Jackson to leave him behind, which his colleague had reluctantly done. Seeing that Bass posed no further threat, Nevill sent a ranger to Round Rock for a wagon and a doctor. While they waited, the ranger and Tucker pressed the outlaw for details. Bass said he had run out of money and "was after a raise."

"When the doctor arrived," Nevill recalled, "he told Bass he couldn't live more than a few hours. Bass ridiculed the idea." Back in Round Rock, the rangers placed the outlaw on a cot outside the Hart House, the town's best hotel.[32]

"He was what the world calls handsome," one newspaper reported, "a man who naturally looked a leader to his fellows; one whom any woman might adore." The story continued, "He breathed heavily, and a subdued groan occasionally escaped his lips. Standing near the cot, and with deep interest regarding its occupant . . . stood Major John B. Jones, the commander of the Texas Rangers, and the High Sheriff of Williamson County. But no woman, no friend of the wounded man, was near."[33]

Dr. C. P. Cochran tried to make the captured outlaw comfortable, but the physician told Jones that Bass, with one of his kidneys destroyed and his intestines perforated by a bullet, had no hope for recovery. Jones, meanwhile, pressed the wounded robber-turned-killer to tell him more about his activities and cronies.

"I tried every conceivable plan . . . but to no purpose," the major later reported.

> About noon on Sunday [July 21], he began to suffer greatly and sent for me to know if I could not give him some relief. I did everything I could for him. Thinking this an excellent opportunity, I said to him, "Bass, you have done much wrong in this world, you now have an opportunity to do some good before you die by giving some information which will lead to the vindication of that justice which you have so often defied and the law which you have constantly violated."
>
> He replied, "No, I won't tell."
>
> "Why won't you?" said I.
>
> "Because it is agin my profession to blow on my pals. If a man knows anything, he ought to die with it in him."[34]

Which is what happened, at about 4:20 that afternoon.

"Sam Bass at least died game," the Lampasas *Daily Times* reported, "and cheated the gallows. This thought must have been some consolation to him as he lay dying, looking at the carpenters who were making his coffin."[35]

Later that year, Adjutant General Steele summarized a book-length episode in two short paragraphs, the second of which concluded, "It is due to Major Jones to say that he obtained the first clue to the robberies, and followed it up until the killing of the leader. . . . During the period in which the hunt was going on it was often frustrated by the ill-timed haste of private detectives and others anxious to get rewards." Afterward, Jones wrote railroads seeking the reward money. He gave Grimes's young widow the outlaw's horse.[36]

John Wesley Hardin, the man behind bars at the state prison in Huntsville for the murder of a former ranger, had earned his outlaw status, but Bass, not Hardin, soon became a Texas folk figure. Only a few months after Bass's death, railroad news butches walked through passenger cars peddling a sensationalist account of the outlaw's career and death at the hands of the Rangers. Bass had been "Robin Hood-ized."[37]

Despite the favorable publicity resulting from the killing of Bass and Barnes by the Rangers, Steele wanted to make sure that Texas lawmakers understood the effectiveness of the Frontier Battalion. His next biennial report contained fourteen letters from county judges and sheriffs written in support of the force. While not rich in particulars, the document summarized Ranger activity for the fiscal year ending August 31, 1878. Rangers had arrested 1,122 people, including 207 for murder or assault to kill. The men had saddled up twenty-eight times to follow Indian trials and made 916 scouts looking for felons and miscreants. In doing so, the state lawmen killed or wounded twenty-eight while losing five of their own with two wounded.[38]

In addition to corralling wanted felons and shooting it out with anyone resisting arrest, the Rangers had brought a measure of stability to the state's judicial system. Company E visited Menard six times between September 1877 and December 1878 to stand by during court proceedings to make sure no group tried to interfere. Establishing camp in Burnet County in May 1878, Lieutenant Reynolds noted in his report to Austin, "Guarding court in Llano." On June 1, the company moved to San Saba for district-court guard duty.[39]

The Ranger image affected more than law and order. Not long after R. G. Kimbell hit Texas from his native Tennessee that late summer of 1878, he met an East Texas girl that "beat the Belle of Tennessee." One night, sitting in her yard under a big moon, he asked her if she would marry him.

As Kimbell later recalled:

She told me that there was another contender, who had said he loved her well enough to die for her, and so I answered that that could then be easily solved—just let him die for her, and I would live for her and we would all be happy. She said on one condition only, would she consent, and that was that if I would agree to prove my love and loyalty to her and to Texas, by joining the Ranger Service, and serving three years, and bring back an honorable discharge. We closed the deal, and I left her that night and was sworn into the service in a few days.[40]

In January 1879, after five years service, Steele stepped down as adjutant general. Newly inaugurated governor Oran Roberts quickly appointed Jones as his replacement. In his first general order as adjutant general, Jones on February 8 instructed company commanders to direct their correspondence and reports to him. Jones did not intend to replace himself with another Frontier Battalion commander—he merged that job into his new position. When the legislature approved a new budget, he would at least have saved the equivalent of his old salary.

Despite the effort Steele had made to show the value of the Rangers, the Sixteenth Legislature reduced Frontier Battalion funding from $150,000 to $100,000. Senators whose districts included the western counties, along with Senator John S. "Rip" Ford, the old warhorse ranger, fought the cut. But the majority of the lawmakers apparently believed, as did at least one newspaper editorial writer, that ever-advancing settlement would take care of the frontier defense problem. "It will take little time for the counties to fill up and be able to protect themselves," one newspaper predicted.[41] Jones at least got some administrative help in the lean new budget. On May 9, General Order Number 11 named Neal Coldwell as battalion quartermaster, continuing his rank of captain.[42] Coldwell and future quartermasters would be responsible for the myriad details it took to keep a Ranger force in the field—personnel matters, payroll, supplies, and forage.

Even though he had not been present at Round Rock, Captain Peak had built a fine reputation. When he came to San Antonio on state business in May 1879, the *Express* noted that "the distinguished commander of Ranger Company B, is at the Menger Hotel." The story, the result of some scribe's daily check of hotel registers, proceeded with more praise for the captain. Though focusing on Peak's accomplishments, the item also reflected most Texans' perception of the Rangers:

> Since Captain Peak took command of the Ranger company he has kept his portion of the state in excellent order; he has hunted down robbers and murderers, driven horse and cattle thieves out of the country, utterly destroyed the business of the "road agents" and restored confidence in the minds of honest men. He has been worth millions of money to the state.[43]

"Public enemies of the Texas people"

After completing his business in San Antonio, Peak returned to West Texas. Since the end of the Red River War, the Comanches and Kiowas had been confined to their reservations near Fort Sill in Indian Territory. But Peak's rangers still scouted for Indians. Having forced those tribes into submission, the U.S. military now had to keep them on the reservation. Though the government hoped to convert the Indians to Christianity, educate their children, and "induce [them] to labor in civilized pursuits,"[44] Uncle Sam did not expect them to surrender all aspects of their culture, and that continued to cause problems for Texas.

In a legislative message on February 10, 1879, Governor Roberts proposed passage of a law "making it a felony for . . . Indians, and all those cooperating with them, or having them in charge under pretense of hunting, to come and be found within the limits of this State, with such heavy penalties as will probably keep them out of it in the future." Indians, the governor continued, "are public enemies of the Texas people, whenever they are found within the limits of the State."[45]

In early June, Fort Sill Indian agent P. B. Hunt granted Black Horse, a Comanche subchief, a fifteen-day leave of absence from the reservation to go buffalo hunting. With supplies and arms furnished by the federal government, Black Horse led twenty-five warriors into Texas.

"Like his white brother, the Indian was prone [at] the slightest temptation to drop back into forbidden paths," Captain Peak later observed. "Black Horse cared much less for shooting buffaloes than he did for wiping out some old scores with the settlers of Texas, and now that he was well armed he could not resist the temptation."

Black Horse knew that if he did not return to the reservation within his allotted time, cavalry would be sent on his trail to escort him back. But the chief had a plan. He stayed in Texas, believing that by claiming poor hunting he could talk the military into granting an extension to his time off the reservation. When a detachment of federal troops found him camped at Double Lakes, a pair of playas on the south plains north of the future town of Big Spring, Black Horse not only gained additional time to hunt, the soldiers gave him more supplies and ammunition.[46]

When Army captain Nicholas Nolan left the rendezvous point to return to Fort Concho in Tom Green County, the Comanches stealthily back-trailed him toward the settlements.

Captain Peak received word on June 29 that a party of Comanches had been detected headed toward populated areas, not the buffalo range. At nine o'clock that night, Corporal Y. Douglass and six rangers left Company B's camp on the Concho near present Paint Rock to scout for Indians. If they did not find any Indian sign, Peak told them, they should scout for water sources.

Along on the scout was blue-eyed, mustachioed W. B. Anglin, a twenty-five-year-old Virginian from a prominent family. Well educated, he had been a ranger for three years. He showed his fellow rangers cartes de visite of his four pretty sisters and read them their letters, a welcome pasttime to men sitting around camp out in the middle of nowhere. "The mother and sisters were always urging him to come home, saying they needed him badly," one of Anglin's friends recalled. "I tried to get him to go to them, but he would put off going."[47]

About a day's ride northwest of Fort Concho, Douglass learned from a rancher that Indians had stolen and killed some horses. The corporal soon cut the Comanches' trail and followed it to their camp. Hoping to prevent their escape, the ranger decided to capture the Indians' horses before attacking.

The corporal quickly discovered that the old chief had him outnumbered, outgunned, and to some extent, outsmarted. Though the Texans did succeed in driving off eight Indian ponies, two rangers had their horses shot from under them and they lost the pack mules burdened with their supplies. Too, the Indians had wounded the horse ridden by the rancher who had accompanied the detachment. Before the rangers could encircle the Indian camp, Black Horse wisely moved to a higher, more defensible position. Assessing the chief's sound tactical move, the corporal decided to pull back for the night.

Black Horse wanted his horses back. The Comanches attacked the Ranger camp during the night, but the seven rangers and a single civilian riding with them held off the Indians. Rebuffed, Black Horse decided to cut his losses and shake the tenacious Texans.

The next morning, the rangers again took up the Comanches' trail. For several days, they followed the raiders from water hole to water hole, covering more than a hundred hot miles of semidesert. Despite the hardships, the men stayed in good humor, particularly the soft-spoken Anglin, "clean in his talk [and] always jolly." On July 1, approaching a reed-ringed buffalo wallow in what is now Midland County, the rangers spotted their two missing pack mules grazing nearby. Correctly wary of sending all of his men to investigate, Douglass split his men, ordering some to approach the small lake head-on and the others to circle around to the other side.

Known for his bravery, Anglin spurred his horse and reached the water hole first, riding straight into a trap. The experienced chief had used the mules to lure the Texans into the open. A volley of rifle fire from Indians hidden in the high vegetation at the edge of the small lake killed Anglin's horse and wounded him. The young ranger disentangled himself from his dead horse, drew his pistol, and got off a shot toward the reeds before a second round of gunfire killed him. The other rangers poured fire into the reeds, but they only occasionally had a visible target. Most of the time the Comanches fired from concealment.

With one ranger already dead and a second horse down, Douglass had no real option other than to pull back. Leaving Anglin where he fell, the rangers turned east for a hard ride back to the Company B camp on the Concho. On the way, the saddle-weary rangers met up with Captain Nolan and his blue-trousered troopers. The corporal ordered two of his men to lead a detail of soldiers under Lieutenant C. R. Ward to the scene of the fight to tend to Anglin's burial, then left with the rest of his detachment to report to Captain Peak.

When the soldiers reached the ambush site, they could read from their tracks that the Indians had left in the direction of their reservation. The rangers wrapped their dead comrade in a saddle blanket and buried him where he died.[48] "I have but little idea that his mother and sisters ever knew what became of him," Anglin's former messmate later declared.

After Peak's report reached Austin, Governor Roberts complained to the federal government about the Comanches' sanctioned incursion to Texas, but nothing came of it. Back on the reservation, Black Horse voiced his own complaint that the Rangers had attacked him without cause.

Beyond the conflicting viewpoints, the incident had a greater significance than anyone realized at the time. Anglin would be the last ranger to die fighting Indians, and Company B's brush with Black Horse marked the final engagement between the Texas Rangers and the Comanches.

Corporal Douglass's scout had not been the Frontier Battalion's finest operation, but the outnumbered rangers had kept Black Horse from reaching the more settled section of the frontier. The long war between Texas and the Comanches had finally ended, but the Rangers hardly had time to notice.

12

"Assist Civil Authorities"

THE FRONTIER BATTALION, 1879–86

When the Rangers came to the Panhandle, Rufe LeFors wanted to join up. The state officers made camp across a creek from his father's land, about a half mile from their ranch headquarters in Crosby County.

"They . . . dug back in a steep clay hill and made them three rather large dug-outs," LeFors recalled, "and lined them on the inside with canvass, and leveled the floor, and packed it down until the floor was hard, then put rugs down . . . , so it looked nice and was very comfortable. Then Capt. [George Washington] Arrington had a smaller dug-out made and fixed up nice for his office."

LeFors tried to enlist in Arrington's company, but the youngster had not had enough birthdays. The captain, a guerrilla fighter in the Civil War who had found it expedient to change his name when he came to Texas, said a ranger had to be at least twenty-one, not twenty.[1]

Arrington had first scouted the High Plains the year before, leaving his camp near Fort Griffin on the Clear Fork of the Brazos in late June. "With his command of twenty-odd men, carrying 40 days' rations," the Fort Griffin *Frontier Echo* reported on July 6, 1879, he had orders to travel

to Sweetwater [Fort Elliott] and assist civil authorities in keeping the peace.

From [Sweetwater] he will make a scout down the foot of the
plains to Blanco Canyon, looking for Indians and desperadoes. The
command will be gone . . . about two months, and the probabilities
are, soon after his return here, they will move camp one hundred or
more miles in a northwest direction. If Captain Arrington should
run across the Indians who are depredating in the state, there will be
hair liftin' for certain.[2]

Arrington returned to Fort Griffin on September 6, 1879, but soon
departed to set up a semipermanent camp at the mouth of Blanco
Canyon in Floyd County, then unorganized. The rangers named their
outpost Camp Roberts in honor of the governor. With Fort Elliott between them and the Indian reservations, and Rangers on scout as well,
ranchers began moving cattle onto land still fertile with buffalo dung.
After Arrington came to the Panhandle, LeFors wrote, "We were not
bothered with Indians any more."[3]

Five years after the creation of the Frontier Battalion, Texas had begun projecting its authority into the last two undeveloped areas of the
state—the Panhandle and the arid, mountainous country west of the
Pecos. The Comanches and Kiowas no longer posed a threat, but in
what Governor Roberts called "that far, wild country," bands of
Apaches still raided occasionally from their reservation at Fort Stanton,
New Mexico.[4] For the most part, the Rangers served as a mounted police force available to back up county sheriffs or to keep the peace in
named but unorganized counties. Indeed, an incident that occurred on
Arrington's first sortie into the Panhandle typified a growing Ranger attitude that when the Frontier Battalion stepped into a situation, they
stood as The Law, no matter the wording of statutes or federal treaties.

The captain and his men still sipped their morning coffee when a
cowboy rode into camp to report that he had seen a party of twenty
Pueblo Indians riding east along the North Fork of the Red River, leading more than a dozen burros loaded with packs. Arrington concluded
the New Mexican Indians must be headed for the Comanche reservation, further supposing their packs held contraband of some sort, possibly weapons.

"The order to saddle was immediately given and in a few minutes the
Rangers were all mounted," LeFors wrote. "Then Cap. Arington [sic]
taken the lead, rode in a fast gallop with the Rangers, two in abrest [sic],

close behind. Cap. Arington wanted to be sure we would over take them before the Indians reached the line of the Indian Territory."

The breaks of the Red River made for rough riding. The rangers trailed the Pueblos nearly all the way to Fort Elliott before catching up with them. As his men surrounded the caravan, Arrington ordered his lieutenant and several privates to check the contents of the Indians' packs. As the captain had suspected, they contained weapons—old needle guns and Sharps rifles.

Intending to escort them back to his camp, Arrington told the Indians to mount up. They had not ridden far when a government scout from the fort appeared. He asked the captain what he planned to do with the Indians, and Arrington said, as LeFors later recalled, that he would "deal with them as he saw proper." At that, the scout urged his horse around, making tracks for Fort Elliott in a cloud of dust.

The rangers had ridden another half dozen miles when a company of cavalry appeared, riding at a gallop in their direction. Seeing it as an attack, Arrington ordered his rangers to dismount and take cover behind their horses. Each ranger pulled his Winchester from its brush-scarred scabbard, wrapped his horse's reins in his left arm, and turned his mount to its right.

The captain walked his horse about ten yards in front of the line, his rifle in his hands. About a hundred yards out, the soldiers slowed. When Arrington raised his lever-action in his right hand, the troopers took it as a directive to stop and they did. At that, Arrington turned his horse and rejoined his men. The state men watched quietly as the ranking cavalry officer trotted to within about twenty feet of them.

"What right have you and your Rangers to take into custody Indians, wards of the government," LeFors remembered the cavalryman saying.

"These are Pueblo Indians," Arrington said, "and are not wards of the government, and are caught taking arms and ammunition in to your bloody Comanches."

"All Indians are under the jurisdiction of the government," the federal officer snapped, "and I demand the immediate surrender of them to the government or I will have to take them by force."

LeFors did not try to reconstruct what Arrington said next, but remembered the gist of it: If the soldiers thought they could take the Pueblos by force, they should go ahead and try. If the soldiers came ten feet closer, the captain added, he would order his men to fire. The Civil

War had been over fifteen years, but Arrington still had little use for Yankees. The army officer could see the hammers pulled back on the rangers' rifles, which the Texans held leveled at his troopers. He studied Arrington's men a few moments longer, then yanked his mount's reins to the side and rode back to his company. After a brief discussion with his men, the soldiers turned and rode back toward the fort.

Arrington escorted the Pueblos to his camp and had them unload the weapons and ammunition. Letting them keep their food and other provisions, he told the Indians to get out of Texas and not come back. A party of rangers then buried the old guns and ammunition.[5]

The incident on the High Plains led to a lively correspondence among the commander of Fort Elliott, the War Department, and Austin, but the cantankerous Ranger captain kept his job. His strong states' rights attitude aside, Arrington's greatest contribution came in exploring this newly opened section of Texas. He provided escorts for surveying parties and, on his long scouts, noted geographic features and located new water sources.

Arrington's most spectacular scout began on December 29, 1879, when he and eleven of his men took the trail of a band of Apaches who had stolen horses from the Slaughter Ranch. For a time the tracks led the rangers south, across Yellow House Canyon near present Lubbock, then up the Caprock and to the west. On the morning of their third day in the field, as Arrington later reported, "I discovered that the trail led off directly west from Double Lakes and into a country that was, at that time, utterly unknown to white man."

The rangers alternately battled cold, thirst, and hunger, moving farther west into the desolate sand dunes of New Mexico. "The sands lay in waves," former ranger James B. Gibson, then an El Paso policeman, recalled more than a half century later, "white almost as snow—most complete picture of desolation I had ever beheld."[6]

Continuing westward, late one day the rangers found an oasis, a lake in the middle of the desert. "We camped at this lake that night, christened it Ranger Lake, and remained there the following day," Arrington later wrote. From all the Indian sign they found, they realized the place had great significance for Indians, a staging area for raids into Texas. The following day, Arrington pressed his command onward, traveling another eighteen to twenty miles before finding a series of four small lakes and more Indian sign.[7]

"We were now in a hostile Indian country with at least 250 miles of desert and plains country between us and our headquarters," Arrington wrote. "Our supplies were running low and our horses were weak, besides I knew from the course and rate we had traveled coming in that we were far beyond the boundary line of Texas, which line was the limit of our jurisdiction. Hence I decided not to follow the trail any further."

The rangers back-trailed themselves, camping for fifteen days at the lake they had named in their honor. Arrington sent three of his men to replenish their shrinking larder with fresh antelope meat, but he dared not expend much ammunition on food. With Indians clearly in the vicinity, the captain knew he could not afford to waste bullets. On January 21, 1880, they left their honor lakeside camp to return to Texas.[8]

By the time they arrived at Camp Roberts on February 6, the rangers had traveled nearly six hundred miles. "We reached headquarters just forty days after leaving there. We had been given up as lost. We had penetrated a vast region never before entered by whites. We had discovered the hiding places of the raiding Indians, causing them to move farther west. Few men, in my opinion, have suffered more than we did on this campaign and lived," Gibson later told an El Paso newspaper writer, using about the same language his old captain had used in describing the expedition.[9]

Reading a newspaper account of Arrington's expedition, Lieutenant Colonel John T. Hatch, commander of Fort Sill, wrote Austin on February 10 asking for "a description of the route taken . . . and if he returned by another route, a description of that also." Referring to Arrington's lake discovery, Hatch wrote, "We have known for some time that there was such a lake, but the great distance from this post has prevented our sending a force to locate it. . . . It is claimed by the Indians that it can only be reached by a march of two days without water."[10]

From another dry corner of Texas, Presidio County attorney John M. Dean wrote Adjutant General Jones on May 21, 1880, asking for rangers. His concern could be summarized in two words: Jesse Evans, leader of a gang of outlaws who figured in New Mexico's Lincoln County War. Evans and one of his cohorts had spent some time behind bars at Fort Stockton in August 1879, but the outlaw had since been released. A Pecos County grand jury indicted him on two counts of assault with intent to murder, but Evans got off with a $5 fine.

Since getting out of jail on April 28, Evans and his fellows had been terrorizing the county. Barely three weeks later, he and four associates robbed a store in the Presidio County town adjacent to Fort Davis, a cavalry post at the mouth of rocky Limpia Canyon. The holdup netted big money—more than $900. By the third week in May local authorities realized they could not handle Evans and his followers.

Jones dispatched a sergeant from the Ranger camp at Ysleta and had Captain Roberts send Sergeant Ed Sieker and nine rangers to Fort Stockton from their camp near Menard. The detail reached the Pecos County seat on June 6—in time to prevent the only jailed member of Evans's gang from being sprung by his colleagues—and moved on with the prisoner to Fort Davis, arriving there June 18.

Near the end of the month, the rangers learned that the Evans gang had been seen on the road leading south to Presidio. Hiring a guide who knew the country, the two Ranger sergeants and four of their men set out after the outlaws. They caught up with them in the Chinati Mountains on July 3, and as Jones later summarized in his report for the year, "a sharp fight ensued." When the shooting stopped, one outlaw and one ranger, George R. Bingham, lay dead, but Evans and two others had been captured.[11]

Most rangers survived their Frontier Battalion career, but the force experienced a high turnover, even among the officers. At their camp at Hackberry Springs in Mitchell County, the rangers of Company B on April 10 unanimously approved a resolution honoring Captain Peak, who had resigned his commission to return to Dallas to work for his father. The document, set down by First Sergeant Ed Hageman, amounted to a codification of the qualities the men themselves believed it took to be a ranger:

> He has performed every duty to the State with promptness and fidelity . . . he has shared with us every hardship and danger, fearlessly and unhesitatingly. In the camp and on the field he has always been prompted by a stern sense of duty, ever ready, ever willing; that he was ever courteous, polite and gentlemanly; ever eager and bold, keen and quiet, urgent and energetic; never daunted, never uncertain, fearless in all things.

The sergeant sent copies of the company resolution to Peak, the adjutant general, and the Galveston *Daily News*.[12]

Riding as a ranger sounded romantic, but it amounted more to boredom interspersed with occasional periods of hard work and even rarer instances of danger. On December 14, 1880, from Camp Musquez near Fort Davis, William Hickman Dunman wrote his niece:

> There has been a great deal of work here but it is over now. The smugglers I spoke of [in a previous letter to his father] . . . we have captured, five of them in number with fifteen mules and horses with 50 boxes of cigars, 3 guns, 2 sixshooters, 3 swords . . . 5 saddles. We did not get any money. They had passed all of it before we made the arrest.

The rangers had made the seizure a week earlier about eighty miles south of Fort Davis, riding as escorts to James A. Tays, a deputy U.S. Customs collector and brother of former ranger John B. Tays.

"There is no Indian news in the country, and I hope we will not be bothered with them soon," Dunman continued.

Shaded by a cluster of live oaks on a creek near the wagon road leading south from Fort Davis, about fourteen miles from the army garrison, the Ranger camp had been established shortly after the Evans gang cleanup. With a bolder-strewn canyon wall behind them for cover, the men lived in nine white canvas tents and two adobe dugouts with thatched roofs. Mitre Peak towered in the distance.

In addition to the pleasant scenery, the rangers also enjoyed their grub, eating better than their horses. For the first time since September, they had a full commissary.

The men may have had plenty to eat, but little to do when not on a scout. One of the rangers had a banjo, and they could always bust a few caps in target practice, but the men did not have much to hold their interest. "This is the dullest country I've ever seen," Dunman continued. "No church, no respectable dances."[13] But for the thinly stretched Ranger force, the dull times seldom lasted long.[14]

"Hoy! Estan los indios"

Residents farther west of Fort Davis would have appreciated a little dullness. In early January 1881, when the westbound stagecoach did not roll into Fort Quitman on time, a party of volunteers rode downriver to find out why. They located the stage in a narrow point in Quitman

Canyon the locals called the Apache Post Office. The name came from the ancient petroglyphs carved in the rock, artwork mistakenly believed to have been done by Apaches. When the men rode up on the stage, they expected to find its occupants slain, but the only fatality was one of the stage's two mules, dead from gunshot wounds. The searchers saw no sign of the driver and his passengers. All the canvas had been cut from the stage, and the vehicle's leather boot shredded. The mailbags had been slashed open and their contents scattered.

The riders followed pony and mule tracks for several miles, expecting at any moment to find the mutilated bodies of the stage's luckless occupants. Not seeing anything further, they turned back toward the military post to report the stage had been ambushed by Indians.

On January 16, 1881, Adjutant General Jones wired Captain George W. Baylor in Ysleta ordering him to investigate the Quitman Canyon incident. Jones authorized the captain, who had been posted near El Paso since the summer of 1879, to recruit four additional rangers and hire Pueblo scouts to pursue the stage attackers. At first, even the old Indian-fighter doubted whether Indians had attacked the stage. That the stage driver and occupants had not been found made Baylor suspicious of an inside job, or a holdup by white outlaws hoping to make their crime look like an Indian depredation.

Baylor left Ysleta with fifteen rangers and ten days' rations the day he got Jones's telegram. Reaching Fort Quitman in two days, Baylor met with the leader of the party that had found the stage. The man assured Baylor that if he rode downriver from the fort, he would cut an Indian trail sooner or later. Baylor concurred, beginning to suspect Indians after all. Twenty-five miles below the fort, the captain picked up a trail. Studying the tracks, the rangers sorted out hoof marks from two barefoot ponies, two unshod mules, and one shod mule, obviously the other mule from the stagecoach. Apaches had attacked the stagecoach, not border bandits.

The next morning, the rangers found a red glove they assumed belonged to one of the stage's occupants. Soon the tracks crossed the river into Mexico, and so did Baylor, not for the first time. In the fall of 1879, at the invitation of local Mexican authorities, he and his men had joined in the Mexican search for the Apache war chief Victorio. He had stayed in Mexico twenty days before the central government in Mexico City learned of the presence of rangers and U.S. troops in their country and ordered that they leave.[15]

Entering Mexico this time on his own hook, Baylor followed the trail to the Indians' first camp after their attack on the stage. The raiders had left behind the carcass of a jaded horse killed for meat and an old pair of moccasins. When he discovered the Indians' next camping place later that day, Baylor found a dead mule and a boot top he surmised came from the driver of the stage. Fifteen to twenty fairly fresh sets of unshod pony and mule tracks led away from the camp site.

The rangers spent a second night in Mexico. Resuming the hunt the next morning, Baylor found that the Indians had turned back into Texas. Their trail now headed north toward the Eagle Mountains. At dusk on January 28, a flock of doves flew over the rangers in the general direction of the trail they followed. Baylor knew the birds sought water, as did the Apaches. Closing in on the Indians, the Ranger captain ordered a fireless camp.

Before dawn, the rangers crawled out of their blankets into the cold. Forced to forgo coffee and food, the men moved out as quietly as they could. They had a hard time at first finding the trail, but "by stooping down with our faces close to the ground, we got the trail off, leading north, along the crest of the mountains."

As Baylor's men crept forward, leading their horses, one of the Pueblos called out in a low voice, *"Hoy! Estan los indios."*

Peering ahead in the early light, Baylor saw campfires on a hill less than a half mile away. Leaving behind five men to guard their horses, the captain and the rest of his men slipped up to within two hundred yards of the Apache party. The Indians had camped on the western side of the hill, but had one shelter on the eastern side. That enabled them to keep watch over the draw between them and the principal approach to their camp.

Baylor split his command, sending Sergeant L. B. Caruthers and seven men to cover one side, while he and newly promoted Lieutenant Charles L. Nevill, along with eleven rangers, took the other side. Using Spanish dagger plants for cover, the men moved single file to within three hundred feet of the main Indian camp. Quietly, they encircled the camp. Kneeling, the men raised their Winchesters and Springfields and "gave the astounded Indians as deliberate a volley as though they had been old veterans," Baylor wrote in his report to Jones. "We got in a second [volley] before they broke, when we charged with a Texas yell and kept it hot for them."

The few shots the Apaches got off went wild. The engagement quickly degenerated into a massacre.

"The Apaches ran like a herd of deer," Baylor continued, "making very little resistance, and each one for himself, unlike our Comanches, who will always turn at bay, no matter against what odds, when their women and children are in danger."

Typically, the body count in Baylor's fight varied with the telling. The generally accepted tally came to four men, two women, and two children. Some of Baylor's men did not like having killed women and children, but the bodies and the blood on the snow did not curb the rangers' appetites.

"We took our breakfast on the ground occupied by the Indians, which we all enjoyed, as we had eaten nothing since dinner the day before," Baylor continued in his report. "Some of the men found horse meat pretty good, while others found venison and roasted weasel good enough."

Plainly, Baylor only regretted not having killed more Indians. If he had only had five men armed with shotguns, he wrote Jones, "I don't believe a single Indian would have escaped." Still, Baylor believed his attack had "broken up a very bad band of Indians that have long depredated in this region. . . . I don't think they will sit down to eat breakfast again without looking around to see if the Rangers are in sight."

The rangers burned what Indian items they did not keep and returned to Ysleta. Lieutenant Nevill escorted the prisoners to the U.S. military at Fort Davis. No one ever found the bodies of the missing stage driver and his passengers.[16]

Baylor and his men did not realize it at the time, but the Rangers had just had their last significant Indian fight. The Frontier Battalion had engaged hostile Indians thirty-two times since 1874, two more skirmishes than the U.S. army had in Texas during the same period. Rangers killed 82 Indians, the army claiming 163 as a result of its campaigns in the state during that time frame.[17]

The military had fielded more men and horses in Texas than the state, but Texans tended to credit the Rangers, not federal soldiers, with eliminating the Indian threat. "The people here are more than ever pleased with the Rangers," Nevill wrote Quartermaster Coldwell after the Apache slaughter. "It is the remark of all that we have killed more Indians in a short time than the 10th Cavalry did all last summer."[18] Though not overtly, Nevill's statement reflected the prevailing racial prejudices of the time. In the Tenth Cavalry, black troopers, popularly called buffalo soldiers, served under white officers. Commanded by Colonel Benjamin Grierson, an officer with a distinguished Civil War record, the Tenth had soldiers at Forts Concho, Davis, and Stockton in West Texas.

Across the Concho River from Fort Concho lay Saint Angela. Despite its nonsecular name, like most army towns Saint Angela existed primarily to cater to the needs of the soldiers, particularly booze and bawds. Not that some townspeople did not have aspirations of propriety and other forms of commercial development, but the army payroll drove the local economy.

On January 31, 1881, a cowboy named Tom McCarty shot and killed one of the Tenth Cavalry's soldiers, Private William Watkins. The cowboy fled the saloon but sentries arrested him when he tried to cross the river. The military held him in the post guardhouse overnight, but in the morning post officials released McCarty to Tom Green County sheriff James D. Spears.

Even though McCarty remained in jail without bond pending trial, soldiers at the fort soon began making threats. Private Watkins had been the second black soldier killed by a white man that month in Saint Angela.

On the afternoon of February 2, a sixty-nine-word printed broadside began circulating in town. "We, the soldiers of the U.S. Army," it began, "do hereby warn the first and last time all citizens and cowboys, etc., of San Angelo and vicinity to recognize our right of way as just and peaceable men. If we do not receive justice and fair play . . . some one will suffer. . . . It has gone too far, justice or death."[19]

The trouble started when the murdered defendant's brother, who looked like McCarty, came to town. When a rumor reached the fort that McCarty had been released from jail, some forty soldiers rushed into town and fired upward of 150 rounds into a local hotel and a store. Despite the lead storm, only one person sustained a minor wound. But a mutinous military contingent had attacked a Texas community. Spurring horseflesh, a messenger left for Mitchell County with a request signed by the district judge, the district attorney, and the sheriff for help from the Rangers "as the Federal soldiers had threatened to burn and pillage the town."[20] Captain Bryan Marsh, a hard-drinking, one-armed Confederate veteran who still had no use for U.S. soldiers, particularly black ones, saddled up his company and left immediately for Tom Green County.

Arriving in Saint Angela on February 5, Marsh established headquarters at a wagon yard, ordered several of his men to protect the jail, scattered rangers strategically around town, and took the rest with him to visit Colonel Grierson. Neither the Ranger captain nor the post commander left an account of their conversation, but it must have been spirited. Jeff Milton, one of Marsh's men, later claimed that Marsh flatly told Grierson that he would kill any soldier, whatever color, who crossed the Concho into Saint Angela without a pass. Taken aback, Grierson supposedly pointed out that he had more soldiers at the fort than the captain had rangers. Marsh reportedly said that he had enough rangers to kill any soldier who did not follow his orders.

Whatever transpired between the two men, Marsh detailed his sergeant to take McCarty to the Kimble County jail in Junction. The local grand jury chose to take no action against the soldiers who had shot up the town and no further incidents occurred.[21]

While in town, the rangers posed for portraits in the studio of pioneer West Texas photographer M. C. Ragsdale. First Sergeant John W. Hoffer made the arrangements. Most of the boys donned coat and cravat for their photograph, but three opted for their regular attire. Ranger Howell Brown posed with hat on and rifle in hand. Despite the racial overtones of the incident that had occasioned the state presence in Tom Green County, the company's black teamster, Jim Werner, stood with the rangers.[22]

Three weeks later, in his monthly report to Adjutant General Jones, Marsh set down in third person the only written account of his company's recent deployment: "Soon after his arrival in town, Capt Marsh called on Col Grierson, Col commanding the Fort, for assistance to help preserve the peace, which was granted."[23] McCarty eventually stood trial in Austin for first-degree murder but a jury acquitted him.

For nearly six years, Texas had what amounted to two Ranger forces, at least on paper. McNelly and his successor, Lee Hall, had never been formally attached to the Frontier Battalion. That changed in March 1881 when the legislature reduced the battalion's $100,000 appropriation by 20 percent. With no funding provided for Hall's Special Company, its official designation, Jones folded the unit into Company F, which had been disbanded in March 1879. That put the battalion back to six companies, but its strength had dropped to 120 men, a loss of twenty-three positions.[24]

More profound change than that soon rolled across Texas at more than thirty miles an hour. Since the summer of 1880, the Texas & Pacific Railroad had been building westward from Fort Worth, laying rails toward a meeting with the eastbound tracks of the Southern Pacific. With the driving of the last spike, Texas would be connected by rail for its entire width, and the United States would have its second transcontinental railroad. The coming of the railroad affected the Rangers in two significant ways: It furthered their transformation into state police officers, and it made it easier for them to do their job by providing faster transportation for both man and horse.

Railroad interests approached the Rangers, still managed on a reactive basis, for help in dealing with the crime problems that came with the freshly laid trackage. "A very rough element numbering sometimes one or two hundred is following at our heels," wrote contractor M. D. Coleman to Captain Roberts, then approaching the end of his Ranger service.[25] With the railroad "now getting into the wild portion of the state we feel insecure without some protection," Coleman continued. Suggesting that Roberts refer the matter to the adjutant general, Coleman said he would like to have "a dozen men or so" made available to escort his construction workers as they moved westward. "We would cheerfully furnish wagons for moving the camp of the Co as the track laying progresses, and in case of disturbances in the new towns springing up in our rear, our locomotives will be at the service of the Co. when required." Colorado City in Mitchell County had quickly become one of the roughest points on the line.[26]

Seeing an opportunity to be his own boss, Ranger Dick Ware resigned to run for sheriff of the newly organized West Texas county. W. P. Patterson, a rancher who had moved to Mitchell County from Coleman in 1879, ran against him. In addition to his ranching, Patterson had an interest in the community's first newspaper, the *Courant*. He may have owned a printing press, but he still lost the election.

Later described as "a man of fine intellect, great will power, and good literary talent," Patterson's only weakness seemed to be alcohol. Honorable, "liberal to a fault," a good friend, he was not a bad man— sober. His electoral defeat, and life in general, did not seem quite so onerous immediately after the warming ingestion of whiskey. That led, however, to errors of judgment, such as the careless discharge of his pistol in town. Several stunts like that got him arrested by the Rangers.

Colorado City having no jail, those taken into custody had to be chained to a mesquite tree. Patterson enjoyed no immunity from that.

About midnight on May 17, Rangers Jeff Milton, J. M. Sedberry, and L. B. Wells heard shooting coming from near the Nip and Tuck Saloon, one of the new town's score or so drinking establishments. The three state officers hoofed it toward the boisterous watering hole. Soon they met up with Patterson and a friend. One of the rangers asked Patterson who had been shooting. Clearly in his cups, Patterson slurred that he did not know. When Sedberry requested Patterson's pistol, intending to sniff it to detect if it had recently been discharged, Patterson replied, "Damn you, you will have to go examine somebody else's pistol."

At that remark, Sedberry and Wells each grabbed one of Patterson's arms. A powerful man, Patterson shook loose from the two rangers long enough to pull the weapon in question and fire at Sedberry. The six-shooter's muzzle blast left Sedberry with powder burns, but the bullet missed. The drunk got no second chance. Milton dropped him dead with a single shot. Driven by adrenaline, poor judgment, or both, Ranger Wells added another bullet after Patterson went down.

Patterson's friends, who also constituted the county's opposing political group, railed against the rangers, and Milton in particular, inside the Nip and Tuck. The same rangers who had guarded a murder suspect from mob action in Saint Angela earlier that year now faced the potential lynching of one of their own. Ranger Milton, backed by his two colleagues, decided to take the bull by the horns and walked into the crowded, smoky saloon. Pointing his Winchester at the more outspoken member of the group, Milton threatened to send him to join his friend Patterson at the funeral parlor if he did not quit his bold talk. The three lawmen then surrendered to Sheriff Ware.

The Mitchell County rancher-editor had not been the only person shot and killed by rangers in 1881. But Patterson's death would have particular significance in the organization's history. The day after the killing, the local justice of the peace leaned toward ordering the three rangers held in jail without bond until their examining trial. Captain Marsh, however, made it clear that the magistrate's ruling would make no difference: "The boys are going to camp with me tonight whether you make their bonds or not, and they will be in court tomorrow." Agreeing with his captain, Milton said, "Hell, I'm not going to jail."

Realizing he had no real choice, the magistrate set the three rangers' bail at $1,500 each. Two local citizens quickly signed as sureties, and the state officers returned to regular duty pending grand jury action.

Adjutant General Jones, well aware of Captain Marsh's volatility, ordered Captain Roberts to Colorado City to assess the situation. Roberts wrote Jones on May 27 that Patterson had been a "drinking man and very troublesome while under the influence." As to threats of retaliation against Milton or the other rangers, some tough talk had occurred, but "I can see nothing ominous of any further serious trouble here."[27] Roberts's judgment proved correct. The only problem arose in the courtroom, where the three rangers, even though they had acted in the line of duty, would be forced to defend themselves against murder charges.

While the Colorado City–based rangers awaited their day in court, rangers stationed farther west watched the advancing railroad like an approaching thunderstorm. "I expect a great deal of trouble on the Pecos when the Railroad reaches there as it is very near the New Mexico line," Lieutenant Nevill wrote Jones from his camp in the Davis Mountains on June 27. "It is reasonable to look for trouble as a great many desperate characters from the States visit that portion of Texas. Then again the Southern Pacific Railroad will be completed at about the same time between here and the Rio Grande." Just back from a scout, Nevill had more worrisome news: "Information reached here that 'Billy, the Kid' was on the Pecos last week with about twenty men. The informer claims to know him, the statement is partially corroborated as quite a number of horses were stolen from the Government troops there last week and is supposed to have been done by the Kid."[28]

The Austin *Daily Statesman* on July 7 reprinted a San Antonio *Express* call for Rangers to be sent to "the Pecos country." A "good company of rangers" should be dispatched "to destroy the desperadoes there, or drive them from the country," the San Antonio newspaper said. The Alamo City daily made its recommendation in response to the reported activities of Billy the Kid, who the anonymous paragrapher referred to only as the "Kid." The writer concluded, "Send out the rangers."

Adjutant General Jones lay too ill to read either Nevill's report or the item in the *Express*. In Austin at four o'clock in the morning on July 19, the forty-seven-year-old Jones died of complications following the second of two operations to treat a liver abscess. The next day's *Statesman* carried a lengthy obituary, concluding that Jones "was distinguished for his gentlemanly, unassuming address, and . . . possessed to a marked degree all the attributes that ennoble and ornament the life of a true man."

The same edition of the capital city newspaper noted in a brief page-one story that a coroner's jury in New Mexico had returned a ruling of justifiable homicide in another death, that of "Billy the kid." The young outlaw had occasionally drifted into Texas, but Jones's Rangers never had the pleasure of his acquaintance. The Kid had died of a bullet from former ranger Pat Garrett the same day Jones succumbed to complications from the infection that had struck him in midyear.

The man who had overseen the Rangers' transition from Indian fighters to peace officers was buried in Austin's Oakwood Cemetery on July 20 with full Masonic rites. The *Daily Statesman* noted that the Reverend G. W. Rogers of the First Baptist Church "delivered an eloquent and impressive funeral oration" but did not elaborate on what the cleric said. The church, the brief story added, had been "appropriately draped, and the ceremonies . . . solemn and imposing." The funeral procession included the governor, "staff heads of departments," a military contingent, and "a large cortege of friends and citizens."[29]

KING TAKES OVER

The governor appointed forty-two-year-old Wilburn Hill King as Jones's successor on July 25. Like Jones, the Georgia native had fought for the Confederacy. Severely wounded in Louisiana during the battle of Mansfield in April 1864, at war's end King commanded Walker's Texas Division. After the Confederacy collapsed, King went to Central America and ran a sugar plantation until 1868. Returning to Texas, he settled in Sulphur Springs. Elected to the Texas House of Representatives, he had served two terms. No champion of the Rangers as a legislator from East Texas, King revised his opinion after taking over his new job.[30]

A hands-on administrator, the new adjutant general soon made his first major personnel decision. Convinced by a report from Coldwell that Marsh was not fit for command, King got rid of Marsh by disbanding Company B in August. King and Coldwell reenlisted the men they wanted to keep, hired new recruits, and promoted Lieutenant S. A. McMurray effective September 1 to replace Marsh as captain.[31]

West of the Pecos, the rangers of Company E still scouted for Indians. A sheepherder had been killed by Indians on the last day of August. Nevill and his men rode out of camp the following day to look for the perpetrators and the sheep they had stolen. Meeting with a detachment of cavalry from Fort Davis, rangers found several dead sheep, but no Indian trail. Two days later, on September 6, Nevill speculated the raiders were afoot, having unsuccessfully tried to steal some horses from the Pruett Ranch.[32]

Nevill's company had an uneventful fall, but their next activity would be out of the ordinary. The lieutenant wrote King that he had been asked to escort a surveying party on a float trip down the Rio Grande. He and four rangers would be leaving on December 13 to travel with an equal number of surveyors. "The river is uninhabited [sic] and Indians are known to frequent that section," Nevill wrote. "The country bordering on the River is so rough, it is impossible to meander it and carry our horses, and as the trip is very risky on account of so small a number of men, I have concluded to lead it myself, which, I hope will be satisfactory to you."[33]

While Nevill and his men rode toward the river, the Texas & Pacific's tracks connected with the Southern Pacific at Sierra Blanca in Hudspeth County on December 15. Transcontinental railroad service along a southern route began the next day.[34]

Not since the days of the republic had Rangers gotten any closer to the water in doing their work than splashing across a stream on horseback. But in January 1882, Lieutenant Nevill and his men had the distinction of being the first and last Texas Rangers in a rowboat to encounter a party of Indians. Floating down the Rio Grande with the surveying party, the rangers and four Indians spotted each other at the same time. The Indians opted not to fight, quickly retreating into Mexico. But they had left some horses behind on the Texas side, and Nevill and his men killed them.

A few days later, the rangers drifted up on another group of Indians who had just crossed into Mexico from the Texas. "Two of them rode back to the edge of the water about 800 yards in front of us," Nevill reported to King on February 4, "but they fled as soon as we pulled into shore for the purpose of landing, they were too far to waste ammunition shooting with Winchesters."

Nevill's sergeant, with extra horses and nine other rangers, met the party at the mouth of Marivillas Creek. The rangers proceeded to San

Francisco Creek, but found no Indian sign. Should he find any Indians on the U.S. side of the river, the lieutenant continued, he would "inform them that they are in Texas."

The river, however, proved far more dangerous than Indians. "I had two accidents on the River," Nevill continued, "on the 23rd of December, a boat turned over, and the 31st my boat ran against a snag in a very swift riffle. I barely escaped drowning, as I had on my pistol and belts, coat and boots. I lost my field glasses and three hundred rounds of ammunition, besides considerable rations lost in the first upset. Eanes and Trentham of my Company also came near drowning, and Mr. Gano [the lead surveyor]."[35]

Late that year, in a general order signed on November 18, 1882, King reduced company strength to fifteen men each effective December 1. That left the battalion with ninety officers and privates—less than a quarter of its original size.[36]

Outgoing Governor Roberts, in his message to the Eighteenth Legislature on January 10, 1883, noted that "the frontiersman no longer fears the tomahawk of the savage Indian." Accordingly, he continued, "the expenses of the police and frontier forces have been reduced to $60,000 for this fiscal year, and their existence at all in a few years will be a thing of the past." Addressing the issue more directly later in his message, the governor said that the adjutant general's report reflected that the Frontier Battalion and Special Force "have done service in arresting criminals and in preserving peace and good order in the western and southwestern portions of the State. Since the Indian depredations have ceased that has been their exclusive business, and, that they might feel and fully understand their full responsibility as peace officers, copies of the digest of the laws have been furnished to the companies."[37]

The state's new governor—the same John Ireland who had literally kicked ex-Governor Davis out of the Capital a decade before—did not propose to write off the Rangers. While agreeing that "the time is rapidly approaching when we will have no frontier," Ireland asserted in a message delivered January 16 that "those familiar with our borders and the enforcement of our laws, will readily concede the fact that the time has not arrived for the disbandment of our State forces."[38] Lawmakers went on to increase the Frontier Battalion appropriation by $10,000 for fiscal 1884 and 1885, upping the authorized strength to 120 officers and men.[39]

After a string of continuances, the murder case against Jeff Milton and the two other rangers stemming from the Colorado City incident finally came to trial in Abilene in November 1883. By this time, Milton had resigned from the Rangers after three years' service. During the trial, the state's principal witness committed suicide, and the jury acquitted all three of the young men. Milton had been represented by H. H. Boone and T. D. Cobbs of Navasota, two competent attorneys hired by his family. Though the Patterson shooting seemed a justifiable use of deadly force to protect the life of another, Boone came up with another defense: The 1874 act creating the Frontier Battalion appeared to give arrest powers only to commissioned officers, not privates.[40] In fact, Adjutant General King had recommended that the legislature amend the law to do away with any ambiguity on that account. Clearly, the intent of the nearly decade-old law had been that all rangers had arrest powers, not merely supervisory officers. But the legislature let the statute stand unchanged. The ambiguity of the law would come back to haunt the Rangers.

With hostile Indians no longer a danger to Texas, the adjutant general's biannual report described the Rangers as "an armed, mounted and active police force, with the same authority as sheriffs, and no more, but not limited to county lines in the exercise of authority."[41] In defining the Ranger force, King also sought to keep it well disciplined.

On January 7, 1884, the general issued General Order Number Thirteen, reminding the rangers of an earlier order still in effect: Rangers could not carry weapons in cities or towns while off duty. Neither could they wear guns in saloons, circuses, or other amusement places unless on duty. Further, rangers "visiting and staying about drinking saloons, gambling houses, or places of prostitution, unless in the performance of public duty" would be summarily discharged. Section V of the order made the broad point:

> Members of the Frontier Battalion must remember that they are in the service for the purpose of assisting the civil authorities and citizens in the suppression of lawlessness and crime and to keep the peace. To carry out this intention, rangers should ever be on the alert to cultivate friendly relations with all civil officers and good citizens, and by their gentlemanly behavior . . . deserve the confidence and esteem of every one.[42]

In comparison to the previous decade, Texas—and its Rangers—had become downright civilized.

"Hell breaks loose in Texas"

Some Texans saw barbed wire as one of the chief agents of that civilization. Meeting in Austin that January, Texas cattle raisers listened as E. R. Lane talked up the relatively new product. "Say what you will," he told the stockmen, "barbed wire is a great civilizer. It has done more for the progress and order, more for the morals and civilization of our people than the law and gospel combined."[43]

The "great civilizer" soon ignited what came to be called the Fence-Cutting War. Mass-produced and therefore inexpensive, barbed wire allowed a landowner to cheaply but effectively close off his holdings. A good, tight fence prevented a landowner's livestock from straying. More important, three strands of wire strung between cedar posts kept other livestock from grazing on that landowner's grass or drinking his water. Since the beginning of the livestock industry in Texas, those necessities had been considered free to all, as ubiquitous as the air men breathed. Wire sliced the open range like so much flank steak, old Indian trails, fresher cattle trails, and even wagon roads suddenly bisected. For the first time in Texas history, if a man wanted land to run cattle on, he had to buy it or lease it.

Landowners liked the new system, but those who preferred the old "free range" days did not. Traditionalists soon found that a pair of wire cutters—popularly called nippers—could reduce someone's new wire fence to so many twisted coils in a matter of seconds. Fences, Texans discovered, did not always make good neighbors.[44]

"HELL BREAKS LOOSE IN TEXAS," a Chicago newspaper blared, reporting that wire cutters had ruined five hundred miles of fence in Coleman County. "The range and soil of Texas belong to the heroes of the South," proclaimed an anonymous note found posted in Coleman after another round of fence cutting.[45]

Hoping to solve the problem with new law, Governor Ireland called a special session of the Eighteenth Legislature. It convened on January 8, 1884, and within a month, but not without stormy debate, lawmakers passed legislation dealing with fence-cutting. Ireland signed an act on February 6 making wire-nipping a felony punishable by up to five years in prison. Another bill required an unlocked gate for every three miles of fence, while an additional new statute prohibited the fencing of land not owned or under lease. The lawmakers stopped short of approving a bill that would have made shooting a fence cutter a justified homicide, but they did appropriate $50,000 to fund the state's enforcement efforts.[46]

On March 6, King pulled a somewhat reluctant Captain Baylor from El Paso County to Brown County to assume temporary command of the Frontier Battalion as major, the first to hold the title since the late John B. Jones. Along with the promotion came orders to cooperate with a cadre of undercover operatives hired directly by the governor to suppress fence-cutting by infiltrating wire-cutting groups such as the Knights of the Knippers.

Agents from Pinkerton's National Detective Agency in Chicago and New Orleans–based Farrell's Commercial Detective Agency soon traveled to west-central Texas to ferret out fence cutters. Using Brownwood as their base, the frontier gumshoes came up with a lot of names, but not enough evidence to hold up in court.

A private operative from Louisiana had better results north of San Angelo in present Coke County, where Representative Thomas L. Odom's newly fenced ninety-thousand-acre ranch at Fort Chadbourne had been repeatedly plagued by wire cutters. The detective had succeeded in planting forty-two-year-old Ben C. Warren into a group of nippers known as the Fish Creek gang for the stream that flowed on the north end of Odom's sprawling ranch. Warren, who lived in the nearby Nolan County community of Hylton, provided the state with the names of those involved in specific instances of fence-cutting in the area and agreed to testify against the offenders. With warrants based on Warren's information, Baylor on May 4 led twenty-five rangers on a sweep netting the arrest of eight suspected fence cutters. When Baylor rounded up the gang, the surprised defendants and their friends noted that Warren now rode as a Texas Ranger. "The men arrested appear to be common loafers and small stockmen," the San Angelo *Standard* reported on May 10.

While that may have been the case, the accused fence cutters did not meekly await their day in court. "With the hope . . . of weakening or defeating the case against themselves," Adjutant General King reported, "these parties . . . have brought damage suits for false imprisonment against Capt. G. W. Baylor . . . and against Col. Odom."

Eight months later, the defendants came up with a more effective solution to their legal difficulties. On the night of February 10, 1885, as Warren, Odom and several others sat around the stove in the lobby of Sweetwater's Central Hotel, someone fired a shot through the window. The bullet grazed Odom and hit the Ranger detective in the face. "The victim never spoke, and died in his chair," the Abilene *Quill* reported. With Warren having been the principal witness in the fence-cutting cases, the state never gained any convictions against the gang members. Nolan County deputies arrested two men for Warren's murder, both of them free on bond on the fence-cutting charges, but neither was ever found guilty.[47]

Even as it faced new problems like fence-cutting, Texas had not forgotten its sixty-year struggle with the Indians—especially the money spent in the process. Congressman Thomas P. Ochiltree introduced a bill on February 20 directing the secretary of war to "examine and audit the accounts and claims of the State of Texas against the United States for moneys expended and indebtedness incurred in organizing, equipping, and paying the volunteer ranger and militia forces" from February 25, 1855, to January 28, 1861, and since October 20, 1865, in frontier defense. While Ochiltree's bill stressed that "nothing in this act shall be construed to commit the government of the United States to the payment of such claims," the sentiment in Texas that Washington should assume some responsibility for the state's efforts at self-defense still remained strong.[48]

In addition to the effort to close out the books on the Indian wars, the state moved to dismantle a long-standing component of frontier protection: pistol-carrying citizens. On April 17, Governor Ireland issued a proclamation "withdrawing the whole territory of Texas from the list of frontier counties, and [extending] the law prohibiting the carrying of six-shooters and other small arms to all parts of the State."[49] Of course, that did not stop outlaws from carrying guns.

GUN SMOKE AT GREEN LAKE

❶rdered to investigate reports of "outlawry, fence cutting, etc.," on July 27, a detachment of four Company D rangers left Camp Leona, four miles south of Uvalde, for a 125-mile ride to Green Lake, a body of water formed by the Llano River in Edwards County thirty-five miles from

Junction. Led by Corporal P. C. Baird, the lawmen stayed off established roads and trails, traveling across open country. They knew well that anytime someone in West Texas saw a group of large shod-horse tracks, word of Rangers being in the area spread quickly "by pony telegraph."

Baird and his men reached the newly acquired sheep ranch of G. B. and W. J. Greer about midnight the following day, July 28. The two brothers, pleased to see the rangers, invited them to bed down in a small cabin about two hundred yards from the lake. Before settling down for the night, the state officers turned their horses over to a ranch hand, who hid their mounts in a cedar brake about two miles away.

The Greers had stretched a barbed-wire fence around their lake, which the summer heat had sucked nearly dry, to keep out stray cattle. But someone kept cutting the fence and watering their stock in what remained of the lake. The Greers suspected four cowboys who had a camp about 250 yards from the other end of the lake.

The Ranger corporal suggested that the Greers repair their fence one more time. Meanwhile, Baird and his men would stay out of sight in their cabin overlooking the lake. Later that morning, the cowboys who had been camping nearby drove a small herd up to the fence gate. When one of the Greers' hands tried to keep the cowboys out, one of them pulled a pistol and threatened to kill him if he did not step aside. Watching from concealment, the corporal had a hard time keeping his men from running out and confronting the gunman. But Baird wanted to catch them cutting the fence, a felony.

Around 4:30 p.m., the same men returned to the lake with another herd. With the rangers observing them from the cabin, the men cut and pulled down a section of fence. As the transgressing cowboys pushed the cattle toward the lake through the new opening, Baird released his men to take position on the fence cutters' flank.

The rangers had succeeded in catching the fence cutters red-handed without giving away their presence. But they had one problem: Riding through the back country to get to the ranch without detection, they had expended a lot of ammunition on rattlesnakes. Baird being the only ranger with a reasonable supply of cartridges, he divided his equally among the others. That done, the corporal made his way to a point on the north side of the lake with a better view of the fence cutters. They spotted him moments later, dismounted, and took cover behind a stone fence.

His Winchester on his shoulder, Baird stood and yelled for the men to surrender.

"Go to hell!" one of them replied.

The corporal saw a puff of gun smoke and felt a burning sensation as a .44 slug left a slight cut under his right arm.

"This opened the ball," Baird recalled. "We answered them shot for shot, when we could get a shot at their heads over the . . . rock fence. . . . This rock wall served them as a complete fortification, in that it also served them with port holes through which to train their guns on me."

Each time they fired, Baird saw the white smoke, heard a buzz, and felt the wind as bullets barely missed him. Some of the cowboys popped high-speed .22s at the rangers. But the state officers proved to be better shots. When the shooting stopped, one of the fence cutters lay dead and his three colleagues sat in leg-irons. Baird threw a saddle blanket over the dead man's face to keep the flies off and sent for a justice of the peace to conduct an inquest.[50]

"Imagine there is no more frontier"

Counting the Green Lake fence cutter, rangers shot and killed seven criminals in 1884. Despite the arrest of numerous other felons and miscreants by the Rangers during the year, when the Nineteenth Legislature convened, Governor Ireland backed off his earlier support of "our State forces" and recommended paring down the Frontier Battalion. "Although this force has, in the last two years, done great service," he told a joint session on January 13, 1885, "I believe that it can be reduced to about fifty men, with the necessary officers."[51]

In his inaugural address a week later, while not specifically mentioning the Rangers, Ireland noted that Texas's border would "continue to recede, our new counties will continue to organize, the six-shooter and the Spencer rifle will disappear, and the people will be able to elect a local government that will afford protection to life and property without having to appeal to a central power to do that for which local officers are created."[52]

Plainly, Ireland had begun to think the Rangers had reached the end of their usefulness, the money appropriated for the battalion's personnel better spent elsewhere. A month later, when word reached Austin that

Mexican bandits had succeeded in making off with a Ranger detachment's horses along the border, a proposal surfaced in the legislature to abolish the battalion. A harsh drought starting in the summer of 1883 had adversely affected the state's economy, and doing away with the Rangers seemed like an effective way to save tax dollars that had become scarce as rain. Too, as one contemporary writer put it, lawmakers in Central and Eastern Texas, "where there has been no frontier for fifty years, imagine there is no more frontier and are in *favor* of cutting down the ranger force."[53]

The still thinly settled western half of the state knew better. "There is work for the rangers yet," the San Angelo *Standard* declared on January 24, "and they had much to do in stopping the recent fence cutting. The time has not yet come for the disbandment of these men and we advocate their being kept in the service of the state." Later that year, the Dallas *Morning News* also weighed in with a lengthy story in support of the Frontier Battalion.[54]

A former sheriff of Comal County and a friend of the governor, Lieutenant George H. Schmitt and his Company C rangers liked staying busy. First assigned to the vastness of the Panhandle, where a ranger might ride a hundred miles without seeing another human, Schmitt sought a transfer to some part of the state offering more work. "I hate to eat the bread of the state without doing some service, and so does every man in my co.," the German-born ranger wrote King.

The ranger's ego matched his strong work ethic. Angling for promotion to captain, Schmitt wrote a friend in the state senate: "I am respected by all citizens who make my acquantance [sic] and my company is under more control and descipline [sic] then [sic] any other co. in the Battalion." Not only that, he continued, "I would sooner die then [sic] [be] called a coward and all the desperados [sic] in this country are afraid of me. I will take them in or kill them."

Schmitt got his captaincy on May 1, 1884, along with orders to move his company farther downstate to Wichita Falls. He posted a detachment in rowdy Vernon and concentrated his efforts on catching outlaws who did their business in Texas only to escape across the Red River into Indian Territory.

Company C Rangers soon thwarted a bank robbery in Wichita Falls when Lieutenant Albert Grimes used a 10-gauge shotgun to end the criminal career of one of two gunmen entering the Panhandle Bank and demanding cash. The rangers under Schmitt also undertook long scouts (Grimes and another ranger rode from Wilbarger County all the way to El Paso and then to New Mexico on the trail of two horse thieves, finally catching one of them back in Texas at Pecos) and dealt with an outbreak of vigilantism in Vernon.

In addition to the hard work he had asked for, Schmitt had to deal with the routine administrative duties all Ranger captains faced. He prepared monthly returns, kept track of state supplies and equipment, fielded requests for assistance from sheriffs and other local officials (often he had to say no because of lack of manpower), fired drunks and misfits, and sparred with headquarters over unpaid expense vouchers and sundry other issues. Unlike some captains, he also had a habit of criticizing his colleagues in letters to Austin. He even once boasted that he could run the Frontier Battalion better than King.[55]

While the legislature debated the fate of the battalion, Andrew Jackson Sowell, who served as a ranger in 1870–71, sold copies of his new book, *Rangers and Pioneers of Texas, with a Concise Account of the Early Settlements, Hardships, Massacres, Battles, and Wars by Which Texas Was Rescued from the Rule of the Savage and Consecrated to the Empire of Civilization*. Written in 1883 and published in San Antonio the following year, the book offered a gripping account of Sowell's participation in the hard fight between eleven rangers and forty-one Indians in Wise County back in 1871. Though his book did not see national distribution, Sowell had written the first Ranger memoir.[56]

The battalion survived the 1885 legislative session, but lawmakers went along with the governor's wishes and reduced its funding from $75,000 to $60,000. At first, King ordered the disbanding of Company F, but a resolution from the Dimmit County Commissioner's Court, asking for rangers to deal with an outbreak of thievery and smuggling by Mexican nationals along the border between Eagle Pass and Laredo, caused the general to change his mind. Effective April 15, King instead eliminated Company A, reduced Company B to eighteen men, and pared the remaining three companies to seventeen men each. The battalion still had five companies, but each had fewer men.[57] In reality, the strength of the Ranger force seldom had anything to do with workload, always the budget. Money might be short, but trouble in Texas continued in ample supply.

Six weeks after the reduction in force, on orders from Company D captain Lamar P. (Lam) Sieker[58], Sergeant Ben Lindsey led a half dozen rangers on a scout along San Ambrosia Creek, some eighty miles up the Rio Grande from Laredo in sprawling Webb County. Looking for two escaped prisoners believed headed for Mexico, the rangers saw in the distance two mounted men trailing a riderless horse. Thinking they had either found the two fugitives or run across a pair of horse thieves, the Ranger patrol trotted to within rifle shot of the men. At that, the two dug the rowels of their spurs into their horses' flanks and galloped off, leaving behind the horse they had been trailing. His suspicions further aroused by their flight, Sergeant Lindsey ordered his men to pursue the unknown riders.

Traversing the muddy creek bottom slowed the sergeant and three of the rangers, but Rangers Ira Aten and Ben C. Riley, who had been leading their pack mules, caught up with the men on a rise and ordered them to surrender. While Aten covered them with his Winchester, Riley walked his horse closer to collect their guns. But the men opened fire, hitting Riley in his shoulder and hip. At that, Aten cut loose with his saddle gun, wounding both shooters. Firing his pistol, Ranger Frank Sieker galloped up on the gunfight only to be shot from his saddle by one of the Mexicans. Just as the sergeant and the other three rangers arrived (one of them suffering from a broken collarbone sustained when his horse slipped and fell in the mud), the wounded Mexicans rode out of sight.

Dismounting only long enough to see that nothing could be done for Sieker, who had died from a bullet in his heart, Lindsey and his three remaining healthy men tracked the Mexicans to a nearby scattering of adobe structures on the Texas side of the Rio Grande. Backed by fifteen armed Mexicans, a man claiming to be a sheriff's deputy refused to turn the two wounded men over to the state officers. The deputy did say he would take the suspects to Laredo, where the sheriff could sort matters out. Outgunned, the sergeant had no other choice but to agree. Aten and two other rangers would travel with the party to the county seat while Lindsey tended to his injured men and saw to the removal of Sieker's body.

When the entourage made it to Laredo on June 1, Sheriff Darrio Gonzales recognized the two men confronted by the rangers as relatives. Even so, he placed them in jail. Within a half hour, however, the sheriff released his kinsmen and arrested the rangers for assault with intent to murder. Lindsey protested that the Mexicans had shot two of his men, and that the rangers had been justified in their use of force to defend themselves when the pair resisted arrest. But the sergeant knew to pick his fights. He had already lost one ranger, his captain's younger brother. Realizing that refusing to be jailed would only lead to more shooting, Lindsey and the other rangers surrendered their weapons and gamely cooled their heels in the Webb County lockup until someone willing to go their bond could be found—a process that took twenty-six days.

The case precipitated a flurry of telegrams and letters between state and local officials, but in the end, neither the Mexicans nor the rangers faced prosecution. All that came of the incident was a compounding of the long-standing cultural friction along the border.

From El Paso to Brownsville, the easily crossed Rio Grande always afforded at least the perception of being a safe haven on one side or the other for outlaws, cattle or horse thieves, smugglers, and the politically disgruntled. That would always mean work for the Rangers.[59]

Rangers had shot it out with suspected criminals often enough along the border and elsewhere, but the growing organized labor movement brought new challenges to the Frontier Battalion. A detachment stood by in Big Spring the year before during a peaceful railroad-workers strike, but when the Knights of Labor struck the Texas & Pacific on March 1, 1886, the situation grew increasingly dicey by the day.

When the railroad, using a scab crew, tried to move a heavily guarded mail train out of Fort Worth on April 3, strikers stopped it at Buttermilk Junction, just south of the city. Gunshots quickly erupted, leaving Tarrant County Deputy Sheriff R. W. (Dick) Townsend dead and two other participants wounded. As word of the violence spread, Fort Worth hardware stores sold out of Winchesters and wholesale violence seemed imminent.

Late that night, when the mayor wired Austin for state help, neither Governor Ireland nor Adjutant General King was in town. Newly promoted to battalion Quarter-master, Lam Seiker, acting adjutant general in King's absence, ordered two Ranger companies to "report in haste to Fort Worth" as the Austin *Daily Statesman* put it. When Ireland telegraphed Seiker from Seguin with orders to send rangers, the former company captain replied that he had already done so and recommended that the governor call out the militia as well. Ireland ordered in 277 state troops.

As soon as they could, both King and the governor traveled by special train to Fort Worth. The show of force, which turned Cowtown into an armed camp for several days, prevented any more trouble but assured further Ranger involvement in labor issues. To King's thinking, the "mad and murderous teachings of Communists and Socialists" lay behind the nascent labor movement.

While condemning "oath bound organizations," King praised the Rangers.

"Quiet and orderly and without uniform of any kind," he wrote, "the sturdy and determined manner and appearance of the Rangers, and their well established character for fearless observance of order made a powerful impression on the minds of the strikers, and had due weight in bringing about . . . peace."

Whenever "lawful and necessary," the general declared, the Rangers would "meet force with force." [60]

13

"I always wanted to join the Rangers"

The Frontier Battalion, 1887–91

Not long after the train left Austin, a twenty-two-year-old store clerk from East Texas struck up a conversation with a fellow passenger. Many of the men sitting around them, he learned, held tickets to Dallas to attend the annual meeting of the Sheriffs' Association of Texas.

A convivial sort, J. Allen Newton soon met William Scott, captain of Ranger Company F.

"I always wanted to join the Rangers," the young man from Jacksonville said after exchanging pleasantries with the state lawman.

"You really mean that, kid?" Scott asked.

"I sure do," Newton replied.

"Well, I'll be wanting a recruit soon. I'll let you know if I need you."

Shortly after that chance encounter in September 1886, a telegram came from Scott. If Newton still wanted to be a ranger, he should come to Brownwood. He resigned his retail position, wrote his girl with the news that he planned on joining the Rangers, and took the train to Fort Worth so he could buy his equipment. The new owner of a six-shooter, a Winchester, two blankets, a saddle, and a bridle, he boarded the train for Brownwood.

Scott met his new hire at the Santa Fe depot. The captain had ridden in from camp with one of his men following in a wagon to carry Newton's tack. Right before they left, Newton realized he had forgotten something.

"Hold on," he said, "we haven't got my trunk."

Scott laughed. His company moved too fast to be toting trunks. Newton would have to store that in Brownwood. The captain told him to leave everything behind except one good suit, an extra shirt, and a pair of canvas duckings. Scott could have added the necessity of a little seasoning to the Ranger laundry list, but that would come soon enough.[1]

Despite Ranger efforts and Governor Ireland's short-lived use of private detectives, fence-cutting had not stopped in Texas, and it had grown increasingly ugly. Brown County rancher L. P. Baugh, one of the first landowners to string barbed wire, found a note tacked to one of his fence posts: "Take down this fence; if you don't, we will cut it and if we cut it and a drop of the cutters [sic] blood is spilled, your life will pay the forfeit." Not easily intimidated, Baugh wrote a reply on the bottom of the paper: "You cowardly cur, this is my fence, and you let it alone." The rancher's reaction did not impress the author of the note. Within a few days, half of Baugh's fence had been snipped between every cedar post.[2]

The fence-cutting on Baugh's place and others in the county continued, the estimated losses in the 956-square-mile county approaching $1 million, a staggering amount for the times. Adjutant General King had ordered Scott on September 16, 1886, to set up camp in the county and put a stop to the cutting.[3]

Hoping to develop useful information, one of Scott's men, Ira Aten, posed as an itinerant cowboy looking for work. Joe Copeland, a local farmer, helped Aten win the fence cutters' confidence. Soon the undercover ranger began collecting the names of fence cutters in the area. Keeping his ears open, Aten eventually learned where the cutters planned to strike next and made his report to Scott.

The captain, Sergeant J. A. Brooks, and Rangers John H. Rogers, Newton, Aten, Jim Carmichael and Billy Treadwell laid a trap for the fence cutters on the ranch of W. M. Baugh, L. P. Baugh's brother, about twelve miles north of town on Jim Ned Creek. The Baughs and three of their hired hands volunteered to join the state officers in the surprise party the night of November 8.

"We waited for them under a clump of big live oak trees," Newton recalled. "It was bright moonlight that night and one of them came walking along with a whiskey bottle in one hand cutting as fast as he could. 'This is fine cutting, ain't it?' he said."[4]

The cutters clipped a mile and a half of fence before running into the rangers. A telegram sent to the Austin *Daily Statesman* the following day reported what happened next:

> At 11 o'clock the cutters were heard coming up the line of the fence. They were permitted to pass a few of those in ambush, but on arriving opposite him, Capt. Scott demanded their surrender, stating they were rangers. His only answer was a pistol shot, then the firing become [sic] rapid on both sides. . . . When the firing ceased one wire cutter was found killed and one mortally wounded, while two made their escape on foot, their horses being captured.

The rangers identified the dead man as Jim Lowell, a constable in the adjoining precinct. Despite his elective office, Lowell had been "an old offender." When the rangers looked closer at his body, they found he had pasted on a false mustache. He died under indictment for fence-cutting, but the case against him had languished on the docket. The rangers took the wounded man, Amos Roberts, into town. A doctor removed a bullet from his chest, but the fence cutter died before sunup. He, too, had been awaiting trial on a previous fence-cutting charge.

As long as they were out, Scott and his men attended to some additional business. "Before morning," the Austin newspaper also reported, "the rangers also captured Bob Hancock, a noted horse thief."[5]

Another shooting nearly broke out in Brownwood later that day. As the state officers walked through town that morning, Will Butler—a deputy sheriff rumored to be a fence cutter—saw Copeland and ordered him to surrender his pistol. Clearly, the cutter crowd had figured out Copeland's role in setting the trap. A ranger standing next to Copeland took exception to the deputy's order and pulled his six-shooter. Sheriff W. N. Adams, in turn, drew his pistol and covered the ranger. A sudden move by any of the three could have precipitated a rapid reduction in the number of peace officers in Brown County that day.

Fortunately, Captain Scott walked up. Quickly assessing the situation, in a reasoning voice he suggested that everyone holster their weapons. Even more fortunately, everyone complied. The captain informed the

Brown County deputy that Copeland had been deputized by the Rangers, which meant he could legally carry a pistol. But to avoid further trouble, the captain told Copeland he no longer had need of his services. Copeland got in his buggy and rode out of town, only to be ambushed as he crossed Salt Creek about seven miles out. The first shots missed, but the noise sent his mules into a panicked run, carrying the Ranger operative safely— if bumpily—home. Copeland survived another attempt on his life nine months later.

A grand jury indicted several persons in connection with the attempted murder of Copeland, but the charges ended up dismissed. A subsequent grand jury returned four other indictments in the case, but those charges also withered. Still, fence-cutting ceased to be a serious problem in Brown County after the shoot-out with the Rangers. Scott's company stayed in the area the rest of the year, using it as a base for scouts in Concho, Lampasas, and McCulloch counties, but no additional fence-cutting occurred.[6]

"The crime of lawless fence cutting is one so easy to commit and so hard to anticipate, prevent or detect," Adjutant General King wrote in his 1886 annual report, "that bad men will be found here and there to attempt it in spite of the penalty of discovery, but it is hoped that it will not take many such bloody scenes as that resulting from the offense in Brown County to practically put an end to this crime."[7]

Local politics caused the Rangers as much trouble as fence-cutting, especially in the South Texas county of LaSalle. In 1886, well-respected former Ranger captain Charles McKinney presided as sheriff there, but he had his hands full dealing with cronies of the sheriff he had defeated at the polls four years earlier. His jurisdiction mostly lonely brush country, McKinney also contended with numerous stock thieves and outlaws. A staunch law-and-order man, the sheriff had the full support of the Rangers. In fact, his successor as Company F captain, Joseph Shely, had proven a bit too partial, injecting his company into the electoral process by persuading Mexicans to vote for McKinney rather than former sheriff William O. Tompkins in a 1884 rematch.

While no one proved Shely did anything improper, in June 1885 King gladly accepted his resignation. But that had no impact on the McKinney–Tompkins rivalry, which climaxed the day after Christmas, 1886, with McKinney's murder at the hands of George Crenshaw and James McCoy, two Tompkins allies. Soon after word of the killing reached

Austin, King ordered Company C Captain Schmitt to Cotulla, the LaSalle county seat.

On the night of January 2, 1887, not long after the rangers arrived, parties unknown rose from concealment and shot and mortally wounded a man named George Hill as he walked down the street in Cotulla. Hill, it developed, was the brother-in-law of one of McKinney's accused killers, Crenshaw. Clearly, his death had been a revenge killing. Before he died, Hill named the two men who had ambushed him and Schmitt's rangers began hunting for them.

With help from an informant, Schmitt laid a trap for Crenshaw that ended in a gun battle with rangers in the brush on January 17, 1887. The accused murderer, who had tried to get off another shot at the rangers even as he lay terminally wounded, died the following day. The same day, McCoy, who had been hiding nearby during the shoot-out, surrendered to Schmitt and his men. The accused killers of Hill gave themselves up to the new sheriff and the Ranger captain on January 25.

"This [the killing of Crenshaw and the arrest of McCoy] has made a great effect on the criminals and they think that we are hell," Schmitt reported to King. Schmitt later received an official commendation from King for the "zeal and energy recently displayed in LaSalle County by Co. C, Frt. Batt., by which the murderers of Sheriff C. B. McKinney . . . were either killed or arrested."[8]

In his message to the Twentieth Legislature on January 11, 1887, lame-duck governor Ireland noted that the "State Troops" had been "of great service during the last two years. In its maintenance a wise economy has prevailed, and in all other respects its management has been satisfactory. The Legislature appropriated $120,000 for the service, and there has been used only the sum of $87,634, leaving an unexpended balance of $32,365." Whenever called upon, the governor continued, the Rangers "responded with alacrity—always acting in subordination, however, to the regular civil authorities."[9]

Six days after Ireland sent his message to the legislature, former ranger Lawrence Sullivan Ross placed his hand on a Bible to be sworn in as governor. Ross had been a good Ranger captain, fought in 135 engagements during the Civil War, and went on to become a popular governor, but he could not keep the legislature from cleaving the Frontier Battalion's budget from $60,000 to $30,000. With no money to fund its operation, Company E, which had moved from near Fort Davis to Murphysville (later renamed Alpine) when the railroad reached there, would be mustered out in April.[10]

THE CONNER GANG

$maller in number, the Rangers hastened across the state from one trouble spot to another. Captain Scott's next assignment necessitated travel to foreign territory for most of his men: deep East Texas. The rangers broke their Brown County camp early in 1887 and rode their horses north to Cisco, a town on the Texas & Pacific Railroad. Two teamsters followed in the company's two supply wagons. From Cisco, the rangers took the train to Marshall, finally reaching Sabine County on March 29.

Local officials had requested state help in tracking down Bill Conner and his seven sons, a family well-known in that part of East Texas simply as the Conner gang. Originally from Florida, Conner and his boys kept to themselves during the Civil War, not inclined to fight for any cause other than their own. Equally disinterested in the legal fineries of land ownership, the old man simply took it for granted that all the property around his cabin belonged to him. But when two men bought acreage encompassing the area where the Conners had been squatting, they did not live to pay their first property-tax assessment. Tried for murder, one of the Conner sons got a life sentence and another, twenty-five years. Their father still awaited trial when the rest of the sons broke all three of them out of jail. The whole clan disappeared into the pines, living off venison, catfish, and whatever they could steal.

One sheriff had already tried to bring them in. When the Conners threw down on him as he rode along a trail through tall timber, they told him to start saying his prayers. Looking down the barrels of their weapons, the county lawman instead made a promise: If they would spare his life, he would go right back to town and turn in his badge. They agreed and that is what he did.

"They terrorized the whole county," Newton recalled. "People were afraid to light their lamps after dark."

When the two prosecutors who had handled the case against the Conners got word that the old man and his sons had threatened them, the officials asked for Rangers. Though local officials felt powerless in dealing with the outlaws, they did convince an acquaintance of the Conners' to lead state lawmen to their hideout. The rangers made camp and awaited the informant's return from a scheduled hunt with the Conners.

Around 2 a.m. on March 31, the man came in and pointed in the direction of the Conners' camp. The rangers drew straws to see who would stay behind to guard their horses and equipment while the rest of the company moved out through the pines, their leggings and spurs left behind so they would not make any noise. The Conners had camped about ten miles south of Hemphill among a stand of pines atop a knoll, an ideal defensive position. The surrounding timber had been cut, meaning anyone approaching had to do so without cover. Scott split his men into two squads and moved toward the high ground in the predawn.

The Conners either suffered from insomnia or expected company. "Quicker than it takes to tell it, [Ranger] Jim Moore of Kerrville was killed, Capt. Scott got shot . . . and [J. H.] Rogers . . . shot in the left side and arm. Bill [Conner], the only Conner to show himself from behind a tree, was killed by Sergeant Brooks," Newton said of the intense gun battle. Ranger bullets wounded another of the Conners and killed their packhorse and four dogs. The rest of the gang escaped in the darkness, disappearing in the timber.

The first word Adjutant General King had of trouble came via telegraph from Nacogdoches at 9:11 a.m., April 2:

> Capt Scott Co F state Rangers & two of his men Brooks & Rogers severely wounded & one man Moore killed dead in a fight with the outlaws Conners . . . yesterday morning A Winchester ball entered apex of Capts left lung & come out at lower border scapular hope to save his life Frank H. Tucker MD.

Tucker, working with two other doctors, kept the captain alive and patched up the other two rangers. Ranger Newton, having survived his second gunfight in less than five months, had been the first to reach Nacogdoches with news of the battle. He wired the state prison at Rusk for tracking dogs, then rejoined his company. Augmented by sheriffs and deputies from adjoining counties, the rangers tried to find the rest of the Conners, but for the time being they had made good their escape. In time, with a $1,000 dead-or-alive price on their heads, three other Conners died at the hands of bounty hunters.

Company F stayed in Hemphill for two months while the captain convalesced.

"The people around there couldn't do enough for us," Newton recalled. "They thought we were real important. They would feed us all the fried chicken we wanted and just begged us to stay longer. . . . The girls, who had never seen anybody but the country boys in their homespun clothes thought 'we were it' in our city clothes."[11]

Finally well enough to travel, Captain Scott came to Austin on May 11, reporting to the adjutant general. "He gives his men unbounded praise for their coolness and the gallantry which they displayed, when every advantage was against them," the Austin *Daily Statesman* reported. "Their record is one of which he is, and he has a right to be, proud. . . . Slight of build, and quiet in manner, Billie Scott would not from a crowd be selected as a typical Texas ranger, but his record is one of dash and gallantry from the very beginning of his connection with the command."[12]

In addition to hunting down fugitives such as the Conners, the Rangers stayed busy investigating stagecoach robberies, a crime that had become so common by the early 1880s that Alexander Sweet, publisher of a humorous newspaper called *Texas Siftings*, wrote, "The traveling public became so accustomed to going through the usual ceremonies [of being relieved of their money and valuables by robbers] that they complained to the stage companies if they came through unmolested. Being robbed came to be regarded as a vested right."[13]

With information gleaned from a jailhouse informant, in 1879 the rangers of companies D and E had broken up the Peg Leg gang, a group of outlaws who got their name from the Peg Leg stage station between Mason and Fort McKavett, not because one of their number had a wooden leg. Three members of the gang died from ranger bullets, with nine others going to prison. No matter this success, the problem did not go away until railroads made stagecoaches obsolete in all but the most remote parts of the state. After San Angelo got rail service in 1888, the Mason *News* observed that "the lone highwayman has gone to California, seeking better fields."[14]

As the Rangers worked to keep the peace despite cuts in funding, the mythical Rangers soon captured the imagination of a generation of youngsters. Dime novelist Prentiss Ingraham, showman Buffalo Bill's press agent, brought out a title immortalizing one of William Cody's cowboy actors, Buck Taylor. With publication of *Buck Taylor, King of the Cowboys; or The Raiders and the Rangers,* Ingraham launched a new series that helped add to the Ranger legend. In the novel, Taylor joins a Ranger company led by one Captain "McNally," a character inspired by the late Leander McNelly. After demonstrating his skill in boxing, wrestling, and wild-bronco riding, Taylor saves the captain's daughter from the Indians. In subsequent titles, Taylor leads a company of "half cowboys, half mounted scout rangers" to deal with cattle rustlers. Like McNelly, Buck Taylor and his "Lasso Rangers' League" dispensed justice roughly, often handling their own adjudication with a rope. Other wrong doers captured by Taylor's Rangers are reported to have "escaped," never to be seen again. Learning of the prisoner deaths, the commander of a nearby army post opines that "to bring law and order here in this country, justice often must be done by illegal methods, and lawless hands work out a certain salvation I suppose."[15]

"RANGERS WILL ATTEND TO ALL KILLING DONE IN THIS LOCALITY"

Ingraham spun his yarns back East, where residents considered themselves relatively civilized. Down on the border, another wordsmith found that freedom of the press had its costs. In Rio Grande City on September 21, 1888, U.S. Customs inspector Victor Sebree, a former ranger, shot and wounded Catarino Garza, publisher of an anti–Porfirio Díaz newspaper called *El Comercio Mexicano.* Sebree also wounded Federico Lopez, a friend of Garza's. After the shooting, Sebree quickly mounted his horse and galloped out of town to the safety of nearby Fort Ringgold as other friends of Garza's blasted away at him. Soon a lynch-minded mob of some two hundred men showed up at the fort demanding that Sebree be handed over to them. The commander of the post ordered the throng off the federal reservation "under penalty of death."

Before the mob cut the telegraph line, Starr County Judge John Kelsey got a wire off to Austin that a "great riot is raging in town here." Governor Ross immediately ordered a company of Rangers, augmented by a Cameron County sheriff's posse, to proceed to the border town. The nearest railroad being a hundred miles away at Laredo, it took the state and county officers three days to get there. When they finally arrived, they found that local officials had defused the situation by promising that Sebree would face trial for shooting Garza. Rangers arrested thirty-four persons for conspiracy and intent to murder, including the slightly wounded Garza, who survived because his gold watch kept a bullet from penetrating his body. Sebree, charged in connection with the shooting, went free on $2,500 bond.

Tensions had been building in Rio Grande City since May, when the sheriff had arrested one Abraham Resendez for theft. Before the case made it to trial, the prisoner tried to escape and Sebree shot and killed him. At least that was Sebree's story. Garza, calling Sebree an "assassin" and "coward," editorialized that the death of the accused robber amounted to cold-blooded murder, not a justified use of deadly force. Sebree, in turn, filed against Garza for criminal libel. A newly enlisted ranger named John R. Hughes arrested the journalist inside a saloon at Realitos, in Duval County, a short time later. But like Sebree, Garza quickly posted bond. Four months later, not satisfied with the progress of his lawsuit against Garza, Sebree shot and wounded him as he sat inside a barbershop in Rio Grande City.[16]

Some rangers exercised their First Amendment rights as well. Following in the footsteps of other rangers who liked to keep the public posted of their activities by writing letters to newspapers, Corporal Walter Durbin wrote from Rio Grande City, "The rangers will attend to all killing done in this locality for the present." It turned out that no additional killing needed to be done, but the Rangers and Garza would meet again.[17]

Elsewhere in the state, the Rangers had to rein in one of their own to defuse an explosive situation in Corsicana. Ranger Aten, still working on the fence-cutting problem, wrote Quartermaster Seiker on October 8 to report he had purchased a supply of dynamite. The ranger told Seiker that he planned to booby-trap fences so they would explode if someone cut a strand of wire. Aten quickly got orders to return to Austin.[18]

Continuing budget problems forced the disbanding of Company C effective November 30, reducing the Rangers to only forty-eight men in three companies: B, D, and F.[19] Maintaining a mounted law enforcement organization in a state as large as Texas cost a lot, but the taxpayers got their money's worth. A report by the Agricultural Bureau of the state's Department of Agriculture, Insurance, Statistics, and History, a study intended to lure new residents to Texas by touting its agricultural possibilities, contained a statistical summary of Frontier Battalion activities from

May 1874 to November 30, 1889. Since the battalion's organization, Rangers had fought fifty-six engagements with either criminals or Indians. Rangers had killed sixty-nine criminals and wounded twenty-seven. Contrary to perception, during six years of Indian fighting (1874–81), Rangers killed only thirty-five Indians, wounded a dozen, and captured four. The cost to the state had been fourteen rangers killed and seventeen wounded.

The number of lives the Rangers took and lost did not, however, accurately reflect the activities of the battalion. Rangers investigated 512 murders and 1,669 instances of livestock thievery. They captured 77 outlaws, 130 escaped convicts, and 13 bandits. (Though the report offers no distinction between outlaw and bandit, it seems likely that *outlaw* meant a criminal with an arrest warrant, a *bandit* being a raider not previously charged with a crime.) Rangers also made 4,870 scouts and 759 escorts. In doing all this, state officers traveled more than a half million miles.[20]

The state report merely offered statistics. Another book published the same year had meat on its bones: Josiah Wilbarger's *Indian Depredations in Texas*. In many Texas homes, only the Bible had more dog-eared passages than Wilbarger's book, which in recounting numerous Indian raids and fights with Texans went a long way toward furthering the Rangers' mystique. Wilbarger gave the late John B. Jones and the Frontier Battalion particular credit for ending the Indian problem in Texas: "There is no doubt that but for the protection given by Major Jones and his little battalion the settlement of many frontier counties would have been greatly retarded, and many defenseless families murdered by the savages."[21]

JAYBIRDS VERSUS WOODPECKERS

By the late 1880s Texans could only read about Indian fighting, but they could still fight each other if they took a mind to. Too much cold beer on a hot, humid afternoon triggered a street fight in downtown Richmond that would alter one ranger's career and eventually claim the life of another. No evidence has been found that either side in what came to be known as the Jaybird-Woodpecker feud had picked August 16, 1889, as the day they would finally resolve their political war. The Battle of Richmond, as some later called it, could better be described as the sudden bursting of a boil, or, in the words of the ranger who tried to prevent the bloodshed, "hell puking."

The animosity that ignited violence in Fort Bend County had been building since the Civil War, its roots enriched in the fertile soil of racism and partisan politics. Representing roughly 90 percent of the county's wealthier white population, the faction known as the Jaybirds considered themselves regular Democrats. The Woodpeckers also called themselves Democrats, but the Jaybirds saw them as Republicans, the still entrenched survivors of a roundly hated Reconstruction regime kept in power by black voters.

The shoot-out could more directly be traced to an outbreak of violence a year earlier, the August 2, 1888, murder of J. M. Shamblin, the leader of the Jaybirds. A little more than a month later, the wounding of another Jaybird led to a September 6 mass meeting that ended with an announcement that several individuals connected to the Woodpeckers had ten hours to leave Fort Bend County in good health. The parties named took the advice, but when the Woodpecker ticket carried the next election, tensions rose again.

On June 21, 1889, Woodpecker tax assessor Kyle Terry killed Jaybird member Ned Gibson in nearby Wharton County with a blast from a side-by-side shotgun. Gibson's brother, Volney, and other Jaybirds swore they would get even, and both factions began buying arms and stocking ammunition.

Responding to a local appeal for help, Adjutant General King sent Captain Frank Jones and seven rangers to Fort Bend County on June 28. A well-respected lawman who had served as a ranger off and on since 1875, Jones met with the leaders of both sides and urged restraint. With work elsewhere, and things still quiet, the captain left on July 10. He detailed Aten, now a sergeant, and three privates to stay behind and maintain a high profile in the county seat until the murder case against Terry came up in district court that fall. The four rangers patrolled the streets of Richmond from daybreak to dark. When one of his men contracted malaria, Aten left him in camp and continued his show of force in town.

The peacekeeping effort held until mid-August. While in camp caring for the still sick ranger, Aten heard a gunshot about six o'clock in the evening on August 16. The sergeant quickly mounted and galloped into town, finding an armed face-off between the two factions. Joined by two of his men, Aten rode between the two groups, urging them to put up their guns and disperse. But things had gone too far. Someone pulled a trigger.

Robie Smith, an innocent young black girl caught by a stray bullet as she crossed a street, died first. Brandishing shotguns, rifles, and pistols, a throng of Jaybirds moved on the courthouse, where the Woodpecker Terry had sought refuge. Within minutes, Sheriff T. J. Garvey, a Woodpecker, lay dead, killed by Jaybird boss Henry Frost, a former ranger who had ridden with Sul Ross in the 1860s. Though he had seven bullets in him, the sheriff had time before he died to mortally wound Frost. A big hole in his stomach, Frost staggered off and managed to kill J. W. Blakely, another Woodpecker. Ranger private Frank Schmidt, with no stake in the fight other than having tried to prevent it, took a bullet in his leg.[22]

Many of the feudists fired until they ran out of ammunition. To stay in the fight, some of them pulled cartridges from the wounded ranger's gunbelt. As soon as he could, Aten made his way to the telegraph office and wired Governor Ross: "Street fight just occurred between the two factions. Many killed. Send militia." County judge J. M. Weston, a Woodpecker who had participated in the fight, sent a shorter message: "Troops needed."

The governor immediately wired the captain of the Houston Light Guard, a component of the state's militia, to entrain his company for Richmond "at once." Ross then prevailed on the railroad to put together a special train and headed for Richmond himself, along with the attorney general.

By daybreak, with the Houston militia unit in town and a second company en route from Brenham, the two factions in Richmond had calmed down. As families mourned and the wounded tossed on their sweat-soaked beds, only black splotches of dried blood on the dirt streets and empty brass shell casings belied the short but intense violence of the previous evening.

Aten believed that if he and the other two rangers had tried to shoot it out with the mob, all of them would have died. He apologized to the governor for not preventing the violence, but Ross assured Aten he had done all that he could, even giving him a cigar. Ross went on to recommend Aten's appointment as Fort Bend County's interim sheriff.[23] While the Rangers had not been able to stave off the Richmond gun battle, reinforcements under Quartermaster Seiker, backed up by militia, kept the two factions in check as Ross worked to mediate the situation.

The Richmond incident marked the end of Aten's Ranger service, and while it did not end the Jaybird-Woodpecker feud, it never again erupted into mob violence. Accepted by both factions, Aten clearly contributed to the easing of tensions, though the former ranger could not be considered totally impartial. When the Jaybirds organized into an association the following October, Aten added his signature to a "constitution" declaring the organization's purpose as being "to confine and unite the white people for the advancement and prosperity of the county."[24]

The spring of 1890, traveling by train to Washington and New York on state business, Governor Ross attracted considerable attention from reporters particularly taken with his having once ridden as a ranger. Because of Ross, the Austin *Daily Statesman* noted, people outside Texas began to realize their vision of Texas as a wild and woolly place had outrun reality. The newspaper continued:

> The enforcement of the laws . . . the protection given property and life have been recognized and the State is in a better condition in every way now than it has ever been in its history. [Ross] is considered a marvel in having succeeded in developing from a ranger boy into a governor. . . . The ranger is, of course, considered . . . as a man who has more fight than polish, more bravery than education. So when they have seen the governor their wonder is great.[25]

When Adjutant General King prepared his 1890 report, he devoted more than nine pages of small type to the Rangers. "In spite of the opinion in many directions to the contrary," he wrote, "the necessity for the active and constant use of the frontier battalion has been pressing and widely extended and the value of their small but potent force has remained undiminished since my last report."

With only three companies amounting to fewer than fifty men, he continued, the battalion had been stretched way too thin. True enough, Indians no longer posed a threat, but "it is still quite a common thing for thieving and murderous Mexicans to invade our territory and to commit outrages upon our border people, and the stealing of stock on the western frontier may be said to be constant and heavy."

In support of his case that the battalion should have the funding to expand, King attached a document listing "Calls For Assistance Of Rangers, Made Directly to the Adjutant General's Office, by Sheriff and Others." From February 25, 1889, when the sheriff of Jeff Davis County requested a Ranger company to assist him in investigating the robbery of a store at Toyah, to October 26, 1890, when officials in Laredo asked for rangers to preserve the peace during a coming election, the department had received fifty-three "calls for assistance." Of those, the department had been unable to send rangers on sixteen occasions.[26]

On January 13, 1891, shortly before leaving office, Ross praised the Rangers in his message to the Twenty-second Legislature. Now down to only thirty-two men, the ranger force had been "the State's puissant right arm in the suppression of lawlessness along the exposed borders." In doing their job, two rangers had been killed and another wounded during the biennium. As of August 31, 1890, the governor reported, $44,285.01 of the Rangers' $60,000 appropriation had been expended.[27]

Ten days after Governor Ross's legislative swan song, Adjutant General King stepped down after a decade of service. "I have worked earnestly and singly for what I believed to be the best interests of the State, its good people and its citizen soldiery, both Militia and Rangers," King said in his last annual report. Indeed, he had. His influence on the organization, which as a legislator he had originally opposed, rivaled Jones's in importance.[28]

A NEW ADJUTANT GENERAL

The new governor, James Stephen Hogg, appointed Woodford Haywood Mabry as King's replacement effective January 22, 1891. A businessman from Jefferson, the thirty-five-year-old Mabry had to accrue his military and law enforcement experience on the job, but he kept a tight rein on the Rangers. Like King, the new adjutant general fought to keep the force out of legislative peril, even succeeding in getting its appropriation increased for the first time in years. Also like his predecessor, Mabry continued the use of nonpaid special rangers to help the dwindling number of rangers in the Frontier Battalion do their job.[29]

No one, however, could accuse Mabry of verbosity. While King prepared detailed annual reports, Mabry's documents tended to be lean. But he championed the Rangers just as effusively. In his first annual report, the new adjutant general wrote, "A Texas Ranger is the synonym for courage and vigilance. A bold rider, a quick eye, and a steady hand, he is the terror of the criminal, and merely his presence has its moral effect and acts as a wholesome restraint."[30]

One man who became a captain shortly after Mabry assumed control of the Rangers would not always be known for his "wholesome restraint," but he and those who would write about him helped to expand and perpetuate the Ranger legend. As a teenager, William Jesse McDonald came to East Texas from Mississippi after the Civil War. Schooled in business at a commercial college in New Orleans, he evolved from merchant to lawman, serving as a deputy sheriff, special ranger, and deputy U.S. marshal. By the mid-1880s he had moved to Hardeman County in northwest Texas.

McDonald, a skinny six-footer and as tough as a telegraph pole, soon proved his effectiveness as a peace officer, but his long-standing friendship with newly elected Governor Hogg is what got him appointed as captain of Company B when S. A. McMurray left the force. McDonald assumed command of the company in Amarillo, a new railroad town in the Panhandle.

Arriving in Amarillo on the Fort Worth & Denver about midnight on January 29, 1891, McDonald found a hotel and went to bed. He had just drifted off when someone awakened him with an urgent wire: Indians had raided Hall County, about a hundred miles to the southeast. His blue eyes smiling, the new captain read the telegram and laughed, assuming some of the rangers in his company had decided to welcome him into state service with a practical joke. It had been a decade since any hostile Indians had caused problems in Texas.

McDonald went back to sleep. But soon other telegrams came, including a dire-sounding message from the railroad superintendent. Still not believing that Indians had dared leave their reservation, McDonald nevertheless realized he had to investigate. The new captain dressed and walked to the telegraph office for more information. After an exchange of messages with the operator in Salisbury, who ended his last transmission with "Good-bye, I'm going now myself," McDonald got the railroad to run a special train trip to Hall County.

When McDonald and his rangers arrived in Salisbury, the town looked abandoned, its populace in hiding. It did not take the captain long to discover the source of the reported Indian outbreak: a tenderfoot had panicked at the sight of a bunch of drunk cowboys raising hell around their campfire. Even so, reports of killing and scalping had swept across the Panhandle like a prairie fire. The Canyon City *Echo* even reported that "state rangers were fighting the Indians and that two or three of the rangers had been killed."[31]

In reality, the rangers only suffered loss of sleep. Failing to see the humor of the situation, McDonald disgustedly returned to Amarillo to get some rest. Downstate, McDonald's Ranger colleagues had a real war to fight.

14

"The glory race of rangers"

THE FRONTIER BATTALION, 1891—99

E. E. Townsend would cheerfully have gone nose to nose with a mountain lion as long as he had his Winchester, but the brush-scarred .45-70 carbine could only do so much.

With Mexican rifle bullets whizzing in his general direction, the ranger squinted down the barrel of his saddle gun and squeezed the trigger. Sand shot up near the feet of Catarino Garza's big paint, but Townsend needed a few more feet out of his rifle. Quickly levering another round, he lined up his sights on the distant horseman and raised the barrel well over his target's big hat, hoping to drop a bullet on him. Too full of adrenaline to feel the kick, he saw another harmless puff of sand as that round, too, fell short.

In growing frustration, Townsend emptied his rifle at the bandit leader, but none of his bullets went where he wanted them. At a hundred yards, he could have put a slug in Garza's chest, at two hundred yards, he could have hit his horse, but at three hundred yards the Mexican sat well out of a Winchester's effective range and gained more distance with every hoofbeat of his horse.

Garza, the newspaperman wounded three years before by former ranger Victor Sebree at Rio Grande City, had decided that lead bullets

could bring political change faster than lead type. "The last of the independent journalists," he wrote, "the most humble of all, puts down today the pen to seize the sword in defense of the people's right."[1] With
some two hundred men, he had invaded Mexico on September 15,
1891—the day before Mexican Independence Day. Mexican troops
quickly drove Garza back into Texas, where despite occasional additional forays into Mexico, his ideological movement eroded into ban-
ditry, particularly in Starr and Duval counties.

As *The Texas Volunteer* reported, "Forced back from the border, unable to obtain shelter in his own home, and equally unable to escape,
Garza was compelled to hide out in the brush. To a man acquainted with
the country, and surrounded by friends . . . this was an easy matter."[2]

The state had no authority to enforce federal neutrality laws, but
when Garza's men started stealing horses from South Texas ranchers,
the Rangers took up his trail. As had been the case with Juan Cortina
more than thirty years earlier, the U.S. military also participated in
the campaign. The state's interest grew more intense on December 22,
when a skirmish between Garzistas and a cavalry patrol claimed the life of
a soldier. As Adjutant General Mabry put it, with the killing of the
solider, "they thus became murderers and amenable to the laws of the
State."[3]

Two Ranger units, Company F (now headed by J. A. Brooks, who had
replaced Scott in the spring of 1888) and Captain J. S. McNeel's Company E, combed the drought-stricken *brasada* looking for Garza and his
supporters over a part of the state that Mabry noted was "nearly equal
in area to the State of Massachusetts." Plagued with poor grazing for
their horses and an irregular supply system, the Rangers had hard duty.[4]

Five of Captain McNeel's rangers had a running fight with Garza and
three of his men near the La Granjenita Ranch in present Brooks
County on December 29, 1891. "We chased them about nine miles in
the brush," Townsend recalled.

> When the shooting started, I fired ten or twelve rifle shots at Garza,
> who was riding a big paint horse, at a distance of about 300 yards. He
> was running at right angle to me. I could see every bullet hit the
> sand, but I simply couldn't connect one of them with him or the
> horse. . . . Their fire was painfully regular and had something to do
> with my nervousness.[5]

At first light on January 6, 1892, rangers and U.S. soldiers engaged the Garzistas again on the La Havana Ranch, twenty miles south of Fort Ringgold in Starr County. Once more, the Mexicans eluded capture.[6]

"The affair has assumed proportions of no small importance," *The Texas Volunteer* declared. "The involving of the United States and Texas troops . . . adds to the interest with which the developments are watched, while the evident probability that it may at any moment be deemed necessary to increase the State forces, and possibly call on the Volunteer Guard, give piquancy to the situation."

But if at all possible, Mabry wanted to handle the situation solely with rangers. He also reminded the two captains and their men to stick to the enforcement of state laws. "You have nothing to do with any violation of the neutrality laws, as they are international questions which Texas must leave to the Federal authorities," Mabry had written Brooks shortly before his January 6 skirmish. "Your command is not to be employed in the capacity of scouts for the United States troops, but will act independently in the performance of your duties. Such action ought to be most effective, because of the nature of the service your command is accustomed to."[7]

Though he had designated Brooks as the ranking captain in the two-company operation, Mabry soon took to the field himself. The adjutant general spent two weeks with the Rangers before returning to Austin in early February. Mabry quickly came to see the difficulties that the Rangers faced:

> The situation was a peculiar one, and the obstacles to a successful [Ranger] raid at one dash were nearly insurmountable. The resident population . . . was composed entirely of Mexicans who claimed citizenship in Texas, but were with singular unanimity in sympathy with the Garza movement and the higher principle which, he claimed, animated him. Being thus friendly, they would, at first, harbor them secretly, act as spies, and notify the revolutionists of any approach of rangers or United States troops.[8]

In another skirmish with rangers on March 22 near the Bennett Ranch, one of the Garzistas shot and killed Ranger Robert Doughty, a scout in Captain McNeel's company. By that time, however, the leader of the failed revolution—facing state and federal prosecution if caught—had escaped from Texas to Costa Rica via New Orleans.[9]

"The so-called Garza revolution," an army officer stationed at Fort Brown wrote a short time later, "has been magnified far beyond actual facts, and has assumed an aspect in the newspapers of the country well calculated to inspire a horror of this border in the minds of their readers. . . . There has been a lot of hunting done by United States troops and Texas Rangers, but with very little result until quite recently, when, Garza having absconded and his plans having utterly failed, the last of his followers have either surrendered or have been captured."[10]

Townsend recalled:

It was not a bloody war, but it was a terribly hard one . . . day and night riding over that vast wilderness of chaparral. . . . One day our company rode 85 miles on horseback and prevented a raid into Mexico. For days, on long scout trips, we were half starved, rode our own horses, furnished our own guns and clothing. For pay we received at the end of each 3 months a State voucher for $90, and to get cash, it was sometimes discounted as much as 10 percent.[11]

Though nothing spectacular came of the campaign, the state and federal presence had clearly succeeded in scattering Garza's followers and forcing him out of the country. Mabry believed the Ranger effort averted significant killing and looting at only moderate expense to the state, much less than calling out the militia would have cost. *The Texas Volunteer* made another point that Mabry could not. In some instances, the magazine noted, "When the fugitives were preparing to assemble, and the Rangers were quietly getting together to rush in on them when they should least expect it, the soldiers marched into the scene, put the wary Mexicans to flight, and upset the plans of the Rangers."[12]

The Garza pursuit had generated more news media attention than results, including firsthand reporting by journalist–soldier of fortune Richard Harding Davis. Within a year, Davis folded his newspaper coverage of the Garza incident into *The West From A Car Window*, a book illustrated by Frederic Remington and published by Harper's. "The West," Davis observed,

is not wholly reconstructed. There are still the Texas Rangers, and in them the man from the cities of the East will find the picturesqueness of the Wild West show and its happiest expression. If they and the sight of cowboys roping cattle do not satisfy him, nothing else will. The Rangers are a semi-militia, semi-military organization of long descent, and with the most brilliant record of border warfare. At the present time their work is less adventurous than it was in the day of Captain McNelly, but the spirit of the first days has only increased with time.[13]

No doubt influenced by Davis's book and the extensive, highly hyped newspaper coverage of the Garza affair that had preceded it, near the end of his life poet Walt Whitman found himself moved to verse in regard to the Texas Rangers. In "Song of Myself," his epic poem, he wrote of the Rangers in lines 880–83:

> They were the glory of the race of rangers;
> Matchless with horse, rifle, song, support, courtship,
> Large, turbulent, generous, handsome, proud, and affectionate
> Bearded, sunburnt, dressed in the free costume of hunters.

Davis's description of the rangers he met in the South Texas brush country proved even more evocative than Whitman's poetry:

Boots above the knee and leather leggings, a belt three inches wide with two rows of brass-bound cartridges, and a slanting sombrero make a man appear larger than he really is; but the Rangers were the largest men I saw in Texas, the State of big men. And some of them were remarkably handsome in a sunburned, broad-shouldered, easy, manly way. They were also somewhat shy with the strangers, listening very intently, but speaking little, and then in a slow, gentle voice; and as they spoke so seldom, they seemed to think what they had to say was too valuable to spoil by profanity.[14]

"Hell Paso"

Responsibility for protecting rural Texas now rested solely on the shoulders of Davis's tanned, "manly" Rangers—the editor of *The Texas Volunteer* found "prairie patrolman" a useful synonym—and local peace officers. In the Panhandle, the army had abandoned Fort Elliott on October 20, 1890, followed in the Trans-Pecos by Fort Davis on July 3, 1891.[15] With

the exception of Fort Sam Houston in San Antonio and coastal artillery in-
stallations in Galveston, only the border remained fortified by the federal
government, the army continuing to maintain a string of garrisons along
or near the Rio Grande from Brownsville to El Paso. The frontier had
faded, but like cockleburs in a horse's tail, vestiges of the Wild West still
hung on in far West Texas and its biggest city, El Paso. Or, as some folks
derisively took to calling the mountain crossroad, "Hell Paso."[16]

"Another corpse floated down the Rio Grande this morning," the El
Paso *Evening Tribune* reported on May 27, 1893. "The fourth in two
weeks."

El Paso had been hard on rangers, too. "Handsome, likable" Sergeant
Charles H. Fusselman, then stationed at Marfa with a detachment of
Company D rangers, had been in town on August 17, 1890, to testify in
federal court when rancher John Barnes hurried to the sheriff's office to
report that Mexican rustlers had killed and cooked one of his calves
and then ridden off with several of his horses. Fusselman, joined by El
Paso policeman and former ranger George Herold, got their horses and
along with Barnes took up the thieves' trail. Riding up on the gang in a
rocky canyon in the Franklin Mountains, the two officers and the
rancher paid no attention to numbers and charged. As they closed in on
the Mexicans, leader Geronimo Parra fired his Winchester at Fusselman. The first shot missed, but Parra's second bullet hit the ranger in
the head, toppling him from his horse. Herold and Barnes, realizing
they had no hope against the larger group of gunmen, spun their horses
around and galloped back to El Paso for help, firing at the Mexicans as
they rode.

"Sheriff [James] White organized a posse of six of the most fearless
men in the county and sent them in pursuit of the thieves and murderers," an El Paso newspaper reported the next day. "A wagonload of provisions follow them and the posse will not return alone."

The posse did return empty-handed, though the officers and volunteers had recovered Barnes's stolen remuda along the Rio Grande, where
it looked as if their quarry had crossed into Mexico. Hearing of the death
of his friend, Ranger corporal John Hughes, in state service since 1887,
caught the next train from Marfa to El Paso. The ranger rode out alone after Fusselman's killer, but could not find him, either. Soon promoted as
Fusselman's successor, Hughes never gave up on the case.[17]

The death of the well-regarded Ranger sergeant convinced Adjutant

General King to move all of Company D from its headquarters at Uvalde to far West Texas. As King explained in his 1889–90 report, "Company D, Capt. Frank Jones, was sent to that section soon after the killing . . . with instructions to establish itself at a point most suitable for reaching and rendering service to the largest number of good citizens."

Barely two weeks earlier, on August 4, 1890, another Company D ranger died in the line of duty in the silver-mining boomtown of Shafter, downriver from El Paso in Presidio County. King summarized the incident:

> During a dance at a Mexican house . . . a difficulty arose in some way between the Mexicans and whites, and during the shooting that occurred, or just afterward, one of the Rangers was killed by the Mexicans. This was Private J. F. Gravis, and his record in the company and from the willing testimony of his Captain, indicate that he was an orderly, faithful, zealous and brave soldier, and his death another serious loss to the Company.

The commander of soon-to-be-closed Fort Davis sent a detachment of cavalry to Shafter until things calmed down. Referring to the killing of Ranger Gravis and three other recent murders in the Big Bend, General David S. Stanley, commander of the Department of Texas, wrote King from his headquarters in San Antonio that "a general state of lawlessness throughout this wild country has given rise to a feeling of much insecurity among the few inhabitants."

King could not argue that the Trans-Pecos was not a dangerous place, but Captain Jones's rangers were doing all they could to tame it. Of the 133 arrests the company made from December 1, 1888, to October 31, 1890, forty-seven were for homicide, more murder arrests than made by the other two companies combined. Nor did companies B and E lose any rangers. In addition to two men killed, Company D had a third ranger seriously wounded. (Not all these arrests took place west of the Pecos, and the wounding of the ranger had been at Richmond, but Jones clearly ran a hardworking outfit.)[18]

In January 1893, some members of the legislature once again brought up the possibility of disbanding the rangers. "We think such action at present by that honorable body would not be prudent, from the fact that the ranger force is of great service in aiding to capture outlaws who have

been forced out of more thickly settled portions of the state to the territory and many of the sparsely settled counties of northwest Texas," the
Amarillo *Northwestern* said in an editorial reprinted in the February 2,
1893 Dallas *Morning News*.

The rangers made it through the legislative session unscathed, and
in the early summer Captain Jones moved his headquarters farther west
from Alpine to Ysleta in El Paso County. Those who had argued a few
months before that the Frontier Battalion had outlived its usefulness
soon got a reminder that Texas still needed peace officers with statewide
jurisdiction.

"BOYS, I AM KILLED"

❶n June 29, 1893, only seven days after relocating in El Paso County,
the captain and four of his men, along with a deputy sheriff, attempted
to serve writs on Jesus and Serverino Olguin, known as thieves on both
sides of the river. Jones also hoped to find Antonio Olguin, a convicted
rapist who had escaped from the state penitentiary in Huntsville. The
Olguin family lived in an adobe compound about thirty miles below El
Paso at a point on the Rio Grande known as Pirate's Island, a well-
named no-man's-land created by a change in the river's course nearly
forty years before. Not finding anyone at the Olguin house but the old
and nearly blind father of the wanted men, the rangers made camp
nearby, intending to resume their search the next day. While breaking
camp early the next morning, they spotted two horsemen who spurred
their mounts and ran as the rangers approached. A subsequent report to
headquarters in Austin told the rest of the story:

> Capt. Jones not knowing he was across the [international] line ran
> them into Tres Jacales Mexico and they entered first house on right
> of the road. Mexicans opened fire. Capt. Jones halted and dis-
> mounted in front of the house and was shot through the leg and fell.
> He sat up & fired two or three shots.

T. F. Tucker, the ranger nearest the captain, asked Jones if he had
been hurt. "Yes, shot all to pieces," Jones said. Before Tucker had time
to say or do anything else, another rifle round thudded into the captain's
chest. "Boys, I am killed," he said, slumping over dead.

Facing intense fire from the Olguins and several dozen of their associates, Tucker and the other rangers held their ground for a while, but finally had to pull back, leaving their captain's body lying in the blazing sun. Tucker, having lost his horse in the fight, had to ride behind another ranger. Corporal Carl Kirchner rode hard ahead of the rest of the detachment for San Elizario, where he wired for help. Sergeant Hughes, who had remained in Brewster County when the rest of the company moved to El Paso County, took the first train to El Paso from Alpine.

The El Paso County sheriff along with former ranger Bazzel Lamar Outlaw, now a deputy U.S. marshal, arrived first with fourteen men. In the meantime, more armed Mexicans had rushed to the Olguin ranch. They clearly had the Texas lawmen outnumbered. Too, the battle had taken place in Mexico. The Texas officers reluctantly had to accept that crossing over to arrest Jones's killers and recover his body would only exacerbate an already volatile situation. The Olguins not being popular in Mexico either, the military commander in Juárez sped troops to the island and arrested them. As soon as he reached the scene, Hughes coordinated what proved to be a difficult effort to get Jones's body back in Texas. He also recovered his captain's rifle, spurs, watch, and money as well as Tucker's mount and gear.[19]

The Mexican government protested what it called an invasion of its territory by Jones and his rangers. The U.S. military investigated the incident for the State Department, and Mabry had the incident thoroughly looked over as well. Both probes concluded that the incursion had been an accident. "The facts show that the ranger detachment did not know that they were invading Mexican territory," Mabry wrote Governor Hogg on September 9. But to Mabry's view, the attack on the rangers had been quite deliberate. "There is no doubt but that Captain Frank Jones and detachment were decoyed into the trap just over the line into Mexico by these criminals, and the plan was to murder not only Jones but his entire detachment."[20]

Though not present at the fight, Alonzo Van Oden, one of Jones's rangers, had arrived in time to attend his captain's funeral at Ysleta. The young ranger wrote in his diary:

Feeling runs high here because the people feel that his death could have been prevented, as one newspaper puts it, "Mingled with the sense of loss at Captain Jones' murder, is the unpleasant feeling that

it was preventable, and should have been prevented by a more adequate provision by the legislature for this indispensable service, and
that body [the legislature] will be regarded as responsible for so needless a sacrifice upon the unholy alter of a so-called economy."[21]

The first Ranger captain to die in the line of duty since the days of
the Republic of Texas, Jones had been considered the Frontier Battalion's top company leader. "Always an active officer," *The Texas Volunteer* had said of Jones six months earlier, "his services have from the
first been most efficient and his record has been a bright one, winning
commendation from his superiors and the warm approval of those
among whom he was located."[22] Jones would be missed, but his successor soon proved equally able as a captain. On July 4, Adjutant General
Mabry promoted the thirty-eight-year-old Hughes to head the company.[23]

Less than a year later, the Rangers lost another of their own. In El
Paso on April 6, 1894, to testify before a grand jury, Private Joe Mc-
Kidrict stood visiting with friends at a print shop when he heard a shrill
police whistle coming from the red-light district. He ran to see if he
could help, finding former Ranger Bazz Outlaw drunk and threatening
people with his pistol outside Tillie Howard's bawdy house. When
McKidrict tried to calm him down, Outlaw shot him in the head and
again when he hit the ground. Constable John Selman in turn shot and
mortally wounded Outlaw.[24]

As one Texas newspaper had predicted, the growth of rail service in
the state meant outlaws would transition from robbing stagecoaches to
trains. Rangers investigated several train robberies, often trailing the
hold-up men for long distances across desolate country.

At about midnight on December 21, 1896, three men armed with
revolvers held up the west-bound Southern Pacific passenger train
about a mile west of Comstock, in Val Verde County. Firing several
shots to make their point, they tied up the engineer and fireman, and
escaped with seventy dollars plus assorted valuables collected from the
passengers.

Arriving in Comstock at 11 a.m. on December 22, Ranger Thalis T.
Cook soon departed on horseback with a posse of deputies and interested citizens to track them down.

Five days later the Dallas *Morning News* reported: "State rangers today arrested and jailed four stockmen, two of whom have been identified, who a week ago . . . held up the Southern Pacific train at Comstock."

That had not been the first time Rangers rode out of Comstock in pursuit of train robbers. In the early fall of 1891, Captain Jones and several of his rangers had cut the trail of a gang suspected of robbing a train near Sanderson in Terrell County. Finally catching up with them near present Ozona in Crockett County, Jones and his men killed two and captured three. The last of the hold-up men tried to outrun the rangers, leading them on an eight-mile chase. John Flint, the gang leader, finally realized he had no hope of outdistancing the lawmen. Stopping long enough to scribble out a quick will, he shot himself in the head.[25]

Captain Hughes's rangers stayed busy in the Trans-Pecos, but the thinly stretched Frontier Battalion had plenty enough work elsewhere. When Texas & Pacific Coal Company president Robert Dickey Hunter cut wages at the T&P CC mines in the vicinity of Thurber in Erath County, the miners staged a work stoppage. "Owing to the troubled conditions among the miners of the United States at this time I ask you to appoint about five special rangers to assist in keeping peace at the mines," Hunter wrote Mabry on June 5.

The adjutant general dispatched Captain McDonald to the coal-mining town seventy-five miles west of Fort Worth to pacify the strike-minded T&P CC workers.[26] Still recovering from wounds suffered in a gunfight six months earlier with Childress County Sheriff John Matthews at Quanah, the captain reached Thurber June 8. He soon found that union agitators from Oklahoma Territory had set up camp at a saloon in adjacent Palo Pinto County. Using complimentary beer to build a crowd, the agitators had been fomenting unrest on the part of the Texas workers. When for safety reasons Hunter began discharging intoxicated miners, the mood of the T&P CC employees deteriorated further. McDonald learned of threats to kill Hunter and his foremen and took seriously a handbill being distributed by the agitators threatening violence against the miners if they did not strike for their rights.

Thurber seemed on the verge of explosion, but McDonald met with both sides and resolutely vowed to maintain order, whatever it took. Only seven months after taking bullets in his neck, shoulder, and a lung, the wiry captain—still full of starch—made it plain that he would brook no trouble. McDonald's resolute manner worked. Both violence and a protracted strike had been averted.[27]

A month later, when President Grover Cleveland used regular army troops to face down railroad workers striking the Pullman Car Company in Chicago, nationwide violence against railroads seemed likely as the newly organized American Railway Union went on strike. Hoping to forestall trouble in Texas, Adjutant General Mabry ordered Brooks, Hughes, and McDonald to deploy their rangers at key rail facilities across the state. The show of force prevented any significant problems in Texas while the national labor issue played out in the courts.[28]

Meanwhile, lack of funding continued to "hamper" the Rangers. In early 1895, Captain Brooks had to cut half his men from the state payroll, reducing his company size from sixteen to eight.

Stopping the fight

Having taken on organized labor and prevailed, the Rangers gained national publicity in 1896 when the state tried to stop a championship fight between Robert Fitzsimmons and Peter Maher, two bare-knuckle pugilists. Determined to prevent the bout from happening on Texas soil, Governor Charles Culberson dispatched Mabry and a contingent of rangers to El Paso.

The first wave arrived February 9. Thirteen rangers, "stalwart, bronzed and determined looking men," stepped off the train and walked to a hotel near the station for breakfast. The men were Mabry, Captains Brooks of Company F and Rogers of Company E, and ten privates. Captain Hughes brought his company up from Ysleta, and Captain McDonald arrived by train from Amarillo with his men. Soon, thirty-two well-armed rangers walked the streets of El Paso.

Though churchgoers applauded the governor's resolve to prevent the boxing match, some local officials and citizens found the invasion of El Paso by state officers offensive. One night the Ranger presence nearly caused a riot. It started when someone provoked Pleas Watson, an East Texan in town on business, and he took a swing at the man outside one of the many saloons on San Antonio Street. Seeing the affray, Ranger "Doc" Losier hastened to arrest Watson. Dispensing with the formalities of an introduction, the ranger made his point by sticking the barrel of his pistol in Watson's belly.

Wrongly figuring Losier for a friend of the man he had punched, Watson twisted to avoid the handgun. That caused Losier's .45 to go off, punching a neat hole in the visiting businessman's coat. But the boisterous out-of-towner did not wait around to ask if Losier knew a good tailor. He ran across the street to the Santa Fe Railroad ticket office, and Losier started shooting for real. Hearing the gunfire, another ranger trotted to the scene. When he saw Losier shooting at a fleeing figure, he and a civic-minded cowboy from New Mexico joined the one-sided gunfight.

Still not realizing he had tangled with state peace officers, Watson turned in the middle of the street, drew two pistols, and returned their fire. That scattered the opposition long enough for him to make it up a stairway between the ticket office and a jewelry store. Safely behind cover, he yelled he would come down "if you fellows will promise not to murder me." The rangers and others agreed to stop shooting and Watson surrendered.

In the morning, passersby counted fifteen bullet holes in the stairs Watson had scampered up. In addition, the glass had been blown out of the Santa Fe office. The ticket agent took the damage in good humor, posting a sign that said, "Take the Santa Fe for Safety."

Recalling the incident years later, El Paso old-timer J. D. Ponder reckoned it "a wonder that several persons were not killed the night 'Doc' Losier started target practice on Pleas Watson, for there was considerable feeling against the rangers and [the rangers] were very angry on account of the criticisms to which they were being subjected." Only "the coolness of the Texas rangers and their refusal to notice their critics" headed off "a bloody riot," Ponder felt.[29]

For the dozens of newspapermen in town to cover the fight and the controversy surrounding it, the Rangers merely added another juicy element to the story.

"The rangers . . . correspond to the militia of any Northern State," reported the New York *World*, "except that the men are mostly graduated cowboys, sheriffs and deputy marshals who are in active service all the time, and whose principal duty is to protect the border."[30]

When the use of the Rangers to prevent the fight had first been threatened in Dallas, the New Orleans *Picayune* informed its readers that the Rangers "know nothing of military red tape, and who quietly and secretly, as cowboys, move about and swoop down upon offenders and all who propose infractions of the law."[31]

The state's show of force in El Paso made it clear to fight promoter

Dan Stuart that he would not be able to pull off the event in Texas. The resourceful showman hit on the idea of staging the match on an island in the Rio Grande across from Langtry—an international no-man's-land. Shortly before midnight on February 20 an eastbound train with two engines and ten passenger cars pulled out of the El Paso depot. Rangers, not knowing Stuart's scheme, joined the promoters and fans on the train, intent on preventing a fight in Texas. Two days later, the state officers stood on a bluff on the Texas side of the river, watching with interest as the disappointingly short fight proceeded beyond their jurisdiction.[32]

In his report to the governor, Mabry praised his men, even though they had not stopped the fight. After all, they had no jurisdiction on an international island. They had "conducted themselves in such manner as to reflect additional credit upon the name of a ranger—always a synonym for courage and duty well performed. They were orderly in manner, determined in mien, fearless and vigilant on duty; they thus naturally incur the displeasure of the law-breakers everywhere."[33] The general dismissed talk that these tough but restrained peace officers had crossed the river to take in the fight as an effort "palpably made to belittle the force." Besides, the rangers could see the boxing match just fine from the Texas side of the river.

The boys of Company B

Barely back from his prizefight duty, on February 25 Captain McDonald and most of his company left Wichita Falls aboard the 1 p.m. train for Fort Worth. When the train stopped at Bellevue, the captain got a telegram from Wichita Falls: Two men had robbed the First National Bank, killed the cashier, and wounded two others. The captain wired for horses to be waiting for him at the station and took the next train back to Wichita Falls. Arriving that evening, the rangers rode out of town to catch up with a posse of local officers and citizens.

Meeting the empty-handed posse members on their way back to town, McDonald declared that he and his men would press on. Inspired by the captain's tenacity, the posse decided to stay on the chase with the rangers. Late that night, the captain and two of his men slipped up on the suspected robbers—Elmer "Kid" Lewis and Foster Crawford—as they rested under a tree near the Red River. Both men held cocked pistols, but after assessing the rangers and posse members, they decided against a shoot-out and surrendered. Back in town, the rangers locked their prisoners in the Wichita County jail and went to get some sleep.

The next day, satisfied that local officers augmented by twenty-five deputized citizens could protect the two prisoners, McDonald left again for Fort Worth. Unfortunately for the two men in jail, the captain had underestimated the determination of local citizens to speed up justice. A mob surrounded the jail, using a telephone pole to break down the back door. They quickly convinced the lone deputy inside of the futility of trying to protect the two prisoners. The vigilantes bound the two bank robbers with ropes, dragged them from their cells, and returned them to the scene of their crime. Outside the bank two wooden boxes had been placed under a telephone pole. Two ropes dangled from the pole's crossarm.

Standing on one of the boxes with a rope around his neck, Lewis showed no fear in his final moments. He cursed the mob until he had no more breath to do so. Taking a different tact, Crawford kept a civil tongue and begged for mercy. As soon as he realized he had no hope of that, he asked for whiskey and got it. But before the drink could have taken effect, Crawford began a suspended sentence not subject to appeal.

When Mabry learned of the double lynching, he ordered McDonald to make a full report on his actions in the affair. The adjutant general accepted McDonald's assertion that he thought the prisoners had been safe, and nothing more came of it. The captain and his men would soon be trying to corral a different sort of mob downstate.[34]

"Mobism" in San Saba County

The lawlessness around San Saba, a Central Texas cattle town about ten miles west of the juncture of the San Saba and Colorado rivers, had been going on for years. The trouble accounted for more murders than any other Texas feud—forty-three homicides eventually being credited to the San Saba "mob." Like the difficulties in Mason County twenty years earlier, the San Saba problem began as vigilantism. But unlike what happened in Mason County, the lawlessness in San Saba mutated from a well-intentioned if extralegal civic effort to get rid of cattle thieves and other undesirables into a convenient means to an end, particularly in the acquisition of land and political power.[35]

In late July 1896, responding to a request from district judge W. M.

Allison as well as discreet pleas from several local citizens, Governor
Culberson ordered the Rangers, as one of the key participants later
wrote, "to put down the mob." The appeal for state intervention came
in the wake of two murders in five weeks, the June 22 killing of T. A.
Henderson and the July 28 murder of William A. James, shot nine times
as he drove his wagon across the Colorado River.

Company B's Sergeant W. John L. Sullivan, with one of his men,
Dudley Barker, took the train from Amarillo to Goldthwaite and met
two rangers from Captain Rogers' Company E, Allen Maddox and Edgar
T. Neal, on August 13. From the Mills County seat, the rangers traveled
by horse to San Saba accompanied by San Saba County sheriff S. E. W.
Hudson.

Sullivan, a tall, thin, full-bearded Mississippian of Irish lineage, later
wrote:

> The people of both factions, especially the mob element, were an-
> tagonistic to us when we first went to San Saba, and our lives were
> in danger. When we four boys pitched our tent at Hannah's Crossing
> [on the Colorado River outside of town] we shook hands with each
> other and made a solemn pledge that we would stay there and do our
> duty if we all had to die together. We vowed that we would arrest
> anybody of either faction whom we caught disobeying the law, and
> that we would die working the lever of our guns before we would
> give up our prisoners, no matter how many men we had to fight.[36]

The Ranger presence gave the county's law-abiding citizenry confidence to speak out against the mob. On August 29, a mass meeting to
discuss the problem drew more than five hundred citizens. "A committee representing every section of the county was named and strong resolutions were reported condemning mobism and lawlessness," the
Dallas *Morning News* reported on September 5.

The San Saba *News*, edited by U. M. Sanderson, courageously came
out editorially against the mob and for the Rangers. "Under the present
unsettled condition of law and order it will not be amiss to station the
rangers at the place most accessible to the old locus operandi of the mob
element," Sanderson had written the month before. "We say it is simply
beyond our power to recognize good citizenship and Christianity with
the spirit of prearranged, deliberate secret assassination. . . . Right can-

not compromise wrong. No man can be a good citizen and encourage by word or action the defiance of law. The Rangers are coming to stay until the lawless element is suppressed."[37]

The mob—which even included preachers—met every month at a place known as Buzzard's Water Hole, not far from the Ranger camp at Hannah's Crossing. A group with more than three hundred members (in one letter to headquarters, Sullivan said it could be as many as a thousand men), the mob was later described by one Ranger biographer as "nothing less than a murder society." Usually gathering under a full moon, the "society" opened with a prayer followed by intonations of secret oaths, then moved on to select targets and plot murder.[38]

When one suspected mob member eventually faced trial, a state's witness captured the essence of the mob's long reign of terror:

"Did you know of an organization of men in San Saba," a prosecutor asked county resident John W. Smith, "and, if so, what was it commonly called?"

The witness replied, "Yes, sir; and it was commonly known as the mob."

Next the prosecutor asked if anyone from that group ever came to his place.

"Yes, sir," Smith replied. "One night about twenty or twenty-five men rode up to my house, and the front one asked if that was where John Smith lived. I told them it was, and they said to me, 'If you don't stop cow stealing, we will break your damned neck,' and then they rode off, and as they went by me one of them said, 'Johnny, we are telling you this for your [own] good."[39]

Smith lived to talk about his experiences with the mob. Others did not, their bodies left perforated with bullets or hanging from trees.

Sullivan soon identified three likely murderers. But, as he reported to Austin, he did not believe he could develop enough evidence for convictions. However, newly elected district attorney W. C. Linden worked vigorously with the Ranger sergeant and his small detail to bring the suspected killers to justice.[40]

The Thirty-third Judicial District grand jury acknowledged that relationship between prosecutor and state law enforcement, reporting to Judge Allison that spring, "The ranger force stationed in [San Saba County] has been of great service in detecting crime, and in arresting the perpetrators; and we feel assured that we have secured testimony before the grand jury which we would not have gotten if the rangers had not been stationed here; and we would insist that every man in our county who is interested in law and order let these efficient officers feel that we are ready and willing to render them all the assistance in our power in bringing criminals to justice."[41]

Despite the panel's optimism, after hearing from 339 witnesses, on October 23, 1896, it only found true bills against two men believed associated with the mob, Matt Ford and George Trowbridge. The indictments alleged they had killed J. R. Turner, postmaster of the small community of Locker, on July 12, 1889, as he plowed his cotton field. Tried on a change of venue in Travis County's Fifty-third District Court beginning February 22, 1897, the case against Ford ended in a hung jury on March 5.[42]

Later that spring, the feisty Sullivan pulled his pistol during a heated courthouse argument with newly elected sheriff A. J. Hawkins, a mob puppet if not a member. One of Sullivan's men prevented a further escalation, and Judge Allison ordered the state officers out of the building. The judge soon wrote Mabry asking for Sullivan's removal from the county, though he wanted even more rangers. Learning of the judge's concerns, McDonald wrote to remind his sergeant that his name was Sullivan, not Caesar, and told him to cut back on his drinking. On May 4, bringing another ranger from his company, the captain arrived in San Saba to take personal command of the situation. Sullivan would stay, but under the direct supervision of his boss.

"If it becomes necessary," Mabry wrote Linden, "the [Ranger] detachment will be increased, until the state asserts its authority over violence and crime. In the history of the Frontier Battalion since 1874, it has yet to be shown that the Rangers have ever been routed, or withdrawn from their post of duty, and I expect that before very long a different feeling will exist in San Saba and adjoining counties."[43]

A second trial on June 14, this time with Trowbridge as defendant, had the same result as the district attorney's first effort, the jury split ten for conviction, two for acquittal. The frustration of seeing suspected mob members escaping punishment took a toll on Sullivan, who had continued drinking heavily despite the warning from his captain. In early July, McDonald demanded and received the lanky sergeant's resignation.[44]

Another round of indictments against alleged mob members that fall never progressed to trial. But working with Linden, the determined young prosecutor, McDonald and his rangers finally succeeded in cutting the head off the snake with the August 26, 1897, arrest of Bill Ogle, a key figure in the gang. Tried in Llano County, Ogle received a life sentence for the killing four years before of Jim Brown, shot off his horse while riding home from church with his wife.[45]

Rangers further solidified their control of the county when a boozed-up mob member confronted Private Barker with a rifle outside the courthouse. The ranger quickly put five bullets in his would-be assailant, laying to rest both the gunman and any future local opposition to the Rangers.[46] In the words of a local historian who had the benefit of interviewing old-timers who had been around during the mob's prime, "Peace had come to dwell in San Saba County."[47]

In "sparsely settled but organized counties" such as San Saba "[in which] a lawless element hold[s] the balance of voting power," Mabry had observed in his report for 1895–96, "it is only the rangers that preserve the peace, restore order, and offer the necessary protection. They represent the majesty of the State, and belong to no faction, and merely their presence often prevents bloodshed, and peace and quiet are restored."

What Mabry did not report, though both McDonald and Sullivan later pointed it out, is what ultimately made San Saba as safe as a Sunday school—eight former rangers settled in the county and married local women. One of those former rangers, Edgar Neal, went on to serve as sheriff for sixteen years.

THE END OF THE RANGERS?

In addition to their work in San Saba County, Mabry reported that the Rangers had arrested 676 criminals, returned 2,856 head of stolen stock to their owners. and assisted civil authorities 162 times. Rangers guarded jails 13 times.

"They [the Rangers] are circumscribed by no county limits," Mabry wrote, "can easily and rapidly move from one section to another and criminals do not care to invite their pursuit. Specially equipped for continued rapid motion, they take up the trail and follow it with a persistency of the sleuth hound, until the criminal is either run out of the country, captured or killed."[48]

Mabry did not have to convince one border newspaper editor of the efficacy of the Rangers. Even though the army continued to garrison the border post of Fort Clark at Brackettville, the proprietor of the Brackettville

News in Kinney County suggested that the next session of the legislature authorize border counties to impose a local tax of ten cents per $100 evaluation to defray the cost of hiring additional rangers.[49]

The newspaper editor's funding idea gained no momentum, but the Rangers did. They scouted 173,381 miles in 1895 and 1896. Though they still spent a lot of time in the saddle, as they had begun to do in the 1880s, they made most of their long trips by train using passes issued by the railroads, either carrying their horses in stock cars or renting or borrowing horses when they arrived at their destination. Where no trains ran, they traveled by stagecoach. Letter mail remained the backbone of their communication system for routine matters, with telegraph and even the telephone for more urgent concerns.[50]

The Rangers no longer had much to do in the urban areas such as Dallas. The largest city in Texas at the time, it had more than forty thousand residents and a competent uniformed police force. But Dallas's most substantial newspaper, the *Morning News*, continued to see the importance of a state law enforcement agency. An unnamed "staff correspondent" in Austin penned a long, favorable piece on the Rangers for the newspaper's July 25, 1896, edition.

"The ranger service is either a necessity or a political luxury," he wrote, "a safeguard to life and property or a product of the pie machine. I believe it is the former, and the recent call on the governor for protection from thieves and assassins in and around San Saba county is a case in point."

The correspondent assessed the Rangers with balance:

I am not contending that the rangers are wingless angels. I am not endorsing everything they have done or have not done. I do not endorse the grand stand play made by the young governor when he sent the frontier guard to El Paso for the purpose of manufacturing political buncombe and corralling the great moral vote. I do not endorse it for the reason that I was there . . . and know of my own knowledge that the rangers were neither needed or wanted. They had no business whatever there at the expense of the people when the local peace officers were equal to every emergency. But it was no fault of theirs. . . . They were simply obeying orders, and aside from all this they have rendered invaluable service to Texas and her people on more occasions than one.

The Dallas journalist also decried the Rangers' low pay: "They are the poorest paid people in the employ of the state. They carry their lives in their hands and encounter dangers and hardships every day." After this broad hint that Texas ought to give its rangers a raise, he concluded, "The service ought to be perpetuated and not in a crippled condition. Its abolishment would be the costliest piece of economy Texas ever practiced." As they had several times before, the Rangers survived the legislative move to abolish the force.[51]

Former adjutant general King made one more contribution to the Rangers in writing their first history, an article in flowery Victorian language that Dudley G. Wooten included in his *Comprehensive History of Texas*. Despite long sentences and paragraphs, King made some salient points, including a treatise on Ranger character:

> A fair share of physical courage may enable an ordinary soldier to execute creditably all that is required of him . . . guided by the judgment and authority of his superior officers . . . in blind obedience to orders; but this was not the case with the Texas Rangers.
>
> The exercise of their functions as peace officers required physical courage as high and true as ever possessed by the most chivalrous soldier, and to this had to be added an individual self-reliance, rare moral courage, comprehensive knowledge of men, steadfastness in the determination to accomplish their purpose, capacity for adapting one's self to all sorts of surroundings and conditions, fertility in resources, quickness of thought in emergencies and a readiness to assume all needed responsibility and to alter plans when such change became necessary. Besides all these notable and excellent qualities, and others which accompanied or grew out of them, the Rangers, in order to meet the requirements and to accomplish to the utmost the duties of their high calling, had to be personally men of good habits, and of upright, honorable conduct.

King had codified what it took to be an effective Ranger.

"The possession of this unusual combination of moral, mental, and manly traits, in connection with their extensive official authority, enabled these men collectively and individually to exert a remarkable power for good wherever they served or were known," King wrote.

In fact, he continued, the Rangers had practically worked themselves out of a job. "We may point with pride to the fact that for years there has been no general disturbance of the public peace in Texas, and no local feuds, riots, mobs, or 'strikes' that caused anything more than a passing flurry, or left behind them any serious or hurtful effects of a permanent nature."[52]

The year before Wooten's Texas history came off the press, an effort had begun to organize an Ex–Texas Rangers Association. In March 1897, all known former rangers received a five-paragraph handbill printed in Austin. "At a meeting of the surviving members of the old Texas Ranger force," it began, "held at Austin, Texas, on the 2nd inst., at which Capt. M. M. Kinney was Chairman and H. G. Lee was Secretary, it was resolved to form an Ex Texas Rangers Association, to be composed of ex Rangers who have been honorably discharged from the service." The flyer said it had further been resolved that the association would have its first meeting in Austin that October. "Rip" Ford also had a hand in organizing the gathering, but a paralyzing stroke on October 1 prevented him from attending the first meeting. The old ranger hung on for a little more than a month, dying on November 3 at the age of eighty-two.[53]

Adjutant General Mabry resigned on May 5, 1898, to serve in the Spanish-American War. Mabry's replacement, A. P. Wozencraft, busied himself overseeing a war-fueled expansion of the Ranger companies to twelve men each. As soon as he had the companies up to strength, the new adjutant general moved them closer to the Rio Grande in the far-fetched event of a Spanish invasion attempt. The ironhanded Mexican president Porfirio Díaz kept the border peaceful, and most rangers soon returned to their regular stations. By mid-June, company size had been pared to eight men each.[54]

Following Wozencraft's resignation, Governor Culberson appointed Thomas Scurry, a Dallas real estate man and Spanish War veteran, as adjutant general on January 17, 1899. A few months shy of his fortieth birthday, Scurry, like King and Mabry, took an active role in his leadership of the Rangers.[55]

The first crisis on Scurry's watch came on March 21, 1899, in Laredo. An outbreak of smallpox, known on the border as *la viruela*, had local residents on edge. When the state health department began a vaccination program, many citizens resisted, not understanding that the quick thrust of a needle into their shoulder could save their lives. Captain Rogers and one of his men traveled from their station at Cotulla to the border city to help enforce a quarantine.

Nearly as fearful of medical intervention on the part of the state as the disease itself, the predominately Mexican-American citizenry grew increasingly uneasy. Rumor had it that the community might resort to arms to prevent local and state officers from removing smallpox patients to a quarantine area. Accordingly, Rogers ordered his sergeant and four men, along with a special ranger, to join him in the operation. When state health officer Dr. W. T. Blount got word that certain parties had stockpiled weapons and ammunition, he notified Sheriff L. R. Ortiz and Rogers. Learning that a local hardware store had received an order for two thousand loads of buckshot, the sheriff got a search warrant for two residences.

The first search went without incident. But at the second house, a conversation between Sheriff Ortiz and owner Agapito Herrera quickly deteriorated into confrontation. When the sheriff grabbed Herrera by the shoulder, two of the man's friends ran inside the house and emerged, as Rogers would recall, "with their Winchesters in a shooting position." Seeing the rifles, Rogers and the two rangers he had with him drew their pistols. The captain fired toward the riflemen and they ran for cover behind a nearby wall. Meanwhile, Herrera pulled free from the sheriff and ducked inside. He came out with a rifle.

Not waiting to see what he intended to do with it, Rogers shot Herrera. Despite a bullet in his breast, the man stayed on his feet, still holding his rifle. At that, as the captain later reported, "shooting . . . became general." From somewhere above, a rifle bullet hit Rogers just below his shoulder, nearly tearing off his right arm. Seeing his captain wounded, private Augie Old shot Herrera in the chest, putting two more bullets in his head for good measure. Herrera's sister, also shooting, took a bullet in her arm. Then a neighbor who had joined the fight toppled from another ranger bullet.

Running out of ammunition, the rangers pulled back toward the Hamilton Hotel, Rogers using his left hand to hold on to his bleeding arm. While doctors began treating the badly wounded captain, the other two rangers and five of their colleagues returned to the scene of the shooting, taking on some twenty armed men. Wounding nine of them, the rangers finally dispersed the mob. The next day, Tenth Cavalry troopers from Fort McIntosh backed up the Rangers with a Gatling gun until the situation calmed down.[56]

The same month, Captain McDonald and two rangers took the train to Columbus, in Colorado County, to defuse a feud between two local factions, the Mark Townsend and Sam Reese families and friends. The other two state lawmen got delayed, leaving McDonald to face the crisis alone. "The district judge and district attorney both informed him that it was impossible to handle the situation," Scurry later reported, "but he told them that he could make the effort, and he gave the members of each faction a limited time in which to get rid of their weapons, stating that he would put those in jail who refused to comply. His order had the desired effect."[57]

McDonald had again upheld the Ranger tradition of feud mitigation, but Scurry saw trouble coming. On January 30, 1899, he sent a letter to McDonald and the other three captains—Brooks, Hughes, and Rogers—urging them "to be prepared to defend the Rangers on the issue of retaining the Frontier Battalion." Noting that the next legislature would be taking up the matter, the adjutant general told his commanders to "be mindful of the things you do, the actions you take, and your service." In other words, make the Rangers continue to look relevant but do not embarrass the service in the process.[58]

Dead twenty-two years, Captain Leander McNelly gained literary immortality in 1899 with publication of N. A. Jennings's partially fictionalized memoir, *A Texas Ranger*. Issued by New York's Charles Scribner's Sons, the book proved popular with readers across the country. Though Jennings had ridden with McNelly for less than eight months, he claimed in his book to have been with the company from its organization. The book had its share of additional inaccuracies, but Jennings deftly captured how rangers thought and acted during the mid-1870s. "I defy anyone to read it without being engaged by its brightness and ranger-swift directness," J. Frank Dobie wrote in the introduction of a later printing of Jennings's book. "The swing of young men in the saddle runs though its pages."[59]

But the book's author viewed its writing from the perspective of an older man. "It is a relief to put on paper the record of the free, out-door existence of by-gone years," Jennings wrote at the end of his book. "I am glad I have done it, for it is well that the history of McNelly's and Hall's Texas Rangers should live after we who made up that body have passed away."[60]

Even so, many of McNelly's "boys" and Frontier Battalion rangers would survive well into the next century. Near the end of his long life, former ranger and San Antonio banker W. W. Collier rounded up his experiences in a memoir he called "Frontier Days or the Old West As I Recall It." His unpublished typescript includes a two-page, single-spaced addendum titled "Some Comments Regarding Rangers and 'The Old West.'"

The Texas Rangers, Collier wrote, "inspired a very wholesome fear in the criminal element. This was partly due to the character of the men in the Service and partly to the support the Governors gave them." The state's chief executives "recognized the necessity of drastic measures against the criminals, so they allowed the Rangers unusual powers as peace officers. . . . Rangers were not under bond and had been told that if they were placed in jeopardy by any Court, any Governor had pardoning power which they could rely upon."

Though rangers had extraordinary authority compared with local and county officers, Collier continued, "At times a man had to be a 'squad' by himself, which was frequently done, with notable success. It was therefore of the utmost importance that each man have self-reliance, courage . . . quick judgment and be equal to any emergency whatsoever." Not every man issued a ranger's commission measured up to Collier's ideal, but "a recruit would soon be eliminated from the Service if he proved lacking in these qualities."

What the Rangers accomplished in post–Civil War Texas, Collier wrote, had been "as necessary and as effectively done as [the work of] their predecessors against the Indian marauders." In fact, to Collier's thinking, "The criminal was by far more dangerous than the Indian and it was more difficult, if not so spectacular, to combat him."[61]

But as the nineteenth century wound down, some Texans viewed the Frontier Battalion as an expensive governmental relic of a vanished era. Modern Texas, many believed, no longer needed the Texas Rangers.

Notes

1. "Ten men . . . to act as rangers"

1. Gregg Cantrell, *Stephen F. Austin: Empresario of Texas* (New Haven and London: Yale University Press, 1999), p. 95. This is the definitive biography of Austin, though it does not dwell on his efforts to defend his colonists from Indians.
2. Eugene C. Barker, *Life of Stephen F. Austin, Founder of Texas, 1793–1836: A Chapter in the Westward Movement of the Anglo-American People* (Austin: Texas State Historical Association, 1949), p. 93.
3. Harold J. Weiss Jr., "Flying Forces: The Origins of the Texas Rangers" (paper delivered at the annual meeting of the Texas State Historical Association, Austin, Texas, March 7, 1997).
4. John L. Davis, *The Texas Rangers: Images and Incidents* (San Antonio: University of Texas Institute of Texan Cultures, 1991), p. 10; Weiss, "Flying Forces."
5. Thomas W. Knowles, *They Rode for the Lone Star: The Saga of the Texas Rangers* (Dallas: Taylor Publishing Company, 1999), p. 10.
6. Boston *News-Letter*, November 13, 1960.
7. Knowles, *They Rode for the Lone Star*, p. 10.
8. Harold J. Weiss Jr., "From Citizen Soldiers to Organized Police: Themes in Texas Ranger History" (paper presented at the thirty-first annual conference of the Western History Association, Austin, Texas, October 16–19, 1991), p. 4.
9. Margaret Maud McKellar, *Life on a Mexican Ranche*, ed. Dolores L. Latorre (Bethlehem, Pa.: Lehigh University Press, 1994), pp. 20–21. For a detailed

though academically dense study of the Spanish legal system in the Southwest, see Charles R. Cutter, *The Legal Culture of New Spain* (Albuquerque: University of New Mexico Press, 1995).

10. D. E. Kilgore, *A Ranger Legacy: 150 Years of Service to Texas* (Austin: Madrona Press, 1973), p. 12.

11. Charles M. Robinson III, *The Men Who Wear the Star: The Story of the Texas Rangers* (New York: Random House, 2000), p. 15.

12. Ibid.

13. Allen G. Hatley, *The Indian Wars in Stephen F. Austin's Colony, 1822–1835* (Austin: Eakin Press, 2001), p. 9.

14. Trespalacios to Austin, in Eugene C. Barker, ed., *The Austin Papers* (Washington: Annual Report of the American Historical Association, 1919), vol. 1, p. 560.

15. Trespalacios to Tumlinson and Kuykendall, January 31, 1823, cited in Kilgore, *Ranger Legacy*, p. 81.

16. Hatley, *Indian Wars*, pp. 84–85, citing Trespalacios to Tumlinson and Kuykendall, Bexar Archives, Roll 74, No. 0116-0117.

17. Stephen F. Austin, *Establishing Austin's Colony*, ed. David B. Gracy III (Austin: Jenkins Publishing Co., 1970), p. 27.

18. J. W. Wilbarger, *Indian Depredations in Texas* (1889; repr., Austin: Eakin Press, State House Books, 1985), p. 198.

19. Kilgore, *Ranger Legacy*, p. 15.

20. *Colorado County Chronicles* (Columbus: Colorado County Historical Commission, 1986), 1:39; *The New Handbook of Texas* (Austin: Texas State Historical Association, 1995), vol. 4, pp. 821–22.

21. Kelly F. Himmel, *The Conquest of the Karankawas and the Tonkawas, 1821–1859* (College Station: Texas A&M University Press, 1999), p. 49.

22. Kilgore, *Ranger Legacy*, p. 18.

23. William B. Dewees, *Letters from an Early Settler of Texas* (1852; repr., Waco: Texian Press, 1968), p. 54; Marshall E. Kuykendall, *They Slept Upon Their Rifles: The Story of the Captain Robert H. Kuykendall Family in America and the Entry of the Family with the Anglo Settlement into Mexican/Texas in Stephen F. Austin's Colony in 1821* (Austin: Nortex Press, 2005), p. 49; Kilgore, *Ranger Legacy*, p. 73.

24. Kuykendall, *They Slept Upon Their Rifles*, pp. 49–50.

25. Kilgore, *Ranger Legacy*, pp. 26–27, 33, 74–77. Tumlinson has often been heralded as the first Texas Ranger to die in the line of duty, but that is overbroad. He was an elected official, more like a modern county judge. His son and fifteen other descendants, however, did become rangers.

26. Ibid., p. 28. Not only was gunpowder scarce, its quality was problematic. The powder available in San Antonio was slow-burning, suitable for Mexican

military muskets, but not for long-barreled rifles designed to discharge a bullet at a higher velocity.

27. Ibid., p. 31. Trespalacios had resigned on April 17, 1823, replaced by Governor Luciano Garcia.
28. Robinson, *Men Who Wear the Star*, p. 19.
29. Walter Prescott Webb, *The Texas Rangers: A Century of Frontier Defense* (Boston: Houghton Mifflin, 1935), p. 10.
30. Kilgore, *Ranger Legacy*, p. 31.
31. Hatley, *Indian Wars*, pp. 32–35.
32. Eugene C. Barker, "The Government of Austin's Colony, 1821–1831," *Southwestern Historical Quarterly*, January 1918, p. 233.
33. Austin, *Establishing Austin's Colony*, pp. 84–85.
34. Cantrell, *Stephen F. Austin*, p. 177.
35. Dewees, *Letters from An Early Settler*, pp. 53–54.
36. Noah Smithwick, *Evolution of a State or Recollections of Old Texas Days*, comp. Nanna Smithwick Donaldson (Austin: W. Thomas Taylor, 1995 printing of 1900 Gammel Book Company edition), p. 73.
37. Hatley, *Indian Wars*, p. 45.
38. Himmel, *Conquest of the Karankawas*, p. 50.
39. Hatley, *Indians Wars*, p. 109.
40. Ibid., pp. 48–52; Barns, Florence Elberta. "Building a Texas Folk-Epic: The Saga of Strap Buckner." *Texas Monthly* (October 1929) pp. 347–357. Buckner, a giant of a man known for his strength and his contentiousness, died in the Battle of Velasco on June 25 or June 26, 1832.
41. J. H. Kuykendall, "Reminiscences of Early Texans," *Southwestern Historical Quarterly* 11 (April 1925): p. 250.
42. Hatley, *Indian Wars*, p. 54. In his study of Indian warfare in colonial Texas, Allen Hatley maintains the members of this small company truly constituted the first Texas Rangers: "The organization of this ranging command is documented, it does not depend on a great leap of faith, as does accepting any earlier ranger organization, and Abner Kuykendall's group actually performed the traditional duties of a ranger command."
43. Natchitoches *Courier*, April 3, 1827.
44. Natchitoches *Courier*, January 23, 1827.
45. Hatley, *Indian Wars*, p. 59.

2. "Chastising . . . menaces to civilised man"

1. Jo Ella Powell Exley, *Frontier Blood: The Saga of the Parker Family* (College Station: Texas A&M University, 2001), p. 33, 46.
2. *New Handbook of Texas*, vol. 5, pp. 623–24. First approved by the Mexican

government in 1825, Robertson's colony had taken nearly nine years to develop, progressing through a series of names, principals, and political intrigue before finally devolving on Robertson on May 22, 1834. The colony extended two hundred miles up the Brazos River, including all or part of thirty present Texas counties. As *empresario*, Robertson settled six hundred families before the outbreak of the Texas Revolution.

3. Ibid., vol. 2, p. 252.

4. Stephen L. Moore, *Savage Frontier: Rangers, Riflemen, and Indian Wars in Texas* (Plano: Republic of Texas Press, 2002), vol. 1, pp. 16–17.

5. Malcolm D. McLean, comp. and ed., *Papers Concerning Robertson's Colony in Texas* (Arlington: University of Texas at Arlington Press, 1983), vol. 10, p. 47.

6. Moore, *Savage Frontier*, p. 20.

7. Ibid., p. 22. The most complete account of the Ranger battalion led by John H. Moore in the summer of 1835 is found in Moore's *Savage Frontier*, pp. 21–29. Captains George W. Barnett, Philip Haddox Coe, Michael R. Goheen, and R. M. Williamson each led a company, joined later in the campaign by R. M. Coleman. Ranger privates received $2 a day for their services, with the compensation for the officers and Colonel Moore commensurate with their rank. At a salary of $170 a month, Moore later received $294.66 for one month and twenty-two days of service. Officers also recovered personal expenses, including the cost of providing beef for their men. By September 13, 1835, all the companies had been mustered out of service. Though this expedition never encountered a large party of Indians, it may have resulted in a higher body count than generally believed. In *Savage Frontier*, p. 29, Moore writes that James C. Neill, Moore's adjutant, inoculated a captured Indian with smallpox virus that summer. What effect this early attempt at biological warfare had is not known, but it is well documented that diseases introduced by whites played havoc with Indians all across the West. The first reported instance of a deliberate attempt to infect Indians with smallpox occurred in Canada in 1763 during the French and Indian War.

8. McLean, *Papers Concerning Robertson's Colony*, vol. 12, pp. 31–32; Eugene C. Barker, ed., "Journal of the Permanent Council (October 11–27, 1835)," *Texas State Historical Association Quarterly* 7 (April 1904): pp. 249–77.

9. Price Daniel and James C. Martin, eds, *Legislative Messages of the Chief Executives of Texas* (Austin: Texas State Library, 1973), vol. 1, p. 6.

10. Ibid., vol. 1, p. 136.

11. John H. Jenkins, general ed., *The Papers of the Texas Revolution, 1835–1836* (Austin: Presidial Press, 1973), vol. 1, p. 203. Cos issued the two-paragraph circular on July 5, 1835.

12. Randy Roberts and James S. Olson, *A Line in the Sand: The Alamo in Blood and Memory* (New York: Free Press, 2001), p. 51.

13. Daniel and Martin, *Legislative Messages*, vol. 1, p. 18.

14. Martha Anne Turner, *Texas Epic: An American Story* (Quanah, Tex.: Nortex Press, 1974), pp. 13–17.

15. Smithwick, *Evolution of a State*, p. 73.

16. John Henry Brown, *The Indian Wars of and Pioneers of Texas* (189-6; repr., Austin: State House Press, 1988), pp. 89–90. Wilbarger told Sarah Hibbins's story first in his *Indian Depredations of Texas* (1889), pp. 220–22, but Brown, relying on an account Tumlinson wrote for him sometime in the 1850s, told it better. Smithwick's version, though his daughter may have refreshed his memory from the Wilbarger book, nevertheless adds perspective. See Moore, *Savage Frontier*, pp. 74–81, for a synthesis of the three primary accounts of the rescue, plus his examination of four Republic of Texas–era audited claims bearing on the incident.

17. Smithwick, *Evolution of a State*, p. 75.

18. Brown, *Indian Wars of and Pioneers of Texas*, p. 90. Tumlinson later claimed he killed the Indian after shooting him with a rifle from twenty-five feet.

19. Ibid.

20. Jenkins, *Papers of the Texas Revolution*, vol. 4, pp. 249–50.

21. Stephen L. Hardin, *Texian Iliad: A Military History of the Texas Revolution* (Austin: University of Texas Press, 1994), p. 109.

22. Daniel and Martin, *Legislative Messages*, vol. 1, pp. 76–77.

23. Jenkins, *Papers of the Texas Revolution*, vol. 4, pp. 249–50.

24. Daughters of the American Revolution, *The Alamo Heroes and Their Revolutionary Ancestors* (San Antonio: 1976), pp. 45, 54–55.

25. http://www.tamu.edu/ccbn/dewitt/dewitt.htm. Tumlinson later fought in the Battle of San Jacinto as a member of Captain William J. E. Heard's company of "citizen volunteers." After the revolution, the former ranger returned to Bastrop County. He eventually settled in DeWitt County, where he made his living as a rancher and land trader. He died in the community of Clinton in 1853, apparently of natural causes.

26. Stephen L. Moore, *Eighteen Minutes: The Battle of San Jacinto and the Texas Independence Campaign* (Lanham, Md.: Republic of Texas Press, 2004), pp. 179–80.

27. Ibid., pp. 453–62.

28. John D. Gray, "Robert McAlpin Williamson," *Texas Ranger Dispatch* 2 (2000), citing Audited Republic Claims, Texas State Archives.

29. *Rachael Plummer's Narrative of Twenty-one Months Servitude as a Prisoner among the Commanchee Indians* (Austin: Jenkins Publishing Company, 1977), pp. 5–7; Exley, *Frontier Blood*, pp. 63–64.

30. Mike Cox, *Texas Ranger Tales II* (Plano: Republic of Texas Press, 1999), pp. 1–12.

31. On December 16, the First Texas Congress appointed Williamson judge of the Third Judicial District, which also made him a member of the republic's Supreme Court. *New Handbook of Texas*, vol. 6, p. 992. The early-day ranger died on December 22, 1859, in Wharton. Duncan W. Robinson, *Judge Robert McAlpin Williamson* (Austin: Texas State Historical Association, 1949), passim.

32. Exley, *Frontier Blood*, pp. 63–64.

33. John H. Jenkins, "Texas Letters and Documents," *Texana* 1 (1963): pp. 57–58.

34. *Niles' Weekly Register*, September 17, 1836, p. 34.

35. Davis, *Texas Rangers*, p. 14.

36. *The Heritage of Blanco County, Texas* (Blanco, Texas: Blanco County News, 1987), p. 195.

37. Gerald S. Pierce, *Texas Under Arms* (Austin: Encino Press, 1969), p. 33.

38. Houston to John Linney, September 18, 1836. Andrew Jackson Houston Papers No. 546, Texas State Archives.

39. Moore, *Savage Frontier*, 197; *Telegraph and Texas Register*, October 14, 1836.

40. Frederick Wilkins, *The Legend Begins: The Texas Rangers, 1823–1845* (Austin: Statehouse Press, 1996), p. 28.

41. *Laws of the Republic of Texas, 1837* (Houston: 1837), pp. 53–54, 74.

42. Pierce, *Texas Under Arms*, p. 46.

43. Dorman H. Winfrey and James M. Day, eds., *The Indian Papers of Texas and the Southwest, 1825–1916* (1966; repr., Austin: Texas State Historical Association, 1995), vol. 1, pp. 22–28.

44. "Today's Rangers Scorned," El Paso *Times*, May 30, 1936, quoting former Frontier Battalion Ranger Michael Bumgardner. He served as a private under Captain W. J. Maltby May 30–December 13, 1874; Frances T. Ingmire, *Texas Rangers Service Records* (St. Louis: Ingmire Publications, 1982), vol. 1., p. 88.

45. *New Handbook of Texas*, vol. 6, p. 112.

46. Charles Adams Gulick Jr., Winnie Allen, Catherine Elliott, and Harriet Smither, eds., *Papers of Mirabeau Bonaparte Lamar* (Austin and New York: Pemberton Press, 1968), vol. 1, pp. 592–95, Benthuysen to Lamar, December 8, 1837.

47. *Writings of Sam Houston*, vol. 1, p. 158; Gerald S. Pierce, "The Army of the Republic of Texas, 1836–1845" (M.A. thesis, University of Mississippi, 1964), pp. 127–28; F. Todd Smith, *The Wichita Indians: Traders of Texas and the Southern Plains, 1540–1845* (College Station: Texas A&M University Press, 2000), p. 141.

48. Stephen L. Moore, *Taming Texas: Captain William T. Sadler's Lone Star Service* (Austin: State House Press, 2000), pp. 287–90. Moore, *Savage Frontier*, Vol. II, pp. 6–7.

49. O. C. Fisher, *It Occurred in Kimble: The Story of a Texas County* (Houston: Anson Jones Press, 1937), pp. 84–85.

3. "UTTERLY FEARLESS AND INVINCIBLE"

1. George Dewey Harmon, *United States Indian Policy in Texas: 1845–1860* (Bethlehem, Pa.: Lehigh University, 1931), pp. 378–79. For an overview on Indian policy during the Republic of Texas era, see Anna Muckleroy, "The Indian Policy of the Republic of Texas," *Southwestern Historical Quarterly* 25 (April 1922): pp. 229–60; 26 (July 1922): pp. 1–29; 26 (October 1922): pp. 128–48; 26 (January 1923): pp. 184–206.

2. Rusk to Roberts, December 25, 1838. Nearly sixty years later, the letter remained in the possession of the Roberts family, passed on from Captain Mark Roberts to his son, T. F. Roberts. The younger Roberts made it available to the Paris correspondent of the Dallas *Morning News*, which published it on October 16, 1897.

3. Harmon, *United States Indian Policy in Texas*, pp. 378–79.

4. Winfrey and Day, *Indian Papers*, vol. 1, pp. 57–59.

5. John H. Jenkins, ed., *Recollections of Early Texas: Memoirs of John Holland Jenkins* (Austin: University of Texas Press, 1958), pp. 186–87; Moore to Secretary of War A. S. Johnston, March 10, 1839, in Winfrey and Day, *Indian Papers of Texas*, vol. 1, pp. 57–59; *New Handbook of Texas*, vol. 4, pp. 821–22. In addition to being the founder of La Grange and a successful agriculturist, Moore never wavered in his willingness to ride after Indians or otherwise fight for what he believed in. He not only participated in the "Come and Take It" skirmish at Gonzales in 1835, he is reported to have designed the Texas banner bearing those defiant words. In the early 1840s, Moore twice raised men to assist in repelling Mexican incursions and even enlisted in Terry's Texas Rangers at the start of the Civil War. Old age kept him out of that sectional catastrophe, but he lived until December 2, 1880. He is buried in the family cemetery in Fayette County. Moore, *Savage Frontier*, Vol. II, pp. 158–168, provides a detailed account of Moore's February 15, 1839, battle with the Comanches.

6. The Battle of Brushy Creek is covered in John H. Jenkins and Kenneth Kesselus, *Edward Burleson: Texas Frontier Leader* (Austin: Jenkins Publishing Co., 1990), pp. 181–85; Wilbarger, *Indian Depredations in Texas*, pp. 146–50; Andrew Jackson Sowell, *Rangers and Pioneers of Texas* (1884; repr., Austin: State House Press, 1991), pp. 54–57; Burleson's report to Secretary of War Albert Sidney Johnston is found in Harriet Smither, ed., *Journals of the Fourth Congress of the Republic of Texas, 1839–1840, to which are added the Relief Laws* (Austin: Von Boeckmann-Jones, n.d.), vol. 3, pp. 112–13.

7. Moore, *Taming Texas*, pp. 165–66, citing Sadler to Lamar, February 22, 1839.

8. William L. Mann, "James O. Rice: Hero of the Battle on the San Gabriels," *Southwestern Historical Quarterly*, July 1951, pp. 30–42, 160. Some sources question whether Flores died in the fight. As Jack Jackson notes in his *Indian Agent: Peter Ellis Bean in Mexican Texas* (College Station: Texas A&M University Press, 2005), p. 268, the Matagorda *Colorado Gazette* of March 28, 1840, reported that "the person supposed to have been Flores was only the commander of a small party who had the papers and baggage of Flores in charge." Jackson, p. 388, also writes that Jack Hays discussed sightings of Flores along the border in January 1844. Though Flores might have survived the battle, the incendiary papers he carried were later published by the U.S. Congress in Senate Executive Document 14, 32nd Cong., 2nd sess., 1852–53, vol. 3. J. W. Wilbarger later concluded in his *Indian Depredations of Texas*, "We can but not think that the fight on the San Gabriel was second only in importance to Texas to the battle of San Jacinto." Moore, *Savage Frontier* Vol. II, pp. 186–199; 202–210 provides a detailed account of this incident and the events leading to it.

9. *Niles' National Register*, July 13, 1839. Moore, *Savage Frontier* Vol. II, pp. 218–227.

10. Wilkins, *Legend Begins*, pp. 50–51.

11. *Niles' National Register*, July 13, 1839.

12. Ira Kennedy, "A Brief History of the Texas Cherokee," *Enchanted Rock Magazine*, February 1996, p. 13.

13. Moore, *Taming Texas*, p. 181–94.

14. Pierce, *Texas Under Arms*, pp. 134, 138.

15. Donaly E. Brice, *The Great Comanche Raid: Boldest Indian Attack of the Texas Republic* (Austin: Eakin Press, 1987), pp. 38–48, 68–70; George R. Nielson, "Matthew Caldwell," *Southwestern Historical Quarterly* 64 (April 1961): pp. 478–502. Felix Huston's account of the Plum Creek fight appeared in the Austin *City Gazette*, August 19, 1840. Dr. Stephen Hardin nicely synthesizes the battle in "Robert Hall: Citizen-Soldier of the Texas Republic," in Ty Cashion and Jesus F. de la Teja, eds., *The Human Tradition in Texas* (Wilmington, Del.: Scholarly Resources, 2001), pp. 45–48. For an overview of Caldwell's life see http://www.tamu.edu/ccbn/dewitt/caldwellmathew.htm. H. H. Williams, "A Veteran of Plum Creek," Dallas *Morning News*, June 4, 1905.

16. Rena Maverick Green, ed., *Samuel Maverick, Texan: 1803–1870, a Collection of Letters, Journals and Memoirs* (San Antonio: 1952), p. 103. Hays and his older brother William, both surveyors, most likely arrived in Texas in late 1837 or early 1838. They presented Sam Houston with a letter of introduction from their uncle Harry Cage dated November 29, 1837. The letter is in the Andrew Jackson Houston Papers at the Texas State Archives, as citied by Robert Utley, *Lone Star Justice: The First Century of the Texas Rangers* (New York: Oxford University Press, 2002), p. 321.

17. John S. Ford, "John C. Hays in Texas" (unpublished manuscript, John Salmon Ford Papers, Center for American History, University of Texas at Austin), p. 5. The primary source on Hays is John C. Caperton's "Sketch of Colonel John C. Hays, Texas Ranger," compiled in 1879. A seventy-seven-page typescript is held at the University of Texas, the original being in the University of California at Berkeley's Bancroft Library. As Utley, *Lone Star Justice*, p. 321, points out, the Caperton manuscript, lacking dates and other specifics, is "rife with hyperbole."

18. Wilkins, *Legend Begins*, pp. 72–74.

19. John Nugent, "Scraps of Early History," San Francisco *Argonaut*, n.d. (1878).

20. Prince Carl of Solms-Braunfels, *Texas, 1844-1845* (Houston: Anson Jones Press, 1936), p. 87.

21. Thomas W. Cutrer, *Ben McCulloch and the Frontier Military Tradition* (Chapel Hill and London: University of North Carolina Press, 1993), p. 48.

22. John H. Jenkins, ed., *Memoirs of John Forester: Soldier, Indian Fighter, and Texas Ranger in the Republic of Texas* (Austin: Jenkins Publishing Co., 1969), p. 12.

23. Wayne Gard, *Frontier Justice* (Norman: University of Oklahoma Press, 1949), p. 221.

24. Cutrer, *Ben McCulloch*, pp. 35–38.

25. Ibid., p. 48.

26. Ford, "John C. Hays in Texas," p. 18.

27. Solms-Braunfels, *Texas*, p. 86. Another European, French *empresario* Henri Castro, said of Hays and his men, "They were equal to any emergency, but such a company can in my opinion only be compared to the old Musketeers of Louis XIV, who represented the chivalrous gentlemen of France. Hays and his men represented the true and chivalrous disinterested American gentleman soldier who at all times was ready to shed the last drop of his blood for his country and the protection of the feeble." Edgar Rivera, "Jack Hays, The Famous Texian Ranger," undated newspaper clipping (ca. March 1884), Center for American History, University of Texas at Austin.

28. "A Biographical Sketch of Captain R. A. Gillespie, In Texas," *Texas Democrat*, October 28, 1846. Born June 12, 1815, in Blount County, Tennessee, Gillespie came with two of his brothers to Texas in 1837, settling in Matagorda. Two years later, the brothers relocated their mercantile business to La Grange. There Gillespie met John Henry Moore, who soon recruited him for an Indian-fighting expedition. Gillespie first rode with Hays in 1843. *New Handbook of Texas*, vol. 3, p. 166.

29. "An Episode of 1841. Fight At Laredo, March 30th, 1841," Laredo *Times*, n.d. (ca. October 1887), reprinting October 1, 1887, letter of P. L. Buquor. In his April 14, 1841, report to Secretary of War Branch T. Archer, published April 22, 1841, in the Austin *Sentinel*, Hays said the fight occurred that

April 7. Buquor, born in New Orleans circa 1821, came to Texas in 1838. He served with Hays in 1840–41 and later was mayor of San Antonio. He died March 15, 1901, in San Antonio. Moore, *Savage Frontier*, Vol. III, pp. 211–216.

30. *Telegraph and Texas Register*, November 28, 1843.

31. Daniel and Martin, *Legislative Messages*, vol. 2, p. 110.

32. An examination of Republic of Texas audited claims in the Texas State Archives by independent historian Sloan Rodgers of Austin, who has done extensive research on the some 300 rangers who served at one time or another with Hays, reveals that Rangers in the early 1840s had more of a law enforcement role than other historians have credited them with. Although Indian fighting and providing protection from Mexican incursions certainly stood as their top priority, rangers of this era spent more time performing law enforcement duties, at least in the sense of looking for cattle thieves, than previously believed. On April 27, 1843, for instance, G. W. Hill, Secretary of War and Marines, informed Thomas Addicks in San Antonio that a number of cattle belonging to Chrisanta La Rocha, "a widow lady," had been stolen "probably by a Party of Marauding Texans." Addicks's orders were to raise "such number of men as may be required" to "pursue and apprehend the offenders and deliver them to the civil authorities for trial and punishment" and to "regain possession of the cattle and return them to their proper owner." Republic of Texas Audited Claims 177–241, Texas State Archives. On another occasion in 1843, Addicks and two other rangers recovered 280 head of cattle stolen from Ignacio Chavez by "ill disposed inhabitants of the River Guadalupe" in Gonzales County. Republic of Texas Audited Claims 177–239, Texas State Archives.

33. Cutrer, *Ben McCulloch*, p. 48.

34. General Adrian Woll to General Isidro Reyes, September 22, 1842, in Joseph Milton Nance, trans. and ed., "Brigadier General Adrian Woll's Report of His Expedition into Texas in 1842," *Southwestern Historical Quarterly* 58, no. 4 (April 1955): pp. 549–50; Miguel A. Lamego, *The Second Mexican-Texas War, 1841–1843* (Hillsboro: Hill Junior College Monograph No. 7, 1972), p. 40. The best overview of Lamar's Santa Fe expedition, the 1841 adventure that triggered Mexican reprisal against Texas, is Noel M. Loomis's *The Texan–Santa Fe Pioneers* (Norman: University of Oklahoma Press, 1958). The basic sources on the second round of conflict between Texas and Mexico are Joseph Milton Nance's *Attack and Counter-Attack: The Texas-Mexican Frontier, 1842* (Austin: University of Texas Press, 1964); Nance and Archie McDonald, *Dare-Devils All: The Texan Mier Expedition, 1842–44* (Austin: Eakin Press, 1998), and Sam W. Haynes, *Soldiers of Misfortune: The Somervell and Mier Expeditions* (Austin: University of Texas Press, 1990).

35. New Orleans *Bulletin*, September 27, 1842.

36. Nelson Lee, *Three Years Among the Comanches* (1859; repr., Norman: University of Oklahoma Press, 1957), with new introduction by Walter Prescott Webb, p. 21.

37. James Wilson Nichols, *Now You Hear My Horn: The Journal of James Wilson Nichols, 1820–1887* (Austin: University of Texas Press, 1967), pp. 122–23.

38. Wilbarger, *Indian Depredations in Texas*, p. 291.

39. Duval's account of the "riding match" between Comanches and rangers first appeared in the late 1860s or early 1870s in *Burke's Weekly*, a publication renamed *Burke's Magazine for Boys and Girls* in 1871. Wilbarger used the piece in his *Indian Depredations of Texas* in 1889. J. Frank Dobie, *John C. Duval: First Texas Man of Letters* (Dallas: Southern Methodist University Press, 1965), pp. 38–39. "Captain Duval was an eye witness to this celebrated 1843 equestrian contest, and the narrative is strictly true," Wilbarger wrote, p. 291.

40. Anson Jones, *Memoranda and Official Correspondence Relating to the Republic of Texas: Its History and Annexation 1826 to 1846* (1859; repr., New York: Arno Press, 1973), p. 252.

41. *Telegraph and Texas Register*, July 12, 1843.

42. Clarksville *Northern Standard*, June 15, 1843.

43. W. Eugene Hollon and Ruth Lapham Butler, eds., *William Bollaert's Texas* (Norman: University of Oklahoma Press, 1956), p. 225.

44. Wilkins, *Legend Begins*, p. 175.

45. Hobart Huson, *A Comprehensive History of Refugio County from Aboriginal Times to 1953* (Woodsboro, Tex.: Rooke Foundation, 1953–55), vol. 1, p. 490.

46. *Telegraph and Texas Register*, March 20, 1844, cited in Wilkins, *Legend Begins*, pp. 176–77.

47. Clarksville *Northern Standard*, July 24, 1844. Hays recounted the Indian fight for someone in Washington-on-the-Brazos, who on June 23 sent a letter containing the details to the Houston *Morning Star*, which published the account on June 29. The *Telegraph and Texas Register* ran the piece on July 3, and by July 24 the Clarksville newspaper carried it. Reid, *Scouting Expeditions of McCulloch's Texas Rangers*, recounts the fight on pp. 109–11, and Lee, *Three Years Among the Comanches*, mentions the fight on pp. 24–26. The engagement came to be called the Battle of Walker's Creek, but the creek may not have had that name until after the battle. Lee wrote that the fight took place at a feature known as The Forks, the confluence of what came to be called Walker's Creek and a fork of Sister Creek. Whether Lee's book is nonfiction or a novel has been debated over the years, but the consensus is that the first part of Lee's narrative is a bona fide memoir, while the portion detailing his supposed Indian captivity is probably somewhat

fictionalized. For a detailed discussion, see John H. Jenkins, *Basic Texas Books* (Austin: Jenkins Publishing Co., 1983), pp. 328–32.

48. Wilkins, *Legend Begins*, pp. 178–85; Kenneth F. Neighbours, "The Battle of Walker's Creek," *West Texas Historical Association Year Book* 41 (October 1965): 121–30; Cox, *Texas Ranger Tales*, pp. 1–16; Bill O'Neal, *Fighting Men of the Indian Wars* (Stillwater, Okla.: Barbed Wire Press, 1991), pp. 137–44; Fayette Robinson, "Captain Samuel Walker," *Graham's Magazine* 32, no. 6 (June 1848): pp. 301–3; Charles Spurlin, "Ranger Walker in the Mexican War," *Military History of Texas and the Southwest* 9, no. 4, pp. 259–79; Thomas Claiborne, "Memoirs of the Past: A Famous Company and the Career and Death of a Gallant Commander," *The Vidette*, April 1, 1886. Born February 24, 1817, in Toaping Castle, Maryland, Walker volunteered for military service in 1836 and fought in Florida during the Seminole Indian War. He came to Texas in 1842 and joined Hays's ranging company in late 1843 or early 1844. Walker survived the lance wound he suffered in Hays's famous fight with the Comanches, just as he had endured imprisonment in Mexico after he and other Texans participating in the ill-conceived 1842 Mier Expedition were captured. When the ranking officer at the Perote prison carried out an order to execute every tenth man, Walker had drawn a white bean in a lottery in which the prize was life. Those holding a black bean soon faced a firing squad. He later escaped from the prison, getting back to Texas in 1843.

49. *Journals of the House of Representatives of the Ninth Congress of the Republic of Texas* (Washington, Texas: Miller & Cushney, Public Printers, 1845), pp. 32–33. Another official account of the fight, based on a letter from Ben McCulloch containing information he received from a messenger dispatched by Hays, is found in Thomas Western to Sam Houston, June 16, 1844, in Winfrey and Day, *Indian Papers*, vol. 2, pp. 72–74.

50. Hockley to Johnson, March 28, 1839, *Papers of Mirabeau Bonaparte Lamar*, vol. 2, pp. 503–5.

51. Wilkins, *Legend Begins*, pp. 65–67; C. F. Eckhardt, *Texas Smoke: Muzzle-Loaders on the Frontier* (Lubbock: Texas Tech University Press, 2001), pp. 96–99.

52. Clarksville *Northern Standard*, July 24, 1844.

53. John C. Caperton, "Sketch of Col. John C. Hays, Texas Ranger," cited in Gard, *Frontier Justice*, p. 218. Flacco was not the only Indian who rode with the Rangers of this era. The Texas Ranger Hall of Fame and Museum in Waco found twenty-six other Indians listed on Ranger muster records from December 1, 1838, through July 12, 1841. With names such as Back Bone, Groundhog, He Throws Them Down, Lightning Bug, and They Have Shot the Dog, these Indians scouted and fought for Texas. http://www.texasranger.org/Library/Hispanic_&_Indian_Rangers.htm.

54. In published accounts of this incident, Acklen is usually spelled *Acklin*, with his middle initial as *H.* Similarly, Carolan's name is misspelled. Exacting research of Republic of Texas audited claims by Sloan Rodgers of Austin, Texas, revealed the correct spelling.

55. Dallas *Semi-Weekly Farm News,* October 12, 1897. Thomas Galbreth, a member of Hays's company at the time of the incident, related the story in this publication.

56. Wilkins, *Legend Begins,* 186–88.

57. Prince Carl of Solms-Braunfels, *Voyage to North America, 1844–45: Prince Carl of Solm's Texas Diary of People, Places, and Events,* trans. from German and notes by Wolfram M. Von-Maszewski (Denton: University of North Texas Press, 2000), pp. 54–55.

58. Dallas *Semi-Weekly Farm News,* October 12, 1897.

59. Solms-Braunfels, *Voyage to North America,* p. 53.

60. Jeff Dykes, *Rangers All: A Catalog and Check List* (College Park, Maryland: Jeff Dykes Western Books, 1968), pp. 111, 144–45.

61. While no conclusive evidence that some of Hays's rangers supplemented their income by collecting bounties on runaway slaves has come to light, it can be shown that at least one of Hays's men became involved in the slave trade not long after leaving the company. On February 11, 1845, someone found the bloody bodies of Simeon Bateman and Matthew Jett near Virginia Point not far from Galveston. Both men had been stabbed to death. Jett, it developed, had only recently left Hays's company after a year's enlistment. He and Bateman, a Gonzales planter, had been on their way to New Orleans "in . . . possession [of] a large sum of money for the purpose of purchasing Negroes and bringing them to Texas." Bateman's overseer, a man named Schultz, had killed the two men in their sleep and escaped with the money. Clarksville *Northern Standard,* February 20, 1845.

62. (Charles W. Webber), "My First Day with the Rangers," *American Review,* March 1845, pp. 280–84. *Niles' National Register,* then a widely circulated weekly, carried a story on Hays, "John C. Hays and His Men," November 28, 1846, pp. 201–2.

63. T. R. Fehrenbach, *Comanches: The Destruction of a People* (New York: Alfred A. Knopf, 1974), pp. 360–61. For more on the Comanches, see Ernest Wallace and E. Adamson Hoebel, *The Comanches: Lords of the South Plains* (Norman: University of Oklahoma Press, 1952); Rupert N. Richardson, *The Comanche Barrier to South Plains Settlement,* rev. ed., ed. Kenneth R. Jacobs (Austin: Eakin Press, 1996); and Thomas W. Kavanagh, *Comanche Political History: An Ethnohistorical Perspective, 1708–1875* (Lincoln: University of Nebraska Press, 1996).

64. Lee, *Three Years Among the Comanches,* p. 13.

65. Three famous fights supposedly involving Hays—the Battle of Bandera Pass,

his solitary stand against Comanches at Enchanted Rock, and a desperate fight with Indians at Paint Rock in present Concho County—may never have happened. Conclusive evidence is lacking for all three of these often-written-about engagements. Wilkins makes a case in his *Legend Begins,* pp. 201–8, that Hays's Bandera Pass and Enchanted Rock encounters amount only to legend. For an examination of the reputed Hays battle at Paint Rock, see Mike Cox, "Battle of the Painted Rocks: Scraping off the Layers," *West Texas Historical Association Year Book* 78 (October 2002): pp. 151–69. But, as John S. "Rip" Ford, who had served under Hays, later wrote, "It must be remembered that in the year 1854 [1857] the Adjutant General's office of Texas was burned, and [in] 1881 the capitol of Texas was consumed by fire. The reports of many military officers were lost, without the possibility of re-production. For that reason it is almost impossible in many instances to give exact dates of military happenings." Ford, "John C. Hays in Texas," p. 6.

4. "Cleaning pistols and grinding knives"

1. Henry W. Barton, *Texas Volunteers in the Mexican War* (Waco: Texian Press, 1970), pp. 5–6; Frederick Wilkins, *The Highly Irregular Irregulars: Texas Rangers in the Mexican War* (Austin: Eakin Press, 1990), p. 23.
2. Joseph Daniels to Anson Jones, Jones, *Memoranda and Official Correspondence,* p. 508.
3. "Horse Stealing," *Texas Democrat,* January 21, 1846.
4. Cutrer, *Ben McCulloch,* p. 64.
5. Corpus Christi *Gazette* Extra, March 8, 1846.
6. Samuel C. Reid, *The Scouting Expeditions of McCulloch's Texas Rangers or, the Summer and Fall Campaign of the Army of the United States in Mexico—1846; including skirmishes with the Mexicans, and an accurate detail of the storming of Monterrey; also, the daring scouts at Buena Vista; together with anecdotes, incidents, descriptions of country, and sketches of the lives of the celebrated partisan chiefs, Hays, McCulloch and Walker* (Philadelphia: G. B. Zieber, 1847), passim. Colonel Truman Cross had gone for a recreational horseback ride on April 10 and not returned. The first combat of the war came on April 21 when a ten-man search party led by Lieutenant Theodric Porter, brother of future admiral David D. Porter, came under attack by Mexican guerrillas. Porter and one of his soldiers fell in the action, but the Americans killed at least three Mexicans. After the skirmish, the American soldiers found Cross's mutilated body. The colonel, as one of his fellow officers wrote the following day, had been "foully assassinated by a party from the other side who were hovering around our camp." For more detail on the events preceding the war and the two-year conflict that followed, see John S. Eisenhower, *So Far from God: The U.S. War with Mexico,*

1846–1848 (New York: Random House, 1989), and Eddie Weems, *To Conquer a Peace: The War Between the United States and Mexico* (Garden City: Doubleday, 1974).

7. Barton, *Texas Volunteers in the Mexican War*, p. 10.

8. Charles D. Spurlin, *Texas Volunteers in the Mexican War* (Austin: Eakin Press, 1998), p. 7.

9. The *Texas Democrat* published Taylor's April 26 letter to the governor on May 6, 1846. Walker's company, Taylor wrote, "is already rendering important service here."

10. Spurlin, *Texas Volunteers*, pp. 8–9; Barton, *Texas Volunteers*, pp. 12–13.

11. Spurlin, *Texas Volunteers*, p. 11.

12. James K. Greer, ed., *Buck Barry, Texas Ranger and Frontiersman* (Waco: Friends of the Moody Texas Ranger Library, 1978), p. 126.

13. Reid, *Scouting Expeditions of McCulloch's Texas Rangers*, p. 38.

14. Barton, *Texas Volunteers*, p. 28.

15. Reid, *Scouting Expeditions of McCulloch's Texas Rangers*, p. 38.

16. Greer, *Buck Barry*, p. 127.

17. Adrian G. Traas, *From the Golden Gate to Mexico City: The U.S. Army Topographical Engineers in the Mexican War, 1846–1848* (Washington: Office of History, Corps of Engineers and Center of Military History, 1993), p. 124.

18. Spurlin, *Texas Volunteers*, p. 15. When word spread of Walker's close call and the loss of his horse at Resaca de la Palma, residents of New Orleans chipped in and bought the ranger a new mount, a five-year-old gelding named Tornado. Walker had become the war's first hero. Wilkins, *Highly Irregular Irregulars*, p. 202, citing letter from the citizens of New Orleans, May 13, 1846, in Walker Papers, Texas State Library.

19. Lawrence R. Clayton and Joseph E. Chance, eds., *The March to Monterrey: The Diary of Lt. Rankin Dilworth* (El Paso: Texas Western Press, 1996), p. 10.

20. Barton, *Texas Volunteers*, p. 33.

21. Spurlin, *Texas Volunteers*, p. 20.

22. Fayette Copeland, *Kendall of the Picayune* (Norman: University of Oklahoma Press, 1943), p. 159.

23. Winfrey and Day, *Indian Papers*, vol. 3, pp. 70–71; Clay Perkins, *The Fort in Fort Worth* (Keller: privately published, 2001), pp. 14–16.

24. Clayton and Chance, *March to Monterrey*, p. 24.

25. Reid, *Scouting Expeditions of McCulloch's Texas Rangers*, pp. 5, 23, 26.

26. Clayton and Chance, *March to Monterrey*, pp. 36–37.

27. S. Compton Smith, *Chile Con Carne; or, The Camp and the Field* (New York: Miller & Curtis, 1857), pp. 324–25.

28. Reid, *Scouting Expeditions of McCulloch's Texas Rangers*, p. 53.

29. Stephen B. Oates, *Visions of Glory: Texans on the Southwestern Frontier* (Norman: University of Oklahoma Press, 1970), pp. 26–27. Rank did not

overawe rangers, either. One Texan told an officer from Ohio, "In our Texas war, an officer was no better than a private . . . but here if we speak to one of these d———d regulars who has a strap on his shirt or one of our own officers familiarly or pretend to dispute his word or differ with him we are treated like dog. Bucked, bucked sir, and I assure you Texans will not be bucked." Paul Foos, *A Short, Offhand Killing Affair: Soldiers and Social Conflict During the Mexican-American War* (Chapel Hill and London: University of North Carolina Press, 2002), p. 90. Despite Taylor's reference to rangers as "licentious vandals," Hays's men won the respect of Assistant Quartermaster Henry Whiting, who reported on the army's effort to buy mules from Mexican citizens at $20 a head. "This call might have been ineffectual, had not a Texan mounted regiment [Hays's] been moving into the quarter whence we expected these mules. The alcaldes have expressed a determination to fulfill the call, if possible." Whiting to Thomas S. Jessup, August 6, 1846, cited in Walter Prescott Webb, *The Texas Rangers in the Mexican War* (Austin: Jenkins Garrett Press, 1975), p. 30.

30. Julian Samora, Joe Bernal, and Albert Pena, *Gunpowder Justice: A Reassessment of the Texas Rangers* (Notre Dame: University of Notre Dame Press, 1979), p. 39.
31. Smith, *Chile Con Carne*, p. 324.
32. Clayton and Chance, *March to Monterrey*, p. 63.
33. Spurlin, *Texas Volunteers*, p. 90; Webb, *Texas Rangers*, p. 51, citing Henderson to Taylor, October 1, 1846. In his after-action report to Taylor, General Henderson wrote of Gillespie, "He had long been employed by the government of Texas in defense of the Western frontier, as the commander of a corps of mounted rangers; and probably no officer ever performed his duty with more activity and efficiency, or with more satisfaction to the country. He was an educated man, and a gentleman by nature." Less than two years later, on February 23, 1848, the Texas legislature took land from Bexar and Travis counties and created a new county named in Gillespie's honor. *New Handbook of Texas*, vol. 3, p. 166.
34. Ford, "John C. Hays in Texas," pp. 29–30; Foos, *Short, Offhand Killing Affair*, citing diary of Daniel Harvey Hill, October 17, 1846. *Niles' National Register* added to Hays's national reputation with the publication of "John C. Hays and His Men," November 28, 1846, pp. 201–2.
35. Spurlin, *Texas Volunteers*, p. 104.
36. Ford, "John C. Hays in Texas," pp. 45–46.
37. (Luther Giddings), *Sketches of the Campaign in Northern Mexico in Eighteen Hundred and Forty-Six and Seven by an Officer of the First Ohio Volunteers* (New York: J. P. Putnam, 1853), 221–22.
38. David Lavender, *Climax at Buena Vista: The American Campaigns in*

Northeastern Mexico, 1846–47 (Philadelphia and New York: J. P. Lippincott, 1966), p. 125.

39. Cox, *Texas Ranger Tales*, pp. 6–7.

40. Charles Edward Chapel, *Guns of the Old West* (New York: Coward-McCann, 1961), pp. 153–57; Eckhardt, *Texas Smoke*, pp. 101–6.

41. Cutrer, *Ben McCulloch*, pp. 96–99. McCulloch's observations come from a little-known letter he wrote two years after Buena Vista to W. R. Scurry as published in Pat R. Clark, *Clarksville and Old Red River County* (Dallas: Mathis, Van Nort, 1937), pp. 246–59.

42. Reid, *Scouting Expeditions of McCulloch's Texas Rangers*, p. 236.

43. Cadmus M. Wilcox and Mary Rachel Wilcox, eds., *History of the Mexican War* (Washington: Church News Publishing Co., 1892), p. 215.

44. Lavender, *Climax at Buena Vista*, pp. 211–13.

45. Clark, *Clarksville and Old Red River County*, p. 258. Major Coffee was not otherwise identified in McCulloch's letter. He may have been referring to Chesley Sheldon Coffey, a lieutenant in the Second Mississippi Rifles.

46. Cutrer, *Ben McCulloch*, p. 103.

47. Henry McCulloch detailed the use of Rangers on the home front during the Mexican War in a letter written to the Dallas *Morning News* from Rockport, Texas, on March 28, 1897. The newspaper published it on April 8 under the headline "About Old Fort Croghan: General Henry E. McCulloch Relates the Circumstances."

48. Reid, *Scouting Expeditions of McCulloch's Texas Rangers*, p. 109. The same year Reid's book appeared, Mississippi-based teacher-lawyer-novelist (and eventually, clergyman) Joseph Holt Ingraham (1809–60) wrote the first book-length piece of Ranger fiction, a novel of the Mexican War called *The Texas Ranger*. Unlike Reid, however, Ingraham's insight into the Rangers came from reading newspaper accounts of the initial Mexican campaigns, not through any firsthand experience. A transplanted Southerner born in Portland, Maine, Ingraham's oeuvre included some eighty novels. Reviewing one of his books, Edgar Allan Poe said the prolific Ingraham's books were written "too minutely, and by far too frequently descriptive." Ingraham's son, Prentiss (1843–1904), later shortened many of his father's works for republication as dime novels by New York's Beadle and Adams publishing house. For more on both Ingrahams, see www.olemiss.edu/depts/general_library/files/archives/exhibits/past/ingrahamex or www.niulib.niu.edu/badndp/ingraham_joseph.

49. Feris A. Bass Jr. and B. R. Brunson, eds., *Fragile Empires: The Texas Correspondence of Samuel Swartwout and James Morgan, 1836–1856* (Austin: Shoal Creek Publishers, 1978), p. 320.

50. Cox, *Texas Ranger Tales*, pp. 8–10. Walker got his wish, though it took nine years. Shortly after his death, his comrades buried him at Huamantla, but after the war his remains were exhumed and returned to San Antonio. On

April 21, 1856, he was reinterred next to Captain Gillespie in the city's Odd Fellows Cemetery. Gillespie's remains had a similar journey, first being buried on the mountainside where he fell, then laid to rest near some cottonwoods on the San Antonio River in San Antonio, and finally in the Odd Fellows Cemetery next to Walker. After restoration, Walker's grave was rededicated on December 6, 2003.

51. Davis, *Texas Rangers*, p. 31.
52. Frank S. Edwards, *A Campaign in New Mexico with Col. Doniphan* (Philadelphia: Carey and Hart, 1847), pp. 154–56.
53. George Winston Smith and Charles Judah, eds., *Chronicles of the Gringos: The U.S. Army in the Mexican War, 1846–1848, Accounts of Eyewitnesses and Combatants* (Albuquerque: University of New Mexico Press, 1968), pp. 40–41.
54. Davis, *Texas Rangers*, pp. 31–32.
55. Ford, "John C. Hays in Texas," pp. 65–66.
56. New Orleans *Picayune*, October 29, 1847, cited in Oates, *Visions of Glory*, p. 37.
57. Ibid., 28–42.
58. Ibid., p. 43.
59. Vicksburg *Daily Whig*, January 11, 1848.
60. Oates, *Visions of Glory*, pp. 46–47.
61. Ford, "John C. Hays in Texas," pp. 86–89.
62. Dudley G., Wooten, ed., *A Comprehensive History of Texas, 1865 to 1897* (Dallas: 1898), vol. 2, p. 338.
63. Ford, "John C. Hays in Texas," pp. 72–73.
64. Winfrey and Day, *Indian Papers*, vol. 3, pp. 87, 96.
65. Ford, "John C. Hays in Texas," p. 56.
66. Dallas *Morning News*, April 8, 1897.
67. John Duff Brown, "Heroes of Texas" (Houston: Union National Bank, 1934), p. 9.
68. Dallas *Morning News*, April 8, 1897.
69. Dr. Ferdinand Herff, *The Regulated Emigration of the German Proletariat with Special Reference to Texas: Being Also a Guide for German Emigrants*, trans. by Arthur L. Finck Jr. (San Antonio: Trinity University Press, 1978), pp. 27–28.
70. Samuel, Highsmith, "San Saba Valley Scout," from the *Texas Democrat*, reprinted in Senate Report No. 171, 30th Cong., 1st sess.
71. James K. Greer, *Colonel Jack Hays: Texas Frontier Leader and California Builder*, rev. ed. (College Station: Texas A&M University Press, 1987), pp. 214–16.
72. Frederick Wilkins, *Defending the Borders: The Texas Rangers, 1848–1861* (Austin: State House Press, 2001), pp. 2–5; *Texas Democrat*, January 28, 1849, reprints Highsmith's December 15, 1848, report on the expedition.

Weakened by the hard scout in West Texas, Highsmith contracted influenza and died in San Antonio on January 10, 1849, at forty-five. Maude Wallis Traylor, "Captain Samuel Highsmith, Ranger," *Frontier Times*, April 1940, pp. 291–302. Hays left Texas for the newly discovered gold fields of California in 1849 and never returned. He became sheriff of San Francisco County and served four years. In 1853, President Franklin Pierce named him surveyor general for California. Successful in ranching and real estate, Hays was one of the founders of Oakland. Active in politics, he attended the Democratic national convention as a delegate in 1876. The man who helped shape the Ranger legend died in Oakland on April 25, 1883. *New Handbook of Texas*, vol. 3, p. 519. Greer's *Colonel Jack Hays*, first published in 1952, still stands as Hays's definitive biography. The 1987 edition includes a new introduction by the author and images and maps not used in the first printing.

73. Winfrey and Day, *Indian Papers*, vol. 3, p. 100.
74. Wilkins, *Defending the Borders*, p. 11.
75. *Nueces Star*, August 25, 1849, cited in Paul Schuster Taylor, *An American-Mexican Frontier: Nueces County, Texas* (Chapel Hill: University of North Carolina Press, 1934), p. 59.
76. Marilyn McAdams Sibley, *Lone Stars and State Gazettes: Texas Newspapers Before the Civil War* (College Station: Texas A&M University Press, 1983), p. 376.
77. Francis D. Allan, comp., *Allan's Lone Star Ballads: A Collection of Southern Patriotic Songs Made During Confederate Times* (1874; repr., New York: Burt Franklin, 1970), p. 24. For more on the Rangers in song and poem, see Stewart Lauterbach and Christina Stopka, comps., *Ranger Songs and Verse: A Collection for the 175th Anniversary Gala of the Texas Rangers* (Waco: Texas Ranger Hall of Fame and Museum, 1998).

5. "The captain believed in drilling his Rangers"

1. The photograph of Ford, discovered by collector John N. McWilliams more than a century after Ford's death, is described in Cox, *Texas Ranger Tales II*, p. 45. For details on Ford's long life, see W. J. Hughes, *Rebellious Ranger: Rip Ford and the Old Southwest* (Norman: University of Oklahoma Press, 1964); Ralph Widener, "John Salmon ('Rip') Ford" (unpublished manuscript, author's collection), is another lengthy study of Ford consulted. The commonly accepted version, as first used by Webb in *The Texas Rangers*, p. 121, is that Ford's nickname stood for "rest in peace" (from the Latin, *requiescat in pace*). Webb says rangers started calling Ford "Rip" because one of his duties as Hays's adjutant included writing letters of notification to family members of Texans who died of wounds or disease during the Mexican War. Ford,

Webb wrote, concluded the letters with "Rest in Peace." But Hughes, p. 79, says Ford probably did not get the nickname until after the war. He also suggests that the meaning was not "rest in peace," but nineteenth-century slang describing someone "always involved in one affair after another." Utley, *Lone Star Justice*, p. 335, agrees with Hughes, noting that the Rangers suffered few casualties during the war and were not overly prone to paperwork. Another possibility is that *Rip* was short for "a ripping fellow," a term first traced to 1838 from *ripping*, a word for "excellent" or "splendid" dating to 1826. See Online Etymology Dictionary at www.etymonline.com. No matter the origin of the nickname, Ford liked it. Recalling having met Ford in 1864, R. H. Williams later wrote, " 'Old Rip,' as he delighted to be called, was fairly popular with most of the people, being hail-fellow-well-met with everybody, free with his money, and equally free with his six-shooter." R. H. Williams, *With the Border Ruffians: Memories of the Far West, 1852–1868*, ed. E. W. Williams (1907; repr., Lincoln: University of Nebraska Press, 1982), p. 365.

2. John Salmon Ford, *Rip Ford's Texas*, ed. Stephen B. Oates (Austin: University of Texas Press, 1963), pp. 142, 145.

3. Ibid., pp. 150–54.

4. Wilbarger, *Indian Depredations in Texas*, p. 616.

5. Ford, *Rip Ford's Texas*, p. 179.

6. DeWitt Clinton Baker, *A Texas Scrap-Book, Made Up of the History, Biography, and Miscellany of Texas and Its People* (New York, Chicago, and New Orleans: A. S. Barnes, 1875), pp. 157–60.

7. Gerald Ashford, "Ranger's Life Often Sure Cure If Comanches Didn't Scalp You," San Antonio *News*, July 6, 1960. Wills's musings were contained in two letters written in 1850–51 acquired from two different dealers by a San Antonio architect and stamp collector.

8. *Senate Journal of the State of Texas* (Austin: 1850), pp. 75–76. For an overview of frontier defense efforts in antebellum Texas, see W. C. Holden, "Frontier Defense, 1846–1860," *West Texas Historical Association Year Book* 6 (1929): pp. 39–71.

9. Clarence Wharton, *History of Texas* (Dallas: Turner Company, 1935), pp. 358, 361.

10. *Senate Journal of the State of Texas, 1851–1852* (Austin: 1852), pp. 38–39; 301–2.

11. Nacogdoches *Chronicle*, August 7, 1852, cited in Harmon, *United States Indian Policy in Texas*, pp. 390–91.

12. Wilkins, *Defending the Borders*, pp. 40, 42.

13. John Wright and William Wright, *Recollections of Western Texas, 1852–55: Descriptive and Narrative, Including an Indian Campaign, 1852–55, Interspersed with Illustrative Anecdotes*, ed. Robert Wooster (Lubbock: Texas Tech University Press, 2001), pp. 55–57.

14. Thomas H. Bradley, *Claims Against the United States,* Senate Executive Document No. 74, 46th Cong., 2nd sess., 1880, pp. 86, 139; Austin *Texas Sentinel,* October 7, 14, and 21, 1854. The formation of the six Ranger companies in Texas did not go unnoticed in the nation's press. The *Texas Sentinel* on October 7 reprinted an item from the St. Louis *Democrat* in which the Missouri newspaper noted, "Our Texas exchanges come to us as usual filled with accounts of bloody murders—not a paper but has chronicled some disgraceful shooting or stabbing affair. We hope that the six companies of Rangers . . . will be recruited from the ranks of these gentlemen of the knife and pistol; and thus society will be relieved of a pest and disgrace, and turn it to a good account for the protection of decent and quiet citizens on the frontier." The editor of the Austin weekly countered with five inches of type in defense of the Rangers. Two sentences, one incomplete, set the tone: "The men composing ranging companies are generally drawn from the laboring, the farming portion of the community. Men who have a reputation to lose at home, and who would scorn a sanguinary act, if not justified, as much as any one."

15. Douglas V. Meed, *Texas Wanderlust: The Adventures of Dutch Wurzbach* (College Station: Texas A&M University Press, 1997), p. 49.

16. Colonel M. L. Crimmins, "General Albert J. Myer: The Father of the Signal Corps," *West Texas Historical Association Year Book* 29 (October 1953): pp. 67–78. The rangers drawing Myer's scorn probably belonged to Captain Charles E. Travis's Company E, which served from December 1, 1854, to April 1, 1855. For more on the Rangers and the army, see Henry W. Barton, "The United States Cavalry and the Texas Rangers," *Southwestern Historical Quarterly* 63, no. 4 (April 1960): pp. 495–510.

17. Bradley, *Claims Against the United States,* p. 139.

18. Callahan claimed to have killed some seventy men in the fight, but the more likely number is four killed, three wounded. Utley, *Lone Star Justice,* p. 96.

19. John W. Sansom, "Captain Callahan's Raid into Mexico," *Hunter's Magazine,* April-May, 1911.

20. Whether slave-hunting figured into the Callahan expedition is inconclusive, but rangers sometimes did go after slaves. As the Galveston *Weekly News* reported on March 25, 1851, "A Negro, belonging to J. P. Caldwell of Brazoria Co. was recently caught near Laredo, by one of the rangers, and lodged in the jail at San Antonio. His master gained possession of him." The slave owner probably was James Peckham Caldwell (1793–1856), who owned a large plantation at Gulf Prairie.

21. James N. Leiker, *Racial Borders: Black Soldiers Along the Rio Grande* (College Station: Texas A&M University Press, 2002), p. 26.

22. Ronnie C. Tyler, "The Callahan Expedition of 1855: Indians or Negroes,"

Southwestern Historical Quarterly 70 (April 1967): pp. 574–85; Ernest C., Shearer, "The Callahan Expedition, 1855," *Southwestern Historical Quarterly* 54 (April 1951): pp. 430–51. Callahan survived his short-lived invasion of Mexico, but did not live to old age. He was shot to death in Blanco County on April 7, 1856, as the result of a "difficulty."

23. *Texas State Gazette,* November 24 and December 15, 1855, cited in David Paul Smith, *Frontier Defense in the Civil War: Texas' Rangers and Rebels* (College Station: Texas A&M University Press, 1992), p. 6.

24. Leona Parrish Carver, *You Can't Get the Coons All Up One Tree: The Life Story of John N. Jones* (Amarillo: Coltharp Printing and Publishing, 1980), pp. 20, 28. Born in Tennessee on February 4, 1835, Jones ran away from home at sixteen and came to Texas lacking "ten cents having a dime in money." Except for fighting in Arkansas for both sides during the Civil War, he spent the rest of his long life in Texas. He died at Cone, Texas, on January 31, 1922. In his crudely written recollection, edited well after his death by his granddaughter, he did not name the captain under whom he served in 1856. Jones is not listed by Ingmire, but Ranger muster rolls are not complete.

25. "The Camp and Field," *Putnam's Monthly Magazine of American Literature, Science and Art,* vol. 10, issue 57, September 1857.

26. Carl H. Moneyhon, *Republicanism in Reconstruction Texas* (Austin: University of Texas Press, 1980), p. 135.

27. Roy L. Swift, *Three Roads to Chihuahua: The Great Wagon Roads That Opened the Southwest, 1823–1883* (Austin: Eakin Press, 1988), pp. 157, 158, 163–66; *A Twentieth Century History of Southwest Texas* (Chicago: Lewis Publishing Co., 1907), vol. 1, pp. 161, 221, 240.

28. Frank W. Johnson, *A History of Texas and Texans,* ed. Eugene C. Barker with the assistance of Ernest William Winkler (Chicago and New York: American Historical Society, 1916), vol. 1, p. 512.

29. Sister Paul of the Cross McGrath, *Political Nativism in Texas, 1825–1860* (Washington: Catholic University of America, 1930), pp. 166–69; Swift, *Three Roads to Chihuahua,* p. 167.

30. *Patchwork of Memories: Historical Sketches of Comanche County, Texas* (Comanche: n.p., 1976), pp. 153–54.

31. *Texas State Gazette* (Austin), January 30, 1858.

32. Bradley, *Claims Against the United States,* p. 33.

33. Cutrer, *Ben McCulloch,* p. 149.

34. *Congressional Globe,* pt. 1, 1857–58, February 1, 1858, pp. 492–97; 873–75.

35. Cutrer, *Ben McCulloch,* pp. 147, 150. As Houston argued in Washington for Ranger funding, Governor Runnels, clearly thinking of politics as well as the state's finances, wrote Ford to remind him that "the people will want to hear of something being done, to hear of Indians and of their being whipped." He admonished the captain to do something quickly as "upon

your reputation and mine the good and welfare of the country depend on something being done to justify the belief of an existing emergency." Still, he admonished Ford not to "augment for any length of time the number of men in service unless absolutely necessary" no matter "the howlings of corrupt and designing or mad men." Runnels told Ford that he felt Ford already had enough men "for all present purposes if properly distributed" and cautioned that he not spend more money than the legislature had appropriated. While the governor wanted action, he seemed to see it more as political necessity than a response to dire need. "If men living on the frontier loose [*sic*] a cow or a Jackass occasionally, only it is because they have placed themselves in a position where they might expect it. It would be better however if that is all the damage done for the State to pay for it, instead of keeping a force at ten times cost under pay." Runnels to Ford, March 10, 1858, http://www.tsl.state.tx.us/governors/earlystate/runnels-ford.html.

36. Ford, *Rip Ford's Texas*, p. 233; "Indian Fight on the Border: Major Fred Kirk Tells of the Last Battle and Death of Iron Jacket," Dallas *Morning News*, April 12, 1897. Kirk claimed that Rangers Bill Terry and Bob Green fired the rifle shots that penetrated Iron Jacket's armor. "I have some of the scales of his armor now," Kirk told a correspondent for the Dallas newspaper. He said the Rangers and friendly Indians killed seventy-six Comanches, calling it "about the hardest fight I was ever in." R. Cotter, "Fighting Indians in 1857," Dallas *Morning News*, August 7, 1892. Ford, Cotter wrote, "was without any doubt one of if not the best and boldest ranger captain the state has produced. His men loved him and had implicit faith in him." By the time Cotter sent his recollection to the Dallas newspaper, only he, Ford, and former second lieutenant W. A. Pitts survived among those who had held rank in the Ranger unit.

37. Dallas *Morning News*, August 7, 1892. One of the Rangers' captives was an eight-year-old Comanche believed to be a son of the slain Iron Jacket. "The boy's name was Nich Po or Little Owl," Cotter wrote. "[He] was cared for by Capt. Ford, who took him to Austin." Ford gave the young Indian to an Austin family who later moved to East Texas. The Comanche never assimilated. "He was an Indian and died one," Cotter recalled.

38. Cox, *Texas Ranger Tales*, pp. 47–49; Adam R. Johnson, "The Battle of Antelope Hills," *Frontier Times*, February 1924, pp. 12–14; Ford reported the details of the fight in a letter to Runnels on May 22, 1858, as cited in Utley, *Lone Star Justice*, p. 337. William Y. Chalfant put Ford's expedition into perspective in *Without Quarter: The Wichita Expedition and the Fight on Crooked Creek* (Norman: University of Oklahoma Press, 1991), pp. 1–37.

39. *Claims Against the United States*, p. 137.

40. J. Marvin. Hunter, " 'Uncle' Ben Dragoo, a Texas Ranger," *Frontier Times*, April 1929, pp. 287–91.

41. Winfrey and Day, *Indian Papers*, vol. 3, Captain John Williams to H. R. Runnels, October 25, 1858, pp. 297–98; Cowan to Runnels, October 28, 1858, John B. Floyd, Protection of the Frontier of Texas, House Executive Doc. 27, (Washington: 1859), p. 69; B. S. Whitaker to Runnels, October 25, 1858, pp. 299–300; Runnels to secretary of war, November 2, 1858; Runnels to Ford, November 2, 1858, p. 304; Cowan to Runnels, November 7, 1858, pp. 306–7; Flora Gatlin Bowles, ed., *A No Man's Land Becomes a County* (Goldthwaite, Tex.: 1958), pp. 35–37; Hartal Langford, Blackwell, *Mills County—the Way It Was* (Goldthwaite, Tex.: Mills County Historical Commission, 1976), pp. 19–22; Linton Otis Pendergrast, "Pioneer Tells of Indian Raids," Fort Worth *Star-Telegram*, October 13, 1930; "Historic Jackson Cabin," *Frontier Times*, January 1927, pp. 30–31; Frank Brown, "Annals of Travis County" (unpublished manuscript, Austin History Center, Austin Public Library), chap. 21, pp. 48–50; Grace Bitner, "R. F. Tankersly and Family, Pioneers of the Concho Valley," *West Texas Historical Association Year Book* 20 (October 1944): pp. 99–108; Candace Cooksey Fulton, "1858 Jackson Crossing Massacre," San Angelo *Standard-Times*, May 17, 1998. The rangers pursuing the Indians who killed the Jacksons may not have had official commissions, but they operated with the governor's blessing. "The Governor warmly approves the formation of minute companies for any emergency that may arise, and has offered to bring them arms, so far as the limited supply remaining on hand will permit," the Belton *Independent* reported (as reprinted in the April 9, 1859, *Texas State Gazette*). By April 1859, Williams and Cowan had been in the field for almost six months, providing food for their men and horses at their own expense. "Capt. Williams is known to us as one among the bravest and best citizens," the *Texas State Gazette* reported on April 16, 1859. "Every one has confidence in him, and he [is] beloved by all for his generosity and friendship. His present service cannot be too highly praised. Lt. Cowan is also a brave man."

42. Ford, *Rip Ford's Texas*, p. 248. On May 7, 1859, the *Texas State Gazette* published a letter in defense of Ford and his unsuccessful second Comanche campaign from someone who signed his name simply as "W." Captain Ford, the writer maintained, had been censured by men who believed "that [Ford], with a single company of Rangers, should immediately check [Indian incursions], and restore peace to a frontier of five hundred miles extent, bounded by mountains as impenetrable as rock, ravines and chaparral can render them." The author continued, "Ford has hitherto rendered efficient services as a Ranger, and all who know him will admit that he is a fighting man. He may not have the capacity [in manpower] to conduct this demi-Guerrilla war at present existing on our frontier, but if the Indians, emboldened by their success, should ever come upon the frontier [en masse], he will do his devoir as boldly as any son of Texas."

43. Ford, *Rip Ford's Texas*, p. xxxiii.

44. Ibid., p. 252; Kenneth Franklin Neighbours, *Robert Simpson Neighbors and the Texas Frontier, 1836–1859* (Waco: Texian Press, 1975), pp. 282–290. A sheriff's posse killed Cornett on May 25, 1860, in Young County.

45. T. R. Havins, *Camp Colorado: A Decade of Frontier Defense* (Brownwood: Brown Press, 1964), p. 83; George Klos, " 'Our People Could Not Distinguish One Tribe from Another': The 1859 Expulsion of the Reserve Indians from Texas," *Southwestern Historical Quarterly* 97, no. 4 (April 1994): 599–619. The most complete study of Texas's reservation experiment is Kenneth Franklin Neighbours's *Robert Simpson Neighbors and the Texas Frontier, 1836–1859* (Waco: Texian Press, 1975).

46. *Claims Against the United States*, p. 43; Patsy McDonald Spaw, *The Texas Senate* (College Station: Texas A&M University Press, 1990), vol. 1, p. 305. In November, a joint resolution of the Legislature authorized Runnels to raise "without delay" a corps of one thousand mounted men designated as Texas Rangers. Term of enlistment was two years. Utley, *Lone Star Justice*, pp. 110–11.

47. *Twentieth Century History of Southwest Texas*, pp. 90–91; Utley, *Lone Star Justice*, p. 110.

48. Jerry Thompson, ed., *Fifty Miles and a Fight: Major Samuel Peter Heintzelman's Journal of Texas and the Cortina War* (Austin: Texas State Historical Association, 1998), pp. 31–32.

49. Ford, *Rip Ford's Texas*, p. 265.

50. *Claims Against the United States*, pp. 143–44.

51. Thompson, *Fifty Miles and a Fight*, pp. 132, 136, 138–41.

52. "Biography of Andrew Nelson Erskine," *Frontier Times*, April 1928, p. 308.

53. Thompson, *Fifty Miles and a Fight*, p. 141.

54. Ibid., p. 142. Heintzelman noted on December 31 that the ranger's election would be that day. "Tobin says that if he is [not] elected he will resign. If he dont keep better orders & do something I will write to the Governor to have the Rangers recalled. They are doing no service and are bringing disgrace upon the country." Ibid., p. 162. Presumably the major referred to Tobin's men, not Ford's better-disciplined command. To the major's chagrin, Tobin won the election by six votes, but his company soon disbanded. That left Ford the ranking ranger in the field.

55. Ibid., p. 155; Heintzelman later estimated Cortina lost more than 10 percent of his 590-men force in the December 27, 1859, fight. Dan R. Manning, "John James Dix: Texas Ranger During the Cortina Campaign," *Texas Ranger Dispatch* 16 (Spring 2005). On February 4, 1860 (Dix said the encounter occurred two days earlier), Cortina tried unsuccessfully to capture the steamboat *Ranchero* at a bend in the river called Las Bolsas. Ford sent rangers into Mexico, which compelled Cortina to withdraw from the area. Cortina would not be heard from in Texas until May 1861, when he tried to

occupy Zapata County. He continued to be a problem to American interests along the border until 1875, when Mexican authorities arrested him and removed him to Mexico City. He died on October 30, 1894, in Atzcapozalco. *New Handbook of Texas*, vol. 2, pp. 343–44. For a different perspective on Cortina, see J. T. Canales, "Juan N. Cortina Presents His Motion for a New Trial" (talk at the Lower Rio Grande Valley Historical Society, San Benito, Texas, October 25, 1951, Lon C. Hill Memorial Library, Harlingen, Texas). The best overview of Cortina is Jerry D. Thompson's *Juan Cortina and the Texas-Mexico Frontier, 1859–1877* (El Paso: University of Texas at El Paso, Texas Western Press, 1994) and Thompson, *Cortina: Defending the Mexican Name in Texas* (College Station: Texas A&M University Press, 2007).

56. Jacob De Cordova, *Texas: Her Resources and Her Public Men* (Philadelphia: 1858), p. 129.

6. "So sad a face"

1. "Old Frontier Events of Long Ago," *Frontier Times*, August 1926, p. 13.
2. J. Evetts Haley, "Charles Goodnight's Indian Recollections," *Frontier Times*, December 1928, pp. 138–39; Doyle Marshall, *A Cry Unheard: The Story of Indian Attacks in and Around Parker County, Texas, 1858–1872* (Aledo, Texas: Annetta Valley Farm Press, 1990), pp. 32–33.
3. June Rayfield Welch, *The Texas Senator* (Waco: Texian Press, 1978), pp. 80, 82.
4. Amelia W. Williams, and Eugene C. Barker, ed., *The Writings of Sam Houston, 1813–1863* (Austin and New York: Pemberton Press, Jenkins Publishing Company, 1970), vol. 7, pp. 381–82.
5. Ibid., p. 385.
6. Spaw, *Texas Senate*, vol. 1, p. 305.
7. Williams and Barker, *Writings of Sam Houston*, vol. 7, p. 411.
8. Ibid., p. 412.
9. Ibid., pp. 503–4.
10. Ibid., p. 513.
11. *Claims Against the United States*, p. 146.
12. *New Handbook of Texas*, vol. 3, pp. 959–60.
13. Johnson, *History of Texas and Texans*, vol. 1, p. 518.
14. Ibid.
15. Margaret Roberts, ed., *Personal Correspondence of Sam Houston* (Denton: University of North Texas Press, 2001), vol. 4, pp. 361–62. Charles Power, Louisa's father, was married to Margaret Houston's sister. A wealthy diamond merchant, Power later wrote Margaret that Johnson had squandered his daughter's inheritance. Author's interview with Margaret Roberts, Huntsville, Texas, March 2, 2002.

16. Houston to John B. Floyd, April 14, 1860, reprinted in *Under Texas Skies* (Austin: Texas Heritage Foundation, September 1953), pp. 4–9.

17. Judith Ann Benner, *Sul Ross: Soldier, Statesman, Educator* (College Station: Texas A&M University Press, 1983), p. 40; Roger N. Conger, "Sul Ross: Waco's Man for All Seasons," *Waco Heritage & History* 8, no. 4 (Winter 1977): pp. 1–16.

18. Roberts, *Personal Correspondence of Sam Houston,* vol. 4, p. 362. Roberts, citing the Johnson Papers at the Center for American History, says Johnson came close to being court-martialed for leaving his Ranger command to marry Power.

19. Austin *State Gazette,* July 21, 1860.

20. Benner, *Sul Ross,* pp. 42–43.

21. *Pioneer Days in the Southwest from 1850–1879: Thrilling Descriptions of Buffalo Hunting, Indian Fighting and Massacres, Cowboy Life and Home Building* (Gutherie, Okla.: State Capital Company, 1909), p. 303. Vantine served in a company recruited in Collin County.

22. Austin *State Gazette,* July 21, 1860; Benner, *Sul Ross,* p. 44.

23. Benner, *Sul Ross,* p. 44.

24. Exley, *Frontier Blood,* p. 148.

25. Benner, *Sul Ross,* pp. 44–45.

26. Ibid., pp. 47, 49.

27. Austin *State Gazette,* November 17, 1860.

28. Benner, *Sul Ross,* p. 49; Marshall, *Cry Unheard,* pp. 32–34.

29. Austin *State Gazette,* November 17, 1860.

30. *Claims Against the United States,* p. 147.

31. Exley, *Frontier Blood,* p. 151.

32. Cynthia Ann Parker's son, Quanah, later maintained that his father, Peta Nacona, had not been the chief killed by Ross's rangers. Nacona died "two or three years" after the recapture of Cynthia Ann Parker and was buried in the Antelope Hills, Parker said. Bill Neeley, *The Last Comanche Chief: The Life and Times of Quanah Parker* (New York: John Wiley & Sons, 1995), p. 62. Robert H. Williams, "The Case for Peta Nacona," *Texana* 10 (1972): pp. 55–72, asserts that the Rangers did kill Nacona.

33. Benner, *Sul Ross,* pp. 56–58; Neeley, *Last Comanche Chief,* p. 60; Jack K. Selden, *Return: The Parker Story* (Palestine, Tex: Clacton Press, 2006) pp. 167–174.

34. Cynthia Ann Parker never assimilated into Anglo culture. She tried several times to rejoin her Comanche family, but never succeeded. Most accounts say she only lived four years after her recapture, but later research showed that enumerators included her in the 1870 U.S. Census. She died in Anderson County about a year later and was buried there. Her son, Quanah, became the last great chief of the Comanches. Unlike his mother, after his people were

relegated to a reservation outside Fort Sill, Indian Territory, Quanah adjusted to white ways. He died February 23, 1911, and was buried at Fort Sill. *New Handbook of Texas*, vol. 5, pp. 61–62; Benner, *Sul Ross*, p. 58.

35. Williams and Barker, *Writings of Sam Houston*, vol. 8, pp. 236–42; Spaw, *Texas Senate*, vol. I, pp. 321–22.

36. Mary H. Nichols ed., *Letters to and from Sidney Green Davidson and His Wife Mary Elizabeth Kuykendall Davidson in the Year 1861* (Ballinger, Tex.: privately published, 1990). The first letter was dated January 30, 1861.

37. Cutrer, *Ben McCulloch*, pp. 189–90; S. G. Davidson to Mary Davidson, February 24, 1861.

38. S. G. Davidson to Mary Davidson, March 4, 1861.

39. Cutrer, *Ben McCulloch*, pp. 189–90.

40. Mary Davidson to S. G. Davidson, March 29, 1861; S. G. Davidson to Mary Davidson, April 6, 1861; Mary to S. G. Davidson, April 9, 1861.

41. Cutrer, *Ben McCulloch*, pp. 189–90.

42. S. G. Davidson to Mary Davidson, June 7 and June 17, 1861; Belton *Democrat*, July 12, 1861. W. N. Alexander, a ranger who witnessed Davidson's death, provided more details of the incident in "Born Under the Lone Star Flag," written in 1908 and included in John M. Elkins's *Indian Fighting on the Texas Frontier* (1929, privately published; repr., Waco: Texian Press, 2000), pp. 115–19. Davidson, born in Tennessee in 1831, married Mary Elizabeth Kuykendall on March 26, 1856, in Bell County. They had three children.

43. Smith, *Frontier Defense in the Civil War*, pp. 42–43.

44. Davis, *Texas Rangers*, p. 47. While Smith's history of the Rangers during the Civil War is the most comprehensive study, historian W. C. Holden provided an earlier overview in "Frontier Defense in Texas During the Civil War," *West Texas Historical Association Year Book* 4 (1928): pp. 16–31. For the interesting experiences of one Confederate Texas Ranger, see Williams, *With the Border Ruffians*, pp. 161–403.

45. Holden, "Frontier Defense in Texas During the Civil War," p. 23–24.

46. McCord came to Texas in 1847 from Abbeville, South Carolina. He was in the surveying party that partitioned Coleman from Travis County in 1856. Three years later he served as a ranger under Edward Burleson, scouting in the area he had helped survey. During the Civil War, he had his headquarters at Camp Colorado, twelve miles from present Coleman. He returned to settle in Coleman County in 1876 following its organization. When he died there in 1914, he was president of Coleman National Bank. Coleman County *Chronicle*, Oct. 25, 1951.

47. Allan, *Allan's Lone Star Ballads*, p. 92.

48. Greer, *Buck Barry*, p. 169.

49. Ibid., p. 175.

50. Carrie J. Crouch, *A History of Young County, Texas* (Austin: Texas State

Historical Association, 1956), pp. 38–41; Kenneth F. Neighbors, "Elm Creek Raid in Young County, 1864," *West Texas Historical Association Year Book* 40 (1964): pp. 83–89.

51. Williams, *With the Border Ruffians*, p. 396.
52. Smith, *Frontier Defense in the Civil War*, pp. 180–2.
53. Ibid., pp. 146–47.
54. I. B. Ferguson, "The Battle of Dove Creek," *Hunter's Magazine*, June 1911. Totten's fight occurred in February 1864.
55. Greer, *Buck Barry*, pp. 186, 193.
56. Michael Reagan Thomasson, "James E. McCord and the Texas Frontier Regiment" (M.A. thesis, Nacogdoches: Stephen F. Austin State University, 1965), pp. 84–87; Ferguson, "Battle of Dove Creek." Barbara Barton, *Ruckus Along the Rivers: True Tales of Early Settlements Along Spring Creek, Dove Creek, and the Conchos* (San Angelo: Anchor Publishing Co., 1997), pp. 3–16; William C. Pool, "The Battle of Dove Creek," *Southwestern Historical Quarterly* 53 April 1950: pp. 367–85; David F. Crosby, "Kickapoo Counterattack at Dove Creek," *Wild West*, December 1999, pp. 50–54, 81.
57. "J. C. Cureton Tells of Famous Battle," *Frontier Times*, January 1946, pp. 59–61.
58. (William Wilson Straley), *Pioneer Sketches Nebraska and Texas* (Hico, Texas: Hico Printing Co., 1915), pp. 25–35.
59. Pete A. Y. Gunter and Robert A. Calvert, eds., *W. R. Strong: His Memoirs*. Denton: Denton County Historical Commission, 1982, p. 34
60. Ferguson, "Battle of Dove Creek."
61. Austin Callan, "Battle of Dove Creek," *Frontier Times*, September 1947, p. 544.
62. Felipe A. Latorre and Dolores L. Latorre, *The Mexican Kickapoo Indians* (Austin: University of Texas Press, 1976), p. 19. The Kickapoo view of the Dove Creek fight is supported by the recollection of participant Wiley Grubbs, who later claimed that he was standing only twenty feet from Captain Totten when he shot down an Indian woman and yelled: "Shoot them all, boys, big, little, old and young, and don't leave one of them to tell the tale." J.M. Franks, *Seventy Years In Texas*, Gatesville, Tex: 1924, p. 32.
63. Gunter and Calvert, *W. R. Strong*, p. 45.
64. Smith, *Frontier Defense in the Civil War*, pp. 173–74.
65. W. C. Nunn, *Texas Under the Carpetbaggers* (Austin: University of Texas Press, 1962), pp. 5–7.
66. Ralph A. Wooster, *Texas and Texans in the Civil War* (Austin: Eakin Press, 1995), p. 95.
67. Smith, *Frontier Defense in the Civil War*, p. 184.
68. Ibid., p. 168.
69. Greer, *Buck Barry*, p. 202.

7. "Filling bloody graves"

1. Kenneth E. Hendrickson Jr., *Chief Executives of Texas: From Stephen F. Austin to John B. Connally, Jr.* (College Station: Texas A&M University Press, 1995), pp. 87–90.
2. Claude Elliott, *Leathercoat: The Life History of a Texas Patriot* (San Antonio: Standard Printing Co., 1938), passim; Spaw, *Texas Senate,* vol. 2, p. 67; Bradley, *Claims Against the United States,* pp. 20–21.
3. David M. Horton and Ryan Kellus Turner, *Lone Star Justice: A Comprehensive Overview of the Texas Criminal Justice System* (Austin: Eakin Press, 1999), p. 97.
4. *Claims Against the United States,* p. 21.
5. Ibid., p. 23.
6. Baker, *Texas Scrap-Book,* pp. 134–35. The *Texas Almanac* estimated five thousand Comanche, Kiowa, and Lipan "could probably put into the field."
7. Hendrickson, *Chief Executives of Texas,* pp. 68, 90.
8. Ibid., pp. 66–68.
9. San Antonio *Daily Express,* March 4, 1870.
10. San Antonio *Daily Express,* March 30, 1870.
11. Spaw, *Texas Senate,* vol. 2, p. 12.
12. San Antonio *Daily Express,* June 16, 1870.
13. *Claims Against the United States,* p. 24.
14. *Report of the Adjutant General, 1875,* p. 3. The Frontier Forces authorized under the June 13, 1870, legislative act cost the state $458,996.51. Steele calculated that amounted to $2.90 per day, per man.
15. A. E. Skinner, "Forgotten Guardians: The Activities of Company C, Frontier Forces, 1870–1871," *Texana,* Summer 1968, pp. 107–21.
16. "The Ledger of Samuel Coleman Lockett," transcribed by Christina Stopka. Unpublished memoir, Texas Ranger Hall of Fame and Museum archives, Waco, Texas.
17. Sowell, *Rangers and Pioneers of Texas,* p. 233.
18. Dobie, *John C. Duval,* p. 17.
19. Sowell, *Rangers and Pioneers of Texas,* p. 233.
20. Ibid., p. 235.
21. "A Ranger Captain," *Voice of the Mexican Border,* November 1933, pp. 137–41.
22. Frankie Davis Glenn, *Capt'n John: Story of a Texas Ranger* (Austin: Nortex Press, 1991), p. 75.
23. J. B. (John) Dunn, *Perilous Trails of Texas* (Dallas: Southwest Press, 1932), passim; Cox, *Texas Ranger Tales II,* pp. 74–84.
24. Cora Melton Cross, "Pleasant Henderson Rice, Reviews Pioneer Days," *Frontier Times,* November 1932, pp. 92–94.
25. *Frontier Times,* July 1928, p. 407.

26. Skinner, "Forgotten Guardians," p. 115; James M. Day, "El Paso's Texas Rangers," *Password* 24, no. 4 (Winter 1979): pp. 156–57.

27. Sowell, *Rangers and Pioneers of Texas*, pp. 298–345.

28. A. C. Hill to Davidson, February 9, 1871, cited in Utley, *Lone Star Justice*, p. 343.

29. Sowell, *Rangers and Pioneers of Texas*, pp. 349-50.

30. Glenn, *Capt'n John*, p. 87.

31. Ibid.

32. Ibid., p. 88.

33. Ibid., p. 78.

34. Skinner, "Forgotten Guardians," p. 117.

35. Barbara Neal Ledbetter, *Indian Raids on Warren—Dubose—Feild—Man Wagon Trains—1871—in Young and Jack Counties.* (Graham, Tex.: privately published, 1992), p. ii.

36. *General Laws*, 1871, pp. 25–27.

37. Sowell, *Rangers and Pioneers of Texas*, pp. 380–81.

38. Ledbetter, *Indian Raids*, p. 64.

39. Ibid., pp. 62–63; Carl H. Moneyhon, *Texas After the Civil War: The Struggle of Reconstruction* (College Station: Texas A&M University Press, 2004), p. 145.

40. Skinner, "Forgotten Guardians," p. 120. The best overview of the Warren Wagon Train episode and its aftermath is Charles M. Robinson III, *The Indian Trial: The Complete Story of the Warren Wagon Train Massacre and the Fall of the Kiowa Nation* (Spokane, Wash.: Arthur H. Clark Co.), 1997.

41. Glenn, *Cap'n John*, pp. 94–95.

42. J. Marvin Hunter, *Pioneer History of Bandera County: Seventy-five Years of Intrepid History* (Bandera, Tex.: Hunter's Printing House, 1922), p. 87.

43. "Horace M. Hall's Letters from Gillespie County," *Southwestern Historical Quarterly* 62, no. 3 (January 1959): p. 349.

44. Baker, *Texas Scrap-Book*, pp. 145–46.

45. Austin *Daily Journal*, April 11, 1873.

46. The state police force did do some good work, its reputation tainted more by politics than fact. For more on this early law enforcement agency, see Ann Patton Baenzinger, "The Texas State Police During Reconstruction: A Reexamination," *Southwestern Historical Quarterly* 72 (April 1969): pp. 470–91; and William T. Field Jr., "The Texas State Police, 1870–1873," *Texas Military History* 5, Fall 1965, pp. 139–41.

47. Austin *Daily Statesman*, March 7, 1873.

48. Mike Cox, *Austin: An Illustrated History* (San Antonio: Historical Publishing Network, 1999), pp. 34–35. For an overview of Reconstruction in Texas, see Moneyhon, *Texas After the Civil War.*

8. "For the Protection of the Frontier"

1. Austin *Daily Statesman*, April 9, 1874.
2. *Messages of Governor Richard Coke to the Legislature*, January 28, 1874, pp. 4–5.
3. Austin *Daily Statesman*, May 12, 1874.
4. Austin *Daily Statesman*, May 10, 1874.
5. *New Handbook of Texas*, vol. 6, p. 79; Major Horace H. Shelton, "Texas Confederate Generals: General William Steele, West Pointer, Indian Fighter, Mexican War Hero, Confederate Leader, Re-Organizer of the Texas Rangers and Restorer of Law and Order in Texas After Reconstruction Days," *Under Texas Skies* (Austin) 3, no. 4, (August 1952): pp. 13–14.
6. Dallas *Weekly Herald*, December 29, 1877. Published under the heading "A Texas Ranger," the story contrasted the mild-mannered Frontier Battalion commander to the "picture of a Texas ranger" painted by "the average architect of a dime novel." The unnamed author of this piece went on to offer his own colorful version of the "ideal of the ranger of the wild frontier of Texas," before asserting that Jones, "a man who is the peer of Walker, Hayes [sic], McCulloch," was "a real, not an imaginary, hero of romance."
7. Austin *Daily Statesman*, May 9, 1874.
8. *New Handbook of Texas*, vol. 3, p. 986. Born December 23, 1834, in Fairfield District, South Carolina, to Henry and Nancy Jones, John B. Jones came with his family to Texas in 1838 when he was four. The family first settled in Travis County, then moved to Matagorda County. His father represented Matagorda County in the congress of the Republic of Texas and also earned a reputation as an Indian fighter. Later, the family moved to Navarro County. Young Jones attended Rutersville College in Fayette County and Mount Zion Collegiate Institute at Winnsboro, South Carolina, then returned to Texas and began farming in Navarro County. He enlisted as a private in Benjamin F. Terry's Eighth Texas Cavalry (better known as Terry's Texas Rangers) at the start of the Civil War, but soon transferred to the Fifteenth Texas Infantry, where he served as adjutant with the rank of captain. After the South's defeat, he and numerous other disaffected Confederates went to Mexico and then Brazil. Unhappy in South America, he returned to Texas and ran for the legislature. He was elected as a representative from Navarro County, but the Republican repatriation board would not allow him to take his seat. "General John B. Jones," Austin *Statesman*, July 20, 1881.
9. Helen Groce to Walter Prescott Webb, April 14, 1933, Webb Papers, Box 2M260, Center for American History, University of Texas at Austin.
10. Frederick Wilkins, *The Law Comes to Texas: Texas Rangers 1870–1901* (Austin: State House Press, 1999), p. 28; T. R. Havins, "Activities of Company

E, Frontier Battalion, Texas Rangers, 1874–1880," *West Texas Historical Association Year Book* 11 (1935): p. 65.

11. William J. Maltby, *Captain Jeff or Frontier Life in Texas with the Texas Rangers* (1906; repr., Waco: Texian Press, 1967), pp. 65–68.

12. "Texas Rangers May Lose Even Their Name." *Frontier Times*, January 1931, p. 157.

13. Austin *Daily Statesman*, May 9, 1874.

14. Havins, "Activities of Company E," p. 65.

15. Adjutant General's Records, Texas State Library and Archives.

16. Leon Metz, *John Wesley Hardin: Dark Angel of Texas* (El Paso: Mangan Books, 1996), pp. 131–40; Havins, "Activities of Company E," pp. 62–63. The papers of Texas's various governors and the records of the Adjutant General's Department contain letter after letter petitioning for rangers in a particular jurisdiction. The Frontier Battalion never had the resources to respond to all the requests for assistance.

17. Walker to Jones, May 30, 1874, Adjutant General's Records, Texas State Library and Archives.

18. Metz, *John Wesley Hardin*, pp. 146–47.

19. Perry had been serving as Blanco County hide inspector, an elected office, when hired to command Company D, which was initially stationed near Mason. He went back to Blanco County after his Ranger service, dying there on October 7, 1898. "The Frontier Battalion—Its Officers," Austin *Daily Statesman*, May 9, 1874; *Heritage of Blanco County*, pp. 194–97; S. P. Elkins, "Served as a Texas Ranger," *Frontier Times*, August 1928, pp. 438–39; 447. Under the minute-company provision of the new frontier protection law, Governor Coke approved formation of a company in El Paso County under Lieutenant Telesforo Montes. Mustered into service May 27, 1874, the minute company had at least two engagements with Indians. Following a raid on September 15, 1874, Montes's Rangers killed two Indians and recovered five stolen horses. Two months later the Rangers pursued a raiding party and killed one Indian while recovering all the stock they had stolen. Day, "El Paso's Texas Rangers," p. 157.

20. Metz, *John Wesley Hardin*, pp. 142–43.

21. Ibid., p. 158.

22. Chuck Parsons and Donaly E. Brice, *Texas Ranger N. O. Reynolds: The Intrepid* (Honolulu: Talei Publishers, 2005), pp. 34–35, citing Austin *Daily Statesman*, July 25 and July 28, 1874.

23. Neeley, *Last Comanche Chief*, p. 90.

24. Ibid.

25. Ibid., p. 91.

26. Stan Hoig, *Kiowas and the Legend of Kicking Bird* (Boulder: University of Colorado Press, 2000), p. 199.

27. Austin *Daily Statesman*, July 19, 1874. Perry had moved his command from Mason County to a location on Celery Springs, six miles northwest of Menardville (present Menard). Parsons and Brice, *Texas Ranger N. O. Reynolds*, p. 29.

28. Havins, "Activities of Company E," p. 66.

29. G. W. Ellington, "When Cattle Trails Were Highways" (unpublished manuscript), pp. 11–13, Ranger Reminiscences, Record Group 401, File 1234-8, Texas State Library and Archives.

30. Wilkins, *Law Comes to Texas*, pp. 42–43; Gillett, *Six Years with the Texas Rangers*, pp. 93–94. Originally from Maryland, thirty-five-year-old S. G. Nicholson attended medical school in New Orleans. He served as Frontier Battalion surgeon, earning $100 a month, until November 30, 1876. He settled for a time in Frio County, then moved to Val Verde County, where he remained in private practice until his death at a sanitarium in Mineral Wells on February 3, 1893. Parsons and Brice, *Texas Ranger N. O. Reynolds*, p. 89.

31. Havins, "Activities of Company E," p. 67.

32. "Indian News," Austin *Daily Statesman*, July 19, 1874.

33. Ibid.

34. "Reminiscences of a Texas Ranger," *Frontier Times*, December 1923, pp. 20–24.

35. Jim McIntire, *Early Days in Texas: A Trip to Hell and Heaven*, ed. and with an introduction and notes by Robert K. DeArment (Norman: University of Oklahoma Press, 1992), pp. 52–53. McIntire (1846–ca. 1910) came to Texas from Ohio and went to work as a cowboy for Jack County rancher J. C. Loving. Though the records show he did not join the Rangers until June 1, 1875, which was after the Lost Valley Fight, he clearly participated in the battle either as a volunteer or special ranger. The same party of Indians had attacked his boss's ranch two days earlier. McIntire served several enlistments in the Rangers through 1878. McIntire wrote his story down in 1902, but it went unpublished for nearly another century. For an overview of McIntire's colorful life, see Robert K. DeArment, "The Frontier Adventures of Jim McIntire," *True West*, February 1999, pp. 10–17.

36. "Reminiscences of a Texas Ranger." In 1970, the Texas Historical Commission placed a marker off U.S. 281 twelve miles northwest of Jacksboro near the site of the battle.

37. Jones to Steele, July 14, 1874, Adjutant General's Records, Texas State Library and Archives. In addition to Jones's official report, all the major Texas newspapers chronicled the Lost Valley fight. Other personal recollections include an August 22, 1874, letter from Ranger Z. T. Wattles published September 2, 1874, in the Corsicana *Observer* and Walter M. Robertson's "The Loss [Lost] Valley Fight," *Frontier Times* 7, no. 3 (December 1929): pp. 100-105.

38. "Indian News," Austin *Daily Statesman*, July 19, 1874.

39. Galveston *Daily News*, January 13, 1875.

40. J. Brett Cruse, "Archeological Investigations at the Battle of Red River Site: New Perspectives on the 1874 Indian Campaign in the Texas Panhandle," *Southwestern Historical Quarterly*, October 2002, pp. 169–92. For an overview of the military's 1874 campaign in Texas see James L. Haley's *The Buffalo War: The History of the Red River Indian Uprising of 1874* (Garden City: Doubleday, 1976). Thomas T. Smith summarized the U.S. army's Indian fighting in Texas in his "U.S. Army Combat Operations in the Indian Wars of Texas, 1849–1881," *Southwestern Historical Quarterly* 99, no. 4 (April 1996): pp. 500-541.

41. *Supplemental Report of the Adjutant General, December 1, 1874*, pp. 6–10; *Report of the Adjutant General, 1876*, pp. 5–9. The Frontier Battalion's appropriation might have been sufficient to sustain its operations without cuts until the next legislative session had it not been for something outside of Jones's control: The act creating the battalion also provided for emergency Ranger companies operated at the county level. Wilkins, *Law Comes to Texas*, pp. 53–55, notes that companies organized and operating in El Paso, Nueces, and Webb counties siphoned money from the frontier protection allocation.

42. "Captured an Indian," *Frontier Times*, March 1929, pp. 245–46. Texas's most famous Indian captive was Santana, placed back in prison at Huntsville on September 17, 1874, for violating his parole by participating in the Red River War. The Kiowa chief languished behind the red brick walls until October 11, 1874, when he killed himself by jumping from the second story of the prison hospital.

43. Frontier Battalion General Order Number 5, October 27, 1874, Adjutant General's Records, Texas State Library and Archives.

44. Havins, "Activities of Company E," pp. 68–69.

45. Maltby, *Captain Jeff*, p. 96.

46. Jones's standards were not uniformly rigid. As Jones's niece Helen Groce later wrote to historian W. P. Webb on April 14, 1933, "Once when he [Jones] came on a visit from the frontier he brought a couple of prairie dogs. . . . He had them in a nice little wooden box, perforated with holes and neat little collars, with chains attached to the box." But the prairie dogs had heads smaller than their necks, and they often escaped. Burrowing into a pile of quilts and blankets, they chewed holes "in each bit of cover." Jones's sister, the girl's mother, "never cared so much for them after that," Groce wrote. When the animals wandered away and never came back, her mother "did not grieve."

47. Beatrice Grady Gay, *"Into the Setting Sun": A History of Coleman County* (Santa Anna, Tex.: n.p., n.d., pp. 119–21. Maltby, *Captain Jeff*, pp. 100–101, told the story differently, maintaining that the Indian had been found the

day after the fight, badly wounded, and died shortly thereafter. He made no mention of the Indian having been kept around camp for a while or having been offered a sporting chance to escape.

48. Jones to Steele, November 24, 1874, published in the Austin *Daily Statesman*, November 28, 1874. Years later, in her *A Woman's Recollections of Six Years in Camp with the Texas Rangers*, p. 17, Luvenia Conway Roberts wrote, "It was contrary to orders to take prisoners, but [Roberts] could not kill a man even an Indian when he was begging for his life. The prisoner suffered agony from fear while in camp, and his expression showed that he expected momentarily to be killed."

49. "Captured an Indian," pp. 245–46.

50. "Outrage at Indian Exhibition on Sabbath," Austin *Daily Statesman*, December 6, 1874.

51. Austin *Daily Statesman*, December 1, 1874.

52. The January 12, 1878, edition of the Fort Worth *Telegram*, cited in Parsons and Brice, *Texas Ranger N. O. Reynolds*, p. 46, reported that "Little Bull, the young Indian chief, kept in the penitentiary as a prisoner of war; died recently of consumption." When Major Jones reduced the size of the battalion for lack of funds, among others he discharged Cooley. He had enlisted in Captain Perry's company on May 25, 1874, and got his discharge notice on December 4. David Johnson, "Scott Cooley—a Byword for Terror," *Quarterly of the National Association for Outlaw and Lawman History* 27, no. 2 (April-June 2003), p. 9.

53. Wilkins, *Law Comes to Texas*, pp. 55–57.

54. Ibid., p. 56. Captains Ikard, Perry, and Stevens, along with one of Perry's lieutenants, also were laid off due to the money shortage. Lieutenant Roberts then assumed command of Company D. Parsons and Brice, *Texas Ranger N. O. Reynolds*, p. 43.

55. Wilkins, *Law Comes to Texas*, pp. 55–56.

56. Austin *Daily Statesman*, December 24, 1874.

57. Wilbarger, *Indian Depredations in Texas*, p. 574; *Report of the Adjutant General, 1875*, pp. 11–12. By September 30, 1875, Frontier Battalion rangers had fought Indians on sixteen occasions, having followed thirty trails. In so doing, they had killed twenty-four Indians and wounded ten. The Rangers had lost two of their own in the Lost Valley fight and had six men wounded. The state had to pay for fourteen Ranger horses killed in action. Rangers recaptured a thousand head of stolen cattle and seventy-eight horses and mules. In addition, they arrested twenty-eight "desperadoes and cattle thieves" and killed three. According to the adjutant general's calculations, all this had cost the state an average of $2.30 a day, per man.

58. Galveston *Daily News*, January 13, 1875.

59. Galveston *Daily News*, January 12, 1875.

60. Davis, *Texas Rangers*, p. 60.

61. *Report of Maj. J. B. Jones, commanding the Frontier Battalion, Texas State Troops, March 1876, Report of the Adjutant General, 1876.*

62. Frontier Battalion General Order Number 10, August 12, 1875, Adjutant General's Records, Texas State Library and Archives.

63. Frontier Battalion General Order Number 11, August 21, 1875, Adjutant General's Records, Texas State Library and Archives.

64. San Antonio *Daily Express,* November 30, 1875.

65. "More About W. B. Anglin," *Frontier Times,* March 1929, p. 224.

9. "Nothing short of an armed force"

1. Victoria *Advocate,* June 4, 1874.

2. Chuck Parsons and Marianne E. Hall Little, *Captain L. H. McNelly—Texas Ranger—the Life and Times of a Fighting Man* (Austin: State House Press, 2001), p. 142.

3. Ibid., p. 137; *Report of the Adjutant General, 1875,* p. 14; Wilkins, *Law Comes to Texas,* p. 85.

4. Parsons and Little, *Captain L. H. McNelly,* passim.

5. Galveston *Daily News,* January 13, 1875.

6. For more on the Taylor-Sutton feud, see Victor M. Rose, *Texas Vendetta: or, The Sutton-Taylor Feud* (New York: J. J. Little, 1880); Sonnichsen, *I'll Die Before I'll Run;* Robert C. Sutton Jr., *The Sutton-Taylor Feud* (Quanah, Tex.: Nortex Press, 1974).

7. Parsons and Little, *Captain L. H. McNelly,* p. 137; Chuck Parsons, *"Pidge": A Texas Ranger from Virginia* (Wolfe City, Tex.: Henington Publishing Co., 1985), pp. 1–4.

8. Napoleon Augustus Jennings, *A Texas Ranger* (New York: Charles Scribner's Sons, 1899), pp. 118–19; George Durham, as told to Clyde Wantland, *Taming the Nueces Strip: The Story of McNelly's Rangers* (Austin: University of Texas Press, 1962), p. 5.

9. Austin *Daily Statesman,* August 11, 1874.

10. Parsons and Little, *Captain L. H. McNelly,* pp. 156–57.

11. Ibid., p. 158.

12. Ibid., pp. 166–67.

13. Taylor, *American-Mexican Frontier,* p. 56; William M. Hager, "The Nueces Town Raid of 1875: A Border Incident," *Arizona and the West* 1 (Spring 1959): 258–70.

14. Austin *Daily Statesman,* April 15, 1874.

15. Ibid.

16. Parsons and Little, *Captain L. H. McNelly,* p. 176.

17. Lindsay Carter, "The Texas Rangers: Interesting Facts About Our Greatest Body of Fighting Men," *Texas Magazine* 3, no. 4 (February 1911): pp. 27–31.

18. Parsons and Little, *Captain L. H. McNelly*, p. 179.

19. Ibid., p. 183.

20. *Report of the Adjutant General, 1875*, pp. 8–13.

21. Ibid.

22. Parsons and Little, *Captain L. H. McNelly*, pp. 192–93.

23. "19th Century Shining Star: James W. Guynn," *Texas Ranger Dispatch* 10, (Summer 2003).

24. Wilkins, *Law Comes to Texas*, p. 89.

25. "19th Century Shining Star," *Texas Ranger Dispatch*.

26. Sara R. Massey, ed., *Black Cowboys of Texas* (College Station: Texas A&M University Press, 2000), pp.104–6, calls Kinchlow "the earliest known African American to be associated with the Special Force or what became McNelly's Rangers."

27. Ibid.

28. *Frontier Times*, September 1932, p. 564.

29. Austin *Daily Statesman*, June 13, 1875.

30. Some writers have interpreted McNelly's "wish you were here" remark as a flip attempt at humor. But the phrase did not acquire its cliché-on-a-postcard meaning until the early twentieth century. Well aware of Steele's military career, McNelly probably was sincere in wishing Steele had been present for the fight.

31. Wilkins, *Law Comes to Texas*, p. 92.

32. Ibid., pp. 95–96.

33. Parsons and Little, *Captain L. H. McNelly*, p. 206.

34. Wilkins, *Law Comes to Texas*, pp. 96–97.

35. Parsons and Little, *Captain L. H. McNelly*, p. 242.

36. Webb, *Texas Rangers*, p. 261, used a different version of this purported soliloquy by McNelly. Webb did not cite this reconstructed speech in his book, but it came in an undated letter from former Ranger William C. Callicott to Webb. Following Webb's death, the letter went to the University of Texas at Austin, where it is among his Texas Ranger papers at the Center for American History. Spelling and basic grammar corrected for easier comprehension.

37. McNelly to Adjutant General Steele, November 22, 1875, and Galveston *Daily News*, December 12, 1875. These are the two prime sources on the Las Cuevas incident.

38. Parsons and Little, *Captain L. H. McNelly*, p. 241.

39. Ibid., pp. 241–42, citing San Antonio *Express*, August 21, 1909.

40. Ibid., citing December 1, 1875, San Antonio *Express*.

41. *Report of the Adjutant General, 1876*, p. 9.

42. Fisher, *It Occurred in Kimble*, p. 82.

43. Erik Rigler, "Frontier Justice in the Days Before NCIC," *FBI Law Enforcement Bulletin*, July 1985, pp. 16–22.

44. Any offenses for which King Fisher may have been guilty became judicially moot on March 11, 1884, when he and former Austin city marshal Ben Thompson died in a flurry of gunshots at Jack Harris's Theater in San Antonio. Ironies abounded in this unsolved double killing. Once considered an outlaw, not long before his demise Fisher had moved to Uvalde and gone to work as a deputy sheriff. Thompson, despite a fondness for gambling and a propensity for excessive drinking, had won election as Austin's city marshal in 1881. He resigned a year later to face trial in San Antonio for killing Bexar County political boss Jack Harris, the owner of the vaudeville theater where he and Fisher would die in the spring of 1884. Good legal representation got Thompson acquitted in Harris's slaying, but the former marshal's death in San Antonio clearly constituted a payback on the part of Harris's cronies. Fisher probably had the misfortune of being in the wrong place at the right time. Bill O'Neal, *Encyclopedia of Western Gunfighters* (Norman: University of Oklahoma Press, 1979), pp. 315–21. For more on King Fisher see O. C. Fisher and Jeff C. Dykes, *King Fisher: His Life and Times* (Norman: University of Oklahoma Press, 1966).

45. Jennings, *Texas Ranger,* p. 235. Jennings came to Texas from New Hampshire in 1874 at eighteen, "my mind . . . inflamed by the highly colored accounts of life in the Lone Star State." He enlisted in McNelly's company on May 26, 1874, and served until February 1, 1877. He left Texas for the East Coast, where he became a journalist.

46. Parsons and Little, *Captain L. H. McNelly,* pp. 272–73; *Report of the Adjutant General, 1876.*

47. Spaw, *Texas Senate,* vol. 2, pp. 243–44.

48. Steele weathered considerable criticism in the press and from some former rangers over discharging McNelly. The adjutant general sent the newspapers a letter explaining his action, his reasons boiling down to the captain's poor leadership, McNelly's frequent health-related absences from his command, medical costs to the state, and a doctor's stipulation that McNelly would not have been fit for service that winter. When newly elected governor Hubbard also questioned Steele's decision, the adjutant general replied with a three-page letter setting forth his case. That letter contained numbers showing that the effectiveness of the company had already increased under Hall's command. The controversy died down, and McNelly's health continued to decline. Parsons and Little, *Captain L. H. McNelly,* pp. 292–96.

49. Beth White, *Goliad Remembered: 1836–1940* (Austin: Nortex Press, 1987), p. 50. Born in Lexington, North Carolina, on October 9, 1849, Jesse Leigh (he later changed *Leigh* to *Lee*) Hall came to Texas with his family in 1869. He spent two years as a schoolteacher, but moved into law enforcement, serving as city marshal in Sherman and later as a Grayson County sheriff's deputy stationed in Denison. He joined McNelly's company on August 10,

1876. For more on Hall, see Dora Neill Raymond, *Captain Lee Hall of Texas* (Norman: University of Oklahoma Press, 1940).

50. Wilkins, *Law Comes to Texas*, pp. 145–46, citing Galveston *Daily News*, August 2, 1877.

51. Ibid., p. 145.

52. Webb, *Texas Rangers*, p. 298.

53. Rick Miller, *Bounty Hunter* (College Station: Creative Publishing Co., 1988), p. 80.

54. Ibid., p. 84.

55. Other sources have the difficulty occurring between Chipley and Bowen, not Swain. In either case, Chipley would have had good reason to be fearful for his life and very interested in getting both men out of Florida.

56. Miller, *Bounty Hunter*, p. 92.

57. New York *Times*, August 25, 1877.

58. Galveston *Daily News*, August 25, 1877.

59. Metz, *John Wesley Hardin*, p. 172.

60. Austin *Daily Statesman*, August 27, 1877; Parsons and Brice, *Texas Ranger N. O. Reynolds*, p. 153.

61. Armstrong and Duncan split the $4,000 reward the state had offered for Hardin, with Hutchinson getting $500 for his assistance. Armstrong received somewhat more credit for the capture than he deserved, but he played a crucial role in keeping Hardin in custody while waiting for a warrant and in protecting Hardin once they returned to Texas. During the struggle preceding the arrest, the lieutenant supposedly threatened to kill anyone who shot Hardin. Duncan's role in the arrest of Hardin was the highlight of his career with the state. He left the Rangers on November 15, 1877, later intimating that the lack of credit he got for capturing Hardin fed into his decision to quit the force.

62. Parsons and Little, *Captain L. H. McNelly*, pp. 297–99. In appreciation of his service in South Texas, the King Ranch spent $3,000 to place a large granite monument on McNelly's grave.

63. Parsons, Chuck. *John B. Armstrong: Texas Ranger and Pioneer Ranchman.* College Station: Texas A&M University Press, 2007, p. 64 citing Goree to Steele, September 1, 1877; R. G., Kimbell, *Ranger Reminiscences*, Record Group 401, 1234-11, Texas State Library and Archives.

64. Miller, *Bounty Hunter*, p. 99.

65. *The Letters of John Wesley Hardin* (Austin: Eakin Press, 2001), pp. 84, 86.

10. "HERE LIES A NOTED COW THIEF"

1. Peter R. Rose and Elizabeth E. Sherry, *The Hoo Doo War: Portraits of a Lawless Time* (Mason, Tex.: Mason County Historical Commission, 2003), p. 5; David Johnson, *The Mason County "Hoo Doo" War, 1874–1902* (Denton:

University of North Texas Press, 2006), passim. Various versions of the text of the note found on Bolt's body have been published, but the sentiment of the message is not ambiguous in any of the accounts.

2. William C. Pool, *A Historical Atlas of Texas* (Austin: Encino Press, 1975), p. 109.

3. Roberts, *Rangers and Sovereignty*, p. 88.

4. *The Lucia Holmes Diary* (Mason, Tex.: Mason County Historical Society, 1985), p. 5.

5. On March 1, 1875, the San Antonio *Daily Herald* managed to find some levity in the Mason County lynching: "We see it stated in an exchange that five men were recently hung at . . . Mason. We are able, thanks to a gentleman who was present, to define the deliberations that took place under the spreading branches of a live oak only a little more definitely. Some unknown parties . . . seized upon the five men who were suspected of being horse thieves, and succeeded in elevating three of the five, when the sheriff put in an appearance. 'Many citizens' thought it best to postpone the obsequies of the rest, and withdrew hastily, after wounding one of the accused, who was waiting for his turn to be an angel. The gentlemen in the tree were cut down, but the other two were [dead]. So instead of five men being hung, only two were hung, and one was shot. For the sake of the reputation of Mason as a law abiding community we hope this correction will be made." Karylon A. Russel and David Johnson, "Backtrailing the 'notorious Baccus brothers,'" *Quarterly of the National Association for Outlaw and Lawman History, Inc.* 29, no. 2 (April-June 2005): pp. 13–17; David Johnson, "Feudal Catalyst: T. P. Williamson," *Quarterly of the National Association for Outlaw and Lawman History, Inc.*, April-June 1998, p. 13. As for Charley Johnson, who survived the lynching, after lying low for a while, he resurfaced and cheekily applied for enlistment in the Frontier Battalion. Jones turned him down. Johnson, *Mason County "Hoo Doo" War*, p. 96, citing Jones to Dan Roberts, October 11, 1875. The author on p. 125 interprets Johnson's attempt to join the Rangers as an infiltration effort on the part of the Cooley–Baird antimob faction, though it could have been a belief that being in the Rangers would be better for his health.

6. Parsons and Brice, *Texas Ranger N. O. Reynolds*, pp. 51–52.

7. C. L. Sonnichsen, *I'll Die Before I'll Run: The Story of the Great Feuds of Texas* (New York: Harper & Brothers, 1951), pp. 95–96. Another account of Williamson's death can be found in the Austin *Daily Statesman*, May 18, 1875.

8. Parsons and Brice, *Texas Ranger N. O. Reynolds*, pp. 56–57.

9. Nannie Moore Kinser to May Kinser Holland, May 16, 1949, in Burnet *Bulletin*, June 6, 1974.

10. Sonnichsen, *I'll Die Before I'll Run*, p. 94.

11. "Horrible Murder at Mason," San Antonio *Daily Herald*, August 18, 1875

(translated from August 17, 1875, Fredericksburg *Freie Presse*) as cited in Parsons and Brice, *Texas Ranger N. O. Reynolds*, pp. 57–58. Cooley did not harm the other two men who had been working with Wohrle. "It is probable that the murderer will evade all earthly punishment as he is evidently the paid assassin of men who will back him up" the newspaper speculated. Cooley had not been on anyone's payroll, but the newspaper proved to be correct in predicting that he would avoid punishment for the killing.

12. John Peters Ringo, born May 3, 1850, in Wayne County, Indiana, came to Texas around 1871 via California and Missouri, to work as a cowboy. He left Texas in 1879, ending up in Arizona, where he died on July 13, 1882. Most historians believe Ringo's death a suicide, though other writers have tried to make it a murder. Two biographies tell his story in detail, each devoting considerable attention to the Hoo Doo War: David Johnson, *John Ringo* (Stillwater, Okla.: Barbed Wire Press, 1996); and Steve Gatto, *Johnny Ringo* (Lansing: Protar House, 2002).

13. Peter Bader, the late Karl Bader's brother, has been credited with killing Baird. On January 13, 1876, John Baird killed Bader. Johnson, "Feudal Catalyst," p. 16; Gatto, *Johnny Ringo*, p. 25.

14. San Antonio *Daily Herald*, September 14, 1875. The quotation comes from a letter dated September 8, 1875, that the newspaper received from Fredericksburg.

15. *Lucia Holmes Diary*, p. 39.

16. As Parsons and Brice show in *Texas Ranger N. O. Reynolds*, pp. 29–30, the state had taken no action on a Mason County official's request for a Ranger presence in the county the year before. Judge Wilson Hey had written Governor Coke from Mason County on June 25, 1874, to report that "parties from Llano & Other Counties" had been "continually depredating upon the Cattle" of Mason County ranchers. Rangers, he implored, could "prevent the citizens from protecting their hard Earnings by taking the Law into their own hand." Johnson, *Mason County 'Hoo Doo' War*, pp. 65–65, maintains that the Rangers accomplished little in Mason County. He is particularly critical of Roberts, who witnessed the lynching in Mason but "made no move to investigate the incident or arrest any of the mob." On p. 78 he writes, "Company D proved worse than useless in suppressing the feud." The next Ranger detachment sent to Mason, elements of Company A, "proved as ineffective as Company D has been," Johnson concluded on p. 146.

17. Johnson, "Scott Cooley," p. 14.

18. *Lucia Holmes Diary*, p. 39.

19. Wilkins, *Law Comes to Texas*, pp. 74–75.

20. Burnet County sheriff John Clymer arrested Cooley and Ringo on December 27, 1875, and transferred them to the Travis County Jail in Austin for safekeeping. Moved to Lampasas County on a change of venue, the outlaw duo es-

caped jail with the assistance of friends on May 4, 1876. Not quite five weeks later, on June 10, 1876, Cooley died in Blanco County. Some said "brain fever" did him in, others speculated that someone poisoned him. Austin *Daily Statesman,* June 13 and August 18, 1876; "Scott Cooley's Grave," *Frontier Times,* February-March 1976, pp. 3–5; Johnson, "Feudal Catalyst," p. 18.

21. Roberts, *Rangers and Sovereignty,* p. 93.
22. Johnson, *Mason County 'Hoo Doo' War, 1874-1902,* pp. 122–125.
23. Rose and Sherry, *Hoo Doo War,* p. 95.
24. Jones to Steele, October 26, 1875, Adjutant General Records, Texas State Library and Archives. Richard Maxwell Brown, *Strain of Violence: Historical Studies of American Violence and Vigilantism* (New York: Oxford University Press, 1975), pp. 248–49, lists the Hoo Doo War as one of twenty-seven vigilante movements in thirty-eight Central Texas counties from 1865 to 1900. Brown postulates up to sixty movements in all, some of which "no trace can be found."
25. Parsons and Brice, *Texas Ranger N. O. Reynolds,* p. 65, citing Steele to Jones, October 27, 1875.
26. Before becoming Mason County's top lawman, Clark may have served for slightly more than a month in a Ranger-like minutemen company in San Saba County in 1872. A former Confederate officer, he fled Texas in 1875 for Missouri, where he died in 1888. For more detail on this key figure in the Hoo Doo War, see Rose and Sherry, *Hoo Doo War,* pp. 107–21. Allen G. Hatley provides an overview of the war in "The Mason County War: Top Texas Feud," *Wild West,* August 2005.
27. Wilkins, *Law Comes to Texas,* p. 76.
28. Roberts, *Woman's Reminiscences,* p. 15.
29. Ibid., p. 29.
30. "The Frontier," Galveston *Daily News,* November 10, 1877.
31. Roberts, *Woman's Reminiscences,* p. 16.
32. Ibid.
33. *The Victorian,* Fifth Annual Calvert Historical Pilgrimage, Robertson County Historical Commission (n.p., n.d.).
34. *Report of the Adjutant General, 1876.*
35. Wilbarger, *Indian Depredations in Texas,* p. 574.
36. Wilkins, *Law Comes to Texas,* pp. 81–82.
37. Roberts, *Woman's Reminiscences,* p. 27.
38. Ibid.
39. Wilkins, *Law Comes to Texas,* p. 82.
40. *Frontier Times,* December 1947, p. 84.
41. Samora, Bernal, and Pena, *Gunpowder Justice,* p. 54; Wilkins, *Law Comes to Texas,* p. 125.
42. Wilkins, *Law Comes to Texas,* p. 125, citing Frontier Battalion Special Order

Number 15, March 20, 1877, Adjutant General's Records, Texas State Library and Archives.

43. Wilbarger, *Indian Depredations in Texas*, p. 576.

44. Fisher, *It Occurred in Kimble*, pp. 196–97.

45. Wilkins, *Law Comes to Texas*, p. 125. The Winchesters clearly made the Sharps obsolete. As Parsons and Brice noted in *Texas Ranger N. O. Reynolds*, p. 92, several of Captain Neal Coldwell's men eagerly awaited Winchesters to replace their single-shot rifles. "Sergeant [N. O.] Reynolds Says that he must have one, but will wait to See if he can get one from the State, before he buys one elsewhere," Coldwell wrote Major Jones on January 7, 1877, from his camp in Frio County. No matter the weapon they carried, rangers liked to shoot. Three days earlier, in his monthly accounting of state property, the captain reported 130 carbine rounds and 130 pistol rounds "expended for game, and target practice."

46. Martha Anne Turner, *Richard Bennent Hubbard: An American Life* (Austin: Shoal Creek Publishers, 1979), pp. 71–72. Hubbard, a Harvard-educated lawyer, had been lieutenant governor under Coke. He succeeded the governor in December 1876 when Coke stepped down to take a seat in the U.S. Senate. A prominent resident of Tyler, Hubbard had come to Texas in 1853 from his native Georgia.

47. Fisher, *It Occurred in Kimble*, p. 208. Parsons and Brice, *Texas Ranger N. O. Reynolds*, pp. 95–96, provide the complete text of Waddill's letter. The ranger was a member of Captain J. C. Sparks's company.

48. Fisher, *It Occurred in Kimbal*, p. 210.

49. Jones to N. O. Reynolds, April 8, 1877, cited in Parsons and Brice, *Texas Ranger N. O. Reynolds*, p. 204.

50. Fisher, *It Occurred in Kimble*, p. 210. As he prepared to descend on Kimble County, Jones wrote Steele on April 12 from Coldwell's camp in Frio County asking that thirty Winchesters be shipped to Fort McKavett for his rangers. Parsons and Brice, *Texas Ranger N. O. Reynolds*, p. 98.

51. Fisher, *It Occurred in Kimble*, pp. 211–12; Parsons and Brice, *Texas Ranger N. O. Reynolds*, pp. 103–4. Not everyone arrested in the roundup proved to be a wrongdoer. County Survey M. J. Denman claimed that a "great many of the arrests made by Jones were of the best citizens of the community, unknown to him, who were soon turned loose." But the Galveston *Daily News* of September 7, 1877, assessed Jones's Kimble County operation more magnanimously: "Here is a county redeemed from lawlessness and crime, and those who have been instrumental in achieving this result are certainly entitled to the thanks of the people of Kimble, their neighbors and the whole State."

52. Brown, *Strain of Violence*, pp. 246–47 termed the Kimble County cleanup "one of the most remarkable episodes in the annals of American law enforcement."

53. Anna J. Pennebacker, *A New History of Texas* (Palestine, Tex.: 1895), p. 289.

54. Marcos Kinevan, *Frontier Cavalryman: Lieutenant John Bigelow with the Buffalo Soldiers in Texas* (El Paso: Texas Western Press, 1997), p. 58.

55. Bill O'Neal, *The Bloody Legacy of Pink Higgins: A Half Century of Violence in Texas* (Austin: Eakin Press, 1999), pp. 37–38.

56. Jerry Sinise, *Pink Higgins, the Reluctant Gunfighter and Other Tales of the Panhandle* (Quanah, Tex.: Nortex Press, 1973), pp. 34–35.

57. Jeff Jackson, "The Horrell-Higgins Feud," Application for Texas State Historical Marker, Texas Historical Commission Library; Frederick Nolan, *Bad Blood: The Life and Times of the Horrell Brothers* (Stillwater, Okla.: Barbed Wire Press, 1994), passim.

58. O'Neal, *Bloody Legacy of Pink Higgins*, p. 49; Chuck Parsons, "But One Shot Was Fired: Sgt. N. O. Reynolds and the Arrest of the Horrells," pp. 131–43, in Sharon Cunningham and Mark Boardman, eds., *Revenge! And Other True Tales of the Old West* (Lafayette, Ind.: Scarlet Mask, 2004).

59. Parsons and Brice, *Texas Ranger N. O. Reynolds*, p. 120.

60. Wilkins, *Law Comes to Texas*, p. 131.

61. Lampasas *Dispatch*, August 9, 1877.

62. Ibid. Parsons and Brice, *Texas Ranger N. O. Reynolds*, pp. 127–28, include the full text of both letters.

63. Turner, *Richard Bennent Hubbard*, p. 82. Following Jones's work, Lampasas settled down considerably, but not the Horrells. Named as accomplices in the May 28, 1878, murder of J. T. Vaughn in Bosque County, Martin and Thomas Horrell died at the hands of vigilantes in an attack on the Bosque County jail at Meridian on December 15, 1878. Only Sam Horrell lived to old age, dying of natural causes on August 3, 1936, in California. Acquitted in the murder of Merritt Horrell, Higgins went on to become a noted range detective, winning a horseback gunfight with a suspected cattle thief on October 1, 1902. He died at sixty-two on December 18, 1913. (His death date is often reported as December 21, since it appears on his tombstone. But as O'Neal pointed out in his *Bloody Legacy of Pink Higgins*, p. 102, that was the day he was buried, not the day he died.)

64. Galveston *Daily News*, September 20, 1877.

11. "A TERROR TO EVIL DOERS"

1. J. J. Bowden, "The Magoffin Salt War," *Password* 7 (Summer 1962): pp. 95–121; C. L. Sonnichsen, *The El Paso Salt War of 1877* (El Paso: Texas Western Press, 1961), passim; *El Paso Troubles in Texas*, House Executive Doc. 93, 45th Cong., 2nd sess., 1878, passim; *Relations of the United States with Mexico*, House Executive Doc. 701, 45th Cong., 2nd sess., 1878, passim; Nancy Hamilton, *Ben Dowell: El Paso's First Mayor* (El Paso: Texas Western

Press, 1976), pp. 51–55; C. F. Ward, "The Salt War of San Elizario, 1877" (M.A. thesis, University of Texas, 1932).

2. Santa Fe *Independent*, October 6, 1877.

3. Wilkins, *Law Comes to Texas*, pp. 136–44.

4. Ibid., p. 138.

5. Walter Kohlberg, *Letters of Ernst Kohlberg, 1875–1877* (El Paso: Texas Western Press, 1973), pp. 68–70.

6. Mrs. O. L., Shipman, "El Paso Rangers Born to Trouble," El Paso *Times*, October 4, 1959.

7. Wilkins, *Law Comes to Texas*, pp. 141–42.

8. Bob Alexander, *Dangerous Dan Tucker: New Mexico's Deadly Lawman* (Silver City, N.M: High Lonesome Books, 2001), p. 37.

9. Leiker, *Racial Borders*, p. 66.

10. Utley, *Lone Star Justice*, pp. 203–4.

11. Alexander, *Dangerous Dan Tucker*, p. 38.

12. San Antonio *Daily Express*, January 1, 1878.

13. *Fugitives from Justice: The Notebook of Texas Ranger Sergeant James B. Gillett*, introd. by Michael D. Morrison (Austin: State House Press, 1997).

14. Ibid., p. 262.

15. Larry D. Ball, "The United States Army and the Big Springs, Nebraska, Train Robbery of 1877," *Journal of the West* 34 (January 1995): pp. 34–45; *New Handbook of Texas*, vol. 1, p. 408.

16. Paula Reed and Grover Ted Tate, *The Tenderfoot Bandits: Sam Bass and Joel Collins, Their Lives and Hard Times* (Tucson: Westernlore Press, 1988), pp. 127–28, 130–31, 137–38.

17. Rick Miller, *Sam Bass & Gang* (Austin: Statehouse Press, 1999), p. 159.

18. Reed and Tate, *Tenderfoot Bandits*, pp. 143–46.

19. Miller, *Sam Bass*, pp. 169–73.

20. Ibid., p. 175.

21. Ibid.

22. Ibid., p. 176.

23. Ibid., p. 192.

24. Ibid., pp. 201–3.

25. Charles L. Martin, *Sketch of Sam Bass, the Bandit: A Graphic Narrative. His Various Train Robberies, His Death, and Accounts of the Deaths of His Gang and Their History* (Norman: University of Oklahoma Press, 1956), p. 108.

26. Ibid., p. 109.

27. Miller, *Sam Bass*, pp. 199–200.

28. Martin, *Sketch of Sam Bass*, p. 123.

29. Cox, *Texas Ranger Tales*, pp. 48–68; James B., Gillett, "Vernon Wilson Was a Ranger," *Frontier Times* 6, no. 7 (April 1929): pp. 257–58; James B. Gillett,

Six Years with the Texas Rangers, 1875–1881 (New Haven: Yale University Press, 1927), pp. 122–23.

30. "How Sam Bass Was Killed," San Antonio *Daily Express*, September 12, 1895. This account is based on an interview with Lee Hall, who related his role in the final days of Bass.

31. "Fort Worth Man Tells of Shooting of Sam Bass," *Frontier Times*, January 1935, pp. 138–39; Cox, *Texas Ranger Tales*, p. 63.

32. Martin, *Sketch of Sam Bass*, pp. 158–59.

33. "Contributor's Club," *Atlantic Monthly*, 43, no. 255 (January 1879): p. 110.

34. Martin, *Sketch of Sam Bass*, p. 158–59. Charles Nevill recalled his roll in the killing of Bass in an interview published by the San Antonio *Daily Express* on December 22, 1901.

35. Lampasas *Daily Times*, July 27, 1878. Bass's demise received extensive newspaper coverage, including one dispatch so loaded with overwriting that an anonymous contributor to *The Atlantic Monthly* later felt compelled to observe, "The coming of the Great American Novel has probably been retarded fifty years by the recent cutting in of a Western newspaper correspondent." After quoting from the piece, which supplied far more adjectives and opinion than fact in reporting Bass's final hours, the critic offered, "None but a genius of first order could have evolved such lofty prose out of so unpromising a subject as a red-handed thief, shot down by officers of the law. Here the pathos and picturesqueness of that modern hybrid, the Moral-Scoundrel, are brought to their legitimate limits. What a delicious dime-novel atmosphere envelops the whole story!" "Contributor's Club," p. 110.

36. *Adjutant General's Report, 1878*, p. 9.

37. J. Frank Dobie, "The Robinhooding of Sam Bass," *True West*, July-August 1958, pp. 8–10, 36. For more on Deputy Sheriff Grimes and the Bass shootout, see "The Killing of 'Caige' Grimes," in Cox, *Texas Ranger Tales: Stories That Need Telling*, pp. 53–68. Despite intense newspaper coverage, several significant questions about the Rangers' confrontation with Bass and his gang have never been answered. Whether Grimes had known that the man he died trying to arrest was Sam Bass or just some cowboy illegally packing a six-shooter remains a mystery. For that matter, Bass told rangers before he died that he did not know if he, Barnes, or Jackson had killed Grimes. Some uncertainty remains over whether Ranger Ware or Ranger Herold (often misidentified as "Harrell," including by this author in *Texas Ranger Tales*) fired the shot that killed Bass, though the general consensus is that Ware killed Barnes and Herold killed Bass. For more on Connor, Herold, and Ware see Parsons and Brice, *Texas Ranger N. O. Reynolds*, pp. 370, 375, 386–87. Another curiosity is why, even though the Round Rock shoot-out took place only a short ride from the capital city, no photographer showed up to take pictures of the wounded Bass, his body, or any of those involved. If any pho-

tographs were taken, none has ever surfaced. More puzzling is that Frank Jackson simply disappeared after the Round Rock shoot-out. In the 1920s, Ranger Captain Frank Hamer got a lead as to Jackson's whereabouts and hoped to finally bring him to justice. But an arrest never materialized, and in 1936, Williamson County dropped the indictment against Jackson.

38. Wilkins, *Law Comes to Texas*, pp. 171–74; H. V. Redfield, *Homicide, North and South: Being a Comparative View of Crime Against the Person in Several Parts of the United States* (Philadelphia: J. B. Lippincott, 1880), pp. 63–85. The 1870s had been extraordinarily bloody. By studying back issues of the Galveston *Daily News,* the state's newspaper of record, Redfield came up with 401 homicides in Texas for 1878. In addition, he found 148 persons had been "severely or dangerously" wounded that year. Estimating that at least 15 percent of those persons later died and assuming another 10 percent of the state's homicides went unreported, Redfield concluded 465 people had been murdered in Texas in 365 days. Sixteen of those victims had been law enforcement officers. By comparison, the Texas death toll exceeded the number of murders reported in Maine, Massachusetts, Michigan, Minnesota, New Hampshire, New York, Pennsylvania, Rhode Island, and Vermont combined. The population of Texas had been 818,579 at the beginning of the decade. Ten years later the state had increased to 1.5 million, but that amounted to only a twelfth of the population of the nine Northern states with fewer murders than Texas. Historian W. C. Holden assessed crime in Texas during the 1870s and 1880s in "Law and Lawlessness on the Texas Frontier: 1875–1890," *Southwestern Historical Quarterly,* October 1940, pp. 188–203. In addition to violent acts on the part of criminals, Brown, *Strain of Violence,* pp. 316–18, lists fifty known vigilante movements in Texas during the nineteenth century and suggests there probably were more.

39. Havins, "Activities of Company E," p. 70. The Frontier Battalion did not solve every law enforcement problem in Texas. A particularly virulent outbreak of vigilantism in Shackelford County ran its course from 1875 to 1878, not withstanding a late and short-lived intervention by the state. Lieutenant George W. Campbell's Company B established camp in the county on April 1, 1877, and his presence subdued the vigilantes (known as the Tin Hat-Band Brigade) for a time. As Robert K. DeArment brings out in his study of the troubles, *Bravo of the Brazos: John Larn of Fort Griffin, Texas* (Norman: University of Oklahoma Press, 2002), the Rangers developed a witness who could have testified before a grand jury about the gang, but the grand jury foreman prevented the appearance. On May 1, 1878, district judge J. R. Fleming and other local officials appealed to Governor Hubbard to remove the Rangers from the county. Clearly, Campbell and his rangers had been making too much progress in identifying the vigilantes, most of them otherwise upstanding citizens. A week later, on orders from the adjutant general, Jones discharged Campbell and most of his

company, leaving only a six-man detachment under Sergeant J. E. Van Riper. Some residents as well as some of the recently discharged rangers wrote Austin to warn of further violence, appealing to Jones to investigate conditions himself. Preoccupied with the search for Sam Bass, and perhaps realizing he had no significant local support, the Frontier Battalion commander left the situation in Sergeant Van Riper's hands. Despite the Ranger presence, when former county sheriff John Larn got arrested by his successor for cattle theft on June 23, 1878, he did not make it through his first night in jail before masked citizens rushed the lockup and shot him to death in his cell. On July 13, six days before the shoot-out with Bass in Round Rock, Jones ordered then Lieutenant George Washington Arrington of Company C to set up camp near Fort Griffin and assist local authorities "in executing process from the courts and in maintaining law and order." Arrington reached Shackelford County on July 31, later reporting that local residents did not have much good to say about "the old Co. of Rangers" and expressing his belief "that at one time nearly everybody belonged to the mob." No further vigilantism occurred in the county.

40. R. G., Kimbell, Ranger Reminiscences, Record Group 401, 1234-11, Texas State Library and Archives. Kimbell enlisted on September 10, 1878, in Pat Dolan's company. A year later, he reenlisted in Dan Roberts's company, serving through August 31, 1880. He re-upped on September 1, 1880, and stayed in the Rangers until November 30, 1880. He may have served one more enlistment. In his narrative he claimed he stayed with the Rangers until 1881, but the record does not reflect that. No matter, as Kimbell wrote, he went to his "Yellow Rose of Texas" and "threw my record in her lap and asked if she were ready to comply with the contract, to which she answered in the affirmative. We were married and started [a] life of happiness on a new plane." Kimbell wrote his recollections at the request of state archivist Harriet Smither in the spring of 1937 while living in Altus, Oklahoma.

41. Spaw, *Texas Senate,* vol. 2 pp. 268–70.

42. Wilkins, *Law Comes to Texas*, p. 176. The last of the original Frontier Battalion captains, Coldwell served as quartermaster until 1883. In addition to the traditional duties involving payroll and supply, Coldwell performed inspections and earned a reputation as an able problem-solver in personnel matters. He settled in Kerr County after leaving the Rangers and lived there until his death on November 1, 1925. He is buried in the Center Point Cemetery.

43. "Captain June Peak, Texas Ranger," *Frontier Times*, September 1927, p. 4.

44. William T. Hagan, *United States–Comanche Relations: The Reservation Years* (New Haven and London: Yale University Press, 1976), p. 147.

45. *Governors' Messages*, pp. 258–59.

46. W. S. Adair, "Captain Peak Recalls Last Indian Fight," Dallas *Semi-Weekly News*, August 31, 1935.

47. "More About W. B. Anglin," *Frontier Times*, March 1929, p. 224.

48. J. Evetts Haley, *Fort Concho on the Texas Frontier* (San Angelo, Tex.: San Angelo *Standard-Times*, 1952), p. 328, citing Peak to Jones, July 5, 1879.

12. "ASSIST CIVIL AUTHORITIES"

1. John Allen Peterson, ed., *"Facts As I Remember Them": The Autobiography of Rufe LeFors* (Austin: University of Texas Press, 1986), pp. 29, 53–54.
2. *Frontier Echo*, July 6, 1879, cited in W. Hubert Curry, *Sun Rising on the West: The Saga of Henry Clay and Elizabeth Smith* (Crosbyton, Tex.: 1979), pp. 173–74.
3. Peterson, *"Facts As I Remember Them,"* p. 29.
4. Roberts to George W. Baylor, July 1879, cited in George Wythe Baylor, *Into the Far, Wild Country: True Tales of the Old Southwest*, ed. Jerry D. Thompson (El Paso: Texas Western Press, 1996), p. 247.
5. Peterson, *"Facts as I Remember Them,"* pp. 55–57.
6. "Former Pecosite Tells of Search for Texas Indians Fifty-Three Years Ago," Pecos *Enterprise*, January 13, 1932.
7. J. Marvin Hunter, "Captain Arrington's Expedition." *Frontier Times*, December 1928, pp. 97–102; George Washington Arrington Papers, Panhandle-Plains Historical Museum, Canyon, Texas.
8. Hunter, "Captain Arrington's Expedition," p. 100.
9. Pecos *Enterprise*, n.d.
10. Jerry Sinise, *George Washington Arrington: Civil War Spy, Texas Ranger, Sheriff and Rancher* (Burnet, Tex.: Eakin Press, 1979), p. 27.
11. Wilkins, *Law Comes to Texas*, pp. 202–3.
12. Ibid., p. 210.
13. Juanita C. Duncan, "Life and Letters of William Hickman Dunman, Texas Ranger," *Frontier Times*, December 1947, pp. 72–79.
14. A series of three photographs taken at the camp near Fort Davis in the early 1880s feature sixteen rangers in flat-brimmed hats with rounded crowns. Clifton Caldwell, whose family sold the land where the camp was located to the Girl Scouts of America in 1946, said he picked up thirty to forty brass shell casings at the site, a mixture of center and rimfire rounds. Over the years, he also found tent pegs and pieces of cast-iron cookware. The photographs were a gift to Caldwell from former Ranger Dogie Wright. Interview with Clifton Caldwell, November 16, 2002, Alpine, Texas.
15. *Report of the Adjutant General, 1880.*
16. Kenneth A. Goldblatt, ed., "Scout to Quitman Canyon: Report of Captain Geo. W. Baylor of the Frontier Battalion," *Texas Military History* 6, no. 2 (Summer 1967): pp. 149–59; Kenneth A. Goldblatt, "Ambush in Quitman Canyon," *Password* 14, no. 4 (Winter 1969): pp. 109–16; Baylor, *Into the Far, Wild Country*, pp. 304–22.

17. Andrew R. Graybill, *Policing the Great Plains: Rangers, Mounties, and the North American Frontier, 1875–1910* (Lincoln: University of Nebraska Press: 2006), p. 35 citing Special Report of the Adjutant-General of the State of Texas, September 1884, appendix and T. T. Smith, "U.S. Army Combat operations," p. 503, 527. U.S. troops 214 Indian captives, the Rangers 6.

18. Wilkins, *Law Comes to Texas*, p. 221.

19. William H. Leckie and Shirley A. Leckie, *Unlikely Warriors: General Benjamin Grierson and His Family* (Norman: University of Oklahoma Press, 1984), p. 271.

20. Susan Miles, "The Soldiers' Riot," *Fort Concho Report* 13 (Spring 1981).

21. Leckie and Leckie, *Unlikely Warriors*, pp. 270–72.

22. "Captain Marsh and His Rangers," *Frontier Times*, April 1929, pp. 300–301.

23. J. Evetts Haley, *Jeff Milton: A Good Man with a Gun* (Norman: University of Oklahoma Press, 1949), p. 38, citing "Monthly Return," Company B, February 28, 1881.

24. Wilkins, *Law Comes to Texas*, p. 224, citing *Report of the Adjutant General*, February 28, 1882.

25. Haley, *Jeff Milton*, pp. 43–44, citing M. D. Coleman to D. W. Roberts, May 30, 1881.

26. Ibid., p. 44; Wilkins, *Law Comes to Texas*, pp. 225–29.

27. Haley, *Jeff Milton*, pp. 52–53.

28. *Voice of the Mexican Border* (1933), p. 177.

29. Austin *Daily Statesman*, July 21, 1881.

30. *New Handbook of Texas*, vol. 3, pp. 1108–9.

31. Wilkins, *Law Comes to Texas*, p. 228. Born in Gallatin, Tennessee, April 25, 1847, McMurry came to Texas after the Civil War to work as a cowboy. He joined the Special Force under Lee Hall in 1877. He gained promotion as a Frontier Battalion captain on September 1, 1881, in Colorado City and served as commander of Company B for a decade. Known for his low-key demeanor, he had a reputation as an effective officer. He died in Louisville, Kentucky, on January 8, 1914, but was taken to St. Louis, Missouri, for burial. Stephens, *Texas Ranger Sketches*, pp. 99–102.

32. *Voice of the Mexican Border*, p. 178.

33. Nevill to King, December 9, 1881, Adjutant General's Records, Texas State Library and Archives.

34. *New Handbook of Texas*, vol. 6, p. 385.

35. *Voice of the Mexican Border*, p. 179. Born April 6, 1855, in Carthage, Alabama, Nevill and his family came to Texas when he was a toddler. At nineteen, armed only with a butcher knife, he joined the Frontier Battalion under Captain Rufus Perry on May 25, 1874. On September 1, 1879, he took command of Company E, promoting to captain in mid-1881. Nevill served until August 31, 1882. On November 7 that year he was elected sheriff of

Presidio County and went through two reelection campaigns, holding office until November 6, 1888. After ranching in partnership with former ranger J. B. Gillett, Nevill moved to San Antonio. He held various positions in the Bexar County government until his death on June 14, 1906. For more on Nevill's long career in the Rangers, see Chuck Parsons, "Charles Liborn Nevill," *Texas Ranger Dispatch* 5 (Fall 2001)

36. Wilkins, *Law Comes to Texas*, p. 236.
37. *Governors' Messages*, pp. 432, 448–49.
38. Ibid., p. 474.
39. *Frontier Times*, November 1932, p. 96.
40. Haley, *Jeff Milton*, pp. 89–90.
41. Wilkins, *Law Comes to Texas*, pp. 240–41.
42. Ibid., pp. 248–49. Rangers could lose their job in other ways, as well. On January 31, 1884, Adjutant General King accepted the forced resignation of Lieutenant W. L. Rudd "on account of his conduct in the town of Gonzales on the evening of the 2nd day of the present month." An investigation by the battalion quartermaster had shown that Rudd "gave up his arms without any effort at resistance, to one or two or three drunken men, who were openly violating the law . . . and retired to his room at their dictation, and made no effort then nor afterwards to arrest said parties or to recover his weapons." As King wrote, "Recklessness and unnecessary risk are not required by the State at the hands of her military forces . . . but good judgment and real courage are essential to success in almost every duty imposed by law upon this force, and a lack of these qualities, when made known, will be deemed a sufficient reason for dismissing any officer or man from the service." *Report of the Adjutant General, 1884*, p. 31.
43. R. D. Holt, "Barbed Wire," *Texas Monthly* September 1929, pp. 174–85; R. D. Holt, "The Introduction of Barbed Wire into Texas and the Fence Cutting War," *West Texas Historical Association Year Book* 6 (1930): pp. 72–88.
44. Henry D. McCallum and Frances T. McCallum, *The Wire That Fenced the West* (Norman: University of Oklahoma Press, 1965), pp. 152–66. The fence-cutting conflict, which to some extent continued for the rest of the nineteenth century, is one of forty-two episodes that historian Richard Maxwell Brown includes in what he terms the Western Civil War of Incorporation, 1850–1919. Brown presented his thesis in "Violence," a chapter in *The Oxford History of the American West*, ed. Clyde A. Milner II et al. (New York: Oxford University Press, 1994), pp. 412–. For another view, see Andrew R. Graybill, "Rural Police and the Defense of the Cattleman's Empire in Texas and Alberta, 1875–1900," *Agricultural History* 79, no. 3 (Summer 2005): pp. 253–80.
45. McCallum and McCallum, *Wire That Fenced the West*, p. 164. In January 1884, forty-five "responsible citizens" of Brown County sent one of their number to Austin to present the governor with a petition listing thirty-four

recent instances of fence-cutting in the county. "We do not wish to suggest to you any remedy for the evils complained of," the petition concluded, "but trust to your superior judgment to save us from anarchy, ruin and blood-shed." Brown County *Banner*, January 24, 1884. Prior entreaty to Adjutant General King netted stockmen no satisfaction, the general believing that fence-cutting should be handled by local authorities. *Report of the Adjutant General, 1884*, pp. 34–43. The free-range movement, meanwhile, gained an unsolicited ally who worsened the situation: rustlers. Cattle thieves did not like barbed fences because, as Holt wrote in his early work on the fence-cutting issue, wire fences were "antagonistic to cow-stealing, as it obstructed the night trail." Holt, "Introduction of Barbed Wire into Texas," p. 81.

46. Spaw, *Texas Senate*, vol. 2, p. 336; *Senate and House Journal of the State of Texas for the Called Session of the 18th Legislature* (Austin, 1884).

47. Utley, *Lone Star Justice*, pp. 235–36; San Angelo *Standard*, February 14, 1885; Austin *Daily Statesman*, February 12 and February 14, 1885; *Report of the Adjutant General*, December 1884, p. 21; Frank D. Jenkins, ed., *Runnels County Pioneers* (Ballinger, Tex.: Ballinger Bicentennial Commission, 1975), pp. 140–41. Born in Conecuh County, Alabama, on March 20, 1825, Thomas Lawson Odom came to Texas with his family in 1853 and settled in San Antonio. After serving in the Confederate Army during the Civil War, he went into the cattle business. In 1876, he and his son, Garland, drove four thousand head of cattle to what was then Runnels County. With $500 in gold, he purchased from the Sam Maverick estate the land around Fort Chadbourne, abandoned by the military in 1867. He and his son added to their holdings, eventually acquiring ninety thousand acres. Odom served as a Runnels County commissioner and in 1882 won election to the legislature. He represented Coleman, Concho, Llano, McCulloch, San Saba, and Runnels counties in the regular session of the Eighteenth Legislature and in the first called session from January 8 to February 6, 1884, playing an active role in getting the fence-cutting law on the books. While the cases against the members of the Fish Creek gang languished on the docket, Ranger operative Ben Warren was filed on for malicious mischief for allegedly killing a cow, a charge most believed to have been trumped up because of his under-cover work. Earlier on the day he was killed, Warren had been tried on the cow-killing charge and acquitted. Odom did not run for reelection. He died March 29, 1897. The ranch he founded, the O D, is still owned by his descendants. Odom and Warren are both buried in the Fort Chadbourne Cemetery.

48. Galveston *Daily News*, February 21, 1884.

49. *Governors' Messages*, p. 515.

50. "Cattle Battle on Edwards Plateau in 1884," *Frontier Times*, March 1932, pp. 249–51; Wilkins, *Law Comes to Texas*, p. 247; *A History of Edwards*

County (Rocksprings, Tex.: 1984), p. 54; author's interview with Harold D. Jobes, Austin, Texas, September 8, 2002. The inquest determined the killing of the suspected fence cutter had been a lawful use of deadly force, but the deceased's survivors filed a civil suit against the Rangers involved and their boss, Captain George W. Baylor. The legal effort went nowhere. The ranch where the shoot-out occurred remained in the Greer family as of 2006, owned by Mary Jane Greer and her son James Lee Greer III. As a youth, James (Jimmy) Greer found five or six empty 44-40 shell casings at the scene of the fight. Though buried on the ranch, the fence-cutter's grave has never been located. Interview with author, January 16, 2006.

51. *Governors' Messages,* pp. 510, 515.

52. Ibid., p. 517.

53. Spaw, *Texas Senate,* vol. 2, p. 353.

54. "The Governor and the State Rangers," Dallas *Morning News,* December 6, 1885.

55. Robert W. Stephens, *Captain George H. Schmitt, Texas Ranger.* Dallas: Privately published, 2006, pp. 31, 49–51, 65; 97–111.

56. For more details on Sowell's book, one of four he would write in his lifetime (1848–1921), see John H. Jenkins, *Basic Texas Books,* pp. 511–13, and Cox, *Texas Ranger Tales,* pp. 306–8.

57. *Report of the Adjutant General, 1886,* pp. 49–50.

58. Lam Sieker served longer in the Frontier Battalion than anyone else. Born on April 8, 1848, in Baltimore, Maryland, he fought for the South in the Civil War. He came to Texas in 1873 and on May 25, 1874, enlisted in Captain C. Rufus Perry's Company D. Staying in the same company for the next eleven years, he made lieutenant in 1881 and on September 1, 1882, was promoted to captain. He held that job until October 15, 1885, when he became battalion quartermaster at Austin. By 1889 he had risen to assistant adjutant general, in which capacity he served until 1895. After a five-year hiatus in private life, he returned to Austin in 1900 and worked in the Adjutant General's Department again until 1905. He died November 13, 1914, in Houston. Robert W. Stephens, *Texas Ranger Sketches* (Dallas: 1972), pp. 144–46.

59. *Report of the Adjutant General, 1886,* pp. 52–53, 60–61; Ira Aten, *Six and One-Half Years in the Ranger Service: The Memoirs of Ira Aten, Sergeant, Company D, Texas Rangers* (Bandera, Tex.: Frontier Times, 1945), pp. 3–4; Austin *Daily Statesman,* June 2, 1885; Utley, *Lone Star Justice,* pp. 244–46; Wilkins, *Law Comes to Texas,* pp. 253–56. Though he would become one of the better known rangers, Aten had been in the Frontier Battalion only a couple of years when the Webb County incident occurred. Born in Cairo, Illinois, in 1862, he came to Texas with his family in 1876 and settled in Round Rock. He later said the Sam Bass shoot-out in 1878 was what got him interested in joining the Rangers. He enlisted in March 1883.

60. Adjutant General's Records, cited in Paul N. Spellman, *Captain John H. Rogers, Texas Ranger* (Denton: University of North Texas Press, 2003), p. 49. For more on Texas labor troubles in the mid-1880s, see Ruth Allen, *The Great Southwest Strike*, University of Texas Publications 4214 (Austin: University of Texas Press, 1942); Graybill, *Policing the Great Plains*, pp. 158–200, treats the Ranger role in nineteenth century labor disputes at length.

13. "I always wanted to join the Rangers"

1. Sarah Ellen Davidge, "Texas Rangers Were Rough and Ready Fighters," *Frontier Times*, November 1935, pp. 125–29.

2. Havins, T. R. *Something About Brown (A History of Brown County, Texas)* (Brownwood, Tex.: Banner Printing Company, 1958), p. 37.

3. Wilkins, *Law Comes to Texas*, p. 268.

4. Davidge, "Texas Rangers," p. 129.

5. Austin *Daily Statesman*, November 11, 1886.

6. Wilkins, *Law Comes to Texas*, pp. 267–69; Havins, *Something About Brown*, pp. 36–40; White, *Promised Land*, pp. 55–57; Spellman, *Captain John H. Rogers*, pp. 40–42; T. C. Smith Jr., *From the Memories of Men* (Brownwood, Tex.: 1954), pp. 29–30. The newspapers favorably portrayed Scott's fight with the fence cutters, but in a letter to headquarters, one of the captain's colleagues begged to differ. German-born Captain George H. Schmitt, the former sheriff and tax assessor-collector of Comal County and a Ranger since 1883, wrote Austin that if Scott had taken more men with him, he could have captured the cutters who escaped. Schmitt also said that he and Captain Jones "are the only Officers who obey Gen. Kings [sic] orders, and run the companies as Economical as possible." Schmitt said that Captain Scott had told him that "Capt McMurray . . . was nothing but a fraud, he never stay [sic] with the company and batting about Fort Worth & Dallas all his time." Wilkins, *Law Comes to Texas*, p. 269, doubted that any of the captains got too much inappropriate spending past state auditors. In something of an irony, given Schmitt's penchant for economical operation of his company, a lack of funds forced its disbandment on November 30, 1887, ending his Ranger career. For more on Schmitt, see Stephens, *Texas Ranger Sketches*, pp. 131–33 and *Captain George H. Schmitt, Texas Ranger*, passim.

7. *Report of the Adjutant General, 1886*, p. 54. Elsewhere in his report, pp. 56–59, King waxed on about fence-cutting, taking both the fence cutters and to some extent the cattle owners to task for their roles in the issue. "The safe solution to this vexed land and fence question will be reached in a lawful way," the general concluded.

8. Stephens, *Captain George H. Schmitt, Texas Ranger*, pp. 173–186.

9. *Governors' Messages*, p. 547.

10. Wilkins, *Law Comes to Texas*, p. 270.

11. Cox, *Texas Ranger Tales II*, pp. 137–39; Davidge, "Texas Rangers"; "On the Sabine: Bloody Battle Between State Rangers and a Gang of Desperadoes," Austin *Daily Statesman*, April 3, 1887. The March fight had not been Scott's first encounter with the Conner family. In February 1886 and again that summer, first as a lieutenant and then as a captain, Scott had scouted the tick-infested backcountry of Sabine County. The first scout netted nothing, but that summer his company arrested two of the Conners. Afterward, the captain reported that he was more than ready to get back to the prairie.

12. "Captain William Scott," Austin *Daily Statesman*, May 12, 1887. Scott resigned from the Rangers April 20, 1888, and bought the Bank Exchange saloon in San Angelo. Wilkins, *Law Comes to Texas*, p. 279; San Angelo *Standard*, April 21, 1888.

13. Cox, *Texas Ranger Tales II*, p. 112. Robert S. Weddle provided a solid overview of the Peg Leg gang in "Peg Leg Station on the San Saba," *Edwards Plateau Historian*, vol. 3–4, 1967–1968, pp. 24–42.

14. Gillett, *Six Years with the Texas Rangers*, pp. 102–4; *Report of the Adjutant General, 1880*, pp. 27, 34; Wilkins, *Law Comes to Texas*, pp. 191–93; John Miller Morris, *A Private in the Texas Rangers: A. T. Miller of Company B, Frontier Battalion* (College Station: Texas A&M University Press, 2001), p. 10. The life of a Frontier Battalion ranger was not all action. After editing a diary kept by his Texas Ranger forebear, Miller concluded, "Despite the dominant legends of sensational frontier violence and lawlessness, the Miller diary entries portray a considerably more polite and socialized state of affairs. Much of an ordinary Texas Ranger's time was spent in routine duties: serving warrants, paperwork, saloon walkthroughs, chasing outlaws, guarding a few hapless prisoners from time to time, looking after the ranger remuda of horses . . . , transporting water, wood, and supplies, and going into town to poke around—to see and be seen."

15. Jones, *Dime Novel Western*, pp. 108–9. *Revolver Billy, the Boy Ranger of Texas* and *Texas Charlie, the Boy Ranger* were two other titles in the series.

16. Elliott Young, *Catarino Garza's Revolution on the Texas-Mexico Border* (Durham and London: Duke University Press, 2004), pp. 65–67; De Leon, *They Called Them Greasers*, pp. 93–94; "The Border Sheriff Now Speaks for Himself," *Frontier Times*, May 1931, pp. 360–68.

17. J. W. Durbin to *The Detective*, as published November 2, 1888, Durbin Scrapbook, author's collection.

18. Webb, *Texas Rangers*, pp. 428–37; Wilkins, *Law Comes to Texas*, pp. 275–77.

19. Wilkins, *Law Comes to Texas*, pp. 279–80.

20. L. L. Foster, *Forgotten Texas Census: First Annual Report of the Agricultural Bureau of the Department of Agriculture, Insurance, Statistics, and History, 1887–1888* (Austin: Texas State Historical Association, 2001), p. 293.

21. Wilbarger, *Indian Depredations in Texas*, p. 575.

22. Stephens, *Texas Ranger Sketches*, pp. 125–31. Frank Schmidt never fully recovered from the gunshot wound he suffered in Fort Bend County. After treatment by several doctors and a lengthy convalescence, he returned for a time to Captain Jones's Uvalde County camp in 1892. But he could not ride a horse and did not care for light duty. The matter of who should pay his medical expenses became controversial. In March 1893, the legislature approved a bill reimbursing the ranger and his family for more than $500 in expenses incurred since his wounding. The twenty-six-year-old ranger died from complications stemming from his wound on June 17, 1893, in Austin. His body was returned to his hometown, St. Louis, Missouri, for burial.

23. Harold Preece, *Lone Star Man: Ira Aten, Last of the Old Texas Rangers* (New York: Hastings House Publishers, 1960), pp. 196–97. Aten opted not to run for sheriff in the 1890 election. He got married in 1892 in Austin and soon moved to the High Plains, becoming sheriff of Castro County in 1893. Following a single two-year term, he went to work as a division foreman on the sprawling XIT Ranch. When the XIT broke up, he moved his wife and children to California in 1904 and lived there for the rest of his long life. He operated an irrigated farm and became active in pushing for the development of water and power in the Imperial Valley. During World War II, at the urging of L. A. Wilke (1897–1984), the author's grandfather, Aten dictated his memoir to a secretary at the El Paso Board of City Development, which Wilke then managed. Aten's manuscript was published by J. Marvin Hunter in 1945 as *Six and One-Half Years in Ranger Service*. The old ranger died on August 5, 1953, at the age of ninety-four.

24. Pauline Yelderman, *The Jay Bird Democratic Association of Fort Bend County: A White Man's Union* (Waco: Texian Press, 1979), pp. 95–111, 133; Wilkins, *Law Comes to Texas*, pp. 287–90. Kyle Terry's murder trial moved to Galveston on a change of venue, where on January 21, 1890, Volney Gibson followed through on his promise of revenge, shooting Terry dead in the Galveston County courthouse. A Galveston grand jury indicted Gibson for murder, but a change of venue moved the case to Bexar County. Before Gibson could face trial, he died of tuberculosis. The Jaybird political organization survived well into the twentieth century, however. By an eight-one decision, the U.S. Supreme Court ruled on May 4, 1953, that Fort Bend County's Jaybird Democratic Association's special primary was unconstitutional. In the litigation the high court had considered on appeal, the president of the association admitted that the primary's intent was to prevent blacks from voting. The Jaybird association finally dissolved in 1959.

25. Austin *Daily Statesman*, May 25, 1890.

26. *Report of the Adjutant General, 1889–1890*, pp. 21–30, 92–94.

27. *Governors' Messages*, p. 686.

28. Wilkins, *Law Comes to Texas*, pp. 295–96. King did much to professionalize the Rangers. Part of that came through trying to hire good men, part came by maintaining good discipline. "As a rule," King wrote in his 1889–90 report, "no man is allowed to join the Ranger service unless he is known or come endorsed as an orderly, sober, discreet and reliable man, and though a mistake may sometimes occur . . . it is not very probable in so small a number of men as one company now includes, and if such a thing should take place as the enlistment of a rash and reckless, or disobedient man, he is discharged as soon as his character is developed." *Report of the Adjutant General, 1899–1890*, p. 25.

29. *New Handbook of Texas*, vol. 4, p. 360; Wilkins, *Law Comes to Texas*, p. 296.

30. *Report of the Adjutant General, 1891*, p. 8.

31. "Lo, the Poor Indian," Canyon City *Echo*, January 31, 1891; Albert Bigelow Paine, *Captain Bill McDonald Texas Ranger: A Story of Frontier Reform* (1909; repr., Austin: State House Press, 1986), pp. 145–48; Harold J. Weiss Jr., " 'Yours to Command': Captain William J. 'Bill' McDonald and the Panhandle Rangers of Texas" (Ph.D. dissertation, Indiana University, 1982).

14. "THE GLORY RACE OF RANGERS"

1. Young, *Catarino Garza's Revolution*, p. 112; Jonathan Gilmer Speed, "The Hunt for Garza," *Harper's Weekly*, January 30, 1892, pp. 103–4. James E. Picher's "Outlawry on the Mexican Border," *Scribner's Magazine* 10, no. 1 (July 1891): pp. 78–87, is reflective of late-nineteenth-century public attitudes concerning the Texas-Mexican border. The author, after tracing the midcentury Cortina troubles and recounting McNelly's exploits of the mid-1870s, concluded with this faulty opinion: "The halcyon days of outlawry upon the Mexican border have passed. . . . Justice on both sides of the border is swifter and surer, and the lawless exploits of the present day may be regarded as the fitful glimmer of an expiring flame."

2. "Among the Rangers," *Texas Volunteer*, vol. 1, no. 4 (February 15, 1892): pp. 1–2. Edited by Robert J. Brown and published in Austin, the monthly tabloid magazine catered to Texas militia members, the Ranger force, and its officers.

3. *Report of the Adjutant General, 1892*, p. 11; Young, *Catarino Garza's Revolution*, pp. 268–70. Ever the revolutionary, Garza died March 8, 1895, in a gun battle on a Panamanian island then part of Colombia. Young, pp. 295–96.

4. *Report of the Adjutant General, 1892*, pp. 10–12.

5. Corpus Christi *Caller*, November 8, 1941.

6. Wilkins, *Law Comes to Texas*, p. 303.

7. "The Border Revolution," *Texas Volunteer*, vol. 1, no. 3 (January 15, 1892): pp. 11–12.

8. *Report of the Adjutant General, 1892*, p. 11.

9. Frontier Battalion, Monthly Return, March 1892, cited in Wilkins, *Law Comes to Texas*, p. 306.

10. Lieutenant W. H. Chatfield, comp., *The Twin Cities of the Border* (New Orleans: 1893), p. 43.

11. *Hearings Before the Committee on Invalid Pensions . . . On H.R. 7899 a Bill Extending the Provisions of Pension Laws Relating to Indian War Veterans to Members of Companies E and F, Frontier Battalion, Texas Rangers*, Washington, 1940.

12. *Report of the Adjutant General, 1892*, p. 12; Gilbert M. Cuthbertson, "Catarino E. Garza and the Garza War," *Texana* 13 (1975): pp. 335–48; Matias Romero, "The Garza Raid and Its Lessons," *North American Review* 155 (September 1892): pp. 324–37; Wilkins, *Law Comes to Texas*, pp. 302–7; *Texas Volunteer*, February 15, 1892, p. 2.

13. Richard Harding Davis, *The West from a Car Window* (New York: Harper & Brothers, 1892), p. 11. Davis was not the only journalist writing about the Rangers that year. *The Texas Volunteer*'s June 15, 1892, issue included a four-and-a-half-page profile by editor Brown on the Frontier Battalion and its men, "The Texas Ranger: A Realistic Review of the Service, and Something of the Men Who Make It." Brown, who had spent two weeks with Captain McNeel's company earlier that year, wrote, "If there is another such organization in the world as the Texas Rangers, it has yet to be identified. Everybody has heard of the Texas Rangers, everywhere has his fame been heralded, and it may be almost as safely asserted that everybody misunderstands him, everywhere are his true characteristics unknown, unappreciated." Unfortunately for his readers, Brown did not succeed in exposing those "unknown, unappreciated" characteristics. After tracing the Frontier Battalion's history, the best he could come up with by way of revealing the true nature of a ranger was to write, "The men who are in the force today are among the staunchest sons that Texas soil ever held . . . while their records tell to the world how well they fill the responsible positions they hold." Brown's greatest achievement in the piece came in serving posterity with biographical sketches of the adjutant general, quartermaster, the four field captains, and many of the rangers.

14. Davis, *West from a Car Window*, p. 13. Even as Davis described the Rangers and their traditional cowboy attire, Adjutant General Mabry gave thought to transforming the Rangers into a uniformed force. The editor of *The Texas Volunteer*, in reporting that the question of uniforming the Rangers had come up, admitted that a uniform was not the best choice for Rangers on a scout in remote country. "But when the rangers are in their permanent camp, when they go on missions into thickly populated sections or into the cities and towns in their territory . . . then they ought, by all means to have a uniform." *Texas Volunteer*, February 15, 1892, p. 17. The March 15, 1892, issue of the magazine, p. 2, carried a letter from Company D captain Frank

Jones saying he favored uniforms for the Rangers: "I believe a uniform would add dignity to the force and not detract from its usefulness in a single particular. We are as easily recognized from our general appearance, shod horses, and pack mules as we would be in uniform. Besides this, men have been known to resist Rangers, claiming that they thought they were citizens banded together for the purpose of lynching." Adjutant General Mabry was quoted in the article as saying that he intended to sound out the other captains on the matter, but nothing ever came of the discussion.

15. *New Handbook of Texas*, vol. 2, p. 1099; Barry Scobee, *Old Fort Davis* (San Antonio: Naylor Co., 1947), p. 85.

16. Former El Paso mayor Sol C. Shutz may have coined the term *Hell Paso*. Looking back on the city's wild and woolly days, a reporter with the El Paso *Times* wrote on June 25, 1916, "At that time it was called 'Hell Paso,' and he [Shutz] said the title was justly earned."

17. "Murderous Thieves," El Paso *Times*, April 18, 1890; Dallas *Morning News*, April 18, 1890; John Middagh, "Proposed Route Would Cross Historic Canyon," El Paso *Times*, August 13, 1959; William CX Handcock, "Ranger's Ranger," *True West*, March-April 1961, pp. 23–25, 45–48; Douglas V. Meed, "Daggers on the Gallows: The Revenge of Texas Ranger Captain 'Boss' Hughes," *True West* 46 (May 1999): pp. 44–49.

18. *Report of the Adjutant General, 1889–1890*, pp. 22–25, 91–93.

19. J. Marvin Hunter, "The Killing of Captain Frank Jones," *Frontier Times*, January 1929, pp. 145–49; Ralph J. Weaver, "The Nine Lives of Captain Frank Jones," *Frontier Times* 34 (Spring 1960): pp. 6–9, 36–40; Wilkins, *Law Comes to Texas*, pp. 310–12.

20. *Report of the Adjutant General, 1893–1894*, pp. 67–68.

21. Ann Jensen, ed., *Texas Ranger's Diary & Scrapbook* (Dallas: Kaleidograph Press, 1936), pp. 71–73. Captain Jones had seen the negative affect that legislative budget-cutting had on the Frontier Battalion and its men. "Of late years the Rangers have been compelled to do killing simply because they were so few in numbers it emboldened fugitives. During the first years of my Ranger service we never went out except there were 8 or 10 men and we never had to kill anyone." Utley, *Lone Star Justice*, p. 266, citing Jones to Mabry, February 17, 1893.

22. "A Rising Ranger," *Texas Volunteer*, vol. 2, no. 2 (December 25, 1892): p. 23. Historian Robert W. Stephens in his *Texas Ranger Sketches*, p. 69, called Frank Jones "perhaps the most intrepid Ranger of his day." Born in Austin on June 12, 1856, Jones had first joined the Frontier Battalion on September 1, 1875, at nineteen. Like many rangers, he would enlist for a year or so, return to civilian life for a while, then reenlist. But after September 1, 1882, he served continuously until his death. He had become a lieutenant in 1884 and a captain on May 1, 1886. Jones's first wife died in 1889, followed in 1890 by

his nine-month-old daughter. In 1892, he married Helen Baylor Gillett, the daughter of former Ranger captain George W. Baylor and ex-wife of former Ranger James B. Gillett. Five of Jones's brothers, Emmett, Gerry, Jim, Pink, and William, all served for a time in the Rangers. Stephens, pp. 63–75.

23. Chuck Parsons, "The Border Boss: John R. Hughes," *Texas Ranger Dispatch* 10 (Summer 2003); Cox, *Texas Ranger Tales*, pp. 132–35. Hughes, born in 1855 in Cambridge, Illinois, grew up in Kansas. At fifteen, Hughes struck out on his own, spending some time in Indian Territory as a cowboy. After participating in several cattle drives from Texas to the railhead in Kansas, he settled in Texas in 1878, running a horse ranch in Williamson County, northwest of Austin. When rustlers stole sixteen of his best animals in 1886, he trailed them to New Mexico, where, in recovering his stock, he killed three of the thieves in a shoot-out. Back in Texas, he became friends with Ranger Ira Aten and, at Aten's urging, joined the force on August 10, 1887. For more on Hughes's long career as a Ranger, see Jack Martin's *Border Boss: Captain John R. Hughes, Texas Ranger* (San Antonio: Naylor Co., 1942; and Austin: State House Press, 1990, with introduction by Mike Cox). In investigating Captain Jones's murder, Hughes developed a list of Olguin family and gang members. Parsons wrote, "The story persists that between eighteen and twenty-one . . . were eventually killed."

24. Robert W. Stephens, *Bullets and Buckshot in Texas* (Dallas: 2002), pp. 33–51. Stephens devotes a chapter to Outlaw (1854?–1894), of whom he writes, "Perhaps no more dangerous and controversial man ever served as a Texas Ranger than the sinister Bazz Outlaw." Though often referred to as "Bass" Outlaw, his full name was Bazzel Lamar Outlaw. The story of the ironically surnamed ranger has become the most commonly used example of a good ranger gone bad, but there were others, some of them never good to start with. Several years before Outlaw came on the scene, El Paso marshal Dallas Stoudenmire asked Captain George Baylor to bar his rangers from coming to town, adding in a letter to the adjutant general that the men stationed in Ysleta were "more ready to aggravate than to preserve the public peace." The marshal went so far as to label rangers "thirty-dollar a month sons of bitches." Ranger C. L. Hathaway responded, "I am a private in the ranks of the Texas Rangers, but I am not a son of a bitch." At that, Stoudenmire backed down a bit, saying, "The Texas Rangers as a body of men are gentlemen, but skunks can get into the service." Leon Claire Metz, *Dallas Stoudenmire: El Paso Marshal* (Austin: Pemberton Press, 1969), pp. 78–79.

25. Jones to Mabry, October 24, 1891, as cited in Wilkins, *The Law Comes to Texas*, pp. 299–300.

26. Michael G. Ehrle, ed., *Childress County Story* (Childress, Tex.: Oxbow Printing, 1971), pp. 58–62; 246–50; Bill Neal, *The Last Frontier: The Story of Hardeman County* (Quanah, Tex.: Hardeman County Historical Society, 1966), pp.

67–69. On the evening of December 9, 1893, Captain McDonald and Childress County sheriff John P. Matthews got into a gunfight near the Fort Worth and Denver railroad depot in Quanah. Both men took a number of bullets, Matthews dying of blood poisoning on December 30. Matthews would have died the day he was shot, but a notebook and two plugs of chewing tobacco stopped two bullets from going into his heart. That much is fact. The rest of the story varies with the telling. Well into the twentieth century, some people in Childress County continued to characterize Matthews's death as an assassination. But even Hardeman County sheriff Richard P. Coffer, an eyewitness who dropped to the ground to get out of the line of fire, could not say with certainty whether Matthews or McDonald fired the first shot. The Fort Worth *Gazette* reported the two lawmen had been feuding since the previous year's Sheriffs' Association of Texas convention in Houston, when Matthews had supposedly made a disparaging remark about Governor Hogg, the man who appointed McDonald to the Rangers. The McDonald-Matthews feud had been deepened by complaints made by Matthews after the Rangers arrested former Motley County sheriff Joe Beckham for absconding with county funds. Tried for murder, the Ranger captain won acquittal on the basis of self-defense and testimony that the shot that killed the sheriff hit him from behind, presumably fired by an unidentified McDonald partisan.

27. Utley, *Lone Star Justice*, p. 259; Marilyn D. Rhinehart, " 'Underground Patriots': Thurber Coal Miners and the Struggle for Individual Freedom, 1888–1903," *Southwestern Historical Quarterly* 92 (April 1989): pp. 509–42. McDonald's intercession in the Thurber labor problem marked the Rangers' third descent on the mining boomtown since December 12, 1888, when Captain Sam A. McMurry went to the mines with ten rangers to keep the peace during a Knights of Labor strike. As the captain reported, his men arrested "a number of them [strikers] for Rioting, Intimidation, [and] Carrying Pistols." With the Rangers as armed referees, management prevailed and McMurry and his men left on June 8, 1889. But the labor organization struck the mines again in July 1890. Once more, McMurry and his rangers came to prevent violence. While the captain succeeded in both instances in living up to Adjutant General King's injunction to remain impartial in labor disputes—he even declined an offer to go on the company's payroll—the perception developed that the Rangers leaned toward management's point of view. Utley, pp. 231–33.

28. Utley, *Lone Star Justice*, pp. 259–60.

29. J. D. Ponder, "When the Santa Fe Windows Were Shot Out; Rangers and Citizens Battle in the Street," El Paso *Times*, December 5, 1920. Ranger Losier later married an El Paso woman. Eventually, they moved to the West Coast, where in 1920 he was a chemistry professor at Stanford University.

30. Leo N. Miletich, *Dan Stuart's Fistic Carnival* (College Station: Texas A&M University Press, 1994), pp. 149–50.

31. Ibid., p. 150.

32. Ibid., p. 175.

33. Dallas *Morning News*, February 28, 1896. Sending most of the Ranger force to the far-western end of Texas had not been cheap. The Dallas newspaper reported on July 24, 1896, that the effort to prevent the prizefight had cost the state $30,000. The Langtry incident got the most attention in the press, but it was not the only time Rangers would try to enforce the state's law against prizefighting. On the night of February 25, 1899, Captain Brooks and several of his rangers watched a fight in Galveston between national contender Joe Choynski and local black pugilist Jack Johnson. Choynski knocked out Johnson in the third round. Brooks and his men then entered the ring and arrested both fighters, but the case never made it past the grand jury. Paul Spellman, *Captain J.A. Brooks, Texas Ranger*, Denton: University of North Texas Press, 2007, pp. 128–129.

34. Paine, *Captain Bill McDonald Texas Ranger*, pp. 199–213; W. J. L. Sullivan, *Twelve Years in the Saddle*, pp. 182–88; McDonald to Mabry, April 4, 1896, cited in Wilkins, *Law Comes to Texas*, pp. 325–28.

35. Ross J. Cox Sr., *The Texas Rangers and the San Saba Mob* (San Saba: C&S Farm Press, 2005), passim; Sonnichsen, *I'll Die Before I'll Run*, pp. 206–31; Wilkins, *Law Comes to Texas*, pp. 328–29. Texas Department of Public Safety Highway Patrol trooper Cox, stationed at San Saba and no relation to the author, devoted years of research to the Rangers and the mob. He demonstrates in this solid work, as had been the case in the Hoo Doo War, that the San Saba County vigilantism extended to other Central Texas counties as well, particularly Brown, McCulloch, and Mills counties. Cox found that mob violence near San Saba County began as early as 1869, when the Williams Ranch community in what is now Mills County supported an Honest Man's Club, which busied itself violently "regulating" those perceived to have been dishonest men. Cox, pp. 5–6. As early as 1878, Ranger lieutenant N. O. Reynolds, in San Saba County to investigate a murder, wrote Major Jones, "Strange people here. Lindsey the man murdered was buried without an inquest. . . . Then had to be disinterred and a jury was hard to find. The verdict—was deceased by a shot fired from shotgun. . . . Only six candidates running for sheriff and not one of them fit for it." Cox, p. 7, citing Reynolds to Jones, October 14, 1878.

36. Sullivan, *Twelve Years in the Saddle*, pp. 198–99. This was not Sullivan's first visit to San Saba County. In San Saba for the fall 1889 term of the district court, Sullivan and two other rangers had their duties interrupted by the murder of Edward R. Hartman, a man who had been trying to dodge the mob for years. Sullivan and his fellow rangers found the body and soon arrested a deputy sheriff, his two sons, and five other men for the murder. Cox, *Texas Rangers and the San Saba Mob*, p. 10. Back in the county seven years later,

Sullivan wrote Adjutant General Mabry on August 15, 1896, "We find things here in pretty bad shape." Eleven days later, the sergeant wrote to headquarters, "I could use two hundred men much better than four." Cox, p. 16.

37. San Saba County *News*, July 31, 1896, editorial reprinted in Cox, *Texas Rangers and the San Saba Mob*, vol. 2, p. 1. An undated clipping c. 1896 that seems to be from another newspaper noted that an "effort will be made to do away with [the Rangers] entirely, as will, also, an effort be made to increase the force and the appropriation. We say increase the force and the appropriation. The west needs the rangers. They are an efficient body of officers. The number of arrests they make and the conspiracies they ferret out are ample verifications of their valuable services to the state." Sullivan Scrapbook, author's collection.

38. Paine, *Captain Bill McDonald Texas Ranger*, p. 221; Cox, *Texas Rangers and the San Saba Mob*, p. 47. Though McDonald credited the mob with at least forty-three killings, Doctor R. D. Forsythe of Mills County estimated at least a hundred men had been killed in McCulloch, Mills, and San Saba counties.

39. Austin *Daily Statesman*, June 10, 1897; Mary Ellen Trowbridge Perry, "Trowbridge Family History," author's collection. This unpublished family history, prepared in 1987 by descendants of suspected mob member George Trowbridge, contains copies of the newspaper stories detailing his 1897 trial, Trowbridge family genealogy, and recollections of life in San Saba County, including family lore about Trowbridge's role in the feud.

40. Cox, *Texas Rangers and the San Saba Mob*, pp. 20, 42. Born July 2, 1862, in Mount Lebanon, Louisiana, W. C. Linden came to Hamilton County, Texas, with his family when he was twelve. He taught school for a few years, read the law, and gained admittance to the bar in Llano County in 1891. A year later he won election as Llano's county attorney. In 1896 he ran for district attorney, representing seven counties, including Llano and San Saba. After completing his second term as district attorney, he moved to Bexar County in 1900 to take up private practice. A decade after the San Saba violence ended, Rebekah Baines and Sam Early Johnson Jr. could not make up their minds on a name for their three-month-old son, born in Blanco County on August 27, 1908. Finally, Johnson proposed naming the boy for his old friend, W. C. Linden. Rebekah agreed to that, as long as they altered the spelling to Lyndon and made his middle name Baines. Johnson, *Family Album*, p. 18. Appointed district attorney in 1913, Linden served until 1916. Nineteen years later, he became Bexar County's assistant district attorney, holding that position until he was eighty. He died on February 9, 1947, at eighty-four.

41. Undated clipping, c. 1897, Sullivan Scrapbook, author's collection.

42. Cox, *Texas Rangers and the San Saba Mob*, pp. 23–24.

43. Ibid., pp. 24–26. Adjutant General Mabry expressed his sentiments to Linden in a letter dated May 17, 1897.

44. Sullivan, probably with the help of a ghostwriter, published his memoir in 1909, the same year a biography of Captain McDonald came out. Despite his prominent role in the San Saba troubles, Sullivan devoted only four pages to the episode in his book. He also failed to mention that the San Saba experience marked the end of his Ranger career. McDonald had become aware that his sergeant seemed to be spending more energy looking for a good fishing hole on the Colorado River than in scouting for outlaws. Indeed, in a poem Sullivan wrote about his time in San Saba, reprinted in Cox, *Texas Rangers and the San Saba Mob*, pp. 21–22, one verse noted, "We made it to the River, and pitched our tent; To have a mess of fish we were all bent." Sullivan also had begun to drink like a fish. On top of that, the ranger imbibed with the wrong people, including the sheriff and others identified with the San Saba mob. On July 4, 1897, the day after Sullivan got so drunk he could not find his way back to Ranger camp, McDonald demanded and received Sullivan's resignation. McDonald to Mabry, July 4, 1897, cited in Utley, *Lone Star Justice*, p. 262. Sullivan carried a special Ranger commission for a time after leaving the Frontier Battalion and spent some of the last years of his life working at the Capitol as a doorkeeper for the Texas House of Representatives. He died on May 21, 1911, and is buried in the Old Round Rock Cemetery in Williamson County, Texas.

45. Ogle was the only person ever convicted of any of the San Saba mob murders, the August 24, 1893, killing of James H. Brown. Found guilty on May 27, 1899, he was sentenced to life in prison. Governor Thomas M. Campbell pardoned him on December 17, 1909. For a while following his release from the penitentiary, Ogle lived in Runnels County. From there he moved to Wichita Falls, where he got hired as city police officer. He worked as a policeman until shortly before his death on August 11, 1934, at the age of sixty-nine. Cox, *Texas Rangers and the San Saba Mob*, vol. 2, p. 97.

46. Ibid., pp. 38–39; Paine, *Captain Bill McDonald Texas Ranger*, pp. 235–36. The incident occurred November 3, 1898, as McDonald attended district court while Ranger Barker stood guard outside the courthouse. James Boren, who had been drinking, showed up and started threatening Barker. When the ranger tried to arrest Boren, he resisted, and Barker shot him.

47. Alma Ward Hamrick, *The Call of the San Saba: A History of San Saba County* (San Antonio: Naylor Co., 1941), pp. 101–4; Sullivan, *Twelve Years in the Saddle*, pp. 197–200. "The Mob was an unpleasant part of our history," Billie Graves wrote in an article on the history of the Locker community published in *San Saba County History, 1856–1983* (San Saba: San Saba County Historical Commission, 1983), p. 458. "As attitudes mellow and priorities change, we choose to forget."

48. *Report of the Adjutant General, 1895–1896,* p. 9.
49. Eagle Pass *Guide,* May 23, 1896; "Protection of Rangers," Dallas *Morning News,* April 2, 1897. The people of Kinney County clearly appreciated the Rangers. When the adjutant general on February 3, 1897, removed the two rangers who had been working the border in that county, cattle theft increased almost immediately. The Kinney County judge wrote Adjutant General Mabry on March 24 to "most respectfully petition . . . that you station two rangers at the Rio Grande boundary of Kinney county, that we might again have immunity from the border thieves."
50. *Report of the Adjutant General, 1895–1896,* p. 9.
51. "The Ranger Service," Dallas *Morning News,* July 25, 1896. On January 16, 1897, the *Morning News* again demonstrated its pro-Ranger stance with an article from Fort Worth, "Favors the Rangers." Former Captain Sam Mc-Murry, in town on business, told a *Morning News* correspondent, "I am sorry to hear some talk of abolishing the appropriation for the state ranger service, and I trust the present legislature will not do this. I have no ax to grind in the matter, for I quit the service for good some six years ago. . . . The legislature, in my opinion, could not make a graver mistake than to wipe out the ranger service." McMurry may not have had an ax to grind, but he did not lack for perspective. A native of Tennessee who came to Texas with his brother in the 1870s to become a cowboy, McMurry joined then lieutenant Lee Hall's company at Clinton in DeWitt County on March 24, 1877. Within three years, the young Southerner had risen in rank to lieutenant. On September 1, 1881, he became captain of newly organized Company B at Colorado City. He served in that capacity for nearly a decade, resigning on January 31, 1891. For more details on this captain, see Stephens, *Texas Ranger Sketches,* pp. 99–102.
52. *Frontier Times,* April 1945, pp. 201–2. About the time King's history of the Rangers appeared in Wooten's 1897 two-volume Texas history, the Chicago *Times-Herald* ran an article on the Rangers by H. S. Canfield. Reprinted in the June 22, 1897, issue of the Dallas *Morning News* under the simple heading "Texas Rangers," the piece noted that the Texas legislature would be considering in special session a $25,000 appropriation for the force. "The smallness of the sum emphasizes the decadence of an arm remarkable for its singularity and efficiency," Canfield wrote. "There is nothing exactly similar among the forces of the world. The mounted constabulary of South Africa bears, perhaps, a closer resemblance that any other, though there are wide divergences." Canfield also expanded on King's characterization of what had come to be regarded as a significant Ranger trait: "In the Texas band the military factor of 'personal equation' is at its strongest and best, because, although under semi-discipline, each member depends pretty much upon himself. Literally his hand guards his head. This teaches self-reliance,

decision, tenacity of purpose and stoicism." Thirteen years before King wrote his Ranger history, one of the men he once supervised had threatened to do the same. "If I ever go out of this buesness [*sic*] I will publish the history of the Battalion," then Lieutenant George Schmitt wrote to his friend State Senator George Pfeuffer on March 24, 1884, as cited in Stephens, *Captain George H. Schmitt, Texas Ranger*, p. 53. Schmitt never followed through on his vow.

53. Cox, *Texas Ranger Tales*, p. 175.

54. *Report of the Adjutant General, 1897–1898*, p. 11. Adjutant General Mabry was not the only man connected to the Rangers who went into the military. Ninety-eight Texans joined the Volunteer Cavalry, better known as the Rough Riders. Of those, as Colonel Theodore Roosevelt later wrote, "Many . . . had served in that famous body of frontier fighters, the Texas Rangers. . . . These rangers needed no teaching. They were already trained to obey and to take responsibility. They were splendid shots, horsemen and trailers." Erma Rogers, "Roosevelt in Texas," *Junior Historian*, November 1958, p. 29.

55. *New Handbook of Texas*, vol. 5, pp. 945–46.

56. Spellman, *Captain John H. Rogers*, pp. 96–102; Cox, *Texas Ranger Tales II*, pp. 142–43. Rogers went by train to San Antonio, where a doctor told him he could save the arm, but would have to remove some of the bone. The operation left the captain with a shorter arm, but after nine weeks of recovery, he rejoined his company. Soon thereafter, he was given a custom-made rifle with a curved stock specially designed to fit his bad shoulder.

57. *Report of the Adjutant General, 1900*, p. 21; Brown, *Strain of Violence*, p. 252. McDonald's presence arguably prevented further violence, but the feud claimed at least eleven lives before it played out in 1906. Sonnichsen's *I'll Die Before I'll Run*, pp. 299–315, still stands as the best overview of the Townsend-Reese feud. For more of the Reese family take on the matter, see John Walter Reese and Lillian Estelle Reese, *Flaming Feuds of Colorado County* (Salado, Tex.: Anson Jones Press, 1962). Columbus did not stay quiet for long after McDonald left on April 1. On May 19, 1899, the day after two Colorado County deputy sheriffs shot and killed Dick Reese and his carriage driver on the Colorado River bridge, Captain J. H. Rogers arrived to put the lid back on the simmering feud. Staying in town a week, the captain disarmed feudist Light Townsend. (Townsend later joined the Rangers.) Rogers left Ranger private Will Wright posted in Columbus through the summer, with no further trouble reported. Paul Spellman covers the Columbus feud in his *Captain J. A. Brooks, Texas Ranger*, Denton: University of North Texas Press, 2007, pp. 109–115.

58. Spellman, *Captain J. A. Brooks, Texas Ranger*, p. 116 citing Scurry to Brooks, Hughes, McDonald, and Rogers, January 30, 1899. The day after

mailing the letter, Scurry wired the captains to suggest that they write the sheriffs in their respective areas to enlist them in the cause of keeping the Frontier Battalion.

59. John H. Jenkins included *A Texas Ranger* in his *Basic Texas Books* (Austin: Jenkins Publishing Co., 1983), pp. 280–84, calling it "one of the most interesting accounts of the life of the Texas Rangers in the late 1870's." In its prepublication promotional material, publisher Charles Scribner's Sons called Jennings's book a "true story of surprising adventures on the Mexican border by a young man who enlisted in the early eighties [*sic*] in a company of Texas Rangers." Going on to claim the book was "as thrilling as a border romance," the advertising copy asserted that the Rangers "were the prototypes of the Rough Riders." For more discussion of *A Texas Ranger*, see Cox, *Texas Ranger Tales*, pp. 295–97, and Jenkins, *Basic Texas Books*, pp. 280–84.

60. Jennings, *Texas Ranger*, p. 321.

61. W. W. Collier, "Frontier Days or the Old West As I Recall It" (unpublished typescript, author's collection), p. 60.

Bibliography

GOVERNMENT DOCUMENTS

Adjutant General's Department of Texas. *Annual and Biennial Reports, 1875–1934.*

Claims Against the United States. Senate Executive Doc. 74. 46th Cong., 2nd sess. Washington: 1880.

Claims for Spoliations by Indians and Mexicans. House Resolution 535. Washington: 1860.

Claims of the State of Texas. House Executive Doc. 277, 42nd Cong., 2nd sess. Washington: 1872.

Claims of the State of Texas. Senate Executive Doc. 19. 45th Cong., 2nd sess. Washington: 1878.

Coke, Richard. *Speech of . . . Indian Policy of the Government.* Washington: 1878.

Daniel, Price, and James C. Martin, eds. *Legislative Messages of the Chief Executives of Texas.* Austin: Texas State Library, 1973.

Depredations on the Frontiers of Texas. House Executive Doc. 39, 42nd Cong., 3d sess. Washington: 1872.

Depredations on the Frontiers of Texas. House Executive Doc. 257, 43rd Cong., 1st sess. Washington: 1874.

Difficulties on the Southwestern Frontier. House Executive Doc. 52. 36th Cong., 1st sess. Washington: 1860.

El Paso Troubles in Texas. House Executive Doc. 93. 45th Cong., 2nd sess. Washington: 1878.

Everett, Edward. *Report of . . . Relative to the Encroachment of the Indians of the U.S. upon the Territory of Mexico.* Senate Executive Doc. 14. Washington: 1853.

Floyd, John B. *Protection of the Frontier of Texas.* House Executive Doc. 27. 35th Cong., 2nd sess. Washington: 1859.

Gammel, Hans Peter Nielson, comp. *The Laws of Texas, 1822–1897.* 10 vols. Austin: Gammel Book Co., 1898.

General Laws of the State of Texas: Passed at the Session of the Fourteenth Legislature Begun and Held at the City of Austin, January 13, 1874. Houston: A. C. Gray, State Printer, 1874.

General Laws of the Twelfth Legislature of the State of Texas. Called Session. Austin: Tracy, Siemering & Co., 1870.

Hearings Before the Committee on Invalid Pensions . . . On H.R. 7899: A Bill Extending the Provisions of Pension Laws Relating to Indian War Veterans to Members of Companies E and F, Frontier Battalion, Texas Rangers . . . Washington: 1940.

Journals of the House of Representatives of the Ninth Congress of the Republic of Texas. Washington, Tex.: Miller & Cushney, Public Printers, 1845.

Laws of the Republic of Texas, 1837. Houston: 1837.

Memorial of the Legislature of Texas, Praying Reimbursement for Defences [sic] *of Her Frontier in 1848.* Senate Miscellaneous Doc. 97. Washington: 1850.

Message of the President of the United States, Communicating, in Compliance with a Resolution of the Senate, a Letter from the Governor of Texas, Concerning the Alleged Hostilities Existing on the Rio Grande, Between the Citizens of the Military Authorities of Mexico and That State. Senate Executive Doc. 21. 36th Cong., 1st sess. Washington: 1860.

Mexican Border Troubles. Message from the President of the United States [Rutherford B. Hayes]. House of Representatives Executive Doc. 13. Washington: 1877.

Ranger Force Order Book. Texas Ranger Division, Texas Department of Public Safety.

Relations of the United States with Mexico. House Executive Doc. 701. 45th Cong., 2nd sess. Washington: 1878.

Reports from the Eighth Military Department–Texas. House Executive Doc. 1. Washington: 1852.

Report of the Commissioner of Indian Affairs for the Year 1857. Washington: 1858.

Report of the Commissioner of Indian Affairs for the Year 1858. Washington: 1859.

Roberts, Governor O. M. *Messages of . . . to the 16th Legislature.* Galveston: 1879.

Senate and House Journal of the State of Texas for the Called Session of the 18th Legislature . . . Jan. 8, 1884. Austin: 1884.

Senate Journal of the State of Texas. Austin: 1850.

Senate Journal of the State of Texas, 1851–1852. Austin: 1852.

Smither, Harriet, ed. *Journals of the Fourth Congress of the Republic of Texas, 1839–1840, to which are added the Relief Laws*. 3 vols. Austin: Von Boeckmann-Jones, n.d.

Special Report of the Adjutant-General of the State of Texas. September 1884. Austin: E. W. Swindells, 1884.

Testimony Taken by the Committee on Military Affairs in Relation to the Texas Border Troubles. House Miscellaneous Doc. 64. 45th Cong., 2nd sess. Washington: 1878.

Texas Frontier Depredations. House Miscellaneous Doc. 37. Washington: 1876.

Texas Frontier Troubles. House Doc. 343. 44th Cong., 1st sess. Washington: 1876.

Texas Indian Depredations. House Miscellaneous Doc. 142. Washington: 1870.

Traas, Adrian G. *From the Golden Gate to Mexico City: The U.S. Army Topographical Engineers in the Mexican War, 1846–1848*. Washington: Office of History, Corps of Engineers and Center of Military History, 1993.

Troubles on the Texas Frontier. House Executive Doc. 81. 36th Cong., 1st sess. Washington: 1860.

United States and Mexican Claims. Senate Executive Doc. 31. 44th Cong., 2nd sess. Washington: 1877.

UNPUBLISHED MATERIAL

Arrington, George Washington. Papers. Panhandle-Plains Historical Museum, Canyon, Texas.

Brown, Frank. "Annals of Travis County." Austin History Center, Austin Public Library.

Collier, W. W., as told to Victoria Hardy Duggan. "Frontier Days or the Old West As I Recall It." December 1938. Typescript in author's collection.

Durbin, Walter. Scrapbook. Author's collection.

Ellington, G. W. "When Cattle Trails Were Highways." Record Group 401, Ranger Reminiscences, File 1234-8, Texas State Library and Archives.

Ford, John S. "John C. Hays in Texas." John Salmon Ford Papers, Center for American History, University of Texas at Austin.

Houston, Andrew Jackson. Papers, No. 546, Texas State Library and Archives.

Kimbell, R. G. Record Group 401, Ranger Reminiscences, File 1234-11, Texas State Archives.

"The Ledger of Samuel Coleman Lockett." Transcribed by Christina Stopka. Texas Ranger Hall of Fame and Museum, Waco, Texas.

Maguire, Jack. "Texas Ranger Personalities." N.d. Author's collection.

Odom, Thomas L. Family papers. Garland Richards Collection, Fort Chadbourne, Texas.

Perry, Mary Ellen Trowbridge, comp. "Trowbridge Family History." 1987. Author's collection.

Sullivan, W. S. J. Scrapbook and papers. Author's collection.

Warren, Harry. "The Porvenir Massacre in Presidio County, Texas, on January 28, 1918." Harry Warren Papers, Archives of the Big Bend, Sul Ross State University, Alpine, Texas.

Webb, Walter Prescott. Papers, Center for American History, University of Texas at Austin.

Widener, Ralph. "John Salmon ("Rip") Ford." Author's collection.

Wilke, L. A. Papers related to Captain John R. Hughes. Author's collection.

Books

Alexander, Bob. *Dangerous Dan Tucker: New Mexico's Deadly Lawman.* Silver City, N.M.: High Lonesome Books, 2001.

———. *Lawmen, Outlaws, and S.O.B.s: Gunfighters of the Old Southwest.* Silver City, N.M.: High Lonesome Books, 2004.

Allan, Francis D., comp. *Allan's Lone Star Ballads: A Collection of Southern Patriotic Songs Made During Confederate Times.* 1874. Reprint, New York: Burt Franklin, 1970.

Allen, Ruth. *The Great Southwest Strike.* University of Texas Publications 4214. Austin: University of Texas Press, 1942.

Anderson, John Q., ed. *Tales of Frontier Texas, 1830–1860.* Dallas: Southern Methodist University Press, 1966.

Aten, Ira. *Six and One-Half Years in the Ranger Service: The Memoirs of Ira Aten, Sergeant Company D, Texas Rangers.* Bandera, Tex.: Frontier Times, 1945.

Austin, Stephen F. *Establishing Austin's Colony.* Ed. David B. Gracy III. Austin: Jenkins Publishing Co., 1970.

Baker, DeWitt Clinton. *A Texas Scrap-Book, Made Up of the History, Biography, and Miscellany of Texas and Its People.* New York, Chicago, and New Orleans: A. S. Barnes, 1875.

Barker, Eugene C., ed. *The Austin Papers.* Annual Report of the American Historical Association. Washington: 1919.

———. *Life of Stephen F. Austin, Founder of Texas, 1793–1836: A Chapter in the Westward Movement of the Anglo-American People.* Austin: Texas State Historical Association, 1949.

Barton, Barbara. *Ruckus Along the Rivers: True Tales of Early Settlements Along Spring Creek, Dove Creek, and the Conchos.* San Angelo, Tex.: Anchor Publishing Co., 1997.

Barton, Henry W. *Texas Volunteers in the Mexican War.* Waco: Texian Press, 1970.

Bass, Feris A., Jr., and B. R. Brunson, eds. *Fragile Empires: The Texas Correspondence of Samuel Swartwout and James Morgan, 1836–1856.* Austin: Shoal Creek Publishers, 1978.

Baugh, Virgil E. *A Pair of Texas Rangers: Bill McDonald and John Hughes.* Washington, Tex.: The Westerners, 1970.

Baylor, George Wythe. *Into the Far, Wild Country: True Tales of the Old Southwest.* Ed. with an introduction by Jerry D. Thompson. El Paso: Texas Western Press, 1996.

Benner, Judith Ann. *Sul Ross: Soldier, Statesman, Educator.* College Station: Texas A&M Press, 1983.

Blackwell, Hartal Langford. *Mills County—the Way It Was.* Goldthwaite, Tex.: Mills County Historical Commission, 1976.

Bowles, Flora Gatlin, ed. *A No Man's Land Becomes a County.* Goldthwaite, Tex.: 1958.

Brandon, Jay. *Law and Liberty: A History of the Legal Profession in San Antonio.* Dallas: Taylor Publishing Co., 1996.

"Brazos." *Life of Robert Hall: Indian Fighter and Veteran of Three Great Wars.* 1898. Reprint, Austin: State House Press. 1992.

Brice, Donaly E. *The Great Comanche Raid: Boldest Indian Attack of the Texas Republic.* Austin: Eakin Press, 1987.

Brooks, Nathan Covington. *A Complete History of the Mexican War: Its Causes, Conduct, and Consequences: Comprising an Account of the Various Military and Naval Operations, from Its Commencement to the Treaty of Peace.* Philadelphia: Grigg, Elliott, 1849.

Brown, John Henry. *The Indian Wars of and Pioneers of Texas.* [189-?] Reprint, Austin: State House Press, 1988.

Brown, Richard Maxwell. *Strain of Violence: Historical Studies of American Violence and Vigilantism.* New York: Oxford University Press, 1975.

Bruce, Leona. *Bannister Was There.* Fort Worth: Branch-Smith, 1968.

Calderon, Roberto R. *Mexican Coal Mining Labor in Texas and Coahuila, 1880–1930.* College Station: Texas A&M University Press, 2000.

Calvert, Robert A., and Arnoldo De Leon. *The History of Texas.* Arlington Heights, Ill.: Harland Davidson, 1990.

Cantrell, Gregg. *Stephen F. Austin: Empresario of Texas.* New Haven and London: Yale University Press, 1999.

Carver, Leona Parrish. *You Can't Get the Coons All Up One Tree: The Life Story of John N. Jones.* Amarillo: Coltharp Printing and Publishing, 1980.

Castleman, Harvey N. *The Texas Rangers: The Story of an Organization That Is Unique, Like Nothing Else in America.* Girard, Kans.: Haldeman-Julius Publications, 1944.

Chadwick, Joseph. *The Texas Rangers: A Concise History of the Most Colorful Law Enforcement Group in the Frontier West.* New York: Monarch Books, 1963.

Chalfant, William Young. *Without Quarter: The Wichita Expedition and the Fight on Crooked Creek.* Norman: University of Oklahoma Press, 1991.

Chapel, Charles Edward. *Guns of the Old West.* New York: Coward-McCann, 1961.

Chatfield, Lieutenant W. H., comp. *The Twin Cities of the Border.* New Orleans: 1893.

Clark, Pat B. *Clarksville and Old Red River County.* Dallas: Mathis, Van Nort, 1937.

Clayton, Lawrence R., and Joseph E. Chance, eds. *The March to Monterrey: The Diary of Lt. Rankin Dilworth.* El Paso: Texas Western Press, 1996.

Colorado County Chronicles. 2 vols. Columbus: Colorado County Historical Commission, 1986.

Copeland, Fayette. *Kendall of the Picayune.* Norman: University of Oklahoma Press, 1943.

Cox, Mike. *Texas Ranger Tales: Stories That Need Telling.* Plano: Republic of Texas Press, 1997.

———. *Texas Ranger Tales II.* Plano: Republic of Texas Press, 1999.

Cox, Ross J., Sr. *The Texas Rangers and the San Saba Mob.* San Saba, Tex.: C&S Farm Press, 2005.

Crouch, Carrie J. *A History of Young County, Texas.* Austin: Texas State Historical Association, 1956.

Cude, Elton. *The Free and Wild Dukedom of Bexar.* San Antonio: Munguia Printers, 1978.

Cunningham, Eugene C. *Famous in the West.* El Paso: 1926.

Cunningham, Sharon, and Mark Boardman, eds. *Revenge! And Other True Tales of the Old West.* Lafayette, Ind.: Scarlet Mask, 2004.

Curry, W. Hubert. *Sun Rising on the West: The Saga of Henry Clay and Elizabeth Smith.* Crosbyton, Tex.: 1979.

Cutrer, Thomas W. *Ben McCulloch and the Frontier Military Tradition.* Chapel Hill and London: University of North Carolina Press, 1993.

Cutter, Charles R. *The Legal Culture of New Spain.* Albuquerque: University of New Mexico Press, 1995.

Daffan, Katie. *Texas Hero Stories: An Historical Reader for the Grades.* Boston: Benj. H. Sanborn, 1908.

Daughters of the American Revolution. *The Alamo Heroes and Their Revolutionary Ancestors.* San Antonio: 1976.

Davis, John L. *The Texas Rangers: Images and Incidents.* San Antonio: University of Texas Institute of Texan Cultures, 1991.

Davis, Richard Harding. *The West from a Car Window.* New York: Harper & Brothers, 1892.

Day, James. *Rangers of Texas.* Waco: Texian Press, 1969.

De Leon, Arnoldo. *They Called Them Greasers.* Austin: University of Texas Press, 1983.

Desmond, H. A. *Texas Knights of the Hill Country: Story of the Texas Rangers.* Kerrville, Tex.: Herring Printing, 1976.

Dewees, William B. *Letters from an Early Settler of Texas.* 1852. Reprint, Waco: Texian Press, 1968.

Dobie, J. Frank. *The Flavor of Texas.* Dallas: Dealey and Lowe, 1936.

———. *John C. Duval: First Texas Man of Letters.* Dallas: Southern Methodist University Press, 1965.

Douglas, C. L. *The Gentlemen in the White Hats: Dramatic Episodes in the History of the Texas Rangers.* Dallas: South-West Press, 1934.

Drago, Harry S. *The Great Range Wars: Violence on the Grasslands.* New York: 1970.

Dunn, J. B. (John). *Perilous Trails of Texas.* Dallas: Southwest Press, 1932.

Durham, George, as told to Clyde Wantland. *Taming the Nueces Strip: The Story of McNelly's Rangers.* Austin: University of Texas Press, 1962.

Dykes, Jeff. *Rangers All: A Catalog and Check List.* College Park, Md.: Jeff Dykes Western Books, 1968.

Eckhardt, C. F. *Texas Smoke: Muzzle-Loaders on the Frontier.* Lubbock: Texas Tech University Press, 2001.

Edwards, Frank S. *A Campaign in New Mexico with Col. Doniphan.* Philadelphia: Carey and Hart, 1847.

Ehrle, Michael G., ed. *Childress County Story.* Childress, Tex.: Oxbow Printing, 1971.

Eisenhower, John S. *So Far from God: The U.S. War with Mexico, 1846–1848.* New York: Random House, 1989.

Elkins, John M. *Indian Fighting on the Texas Frontier.* 1929. Reprint, rev. ed., Waco: Texian Press, 2000.

Elliott, Claude. *Leathercoat: The Life History of a Texas Patriot.* San Antonio: Standard Printing Co., 1938.

Erath, George B., dictated to and arranged by Lucy A. Erath. *Memoirs of Major George Bernard Earth.* Ed. E. W. Winkler. 1923. Reprint, Waco: Bulletin Number Three of the Heritage Society of Waco, 1956.

Exley, Jo Ella Powell. *Frontier Blood: The Saga of the Parker Family.* College Station: Texas A&M University, 2001.

Farrow, Marion Humphreys. *Troublesome Times in Texas.* San Antonio: Naylor Co., 1957.

Fehrenbach, T. R. *Comanches: The Destruction of a People.* New York: Alfred A. Knopf, 1974.

Fisher, O. C. *It Occurred in Kimble: The Story of a Texas County.* Houston: Anson Jones Press, 1937.

Fisher, O. C., and Jeff C. Dykes. *King Fisher: His Life and Times*. Norman: University of Oklahoma Press, 1966.

Foos, Paul. *A Short, Offhand Killing Affair: Soldiers and Social Conflict During the Mexican-American War*. Chapel Hill and London: University of North Carolina Press, 2002.

Ford, John Salmon. *Rip Ford's Texas*. Ed. Stephen B. Oates. Austin: University of Texas Press, 1963.

Foster, L. L. *Forgotten Texas Census: First Annual Report of the Agricultural Bureau of the Department of Agriculture, Insurance, Statistics, and History, 1887–1888*. Austin: Texas State Historical Association, 2001.

Franks, J. M. *Seventy Years In Texas*. Gatesville, Tex.: Privately Published, 1924.

Friends of the Moody Texas Ranger Library. *The Texas Ranger Annual*. 3 vols. Waco, 1982–84.

Fugitives from Justice: The Notebook of Texas Ranger Sergeant James B. Gillett. Introd. by Michael D. Morrison. Austin: State House Press, 1997.

Fulmore, Z. T. *The History and Geography of Texas as Told in County Names*. 1915. Reprint, Austin: Steck Company, 1935.

Furman, Necah Stewart. *Walter Prescott Webb: His Life and Impact*. Albuquerque: University of New Mexico Press, 1976.

Gard, Wayne. *Frontier Justice*. Norman: University of Oklahoma Press, 1949.

———. *Sam Bass*. Boston: Houghton Mifflin, 1936.

Gatto, Steve. *Johnny Ringo*. Lansing: Protar House, 2002.

Gay, Beatrice Grady. *"Into the Setting Sun": A History of Coleman County*. Santa Anna: n.p., n.d.

[Giddings, Luther]. *Sketches of the Campaigns in Northern Mexico by an Officer of the First Ohio Volunteers*. New York: Putnam, 1853.

Gillett, James B. *Six Years with the Texas Rangers, 1875 to 1881*. Austin: Von-Boeckmann Jones, 1921.

———. *Six Years with the Texas Rangers, 1875–1881*. Ed., with an introduction by M. M. Quaife. New Haven: Yale University Press, 1925.

Gilliland, Maude T. *Wilson County Texas Rangers, 1837–1977*. Brownsville, Tex.: Springman-King Co., 1977.

Glenn, Frankie Davis. *Capt'n John: Story of a Texas Ranger*. Austin: Nortex Press, 1991.

Graham, Don. *Kings of Texas: The 150-Year Saga of an American Ranching Empire*. New York: John Wiley and Sons, 2003.

Graybill, Andrew R. *Policing the Great Plains: Rangers, Mounties, and the North American Frontier, 1875–1910*. Lincoln: University of Nebraska Press, 2006.

Green, Rena Maverick, ed. *Samuel Maverick, Texan, 1803–1870: A Collection of Letters, Journals and Memoirs*. San Antonio, 1952.

Greer, James Kimmins. *Colonel Jack Hays: Frontier Leader and California Builder*. New York: 1952.

——, ed. *A Texas Ranger and Frontiersman: The Days of Buck Barry in Texas, 1845–1906*. Dallas: Southwest Press, 1932.

Gulick, Charles Adams, Jr., Winnie Allen, Catherine Elliott, and Harriet Smither, eds. *Papers of Mirabeau Bonaparte Lamar*. Austin and New York: Pemberton Press, 1968.

Gunter, Pete A. Y., and Robert A. Calvert, eds. *W. R. Strong: His Memoirs*. Denton: Denton County Historical Commission, 1982.

Hagan, William T. *United States–Comanche Relations: The Reservation Years*. New Haven and London: Yale University Press, 1976.

Haley, James L. *The Buffalo War: The History of the Red River Indian Uprising of 1874*. Norman: University of Oklahoma Press, 1985.

——. *Passionate Nation: The Epic History of Texas*. New York: Free Press, 2006.

Haley, J. Evetts. *Fort Concho on the Texas Frontier*. San Angelo, Tex.: San Angelo *Standard-Times*, 1952.

——. *Jeff Milton: A Good Man with a Gun*. Norman: University of Oklahoma Press, 1949.

Hamilton, Nancy, *Ben Dowell: El Paso's First Mayor*. El Paso: Texas Western Press, 1976.

Hamrick, Alma Ward. *The Call of the San Saba: A History of San Saba County*. San Antonio: Naylor Co., 1941.

Hardin, Stephen L. *The Texas Rangers*. London: Osprey Publishing, 1991.

——. *Texian Iliad: A Military History of the Texas Revolution*. Austin: University of Texas Press, 1994.

Harmon, George Dewey. *United States Indian Policy in Texas: 1845–1860*. Bethlehem, Pa.: Lehigh University, 1931.

Harris, Charles H., III, and Louis R. Sadler. *The Texas Rangers and the Mexican Revolution*. Albuquerque: University of New Mexico Press, 2004.

Hatley, Allen G. *The Indian Wars in Stephen F. Austin's Colony, 1822–1835*. Austin: Eakin Press, 2001.

Hausenfluke, Gene. *Texas Ranger Sesquicentennial Anniversary, 1823–1973*. Fort Worth: Heritage Publications, 1973.

Havins, T. R. *Something About Brown (A History of Brown County, Texas)*. Brownwood, Tex.: Banner Printing Company, 1958.

Haynes, Sam W. *Soldiers of Misfortune: The Somervell and Mier Expeditions*. Austin: University of Texas Press, 1990.

Hendrickson, Kenneth E., Jr. *Chief Executives of Texas: From Stephen F. Austin to John B. Connally, Jr.* College Station: Texas A&M University Press, 1995.

Henry, Will. *The Texas Rangers*. New York: Random House, 1957.

Herff, Dr. Ferdinand. *The Regulated Emigration of the German Proletariat with Special Reference to Texas: Being Also a Guide for German Emigrants*. Trans. Arthur L. Finck Jr. San Antonio: Trinity University Press, 1978.

The Heritage of Blanco County, Texas. Blanco, Tex.: Blanco County News, 1987.

Himmel, Kelly F. *The Conquest of the Karankawas and the Tonkawas, 1821–1859*. College Station: Texas A&M University Press, 1999.

Hoig, Stan. *Kiowas and the Legend of Kicking Bird*. Boulder: University of Colorado Press, 2000.

Hollon, W. Eugene. *Frontier Violence: Another Look*. New York: Oxford University Press, 1974.

Hollon, W. Eugene, and Ruth Lapham Butler, eds. *William Bollaert's Texas*. Norman: University of Oklahoma Press, 1956.

Horton, David M., and Ryan Kellus Turner. *Lone Star Justice: A Comprehensive Overview of the Texas Criminal Justice System*. Austin: Eakin Press, 1999.

Howard, Robert West, ed. *This Is the West*. New York: 1977.

Hughes, W. J. *Rebellious Ranger: Rip Ford and the Old Southwest*. Norman: University of Oklahoma Press, 1964.

Hunter, J. Marvin. *Jack Hays: The Intrepid Texas Ranger*. Bandera, Tex.: n.d.

Huson, Hobart. *A Comprehensive History of Refugio County from Aboriginal Times to 1953*. Woodsboro, Tex.: Rooke Foundation, 1953–55.

Hyde, George E. *Rangers and Regulars*. Denver: 1933. Reprint, Columbus: 1952.

Ingmire, Frances Terry. *Texas Ranger Service Records, 1847–1900*. St. Louis: privately printed, 1982.

Jackson, Jack. *Indian Agent: Peter Ellis Bean in Mexican Texas*. College Station: Texas A&M University Press, 2005.

Jenkins, John H., ed. *Memoirs of John Forester: Soldier, Indian Fighter, and Texas Ranger in the Republic of Texas*. Austin: Jenkins Publishing Co., 1969.

———, ed. *The Papers of the Texas Revolution, 1835–1836*. Austin: Presidial Press, 1973.

———, ed. *Recollections of Early Texas: Memoirs of John Holland Jenkins*. Austin: University of Texas Press, 1958.

Jenkins, John H., and Kenneth Kesselus. *Edward Burleson: Texas Frontier Leader*. Austin: Jenkins Publishing Co., 1990.

Jennings, Napoleon Augustus. *A Texas Ranger*. New York: Charles Scribner's Sons, 1899.

Jensen, Ann, ed. *Texas Ranger's Diary & Scrapbook*. Dallas: Kaleidograph Press, 1936.

Johnson, David. *The Mason County "Hoo Doo" War, 1874–1902*. Denton: University of North Texas Press, 2006.

Johnson, David R. *American Law Enforcement: A History*. Wheeling, Ill.: Forum Press, 1981.

Johnson, Frank W. *A History of Texas and Texans*. Ed. Eugene C. Barker with the assistance of Ernest William Winkler. Chicago and New York: American Historical Society, 1916.

Jones, Anson. *Memoranda and Official Correspondence Relating to the Republic of Texas: Its History and Annexation, 1826 to 1846*. 1859. Reprint, New York: Arno Press, 1973.

Jones, Daryl. *The Dime Novel Western*. Bowling Green, Ohio: Bowling Green State University Popular Press, 1978.

Kaiser, Frank C. *Reminiscences of a Texas Ranger*. Ed. and annotated by A. E. Skinner. Austin: privately printed, 1967.

Keating, Bern. *An Illustrated History of the Texas Rangers*. New York: Rand McNally, 1975.

Kilgore, D. E. *A Ranger Legacy: 150 Years of Service to Texas*. Austin: Madrona Press, 1973.

Kinevan, Marcos. *Lieutenant John Bigelow with the Buffalo Soldiers in Texas*. El Paso: Texas Western Press, 1997.

Knowles, Thomas W. *They Rode for the Lone Star: The Saga of the Texas Rangers*. Dallas: Taylor Publishing Company, 1999.

Kohlberg, Walter. *Letters of Ernst Kohlberg, 1875–1877*. El Paso: Texas Western Press, 1973.

Kuykendall, Marshall E. *They Slept Upon Their Rifles: The Story of the Captain Robert H. Kuykendall Family in America and the Entry of the Family with the Anglo Settlement into Mexican/Texas in Stephen F. Austin's Colony in 1821*. Austin: Nortex Press, 2005.

Lamego, Miguel A. *The Second Mexican-Texas War, 1841–1843*. Hillsboro, Tex.: Hill Junior College Monograph No. 7, 1972.

Lauterbach, Stewart, and Christina Stopka, comps. *Ranger Songs and Verse: A Collection for the 175th Anniversary Gala of the Texas Rangers*. Waco: Texas Ranger Hall of Fame and Museum, 1998.

Lavender, David. *Climax at Buena Vista: The American Campaigns in Northeastern Mexico, 1846–47*. Philadelphia and New York: J. P. Lippincott Co., 1966.

Leckie, William H., and Shirley A. Leckie. *Unlikely Warriors: General Benjamin Grierson and His Family*. Norman: University of Oklahoma Press, 1984.

Ledbetter, Barbara Neal. *Indian Raids on Warren—Dubose—Feild—Man Wagon Trains—1871—in Young and Jack Counties*. Graham, Tex.: privately published, 1992.

Lee, Nelson. *Three Years Among the Comanches: The Narrative of Nelson Lee the Texas Ranger Containing a Detailed Account of His Captivity Among the Indians, His Singular Escape Through the Instrumentality of His Watch, and Fully Illustrating Indian Life as It Is on the War Path and in*

Camp. 1859. Reprint, ed. with introduction by Walter Prescott Webb, Norman: University of Oklahoma Press, 1957.

Leiker, James N. *Racial Borders: Black Soldiers Along the Rio Grande*. College Station: Texas A&M University Press, 2002.

Lewis, Tracy. *Along the Rio Grande*. New York: 1916.

Loomis, Noel M. *The Texan–Santa Fe Pioneers*. Norman: University of Oklahoma Press, 1958.

The Lucia Holmes Diary. Mason: Mason County Historical Society, 1985.

McCallum, Henry D., and Frances T. McCallum. *The Wire That Fenced the West*. Norman: University of Oklahoma Press, 1965.

McGiffin, Lee. *Ten Tall Texans: Tales of the Texas Rangers*. New York: Lee and Shepard Company, 1956.

McGrath, Sister Paul of the Cross. *Political Nativism in Texas, 1825–1860*. Washington, D.C.: Catholic University of America, 1930.

McIntire, Jim. *Early Days in Texas: A Trip to Hell and Heaven*. Ed. with an introduction and notes by Robert K. DeArment. Norman: University of Oklahoma Press, 1992.

McKellar, Margaret Maud. *Life on a Mexican Ranche*. Ed. Dolores L. Latorre. Bethlehem, Pa.: Lehigh University Press, 1994.

McLean, Malcolm D., comp. and ed. *Papers Concerning Robertson's Colony in Texas*. 19 vols. Fort Worth: Texas Christian University Press, 1974–76; Arlington: University of Texas at Arlington Press, 1974–87.

Maltby, Jeff. *Captain Jeff, or Frontier Life in Texas with the Texas Rangers*. Colorado, Tex.: Whipkey Printing Co., 1906. Facsimile reprint, Waco: Texian Press, 1967.

Marshall, Doyle. *A Cry Unheard: The Story of Indian Attacks in and around Parker County, Texas, 1858–1872*. Aledo, Tex.: Annetta Valley Farm Press, 1990.

Martin, Charles L. *Sketch of Sam Bass, the Bandit: A Graphic Narrative. His Various Train Robberies, His Death, and Accounts of the Deaths of His Gang and Their History*. Norman: University of Oklahoma Press, 1956.

Martin, Jack. *Border Boss: Captain John R. Hughes, Texas Ranger*. San Antonio: Naylor Co., 1942.

Mason, Herbert Malloy, Jr. *The Texas Rangers*. New York: Meredith Press, 1967.

Mason-Manheim, Madeline. *Riding for Texas: The True Adventures of Captain Bill McDonald of the Texas Rangers*. New York: Reynal & Hitchcock, 1936.

Massey, Sara R., ed. *Black Cowboys of Texas*. College Station: Texas A&M University Press, 2000.

Meed, Douglas V. *Texas Wanderlust: The Adventures of Dutch Wurzbach*. College Station: Texas A&M University Press, 1997.

Metz, Leon Claire. *Dallas Stoudenmire: El Paso Marshal*. Austin: Pemberton Press, 1969.

————. *John Wesley Hardin: Dark Angel of Texas*. El Paso: Mangan Books, 1996.

Miletich, Leo N. *Dan Stuart's Fistic Carnival*. College Station: Texas A&M University Press, 1994.

Miller, Rick. *Bounty Hunter*. College Station: Creative Publishing Co., 1988.

————. *Sam Bass & Gang*. Austin: State House Press, 1999.

Mills, Susie. *Legend in Bronze: The Biography of Jay Banks*. Dallas: 1982.

Moneyhon, Carl H. *Republicanism in Reconstruction Texas*. Austin: University of Texas Press, 1980.

————. *Texas After the Civil War: The Struggle of Reconstruction*. College Station: Texas A&M University Press, 2004.

Moore, Stephen L. *Eighteen Minutes: The Battle of San Jacinto and the Texas Independence Campaign*. Lanham, Md.: Republic of Texas Press, 2004.

————. *Savage Frontier: Rangers, Riflemen, and Indian Wars in Texas*. Vol. 1, 1835–37. Plano: Republic of Texas Press, 2002.

————. *Savage Frontier*. Vol. II Denton: University of North Texas Press, 2006.

————. *Savage Frontier*. Vol. III Denton: University of North Texas Press, 2007.

Morgan, Linda Buckles. *The Road to Erath: Following the Footsteps of the Thompson and Hollis Families to Erath County, Texas*. Kearney, Neb: Morris Publishing, 2000.

Morris, John Miller. *A Private in the Texas Rangers: A. T. Miller of Company B, Frontier Battalion*. College Station: Texas A&M University Press, 2001.

Nance, Joseph Milton. *Attack and Counter-Attack: The Texas-Mexican Frontier, 1842*. Austin: University of Texas Press, 1964.

Nance, Joseph Milton, and Archie McDonald. *Dare-Devils All: The Texan Mier Expedition, 1842–44*. Austin: Eakin Press, 1998.

Neal, Bill. *The Last Frontier: The Story of Hardeman County*. Quanah, Tex.: Hardeman County Historical Society, 1966.

————. *Getting Away With Murder on the Texas Frontier*. Lubbock: Texas Tech University Press, 2006.

Neeley, Bill. *The Last Comanche Chief: The Life and Times of Quanah Parker*. New York: John Wiley & Sons, 1995.

Neighbours, Kenneth Franklin. *Robert Simpson Neighbors and the Texas Frontier, 1836–1859*. Waco: Texian Press, 1975.

Nichols, James Wilson. *Now You Hear My Horn: The Journal of James Wilson Nichols, 1820–1887*. Austin: University of Texas Press, 1967.

Nichols, Mary H., ed., *Letters to and from Sidney Green Davidson and His Wife Mary Elizabeth Kuykendall Davidson in the Year 1861*. Ballinger, Tex.: privately published, 1990.

Nolan, Frederick. *Bad Blood: The Life and Times of the Horrell Brothers*. Stillwater, Okla.: Barbed Wire Press, 1994.

Nunn, W. C. *Texas Under the Carpetbaggers*. Austin: University of Texas Press, 1962.

Oates, Stephen B. *Visions of Glory: Texans on the Southwestern Frontier*. Norman: University of Oklahoma Press, 1970.

O'Neal, Bill. *The Bloody Legacy of Pink Higgins: A Half Century of Violence in Texas*. Austin: Eakin Press, 1999.

———. *Encyclopedia of Western Gunfighters*. Norman: University of Oklahoma Press, 1979.

———. *Fighting Men of the Indian Wars*. Stillwater, Okla.: Barbed Wire Press, 1991.

The Oxford History of the American West. Ed. Clyde A. Milner II et al. New York: Oxford University Press, 1994.

Paine, Albert Bigelow. *Captain Bill McDonald Texas Ranger: A Story of Frontier Reform*. New York: Little & Ives, 1909.

Parsons, Chuck. *John B. Armstrong, Texas Ranger and Pioneer Ranchman*. College Station: Texas A&M University Press, 2007.

———. *The Capture of John Wesley Hardin*. College Station: Creative Publishing Co., 1978.

———. *"Pidge": A Texas Ranger from Virginia*. Wolfe City, Tex.: Henington Publishing Co., 1985.

Parsons, Chuck, and Donaly E. Brice. *Texas Ranger N.O. Reynolds: The Intrepid*. Honolulu: Talei Publishers, 2005.

Parsons, Chuck, and Marianne E. Hall Little. *Captain L. H. McNelly—Texas Ranger—the Life and Times of a Fighting Man*. Austin: State House Press, 2001.

Patchwork of Memories: Historical Sketches of Comanche County, Texas. Comanche: n.p., 1976.

Pennebacker, Anna J. *A New History of Texas*. Palestine, Tex.: 1895.

Peterson, John Allen, ed. *"Facts as I Remember Them": The Autobiography of Rufe LeFors*. Austin: University of Texas Press, 1986.

Pieratt, Shirley Insall. *Cade Insall, Texas Ranger . . . and His People*. San Antonio: privately published, 1983.

Pierce, Gerald S. *Texas Under Arms*. Austin: Encino Press, 1969.

Pike, James. *The Scout and Ranger: Being the Personal Adventures of Corporal Pike of the Fourth Ohio Cavalry. As a Texas Ranger, in the Indian Wars, Delineating Western Adventure; Afterward a Scout and Spy, in Tennessee, Alabama, Georgia, and in the Carolinas . . . Fully Illustrating the Secret Service*. Cincinnati and New York: J. R. Hawley, 1865. Reprint, New York: Da Capo, 1972.

Pioneer Days in the Southwest from 1850–1879: Thrilling Descriptions of Buffalo Hunting, Indian Fighting and Massacres, Cowboy Life and Home Building. Guthrie, Okla.: State Capital Company, 1909.

Pool, William C. *A Historical Atlas of Texas*. Austin: Encino Press, 1975.

Prassel, Frank Richard. *The Western Peace Officer: A Legacy of Law and Order.* Norman: University of Oklahoma Press, 1972.

Preece, Harold. *Lone Star Man: Ira Aten, Last of the Old Texas Rangers.* New York: Hastings House, 1960.

Rachael Plummer's Narrative of Twenty-one Months' Servitude as a Prisoner among the Commanchee Indians. Austin: Jenkins Publishing Company, 1977.

Raht, Carysle Graham. *The Romance of Davis Mountains and Big Bend Country.* Odessa, Tex.: Rahtbooks Co., 1963.

Raine, William MacLeod. *45-Caliber Law: The Way of Life of the Frontier Peace Officer.* Evanston, Ill.: Row Petersen, 1941.

Ramsdell, Charles William. *The Frontier and Secession.* New York: Columbia University Press, 1914.

Raymond, Dora Neill. *Captain Lee Hall of Texas.* Norman: University of Oklahoma Press, 1940.

Redfield, H. V. *Homicide, North and South: Being a Comparative View of Crime Against the Person in Several Parts of the United States.* Philadelphia: J. B. Lippincott, 1880.

Reed, Paula, and Grover Ted Tate. *The Tenderfoot Bandits: Sam Bass and Joel Collins, Their Lives and Hard Times.* Tucson: Westernlore Press, 1988.

Reid, Samuel C. *The Scouting Expeditions of McCulloch's Texas Rangers or, the Summer and Fall Campaign of the Army of the United States in Mexico— 1846; including skirmishes with the Mexicans, and an accurate detail of the storming of Monterrey; also, the daring scouts at Buena Vista; together with anecdotes, incidents, descriptions of country, and sketches of the lives of the celebrated partisan chiefs, Hays, McCulloch and Walker.* Philadelphia: G. B. Zieber, 1847.

Remington, Frederic. *How the Law Got into the Chaparral: Conversations with Old Texas Rangers.* Ed. John H. Jenkins. Austin: Jenkins Publishing Co., 1987.

Roberts, Daniel Webster. *Rangers and Sovereignty.* San Antonio: Wood Printing & Engraving Co., 1914.

Roberts, Mrs. D. W. *A Woman's Reminiscences of Six Years in Camp with the Texas Rangers.* Austin: Von Boeckmann-Jones, 1928.

Roberts, Randy, and James S. Olson. *A Line in the Sand: The Alamo in Blood and Memory.* New York: Free Press, 2001.

Robinson, Charles M., III. *The Indian Trial: The Complete Story of the Warren Wagon Train Massacre and the Fall of the Kiowa Nation.* Spokane, Wash.: Arthur H. Clark Co., 1997.

———. *The Men Who Wear the Star: The Story of the Texas Rangers.* New York: Random House, 2000.

Robinson, Duncan W. *Judge Robert McAlpin Williamson*. Austin: Texas State Historical Association, 1949.

Rose, Peter R., and Elizabeth E. Sherry. *The Hoo Doo War: Portraits of a Lawless Time*. Mason, Tex.: Mason County Historical Commission, 2003.

Rose, Victor M. *The Life and Services of Gen. Ben McCulloch*. Philadelphia: Pictorial Bureau of the Press, 1888.

———. *Texas Vendetta: or, The Sutton-Taylor Feud*. New York: J. J. Little, 1880.

Samora, Julian, Joe Bernal, and Albert Pena. *Gunpowder Justice: A Reassessment of the Texas Rangers*. Notre Dame: University of Notre Dame Press, 1979.

San Saba County Historical Commission. *San Saba County History, 1856–1983*. San Saba, Tex.: San Saba Historical Commission, 1983.

Schreiner, Charles, III, ed. *A Pictorial History of the Texas Rangers*. Mountain Home, Tex.: YO Ranch, 1969.

Scobee, Barry. *Old Fort Davis*. San Antonio: Naylor Co., 1947.

Selden, Jack K. *Return: The Parker Story*. Palestine, Tex: Clacton Press, 2006.

Sibley, Marilyn McAdams. *Lone Stars and State Gazettes: Texas Newspapers Before the Civil War*. College Station: Texas A&M University Press, 1983.

Sinise, Jerry. *George Washington Arrington*. Burnet, Tex.: Eakin Press, 1979.

———. *Pink Higgins, the Reluctant Gunfighter, and Other Tales of the Panhandle*. Quanah, Tex.: Nortex Press, 1973.

Smith, Cornelius C., Jr. *William Sanders Oury: History-Maker of the Southwest*. Tucson: University of Arizona Press, 1967.

Smith, David Paul. *Frontier Defense in the Civil War: Texas' Rangers and Rebels*. College Station: Texas A&M University Press, 1992.

Smith, F. Todd. *The Wichita Indians: Traders of Texas and the Southern Plains, 1540–1845*. College Station: Texas A&M University Press, 2000.

Smith, George W., and Charles Judah. *Chronicles of the Gringos: The U.S. Army in the Mexican War, 1846–1848*. Albuquerque: University of New Mexico Press, 1968.

Smith, S. Compton. *Chile Con Carne; or The Camp and the Field*. New York: Miller & Curtis, 1857.

Smith, T. C., Jr. *From the Memories of Men*. Brownwood, Tex.: 1954.

Smithwick, Noah. *Evolution of a State or Recollections of Old Texas Days*. Comp. Nanna Smithwick Donaldson. Gammel Book Company, 1900. Reprint, Austin: W. Thomas Taylor, 1995.

Solms-Braunfels, Prince Carl of. *Texas, 1844–1845*. Houston: Anson Jones Press, 1936.

———. *Voyage to North America, 1844–45: Prince Carl of Solms' Texas Diary of People, Places, and Events*. Trans. from German and notes by Wolfram M. Von-Maszewski. Denton: University of North Texas Press, 2000.

Sonnichsen, C. L. *The El Paso Salt War of 1877.* El Paso: Texas Western Press, 1961.

———. *I'll Die Before I'll Run: The Story of the Great Feuds of Texas.* New York: Harper & Brothers, 1951.

Sowell, A. J. *Rangers and Pioneers of Texas, with a Concise Account of the Early Settlements, Hardships, Massacres, Battles, and Wars.* 1884. Reprint, ed., new introduction by Mike Cox, Austin: State House Press, 1991.

Spaw, Patsy McDonald. *The Texas Senate.* Vol. 1. College Station: Texas A&M University Press, 1990; vol. 2, 1999.

Spellman, Paul. *Captain J. A. Brooks, Texas Ranger.* Denton: University of North Texas Press, 2007.

——— N. *Captain John H. Rogers, Texas Ranger.* Denton: University of North Texas Press, 2003.

Stamps, Roy, and Jo Ann Stamps, comps. *The Letters of John Wesley Hardin.* Austin: Eakin Press, 2001.

Stephens, Robert W. *Bullets and Buckshot in Texas.* Dallas: 2002.

———. *Captain George H. Schmitt Texas Ranger.* Dallas: Privately published, 2006.

———. *Texas Ranger Indian War Pensions.* Quanah, Tex.: 1975.

———. *Texas Ranger Sketches.* Privately printed, 1972.

———. *The Texas Rangers: An American Legend.* Rogers, Ark.: 1973.

———. *W. Walter Durbin: Texas Ranger and Sheriff.* Clarendon, Tex.: 1970.

Sterling, William Warren. *Trails and Trials of a Texas Ranger.* 1959. Reprint, Norman: University of Oklahoma Press, 1969.

(Straley, William Wilson). *Pioneer Sketches of Texas and Nebraska.* Hico, Tex.: Hico Printing Co., 1915.

Sullivan, W. John L. *Twelve Years in the Saddle for Law and Order on the Frontiers of Texas.* Austin: Von Boeckmann-Jones, 1909.

Sutton, Robert C., Jr. *The Sutton-Taylor Feud.* Quanah, Tex.: Nortex Press, 1974.

Swift, Roy L. *Three Roads to Chihuahua: The Great Wagon Roads That Opened the Southwest, 1823–1883.* Austin: Eakin Press, 1988.

Taylor, Drew Kirksey. *Taylor's Thrilling Tales of Texas, Being the Experience of Drew Kirksey Taylor, Ex–Texas Ranger and Peace Officer on the Border of Texas.* N.p., [1926].

Taylor, Paul Schuster. *An American-Mexican Frontier: Nueces County, Texas.* Chapel Hill: University of North Carolina Press, 1934.

Texas State Historical Association. *The New Handbook of Texas.* 6 vols. Austin: Texas State Historical Association, 1995.

Thompson, Cecilia. *History of Marfa and Presidio County, Texas, 1535–1946.* 2 vols. Austin: Nortex Press, 1985.

Thompson, Jerry, ed. *Fifty Miles and a Fight: Major Samuel Peter Heintzel-*

man's Journal of Texas & the Cortina War. Austin: Texas State Historical Association, 1998.

———, ed. *Into the Far, Wild Country: True Tales of the Old Southwest*. El Paso: Texas Western Press, 1996.

———, ed. *Juan Cortina and the Texas-Mexico Frontier, 1859–1877*. El Paso: University of Texas at El Paso, Texas Western Press, 1994.

Thompson, Karen R. *Round Rock, Texas: From Cowboys to Computers*. Austin: Nortex Press, 2002.

Toepperwein, Herman. *Texas Rangers*. San Antonio: Hall of Texas History, 1968.

Turner, Martha Anne. *Richard Bennent Hubbard: An American Life*. Austin: Shoal Creek Publishers, 1979.

———. *Texas Epic: An American Story*. Quanah, Tex.: Nortex Press, 1974.

A Twentieth Century History of Southwest Texas. Chicago: Lewis Publishing Co., 1907.

Van Oden, Alonzo. *Texas Ranger's Diary & Scrapbook*. Ed. Ann Jensen. Dallas: Kaleidograph Press, 1936.

Wallace, Ernest, and E. Adamson Hoebel. *The Comanches: Lords of the South Plains*. Norman: University of Oklahoma Press, 1952.

Webb, Walter Prescott. *The Texas Rangers: A Century of Frontier Defense*. Boston: 1935.

———. *The Texas Rangers in the Mexican War*. Austin: Jenkins Garrett Press, 1975.

Weems, Eddie. *To Conquer a Peace: The War Between the United States and Mexico*. Garden City, N.Y.: Doubleday, 1974.

Welborn, C. A. *History of the Red River Controversy: The Western Boundary of the Louisiana Purchase*. Quanah, Tex.: Nortex Offset Publications, 1973.

Wharton, Clarence. *History of Texas*. Dallas: Turner Company, 1935.

Wilbarger, J. W. *Indian Depredations in Texas*. 1889. Reprint, Austin: Eakin Press, State House Books: 1985.

Wilcox, Cadmus M. *History of the Mexican War*. Ed. Mary Rachel Wilcox. Washington, D.C.: Church News Publishing Co., 1892.

Wilkins, Frederick. *Defending the Borders: The Texas Rangers 1848–1861*. Austin: State House Press, 2001.

———. *The Law Comes to Texas: The Texas Rangers, 1870–1901*. Austin: State House Press, 1999.

———. *The Legend Begins: The Texas Rangers, 1823–1845*. Austin: State House Press, 1996.

Williams, Amelia W., and Eugene C. Barker, eds. *The Writings of Sam Houston, 1813–1863*. Austin and New York: Pemberton Press, Jenkins Publishing Co., 1970.

Williams, R. H. *With the Border Ruffians: Memories of the Far West, 1852–1868*. Ed. E. W. Williams. 1907. Reprint, Lincoln: University of Nebraska Press, 1982.

Winfrey, Dorman H., and James M. Day, eds. *The Indian Papers of Texas and the Southwest, 1825–1916*. 5 vols. 1966. Reprint, Austin: Texas State Historical Association, 1995.

Wooster, Ralph A. *Texas and Texans in the Civil War.* Austin: Eakin Press, 1995.

Wooten, Dudley G., ed. *A Comprehensive History of Texas, 1865 to 1897.* 2 vols. Dallas: 1898.

Wright, John, and William Wright. *Recollections of Western Texas, 1852–55: Descriptive and Narrative, Including an Indian Campaign, 1852–55, Interspersed with Illustrative Anecdotes.* Ed. Robert Wooster. Lubbock: Texas Tech University Press, 2001.

Yelderman, Pauline. *The Jay Bird Democratic Association of Fort Bend County: A White Man's Union.* Waco: Texian Press, 1979.

Young, Elliott. *Catarino Garza's Revolution on the Texas-Mexico Border.* Durham and London: Duke University Press, 2004.

Zamora, Emilio, Cynthia Orozco, and Rodolfo Rocha, eds. *Mexican Americans in Texas History: Selected Essays.* Austin: Texas State Historical Association, 2000.

Articles

Ball, Larry D. "The United States Army and the Big Springs, Nebraska, Train Robbery of 1877." *Journal of the West* 34 (January 1995): pp. 34–45.

Barnes, Florence Elberta, "Building a Texas Folk-Epic: The Saga of Strap Buckner." *The Texas Monthly*, October 1929, pp. 347–357.

Barker, Eugene C. "The Government of Austin's Colony, 1821–1831." *Southwestern Historical Quarterly* 21, no. 3 (January 1918): pp. 223–52.

Barton, Henry W. "The United States Cavalry and the Texas Rangers." *Southwestern Historical Quarterly* 63, no. 4 (April 1960): pp. 495–510.

"The Border Sheriff Now Speaks for Himself," *Frontier Times*, May 1931, pp. 360–68.

Bowden, J. J. "The Magoffin Salt War." *Password* 7 (Summer 1962): pp. 95–121.

(Brown, Robert J.) "Among the Rangers." *Texas Volunteer* 1, no. 4 (February 15, 1892): pp. 1–2.

———. "The Border Revolution." *Texas Volunteer* 1, no. 3 (January 15, 1892): pp. 11–12.

———. "Here's Garza Again." *Texas Volunteer* 1, no. 10 (August 15, 1892): p. 14.

——. "The Texas Ranger: A Realistic Review of the Service, and Something of the Men Who Make It." *Texas Volunteer* 1, no. 8 (June 15, 1892): pp. 4–7.

——. "Uniforming the Rangers." *Texas Volunteer* 1, no. 4 (February 15, 1892): p. 17.

——. "Uniforms for the Rangers." *Texas Volunteer* 1, no. 5 (March 15, 1892): p. 2.

Callan, Austin. "Battle of Dove Creek." *Frontier Times*, September 1947, p. 544.

"The Camp and Field." *Putnam's Monthly Magazine of American Literature, Science and Art*, vol. 10, no. 57 (September 1857).

Canales, J. T. "Juan N. Cortina: Bandit or Patriot?" An Address Before the Lower Rio Grande Valley Historical Society, San Benito, Texas, October 25, 1951.

"Captain June Peak, Texas Ranger." *Frontier Times*, September 1927, p. 4.

"Captain Marsh and His Rangers." *Frontier Times*, April 1929, pp. 300–301.

Carter, Lindsay. "The Texas Rangers: Interesting Facts About Our Greatest Body of Fighting Men." *Texas Magazine* 3, no. 4 (February 1911).

"Cattle Battle on Edwards Plateau in 1884." *Frontier Times*, March 1932, pp. 249–51.

"Cattle Raid on the Texas Border." *Harper's Weekly*, January 13, 1874.

Claiborne, Thomas. "Memoirs of the Past: A Famous Company and the Career and Death of a Gallant Commander." *Vedette*, April 1886, pp. 12–15.

"Contributor's Club." *Atlantic Monthly* 43, no. 255 (January 1879): p. 110.

Cox, Mike. "Battle of the Painted Rocks: Scraping off the Layers." *West Texas Historical Association Year Book* 78 (October 2002), pp. 151–69.

——. "Texas Rangers: From Horses to Helicopters." *Texas Almanac, 2000–2001*. Dallas: Belo Communications, 2001, pp. 23–28.

Crimmins. Colonel M. L. "General Albert J. Myer: The Father of the Signal Corps." *West Texas Historical Association Year Book* 29 (October 1953): pp. 67–78.

——. "The Mescalero Apaches." *Frontier Times*, September 1931, pp. 551–61.

Crosby, David F. "Kickapoo Counterattack at Dove Creek." *Wild West*, December 1999, pp. 50–54, 81.

Cruse, J. Brett. "Archeological Investigations at the Battle of Red River Site: New Perspectives on the 1874 Indian Campaign in the Texas Panhandle." *Southwestern Historical Quarterly* 106, no. 2 (October 2002): pp. 169–92.

Cuthbertson, Gilbert M. "Catarino E. Garza and the Garza War." *Texana* 13 (1975): pp. 335–48.

Davidge, Sarah Ellen. "Texas Rangers Were Rough and Ready Fighters." *Frontier Times*, November 1935.

Day, James M. "El Paso's Texas Rangers." *Password* 24, no. 4 (Winter 1979): pp. 153–72.

Dobie, J. Frank. "The Robinhooding of Sam Bass." *True West,* July-August 1958, pp. 8–10, 36.

Duke, J. K. "Bad Men and Peace Officers of the Southwest." *West Texas Historical Association Year book* 8 (1932): pp. 51–61.

Duncan, Juanita C. "Life and Letters of William Hickman Dunman, Texas Ranger." *Frontier Times,* December 1947, pp. 72–79.

Elkins, S. P. "Served as a Texas Ranger." *Frontier Times,* August 1928, pp. 438–39, 447.

Ferguson, I. B. "The Battle of Dove Creek." *Hunter's Magazine,* June 1911.

Fletcher, Henry T. "Violent Early Days of Big Bend Section Recalled." *Frontier Times,* May 1934, pp. 355–57.

"Fort Worth Man Tells of Shooting of Sam Bass." *Frontier Times,* January 1935, pp. 138–39.

Gillett, James B. "Vernon Wilson Was a Texas Ranger." *Frontier Times* 6, no. 7 (April 1929): pp. 257–58.

Godbold, Mollie Moore. "Comanche and the Hardin Gang." *Southwestern Historical Quarterly* 67 (July 1963): pp. 55–77; (October 1963), pp. 247–66.

Goldblatt, Kenneth A. "Ambush in Quitman Canyon." *Password* 14, no. 4 (Winter 1969): pp. 109–16.

———, ed. "Scout to Quitman Canyon: Report of Captain Geo. W. Baylor of the Frontier Battalion." *Texas Military History* 6, no. 2 (Summer 1967): pp. 149–59.

Gray, John D. "Robert McAlpin Williamson." *Texas Ranger Dispatch* 2 (2000).

Graybill, Andrew R. "Rural Police and the Defense of the Cattleman's Empire in Texas and Alberta, 1875–1900." *Agricultural History* 79, no. 3 (Summer 2005): pp. 253–80.

———. "Texas Rangers, Canadian Mounties, and the Policing of the Transnational Industrial Frontier, 1885–1910." *Western Historical Quarterly,* vol. 35, No. 2, Summer 2004, pp. 167–191.

Hager, William M. "The Nueces Town Raid of 1875: A Border Incident." *Arizona and the West* 1 (Spring 1959): pp. 258–70.

Haley, J. Evetts. "Texas Ranger." *The Shamrock,* Fall 1963.

Handcock, William CX. "Ranger's Ranger." *True West,* March-April 1961, pp. 23–25; 45–48.

Hardin, Stephen L. "Robert Hall: Citizen-Soldier of the Texas Republic." In *The Human Tradition in Texas,* ed. Ty Cashion and Jesus F. de la Teja. Wilmington, Del.: Scholarly Resources, 2001, pp. 35–54.

Hatley, Allen G. "The Mason County War: Top Texas Feud." *Wild West,* August 2005.

Havins, T. R. "Activities of Company E, Frontier Battalion, Texas Rangers, 1874–1880." *West Texas Historical Association Year Book* 11 (1935): pp. 62–72.

Holden, W. C. "Frontier Defense, 1846–1860." *West Texas Historical Association Year Book* 5 (1929): pp. 39–71.

———. "Frontier Defense in Texas During the Civil War." *West Texas Historical Association Year Book* 4 (1928): pp. 16–31.

———. "Law and Lawlessness on the Texas Frontier: 1875–1890." *Southwestern Historical Quarterly*, October 1940, pp. 188–203.

Holt, R. D. "Barbed Wire." *Texas Monthly*, September 1929, pp. 174–85.

———. "The Introduction of Barbed Wire into Texas and the Fence Cutting War." *West Texas Historical Association Year Book* 6 (1930): pp. 72–88.

"Horace M. Hall's Letters from Gillespie County." *Southwestern Historical Quarterly* 62, no. 3 (January 1959).

"The Hudson Pension Bill." *Frontier Times*, May 1928, pp. 334–35.

Hunter, J. Marvin. "Captain Arrington's Expedition." *Frontier Times*, December 1928, pp. 97–102.

———. "The Killing of Captain Frank Jones." *Frontier Times*, January 1929.

———. "Texas Rangers Are Still Active." *Frontier Times*, July 1945, pp. 294–98.

———. "'Uncle' Ben Dragoo, a Texas Ranger." *Frontier Times*, April 1929, pp. 287–91.

"The Indian: What We Should Do With Him." *Harper's Monthly*, April 1870.

"J. C. Cureton Tells of Famous Battle." *Frontier Times*, January 1946.

Jenkins, John H. "Texas Letters and Documents." *Texana* 1 (1963): pp. 57–58.

Johnson, Adam R. "The Battle of Antelope Hills." *Frontier Times*, February 1924, pp. 12–14.

Johnson, David. "Feudal Catalyst: T. P. Williamson." *Quarterly of the National Association for Outlaw and Lawman History, Inc.*, April-June 1998.

———. "Scott Cooley—a Byword for Terror." *Quarterly of the National Association for Outlaw and Lawman History, Inc.* 27, no. 2 (April-June 2003).

Kennedy, Ira. "A Brief History of the Texas Cherokee." *Enchanted Rock Magazine*, February 1996, p. 13.

King, W. H. "The Texas Ranger Service." In Dudley Wooten, *A Comprehensive History of Texas*. Vol. 2. II. Dallas: William Scarff, 1898.

Klos, George. "'Our People Could Not Distinguish One Tribe from Another': The 1859 Expulsion of the Reserve Indians from Texas." *Southwestern Historical Quarterly* 97, no. 4 (April 1994): pp. 599–619.

Kuykendall, J. H. "Reminiscences of Early Texas." *Southwestern Historical Quarterly* 11 (January 1903): pp. 236–53.

Mann, William L. "James O. Rice: Hero of the Battle on the San Gabriels." *Southwestern Historical Quarterly* 55 (July 1951): pp. 30–42.

Manning, Dan R. "John James Dix: Texas Ranger During the Cortina Campaign." *Texas Ranger Dispatch* 16 (Spring 2005).

Meed, Douglas V. "Daggers on the Gallows: The Revenge of Texas Ranger Captain 'Boss' Hughes." *True West* 46 (May 1999): pp. 44–49.

Miles, Susan. "The Soldiers' Riot." *Fort Concho Report* 13 (Spring 1981): pp. 1–20.

"More About W. B. Anglin." *Frontier Times*, March 1929, p. 224.

Muckleroy, Anna. "The Indian Policy of the Republic of Texas." *Southwestern Historical Quarterly* 25 (April 1922): pp. 229–60; 26 (July 1922): pp. 1–29; 26 (October 1922): pp. 128–48; 26 (January 1923): pp. 184 206.

Nance, Joseph Milton, trans. and ed. "Brigadier General Adrian Woll's Report of His Expedition into Texas in 1842." *Southwestern Historical Quarterly* 58, no. 4, (April 1955).

Neighbors, Kenneth F. "The Battle of Walker's Creek." *West Texas Historical Association Year Book* 41 (October 1965): pp. 121–30.

———. "Elm Creek Raid in Young County, 1864." *West Texas Historical Association Year Book* 40 (October 1964): pp. 83–89.

Nielson, George R. "Matthew Caldwell." *Southwestern Historical Quarterly* 64 (April 1961), pp. 478–502.

"19th Century Shining Star: James W. Guynn." *Texas Ranger Dispatch* 10 (Summer 2003).

Parsons, Chuck. "The Border Boss: John R. Hughes." *Texas Ranger Dispatch* 10 (Summer 2003).

———. "Charles Lilborn Nevill." *Texas Ranger Dispatch* 5 (Fall 2001).

Pilcher, James E. "Outlawry on the Mexican Border." *Scribner's Magazine* 10, no. 1 (July 1891): pp. 78–87.

Pool, William C. "The Battle of Dove Creek." *Southwestern Historical Quarterly* 53 (April 1950): pp. 367–85.

Preece, Harold. "Ben McCulloch, Bachelor of Wars." *Texas Rangers* 33, no. 1 (March 1949): p. 79.

———. "Buck Barry—Death on Horse Thieves." *Texas Rangers* 32, no. 3 (November 1948): p. 84.

———. "The Conquerin' Kid." *Texas Rangers* 43, no. 1 (June 1951): p. 91.

———. "Senor El Colt." *Texas Rangers* 34, no. 1 (March 1949): p. 82.

———. "Top Man." *Texas Rangers* 36, no. 2 (October 1949): p. 64.

Ramsdell, Charles William. "The Frontier and Secession," offprint. *Studies in Southern History and Politics* (New York: Columbia University Press, 1914).

"A Ranger Captain." *Voice of the Mexican Border*, November 1933, pp. 137–41.

"Reminiscences of a Texas Ranger." *Frontier Times*, December 1923.

Rhinehart, Marilyn D. " 'Underground Patriots': Thurber Coal Miners and the Struggle for Individual Freedom, 1888–1903." *Southwestern Historical Quarterly* 92 (April 1989): pp. 509–42.

Rigler, Erik. "Frontier Justice in the Days Before NCIC." *FBI Law Enforcement Bulletin*, July 1985, pp. 16–22.

"A Rising Ranger." *Texas Volunteer* 2, no. 2 (December 25, 1892): p. 23.

Robinson, Fayette. "Captain Samuel Walker." *Graham's Magazine* 32, no. 6 (June 1848): pp. 301–3.

Romero, Matias. "The Garza Raid and Its Lessons." *North American Review* 155 (September 1892): pp. 324–37.

Russel, Karylon A., and David Johnson. "Backtrailing the 'Notorious Baccus Brothers.'" *Quarterly of the National Association for Outlaw and Lawman History, Inc.* 29, no. 2 (April-June 2005): pp. 13–17.

Sansom, John W. "Captain Callahan's Raid into Mexico." *Hunter's Magazine*, April-May 1911.

"Scott Cooley's Grave." *Frontier Times*, February-March 1976, pp. 3–5.

Shearer, Ernest C. "The Callahan Expedition, 1855." *Southwestern Historical Quarterly* 54 (April 1951): pp. 430–51.

Sheffy, Lester Fields. "The Arrington Papers." *Panhandle-Plains Historical Review* 1, no. 1 (1928).

Shelton, Major Horace H. "Texas Confederate Generals: General William Steele, West Pointer, Indian Fighter, Mexican War Hero, Confederate Leader, Re-Organizer of the Texas Rangers and Restorer of Law and Order in Texas After Reconstruction Days." *Under Texas Skies* (Austin) 3, no. 4 (August 1952): pp. 13–14.

Skinner, A. E. "Forgotten Guardians: The Activities of Company C, Frontier Forces, 1870–1871." *Texana* 6, no. 2 (Summer 1968).

Smith, Thomas T. "U.S. Army Combat Operations in the Indian Wars of Texas, 1849–1881." *Southwestern Historical Quarterly* 99, no. 4 (April 1996): pp. 500–541.

Speed, Jonathon Gilmer. "The Hunt for Garza." *Harper's Weekly*, January 30, 1892, pp. 103–4.

Spurlin, Charles. "Ranger Walker in the Mexican War." *Military History of Texas and the Southwest* 9, no. 4 (1971): pp. 259–79.

Taylor, Maude Wallis. "Captain Samuel Highsmith, Ranger." *Frontier Times*, April 1940, pp. 291–302.

"Texas Rangers and Their Great Leaders." *Frontier Times*, August 1938.

"The Texas Rangers Brought Law and Order." *Frontier Times*, July 1935, pp. 425–28.

Townsend, E. E. "Rangers and Indians in the Big Bend Region." *Sul Ross State Teachers College Bulletin* (Alpine, Texas) 56, no. 6 (December 1, 1935): pp. 43–48.

Tyler, Ronnie C. "The Callahan Expedition of 1855: Indians or Negroes." *Southwestern Historical Quarterly* 70 (April 1967): pp. 574–85.

Virgines, George E. "Heraldry of the Texas Rangers." *Password* 37, no. 2 (Summer 1992): pp. 83–88.

Weaver, Ralph J. "The Nine Lives of Captain Frank Jones." *Frontier Times* 34 (Spring 1960): pp. 6–9, 36–40.

Webb, Walter Prescott. "George W. Arrington: The Iron-handed Man of the Panhandle." *Panhandle-Plains Historical Review* 8 (1935).

Weiss, Harold J., Jr. "Organized Constabularies: The Texas Rangers and the Early State Police Movement in the American Southwest." *Journal of the West* 34 (January 1995): pp. 29–30.

———. "The Texas Rangers Revisited: Old Themes and New Viewpoints." *Southwestern Historical Quarterly* 97, no. 4 (April 1994): pp. 620–40.

White, Grace Miller. "Captain John E. Elgin, Texian." *Frontier Times*, May 1944, pp. 337–40.

Whitehead, Ruth, "That Bloody Fence-Cutting War." *The West*, vol. 12, no. 1, December 1969, pp. 20–21, 64–66.

Williams, H. H., "A Veteran of Plum Creek." Dallas *Morning News*, June 4, 1905.

Williams, Robert H. "The Case for Peta Nacona." *Texana* 10 (1972): pp. 55–72.

Winterfield, Charles. "My First Day with the Rangers, by a Kentuckian." *American Review*, March 1845, pp. 280–88.

Theses and Dissertations

Pierce, Gerald S. "The Army of the Republic of Texas, 1836–1845." M.A. thesis, University of Mississippi, 1964.

Thomasson, Michael Reagan. "James E. McCord and the Texas Frontier Regiment." M.A. thesis, Stephen F. Austin State University, 1965.

Ward, C. F. "The Salt War of San Elizario, 1877." M.A. thesis, University of Texas, 1932.

Weiss, Harold J., Jr. " 'Yours to Command': Captain William J. 'Bill' McDonald and the Panhandle Rangers of Texas." Ph.D dissertation, Indiana University, 1982.

NEWSPAPERS

Austin *City Gazette*
Austin *Daily Journal*
Austin *Statesman*
Austin *Texas Democrat*
Austin *Texas Sentinel*
Austin *Texas State Gazette*
Boston *News-Letter*
Brown County *Banner*
Burnet *Bulletin*
Canyon City *Echo*
Clarksville *Northern Standard*
Coleman County *Chronicle*
Corpus Christi *Caller-Times*
Corpus Christi *Gazette*
Dallas *Morning News*
Dallas *Semi-Weekly Farm News*
Dallas *Times-Herald*
Dallas *Weekly Herald*
Eagle Pass *Guide*
El Paso *Herald-Post*
El Paso *Times*
Fort Worth *Star-Telegram*
Galveston *News*

Galveston *Weekly News*
Houston *Chronicle*
Houston *Post*
Lampasas *Daily Times*
Lampasas *Dispatch*
Laredo *Times*
Leslie's Illustrated Weekly Newspaper
Natchitoches *Courier*
New Orleans *Bulletin*
New York *Times*
Niles' Weekly Register
Pecos *Enterprise*
San Angelo *Standard-Times*
San Antonio *Daily Herald*
San Antonio *Express*
San Antonio *News*
San Francisco *Argonaut*
San Saba *News*
Santa Fe *Independent*
Telegraph and Texas Register
Vicksburg *Daily Whig*
Victoria *Advocate*

Index

Navasota River, 42, 45, 56
Neal, Edgar T., 366, 369
Nebraska Territory, 145
Neighbors, Robert S., 132–34, 152,
    153
Neill, James C., 380n7
Nelson, G. H., 142
Nelson, James, 26
Neri de Bastrop, Felipe Enrique, 27
Nevill, Charles L., 295, 297, 313, 314,
    319, 321–22, 427n35
Newman, Joseph, 31
New Mexico, 84, 278, 288–89, 306,
    308
New Orleans, 25, 27, 106–7, 112
New Spain, 23–24
newspapers and journalists, at wars,
    106–7
Newton, J. Allen, 334–36, 340–41
Nichols, James Wilson, 87
Nicholson, S. G., 224, 410n30
Nich Po or Little Owl, 399n37
Noakes, Thomas J., 244
No-ko-aht, 183
Nolan, Nicholas, 301, 303
Norris, James M., 176
Northern Standard (newspaper), 106
Northington, E. A., 243
North Leon, 151
Nowlin, James C., 193
Nueces County raid, 244–45
Nueces River, 93, 103, 112, 126, 129,
    133
Nueces Strip, 126, 244–51
Nuecestown, 244
Nugent, John, 78

Ochiltree, Thomas P., 326
Odd Fellow Cemetery, San Antonio,
    394n50
Odom, Thomas L., 325–26, 429n47
O'Dorne, Jim, 198
Ogle, Bill, 369, 441n45
Old, Augie, 373

Old Forgit (a Ranger), 198
Olguin, Antonio, 358
Olguin, Jesus and Serverino, 358–59
Olguin family, 437n23
Onion Creek, 72
Only Son (schooner), 27–28
Ordinance Establishing a Provisional
    Government, 46
Organic Law, 46
Ormsby, W. L., 113
Ortiz, L. R., 373
Outlaw, Bazzel Lamar, 359, 360,
    437n24
outlaws, 30–31

Paint Creek, 201
Paint Rock, 275
    encounter at, 390n65
Palo Alto, 155
Palo Alto, battle of, 105
Palo Alto Prairie, 249
Palo Duro Canyon, 229
Palo Pinto County, 143, 152, 166,
    194
Panhandle, the, 220–22, 229, 305–9,
    329, 349–50, 355
Panic of 1873, 208
Parker, Benjamin, 56–57
Parker, Cynthia Ann (Naudah,
    "Cincee Ann"), 57, 170, 221,
    403n34
Parker, Daniel, 41–42, 45
Parker, Isaac, 57, 170
Parker, James W., 56, 57, 59
Parker, John, 57
Parker, John (boy), 57
Parker, Quanah (Comanche chief),
    221–22, 403n32, 403n34
Parker, Silas M., 45, 56–57
Parker clan, 56
Parker County, 164, 166
Parker massacre, 56–57
Parra, Geronimo, 356
Paso del Norte (Juárez), 283